STUDY GUIDE

STUDY GUIDE

to accompany

ESSENTIALS OF
ECONOMICS

THIRD EDITION

Krugman • Wells
Graddy

Elizabeth Sawyer Kelly

University of Wisconsin-Madison

WORTH PUBLISHERS
A Macmillan Higher Education Company

Study Guide
by Elizabeth Sawyer Kelly
to accompany
Krugman/Wells/Graddy: Essentials of Economics, Third Edition

ISBN 13: 978-1-4641-4338-0
ISBN 10: 1-4641-4338-2

First Printing

Printed in the United States of America

Worth Publishers
41 Madison Avenue
New York, NY 10010
www.wortheconomics.com

Contents

Preface

This Study Guide is designed for use with **Essentials of Economics, Third Edition** by Paul Krugman, Robin Wells, and Kathryn Graddy. It is intended to help you evaluate your understanding of the material covered in the textbook and thereby reinforce the key concepts you need to learn.

For each chapter, the Study Guide is organized as follows:

Before You Read the Chapter
- Summary: an opening paragraph that provides a brief overview of the chapter.
- Objectives: a numbered list outlining and describing the material that you should have learned in the chapter. These objectives can be easily used as a study tool.
- Key Terms: a list of bold key terms with their definitions. This section includes room for note-taking.

After You Read the Chapter
- Tips: a numbered list of learning tips with graphical analysis.
- Worked Problems: a new set of worked-out problems that take the student step-by-step through a particular problem/exercise.
- Problems and Exercises: a set of 10-15 comprehensive problems.

Before You Take the Test
- Chapter Review Questions: a set of approximately 30 multiple-choice questions that focus on the key concepts from the text that you should grasp after reading the chapter. These questions are designed for quick exam preparation.

Answer Key
- Answers to Problems and Exercises: detailed solutions to the Problems and Exercises in the Study Guide.
- Answers to Chapter Review Questions: solutions to the multiple-choice questions in the Study Guide—along with thorough explanations.

Answers as well as explanatory solutions can be found at the end of each chapter. Students often use an answer section to simply check if they have gotten the "right" answer. I caution you to use the answer section accompanying each chapter with an eye to getting the highest possible value from the exercises provided. In economics, the reasoning used in coming to conclusions and correctly modeling the problems are as important as coming to an accurate answer. Explanations for each problem have been provided in order for you to check that your understanding of the concepts has been appropriately applied.

The study of economics has the potential of altering the way you evaluate and understand the world. I hope that your use of this guide will help you in your study of basic microeconomics principles and will provide a jumping-off point for further study in the economics field.

Elizabeth Sawyer Kelly

First Principles

BEFORE YOU READ THE CHAPTER

Summary

This chapter provides a brief overview of 12 general principles underlying the study of economics. These principles are explored and discussed at greater length as you work your way through the text. This first chapter indicates the breadth and depth of economics as a course of study by delineating these 12 principles, which describe how individuals make choices and how individual choices interact.

Chapter Objectives

This chapter introduces a set of principles that will guide your study of economics.

Objective #1. Resources—land, labor, capital, and human capital—are scarce, so individuals as well as societies must make choices about how to use these resources.

Objective #2. The opportunity cost, or the real cost of something, is what you must give up to get it.

Objective #3. Decisions about how much to produce and how much to consume are made at the margin. These decisions invariably involve a trade-off, or a comparison of the costs and benefits of producing more or consuming more.

Objective #4. People usually exploit opportunities to make themselves better off—in other words, people respond to incentives.

Objective #5. There are gains from trade.

Objective #6. Markets move toward equilibrium, a situation in which no individual would be better off doing something different.

Objective #7.   Resources should be used as efficiently as possible to achieve society's goals. However, there is a trade-off between efficiency and equity: decisions based solely on efficiency may be highly inequitable.

Objective #8.   Markets usually lead to efficiency.

Objective #9.   When markets fail to achieve efficiency, government intervention can improve society's welfare. Markets may fail due to (1) the existence of side effects from individual actions that are not accounted for in the market; (2) the prevention of mutually beneficial trades by an individual or individuals so they can capture a greater share of resources; or (3) the inability of the market to efficiently produce some goods, due to the nature of these goods.

Objective #10.   One person's spending is another person's income.

Objective #11.   Spending sometimes gets out of line with the economy's capacity to produce goods and services. It is possible for the economy's spending to be less than, or greater than, the current level of production.

Objective #12.   Government policies can change the level of spending in an economy.

Key Terms

economy a system for coordinating society's productive activities.

economics the social science that studies the production, distribution, and consumption of goods and services.

market economy an economy in which decisions about production and consumption are made by individual producers and consumers.

invisible hand the way in which the individual pursuit of self-interest can lead to good results for society as a whole.

microeconomics the branch of economics that studies how people make decisions and how these decisions interact.

market failure when the individual pursuit of self-interest leads to bad results for society as a whole.

recession a downturn in the economy.

macroeconomics the branch of economics that is concerned with overall ups and downs in the economy.

economic growth the growing ability of the economy to produce goods and services.

individual choice the decision by an individual of what to do, which necessarily involves a decision of what not to do.

resource anything, such as land, labor, and capital, that can be used to produce something else; includes natural resources (from the physical environment) and human resources (labor, skill, intelligence).

Notes

Key Terms *(continued)*

scarce in short supply; a *resource* is scarce when there is not enough of the resources available to satisfy all the various ways a society wants to use them.

opportunity cost the real cost of an item: what you must give up in order to get it.

trade-off a comparison of costs and benefits of doing something.

marginal decision a decision made at the "margin" of an activity to do a bit more or a bit less of an activity.

marginal analysis the study of *marginal decisions*.

incentive anything that offers rewards to people who change their behavior.

interaction (of choices) my choices affect your choices, and vice versa; a feature of most economic situations. The results of this interaction are often quite different from what the individuals intend.

trade in a market *economy*, individuals provide goods and services to others and receive goods and services in return.

gains from trade by dividing tasks and trading, people can get more of what they want through *trade* than they could if they tried to be self-sufficient.

specialization each person specializes in the task that he or she is good at performing.

equilibrium an economic situation in which no individual would be better off doing something different.

efficient description of a market or *economy* that takes all opportunities to make some people better off without making other people worse off.

equity fairness; everyone gets his or her fair share. Since people can disagree about what is "fair," equity is not as well defined a concept as efficiency.

▮ AFTER YOU READ THE CHAPTER

Tips

Tip #1. The study of economics is cumulative. You should master each topic as it is presented since later topics build on earlier topics.

Tip #2. Pay attention to new vocabulary and make sure you know, understand, and can apply these terms. Your instructor will expect you to do more than just define the terms: you must also be able to indicate through your work an ability to apply these terms in a meaningful manner.

Tip #3.   Plan to spend time every day studying economics. Review your lecture notes, review the vocabulary, work on the practice questions, and identify what questions you have about the material. Once you formulate your questions, seek out answers by returning to your text, your lecture notes, your classmates, or your professor.

Tip #4.   Think about the topics that might be on an exam and the kinds of questions that might be asked about these topics—questions that are strictly definitional, questions that apply the definitions in a problem-solving setting, and questions that force you to really think about the material and apply your knowledge. Most college-level exams include questions designed to make you think about the material.

Tip #5.   You might find it helpful to create a set of flash cards to help you study. For this chapter, the set of flash cards would include a card for each principle and a card for each new vocabulary word. On the vocabulary cards, put the word on one side of the card and its definition on the other. In the upper corner of each card, note the chapter the card comes from— for example, you might write "Ch. 1" on the cards for this chapter to remind you where this material was first presented. Then, make a point of reviewing these flash cards throughout the day until you feel confident you have absorbed this material.

Tip #6.   Your study of economics is applicable to the real world. As you read or listen to the news, try to apply your new knowledge of economics to your understanding of these world events.

WORKED PROBLEMS

1. In each of the following situations identify the cost or the benefit that the market does not take into account in determining the optimal amount of the good. For example, when Joe drives to work during rush hour, his driving adds to the traffic congestion: Joe imposes a cost on all the other drivers that the market and Joe do not take into account when deciding whether he should drive during rush hour.
    a. Mary drinks several alcoholic drinks and then gets into her car to drive home. Mary's actions increase the risk of car accidents that may injure Mary as well as other people. In addition, Mary's actions may also lead to other types of property damage.
    b. Jerry picks up litter along his route to work.
    c. Sarah decides to paint the outside of her house lime green. Most of Sarah's neighbors strongly dislike her choice of color since they fear that their property values are apt to fall after Sarah paints her home lime green.
    d. Ying smokes two packs of cigarettes a day at her place of employment even though she knows smoking will likely create health consequences for her as well as anyone else who breathes her second-hand smoke.

    STEP 1: For each of the situations think about a cost or a benefit that the transaction involves that will not be considered by the market.

    Review the section "Interaction: How Economics Work" on pages 10–16.

    a. Mary imposes a cost on other members of society when she drinks and then drives. Her driving while intoxicated poses distinct risks to her and to others who may be on her route. Mary, if intoxicated, may make poor decisions that result in a car accident that may injure her as well as other individuals. Her driving while impaired also poses greater risk of property damage due to driving error.

b. Jerry provides a benefit to other members of society when he collects litter: thanks to Jerry's uncompensated efforts, the route is aesthetically more pleasing to everyone traveling the route.

c. Sarah imposes a cost on her neighbors when she paints the exterior of her house lime green. Her actions are apt to decrease the property values of her neighbors.

d. Ying imposes a cost on society by her choice of smoking: she is likely to experience greater health risks and costs that will not necessarily be borne just by her. In addition, her actions result in air pollution that creates costs to those who are not smoking but who are exposed to Ying's smoking.

2. This chapter introduces four general principles that underlie the economics of individual choice: (1) resources are scarce; (2) the real cost of something is what you must give up to get it; (3) "how much?" is a decision at the margin; and (4) people usually exploit opportunities to make themselves better off. In each of the following situations identify which of these principles is being illustrated. More than one principle may be illustrated in a particular example.

    a. Peter is trying to decide whether he should spend the afternoon working on the sailboat he is building or whether he should spend the afternoon studying for his economics exam.

    b. Carolyn has realized that she can earn $20 an hour babysitting while attending law school. Any other job she might be able to fit into her schedule would only pay $15 an hour.

    c. Katherine would like to fly to Costa Rica for a week and she would like to replace her snow tires on her car. Either choice Katherine makes will cost $400 and she only has $400 to spend.

    d. Mark decides to work as a canoe guide for the summer and therefore turns down the opportunity of working in Arizona.

    e. Susie is debating how many servings of cake she is going to eat at her cousin's wedding reception.

STEP 1: **For each of the situations think about which principle or principles apply to the scenario.**

Review the section "Principles that Underlie Individual Choice: The Core of Economics" on pages 4–10.

a. Faced with this decision, Peter is aware that resources are scarce and that he has only one afternoon available and thus cannot do both activities. He also recognizes that the real cost of doing something is measured by what must be given up: he can work on his sailboat but the cost to him of this choice is not studying for his economics exam. Or, he can study for his economics exam, but the cost to him of this choice is not working on his boat.

b. Carolyn when deciding to babysit is exploiting the opportunity to make herself better off. Babysitting offers her the highest wage per hour that she can command while in law school.

c. Katherine faces scarce resources (only $400) as well as the recognition that the real cost of doing something is measured by what must be given up. Katherine can go to Costa Rica, but she must give up new snow tires in order to take the trip.

d. Since Mark must choose between the canoe guide position and the job in Arizona, he is faced with the first and second principle: resources are scarce (he has limited available time) and the real cost of doing something is measured by what must be given up.

e. Susie's decision about how much wedding cake to eat is a decision made at the margin: Susie considers how much enjoyment or benefit she will get from an additional piece of cake versus the cost of eating another piece. If the benefit is greater than the cost, then Susie will eat an additional piece of cake.

3. In January 2009, Flight 1549, the "Miracle on the Hudson," crashed after Canadian geese struck the airplane. Amazingly no one on board was killed, but the accident did lead to the Federal Aviation Administration ordering a review of wildlife hazards at all major American airports. In some locales, substantial populations of Canadian geese were identified and orders were given to kill these geese. The "how much?" principle is useful in analyzing many situations. Use this principle to provide an analysis of the steps you would advocate that officials take in deciding what the optimal number of geese is for the area around an airport.

STEP 1: **In formulating your answer to this question, think about the benefit of a small change in the number of geese and the cost of this small change in the number of geese.**

Review the section "'How Much?' Is a Decision at the Margin" on pages 7–8.

The "how much?" principle advises that each decision should be made at the margin at which we consider the benefit of a small change relative to the cost of that small change. In the case of the Canadian geese, we would want to start with an analysis of the cost of the current flock sizes as it relates to aviation operation, and then consider what the marginal benefit of a reduction in the Canadian geese population in the area would be, as well as what the marginal cost of that reduction would be. Provided that the marginal benefit was greater than the marginal cost, then it would make sense to reduce the Canadian geese population. But, if the marginal benefit proved smaller than the marginal cost, then it would not make sense to reduce the Canadian geese population.

4. Suppose you are on a Board of Directors for an organization and that your Board is currently trying to hire an Administrative Assistant to assist in a broad range of responsibilities for your group. You advertise the job, its responsibilities, and its salary range and then you begin to receive applications from prospective employees. In reviewing the résumés, you realize that none of the applicants has the necessary experience or skill set that you seek. Analyze this situation and what you think you should do to rectify it.

STEP 1: **Think about which principle or principles is applicable to this question as you formulate your answer.**

Review the section "Markets Move Toward Equilibrium" on pages 12–13. Recall the statement, "markets usually reach equilibrium via changes in prices, which rise or fall until no opportunities for individuals to make themselves better off remain" (page 12) when answering this question.

People applying for the job know what skills you are looking for and what the salary range is. If you are not getting applicants with those skills, it suggests that you are offering a salary that is too low. By adjusting the salary level upward you should begin to see a group of prospective employees that possess greater skills and more experience.

5. Suppose that a new government is elected and that on taking office these political leaders mandate that everyone in their society receive the same wage per hour. Discuss the equity of this decision as well as its efficiency.

STEP 1: One of the ideas that your course of study in economics will expose you to is the trade-off between equity and efficiency. A policy may prove to be highly efficient but inequitable or highly equitable but quite inefficient. In the example, identify both the equity and efficiency aspects of the proposed policy.

Review the section "Resources Should Be Used Efficiently to Achieve Society's Goals" on pages 13–14.

With regard to equity, this mandate seeks to treat everyone equally: all people get the same wage per hour irrespective of what work they are doing. Some members of this society might feel that this is still inequitable since, for example, some jobs are harder to perform than others, some jobs require far more training than others, and some jobs are riskier than others. Income equity among all members of a society poses some definitional and operational challenges. With regard to efficiency, if everyone receives the same wage per hour, then there will be little incentive to work hard. Most members of the society will choose to work less intensely, and this will therefore result in less total output for the society and a reduction in overall living standard.

6. In recent years, the U.S. government has sought to keep interest rates low through the actions of the Federal Reserve Bank as well as by implementing a major government spending program. Briefly discuss what the intent of these programs has been.

STEP 1: Identify which of the principles introduced in the chapter seem most relevant with regard to this question.

Review the section "Economy-Wide Interactions" on pages 17–19. In particular pay close attention to the sections "Overall Spending Sometimes Gets Out of Line with the Economy's Productive Capacity" on pages 17–18 and "Government Policies Can Change Spending" on page 18.

In light of the financial crisis that began in 2007, the government has tried to pursue monetary and fiscal policies that would soften the recessionary impact. By pursuing monetary policies that would keep interest rates low, the Federal Reserve Bank hoped to stimulate consumer and business spending that is affected by the level of the interest rate. In addition, the government increased its expenditures on goods and services in order to help maintain a higher level of spending than would otherwise have occurred during the months after the financial crisis.

Problems and Exercises

1. For each of the following situations describe the opportunity costs of each decision.
   a. Sarah considers two options for Saturday night: she can attend a concert that costs $10 per ticket or she can go to the free movie offered at the student union. She decides to attend the concert.

b. A new business in town debates paying $20,000 for a prime location versus $10,000 for a less perfect location. The business estimates that it will eventually serve the same number of customers in either location, but that it will take six months before the suboptimal location provides the same outcome as the prime location. The business decides to purchase the $10,000 property.

c. Jamie is given a choice for his next holiday from school: he can be an unpaid intern at a company or he can earn $2,000 working as a camp counselor. He decides to take the internship.

d. Roberto is studying for two midterms this week. He figures he has 20 available hours to study for both midterms. If he studies all 20 hours for the economics exam he will undoubtedly get an A on the exam, but he will at best make a C on his organic chemistry test. If he studies all 20 hours for the organic chemistry test he will get an A on the organic chemistry exam, but he will likely earn a D on his economics test. Roberto decides to devote all of his available time to economics since he has determined that he does not wish to pursue a premed major.

2. The following table presents the possible combinations of study time available to Roberto this week as he prepares for his two midterms (one in economics and the other in organic chemistry). Assume Roberto has 20 hours available to study and that he will use all 20 hours studying economics and chemistry.

Hours of study time spent on economics	Hours of study time spent on organic chemistry	Grade in economics	Grade in organic chemistry
0	20	60	90
5	15	70	85
10	10	80	75
15	5	86	73
20	0	90	70

Roberto currently plans to study 10 hours for economics and 10 hours for organic chemistry.

a. If he alters his plan and studies 15 hours for economics, what is the opportunity cost of that decision?

b. If he alters his plan and studies 15 hours for organic chemistry, what is the opportunity cost of that decision?

c. If he alters his plan and studies 20 hours for economics, what is the opportunity cost of that decision?

d. If he alters his plan and studies 20 hours for organic chemistry, what is the opportunity cost of that decision?

3. a. Joe is trying to decide whether to have another piece of cake at dinner tonight. Describe how Joe can use the principle of marginal analysis to decide whether to eat this piece of cake.

b. A local government is debating whether to institute a stricter recycling ordinance for their community. Suppose the cost of the additional recycling restrictions is $500,000 a year due to the need to have additional labor and capital available to meet the demands of the new ordinance. This community uses marginal analysis to make their decisions and decides to adopt this stricter recycling ordinance. What do you know about the benefits this community will receive from implementing this ordinance?

c. Susy is recovering from knee surgery and has a number of exercises she needs to do each day to enhance that recovery. These exercises are tedious and at times painful. If Susy uses the principle of marginal analysis to make her decisions, what must be true about the costs and benefits of doing these exercises if Susy is to do them on a daily basis?

4. The two health insurance organizations in a community are trying to encourage their members to embrace healthier lifestyles. Healthlines is willing to pay 25% of the class fee for exercise classes offered at the local gym. Longhealth is willing to refund 50% of the class fee at the end of the class, provided that the instructor signs a form verifying that the member has attended at least 80% of the classes. Which fee structure is likely to result in the larger improvement in lifestyle choices? Explain the reasoning that underlies your answer.

5. Matt and Sarah are teenagers in Everycity, USA. Both of their families are concerned about their teenagers staying out late. Matt's family has a rule that if he returns home after midnight (even one minute late!) he loses his driving privileges for two weeks and cannot go out during that time. Sarah's family does not have a rule. Instead, before she goes out for the evening, Sarah and her family negotiate an expected time of return and Sarah then strives to honor this agreement. When she is running later than expected she calls her family so they will not be unduly worried. Compare and contrast these two approaches, paying particular attention to the set of incentives that the two approaches offer Matt and Sarah.

6. Suppose that Bill and Mary are the only individuals living in a community and that this community has no contact with the rest of the world. Bill grows tomatoes and corn while Mary grows wheat and onions. How does trade between Bill and Mary benefit both of them?

7. Wisconsin produces cheese and corn while Georgia produces peaches and peanuts. How does trade between these two states benefit the individuals who live in those states?

8. **a.** Pedro enjoys getting a cup of coffee on his way to campus each morning. He can get a cup at Joe's for $1.50 or he can get a cup at Mary's for $2.00. The coffee is equivalent at both places and the waiting time in line is equivalent as well. Is this an equilibrium situation? Explain your answer.

b. Suzanne eats a hamburger for lunch every Wednesday. She can purchase her hamburger at the Big Bun for $5.50 or she can purchase a similar hamburger at The Real McCoy for $7.00. Is this an equilibrium situation? Explain your answer.

9. **a.** The cafeteria at your college offers two desserts each night: soft-serve ice cream and some kind of cake or pie. Each night the cafeteria runs out of the soft-serve ice cream and finds that it has a surplus of the cake or pie. Is this situation efficient? Explain your answer.

b. A community provides bus service to its residents and charges $2 per ride. At this price, 98% of residents refuse to ride the buses and instead drive their cars. The community has serious air pollution problems from automobile emissions. Is this an efficient situation? Explain your answer.

c. A community ponders implementing a no-smoking ordinance that would eliminate smoking in all businesses, government offices, and public places. Smokers are upset and argue that their rights are being violated by this proposed ordinance. An independent analyst estimates that the benefits of the ordinance will be $100,000 a year, while the cost of implementing the ordinance will be $40,000. Would it be efficient to implement the ordinance? Explain your answer.

10. France is debating a change in its unemployment insurance policy. Historically the country has been willing to provide generous benefits to the unemployed for a substantial period. The country is now debating whether to reduce the length of time that unemployed people can collect these benefits. Comment on the efficiency and equity aspects of this proposed change in policy.

11. The government of a country decides to mandate that all people younger than 25 years old must be in school and must pursue a college education. The government also passes the necessary legislation to fund this education for all of its citizens. Comment on the efficiency and equity aspects of this proposed policy.

12. Government sometimes intervenes to alter people's decisions. For each of the following situations, comment on how the government intervention provides an incentive to change behavior and what the desired change in behavior is.

   a. The government offers a free bus pass to all citizens living in metropolitan areas.

   b. The government offers individuals an income tax refund of $2,000 a year if they reduce the number of cars they own in their household by one car.

   c. The government requires all children younger than 16 years old to be in school, and failure to comply results in the child's guardian being sent to jail.

   d. The college you attend requires you to have an up-to-date immunization record before you can move into your dormitory.

13. A community sits on a rocky seacoast and each year several large ships run up against the rocks and sink. The community would benefit from installing a lighthouse, but the lighthouse has not been built because no individuals are willing to pay for the construction of this lighthouse, knowing that once the lighthouse is built they can enjoy it even if they did not contribute to its construction. Is there a solution to this problem? Explain your answer.

14. An economy experiences a recession in which the level of production of goods and services is lower than the level the economy is capable of producing. As the level of production falls, people decrease their level of spending. What can you conclude in general about the level of people's income in this economy?

15. An economy has a fixed amount of resources available to it during any given period. If there is too much spending in the economy during this time, how will the economy respond?

16. What can the government do to alter the level of spending during a recession? What can the government do to alter the level of spending during a period of inflation?

■ BEFORE YOU TAKE THE TEST

Chapter Review Questions

1.   Camillo is offered two jobs: one pays a salary of $30,000 per year and offers four weeks of vacation, and the other job pays a salary of $32,000 per year and offers two weeks of vacation. What is the opportunity cost for Camillo of taking the job offering $32,000 per year?

   a. $2,000 plus two weeks of vacation per year

   b. $2,000 per year

   c.   two weeks of vacation per year

   d. $30,000 plus two weeks of vacation per year

2.   Ning decides to attend a special speaker presentation tonight at her college instead of staying in her dorm and listening to her music collection. Which of the following statements is true?

   a.   Ning faces no opportunity cost with regard to her decision since listening to music or attending the speaker are both free events.

   b.   The opportunity cost of Ning's decision is so small that it is not worth calculating.

   c.   The opportunity cost of Ning's decision is the loss of her evening of music listening.

   d.   The opportunity cost of Ning's decision includes the cost associated with hearing the speaker.

3.   A firm is debating the purchase of an additional piece of machinery. The firm estimates that the machine will enable them to increase their revenue by $1,000 a month, but it will increase their monthly costs by $750. This firm applies the principle of marginal analysis and decides that

   a.   it should purchase the machine since the benefits from this additional equipment exceed the costs.

   b.   it should not purchase the machine since the benefits from this additional equipment are less than the costs.

4.   Marie is training for a triathlon. She will need to be able to swim, bike, and run to compete successfully. On Tuesdays, Thursdays, and Saturdays she always swims, while on Mondays and Fridays she runs. On Wednesdays she bikes. On Sundays she can choose to rest, bike, swim, or run. When Marie chooses to rest on Sundays it must be the case that

   a.   Marie is lazy and not pushing herself to her fullest potential.

   b.   Marie perceives that the benefit of a day of rest exceeds the cost of a day of rest.

   c.   Marie has lost sight of her goal to compete successfully in the triathlon.

   d.   Marie is not able to compare the benefits and costs associated with biking, swimming, and running.

5.   Scarcity of resources implies that

   a.   people can do whatever they want and do not need to worry about making choices.

   b.   life involves making choices about how to best use these scarce resources.

   c.   societies need to invest time and money to discover more resources.

   d.   only very wealthy individuals are not constrained by their resources.

6. Each day people make decisions about what to wear, what to eat, or where to work
   a. since they all face constraints that mean they cannot do everything they would like to do.
   b. without regard to the level of resources that are available to them.

7. The university in Smart, USA, has a parking problem and is looking into programs to alleviate the parking shortage. Which of the following ideas is likely to decrease by the greatest amount the number of cars parking on campus each day?
   a. Faculty and staff at the university all receive free parking permits.
   b. Faculty and staff at the university all pay a set fee per year for parking permits.
   c. Faculty and staff at the university must pay an hourly fee for each hour that they park on campus.
   d. Faculty and staff are exempt from any parking policies at the university since they need to be able to come to campus to do their jobs.

8. Salespeople working at Department Store of Suburbia are offered two compensation plans. Plan A pays the worker $4.00 per hour plus a 5% sales commission on the total dollar value of sales that this worker makes. Plan B pays the worker $6.00 per hour and does not include a sales commission. Total sales per hour per salesperson averages $100. Which of the following statements is true?
   a. Plan A will result in the salespeople being less helpful to customers than does plan B.
   b. Plan A will result in the salespeople being more helpful to customers than does plan B.

9. Trade between two individuals
   a. rarely is beneficial.
   b. usually benefits only one of the trading partners.
   c. usually requires some form of coercion.
   d. is beneficial to both of the individuals.

10. Trade between two countries
   a. always benefits the economically wealthier country more than the economically weaker country.
   b. usually benefits only one of the trading partners.
   c. usually is the result of some form of coercion.
   d. is beneficial to both of the countries.

11. An equilibrium
   a. is a situation in which people have exploited all opportunities to make themselves better off.
   b. is a situation in which no individual would be better off doing something different.
   c. usually is reached through changes in prices, which increase or decrease until there are no longer opportunities for individuals to make themselves better off.
   d. Answers (a), (b), and (c) are all true.

12. A situation is efficient when
   a. it is producing the maximum gains from trade that are possible given the resources available.
   b. the price of the good under consideration is as low as possible.
   c. one person is made better off even if some other person is made worse off.
   d. one group of people are made better off even if it harms some other group of people.

13. A college keeps its library open all night throughout the semester even though students study in the library after midnight only in the weeks immediately before midterms and final exams. This situation is
    a. efficient, since no one can be made better off with the available resources.
    b. inefficient, since the college could close the library after midnight for those weeks that are not right before the midterms or final exams and use the freed-up resources to provide other, more highly valued, services.
    c. too much of an administrative headache to solve.
    d. equitable, since it does not discriminate between different weeks in the semester.

14. A government policy gives everyone under 30 years of age a subsidy no matter what their level of income. From the perspective of the people under 30, this policy
    a. may be equitable, since it guarantees everyone under 30 the same level of subsidy, but it is probably not efficient.
    b. is efficient, since the government simply writes a check for the same amount to everyone under 30.

15. A government policy gives everyone under 30 years of age a subsidy no matter what their level of income. But, if you are a member of the ethnic group that runs the government, you receive a subsidy that is twice the size of the subsidy paid to people who do not belong to this ethnic group. From the perspective of the people under 30, this policy
    a. is inequitable, since the individual's ethnic identity alters the level of the subsidy available to the individual.
    b. is equitable, since each person under 30 is treated the same as every other person under 30 in their ethnic group.

16. Government intervention in a market
    a. is never a good idea.
    b. can improve an outcome if the market fails to provide the good or the right amount of the good.
    c. should not occur if there are side payments from the provision of the good that the market does not include.
    d. always reduces the level of efficiency.

17. When one group of people in an economy decreases their spending, this will
    a. have no effect on the level of income of other people in the economy.
    b. increase the level of income of other people in the economy.
    c. decrease the level of income of other people in the economy.
    d. lead to inflationary pressures in this economy.

18. When one group of people in an economy increases their spending, this will
    a. have no effect on the level of income of other people in the economy.
    b. increase the level of income of other people in the economy.
    c. decrease the level of income of other people in the economy.
    d. lead to inflationary pressures in this economy.

19. When there is too much spending in an economy relative to production, this leads to
    a. a recession in that economy.   b. inflation in that economy.

20. In a recession, the government can increase the level of spending in the economy by
    a. decreasing taxes.   b. decreasing government spending.

■ ANSWER KEY

Answers to Problems and Exercises

1. **a.** Sarah's decision to attend the concert has two opportunity costs: attending the concert means that she will be unable to attend the movie, and in addition, to attend the concert she must pay $10 for a ticket. Her decision to attend the concert means that she is giving up whatever she could have purchased with the $10.

b. The business gives up $10,000 to get the property, but this is not an opportunity cost since the business must have a business location to exist. However, there is an opportunity cost to this decision: the business gives up the additional business it would have gotten at the prime location during the first six months.

c. When he decides to take the internship, Jamie incurs an opportunity cost of $2,000, since he is giving up this income to work in the intern position.

d. Roberto's opportunity cost with regard to his studying is his diminished grade in organic chemistry. (Obviously Roberto might want to consider some combination of studying that allows him to prepare for both exams, but this question did not offer that possibility.)

2. Remember that opportunity cost measures what is given up, so when Roberto studies more for his economics exam, he is giving up time he could devote to his organic chemistry exam. This decision will therefore affect his organic chemistry grade. Similarly, if Roberto devotes more time to studying for his organic chemistry exam, then he will be giving up points on his economics exam.

a. The opportunity cost of studying 15 hours for the economics exam instead of 10 hours is two points on the organic chemistry exam.

b. The opportunity cost of studying 15 hours for the organic chemistry exam instead of 10 hours is ten points on the economics exam.

c. The opportunity cost of studying 20 hours for the economics exam instead of 10 hours is five points on the organic chemistry exam.

d. The opportunity cost of studying 20 hours for the organic chemistry exam instead of 10 hours is twenty points on the economics exam.

3. **a.** Joe will want to think about the benefits of eating another slice of cake (tastes good, delays the start of his studying, prolongs the amount of time he can spend with his friends) to the costs of eating another slice of cake (an additional hour of exercise to maintain a steady weight, a feeling of guilt, an unhealthy balance in his diet). If Joe decides that the costs associated with the additional slice of cake outweigh the benefits, he will decide not to eat the cake. But if he decides that the benefits outweigh the costs, he will eat the cake.

b. Since the community enacts the ordinance, it must be the case that the benefits from the new ordinance outweigh the costs; in other words, the community must anticipate that this ordinance will generate more than $500,000 worth of benefits to their community.

c. Susy must perceive that the benefits of doing the exercises each day are greater than the costs of doing them every day.

4. Longhealth's policy rewards people who not only sign up for the class but also participate in the class. If the goal is to alter people's lifestyle choices toward more exercise, then Longhealth's policy offers the better set of incentives. Although Healthlines subsidizes the exercise class, it does not provide any incentive to ensure that members actually attend and participate in the class.

5. The incentives Matt faces are quite clear: being late carries a major penalty, so Matt will try hard to make sure he gets home on time. This may lead Matt to drive faster than is optimal in order to avoid his family's wrath. Unfortunately, the set of incentives offered to Matt may get him home early on most nights, but it may also result in a tragic outcome if he is running late. Sarah, on the other hand, faces a set of incentives that encourages her growth by forecasting what she is going to do, taking responsibility for what she is doing, and recognizing that even a well-planned evening may run late. Sarah knows that she is responsible for getting in at the time she agreed to, but she also knows that if she is running late she need not speed to get home.

6. Without trade, Bill would have only tomatoes and corn to eat; by trading, Bill gets more variety in his diet. This argument is also true for Mary, who would have only wheat and onions to eat if she did not trade with Bill.

7. Without trade, both states would have less variety in the goods available to their residents. With trade, Wisconsin residents can enjoy Georgia peaches and peanuts and Georgia residents can enjoy Wisconsin cheese and corn.

8. a. This is not an equilibrium situation. If the coffee is equivalent and the waiting times the same, then people should go to Joe's for the less expensive cup of coffee. One would anticipate that over time the price at Mary's will fall and that the price at Joe's will rise until the two prices converge.

   b. This is not an equilibrium situation. If the hamburgers are equivalent, then people should go to the Big Bun for the less expensive hamburger. One would anticipate that over time the price of hamburgers at the two restaurants will converge at a single price.

9. a. This is not an efficient situation, since clearly the cafeteria is failing to provide the type of dessert that is preferred by the students. The cafeteria could make students better off by providing a larger amount of soft-serve ice cream and a smaller amount of cake or pie.

   b. If we assume that the air pollution seriously affects the quality of life in this community, then this is not an efficient situation. If the community drove less and rode the bus more, then the quality of life would be enhanced in the community and people would be better off. The community might be able to move toward this outcome by reducing the price of bus transportation dramatically and by instituting other types of charges for those who opt to travel by car.

   c. Yes, it would be efficient to implement this ordinance. It would even be possible to compensate the smokers for their loss of rights and still have the benefits from the ordinance exceed the costs of the ordinance.

10. The proposed policy moves the country toward a more efficient outcome, since a reduction in the length of time that unemployed people can collect benefits will encourage the unemployed to resume work and therefore result in fewer wasted resources. People may feel that this policy change is unfair, however, since historically the country has been willing to provide more generous support to the unemployed.

11. Because this policy covers all individuals within the designated group, it is equitable, but it is highly inefficient since it requires everyone to do the same thing regardless of their interests and abilities. To implement this policy also requires a large amount of resources that the government could use in alternative ways. For example, the government might want to provide job training in fields that would be beneficial to the economy but are not taught in a college curriculum (for example, carpentry, mechanical repair, drafting).

12. a. The government subsidizes bus ridership by providing free bus passes, which reduces the cost of riding the bus while increasing the cost of using a car. The government wishes to encourage people to use the bus system more and the private transportation system less.

b. The government provides a financial reward for altering your household's car usage. By reducing the number of cars in each household, the government hopes to reduce the number of miles driven and thus the emissions from automobiles.

c. The government's incentive here is a negative incentive. Guardians do not wish to serve time in jail, and their wish to avoid this outcome will result in their children going to school.

d. The college wants to reduce the risk of transmission of highly communicable diseases in the dormitories. It limits your ability to engage in student activities until you can provide proof that you are immunized.

13. In this case, the lighthouse will not be built through the contributions of individuals in the community. The market will fail to provide the lighthouse, but the government can intervene by imposing a tax for the construction of the lighthouse and then providing these funds to the community for the construction.

14. When people reduce their spending and purchase fewer goods and services, the level of income that other people in the economy earn is reduced since the purchases by one group of people represent income for another group of people. In a recession, the level of spending and the level of income fall in an economy.

15. With a fixed amount of resources in an economy during a given period, there is a limit to the amount of goods and services the economy can produce. If spending is greater than this economic capacity, then this puts pressure on the prices of goods and services to rise, leading to inflationary pressures. Too much spending in an economy results in inflation.

16. A recession implies that the level of spending in the economy is too low. The government can stimulate spending by decreasing the level of taxes, by increasing the level of government spending, or by having the central bank increase the money supply. When there is inflation in an economy, the government can slow down spending by increasing the level of taxes, by decreasing the level of government spending, or by having the central bank decrease the money supply. The textbook will discuss these issues in much greater detail in subsequent chapters.

Answers to Chapter Review Questions

1. **Answer c.** The opportunity cost of taking the job includes what must be given up. In this case, Camillo is giving up two weeks of vacation since the other job offers four weeks of vacation instead of two weeks. He is not giving up any salary when he selects the job paying $32,000.

2. **Answer c.** Ning's opportunity cost is measured by what she must give up when she chooses to do something else. In this case, when Ning decides to attend the lecture she is giving up a night of listening to music in her dorm room.

3. **Answer a.** The firm should purchase this equipment since the addition to revenue ($1,000 a month) is greater than the addition to cost ($750 a month).

4. **Answer b.** In making a decision about whether to run, swim, bike, or rest, Marie should compare the benefits she gets from additional exercise to the costs she incurs from this additional exercise. When she elects to rest, she perceives that the additional costs of the exercise exceed the additional benefits of the exercise.

5. **Answer b.** When resources are scarce, this implies that people and societies must make decisions about how to use those scarce resources since the scarcity of resources is a constraint on production and consumption.

6. **Answer a.** People must make decisions every day because they do not have an infinite amount of time, income, or resources that would allow them to do everything they might want to do.

7. **Answer c.** To get the university community to curtail their parking on campus by the greatest amount, the university should adopt a program that makes drivers aware of the cost of bringing a car on campus every time they drive on campus. Thus, charging an hourly parking fee is the best choice offered, since this fee will serve to remind drivers that bringing a car to campus will cost them something each time they drive on campus and park. In contrast, a single annual fee does not reward the purchaser for reducing the number of times they park on campus during the year; free parking indicates that parking on campus does not cost anything and will result in people parking on campus more often; and exempting the staff from parking fees eliminates incentives to get staff to think about alternatives to driving on campus and parking.

8. **Answer b.** When salespeople are awarded the base salary plus a commission, they are encouraged to be helpful to shoppers in the hope of boosting their sales figures. When offered a flat hourly rate, they have no incentive to provide helpful service beyond the minimum required by the store, since their compensation will not be affected by their extra effort.

9. **Answer d.** Individuals who elect to trade with each other do so because the trade is beneficial to them. As long as trade is a choice, then the decision to trade with each other must indicate that the trade is beneficial to both parties.

10. **Answer d.** Countries that elect to trade with each other do so because the trade is beneficial to them. As long as trade is a choice, then the decision to trade with each other must indicate that the trade is beneficial to both parties.

11. **Answer d.** All three of these responses describe equilibrium. They are true either by definition or by implication.

12. **Answer a.** Answers (c) and (d) are essentially the same answer, with answer (c) focusing on the individual while answer (d) focuses on the group: both are incorrect. That leaves answers (a) and (b): a situation is efficient when no one can be made better off through a different outcome. This implies that the maximum gains from trade are achieved when a situation is efficient, and this does not necessarily occur when price is as low as possible.

13. **Answer b.** Since college students do not use the library throughout the semester in the early morning hours, the college is not using its scarce resources efficiently when it elects to keep the library open all night. It would be more efficient to open the library all night only during those weeks when students would actually avail themselves of these hours.

14. **Answer a.** This policy treats everyone under 30 equally and so it is an equitable policy from that perspective. However, the policy is not efficient since it does not consider whether this is an efficient use of the resources involved.

15. **Answer a.** This policy is not equitable since it does not treat everyone under 30 equally: instead it discriminates on the basis of ethnicity.

16. **Answer b.** This is a definitional statement. Answer (a) is incorrect since there are times when government intervention is helpful (for example, regulation of certain industries or laws restricting pollution); answer (c) is incorrect since government intervention may be called for when there are side payments that the market does not account for; and answer (d) is incorrect since there are occasions when government intervention can improve the efficiency of the market.

17. **Answer c.** This is true by definition. If spending is reduced by one group in an economy, then some other individuals in the economy will not receive as much income as they initially did due to this reduction in the other group's spending.

18. **Answer b.** This is true by definition. An increase in spending in an economy indicates that some people in that economy will receive that additional spending and, hence, their incomes will rise.

19. **Answer b.** When spending increases at a faster pace than the production of goods and services, then this leads to upward pressure on the prices of those goods and services. Hence, this spending will lead to inflation.

20. **Answer a.** If the government decreases taxes, this tax decrease results in people having higher net incomes and, therefore, more income available to spend. This leads to greater spending. In contrast, if the government decreases government spending, there is less spending in the economy.

chapter 2

Economic Models: Trade-offs and Trade

Summary

This chapter introduces the concept of model building and then discusses two different economic models, the model of production possibility frontiers and the model of comparative advantage. Models are a simplified representation of reality, and the study of economic models will be a crucial aspect of your study of economics. The two models presented in this chapter provide a simplified framework for discussing the concept of opportunity cost, trade-offs, scarcity, efficiency, and gains from trade. This chapter uses the production possibility frontier model to discuss comparative advantage and the gains that are possible through trade. The chapter also presents the circular flow diagram as a way to describe a simple economy and, in addition, discusses the distinction between positive and normative economics.

Chapter Objectives

Objective #1. A model is a simplified representation of reality that is used to better understand real-life situations. Underlying every model is a set of assumptions.

Objective #2. The production possibility frontier is a model that represents the production possibilities available to an individual or to an economy. The production possibility frontier model assumes that the individual (or country) has a set amount of resources, a set level of technology, and a set amount of time, and then the production possibility frontier delineates a set of points that indicate the maximum amount of two goods that can be produced by this individual (or country) given their resources, technology, and available time. For simplicity, this Study Guide refers to production possibility frontiers in terms of production by countries rather than individuals, but the arguments made from the perspective of countries also hold for individuals. Figure 2.1 illustrates a linear production possibility frontier for a country, where the frontier indicates the maximum amount of goods X and Y that can be produced from the available resources and technology. Points *A* and *B* are points that lie on the production possibility frontier and are feasible production points for this country. Points *C* and *D* are points that lie inside the production possibility frontier: this country can produce these points—they are feasible—but the country is not using its available resources fully. Points *C* and *D* are therefore feasible points, but not efficient points. Points *E* and *F* lie outside the production possibility frontier and are therefore not feasible points of production for this country.

Figure 2.1

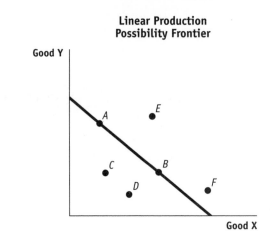

Linear Production
Possibility Frontier

Objective #3. The simplest version of this production possibility frontier model assumes that the frontier is linear and thus has a constant slope. This implies that the opportunity cost of producing another unit of the good measured on the *x*-axis stays the same as you move along the production possibility frontier. In Figure 2.2, the opportunity cost of moving from point *A* to point *B* and the opportunity cost of moving from point *C* to point *D* are illustrated. Remember that opportunity cost measures what you give up to get something: thus, when moving from point *A* to point *B*, opportunity cost is measured in terms of good Y, the good you give up to get more of good X; whereas, when moving from point *C* to point *D*, opportunity cost is measured in terms of good X, the good you give up to get more of good Y. The lines that are bold in Figure 2.2 indicate the opportunity cost of moving from point *A* to point *B* or from point *C* to point *D*.

Figure 2.2

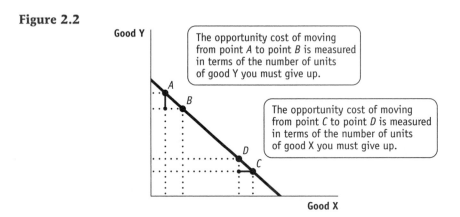

Objective #4. A more realistic production possibility frontier is one that is bowed out from the origin: this implies that as the country produces more and more of one of the goods, the opportunity cost of producing this good increases. The production possibility frontier has this shape due to specialization of resources: some of the resources available to the country are more suited to produce good X than they are good Y. When the country decides to increase the production of one type of good, the first few units can be produced at relatively low opportunity cost, since resources can be shifted from the production of one good to the production of the other good that are not particularly well suited to the production of the first good. However, the opportunity cost eventually will rise since the increased production of this good eventually will require the use of resources that are ill-suited to produce this good. Figure 2.3 illustrates a bowed-out production possibility frontier and the opportunity cost of getting one more unit of the good measured on the *x*-axis. Notice that as we get more and more units of good X, the opportunity cost of each additional unit of X is larger than the opportunity cost of the preceding unit.

Figure 2.3

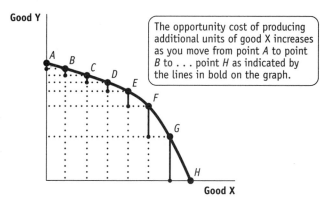

Objective #5. There are two types of efficiency to discuss with respect to production possibility frontiers: productive efficiency and allocative efficiency. Productive efficiency refers to producing at a point that lies on the production possibility frontier. Points that lie inside the frontier are inefficient, since it is possible to increase the level of production from the given set of resources. Allocative efficiency refers to producing the right mix of goods from the available resources. For an economy to be allocatively efficient, it must allocate its resources in such a way as to make consumers as well off as possible. Another way of saying this is that an allocatively efficient economy produces the mix of goods that people want.

Objective #6. For an economy to be efficient, it must achieve productive and allocative efficiency: it must not waste resources and it must produce the right mix of goods.

Objective #7. The production possibility frontier illustrates scarcity in that there are points of production that cannot be produced because the level of resources and/or technology constrain production. The production possibility frontier illustrates trade-offs: getting more of good X requires giving up some of good Y.

Objective #8. Economic growth can be illustrated with the production possibility frontier model. When the frontier shifts away from the origin, this means that the represented economy can now produce more of good X and good Y. The production possibility frontier shifts out when there are increases in resources or increases in the available level of technology.

Objective #9. The model of production possibility frontiers can also be used to illustrate the gains from trade, which is referred to as the model of comparative advantage. This model assumes that there are two countries, that there are two goods that the countries produce, and that each country has a set amount of resources, technology, and time available to them. Furthermore, this model assumes that the two countries have different opportunity costs of production. In this model, countries benefit from specializing in the production of that good for which they have the comparative advantage, or lower opportunity cost of production, and then trade with each other. Countries do not have to have absolute advantage in production to benefit from trade: the benefits from trade only require that countries have different opportunity costs of production for the two goods and that each country specialize in producing the good that it can produce at lower opportunity cost relative to the other country.

Objective #10. The simple circular flow diagram of the economy can be used to describe the relationship between firms and households. In this simple circular-flow diagram, households provide factors of production to firms, while firms provide goods and services to households.

Objective #11. Positive economics is factual and descriptive, whereas normative economics is about what ought to be or what should be. Positive economics is objective and can be tested for accuracy, and it often involves forecasting. Normative economics is subjective and prescriptive, and it is value based. However, it is possible to rank normative policies designed to achieve a certain prescription on the basis of the efficiency of each policy.

Objective #12. Economists may come to different conclusions because they have different values or because they use different economic models.

Key Terms

model a simplified representation of a real situation that is used to better understand real-life situations.

other things equal assumption in the development of a model, the assumption that all relevant factors except the one under study remain unchanged.

production possibility frontier illustrates the trade-offs facing an economy that produces only two goods. It shows the maximum quantity of one good that can be produced for any given quantity produced of the other.

factors of production the *resources* used to produce goods and services. Labor and capital are examples of factors.

technology the technical means for producing goods and services.

comparative advantage the advantage conferred on an individual or nation in producing a good or service if the *opportunity cost* of producing the good or service is lower for that individual or nation than for other producers.

absolute advantage the advantage conferred on an individual or nation has in producing a good or service if the individual or nation is better at producing it than other producers.

barter people directly exchange goods or services that they have for goods or services that they want.

circular-flow diagram represents the transactions in an *economy* by two kinds of flows around a circle: flows of physical things such as goods or labor in one direction and flows of money to pay for these physical things in the opposite direction.

household a person or a group of people that share their income.

firm an organization that produces goods and services for sale.

markets for goods and services markets in which *firms* sell goods and services that they produce to *households*.

factor markets markets in which *firms* buy the *resources* they need to produce goods and services.

Notes

Key Terms *(continued)*

income distribution the way in which total income is divided among the owners of the various factors of production.

positive economics the branch of economic analysis that describes the way the *economy* actually works.

normative economics the branch of economic analysis that makes prescriptions about the way the *economy* should work.

forecast a simple prediction of the future.

variable a quantity that can take on more than one value.

horizontal axis the horizontal number line of a graph along which values of the *x*-variable are measured; also referred to as the *x-axis*.

x-axis the horizontal number line of a graph along which values of the *x*-variable are measured; also referred to as the *horizontal axis*.

vertical axis the vertical number line of a graph along which values of the *y*-variable are measured; also referred to as the *y-axis*.

y-axis the vertical number line of a graph along which values of the *y*-variable are measured; also referred to as the *vertical axis*.

origin the point where the axes of a two-variable graph meet.

causal relationship the relationship between two variables in which the value taken by one variable directly influences or determines the value taken by the other variable.

independent variable the determining variable in a causal relationship.

dependent variable the determined variable in a causal relationship.

curve a line on a graph, which may be curved or straight, that depicts a relationship between two variables.

linear relationship the relationship between two variables in which the *slope* is constant and therefore is depicted on a graph by a *curve* that is a straight line.

nonlinear relationship the relationship between two variables in which the *slope* is not constant and therefore is depicted on a graph by a *curve* that is not a straight line.

positive relationship a relationship between two variables in which an increase in the value of one variable is associated with an increase in the value of the other variable. It is illustrated by a *curve* that slopes upward from left to right.

negative relationship a relationship between two variables in which an increase in the value of one variable is associated with a decrease in the value of the other variable. It is illustrated by a *curve* that slopes downward from left to right.

horizontal intercept the point at which a *curve* hits the *horizontal axis*; it indicates the value of the *x*-variable when the value of the *y*-variable is zero.

Key Terms *(continued)*

vertical intercept the point at which a *curve* hits the *vertical axis;* it shows the value of the *y*-variable when the value of the *x*-variable is zero.

slope a measure of how steep a line or curve is. The slope of a line is measured by "rise over run"—the change in the *y*-variable between two points on the line divided by the change in the *x*-variable between those same two points.

nonlinear curve a curve in which the *slope* is not the same between every pair of points.

absolute value the value of a number without regard to a plus or minus sign.

tangent line a straight line that just touches a *nonlinear curve* at a particular point; the *slope* of the tangent line is equal to the slope of the nonlinear curve at that point.

maximum the highest point on a *nonlinear curve,* where the *slope* changes from positive to negative.

minimum the lowest point on a *nonlinear curve,* where the *slope* changes from negative to positive.

time-series graph a two-variable graph that has dates on the *horizontal axis* and values of a variable that occurred on those dates on the *vertical axis*.

scatter diagram a graph that shows points that correspond to actual observations of the *x*- and *y*-variables; a *curve* is usually fitted to the scatter of points to indicate the trend in the data.

pie chart a circular graph that shows how some total is divided among its components, usually expressed in percentages.

bar graph a graph that uses bars of varying height or length to show the comparative sizes of different observations of a variable.

truncated cut; in a truncated axis, some of the range of values are omitted, usually to save space.

omitted variable an unobserved *variable* that, through its influence on other variables, creates the erroneous appearance of a direct *causal relationship* among those variables.

reverse causality the error committed when the true direction of causality between two *variables* is reversed, and the *independent variable* and the *dependent variable* are incorrectly identified.

Notes

![] AFTER YOU READ THE CHAPTER

Tips

Tip #1. This chapter introduces the concept of models. This is a crucial concept that forms the basis of the majority of material you will study in the rest of the course. In working with models, it is important to understand the simplifying assumptions underlying whatever model you are using.

Tip #2. Many of the models you will encounter in this course make the other things equal assumption, which means that the model considers only one change at a time while holding everything else constant. Make sure you understand this basic assumption before working with the models introduced in the chapter.

Tip #3. Economic models can be described verbally, but they can also be represented by graphs or equations. You will want to be comfortable working with all three types of representations. The appendix to Chapter 2 provides an introduction to graphs in economics.

Tip #4. Throughout the course you will find it helpful to be able to sketch graphs to illustrate the ideas you are analyzing. You should practice making precise, numerically significant graphs, but you also should practice less formal graphs that sketch the nature of the relationship rather than the precise mathematical relationship.

Tip #5. Opportunity cost can be measured using the production possibility frontier model. To do this calculation, pick a point on the production possibility frontier and identify how much of each good is being produced. Then pick a second point on the production possibility frontier and identify the new levels of production. The opportunity cost is measured as the number of units of the good you must give up to get more of the other good. Note that both points must be on the production possibility frontier. Figure 2.4 illustrates the measurement of opportunity cost when moving from point A to point B. In this example, the opportunity cost is measured as the amount of good Y, $Y_1 - Y_2$, that must be given up to increase the production of good X from its initial value of X_1 to the new level X_2. The bold line indicates the amount of good Y that is given up to increase the production of good X from X_1 to X_2.

Figure 2.4

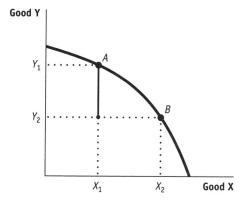

Tip #6. You should practice working with the models and with specific techniques introduced with each model. For instance, you should be comfortable calculating opportunity cost using the production possibility frontier model. You also should be comfortable comparing the opportunity cost of production for two countries and deciding which good each country should specialize in producing.

Tip #7. If you are using flash cards, make sure you include the following cards: (a) a linear production possibility frontier indicating feasible and infeasible points as well as efficient and inefficient points, (b) a production possibility frontier bowed out from the origin showing these same concepts, and (c) an example of comparative advantage that illustrates two countries and then calculates each country's comparative advantage. Also, don't forget to include a card for each new vocabulary word as well as the chapter heading on each card.

Tip #8. Calculating opportunity cost in a problem is often challenging for students initially. Let's explore a fail-safe method for this calculation based on a linear production possibility frontier (this is the type of production possibility frontier that we will use in the comparative advantage model). First, construct the production possibility frontier and, since it is linear, calculate the slope of the frontier. Then use this slope measure to generate the opportunity costs you want: the opportunity cost of producing one more unit of the good measured on the *x*-axis is given by the slope, since the slope tells us the change in the *y*-variable divided by the change in the *x*-variable. Thus, if the slope of the production possibility frontier is –2, then the opportunity cost of producing an additional unit of good X is 2 units of good Y. To find the opportunity cost of the good produced on the *y*-axis, we simply need to use the reciprocal of the slope. Thus, if the slope of the linear production possibility frontier is –2, then the opportunity cost of producing one more unit of good Y is ½ unit of good X, since this is the amount of good X we must give up to get one more unit of good Y. The problems in this chapter will give you a chance to practice this reasoning and this technique.

Tip #9. Once you can calculate the opportunity cost of producing good X or good Y, then you can compare the opportunity costs faced by two countries. The model of comparative advantage illustrates that countries will benefit from trade when they specialize and produce the good that has the lowest opportunity cost of production relative to the other country.

Tip #10 [From Appendix]: It will be important for you to be comfortable graphing the relationship between two variables. If any of the material in the Appendix is new or challenging to you, make sure to work on mastering it, since your performance in the course will depend on your ability to use these mathematical tools.

Tip #11 [From Appendix]: Practice plotting linear equations with two variables in a graph: make sure you can calculate the slope of a straight line drawn on a graph and that you understand why the slope of a curved line is not constant.

Tip #12 [From Appendix]: The Appendix provides examples of several different ways to graph numerical data: make sure to familiarize yourself with time-series graphs, scatter diagrams, pie charts, and bar graphs. If you find the information presented in these graphs difficult to interpret, ask your instructor for help. Your ability to handle mathematical representations in this course is important: make sure you understand fully the material presented in the Appendix and, if you do not understand it, seek assistance.

WORKED PROBLEMS

1. People often face trade-offs about the use of their resources. In this problem, Joe can produce either bicycles or sweaters. The following points lie on Joe's production possibility frontier and represent points where Joe is maximizing his production of the two goods based on his available resources, technology, and time. Assume that Joe's production possibility frontier for these two goods is linear.

Production point	Bicycles per year	Sweaters per year
A	160	20
B	120	40
C	60	70
D	40	80

a. Draw a graph of Joe's production possibility frontier. In your graph measure bicycles on the *y*-axis and sweaters on the *x*-axis.

STEP 1: Draw a graph of Joe's production possibility frontier using the given points in the table. The following figure provides a graph of Joe's production possibility frontier based on the points given in the provided table.

Review the section "Models in Economics: Some Important Examples" on pages 26–40, the section "Trade-offs: The Production Possibility Frontier" on pages 27–32 (along with Figure 2-1 on page 28), and "Chapter 2 Appendix: How Graphs Work" on pages 51–54.

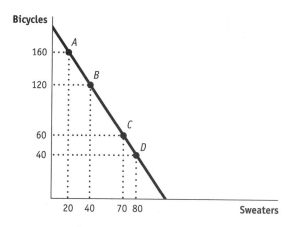

b. Write an equation for Joe's production possibility frontier.

STEP 2: Use the slope-intercept form to write an equation for Joe's production possibility frontier. The slope-intercept form is given as *y = mx + b,* where *y* is the variable measured on the vertical axis (in this case bicycles, *B*), *x* is the variable measured on the horizontal axis (in this case sweaters, *S*), *m* is the slope of the equation, and *b* is the *y*-intercept.

Review "Chapter 2 Appendix: Graphs in Economics" on pages 51–68.

To write the equation for Joe's production possibility frontier, you will need to know the slope of the frontier as well as the *y*-intercept for the frontier. Since the frontier is linear, the slope will be constant and equal to the change in the bicycles divided by the change in sweaters. Thus, moving from point A to point B, the slope is equal to $(160 - 120)/(20 - 40) = -2$. To find the y-intercept, you can use the general formula for a linear equation, $y = mx + b$, and substitute in the slope measure you just computed for m, and replace the y and x with B and S (where B is the number of bicycles and S is the number of sweaters). Thus, $y = mx + b$ is now $B = -2S + b$. To find the y-intercept, b, you need to replace (S,B) with values that you know are on the line. For example, you know that point A is on the line and that point A consists of 20 sweaters and 160 bicycles. Thus, $B = -2S + b$ can be written as $160 = -2(20) + b$. Solving for b, you will find that $b = 200$. You can use any of the points you are given in the table to find this y-intercept: the only requirement is that the point must lie on the production possibility frontier. The following figure illustrates Joe's production possibility frontier while identifying both the y-intercept and the x-intercept (to find the x-intercept, use the basic formula $B = -2S + 200$ and substitute $B = 0$ into this equation: thus, $S = 100$).

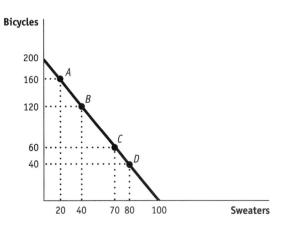

c. Consider each of the following production points and determine whether the production point is (1) feasible and efficient; (2) feasible and inefficient; or (3) infeasible (that is, the point lies beyond the production possibility frontier). (Hint: You may find the equation you wrote in part (b) helpful in determining the attributes of these production points.)

   i. 30 sweaters and 150 bicycles

   ii. 15 sweaters and 170 bicycles

   iii. 90 sweaters and 15 bicycles

   iv. 75 sweaters and 55 bicycles

STEP 3: Using the equation for Joe's production possibility frontier you found in part (b), check each of the previously mentioned points to see if they lie on his production possibility frontier, lie beyond his production possibility frontier, or lie inside his production possibility frontier.

Review the section "Trade-offs: The Production Possibility Frontier" on pages 27–32 and the section "Efficiency" on pages 29–30.

    i. This point is infeasible. To see this, use the equation you found in part (b) and plug in the value for S. Thus, $B = -2S + 200$ and you are told that sweater production is 30. So, $B = -2(30) + 200 = 140$. The maximum number of bicycles that can be produced when 30 sweaters are produced is 140 and not 150. The point (30, 150) lies beyond Joe's production possibility frontier and therefore is not feasible.

    ii. This point is feasible and efficient. To see this, use the equation from part (b) and this point. Thus, $B = -2(15) + 200 = 170$. The point (15, 170) lies on Joe's production possibility frontier: it is both feasible and efficient.

    iii. This point is feasible but inefficient. To see this, use the equation from part (b) and this point. Thus, $B = -2(90) + 200 = 20$. The point (90, 15) lies inside Joe's production possibility frontier since the point (90, 20) lies on his frontier. This point is therefore feasible but inefficient.

    iv. This point is infeasible. To see this, use the equation from part (b) and this point. Thus, $B = -2(75) + 200 = 50$. The point (75, 55) lies outside Joe's production possibility frontier since the point (75, 50) lies on his frontier. This point is therefore not feasible.

  d. Suppose that Joe experiences an improvement in his sweater-making technology so that he can now produce twice as many sweaters as he could initially. Assume that his ability to produce bicycles has not changed. Draw this new production possibility frontier for Joe and then write an equation for this new production possibility frontier.

STEP 4: **Draw Joe's new production possibility frontier and compare it to his original production possibility frontier.**

Review the section "Economic Growth" on pages 31–32 and Figure 2-3 on page 31.

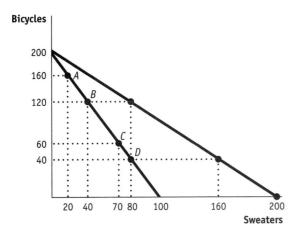

The equation for this new production possibility frontier is $B = -S + 200$.

2. The following graph depicts Susie's production possibility frontier for producing widgets and gadgets. In this problem assume that Susie is initially producing only widgets and no gadgets.

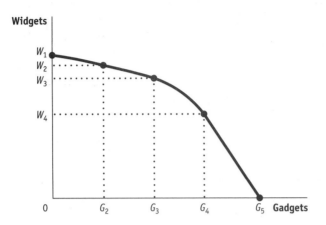

Use this graph to evaluate Susie's opportunity cost of moving from one point of her production possibility frontier to another point on it.

    a. What is Susie's opportunity cost of producing G_2 units of gadgets if she is currently producing zero gadgets?

STEP 1: For questions (a), (b), and (c), refer to the previous graph and measure Susie's opportunity cost by what she must give up when moving from one point on her production possibility frontier to another point on it.

Review the section "Opportunity Cost" on pages 30–31 and Figure 2-2 on page 30.

The opportunity cost of producing G_2 units of gadgets is the number of widgets that must be given up. Initially, Susie is producing W_1 widgets and 0 gadgets. When Susie moves along her production possibility frontier to produce G_2 units of gadgets, she finds that she must decrease her widget production to W_2. The opportunity cost of this gadget production is therefore equal to $(W_1 - W_2)$ units of widgets.

    b. Suppose that Susie is now producing G_2 units of gadgets and that she is producing at a point on her production possibility frontier. What is the opportunity cost of producing G_3 units of gadgets?

The opportunity cost of producing G_3 units of gadgets is the number of widgets that must be given up. Using the same logic as in the answer to part (a), this opportunity cost can be calculated as the distance $(W_2 - W_3)$ since this distance measures the number of widgets that Susie must give up in order to increase her gadget production from G_2 units to G_3 units.

    c. Suppose that Susie is now producing G_3 units of gadgets and that she is producing at a point on her production possibility frontier. What is the opportunity cost of producing G_4 units of gadgets?

The opportunity cost of producing G_4 units of gadgets is the number of widgets that must be given up. Using the same logic as in the answer to part (a), this opportunity cost can be calculated as the distance $(W_3 - W_4)$ since this distance measures the number of widgets that Susie must give up in order to increase her gadget production from G_3 to G_4 units.

d. What happens to Susie's opportunity cost of producing gadgets as she decides to produce increasing amounts of gadgets? Provide a verbal explanation and then use the preceding graph to illustrate what happens to Susie's opportunity cost as she produces more and more gadgets.

STEP 2: Refer to the graph and use it to see what happens to Susie's opportunity cost as she increases her production of gadgets by one unit at a time, starting with zero units of gadgets. Remember that her opportunity cost of producing a gadget is measured by the number of widgets she must give up.

Review the section "Opportunity Cost" on pages 30–31 and Figure 2-2 on page 30.

As Susie produces more and more gadgets, her opportunity cost increases. Since her production possibility frontier is bowed outward from the origin, this indicates that Susie's available resources are specialized, with some of those resources being more suited to widget production while others are more suited to gadget production. This idea of increasing opportunity cost is illustrated on the following graph.

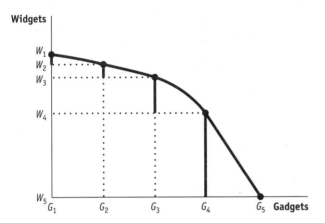

Notice that the bold vertical lines get longer and longer as we move from 0 units of gadgets to a larger level of gadget production (e.g., G_4). The length of the bold vertical lines measures the opportunity cost of that level of gadget production: for example, the opportunity cost of moving from 0 units of gadgets to G_2 units of gadgets is given by the vertical distance ($W_1 - W_2$).

e. Suppose that Susie had initially produced only gadgets and no widgets. Does the opportunity cost of producing widgets increase as Susie increases her widget production by one unit at a time, from 0 units of widgets to W_1 units of widgets? Use a graph to illustrate your answer.

STEP 3: Now, you want to use the graph to think about moving from the point that corresponds to G_5 units of gadgets and 0 units of widgets to the point that corresponds to 0 units of gadgets and W_1 units of widgets. As you move upward along the curve increasing widget production by one unit at a time, remember that the opportunity cost of this increased widget production will be measured by the number of gadgets that must be given up.

Review the section "Opportunity Cost" on pages 30–31 and Figure 2-2 on page 30.

The law of increasing opportunity cost holds if Susie moves from producing only gadgets to producing a mix of gadgets and widgets. The following graph illustrates this idea by considering changing the production of widgets by one unit at a time. Notice that in this case the opportunity cost is measured as a horizontal distance, since increasing widget production implies giving up gadget production: thus, the opportunity cost of producing widgets is measured by the number of gadgets that must be given up.

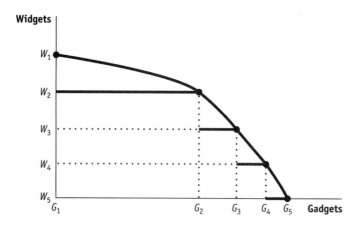

3. The following provides a numerical example of how trade is advantageous to two countries that decide to trade with each other. Suppose there are two countries, Arcadia and Supreme, that produce bricks and windows. Arcadia and Supreme use only labor to produce these two goods, and each country has 200 units of available labor. The following table provides information about the number of hours of labor needed in each country to produce one unit of bricks or one unit of windows.

	Hours of labor to produce one brick	Hours of labor to produce one window
Arcadia	2 hours of labor	4 hours of labor
Supreme	5 hours of labor	2 hours of labor

Use the table's information to draw production possibility frontiers for Arcadia and for Supreme. In your graph, measure bricks on the *x*-axis and windows on the *y*-axis. Then use your graph to find each country's opportunity cost of producing one brick. Identify each country's comparative advantage. Finally, calculate a range of prices for one brick in terms of windows.

STEP 1: Draw and label the production possibility frontiers for Arcadia and Supreme.

Review the section "Trade-offs: The Production Possibility Frontier" on pages 27–32 and Figure 2-1 on page 28.

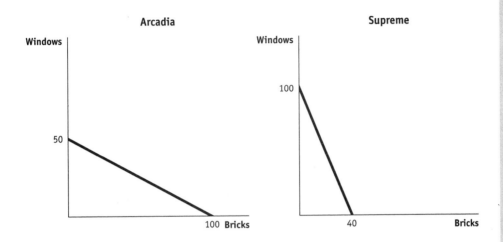

STEP 2: Find each country's opportunity cost of producing one brick, as measured by the number of windows that must be given up when the country produces one additional brick.

Review the section "Trade-offs: The Production Possibility Frontier" on pages 27–32 (along with Figure 2-1 on page 28) and the section "Opportunity Cost" on pages 30–31.

The opportunity cost of producing one brick for Arcadia is ½ of a window. To see this, remember that the slope of the production possibility frontier tells you how many units of the good on the *y*-axis must be given up in order to get one more unit of the good on the *x*-axis. Since the slope of Arcadia's production possibility frontier is equal to –1/2, we know that the opportunity cost of one more brick is equal to ½ of a window. The opportunity cost of producing one brick for Supreme is 2.5 windows.

STEP 3: Identify each country's comparative advantage by comparing its opportunity cost of production for each good: a country has the comparative advantage in producing the good when its opportunity cost of producing the good is lower than the other country's opportunity cost of producing the good.

Review the section "Comparative Advantage and Gains from Trade" on pages 33–36, Figure 2-5 on page 35, and Table 2-2 on page 34.

Arcadia has the comparative advantage in producing bricks, since Arcadia can produce an additional brick at lower opportunity cost than can Supreme. One additional brick costs Arcadia ½ of a window, while it costs Supreme 2.5 windows: Arcadia can produce bricks at lower opportunity cost and therefore has a comparative advantage in brick production.

STEP 4: Find the range of prices for one brick in terms of windows.

Review the section "Comparative Advantage and Gains from Trade" on pages 33–36, Figure 2-5 on page 35, and Tables 2-1 and 2-2 on page 34.

Arcadia is willing to produce bricks for any price equal to or greater than ½ of a window. Supreme is willing to purchase one brick for any price equal to or less than 2.5 windows. The range of prices for one brick will therefore fall between ½ of a window and 2.5 windows.

4. All countries face scarcity of resources and must therefore make tough decisions about what they should produce. Consider the following example about the allocation of resources toward health care. Suppose that a kidney transplant costs $50,000, while immunizations against major childhood diseases cost $500 per child. Assume that a country has a total of $10 million available for these two programs and that there is no issue with regard to procuring the necessary kidneys for transplants. Use the provided information to construct the country's production possibility frontier, placing childhood immunizations on the horizontal axis and kidney transplants on the vertical axis. Use your graph to measure the opportunity cost of producing an additional kidney transplant as well as the opportunity cost of producing an additional childhood immunization. Use this example to discuss the trade-offs that an economy faces with regard to the production of these two goods.

STEP 1: Use the given information to construct a production possibility frontier for these two goods. Then use this figure to measure the opportunity cost of producing an additional unit of either good.

Review the section "Trade-offs: The Production Possibility Frontier" on pages 27–32 and Figure 2-1 on page 28.

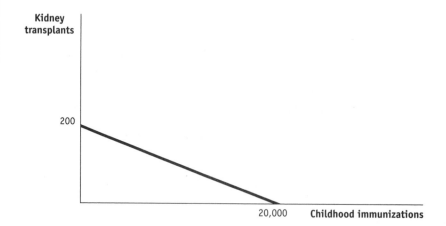

The opportunity cost of a kidney transplant is 100 immunizations. The opportunity cost of an immunization is (1/100) of a kidney transplant.

STEP 2: Use this example to discuss the trade-offs an economy faces with regard to the production of these two goods.

Review the section "Efficiency" on pages 29–30 and the section "Opportunity Cost" on pages 30–31.

If a country is faced with a limited amount of resources, it cannot produce an unlimited amount of goods and services. In this example, the country has only so many financial resources available for the production of kidney transplants and immunizations: the country will have to decide how to allocate these scarce resources, and in allocating these scarce resources it will face a trade-off in which the decision to produce more kidney transplants implies a decision to provide fewer immunizations and vice-versa.

5. In your study of economics, it is helpful to practice certain mathematical techniques. With this example, practice the mathematics reviewed in the Appendix to Chapter 2. Use the production possibility frontier you constructed in problem 4 to determine whether the following production combinations are feasible and efficient (that is, the point lies on the production possibility frontier), are feasible and inefficient (that is, the combination lies inside the production possibility frontier), or are not feasible (that is, the combination lies beyond the production possibility frontier).
    a. 400 immunizations and 190 kidney transplants
    b. 10,000 immunizations and 100 kidney transplants
    c. 1,800 immunizations and 182 kidney transplants
    d. 3,200 immunizations and 170 kidney transplants

STEP 1: **Write a mathematical equation expressing the relationship between kidney transplants (K) and childhood immunizations (I). Use this equation to evaluate each of the preceding combinations.**

Review the section "Trade-offs: The Production Possibility Frontier" on pages 27–32, the section "Two-Variable Graphs" on pages 51–53, and the section "Curves on a Graph" on pages 53–54 of Chapter 2 Appendix.

The equation for the linear production possibility frontier you found in problem 4 is $K = 200 - (1/100)I$, where K is kidney transplants and I is immunizations.
    a. You can then substitute the immunization value into the formula to calculate the maximum number of kidney transplants that are possible given this level of immunizations. Thus, $K = 200 - (1/100)(400)$, or $K = 196$. The combination of 400 immunizations and 190 kidney transplants must be feasible but inefficient, since it is possible to produce 400 immunizations and 196 kidney transplants.
    b. Use the same technique: when this economy produces 10,000 immunizations, it can produce a maximum of 100 kidney transplants. This combination is feasible and efficient.
    c. Use the same technique: when this economy produces 1,800 immunizations, it can produce a maximum of 182 kidney transplants. This combination is feasible and efficient.
    d. Use the same technique: when this economy produces 3,200 immunizations, it can produce a maximum of 168 kidney transplants. The combination of 3,200 immunizations and 170 kidney transplants is not feasible.

6. Let's continue practicing the interpretation of the numerical relationship depicted in a production possibility frontier. Using the production possibility frontier you constructed in problem 4, determine the maximum number of kidney transplants this country can produce this year given the following levels of childhood immunizations.
    a. 3,000 immunizations
    b. 4,500 immunizations
    c. 6,800 immunizations
    d. 18,000 immunizations

STEP 1: Use the mathematical equation expressing the relationship between kidney transplants (*K*) and childhood immunizations (*I*) that you wrote in problem (5). Use this equation to evaluate the maximum number of kidney transplants this economy can produce when it produces a given level of childhood immunizations.

Review the section on "Trade-offs: The Production Possibility Frontier" on pages 27–32, the section "Two-Variable Graphs" on pages 51–53, and the section "Curves on a Graph" on pages 53–54 of Chapter 2 Appendix.

The equation for the linear production possibility frontier you found in problem (4) is $K = 200 - (1/100)I$, where *K* is kidney transplants and *I* is immunizations.

a. Substitute the immunization value into the formula to calculate the maximum number of kidney transplants that are possible given this level of immunizations. Thus, $K = 200 - (1/100)(3,000) = 170$ kidney transplants.

b. Use the same technique to determine the maximum number of kidney transplants this country can produce when it produces 4,500 immunizations: the maximum number of kidney transplants it can produce is 155.

c. Use the same technique to determine the maximum number of kidney transplants this country can produce when it produces 6,800 immunizations: the maximum number of kidney transplants it can produce is 132.

d. Use the same technique to determine the maximum number of kidney transplants this country can produce when it produces 18,000 immunizations: the maximum number of kidney transplants it can produce is 20.

Problems and Exercises

1. Suppose that you wish to travel from your college campus to a nearby community. You go online to download a map to guide you on your trip. How is this map an example of a model? How does it simplify reality? How do you evaluate whether or not your map helps you better understand the world?

2. The production possibilities frontier model holds resources, technology, and the time period constant in order to construct a path of points that represents the maximum amount of two goods an economy can produce, given the constraints of their resources and technology during the given time period. This model allows us to consider the effect of an increase in resources while holding everything else constant. In this example, what is it that we are holding constant? Describe the effect of this change in resources on this economy's production possibility frontier.

3. Suppose you are stranded on an island by yourself and must therefore produce all the goods you consume. You consume clams and mangos exclusively. If you devote all your available time to harvesting clams, you can harvest 100 clams in a week. If you devote all your available time to collecting mangos, you can find 200 mangos in a week.

   a. Imagine it is possible for you to divide your time between harvesting clams and collecting mangos and that you can even find fractional amounts of both goods. Draw a sketch of your production possibility frontier for a week, placing mangos on the x-axis and clams on the y-axis.

b. Now, sketch your production possibility frontier for a two-week period. Describe what happens to your production possibility frontier when you increase the amount of time available for production.

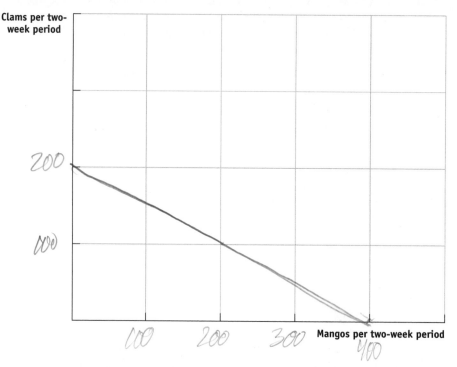

c. Now, imagine you invent a clam rake that enhances your ability to harvest clams. With this invention you are able to increase your clam harvest to a maximum of 200 clams a week if you spend all your time on clams. Your invention has no effect on your ability to collect mangos. Sketch your new production possibility frontier. Describe in words the effect of a change in technology that affects the ability to produce one of the goods, but not both of the goods.

d. Suppose you have your clam rake and, in addition, you procure knowledge over time that enhances your ability to collect mangos. Your ability to gather mangos increases to 300 mangos a week due to this knowledge. Sketch your new production possibility frontier based on this knowledge and your use of the clam rake. In effect you have experienced a change in technology that has a positive effect on the production of both goods. Describe in words the effect of this change on the production possibility frontier.

Clams per week

Mangos per week

4. Let's return to the example given in problem 3.

   a. What is the opportunity cost of harvesting a clam, given the original information in problem 3?

   b. What is the opportunity cost of collecting a mango, given the original information in problem 3?

   c. What is the slope of the production possibility frontier that you sketched in your answer to problem 3a? How does this slope measure relate to the answers you provide in parts (a) and (b) of this question?

   d. What happened to the slope of the production possibility frontier once you invent the clam rake (question 3c)? What happens to the opportunity cost of harvesting clams once you invent the clam rake? What happens to the opportunity cost of collecting mangos once you invent the clam rake?

5. The country of Orange manufactures sofas and lamps. With its available resources and technology, in a year Orange can manufacture 1,000 sofas and 0 lamps or 0 sofas and 250 lamps. It can also manufacture any combination of sofas and lamps that lie on the straight line connecting these two points.

a. Sketch Orange's production possibility frontier, placing sofas on the *y*-axis and lamps on the *x*-axis.

b. Fill in the following table by listing some of the feasible and efficient combinations of production available to Orange each year, given its resources and technology.

Combination	Number of lamps possible	Number of sofas possible
A	0	
B	50	
C		500
D		200
E	225	
F	250	

c. What is the slope of the production possibility frontier for Orange?

d. What is Orange's opportunity cost of producing one additional sofa?

e. What is Orange's opportunity cost of producing one additional lamp?

f. What is the value of the *y*-intercept for Orange? (Hint: In this example the *y*-intercept is the number of sofas Orange can produce if it does not produce anything else.)

g. Write an equation for the production possibility frontier for Orange, using *S* to stand for sofas and *L* to stand for lamps. Write this equation in *y*-intercept form. (Hint: This means that the equation will be written with *S* on the left-hand side of the equation, where the *S* stands for the value of the variable measured on the vertical axis of your sketch.) Verify that each of the combinations you found in part (b) of this problem are true in the equation you wrote.

6. The country of Utopia produces two goods from its available resources and technology. The only resource that Utopia has is labor. It takes 3 hours of labor to produce 2 widgets and 4 hours of labor to produce 1 gadget. For this question, assume that the production possibility frontier for Utopia is a straight line.

a. Sketch the production possibility frontier for the country of Utopia. (Hint: To do this you must first decide on a relevant time period. You might pick 120 hours, or 1,200 hours, or 1.2 million hours as your labor constraint, for example, and then you would sketch your production possibility frontier based on this amount of available time and labor.) Draw your production possibility frontier with widgets on the *y*-axis and gadgets on the *x*-axis.

Widgets

Gadgets

b. What is the slope of your production possibility frontier?

c. What is the opportunity cost of producing an additional widget in Utopia?

d. What is the opportunity cost of producing an additional gadget in Utopia?

7. The country of Jonesville produces two goods from its available resources and technology. The only resource that Jonesville has is labor. The following table gives the amount of labor necessary to produce a widget or a gadget. For this question assume that the production possibility frontier for Jonesville is a straight line.

	Number of hours of labor needed to produce a gadget	Number of hours of labor needed to produce a widget
Jonesville	2	5

a. Suppose that you want to draw a production possibility frontier for Jonesville. What must you do first to draw your sketch?

b. Sketch the production possibility frontier for Jonesville assuming that Jonesville has 120 hours of labor available. Place gadgets on the *x*-axis and widgets on the *y*-axis.

c. What is the slope of the production possibility frontier?

d. What is the opportunity cost of producing an additional gadget?

e. What is the opportunity cost of producing an additional widget?

f. Suppose that Jonesville has 240 hours of labor instead of 120 hours of labor. Does this affect the opportunity cost of producing widgets or gadgets? Explain your answer.

8. The following table provides six possible production combinations that Smithtown can produce from their available resources and technology during this year. Assume that Smithtown only produces bicycles and tents from their available resources.

Combination	Bicycles	Tents
A	100	0
B	90	10
C	70	25
D	40	36
E	10	42
F	0	44

a. Sketch Smithtown's production possibility frontier. Measure bicycles along the *x*-axis and tents along the *y*-axis.

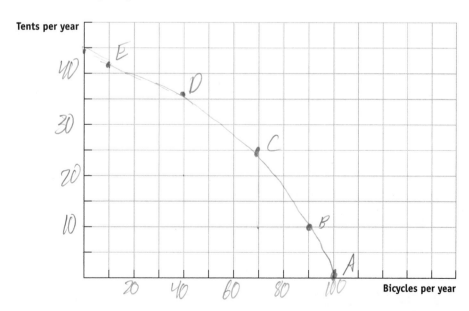

   b. Suppose Smithtown is currently producing at combination *C*. If Smithtown chooses to produce at combination *B*, what is the opportunity cost of moving from combination *C* to combination *B*?

   c. Suppose Smithtown is currently producing at combination *C*. If Smithtown chooses to produce at combination *D*, what is the opportunity cost of moving from combination *C* to combination *D*?

   d. Smithtown's production possibility frontier is not linear. Provide an explanation for why it is not linear.

9. Suppose an economy produces two goods in a year using its available resources and technology. This economy's resources are specialized.

   a. Describe the general shape of this economy's production possibility frontier.

   b. If this economy currently produces only one of these two goods, what do you know must be true about the opportunity cost of producing more and more units of the good that is not being currently produced?

   c. If this economy is to be productively efficient, what must be true about its production of these two goods?

   d. If this economy is to be allocatively efficient, what must be true about its production of these two goods?

e. Suppose this economy is deemed to be efficient. What must occur for this statement to be true?

10. Economists believe that specialization and trade are beneficial when they are based on comparative advantage. Briefly explain why economists believe this to be true.

11. There are two islands in the middle of the ocean and these two islands produce fish and baskets. Big Island can produce either 100 fish per day and 0 baskets per day or 0 fish per day and 200 baskets per day. Big Island can also produce any combination of fish and baskets that lies on its linear production possibility frontier. Small Island can produce either 80 fish per day and 0 baskets per day or 0 fish per day and 80 baskets per day. Like Big Island, Small Island has a linear production possibility frontier.

a. Sketch two graphs. Sketch Big Island's production possibility frontier on the first graph, and sketch Small Island's production possibility frontier on the second graph. Place fish/day on the y-axis and baskets/day on the x-axis.

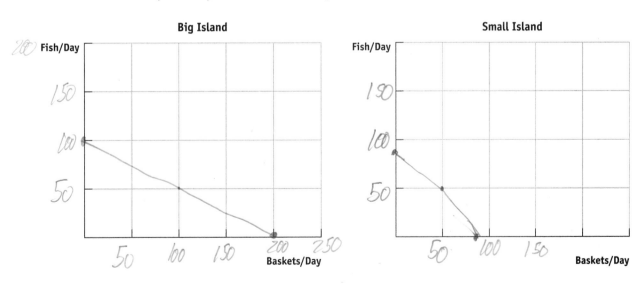

b. What is the slope of Big Island's production possibility frontier?

c. What is the slope of Small Island's production possibility frontier?

d. What is the opportunity cost of producing an additional basket on Big Island? What is the opportunity cost of producing an additional basket on Small Island? Which island can produce baskets at lower opportunity cost?

e. What is the opportunity cost of producing an additional fish on Big Island? What is the opportunity cost of producing an additional fish on Small Island? Which island can produce fish at lower opportunity cost?

f. What good should Big Island specialize in producing?

g. What good should Small Island specialize in producing?

12. There are two islands in the middle of the ocean, and these two islands produce fish and baskets. Big Island can produce either 100 fish per day and 0 baskets per day or 0 fish per day and 200 baskets per day. Big Island can also produce any combination of fish and baskets that includes these two combinations and lies on its linear production possibility frontier. Small Island can produce either 80 fish per day and 0 baskets per day or 0 fish per day and 80 baskets per day. Like Big Island, Small Island has a linear production possibility frontier. Currently there is no trade between the two islands. The current production for both islands is given in the following table.

Initial production	Fish	Baskets
Big Island	80	40
Small Island	30	50
Total production	110	90

a. Is Big Island producing at a productively efficient point? Explain your answer.

b. Is Small Island producing at a productively efficient point? Explain your answer.

Referring back to question 11, let's analyze what happens to total production if these islands decide to specialize and trade according to their comparative advantage.

c. Suppose that Big Island decides to produce 50 baskets instead of 40 baskets. How many fish will Big Island be able to produce if its basket production is increased to 50 baskets?

d. Suppose that Small Island decides to produce 40 fish instead of 30 fish. How many baskets will Small Island be able to produce if its fish production is increased to 40 fish?

e. Fill in the following table showing the new levels of production, given the information in parts (c) and (d).

New production	Fish	Baskets
Big Island		50
Small Island	40	
Total production		

f. Do specialization and trade benefit both islands in this example? Explain your answer.

Referring back to question 11, let's analyze what happens to total production if these islands decide to specialize and trade without regard to their comparative advantage.

g. Suppose that Big Island decides to produce 30 baskets instead of 40 baskets. How many fish will Big Island be able to produce if its basket production is decreased to 30 baskets?

h. Suppose that Small Island decides to produce 20 fish instead of 30 fish. How many baskets will Small Island be able to produce if its fish production is decreased to 20 fish?

i. Fill in the following table showing the new levels of production given the information in parts (g) and (h).

New production	Fish	Baskets
Big Island		30
Small Island	20	
Total production		

j. Do specialization and trade benefit both islands in this example? Explain your answer.

k. What must be true for specialization and trade to be beneficial? (Hint: Before you write your answer, think about the two examples in this problem and how they differ.)

13. Suppose that Jane and Bob live on an island far away from any other countries. Jane and Bob both produce widgets and gadgets from their available resources, but they do not currently trade with each other. The table that follows gives the number of hours of labor needed to produce one widget or one gadget for Bob and Jane. For this example, let's assume that Jane and Bob each have 120 hours of labor time.

	Hours of labor needed to produce a widget	Hours of labor needed to produce a gadget
Bob	2	4
Jane	3	1.5

a. Sketch two graphs: on the first graph draw Bob's production possibility frontier and on the second graph draw Jane's production possibility frontier. Place widgets on the *y*-axis and gadgets on the *x*-axis. Label both graphs carefully.

Bob's Production Possibility Frontier

Widgets

Gadgets

Jane's Production Possibility Frontier

Widgets

Gadgets

CHAPTER 2 ECONOMIC MODELS: TRADE-OFFS AND TRADE **53**

b. Suppose that Bob and Jane devote half of their labor time to producing gadgets and half to producing widgets. Fill in the following table based on this allocation of labor.

Initial production	Widgets	Gadgets
Bob		
Jane		
Total production		

c. What is Bob's opportunity cost of producing an additional gadget? What is Jane's opportunity cost of producing an additional gadget? Who can produce gadgets at lower opportunity cost?

d. What is Bob's opportunity cost of producing an additional widget? What is Jane's opportunity cost of producing an additional widget? Who can produce widgets at lower opportunity cost?

e. Bob and Jane decide to specialize and trade. What good should Bob specialize in producing?

f. Bob and Jane decide to specialize and trade. What good should Jane specialize in producing?

g. Bob and Jane specialize according to each's comparative advantage and they give us this partially filled-in table that provides some information about their production. Fill in the missing information, assuming that Bob and Jane are both productively efficient.

New production	Widgets	Gadgets
Bob	46	
Jane		60
Total production		

14. Decide whether each of the following statements is a normative statement or a positive statement, then explain your answer.

a. The gasoline tax is projected to yield $10 million in tax revenue next year.

b. If the gasoline tax was raised by 10 cents per gallon, the tax revenue from this tax would increase by 4%.

c. The state should raise the gasoline tax for the coming year. An increase in the tax will reduce congestion and smog, which is more important than the cost to commuters if they shift from private car transportation to public transportation.

d. Mandatory school enhances the work skills of students.

e. The age of mandatory school attendance should be extended, since this will provide greater benefits to our economy.

f. An extension of mandatory school attendance will increase government education costs by $2 million for the state.

15. Economists sometimes disagree about positive economics, but more often they disagree about normative economics. Briefly define both of these terms and then explain why economists do not always agree.

16. Why must the circular-flow diagram include two flows moving in opposite directions? In your answer identify what each of these flows is.

17. Suppose you are told that each additional inch of height results in an increase of five pounds in weight. What can you conclude from this information about the relationship between height and weight?

18. Suppose you are told that the points $(x, y) = (15, 30)$ and $(x, y) = (-5, 10)$ both sit on the same straight line.

   a. From this information, calculate the slope of the line.

   b. Draw a quick sketch of this line and be sure to mark and identify both of these two points on the line.

   c. Write an equation for this line.

   d. What is the y-intercept of this line?

19. Suppose that you know that the slope of a straight line is -10 and the line also contains the point $(x, y) = (10, 0)$.

   a. What is the equation for this line given this information?

   b. What is the x-intercept of this line?

   c. What is the y-intercept of this line?

▌ BEFORE YOU TAKE THE TEST

Chapter Review Questions

1. Models
    a. are an exact replica of reality.
    b. bear no resemblance to real life.
    c. are a simplification of the real world.
    d. are made more complicated by the assumptions that underlie the model.

2. There are a limited number of possible economic models.
    a. True
    b. False

3. The other things equal assumption means that
    a. all economic models hold the same variables constant.
    b. all economic models change only one variable at a time, and that variable is always the same for all economic models.
    c. only one variable is allowed to change in a model at a time so that the analyst using the model can focus on the effect of that change on the model.
    d. lots of variables are allowed to change in a model at one time so that the analyst using the model can focus on the effect of all these changes on a single variable of interest.

4. Suppose Mike has a linear production possibility frontier in the production of potatoes and tomatoes. If Mike devotes all his time to the production of potatoes, he can produce 1,000 pounds of potatoes a year; if he devotes all his time to the production of tomatoes, he can produce 2,000 pounds of tomatoes a year. Which of the following combinations of potatoes and tomatoes are not feasible for Mike?
    a. 1,000 pounds of potatoes and 2,000 pounds of tomatoes per year
    b. 1,000 pounds of potatoes and 0 pounds of tomatoes per year
    c. 0 pounds of potatoes and 2,000 pounds of tomatoes per year
    d. 500 pounds of potatoes and 1,000 pounds of tomatoes per year

5. Suppose Mike has a linear production possibility frontier in the production of potatoes and tomatoes. If Mike devotes all his time to the production of potatoes, he can produce 1,000 pounds of potatoes a year; if he devotes all his time to the production of tomatoes, he can produce 2,000 pounds of tomatoes a year. Which of the following combinations of potatoes and tomatoes are not efficient for Mike?
    a. 500 pounds of potatoes and 500 pounds of tomatoes per year
    b. 500 pounds of potatoes and 1,000 pounds of tomatoes per year
    c. 750 pounds of potatoes and 500 pounds of tomatoes per year
    d. 250 pounds of potatoes and 1,500 pounds of tomatoes per year

6. Utopia has a linear production possibility frontier in the production of widgets and gadgets. It can produce three gadgets per hour of labor time or four widgets per hour of labor time. What is the opportunity cost of producing one widget in Utopia?
    a. 3 gadgets
    b. 4 widgets
    c. ¾ of a gadget
    d. ⅘ of a gadget

7. Jonesville produces widgets and gadgets and its production possibility frontier is linear. The following table provides the number of units of labor necessary to produce 1 gadget or 1 widget in Jonesville.

	Number of hours of labor needed to produce a gadget	Number of hours of labor needed to produce a widget
Jonesville	5	10

Suppose that Jonesville has 100 hours of labor. What is the maximum number of widgets it can produce?

a. 10 widgets

b. 20 widgets

c. 1 widget

d. 100 widgets

8. Jonesville produces widgets and gadgets and its production possibility frontier is linear. The following table provides the number of units of labor necessary to produce 1 gadget or 1 widget in Jonesville.

	Number of hours of labor needed to produce a gadget	Number of hours of labor needed to produce a widget
Jonesville	5	10

Suppose that Jonesville has 100 hours of labor. What is the maximum number of gadgets and widgets it can produce if it devotes half of its labor time to the production of gadgets and half of its labor time to the production of widgets?

a. 20 gadgets and 5 widgets

b. 10 gadgets and 5 widgets

c. 5 gadgets and 20 widgets

d. 5 gadgets and 10 widgets

9. Jonesville produces widgets and gadgets and its production possibility frontier is linear. The following table provides the number of units of labor necessary to produce 1 gadget or 1 widget in Jonesville.

	Number of hours of labor needed to produce a gadget	Number of hours of labor needed to produce a widget
Jonesville	5	10

Suppose that Jonesville initially has 100 hours of labor. What happens to the opportunity cost of producing a widget if Jonesville's labor resource increases to 200 hours of labor?

a. The opportunity cost of producing a widget decreases.

b. The opportunity cost of producing a widget increases.

c. The opportunity cost of producing a widget does not change.

d. The opportunity cost of producing a widget may increase, decrease, or remain unchanged depending on the number of gadgets that are produced in Jonesville.

10. Jonesville produces widgets and gadgets and its production possibility frontier is linear. The following table provides the number of units of labor necessary to produce 1 gadget or 1 widget in Jonesville.

	Number of hours of labor needed to produce a gadget	Number of hours of labor needed to produce a widget
Jonesville	5	10

Suppose that Jonesville has 100 hours of labor. Which of the following combinations of gadgets and widgets is not feasible for Jonesville to produce?

a. 4 gadgets and 8 widgets   c. 8 gadgets and 6 widgets

b. 7 gadgets and 7 widgets   d. 0 gadgets and 10 widgets

11. Utopia has a linear production possibility frontier in the production of widgets and gadgets. It can produce 3 gadgets per hour of labor time or 4 widgets per hour of labor time. Suppose that Utopia has 120 hours of labor time and that it chooses to divide its labor time equally between the production of widgets and gadgets. What is the maximum number of widgets Utopia can produce given this decision?

a. 480 widgets   c. 60 widgets

b. 240 widgets   d. 15 widgets

12. Suburbia has a production possibility frontier bowed out from the origin for the two goods, guns and butter, that Suburbia produces from its available resources and technology. The following table describes six points that lie on Suburbia's production possibility frontier.

Combination	Number of guns	Pounds of butter
A	0	80
B	10	75
C	20	65
D	30	50
E	40	30
F	50	0

Suppose Suburbia is initially producing at point D. What is the opportunity cost of moving to point E?

a. 10 guns

b. 40 guns

c. 20 pounds of butter

d. 30 pounds of butter

13. Suburbia has a production possibility frontier bowed out from the origin for the two goods, guns and butter, that Suburbia produces from its available resources and technology. The following table describes six points that lie on Suburbia's production possibility frontier.

Combination	Number of guns	Pounds of butter
A	0	80
B	10	75
C	20	65
D	30	50
E	40	30
F	50	0

Suppose Suburbia is initially producing at point D. What is the opportunity cost of moving to point B?
a. 25 pounds of butter
b. 20 guns
c. 10 guns
d. 75 pounds of butter

14. Suburbia has a production possibility frontier bowed out from the origin for the two goods, guns and butter, that Suburbia produces from its available resources and technology. The following table describes six points that lie on Suburbia's production possibility frontier.

Combination	Number of guns	Pounds of butter
A	0	80
B	10	75
C	20	65
D	30	50
E	40	30
F	50	0

Suburbia is currently producing 50 pounds of butter and 20 guns. This combination is
a. allocatively efficient, since butter is tastier than guns.
b. productively efficient, since it is a feasible point for Suburbia to produce.
c. infeasible, because Suburbia cannot produce this combination given its resources and technology.
d. feasible but inefficient, since it is a combination that lies inside the production possibility frontier.

15. Which of the following statements is true?
    I. Points that lie on the production possibility frontier are allocatively efficient.
    II. Points that lie on the production possibility frontier are productively efficient.
a. Statement I is true.
b. Statement II is true.
c. Statements I and II are true.
d. Statements I and II are false.

16. An economy is allocatively efficient provided that

    a. it produces at any point along its production possibility frontier.

    b. it produces the right mix of goods from its available resources.

    c. no resources are wasted.

    d. All of the statements are true of allocative efficiency.

17. Suppose there are two countries, Texia and Urbania, that produce food and clothing and currently do not trade. Both countries have linear production possibility frontiers. Texia, if it devotes all of its resources to food production, can produce 1,000 units of food this year and 0 units of clothing. If Texia devotes all of its resources to clothing production this year, it can produce 500 units of clothing and 0 units of food. Urbania can either produce 500 units of food this year and 0 units of clothing, or it can produce 200 units of clothing this year and 0 units of food. _____ has the absolute advantage in the production of clothing, and _____ has the absolute advantage in the production of food.

    a. Texia; Texia   c. Urbania; Texia

    b. Texia; Urbania   d. Urbania; Urbania

18. Suppose there are two countries, Texia and Urbania, that produce food and clothing and currently do not trade. Both countries have linear production possibility frontiers. Texia, if it devotes all of its resources to food production, can produce 1,000 units of food this year and 0 units of clothing. If Texia devotes all of its resources to clothing production this year, it can produce 500 units of clothing and 0 units of food. Urbania can either produce 500 units of food this year and 0 units of clothing, or it can produce 200 units of clothing this year and 0 units of food. _____ has the comparative advantage in the production of clothing, and _____ has the comparative advantage in the production of food.

    a. Texia; Texia   c. Urbania; Texia

    b. Texia; Urbania   d. Urbania; Urbania

19. Suppose there are two countries, Texia and Urbania, that produce food and clothing and currently do not trade. Both countries have linear production possibility frontiers. Texia, if it devotes all of its resources to food production, can produce 1,000 units of food this year and 0 units of clothing. If Texia devotes all of its resources to clothing production this year, it can produce 500 units of clothing and 0 units of food. Urbania can either produce 500 units of food this year and 0 units of clothing, or it can produce 200 units of clothing this year and 0 units of food. Each country devotes half of its resources to the production of food and half of its resources to the production of clothing. Total clothing production is equal to _____, and total food production is equal to _____.

    a. 600; 500   c. 100; 250

    b. 250; 500   d. 350; 750

20. Suppose there are two countries, Texia and Urbania, that produce food and clothing and initially do not trade. Both countries have linear production possibility frontiers. Texia, if it devotes all of its resources to food production, can produce 1,000 units of food this year, and 0 units of clothing. If Texia devotes all of its resources to clothing production this year, it can produce 500 units of clothing and 0 units of food. Urbania can either produce 500 units of food this year and 0 units of clothing, or it can produce 200 units of clothing this year and 0 units of food. Suppose that Texia and Urbania decide to specialize and trade. If Texia increases its clothing production to a total of 400 units, how many units of food will Texia be able to produce if it is productively efficient?

    a. 100 units   c. 300 units

    b. 200 units   d. 400 units

21. Specialization and trade benefit
   a. usually only one of the trading partners.
   b. the wealthier country more than the poorer country.
   c. the poorer country more than the wealthier country.
   d. both countries if they specialize according to their comparative advantage.

22. Which of the following statements is true about positive economics?
   I. Positive economics is about how the world should work.
   II. Positive economics is about how the world works.
   III. Positive economics is descriptive.
   a. Statements I, II, and III are all true.
   b. Statements I and III are true.
   c. Statements II and III are true.
   d. Statement II is true.

23. Which of the following statements is an example of normative economics?
   I. The United States should pass a value-added tax, since this is a tax that will work best for the country.
   II. A value-added tax will add $10 billion to the administrative costs of the U.S. tax system.
   III. A value-added tax will increase the economic burden of taxes on poor people by 15%.
   a. Statements I, II, and III are all examples of normative economics.
   b. Statements I and III are examples of normative economics.
   c. Statements I and II are examples of normative economics.
   d. Statement I is an example of normative economics.

24. In the simple circular-flow diagram presented in the chapter there are only two types of inhabitants in the economy. These two types are
   a. money earners and money savers.
   b. households and firms.
   c. resources and outputs.
   d. governments and individuals.

25. The simple circular-flow diagram presented in the chapter illustrates two markets: the markets for
   a. households and firms.
   b. government services and foreign-produced goods.
   c. money and physical times.
   d. goods and services and the market for factors of production.

26. A positively sloped line indicates that as one variable increases, the other variable
   a. stays the same.
   b. increases.
   c. decreases.
   d. may increase, decrease, or remain unchanged.

27. A negatively sloped line indicates that as one variable increases, the other variable
   a. stays the same.
   b. increases.
   c. decreases.
   d. may increase, decrease, or remain the same.

ANSWER KEY

Answers to Problems and Exercises

1. The map is an example of a model because it simplifies the real world while trying to enable the user to better understand that world. It simplifies the real world by leaving out many things—for example, your map may only show the main roads in your community, or it might leave out major landmarks that you might find helpful, such as park and school names. The map is helpful to you provided it enables you to get from your starting point to your destination. Although it simplifies the real world, it should still provide key insights into that world.

2. Technology and the time period are being held constant so that we can focus on the effect of a change in the level of resources on this economy's production possibility frontier. If resources increase, we would expect the production possibility frontier to shift out because the economy should be able to produce more of both goods now that there are more resources to work with.

3. **a.**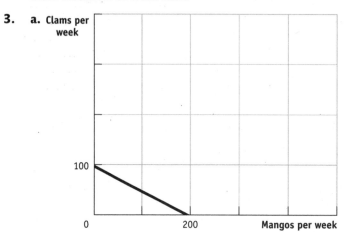

   b. An increase in the time period, holding everything else constant, increases the level of production.

   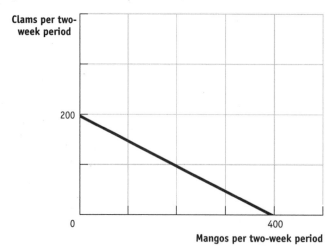

c. The invention of the clam rake shifts the production possibilities frontier out along the clam axis since it is now possible to produce more clams in the same time period.

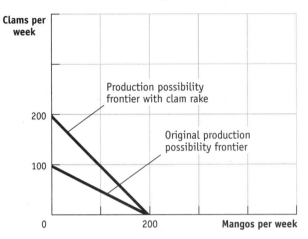

d. Technological change shifts the production possibility frontier away from the origin and therefore results in the possibility of greater production of both goods.

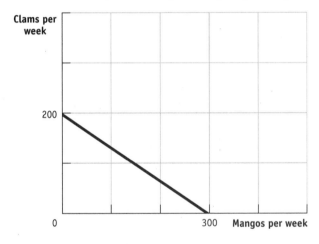

4.   a. The opportunity cost of harvesting a clam is measured in terms of the number of mangos you must give up when you harvest a clam. In the original example, you must give up 2 mangos for every clam you harvest.

b. The opportunity cost of collecting a mango is measured in terms of the number of clams you must give up when you collect a mango. In the original example, you must give up ½ clam for every mango you collect.

c. The slope of the production possibility frontier is $-\frac{1}{2}$ (remember, you calculate this as the rise/run, or the change in the y-variable divided by the change in the x-variable). The slope tells us what the change in the y-variable is for a 1-unit change in the x-variable. In this case, the slope tells us what the change in the number of clams is for a 1-unit change in mangos: when mango collection increases by 1 unit, then clam harvesting decreases by ½ of a unit; when mango collection decreases by 1 unit, then clam harvesting increases by ½ of a unit. The negative sign of the slope tells us that these two variables move in opposite directions: an increase in mangos requires a decrease in clams, or a decrease in mangos requires an increase in clams. The slope measure tells us what the opportunity cost of one more mango is, since mangos are measured on the horizontal axis in this example. If we take the reciprocal of the slope (in this case, –2), it would give us the opportunity cost of producing one more unit of the good on the y-axis. In this case, harvesting one more clam has an opportunity cost of 2 mangos since that is the amount of mangos we must give up to get one more clam.

d. The invention of the clam rake changed the slope of the production possibility frontier from –½ to –1 and therefore changed the opportunity cost of producing both goods. The opportunity cost of collecting a mango is now 1 clam and the opportunity cost of harvesting one clam is 1 mango.

5. **a.**

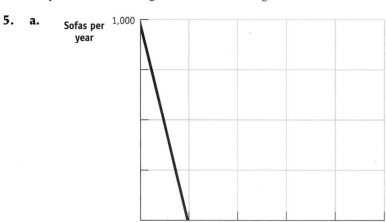

b.

Combination	Number of lamps possible	Number of sofas possible
A	0	1,000
B	50	800
C	125	500
D	200	200
E	225	100
F	250	0

c. The slope of the production possibility frontier is –4 (you can find this by looking at the rise/run, or in this case, –1,000/250).

d. The opportunity cost of producing one more sofa is ¼ of a lamp. (Hint: Remember that because sofas are measured on the y-axis, you can find the opportunity cost by taking the reciprocal of the slope measure.)

e. The opportunity cost of producing one more lamp is 4 sofas. (Hint: Remember that because lamps are measured on the x-axis, you can find the opportunity cost by using the slope measure.)

f. The y-intercept is 1,000, since if Orange uses all of its resources and technology to produce sofas, this is the maximum number of sofas it can produce in a year.

g. The equation for Orange's production possibility frontier is $S = 1,000 - 4L$. You can verify that all the combinations work in this equation by substituting the value of the number of lamps in one of the combinations and verifying that the equation generates the number of sofas you found in the table. For example, if L equals 225, then $S = 1,000 - 4(225)$ or $S = 100$ (the value you found in the table).

6.   a. To draw the production possibility frontier, you first need to identify the number of hours of labor that Utopia has available. Since it takes 3 hours of labor to produce 2 widgets (or 1.5 hours of labor to produce 1 widget) and 4 hours of labor to produce 1 gadget, you will find it helpful to select an amount of time that is divisible by both three and four. So, for instance, 12 hours would work, as would 120 hours, or 240 hours, or an infinite number of other numbers that are divisible by both three and four. For our sketch let's suppose that there are 120 hours of labor available to Utopia and that its citizens can produce either widgets or gadgets or some combination of the two goods. If they devote all of their labor time to widget production, they can produce 80 widgets since (120 hours of labor/3 hours of labor) × (2 widgets) = 80 widgets. If they devote all of their labor time to gadget production, they can produce 30 gadgets since (120 hours of labor/4 hours of labor) × (1 gadget) = 30 gadgets. The following graph illustrates Utopia's production possibility frontier.

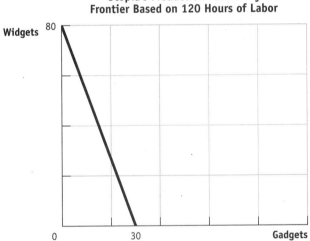

Utopia's Production Possibility Frontier Based on 120 Hours of Labor

The values of your intercepts will be different depending on the number of hours of labor you assume Utopia has, but the slope of the production possibility frontier should be the same as in the figure shown.

b. The slope of the production possibility frontier is –8/3.

c. The opportunity cost of producing an additional widget in Utopia is 3/8 of a gadget.

d. The opportunity cost of producing an additional gadget in Utopia is 8/3 of a widget.

7.   a. You must first decide how much labor Jonesville has so that you can calculate the maximum amount of widgets and gadgets Jonesville can produce. Since you know gadgets take 2 hours of labor and widgets take 5 hours of labor, you will want to pick a number of hours that is divisible by both two and five. For example, 10 hours would work, or 100 hours, or 20 hours, or 2,000 hours—there is an infinite number of labor quantities that would work in constructing this production possibility frontier.

b.

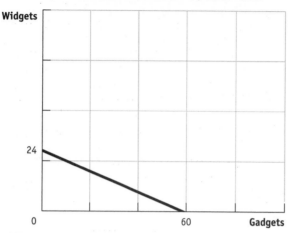

Production Possibility Frontier for Jonesville Based on 120 Hours of Labor

c. The slope of the production possibility frontier is –24/60, or –4/10, or –0.4.

d. Recall that you can use the slope measure to quickly find the opportunity cost of producing one more unit of the good measured on the *x*-axis. To produce one more gadget, you must give up 0.4 of a widget, therefore the opportunity cost of an additional gadget is 0.4 of a widget.

e. Recall that you can use the reciprocal of the slope measure to quickly find the opportunity cost of producing one more unit of the good measured on the *y*-axis. To produce one more widget, you must give up 1/0.4 gadgets, therefore the opportunity cost of an additional widget is 2.5 gadgets.

f. If Jonesville has an increase in the amount of labor available to use in producing gadgets and widgets, it can produce more gadgets and more widgets. That is, Jonesville's production possibility frontier will shift out from the origin. But the slope of the new production possibility frontier will be the same as the one drawn based on 120 hours of labor, thus the opportunity cost of producing widgets or gadgets will not change for Jonesville.

8. a.

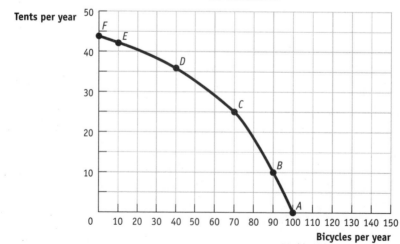

Production Possibility Frontier for Smithtown

b. The opportunity cost of moving from point *C* to point *B* is measured in terms of the number of units of production you give up. In this case you give up 15 tents, so this is the opportunity cost.

c. The opportunity cost of moving from point *C* to point *D* is 30 bicycles.

d. Smithtown's resources are not equally well suited to produce bicycles and tents. If Smithtown initially devotes all of its resources to producing bicycles, then some of its resources that are currently going into the production of bicycles are not particularly productive at producing bicycles. Smithtown can move some of these resources away from bicycle production and into tent production without decreasing its bicycle production significantly. However, as Smithtown decides to produce more and more tents, this will eventually require moving resources that are well suited to bicycle production into tent production where they are less productive. This specialization of resources results in a production possibility frontier that is bowed out from the origin.

9. **a.** This economy's production possibility frontier must be bowed out from the origin if the economy's resources are specialized: this implies that the opportunity cost of producing more and more units of one of the goods increases because increased production of this good requires the economy to use resources that would be more productive producing the other good.

b. The opportunity cost of producing more and more units of the good will increase due to the shape of the production possibility frontier, which is bowed out from the origin.

c. To be productively efficient, this economy must be producing at a point that is located on the production possibility frontier.

d. To be allocatively efficient, this economy must be producing at a point that represents the optimal mix of these two goods for the economy.

e. To be efficient, the economy must be both productively and allocatively efficient—that is, it must produce not only on the production possibility frontier, but it must also produce the right mix of goods.

10. Economists believe that specialization and trade based on comparative advantage result in a greater level of production than is possible without specialization and trade. Economists argue that, so long as opportunity costs differ, specialization in the production of the good that has a lower opportunity cost will enhance the overall level of production available and will therefore be beneficial.

11. **a.**

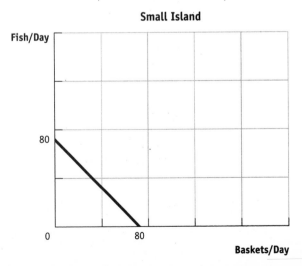

b. The slope of Big Island's production possibility frontier is –½.

c. The slope of Small Island's production possibility frontier is –1.

d. The opportunity cost of producing an additional basket for Big Island is ½ of a fish. The opportunity cost of producing an additional basket for Small Island is 1 fish. Big Island can produce an additional basket at a lower opportunity cost than can Small Island.

e. The opportunity cost of producing an additional fish for Big Island is 2 baskets. The opportunity cost of producing an additional fish for Small Island is 1 basket. Small Island can produce an additional fish at a lower opportunity cost than can Big Island.

f. Big Island should specialize in producing baskets, since it can produce baskets at a lower opportunity cost than can Small Island.

g. Small Island should specialize in producing fish, since it can produce fish at a lower opportunity cost than can Big Island.

12. **a.** Big Island is producing at a productively efficient point because 80 fish and 40 baskets lies on its linear production possibility frontier.

b. Small Island is producing at a productively efficient point because 30 fish and 50 baskets lies on its linear production possibility frontier.

c. Big Island will be able to produce 75 fish. The easiest way to calculate this answer is to write an equation for Big Island's production possibility frontier: $F = (-\frac{1}{2})B + 100$, where F is the symbol for fish and B is the symbol for baskets. Thus, if $B = 50$, then F must equal 75 according to this equation.

d. Small Island will be able to produce 40 baskets. The easiest way to calculate this answer is to write an equation for Small Island's production possibility frontier: $F = (-1)B + 80$, where F stands for fish and B stands for baskets. Thus, if $F = 40$, then B must equal 40.

e.

New production	Fish	Baskets
Big Island	75	50
Small Island	40	40
Total production	115	90

f. Specialization and trade are beneficial to both islands, since the total production of fish is increased to 115 fish instead of the original 110. This change in fish production does not change the level of basket production. Thus, the two islands can increase the amount of goods available to them if they specialize according to their comparative advantage and then trade with each other.

g. Big Island will be able to produce 85 fish. The easiest way to calculate this answer is to write an equation for Big Island's production possibility frontier: $F = (-\frac{1}{2})B + 100$, where F is the symbol for fish and B is the symbol for baskets. Thus, if $B = 30$, then F must equal 85 according to this equation.

h. Small Island will be able to produce 60 baskets. The easiest way to calculate this answer is to write an equation for Small Island's production possibility frontier: $F = (-1)B + 80$, where F stands for fish and B stands for baskets. Thus, if $F = 20$, then B must equal 60.

i.

New production	Fish	Baskets
Big Island	85	30
Small Island	20	60
Total production	105	90

j. Specialization and trade are not beneficial to both islands in this example, since the total production of fish decreased to 105 fish instead of the original 110. This change in fish production does not change the level of basket production. Thus, the two islands decrease the amount of goods available to them when they specialize and trade with each other without paying attention to their comparative advantage.

k. For specialization and trade to be beneficial for two countries, they must have different opportunity costs of production, and they must also specialize according to their comparative advantage.

13. a.

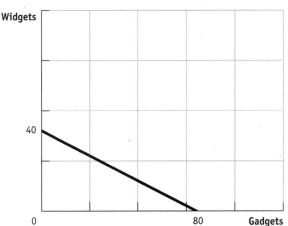

b.

Initial production	Widgets	Gadgets
Bob	30	15
Jane	20	40
Total production	50	55

c. Bob's opportunity cost of producing an additional gadget is 2 widgets, whereas Jane's opportunity cost of producing an additional gadget is ½ of a widget. Jane can produce gadgets at a lower opportunity cost than can Bob.

d. Bob's opportunity cost of producing an additional widget is ½ of a gadget, whereas Jane's opportunity cost of producing an additional widget is 2 gadgets. Bob can produce widgets at a lower opportunity cost than can Jane.

e. Bob should specialize in producing widgets.

f. Jane should specialize in producing gadgets.

g.

Initial production	Widgets	Gadgets
Bob	46	7
Jane	10	60
Total production	56	67

14. a. Positive: this statement is a forecast of the tax revenue from the gasoline tax. It is verifiable and hence positive.

b. Positive: this is also a forecast, and although it may be wrong, it can be verified through the data once the data are available.

c. Normative: this is a value statement that reflects one person's viewpoint of the way the world should work. It is not refutable since it reflects a person's opinion and not a set of facts.

d. Positive: this statement can be tested for its accuracy.

e. Normative: this statement reflects the opinions of the speaker.

f. Positive: this is a forecast.

15. Positive economics is descriptive, whereas normative economics is prescriptive—that is, positive economics is objective and expresses how the world works, while normative economics is subjective and expresses how the world should work. Economists may differ because of positive economics: they may use different models with different assumptions that lead to different conclusions. Economists may also disagree over normative economics: economists may not share the same values and will therefore reach different conclusions about how the world should work. Economists can evaluate alternative policies in terms of their efficiency at reaching stated goals.

16. The circular-flow diagram is a simplified representation of the economy. There is a flow of physical items like goods, services, labor, and raw materials that moves in one direction around the circle, and the flow of money to pay for these physical things moves in the opposite direction around the circle.

17. Height and weight are positively related: this implies that as height increases, weight increases or as height decreases, weight decreases. A graph of the relationship between height and weight would show an upward-sloping line.

18. a. The slope of the line is equal to the rise/run = (the change in Y)/(the change in X) = $(30 - 10)/[15 - (-5)] = 20/(20) = 1$.

b.

c. The general slope intercept form of an equation is $y = mx + b$, where m is the slope of the line and b is the y-intercept of the line. We know from part (a) that the slope of the line is 1. Hence, $y = x + b$. To find b, use one of the given points. Thus, $30 = 15 + b$ implies that b is equal to 15. The equation for the line is therefore $y = x + 15$.

d. From part (c), we know that the y-intercept of the line is 15.

19. a. To find the equation for this line, recall that the general slope intercept form is $y = mx + b$, where m is the slope and b is the y-intercept. You know that the slope is equal to -10, so you can rewrite this equation as $y = -10x + b$. To find b, simply substitute the point $(x, y) = (10, 0)$ into this equation. Thus, $0 = -10(10) + b$, or $b = 100$. The equation for the line is therefore $y = -10x + 100$.

b. The y-intercept for this line is 100 since when x is equal to zero, the y value is 100.

c. To find the x-intercept of the line, you could use the equation from part (a): $y = -10x + 100$ and use 0 as the value for y. When y is equal to zero, then x is equal to 10. Alternatively, you might recognize that the point $(x, y) = (10, 0)$ already tells you the x-intercept: when the value of y is zero, then the value of x is 10.

Answers to Chapter Review Questions

1. **Answer c.** This is a simple definition of "model."

2. **Answer b.** This is not a true statement, since there are an infinite number of possible models. Models can vary, for example, due to their focus of attention, their underlying assumptions, and their degree of complexity.

3. **Answer c.** The assumption "other things equal" implies that everything else is being held equal or constant while considering the effect of changing one variable. Answer (a) is incorrect, since different economic models have different economic variables. Answer (b) is incorrect since different variables may be varied in different models or even within a particular model. Answer (d) is incorrect with regard to the other things equal assumption, which is used to isolate the effect of a single change on the rest of the model.

4. **Answer a.** Mike can produce 1,000 pounds of potatoes and 0 pounds of tomatoes a year, or he can produce 2,000 pounds of tomatoes and 0 pounds of potatoes a year. His resources do not allow him to produce a combination of 1,000 pounds of potatoes and 2,000 pounds of tomatoes in a year. Thus, answer (a) is not feasible, while answers (b) and (c) are feasible. Answer (d) is also feasible, since if Mike devotes half of his resources this year to producing potatoes and half of his resources this year to producing tomatoes, he will be able to produce 500 pounds of potatoes and 1,000 pounds of tomatoes this year.

5. **Answer a.** Any combination of production of potatoes and tomatoes that lies on Mike's linear production possibility frontier is an efficient combination. An inefficient combination must lie inside his production possibility frontier. His linear production possibility frontier includes the two points (1,000 pounds of potatoes, 0 pounds of tomatoes) and (0 pounds of potatoes, 2,000 pounds of tomatoes), and we can use these two points to write an equation for his production possibility frontier. If potatoes are measured on the y-axis and are denoted by P, and tomatoes are measured on the x-axis and denoted by T, then Mike's production possibility frontier is $P = 1,000 - \frac{1}{2}T$. Substitute the number of tomatoes provided in each answer into this equation to calculate the number of potatoes Mike can produce when he produces that level of tomatoes. Thus, for answer (b), when Mike produces 1,000 pounds of tomatoes, the equation states that he will be able to produce 500 pounds of potatoes, which is the number of potatoes given in answer (b). Answers (c) and (d) also fit the equation. Thus, answers (b), (c), and (d) all identify production combinations that are on the production possibility frontier. But answer (a) does not fit the equation: when Mike produces 500 pounds of tomatoes, the equation says that he will be able to produce 750 pounds of potatoes, while answer (a) says that he will produce 500 pounds of potatoes. The combination in answer (a) is a combination that lies inside Mike's production possibility frontier.

6. **Answer c.** Since in Utopia 4 widgets can be produced in the same amount of labor time as 3 gadgets, then 1 widget can be produced in the same amount of labor time as ¾ of a gadget. Thus, the opportunity cost of producing 1 widget is measured by the number of gadgets that must be given up, in this case ¾ of a gadget.

7. **Answer a.** Jonesville uses all of its labor to produce widgets. With 100 hours of labor, it can produce 10 widgets since the production of each widget takes 10 hours of labor.

8. **Answer b.** When Jonesville devotes 50 hours of labor to widget production, it can produce 5 widgets. When Jonesville devotes 50 hours of labor to gadget production, it can produce 10 gadgets. Thus, when Jonesville divides its labor evenly between widget and gadget production, the maximum number of gadgets it can produce is 10 while the maximum number of widgets it can produce is 5.

9. **Answer c.** Since the number of hours needed to produce each widget and each gadget has not changed in Jonesville, the opportunity cost of producing these goods does not change. Jonesville does see its linear production possibility frontier shift out due to the

increase in the amount of available labor, but the new production possibility frontier has the same slope as the original production possibility frontier.

10. **Answer b.** A combination of gadgets and widgets is not feasible for Jonesville if that combination lies outside of its production possibility frontier. If gadgets are measured on the vertical axis and widgets are measured on the horizontal axis, then the production possibility frontier can be written as $G = 20 - 2W$, where G is the symbol for gadgets and W is the symbol for widgets. Answer (a) lies on the production possibility frontier, since $G = 20 - 2(8) = 4$. Answer (c) lies on the production possibility frontier, since $G = 20 - 2(6) = 8$. Answer (d) lies on the production possibility frontier, since $G = 20 - 2(10) = 0$. Answer (b) does not lie on the production possibility frontier nor does it lie inside the production possibility frontier: $G = 20 - 2(7) = 6$, but the answer in (b) has gadgets equal to 7 and not 6. The combination of 7 widgets and 7 gadgets lies beyond the production possibility frontier for Jonesville.

11. **Answer b.** Utopia plans to devote 60 hours of labor to the production of widgets. If the production of 4 widgets takes 1 hour of labor time, then 60 hours of labor is enough labor to produce 240 widgets.

12. **Answer c.** The opportunity cost of moving from point D to point E is measured by what Suburbia must give up when it makes this move. At point D, Suburbia has 50 pounds of butter, while at point E Suburbia has only 30 pounds of butter; thus, when moving from point D to point E, Suburbia must give up 20 pounds of butter. Notice that when measuring the opportunity cost of moving from one point of a production possibility frontier to another point on the production possibility frontier, it is important to provide the unit of measurement as well as the numerical value.

13. **Answer b.** The opportunity cost of moving from point D to point B is measured by what Suburbia must give up when it makes this move. In this case, Suburbia is giving up guns to get more butter. Moving from point D to point B, Suburbia gives up 20 guns.

14. **Answer d.** From the table, we know that Suburbia can produce 50 pounds of butter and 30 guns (point D on the production possibility frontier). When Suburbia produces 50 pounds of butter and 20 guns, it is producing at a point that is inside its production possibility frontier and hence it is producing at a feasible but inefficient point, since the point does not lie on the production possibility frontier. Alternatively, Suburbia could produce 20 guns and 65 pounds of butter (point C) according to the table. Its choice of 20 guns and 50 pounds of butter is also not efficient from this perspective.

15. **Answer b.** Allocative efficiency focuses on producing the right mix of goods and services. Without additional information, we cannot identify which point is the allocatively efficient point on the production possibility frontier. "Productively efficient" refers to the maximum production feasible from the available resources. All points on the production possibility frontier are productively efficient.

16. **Answer b.** This is true by definition.

17. **Answer a.** Given the resources that Texia and Urbania have this year, Texia is able to produce more food and more clothing than Urbania this year.

18. **Answer b.** For every unit of clothing that Texia produces it must give up 2 units of food, while for Urbania the opportunity cost of producing 1 unit of clothing is 2.5 units of food. Thus, the opportunity cost of producing clothing is lower for Texia than it is for Urbania. Texia therefore has the comparative advantage in producing clothing while Urbania has the comparative advantage in producing food.

19. **Answer d.** When Texia devotes half of its resources to food production and half of its resources to clothing production, it can produce 500 units of food and 250 units of clothing. When Urbania devotes half of its resources to food production and half of its

resources to clothing production, it can produce 250 units of food and 100 units of clothing. Thus, under this arrangement, total food production is 750 units and total clothing production is 350 units.

20. **Answer b.** Texia's production possibility frontier can be written as $F = 1,000 - 2C$, where F is the number of units of food and C is the number of units of clothing. When Texia produces 400 units of clothing, the maximum amount of food it can produce is 200 units: $F = 1,000 - 2(400) = 200$.

21. **Answer d.** The logic of comparative advantage is that both trading parties benefit through specialization and trade based on their comparative advantage.

22. **Answer c.** Positive economics is objective, factual, and can be subject to proof. In contrast, normative economics is subjective and expresses what ought to happen or what should happen. Statements II and III are both statements that describe positive economics, since positive economics describes and analyzes how the world works.

23. **Answer d.** Normative economics is subjective and value oriented. Both statements II and III are positive statements that can be evaluated as to their factual accuracy. Statement I is a normative statement since it expresses someone's subjective opinion and therefore cannot be proven true or false.

24. **Answer b.** The simple circular-flow diagram depicts the relationship between households and firms, with firms providing goods and services to households while households provide factors of production to firms.

25. **Answer d.** There are two markets represented in the simple circular-flow diagram: the market for goods and services, where households buy the goods and services they want from firms; and the market for factors of production, where firms buy the resources they need to produce goods and services.

26. **Answer b.** A positively sloped line is one in which the relationship between the two variables depicted is such that an increase in the value of one variable is accompanied by an increase in the value of the other variable. Or, conversely, a decrease in the value of one variable is accompanied by a decrease in the value of the other variable.

27. **Answer c.** A negatively sloped line indicates that the two variables are inversely related: as the value of one variable increases, the value of the other variable decreases.

chapter 3

Supply and Demand

BEFORE YOU READ THE CHAPTER

Summary

Chapter 3 describes a competitive market and then develops the model of supply and demand for this type of market. The chapter describes the demand and supply curves, explains the distinction between movements along a curve versus a shift of the curve, discusses the primary determinants of supply and demand, and defines the meaning of equilibrium in this model. The chapter also discusses how a market eliminates shortages and surpluses through changes in price and quantity so that the market returns to its equilibrium.

Chapter Objectives

Objective #1. A competitive market is a market that has many buyers and many sellers of the same good or service. No buyer or seller can affect the price of the good or service in a competitive market.

Objective #2. A demand schedule shows the relationship between possible prices of the good or service and the quantity of that good or service demanded at those different prices. As the price increases, the quantity demanded decreases: price and quantity demanded are inversely related to each other. A demand curve is the graphical representation of the demand schedule. The demand curve is drawn with the price of the good on the vertical axis and the quantity demanded on the horizontal axis. Demand curves usually slope downward: this is referred to as the "law of demand." Demand refers to the entire demand curve, while quantity demanded refers to a specific quantity demanded at a specific price. Figure 3.1 illustrates a demand curve as well as the quantity demanded (Q_1) at the price (P_1). Notice that as the price of the good decreases from P_1 to P_2, the quantity demanded increases from Q_1 to Q_2, thus illustrating the inverse relationship between the quantity demanded of the good and the price of the good.

Figure 3.1

Objective #3. The quantity demanded depends on many factors, but the primary determinants of the quantity demanded are the price of the good, the changes in the price of related goods, and changes in income, tastes, expectations, and the number of consumers. A change in the price of the good, holding everything else constant, will cause a movement along the curve and a change in the quantity demanded. A change in any other determinant of demand, holding everything else constant, will cause a shift in the demand curve. At any given price, the quantity demanded will increase when demand shifts to the right and decrease when demand shifts to the left. Figure 3.1 illustrates the concept of a movement along the demand curve. Holding everything else constant, an increase (or decrease) in the price of the good will cause the quantity demanded to decrease (or increase). There is a movement along the demand curve. But, if the price is held constant and some other factor that influences demand changes, then there will be a shift in the demand curve. Figure 3.2 illustrates an increase in demand where the demand curve shifts from D_1 to D_2: at every price, a greater quantity of the good is demanded since demand has increased (the quantity demanded changes from Q_1 to Q_2). For example, suppose tastes and preferences for the good increase, holding everything else constant: this will cause the demand curve to shift to the right as illustrated in Figure 3.2.

Figure 3.2

Objective #4. The chapter discusses several kinds of specific types of goods.

- Two goods are substitutes if a decrease in the price of one of the goods causes a decrease in the demand for the other good. As the price of the first good decreases, people increase the quantity of this good they demand, which results in a reduction in the overall demand for the other, substitute good. Two goods are complements if a decrease in the price of one of the goods causes an increase in the demand for the other good. As the price of the first good decreases, people increase the quantity of this good they demand, which results in an increase in the overall demand for the other, complementary, good.

- A good is a normal good if a decrease in income causes a decrease in the demand for the good. A good is an inferior good if a decrease in income causes an increase in the demand for the good.

Objective #5.   A market demand curve illustrates the combined quantity demanded by all consumers in the market. The market demand curve is found by horizontally adding together the individual demand curves. At each price the quantity demanded by each individual is added together to give the total quantity demanded at that price. Figure 3.3 illustrates this horizontal summation of the individual demand curves to create a market demand curve. For simplicity, it assumes there are only two demanders of the good in the market. The figure illustrates the demand for each of these individuals and then, for the market demand curve, it adds up the quantity demanded by the two individuals at a particular price. By repeating this horizontal addition for different prices, it is possible to create the market demand curve. Notice that the market demand curve depicted in Figure 3.3 is composed of two straight line segments: when the price is equal to or greater than P_3, Individual Two does not demand the good: the good is too expensive. Thus, the market demand is composed of a segment from P_1 to P_3 that just reflects Individual One's demand, while the segment starting at P_3, and for all prices lower than P_3, includes demand from both Individual One and Individual Two.

Figure 3.3

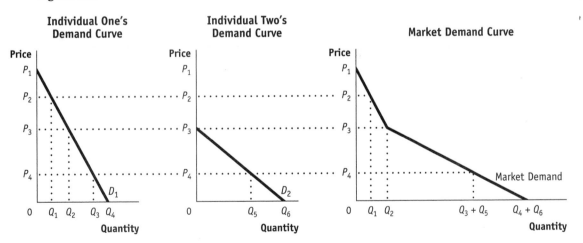

Objective #6.   The quantity of a good or service supplied by a producer depends on the price producers are offered for their product. The supply schedule illustrates the relationship between various prices and the quantity of the good supplied at each of these prices. Generally speaking, the quantity supplied increases as the price increases, holding everything else constant. A supply curve is the graphical representation of a supply schedule. Usually a supply curve is upward sloping: the quantity supplied increases as the price increases. Figure 3.4 illustrates a supply curve as well as the quantity supplied (Q_1) at the price (P_1). Notice that as the price of the good decreases from P_1 to P_2, the quantity supplied decreases from Q_1 to Q_2, thus illustrating the positive relationship between the quantity supplied of the good and the price of the good.

Figure 3.4

Objective #7. The quantity supplied depends on many factors, but the primary determinants of the quantity supplied are the price of the good, the price of its inputs, the price of related goods, and changes in technology, expectations, and the number of producers. A change in the price of the good causes a movement along the supply curve; a change in one of the other supply determinants, other than price, causes a shift in the supply curve. A rightward shift in the supply curve is an increase in supply; a leftward shift in the supply curve is a decrease in supply. An increase in the price of inputs, holding everything else constant, will cause a decrease in supply. This means that the supply curve shifts to the left, and at every price the quantity supplied is now less than it was initially. Figure 3.4 illustrates the concept of a movement along the supply curve. Holding everything else constant, an increase (or decrease) in the price of the good will cause the quantity supplied to increase (or decrease). There is a movement along the supply curve. But if the price is held constant and some other factor that influences supply changes, then there will be a shift in the supply curve. Figure 3.5 illustrates an increase in supply where the supply curve shifts from S_1 to S_2. At every price, a greater quantity of the good is supplied since supply has increased (the quantity supplied changes from Q_1 to Q_2). For example, suppose the price of an input decreases, holding everything else constant: this will cause the supply curve to shift to the right, as illustrated in Figure 3.5. But if the price is held constant and some other factor that influences supply changes, then there will be a shift in the supply curve.

Figure 3.5

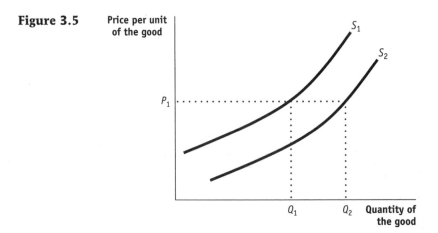

Objective #8. Two goods are substitutes in production when an increase in the price of one of these goods results in greater production of this good and reduced production of the other good. Two goods are complements in production when an increase in the price of one of these goods results in greater production of both goods.

Objective #9. The market supply curve is found by horizontally adding together the individual supply curves. At each price, the quantity supplied by each firm is added together to create the market supply curve. As the number of individual producers increases, there is an increase in supply. Figure 3.6 illustrates this horizontal summation of the individual supply curves to create a market supply curve. For simplicity it assumes there are only two providers of the good in the market. The figure illustrates the supply curve for each of these two firms. Then, for the market supply curve, it adds up the quantity supplied by the two firms at a particular price. By repeating this horizontal addition for different prices, it is possible to create the market supply curve. Notice that the market supply curve depicted in Figure 3.6 is composed of two straight line segments: when the price is equal to or less than P_1, Firm 2 does not supply the good: the price is too low for the firm to be willing to supply it. Thus, the market supply is composed of a segment for prices up to P_1 that reflects just Firm 1's supply, while the segment starting at P_1, and for all prices greater than P_1, includes supply from both Firm 1 and Firm 2.

Figure 3.6

Objective #10. A competitive market is in equilibrium at the price at which the quantity demanded equals the quantity supplied. This price is called the equilibrium price. The quantity associated with this equilibrium price is called the equilibrium quantity. The equilibrium price is the market-clearing price, since at this price the quantity demanded equals the quantity supplied. The equilibrium in a market occurs at the point of intersection between the demand and supply curves. Figure 3.7 illustrates a market in equilibrium. At price P_1, the quantity demanded (Q_d) of the good is equal to the quantity supplied (Q_s) of the good.

Figure 3.7

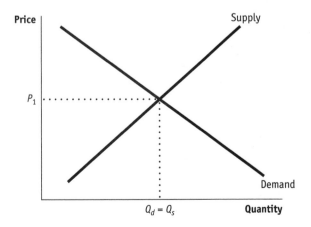

Objective #11. At a given price, if the quantity supplied of the good is greater than the quantity demanded of the good, there is a surplus, or excess supply, in the market. If there is excess supply, prices will fall until the quantity supplied equals the quantity demanded. At a given price, if the quantity supplied of the good is less than the quantity demanded of the good, there is a shortage, or excess demand, in the market. If there is excess demand, prices will rise until the quantity supplied equals the quantity demanded. Figure 3.8 illustrates disequilibrium: when the price is P_2, there is excess supply in the market since the quantity supplied of the good is equal to Q_2, while the quantity demanded in the market is equal to Q_3; when the price is P_3, there is excess demand in the market since the quantity supplied of the good is equal to Q_4, while the quantity demanded in the market is equal to Q_5. When there is excess supply in the market, price decreases until the market is restored to equilibrium: note that as the price decreases from P_2 toward P_1, there is a movement along both the demand and the supply curves. When there is excess demand in the market, price increases until the market is restored to equilibrium: note that as the price increases from P_3 toward P_1, there is a movement along both the demand and the supply curve.

Figure 3.8

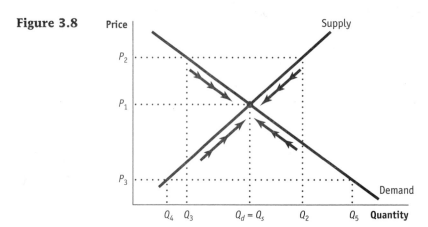

Objective #12. A shift in the demand curve, holding everything else constant, causes a change in the equilibrium price and quantity. The shift in the demand curve causes a movement along the supply curve. An increase in demand leads to a rise in both the equilibrium price and equilibrium quantity. A decrease in demand leads to a fall in both the equilibrium price and equilibrium quantity. A shift in the supply curve, holding everything else constant, causes a change in the equilibrium price and quantity. The shift in the supply curve causes a movement along the demand curve. An increase in supply leads to a fall in the equilibrium price and a rise in the equilibrium quantity. A decrease in supply leads to a rise in the equilibrium price and a fall in the equilibrium quantity. Figure 3.9 illustrates the effect of an increase in demand on the market equilibrium: the increase in demand causes both the equilibrium price and the equilibrium quantity to increase. Figure 3.10 illustrates the effect of an increase in supply on the market equilibrium: the increase in demand causes the equilibrium price to decrease, while the equilibrium quantity increases.

Figure 3.9

Figure 3.10

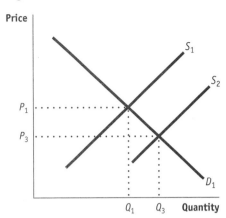

Objective #13. If demand and supply both change simultaneously but without specific information about the relative magnitude of these changes, there will be ambiguity about the value of either the new equilibrium price or the new equilibrium quantity. The four possible outcomes of these changes are summarized in Table 3.1.

Table 3.1

Shift in demand	Shift in supply	Effect on equilibrium price	Effect on equilibrium quantity
Right	Left	Increase	Ambiguous
Right	Right	Ambiguous	Increase
Left	Left	Ambiguous	Decrease
Left	Right	Decrease	Ambiguous

Figure 3.11 illustrates the first case in Table 3.1. Both the demand and the supply curves shift: the demand curve shifts to the right and the supply curve to the left. Figure 3.11 illustrates three possible outcomes that might occur with these two simultaneous shifts: note that in each illustration we know with certainty that the equilibrium price increases, but when we compare the three illustrations we see that the equilibrium quantity may increase, decrease, or remain the same. You should practice by drawing the other three examples given in the table.

Figure 3.11

Key Terms

competitive market a market in which there are many buyers and sellers of the same good or service, none of whom can influence the price at which the good or service is sold.

supply and demand model a model of how a *competitive market* works.

demand schedule a list or table showing how much of a good or service consumers will want to buy at different prices.

quantity demanded the actual amount of a good or service consumers are willing to buy at some specific price.

demand curve a graphical representation of the *demand schedule*, showing the relationship between quantity demanded and price.

law of demand a higher price for a good or service, other things equal, leads people to demand a smaller quantity of that good or service.

shift of the demand curve a change in the *quantity demanded* at any given price, represented graphically by the change of the original *demand curve* to a new position, denoted by a new demand curve.

movement along the demand curve a change in the *quantity demanded* of a good that results from a change in the price of that good.

Notes

Key Terms *(continued)*

substitutes pairs of goods for which a rise in the price of one of the goods leads to an increase in the demand for the other good.

complements pairs of goods for which a rise in the price of one good leads to a decrease in the demand for the other good.

normal good a good for which a rise in income increases the demand for that good—the "normal" case.

inferior good a good for which a rise in income decreases the demand for the good.

individual demand curve a graphical representation of the relationship between *quantity demanded* and price for an individual consumer.

quantity supplied the actual amount of a good or service producers are willing to sell at some specific price.

supply schedule a list or table showing how much of a good or service producers will supply at different prices.

supply curve a graphical representation of the *supply schedule*, showing the relationship between *quantity supplied* and price.

shift of the supply curve a change in the *quantity supplied* of a good or service at any given price, represented graphically by the change of the original *supply curve* to a new position, denoted by a new supply curve.

movement along the supply curve a change in the *quantity supplied* of a good that results from a change in the price of that good.

input a good or service used to produce another good or service.

individual supply curve a graphical representation of the relationship between *quantity supplied* and price for an individual producer.

equilibrium price the price at which the market is in *equilibrium*, that is, the quantity of a good or service demanded equals the quantity of that good or service supplied; also referred to as the *market-clearing price.*

equilibrium quantity the quantity of a good or service bought and sold at the *equilibrium* (or *market-clearing*) *price.*

market-clearing price the price at which the market is in *equilibrium*, that is, the quantity of a good or service demanded equals the quantity of that good or service supplied; also referred to as the *equilibrium price.*

surplus the excess of a good or service that occurs when the quantity supplied exceeds the quantity demanded; surpluses occur when the price is above the *equilibrium price.*

shortage the insufficiency of a good or service that occurs when the quantity demanded exceeds the quantity supplied; shortages occur when the price is below the *equilibrium price.*

■ AFTER YOU READ THE CHAPTER

Tips

Tip #1. A full understanding of this chapter is critical for your study of economics. The model of supply and demand is used repeatedly in a variety of settings throughout the remainder of this course. You should work with the material in this chapter until you are confident that you know it well and that you understand the techniques, vocabulary, and information in the chapter. Pay particular attention to the distinction between supply and the quantity supplied, demand and the quantity demanded, and shifts of a curve versus movements along a curve. You also should know the determinants of demand and the determinants of supply, and fully understand the meaning of equilibrium in a market and how to find the equilibrium price and equilibrium quantity.

Tip #2. A demand curve is usually downward sloping. The negative slope of a demand curve implies that the quantity demanded of a good or service is inversely related to its price. Another way to express this idea is that as the price of the good decreases, holding everything else constant, consumers will want to buy more units of the good. Figure 3.12 illustrates this law of demand: at P_1, Q_1 units of the good are demanded; as the price of the good falls from P_1 to P_2, the quantity demanded of the good increases from Q_1 to Q_2.

Figure 3.12

Tip #3. A supply curve is usually upward sloping. The positive slope of a supply curve implies that the quantity supplied of a good or service is directly related to its price. Another way to express this idea is that as the price of the good decreases, holding everything else constant, producers will want to supply fewer units of the good. Figure 3.13 illustrates this idea: at P_1, Q_1 units of the good are supplied; as the price of the good falls from P_1 to P_2, the quantity supplied of the good decreases from Q_1 to Q_2.

Figure 3.13

Tip #4. A demand curve illustrates the relationship between the price of the good and the quantity demanded at each specific price. In drawing the demand curve, the other determinants of demand are held constant; this constancy is referred to as the other things equal assumption. This assumption allows economists to consider a change in a single variable while holding all other potentially important variables constant. In the examples throughout the remainder of the course, we typically consider a single change in a situation while holding the other variables constant. Students often struggle with this concept and have trouble working with the model of supply and demand because they do not limit themselves to considering a single change at a time.

Tip #5. Besides the price of the good, the quantity demanded of a good is affected by the following variables: changes in the price of related goods, changes in income, changes in tastes and preferences, changes in expectations, and changes in the number of consumers. You will need to know this list of variables as well as how each of these variables affects the demand curve.

Tip #6. A supply curve illustrates the relationship between the price of the good and the quantity supplied at each specific price. In drawing the supply curve, the other determinants of supply are held constant; this constancy is another example of the other things equal assumption.

Tip #7. Besides the price of the good, the quantity supplied of a good is affected by the following variables: changes in input prices, changes in the price of related goods, and changes in technology, expectations, and the number of producers. You need to know this list of variables as well as how each of these variables affects the supply curve.

Tip #8. Economists make a distinction between demand and the quantity demanded. The quantity demanded refers to a specific quantity associated with a specific price (as in Figure 3.12, where Q_1 is associated with P_1 and Q_2 is associated with P_2). Demand refers to the entire demand curve. Although this may sound like a matter of semantics, economists view this distinction as highly important. Economists make the same distinction between supply and the quantity supplied. The quantity supplied refers to a specific quantity associated with a specific price (as in Figure 3.13, where Q_1 is associated with P_1 and Q_2 is associated with P_2). Supply refers to the entire supply curve.

Tip #9. Economists also make a distinction between a movement along a curve and a shift of the curve. A movement along a curve is caused by a change in the good's price, while a shift in a curve is caused by a change in some variable other than the price of the good.

- Figure 3.14 illustrates this distinction for a demand curve. There is a movement from point *A* to point *B* when the price decreases from P_1 to P_2, and there is a shift in the demand curve from D_1 to D_2 due to a change in some other determinant of demand. A shift causes the quantity demanded of the good to change at every price—for example, at P_1 in Figure 3.14, the shift causes the quantity demanded to increase from Q_1 to Q_3 (compare point *A* to point *C*). Figure 3.14 illustrates an increase in demand when the demand curve shifts to the right from D_1 to D_2. A decrease in demand would be illustrated by the demand curve shifting to the left (in Figure 3.14, this would be a shift from D_2 to D_1).

Figure 3.14

- Figure 3.15 illustrates this distinction for a supply curve. There is a movement from point A to point B when the price decreases from P_1 to P_2, and there is a shift in the supply curve from S_1 to S_2 due to a change in some other determinant of supply. A shift causes the quantity supplied of the good to change at every price—for example, at P_1 in Figure 3.15, the shift causes the quantity supplied to increase from Q_1 to Q_3 (compare point A to point C). Figure 3.15 illustrates an increase in supply when the supply curve shifts to the right from S_1 to S_2. A decrease in supply would be illustrated by the supply curve shifting to the left (in Figure 3.15 this would be a shift from S_2 to S_1).

Figure 3.15

Tip #10. Students initially find it easier to understand the concepts of substitutes and complements if they think about concrete examples. (In Chapter 6, the concept of cross-price elasticity of demand will provide a formal way to determine if two goods are substitutes or complements.) For example, consider soft drinks and popcorn. Two different brands of soft drinks are substitutes: holding all other demand determinants constant, if the price of one brand increases, then the demand for the other soft drink will increase since it is now relatively cheaper and the two goods can easily serve as substitutes for each other. In contrast, if the price of soft drinks increases, holding everything else constant, then the demand for popcorn will decrease. Popcorn and soft drinks are consumed together: they are complements to each other, which implies that if one of these goods gets more expensive (and, therefore, you move upward along that good's demand curve), the quantity demanded of that good decreases. This in turn leads to a decrease in the demand for the complementary good. Questions about substitutes and complements are far easier to interpret if you take the time to think of two specific goods.

Tip #11. You will find it easier to understand questions about normal and inferior goods if you think of specific examples. (In Chapter 6, the concept of income elasticity of demand will provide a formal way to determine if a good is a normal or an inferior good.) A normal good is a good that you will choose to increase the quantity demanded at every price as your income increases (demand shifts to the right as income increases). For example, as your income increases you will increase the quantity demanded of vacations, car travel, and recreation. An inferior good is a good that you will choose to decrease the quantity demanded at every price as your income increases (demand shifts to the left as income increases). For example, as your income increases you will likely consume fewer fast-food restaurant meals or generic pasta dinners.

Tip #12. A shift in the demand or supply curve causes a movement along the supply or demand curve. Figure 3.16 illustrates this idea for a demand curve shift. Notice that when demand shifts to the left (a decrease in demand) this causes a movement along the supply curve: the equilibrium price falls from P_1 to P_2 and the equilibrium quantity falls from Q_1 to Q_2.

Figure 3.16

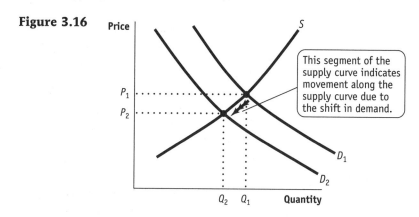

Figure 3.17 illustrates this idea for a supply curve shift. Notice that when supply shifts to the right (an increase in supply) this causes a movement along the demand curve: the equilibrium price falls from P_1 to P_2 and the equilibrium quantity increases from Q_1 to Q_2.

Figure 3.17

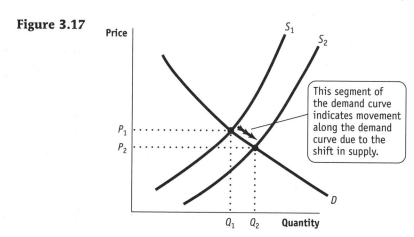

Tip #13. The market equilibrium occurs at the point of intersection of the demand and supply curves. Figure 3.18 indicates that equilibrium at point E, where the equilibrium price is P_1 and the equilibrium quantity is Q_1. If the price is greater than the equilibrium price, there is excess supply, or a surplus, in the market. Figure 3.18 illustrates a situation of excess supply at the price P_2. Note that at price P_2 the quantity supplied is Q_3, while the quantity demanded is Q_2. If the price is less than the equilibrium price, there is excess demand, or a shortage, in the market. Figure 3.18 illustrates a situation of excess demand at the price P_3. Note that at price P_3 the quantity supplied is Q_4, while the quantity demanded is Q_5.

Figure 3.18

Tip #14. If you are given an equation for the demand curve and an equation for the supply curve, you can solve these two equations for the equilibrium price and equilibrium quantity. For example, suppose demand is given by the equation $P = 10 - Q$ and supply is given by the equation $P = Q$. To find the equilibrium, recall that in equilibrium the quantity demanded equals the quantity supplied; thus, $10 - Q = Q$, or the equilibrium quantity equals 5. Replace Q in either equation with 5 and you will find that the equilibrium price is 5.

Tip #15. Often a quick sketch of a demand and supply curve is all that you need to answer questions about the effect of a change in the market on the equilibrium price or equilibrium quantity. Practice drawing a quick representation of the demand and supply curves as you do this chapter's problems, recognizing that you do not always need a precisely plotted graph to find a solution or to guide your solution of a problem.

Tip #16. As always, if you are making a set of flash cards, make one for each new definition or concept and then review these cards (as well as the cards from the earlier chapters).

1. The supply and demand model is often used to analyze the effect of a change in the market on the equilibrium price and quantity of a good. Consider each of the following markets and the given situation to determine whether the demand and/or supply curve shift(s), and what the impact on the equilibrium price and equilibrium quantity will be relative to the initial equilibrium price and equilibrium quantity. For any shift in the demand or supply curve, indicate whether the curve shifts to the left or to the right. The examples are given in a table to help you consolidate your answers.

Market under consideration	Situation	Shift or movement along the demand curve	Shift or movement along the supply curve	Effect on equilibrium price	Effect on equilibrium quantity
Automobile market	War in the Middle East disrupts petroleum exports substantially	*SL – rise in price for comp leads to dec in demand*	*m Left*	*down*	*down*
Pizza market	Price of cheese increases	*m left*	*S Left*	*up*	*down*
Shampoo market	Health advisors release study showing danger of frequent hair washing	*Shift left*	*m left*	*down*	*down*
Oil market	Oil-producing countries form cartel and agree to restrict output	*m r → Shift left*	*Shift left*	*up*	*down up*
Insulation market	Homeowners granted tax credit for installing home insulation	*Shift right*	*m right*	*up*	*up*

STEP 1: For each of the situations, draw the initial market situation and then label the initial equilibrium price and equilibrium quantity.

Review the section "Supply, Demand, and Equilibrium" on pages 87–91.

STEP 2: Next look at the situation and decide whether the situation will cause a movement or a shift of the demand curve, or a movement or a shift of the supply curve. Draw the appropriate shift on your base graph.

Review the section "Shifts of the Demand Curve" on pages 72-74, the section "Understanding Shifts of the Demand Curve" on pages 74-79, the section "Shifts of the Supply Curve" on pages 81-82, and the section "Understanding Shifts of the Supply Curve" on pages 82-86.

STEP 3: Mark the new equilibrium price and equilibrium quantity and then compare the new equilibrium to the initial equilibrium. For example, when war in the Middle East disrupts petroleum exports substantially, this will cause the price of gas to rise, and since cars and gas are complements, the demand for cars will shift to the left due to the increase in the price of gas. As demand shifts left, there is a movement along the supply curve, resulting in a reduction in the equilibrium quantity and the equilibrium price of cars.

Review the section "Changes in Supply and Demand" on pages 92-97.

STEP 4: Record your answers on the given table.

Market under consideration	Situation	Shift or movement along the demand curve	Shift or movement along the supply curve	Effect on equilibrium price	Effect on equilibrium quantity
Automobile market	War in the Middle East disrupts petroleum exports substantially	Demand shifts left as the price of gas rises: cars and gas are complements	Movement along the supply curve as price falls	Decrease in the price of cars	Decrease in the quantity of cars
Pizza market	Price of cheese increases	Movement along the demand curve as price increases	Supply shifts left since cheese is an input in making pizza	Increase in the price of pizza	Decrease in the quantity of pizza
Shampoo market	Health advisors release study showing danger of frequent hair washing	Demand shifts left due to change in tastes and preferences for washing hair: people wish to wash their hair less often at any price of shampoo after the study	Movement along the supply curve as the price of shampoo falls	Decrease in the price of shampoo	Decrease in the quantity of shampoo

Market under consideration	Situation	Shift or movement along the demand curve	Shift or movement along the supply curve	Effect on equilibrium price	Effect on equilibrium quantity
Oil market	Oil-producing countries form cartel and agree to restrict output	Movement along the demand curve due to the shift in the supply curve	Supply shifts left due to the cartel restricting output at every price	Increase in the price of oil	Decrease in the quantity of oil
Insulation market	Homeowners granted tax credit for installing home insulation	Demand shifts right due to the government subsidizing consumption of home insulation: at every price, the quantity of insulation demanded increases	Movement along the supply curve due to the shift in demand curve	Increase in the price of home insulation	Increase in the quantity of home insulation

2. In the market for corn flakes, the price of cardboard used in packing the cereal has risen at the same time that the Surgeon General releases a report detailing the dangers of a diet high in corn products. What happens to the equilibrium price and equilibrium quantity relative to the equilibrium before these two changes?

STEP 1: **First identify that there are two different changes occurring in the market for corn flakes: the price of cardboard used in packing the cereal is increasing, and the Surgeon General has released a report that reveals the danger of eating corn products. In this question you will want to model each of these changes to see what the overall effect is in the market for corn flakes.**

Review the section "Simultaneous Shifts of Supply and Demand Curves" on pages 94–97.

STEP 2: **Draw the initial market situation and label the initial equilibrium price and equilibrium quantity. The figure that follows illustrates the initial situation.**

Review the section "Supply, Demand, and Equilibrium" on pages 87–91.

STEP 3: Consider the change in the price of cardboard: this is an input used to produce a box of corn flakes, and thus an increase in the price of cardboard will cause the supply curve for corn flakes to shift to the left. Draw the appropriate shift on your base graph and label it clearly. The figure that follows illustrates this shift.

Review the section "Shifts of the Supply Curve" on pages 81-82 and the section "Understanding Shifts of the Supply Curve" on pages 82-86.

STEP 4: Next, consider the Surgeon General's report: people will decrease the quantity of corn flakes they demand at every price once this report is released. This will cause the demand curve to shift to the left. But we are not told the magnitude of the shift: a small shift will cause the equilibrium price to rise, while the equilibrium quantity will fall (the intersection of D_2 and S_2, with the equilibrium occurring at Q_2 and P_2); a moderate shift might cause the equilibrium price to remain at its initial level, while the equilibrium quantity falls (the intersection of D_2' and S_2, with the equilibrium occurring at Q_2' and $P_2' = P_1$); and a large shift would cause the equilibrium price to fall, while the equilibrium quantity also falls (the intersection of D_2'' and S_2, with the equilibrium occurring at Q_2'' and P_2''). Price is therefore indeterminate, while quantity will definitely decrease with these two changes in the market for corn flakes. Study the following figure carefully to see this concept.

Review the section "Shifts of the Demand Curve" on pages 72-74, the section "Understanding Shifts of the Demand Curve" on pages 74-79, the section "Changes in Supply and Demand" on pages 92-97, and the section "Simultaneous Shifts of Supply and Demand Curves" on pages 94-97.

3. In the market for chocolate, people read that the consumption of chocolate has major health benefits. At the same time, the cost of growing and harvesting cocoa beans increases. What happens to the equilibrium price and equilibrium quantity relative to the equilibrium before these two changes?

STEP 1: First, identify that there are two different changes occurring in the market for chocolate: eating chocolate provides health benefits and the cost of growing and harvesting cocoa beans increases. In this question, you will want to model each of these changes to see what the overall effect is in the market for chocolate.

Review the section "Simultaneous Shifts of Supply and Demand Curves" on pages 94-97.

STEP 2: Draw the initial market situation and label the initial equilibrium price and equilibrium quantity. The following figure illustrates the initial situation.

Review the section "Supply, Demand, and Equilibrium" on pages 87-91.

STEP 3: Consider the change in the cost of growing and harvesting cocoa beans: cocoa beans are an input used to produce chocolate, and thus an increase in the price of cocoa beans will cause the supply curve for chocolate to shift to the left. Draw the appropriate shift on your base graph and label it clearly. The figure that follows illustrates this shift.

Review the section "Shifts of the Supply Curve" on pages 81-82 and the section "Understanding Shifts of the Supply Curve" on pages 82-86.

STEP 4: Next, consider the health benefits from consuming chocolate: this will cause the quantity demanded of chocolate to increase at every price. Thus, the demand curve for chocolate will shift to the right. But we are not told the magnitude of the shift:

- A small shift will cause the equilibrium price to rise while the equilibrium quantity will fall (the intersection of D_2 and S_2, with the equilibrium occurring at Q_2 and P_2)

- A moderate shift might cause the equilibrium price to rise while the equilibrium quantity remains at its initial level (the intersection of D_2' and S_2, with the equilibrium occurring at P_2' and $Q_2' = Q_1$)

- A large shift would cause the equilibrium price to rise while the equilibrium quantity also rises (the intersection of D_2'' and S_2, with the equilibrium occurring at Q_2'' and P_2'').

Price will definitely increase while quantity is indeterminate with these two changes in the market for chocolate.

Study the following figure carefully to see this concept.

Review the section "Shifts of the Demand Curve" on pages 72–74, the section "Understanding Shifts of the Demand Curve" on pages 74–79, the section "Changes in Supply and Demand" on pages 92–97, and the section "Simultaneous Shifts of Supply and Demand Curves" on pages 94–97.

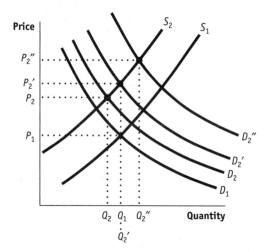

4. Suppose you are told that the initial demand curve for good X is $P = 100 - Q$. You are then told that incomes increase in this economy and that good X is a normal good. If you know that the quantity demanded of good X changes by 5 units at every price, what is the equation for the new demand curve?

STEP 1: Start by drawing a graph of the initial demand curve. The figure that follows illustrates this demand curve.

Review the section "The Demand Schedule and the Demand Curve" on pages 71–72, and Figure 3-1 on page 71.

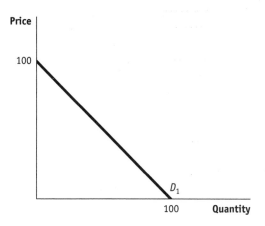

STEP 2: You are told that incomes increase in this economy and that this is a normal good. A change in income will cause the demand curve to shift: since incomes increase and the good is a normal good, the demand curve will shift to the right.

Review the section "Shifts of the Demand Curve" on pages 72–74.

STEP 3: Calculate the exact location of the new demand curve. You know that, at every price, 5 more units are being demanded than were demanded initially. Thus, if the price was initially $0, the quantity demanded was initially 100 units (use the demand equation to get the quantity demanded when the price is $0). Now, at a price of $0, the original 100 units plus an additional 5 units will be demanded. Thus, you know that the point $(Q,P) = (105,\$0)$ sits on the new demand curve. The new demand curve has the same slope as the original demand curve, so all you need to find is the new y-intercept: use the point you know that is on the new demand curve to find this y-intercept. Thus, $P = b - Q$, and when $Q = 105$ and $P = \$0$, then $b = 105$. Thus, the new demand equation is $P = 105 - Q$. The figure that follows illustrates the new demand curve, D_2, along with the initial demand curve. Alternatively, the initial demand curve can be written as $Q = 100 - P$. The new demand curve has the same slope as the initial demand curve and an x-intercept of 105: thus, the new demand curve can be written as $Q = 105 - P$.

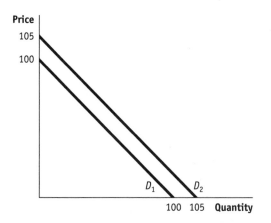

5. Suppose you are told that each firm in an industry is identical and that there are two firms in the industry. Furthermore, you are told that one firm's supply curve is given by the equation $P = 10 + 2Q$. Find the market supply curve in this industry.

STEP 1: To find the market supply curve, you will want to horizontally add all the individual supply curves of the firms in the industry. This will be relatively easy if you draw three horizontally aligned graphs where the first graph illustrates Firm 1's supply curve, the second graph illustrates Firm 2's supply curve, and the third graph illustrates the market supply curve. The following figure represents this concept.

Review the section "Shifts of the Supply Curve" on pages 81–82, and Figure 3-10 on page 84.

STEP 2: To find the market supply curve, you will want to horizontally add all the individual supply curves of the firms in the industry. Use your sketch to help you write this equation.

Review the section "Shifts of the Supply Curve" on pages 81–82, and Figure 3-10 on page 84.

From the third graph you can see- that the y-intercept is 10. You can also calculate the slope of the market supply curve as the change in price divided by the change in quantity. Using the points (0, 10) and (10, 20), the slope is equal to 1. The market supply curve can thus be written as $P = Q + 10$.

Problems and Exercises

1. Why is the assumption that there are many buyers and many sellers in a competitive market important?

2. You are given the following information about demand in the competitive market for bicycles.

Price per bicycle	Quantity of bicycles demanded per week
$100	0
80	100
60	200
40	500
20	800
0	1,000

a. Graph this demand schedule, placing price on the vertical axis and quantity on the horizontal axis.

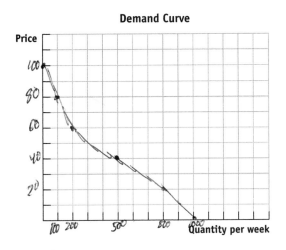

b. Suppose the price is initially $40. If the price rises by $20, what happens to the quantity demanded?

decreases by 300

c. Suppose the price is initially $40. If the price falls by $40, what happens to the quantity demanded?

goes up to 100

3. For each of the situations in the following table, fill in the missing information. First, determine whether the situation causes a shift or a movement along the demand curve; then, if it causes a shift, determine whether the demand curve shifts to the right or to the left.

Situation	Specified market	Movement or shift	Rightward or leftward shift in demand
People's income increases	Market for exotic vacations	shift	right
People's income decreases	Market for goods sold in secondhand shops	shift	left r
Price of bicycles increases	Market for bicycles	m	right
Price of tennis balls increases	Market for tennis racquets	shift	right left
Price of movie tickets decreases	Popcorn at movie theaters	shift	left right
Popularity of music-playing device increases	Market for music-playing devices	shift	r
Popularity of branded clothing items decreases	Market for brand-name designer clothing	shift	left
Winter clothing to go on sale next month	Market for winter clothing	shift	left
Increase in urban residents	Market for apartments in urban areas	shift	right

4. Suppose a market has three consumers (this will simplify the work you need to do!): Joe, Maria, and Chao. Their demand schedules are given in the following table.

Price	Quantity demanded by Joe	Quantity demanded by Maria	Quantity demanded by Chao
$0	10	20	5
1	8	16	4
2	6	12	3
3	4	8	2
4	2	4	1

a. In the following graphs, sketch a graph of Joe's demand curve, Maria's demand curve, and Chao's demand curve. Then sketch the market demand curve based on the demand of these three individuals.

Joe's Demand

Maria's Demand

Chao's Demand

Market Demand

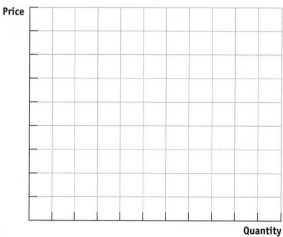

b. Summarize the market demand curve you found by filling in the following table.

Price	Quantity demanded in market
$0	
1	
2	
3	
4	

5. The following graph represents the supply curve for the production of widgets in Town Center.

a. At a price of $20, how many widgets are producers willing to supply?

b. At a price of $40, how many widgets are producers willing to supply?

c. Suppose there are ten widget producers in Town Center and that the price of widgets is $50. If each widget producer produces exactly the same number of widgets as every other widget producer, how many widgets will each producer produce at this price?

d. Suppose the price is initially $30 but then falls to $20. What is the change in the quantity supplied?

e. Suppose the price is initially $30 but then increases to $50. What is the change in the quantity supplied?

f. What price must suppliers receive to be willing to supply 80 widgets?

g. What price must suppliers receive to be willing to supply 40 widgets?

h. What does the slope of a typical supply curve imply about the relationship between price and the quantity supplied?

6. For each of the situations in the following table, fill in the missing information: first, determine whether the situation causes a shift or a movement along the supply curve; then, if it causes a shift, determine whether the supply curve shifts to the right or to the left.

Situation	Specified market	Movement or shift	Rightward or leftward shift in supply
Labor costs for air travel and cruise ships increase	Market for exotic vacations	shift	left
Prices of office equipment and phone service rise by 40%	Market for call center services	shift	left
Price of bicycles increases	Market for bicycles	m	
Price of leather boots increases	Market for beef products	shift	right
Price of leather boots increases	Market for leather belts	shift	left
New technology for music-playing device revealed	Market for music-playing devices	shift	right
Price of brand-name designer clothing increases	Market for brand-name designer clothing	m	
Stock market prices expected to fall next quarter	Stock market today	shift	right
Increase in number of coffee shop owners in the metro area	Market for coffee shops in the metro area	shift	right

7. The following table provides the demand and supply schedules for Healthy Snacks, Inc.

Price	Quantity demanded	Quantity supplied
$ 0	1,000	0
10	800	125
20	600	275
30	400	400
40	200	550
50	0	675

a. Draw a sketch of the demand and supply curves for Healthy Snacks, Inc. Don't worry about drawing a precise graph but instead focus on drawing a simple rendering of the underlying relationships captured in the previous table. This drawing should be accurate with regard to x-intercepts and y-intercepts, and it should also indicate the point of equilibrium.

Demand and Supply Curves for Healthy Snacks, Inc.

b. From the table, what are the equilibrium price and the equilibrium quantity in this market? Indicate these on your graph.

$$Ep = 30$$
$$Eq = 400$$

c. Fill in the following table based on the data given to you. Assume that for each row in the table, the price is as given and that you are calculating the number of units of excess demand or excess supply. (Hint: Some of the cells in your table will be left empty—for example, if there is excess supply, then there isn't excess demand.)

Price	Excess Demand	Excess Supply
$ 0	1000	
10	675	
20	325	
30		
40		350
50		675

d. Why is a situation of excess demand referred to as a shortage? Explain using a simple graph to illustrate your answer.

b/c more Q_D
than Q_S → not enough → shortage

Shortage

e. Why is a situation of excess supply referred to as a surplus? Explain using a simple graph to illustrate your answer.

8. Use the following graph to answer this next set of questions. The graph illustrates the competitive market for garbage cans in Cleantopia.

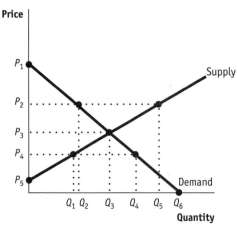

a. What is the equilibrium price in this market?

b. What is the equilibrium quantity in this market?

c. Suppose the current price of garbage cans in Cleantopia is P_2. Describe this market in detail and explain what you think will happen in this market.

d. Suppose the current price of garbage cans in Cleantopia is P_4. Describe this market in detail and explain what you think will happen in this market.

e. Suppose at the current market price the quantity demanded equals Q_4. Describe this market and identify the quantity supplied given this information. What do you expect will happen in this market?

f. Suppose at the current market price the quantity supplied equals Q_5. Describe this market and identify the quantity demanded given this information. What do you expect will happen in this market?

g. At what price is the quantity demanded equal to zero? What does it mean to have the quantity demanded equal to zero?

h. At what price is the quantity supplied equal to zero? What does it mean to have the quantity supplied equal to zero?

9. The competitive market for bicycles in Pedal City is described by the demand curve $P = 2,000 - 2Q$ and the supply curve $P = 6Q$. There are 20 bicycle manufacturers in Pedal City and each of these manufacturers produces the same number of bicycles as every other manufacturer.

a. Using the two equations for the demand and supply curves, fill in the following table describing the demand and supply schedules for bicycles in Pedal City.

Price	Quantity demanded	Quantity supplied
$ 0	1000	0
240	880	40
480	760	80
720	640	120
960	520	160
1,200	400	200
1,440	280	240
1,680	160	280
1,920	40	320

$6Q = 2000 - 2Q$
$8Q = 2000$
$Q = 250$

b. Examine the table you created in (a) and provide a range of prices that you expect the equilibrium price to fall between. Why do you expect the equilibrium price to fall within this range?

c. Sketch a graph of the demand and supply curves for bicycles in Pedal City.

Market for Bicycles in Pedal City

d. If the current price for bicycles is $240, how many bicycles will be supplied in Pedal City and how many bicycles will a single manufacturer produce? At a price of $240, how many bicycles will be demanded? At a price of $240, is the market in equilibrium? Explain your answer.

e. If the current price for bicycles is $480, how many bicycles will be supplied in Pedal City and how many bicycles will a single manufacturer produce? At a price of $480, how many bicycles will be demanded? At a price of $480, is the market in equilibrium? Explain your answer.

f. If the current price for bicycles is $1,680, how many bicycles will be supplied in Pedal City and how many bicycles will a single manufacturer produce? At a price of $1,680, how many bicycles will be demanded? At a price of $1,680, is the market in equilibrium? Explain your answer.

g. Calculate the equilibrium price and the equilibrium quantity in the market for bicycles in Pedal City.

10. For each of the following situations, sketch a graph of the initial market demand (D_1) and supply (S_1) curves and indicate the initial equilibrium price (P_1) and equilibrium quantity (Q_1). Then sketch any changes in the market demand (D_2) and supply (S_2) curves and indicate the new equilibrium price (P_2) and equilibrium quantity (Q_2). For each situation, identify which curve(s) shift and whether there is a movement along the demand or supply curves.

a. The price of gasoline increases by 40%. What happens in the market for bicycles?

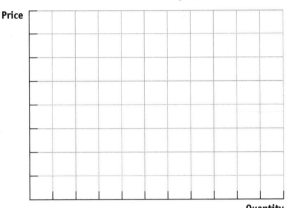

b. The price of gasoline increases by 40%. What happens in the market for fuel-inefficient SUVs?

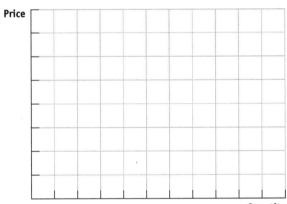

c. New technology for music-playing devices is developed. What happens in the market for music-playing devices?

d. The price of labor decreases. What happens in the market for fast-food restaurants?

Market for Fast-Food Restaurants

e. Income increases and good X is a normal good. What happens in the market for good X?

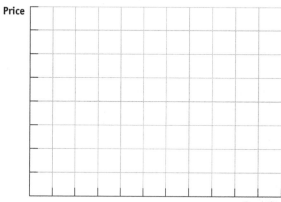

Market for Good X

f. Income increases and good X is an inferior good. What happens in the market for good X?

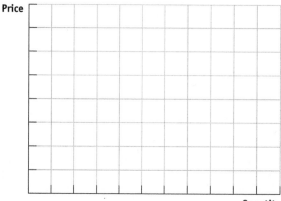

Market for Good X

11. You are given the following information about the demand and supply schedules for gadgets in Micro Town. Assume that gadgets in Micro Town are produced in a competitive market.

Price	Quantity demanded	Quantity supplied
$ 0	100	0
2	80	20
4	60	40
6	40	60
8	20	80
10	0	100

a. From the data provided in the table, write an equation expressing the demand schedule and an equation expressing the supply schedule.

b. Using the equations you wrote in part (a), find the equilibrium price and the equilibrium quantity in this market.

c. Now suppose that the quantity demanded increases by 20 units at every price and that the quantity supplied increases by 40 units at every price. What happens to the equilibrium price and equilibrium quantity in this market relative to the initial levels of the equilibrium price and equilibrium quantity? (Hint: You might find it helpful to draw a sketch of the original demand curve and then the new demand curve to help guide you in your work. Then, once you have the new demand curve equation, you could draw a sketch of the original supply curve and the new supply curve to help you calculate the new supply curve equation.)

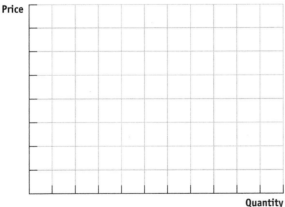

Price

Quantity

d. Now suppose that the quantity demanded increases by the same amount as in part (c), but that the quantity supplied increases by only 10 units at every price. What happens to the equilibrium price and the equilibrium quantity in this market relative to the initial levels of the equilibrium price and equilibrium quantity?

e. In parts (c) and (d), the demand and supply curves shifted to the right. If you knew the direction of these shifts but did not know the size or magnitude of the shift, what would you know about the new equilibrium price and quantity?

12. Let's generalize the findings of question 11 for four different situations in which both the demand and supply curves shift at the same time. In each of these situations we assume that we know the direction of the shift but not the size of the shift. Fill in the following table for each of the possible situations. The first situation (the one in question 11) has already been done for you.

Situation	Effect on equilibrium price	Effect on equilibrium quantity
Demand shifts to the right and supply shifts to the right	May increase, decrease, or remain the same	Increases
Demand shifts to the left and supply shifts to the left		
Demand shifts to the right and supply shifts to the left		
Demand shifts to the left and supply shifts to the right		

BEFORE YOU TAKE THE TEST

Chapter Review Questions

1. Competitive markets are characterized as having
   a. many buyers and a single seller.
   b. many buyers and a few sellers.
   c. many buyers and many sellers.
   d. a few buyers and many sellers.

2. Sue goes to the store to purchase a bottle of shampoo. When she gets to the store she discovers that her brand of shampoo is on sale for $4 a bottle instead of the usual $5.99 per bottle. According to the law of demand, we can expect that
   a. Sue will purchase one bottle of shampoo.
   b. Sue will not purchase the shampoo.
   c. Sue will likely purchase more than one bottle of shampoo.
   d. Sue will substitute away from her usual brand of shampoo and instead purchase an alternative brand.

3. The law of demand states that the quantity demanded is an inverse function of its price. This means that
   a. as price increases, the quantity demanded decreases.
   b. as price increases, the quantity demanded increases.
   c. the demand curve shifts to the left with increases in price.
   d. the demand curve shifts to the right with increases in price.

4. Consider the market for mangos. Suppose researchers discover that eating mangos generates large health benefits. Which of the following statements is true?
   a. This discovery will not affect the market for mangos.
   b. This discovery will cause the demand for mangos to shift to the right.
   c. This discovery will cause the price of mangos to decrease due to a movement along the demand curve for mangos.
   d. This discovery will cause a movement along the demand curve for mangos.

5. Consider the demand curve for automobiles. An increase in the price of automobiles due to a leftward shift in the supply curve will
   a. cause a movement along the demand curve for automobiles.
   b. result in an increase in the quantity of automobiles demanded.
   c. have no effect on the quantity of automobiles demanded, since the change occurred on the supply side of the model.
   d. Answers (a) and (b) are both true statements.

6. The prices of flat-screen TVs are expected to fall next year. Which of the following statements about the market for flat-screen TVs this year are true?
   I. Consumers will decrease their demand for flat-screen TVs at all prices this year in anticipation of the decrease in flat-screen TV prices next year.
   II. Flat-screen TV prices today are likely to decrease due to these expectations.
   III. Flat-screen TV prices today are likely to increase due to these expectations.
   a. Statement I is true.
   b. Statement II is true.
   c. Statement III is true.
   d. Statements I and II are true.
   e. Statements I and III are true.

7. Peanut butter and jelly are considered to be complements in the diet of many people. Holding everything else constant, if the price of peanut butter increases, then the demand for
   a. peanut butter will shift to the left.
   b. peanut butter will shift to the right.
   c. jelly will shift to the left.
   d. jelly will shift to the right.

8. Ham and turkey are considered to be substitutes in the diet of many people. Holding everything else constant, if the price of ham decreases, then the demand for
   a. turkey will shift to the left.
   b. turkey will shift to the right.
   c. ham will shift to the left.
   d. ham will shift to the right.

9. Consider two goods: good X and good Y. Holding everything else constant, the price of good Y increases and the demand for good X decreases. Good X and good Y are
   a. complements.
   b. substitutes.
   c. not related to each other.

10. Consider two goods: good X and good Y. Holding everything else constant, the price of good Y decreases and the demand for good X decreases. Good X and good Y are
    a. complements.
    b. substitutes.
    c. not related to each other.

11. Holding everything else constant, Jon's income increases. If Jon's demand for good X decreases, then it must be the case that good X is a(n)
    a. inferior good.
    b. normal good.
    c. complement.
    d. substitute.

12. Jon's income increases by 10% this year while his purchases of steak increase by 4% this year over last year's purchases of steak. Holding everything else constant, Jon considers steak to be a(n)
    a. inferior good.
    b. normal good.
    c. complement.
    d. substitute.

13. Smalltown experiences an increase in its population due to the economic opportunities available there. This event is likely to
    a. cause the demand curve for many products in Smalltown to shift to the right.
    b. cause the demand curve for many products in Smalltown to shift to the left.
    c. have little effect on the demand for products in Smalltown.
    d. cause the supply curve for many products in Smalltown to shift to the left.

14. A market is initially composed of 100 buyers. Holding everything else constant, if an additional 100 buyers join this market, then this will
    a. have no effect on the market demand curve since there is a limit to how many units of the good can be demanded at any price.
    b. cause the market demand curve to shift to the left since the good's price will necessarily increase when there are more buyers.
    c. cause the market demand curve to shift to the right as the additional demand of these new consumers is added to the initial demand curve.
    d. cause a movement along the demand curve as the price of the good rises due to the increase in the number of buyers.

15. Consider a market composed of three consumers: Peter, Anya, and Pablo. The market demand schedule is given in the table that follows. Which of the possible individual demand schedules provided in the answer selection is most likely to correspond to this market demand schedule?

Price	Market quantity demanded
$10	100
20	75
30	50
40	25

a.

Price	Quantity demanded by Peter	Quantity demanded by Anya	Quantity demanded by Pablo
$10	25	25	40
20	20	20	35
30	15	14	16
40	10	10	5

b.

Price	Quantity demanded by Peter	Quantity demanded by Anya	Quantity demanded by Pablo
$10	25	25	50
20	20	15	35
30	15	10	25
40	10	10	5

c.

Price	Quantity demanded by Peter	Quantity demanded by Anya	Quantity demanded by Pablo
$10	25	25	55
20	15	20	35
30	10	15	20
40	5	10	5

d.

Price	Quantity demanded by Peter	Quantity demanded by Anya	Quantity demanded by Pablo
$10	25	25	50
20	20	20	35
30	15	15	20
40	10	10	5

16. Consider a supply curve. When the price of the good increases, then this results in a movement along the supply curve resulting in a greater

a. supply of the good.

b. quantity supplied.

17. The cost of ground beef used to produce Fast Wally's hamburgers increases. Holding everything else constant, this will result
   a. in the supply curve shifting to the left.
   b. in the supply curve shifting to the right.
   c. in a movement along the supply curve to a smaller quantity supplied.
   d. in a movement along the supply curve to a greater quantity supplied.

18. The cost of raw materials used to produce Ever Strong Batteries decreases. Holding everything else constant, this will result
   a. in the supply curve shifting to the left.
   b. in the supply curve shifting to the right.
   c. in a movement along the supply curve to a smaller quantity supplied.
   d. in a movement along the supply curve to a greater quantity supplied.

19. Input prices decrease for a manufacturer. Holding everything else constant, this implies that at any given price the manufacturer will supply
   a. more of the good.
   b. less of the good.

20. A manufacturer produces two different products from its fixed set of resources. When the manufacturer increases the production of the first good, it must necessarily reduce the level of production of the second good due to these fixed resources. These two goods are
   a. complements in production.
   b. substitutes in production.

21. A sawmill operator produces lumber used in the construction industry as well as sawdust used for pet bedding. An increase in the supply of lumber is likely to
   a. increase the supply of sawdust, since lumber and sawdust are complements in production.
   b. decrease the supply of sawdust, since lumber and sawdust are complements in production.
   c. increase the supply of sawdust, since lumber and sawdust are substitutes in production.
   d. decrease the supply of sawdust, since lumber and sawdust are substitutes in production.

22. Research and development result in the discovery of a new technology for electricity generation. Holding everything else constant, this discovery will
   a. increase the supply of electricity.
   b. increase the quantity supplied of electricity.
   c. decrease the supply of electricity.
   d. decrease the quantity supplied of electricity.

23. The sawmill industry expects lumber prices to rise next year due to growing demand for the construction of new homes. Holding everything else constant, this expectation will shift
   a. the supply curve for lumber this year to the left.
   b. the supply curve for lumber this year to the right.

24. The following graph illustrates the supply curve for the competitive market for widgets. Currently there are 16 producers in this market and each producer produces exactly the same number of widgets as every other producer. Suppose the price of widgets is $40. If all the producers continue to produce the same number as every other producer, what will be the level of production for each producer?

a. 8 widgets

b. 10 widgets

c. 5 widgets

d. 20 widgets

25. The market demand curve for a product is the horizontal summation of the individual demand curves for the product, holding the

a. quantity demanded constant.

b. price constant.

26. Which of the following statements is true about equilibrium in a competitive market for a good?

    I. In equilibrium, the quantity demanded equals the quantity supplied.

    II. The equilibrium price and the equilibrium quantity correspond to the price and quantity at which the demand curve intersects the supply curve.

    III. In equilibrium, every consumer who wishes to consume the product is satisfied.

a. Statement I is true.

b. Statement II is true.

c. Statement III is true.

d. Statements I and II are true.

e. Statements I, II, and III are true.

27. The competitive market for widgets is described in the following table.

Price	Quantity demanded	Quantity supplied
$ 0	400	0
20	300	100
40	200	200
60	100	300
80	0	400

If the current price is $20, then there is a(n)
a. excess supply of 200 widgets.
b. shortage of 200 widgets.
c. excess demand of 100 widgets.
d. surplus of 100 widgets.

28. The competitive market for widgets is described in the following table.

Price	Quantity demanded	Quantity supplied
$ 0	400	0
20	300	100
40	200	200
60	100	300
80	0	400

If the current price is $60, then there is a(n)
a. excess supply of 200 widgets.
b. excess demand of 200 widgets.
c. shortage of 100 widgets.
d. surplus of 100 widgets.

29. The competitive market for widgets is described in the following table.

Price	Quantity demanded	Quantity supplied
$ 0	400	0
20	300	100
40	200	200
60	100	300
80	0	400

The equilibrium quantity in this market is _____ and the equilibrium **price is**
_____ .

a. 300 widgets; $20
b. 200 widgets; $20
c. 200 widgets; $40
d. 200 widgets; $60

30. The competitive market for widgets is described in the following table. Furthermore, **you**
are told that both the demand curve and the supply curve are linear.

Price	Quantity demanded	Quantity supplied
$ 0	400	0
20	300	100
40 /	200	200
60	100	300
80	0	400

Which of the following equations is the demand equation for widgets?
a. $Q = 80 - 5P$
b. $P = 80 - 5Q$
c. $Q = 400 - 5P$
d. $Q = 1/5P$

31. The competitive market for widgets is described in the following table. Furthermore, **you**
are told that both the demand curve and the supply curve are linear.

Price	Quantity demanded	Quantity supplied
$ 0	400	0
20	300	100
40	200	200
60	100	300
80	0	400

Which of the following equations is the supply equation for widgets?
a. $P = 5Q$
b. $P = 1/5Q$
c. $Q = 1/5P - 100$
d. $Q = 100 + 1/5Q$

$100 = 100 + 1/5(600) =$

32. Use the following graph of a competitive market for candles to answer this question.

Market for Candles

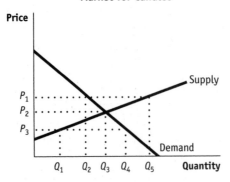

At a price of P_1, there is an
a. excess supply of the good equal to $Q_2 - Q_5$.
b. excess supply of the good equal to $Q_5 - Q_2$.
c. excess supply of the good equal to $Q_3 - Q_2$.
d. excess demand for the good equal to $Q_3 - Q_2$.

33. Use the following graph of a competitive market for candles to answer this question.

Market for Candles

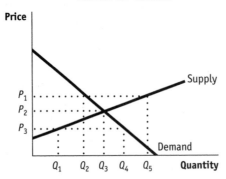

At a price of P_3, there is an
a. excess demand for the good of $Q_4 - Q_1$.
b. excess demand for the good of $Q_1 - Q_4$.
c. excess demand for the good of $Q_3 - Q_2$.
d. excess supply of the good of $Q_3 - Q_2$.

34. In the competitive market for candles, there is an increase in the number of people purchasing candles and a decrease in the cost of beeswax, a major ingredient in the production of candles. Which of the following statements is true?
a. The equilibrium price and the equilibrium quantity of candles will increase.
b. The equilibrium price and the equilibrium quantity of candles will decrease.
c. The equilibrium price may increase, decrease, or remain the same, but the equilibrium quantity will increase.
d. The equilibrium quantity may increase, decrease, or remain the same, but the equilibrium price will increase.

35. Consumers in Mayville consider houses and apartments to be substitutes. There is an increase in the price of houses in Mayville at the same time three new apartment buildings are opened there. In the market for apartments in Mayville
    a. the equilibrium price will rise relative to its level before these two events.
    b. the equilibrium price will fall relative to its level before these two events.
    c. the equilibrium quantity will rise relative to its level before these two events.
    d. the equilibrium quantity will fall relative to its level before these two events.

36. The production of good X requires labor inputs and therefore the price of good X is directly affected by labor costs. Suppose that the price of labor increases while simultaneously people's income rises. If good X is a normal good, then we know in the market for good X
    a. the equilibrium price will increase and the equilibrium quantity may increase, decrease, or remain the same relative to their initial levels.
    b. the equilibrium price will decrease and the equilibrium quantity may increase, decrease, or remain the same relative to their initial levels.
    c. the equilibrium quantity will increase and the equilibrium price may increase, decrease, or remain the same relative to their initial levels.
    d. the equilibrium quantity will decrease and the equilibrium price may increase, decrease, or remain the same relative to their initial levels.

37. People's income rises, while simultaneously there is a technological advance in the production of good X. Good X is an inferior good. Given this information, we know in the market for good X
    a. the equilibrium price will increase and the equilibrium quantity may increase, decrease, or remain the same relative to their initial levels.
    b. the equilibrium price will decrease and the equilibrium quantity may increase, decrease, or remain the same relative to their initial levels.
    c. the equilibrium quantity will increase and the equilibrium price may increase, decrease, or remain the same relative to their initial levels.
    d. the equilibrium quantity will decrease and the equilibrium price may increase, decrease, or remain the same relative to their initial levels.

38. The price of bubble gum increases at the same time that sugar, a major ingredient in candy, gets more expensive. If candy and bubble gum are substitutes, what happens to the equilibrium price and the equilibrium quantity in the market for candy?
    a. The equilibrium price will increase and the equilibrium quantity may increase, decrease, or remain the same relative to their initial levels.
    b. The equilibrium price will decrease and the equilibrium quantity may increase, decrease, or remain the same relative to their initial levels.
    c. The equilibrium quantity will increase and the equilibrium price may increase, decrease, or remain the same relative to their initial levels.
    d. The equilibrium quantity will decrease and the equilibrium price may increase, decrease, or remain the same relative to their initial levels.

ANSWER KEY

Answers to Problems and Exercises

1. This assumption results in a market situation in which no buyer (or group of buyers) and no seller (or group of sellers) can affect the market price. In a competitive market, the interaction of demand and supply determines the equilibrium price and the equilibrium quantity rather than the behavior of a particular buyer and/or seller.

2. **a.**

Demand Curve

b. If the price rises to $60, the quantity demanded will fall by 300 units, from 500 bicycles to 200 bicycles.

c. If the price falls to $0, the quantity demanded will increase by 500 units, from 500 bicycles to 1,000 bicycles.

3.

Situation	Specified market	Movement or shift	Rightward or leftward shift in demand
People's income increases	Market for exotic vacations	Shift	Rightward
People's income decreases	Market for goods sold in secondhand shops	Shift	Rightward
Price of bicycles increases	Market for bicycles	Movement	
Price of tennis balls increases	Market for tennis racquets	Shift	Leftward
Price of movie tickets decreases	Popcorn at movie theaters	Shift	Rightward
Popularity of music-playing device increases	Market for music-playing devices	Shift	Rightward
Popularity of branded clothing items decreases	Market for brand-name designer clothing	Shift	Leftward
Winter clothing to go on sale next month	Market for winter clothing	Shift	Leftward
Increase in urban residents	Market for apartments in urban areas	Shift	Rightward

4. **a.** Note: these sketches are not drawn to scale, since they are meant to be a guide rather than a perfect mathematical rendering of the data in the table. To find the market demand curve, hold price constant and ask how many units are demanded by all the consumers at this price. For example, at a price of $3, Joe demands 4 units, Maria demands 8 units, and Chao demands 2 units, for a total market demand of 14 units at a price of $3. Repeat this for another price (e.g., for a price of $4, Joe demands 2 units, Maria demands 4 units, and Chao demands 1 unit, for a total market demand of 7 units).

Joe's Demand

Maria's Demand

Chao's Demand

Market Demand

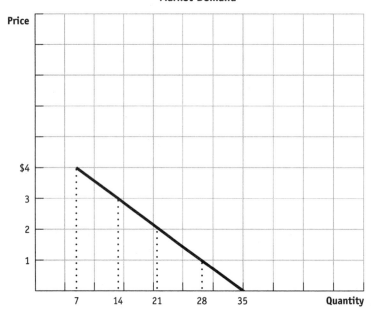

b. Summarize the market demand curve you found by filling in the following table.

Price	Quantity demanded in market
$0	35
1	28
2	21
3	14
4	7

5. **a.** At a price of $20, producers are willing to supply 40 units.

   b. At a price of $40, producers are willing to supply 80 units.

   c. At a price of $50, 100 widgets are supplied. Thus, if there are ten producers producing exactly the same number of widgets, then each producer must produce 10 widgets.

   d. When price falls from $30 to $20, the number of widgets supplied decreases by 20 widgets (from 60 widgets to 40 widgets).

   e. When price rises from $30 to $50, the number of widgets supplied increases by 40 widgets (from 60 widgets to 100 widgets).

   f. Suppliers are willing to supply 80 widgets if the price is $40.

   g. Suppliers are willing to supply 40 widgets if the price is $20.

   h. The typical supply curve is upward sloping: its slope is positive. This implies that the quantity supplied increases when price increases and that the quantity supplied decreases when price decreases.

6.

Situation	Specified market	Movement or shift	Rightward or leftward shift in supply
Labor costs for air travel and cruise ships increase	Market for exotic vacations	Shift	Leftward
Prices of office equipment and phone service rise by 40%	Market for call center services	Shift	Leftward
Price of bicycles increases	Market for bicycles	Movement	
Price of leather boots increases	Market for beef products	Shift	Rightward
Price of leather boots increases	Market for leather belts	Shift	Leftward
New technology for music-playing device revealed	Market for music-playing devices	Shift	Rightward
Price of brand-name designer clothing increases	Market for brand-name designer clothing	Movement	
Stock market prices expected to fall next quarter	Stock market today	Shift	Rightward
Increase in number of coffee shop owners in the metro area	Market for coffee shops in the metro area	Shift	Rightward

7. a.,b. Equilibrium occurs at the price at which the quantity demanded equals the quantity supplied. From the following table, we can see that the quantity demanded equals the quantity supplied at a price of $30. The equilibrium price is thus $30 and the equilibrium quantity is 400 units. This point is illustrated in the graph in part (d).

c.

Price	Excess demand	Excess supply
$ 0	1,000 units	
10	675 units	
20	325 units	
30	Equilibrium	Equilibrium
40		350 units
50		675 units

d. When there is excess demand this means that the quantity demanded by consumers is greater than the quantity supplied by producers. The market for some reason does not provide an adequate amount of the good, and thus there is a shortage of the good. The following figure illustrates a shortage at a price of P_1. Note that at P_1, the quantity demanded is Q_1, the quantity supplied is Q_2, and the excess demand is equal to $Q_1 - Q_2$. When a market has excess demand, this implies that the current price of the good is less than the market-clearing price.

Illustration of a Situation of Excess Demand, or a Shortage

e. When there is excess supply this means that the quantity demanded by consumers is less than the quantity supplied by producers. The market for some reason provides too much of the good, and there is thus a surplus of the good. The following figure illustrates a surplus at a price of P_1. Note that at P_1, the quantity demanded is Q_1, the quantity supplied is Q_2, and the excess supply is equal to $Q_2 - Q_1$. When a market has excess supply of a good, this implies that the current price in the market is greater than the market-clearing price.

Illustration of a Situation of Excess Supply, or a Surplus

The arrow segment represents the excess supply, or surplus, of the good at the price of P_1.

8. a. The equilibrium price in this market is P_3, since the quantity demanded (Q_3) equals the quantity supplied (Q_3) at this price.

b. Q_3.

c. At P_2 there is an excess supply, or surplus, of the good, since the quantity supplied equals Q_5 while the quantity demanded equals Q_2. The price should fall toward the equilibrium price. As the price falls, consumers will increase the quantity demanded of the good, while producers will decrease the quantity supplied of the good until the price reaches the point at which the quantity demanded equals the quantity supplied.

d. At P_4 there is an excess demand, or shortage, for the good, since the quantity supplied equals Q_1 while the quantity demanded equals Q_4. The price should rise toward the equilibrium price. As the price increases, consumers will reduce the quantity demanded of the good while producers will increase the quantity supplied of the good until the price reaches the point where the quantity demanded equals the quantity supplied.

e. When the quantity demanded is equal to Q_4, this implies that the current price in the market is P_4, which is the situation of excess demand described in part (d).

f. When the quantity supplied is equal to Q_5, this implies that the current price in the market is P_2, which is the situation of excess supply described in part (c).

g. At P_1 the quantity demanded is equal to zero. This implies that at a price of P_1 the price is too high for consumers to be willing to demand the product.

h. At P_5 the quantity supplied is equal to zero. This implies that at a price of P_5 the price is too low for producers to be willing to supply the good.

9. a.

Price	Quantity demanded	Quantity supplied
$ 0	1,000	0
240	880	40
480	760	80
720	640	120
960	520	160
1,200	400	200
1,440	280	240
1,680	160	280
1,920	40	320

b. Examination of the previous table reveals that prices less than or equal to $1,440 result in a situation of excess demand, while prices greater than or equal to $1,680 result in a situation of excess supply. Thus, the equilibrium price will fall somewhere in the range of $1,440 to $1,680 in this market.

c.

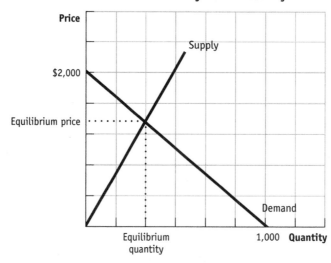

Market for Bicycles in Pedal City

d. At a price of $240, 40 bicycles will be supplied and each manufacturer will produce 2 bicycles. At a price of $240, 880 bicycles will be demanded. The market is not in equilibrium, since there is an excess demand for bicycles.

e. At a price of $480, 80 bicycles will be supplied and each manufacturer will produce 4 bicycles. At a price of $480, 760 bicycles will be demanded. The market is not in equilibrium, since there is an excess demand for bicycles.

f. At a price of $1,680, 280 bicycles will be supplied and each manufacturer will produce 14 bicycles. At a price of $1,680, 160 bicycles will be demanded. The market is not in equilibrium, since there is an excess supply of bicycles.

g. Since $P = 2,000 - 2Q$ and $P = 6Q$, we can use this information to write $2,000 - 2Q = 6Q$. Solving this equation gives us the equilibrium quantity of 250 bicycles. Substituting this quantity into either the demand equation or the supply equation yields the equilibrium price: $P = 2,000 - 2(250) = \$1,500$, or $P = 6(250) = \$1,500$.

10. a. Gasoline and bicycles are substitutes for each other. When the price of gasoline rises, people substitute away from gasoline toward bicycle transportation. This is illustrated in the following graph with the demand curve for bicycles shifting to the right, resulting in a higher equilibrium price (P_2) and a higher equilibrium quantity (Q_2). Note that there is a shift in the demand curve and a movement along the supply curve.

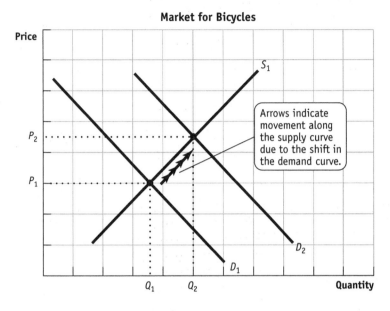

Market for Bicycles

b. Gasoline and SUVs are complements for each other. When the price of gasoline rises, people find that driving SUVs is relatively more expensive and therefore decrease their demand for SUVs at every price. This is illustrated in the following graph with the demand curve for SUVs shifting to the left, resulting in a lower equilibrium price (P_2) and a lower equilibrium quantity (Q_2). Note that there is a shift in the demand curve and a movement along the supply curve.

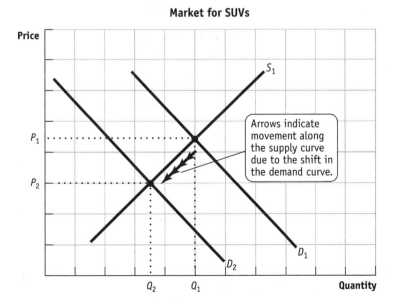

Market for SUVs

c. New technology shifts the supply curve to the right from S_1 to S_2. This causes a movement along the demand curve and results in a decrease in the equilibrium price and an increase in the equilibrium quantity. This is illustrated in the following graph.

Market for Music-Playing Devices

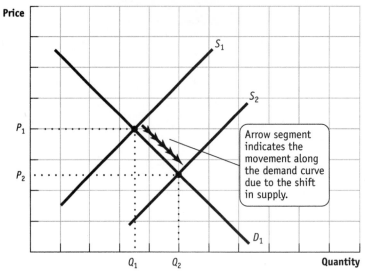

d. When the price of labor decreases, this causes the supply of the good to shift to the right since labor is an input in the production of fast-food meals. This results in a movement along the demand curve and a decrease in the equilibrium price and an increase in the equilibrium quantity.

Market for Fast-Food Restaurants

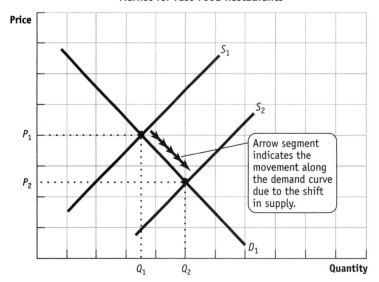

e. An increase in income shifts the demand curve to the right if the good is a normal good. This shift in demand causes a movement along the supply curve and an increase in both the equilibrium price and the equilibrium quantity.

Market for Good X

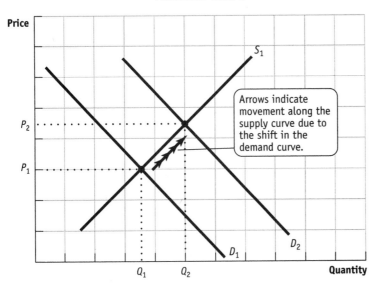

f. An increase in income shifts the demand curve to the left if the good is an inferior good. This shift in demand causes a movement along the supply curve and a decrease in both the equilibrium price and the equilibrium quantity. The following graph illustrates this situation.

Market for Good X

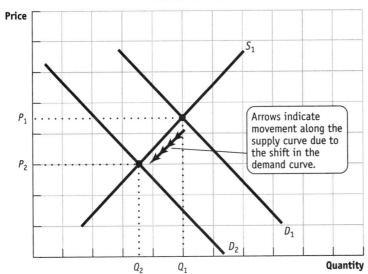

11. a. The demand equation is $P = 10 - (1/10)Q$ and the supply equation is $P = (1/10)Q$.

   b. Solving the two equations from part (a), we find that the equilibrium price equals $5 and the equilibrium quantity equals 50.

c. To find the new equilibrium price and quantity, we need to know the new demand and supply curves. Draw a sketch of the original demand curve and the new demand curve (shifted to the right at every price by 20 units) to guide you in your calculations. The following figure illustrates this sketch.

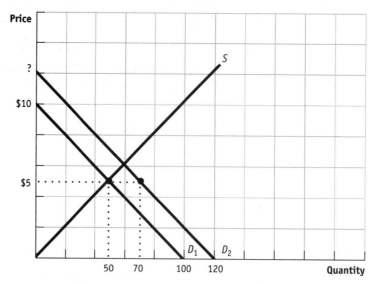

We know from part (b) that the initial equilibrium is at price $5 and the equilibrium quantity is 50, which gives us two points on the new demand curve: (70, 5) and (120, 0). We also know that the new demand curve is parallel to the original demand curve and thus has the same slope as the original demand curve. But we do not know the y-intercept for the new demand curve. To find the equation, let's write the new equation as $P = b - (1/10)Q$. This equation has the same slope as the original demand curve, but has not yet identified the y-intercept. To find the value of b, let's substitute the coordinates of one of the points we know is on D_2: thus, using (70, 5) yields $5 = b - (1/10)70$, or $b = 12$. So our new demand curve equation is $P = 12 - (1/10)Q$. Use the same technique to find the new supply curve equation. The graph that follows sketches the original demand and supply curve and also the new supply curve, which illustrates an increase of 40 units in the quantity supplied at every price. We know the coordinates of two points on this new supply curve—(40, 0) and (90, 5)—and we also know that the new supply curve has the same slope as the original supply curve. So we can rewrite the new supply curve as $P = b + (1/10)Q$ and then use one of our known points to solve for b, the y-intercept. Thus, using (90, 5) we get $5 = b + (1/10)90$, or $b = -4$, and the new supply curve is $P = (1/10)Q - 4$.

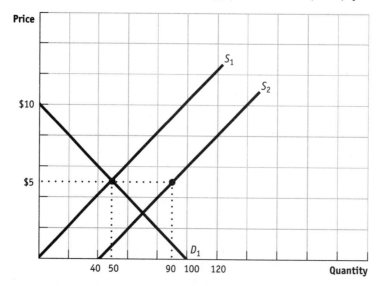

Using the new demand curve and new supply curve, we can easily solve for the equilibrium price and the equilibrium quantity in this market. Since $P = 12 - (1/10)Q$ and $P = (1/10)Q - 4$, we have $12 - (1/10)Q = (1/10)Q - 4$, or the equilibrium quantity (Q) equals 80. Then, replacing Q with 80 in either the demand or supply equation, we find that the equilibrium price (P) equals 4. In this case, the equilibrium price decreases relative to its initial level, while the equilibrium quantity increases relative to its initial level.

d. Since the change in the quantity demanded at each price is the same as in part (c), we know that the new demand curve can be written as $P = 12 - (1/10)Q$. But we need to use the same technique we employed in part (c) to find the new supply curve. When you do this, you will find that the new supply curve equation is $P = (1/10)Q - 1$. Solving these two equations for the equilibrium price and the equilibrium quantity, we find that the new equilibrium price is 5.5 while the new equilibrium quantity is 65 units. In this case, the equilibrium price and the equilibrium quantity increase relative to their initial quantities.

e. You would know with certainty that the equilibrium quantity increased, but you would not know if the equilibrium price increased, decreased, or remained the same, since you do not know the magnitude of the shifts in the demand and supply curves.

12.

Situation	Effect on equilibrium price	Effect on equilibrium quantity
Demand shifts to the right and supply shifts to the right	May increase, decrease, or remain the same	Increases
Demand shifts to the left and supply shifts to the left	May increase, decrease, or remain the same	Decreases
Demand shifts to the right and supply shifts to the left	Increases	May increase, decrease, or remain the same
Demand shifts to the left and supply shifts to the right	Decreases	May increase, decrease, or remain the same

Answers to Chapter Review Questions

1. **Answer c.** This is a definitional statement.

2. **Answer c.** The law of demand states that as the price of the good decreases, the quantity demanded of the good increases. Since the shampoo is on sale, its price has fallen and the law of demand suggests that the quantity demanded should therefore increase.

3. **Answer a.** This is a definitional statement. An inverse function of two variables means that an increase in one of the variables will result in a decrease in the other variable, or a decrease in one of the variables will result in an increase in the other variable. The law of demand states that as the price of the good increases, the quantity demanded of the good decreases; thus, price and quantity are inversely related.

4. **Answer b.** This research finding is likely to result in an increase in tastes and preferences for mangos, which will cause the demand curve for mangos to shift to the right.

5. **Answer a.** A leftward shift in the supply curve, holding everything else constant, will cause the price of the good to increase. This increase in price will result in a movement along the demand curve, since as the price increases, the quantity demanded of the good decreases.

6. **Answer d.** The expected fall in flat-screen TV prices next year will cause the demand curve for flat-screen TVs this year to shift to the left as consumers decrease the quantity of flat-screen TVs they demand at every price. This will result in a movement along the supply curve for flat-screen TVs this year. This price expectation should result in a decrease in the price of flat-screen TVs this year.

7. **Answer c.** Since peanut butter and jelly are considered complements in this example, an increase in the price of peanut butter will cause the demand curve for jelly to shift to the left, since as fewer units of peanut butter are demanded due to the higher price of peanut butter, fewer units of jelly will also be demanded at any given price for jelly.

8. **Answer a.** Since ham and turkey are substitutes, when the price of ham decreases, this causes the quantity of ham demanded to increase. As more units of ham are demanded, fewer units of turkey are demanded at every price. The demand for turkey therefore shifts to the left.

9. **Answer a.** When the price of good Y increases, there is a decrease in the quantity demanded of good Y. Since the demand for good X decreases, this implies that good Y and good X are consumed together; thus good X and good Y are complements.

10. **Answer b.** When the price of good Y decreases, there is an increase in the quantity demanded of good Y. Since the demand for good X increases when the quantity demanded of good Y decreases, this implies that good X is a substitute for good Y.

11. **Answer a.** When Jon's income increases, the quantity of good X he demands at any given price falls, which implies that good X is an inferior good.

12. **Answer b.** Both Jon's income and the quantity of steak he demands increase; therefore steak is a normal good.

13. **Answer a.** An increase in population shifts the demand curve to the right, since the increase in population implies a larger number of consumers of the product.

14. **Answer c.** An increase in the number of buyers causes the quantity demanded of the good to increase at every price, and the demand curve shifts to the right.

15. **Answer d.** To find the market demand curve, hold price constant and then add the quantity of the good demanded by each of the consumers. Thus, if the price of the good is $10, then, according to the table provided in the question, the total of Peter's, Anya's, and Pablo's demand must add up to 100 units.

16. **Answer b.** This question is asking you to recall that a change in the price of the good, holding everything else constant, results in a movement along the curve. This movement along the curve causes a change in the quantity supplied and not a change in the supply curve.

17. **Answer a.** Ground beef is an input in the production of Fast Wally's hamburgers. When ground beef gets more expensive, this increases the cost of producing hamburgers, which causes the supply curve to shift to the left.

18. **Answer b.** When the cost of raw materials decreases, more batteries can be produced at any given price. This decrease in the cost of raw materials causes the supply curve for batteries to shift to the right.

19. **Answer a.** When input prices decrease, producers are willing to supply more units of the good at every price.

20. **Answer b.** Since an increase in the production of one of the goods results in a decrease in the production of the other good, these two goods must be substitutes in production.

21. **Answer a.** Sawdust and lumber are complements in production. As the producer increases its production of lumber, the production of sawdust is also increased since sawdust is a by-product of lumber production.

22. **Answer a.** New technology causes the supply curve to shift to the right, resulting in an increase in the quantity supplied of the good at every price.

23. **Answer a.** The sawmill industry will want to decrease the supply of lumber it provides to the market this year due to its expectation that next year's lumber prices will be higher. At every price, the quantity of lumber supplied this year will be decreased, and the supply curve for lumber this year shifts to the left.

24. **Answer c.** When the price is $40, 80 widgets are produced. Since there are 16 producers in this market and each of these producers produces the same number of widgets, this implies that each producer must be producing 5 widgets.

25. **Answer b.** This is a definitional statement. The market demand curve is found by holding price constant and then adding together the quantities demanded by each consumer in the market. This process is repeated for other prices.

26. **Answer d.** The first two statements are fairly straightforward, but statement III may be somewhat appealing at first glance. At equilibrium, however, even though the quantity demanded equals the quantity supplied, this does not imply that every potential consumer of the good is consuming the good. Those consumers who would like to consume the good, but who are unwilling to pay the equilibrium price, will not consume the good.

27. **Answer b.** At a price of $20, 300 widgets are demanded while 100 widgets are supplied. Thus, at a price of $20 there is an excess demand, or shortage, of 200 widgets.

28. **Answer a.** At a price of $60, 100 widgets are demanded while 300 widgets are supplied. Thus, at a price of $60 there is an excess supply, or surplus, of 200 widgets.

29. **Answer c.** The equilibrium quantity is the quantity at which demand equals the quantity supplied. The equilibrium quantity is 200 widgets, and the equilibrium price is $40.

30. **Answer c.** To find the demand curve, you can either plot the demand curve (although this is time-consuming) or you can calculate the slope (rise/run = $-20/100 = -1/5$) and then use the slope-intercept form, $y = mx + b$, to write the equation. Thus, $P = (-1/5)Q + 80$, or solving for Q, $Q = 400 - 5P$.

31. **Answer b.** To find the supply curve, you can either plot the supply curve (although this is time-consuming) or you can calculate the slope (rise/run = $20/100 = 1/5$) and then use the slope-intercept form, $y = mx + b$, to write the equation. Thus, $P = (1/5)Q + 0$.

32. **Answer b.** At P_1 the quantity demanded is Q_2 units, while the quantity supplied is Q_5 units. The quantity supplied is greater than the quantity demanded at P_1: this excess supply is equal to $Q_5 - Q_2$.

33. **Answer a.** At P_3 the quantity demanded is Q_4 units while the quantity supplied is Q_1 units. The quantity demanded is greater than the quantity supplied at P_3: this excess demand is equal to $Q_4 - Q_1$.

34. **Answer c.** Since we do not know the relative magnitude of the shifts in the demand and supply curves, we cannot know for certain what happens to both the equilibrium price and the equilibrium quantity. The demand curve shifts to the right with the increase in the number of people purchasing candles, and the supply curve also shifts to the right with the decrease in the price of beeswax, one of the inputs in candle production. The equilibrium quantity will increase, but the equilibrium price may increase, decrease, or remain the same depending on the relative magnitude of the shifts in the two curves.

35. **Answer c.** The demand curve for apartments shifts to the right with the increase in the price of houses (houses and apartments are substitute goods for consumers in Mayville), while the supply curve for apartments also shifts to the right with the opening of the new apartment buildings. Since we do not know the magnitude of the shifts in the demand and supply curves, we know that the equilibrium quantity is now larger, but the equilibrium price may increase, decrease, or remain the same with these shifts in the demand and supply curves.

36. **Answer a.** The demand curve for good X shifts to the right, since good X is a normal good and income has increased. At the same time, the supply curve for good X shifts to the left since the price of labor has increased. These two shifts result in the equilibrium price increasing, while the equilibrium quantity may have increased, decreased, or remained the same depending on the magnitude of the shifts in the demand and supply curves.

37. **Answer b.** Since good X is an inferior good, the increase in income results in the demand curve for good X shifting to the left. At the same time, the technological advance causes the supply curve for good X to shift to the right. The equilibrium price will decrease, but the equilibrium quantity may increase, decrease, or remain the same depending on the magnitude of the shifts in the demand and supply curves.

38. **Answer a.** The supply curve for candy shifts to the left with the increase in the price of sugar, while the demand curve for candy shifts to the right with the increase in the price of bubble gum. The equilibrium price will increase, but the equilibrium quantity may increase, decrease, or remain the same depending on the magnitude of the shifts in the demand and supply curves.

chapter 4

The Market
Strikes Back

▮ BEFORE YOU READ THE CHAPTER

Summary

This chapter develops the concepts of producer surplus, consumer surplus, and total surplus and then illustrates the connection between these concepts and the demand and supply model. The chapter also explains how total surplus can be used to show the gains from trade and to evaluate the efficiency of a market.

This chapter also develops the ideas of price controls and quantity controls in competitive markets and then illustrates how the implementation of these types of controls reduces the efficiency of a market. In particular, the chapter discusses effective price ceilings, whereby the government sets the price of the good below the equilibrium price; effective price floors, whereby the government sets the price of the good above the equilibrium price; and quantity controls, whereby the government limits the amount of the good available to a level lower than the equilibrium level of output. The chapter also discusses the distributional impact of market interventions.

Chapter Objectives

Objective #1. The demand and supply model illustrates how much consumers and producers gain from participating in a market. A consumer's willingness to pay refers to the maximum price the consumer would pay to purchase an item. The demand curve is defined by the willingness of consumers to pay.

Objective #2. An individual's consumer surplus is the difference between the individual's willingness to pay and the price he/she pays for the good: consumer surplus measures the net gain the consumer receives when he/she purchases the good. Total consumer surplus is the sum of the individual consumer surpluses achieved by all the buyers of the good. Total consumer surplus is equal to the area under the demand curve but above the price.

- The area of consumer surplus is a triangle for a smooth demand curve or a series of rectangles for a step-shaped demand curve.

- Holding everything else constant, a decrease in price increases consumer surplus while an increase in price decreases consumer surplus.

Objective #3. The seller's price is the lowest price the seller is willing to sell the good for. Individual producer surplus is the difference between the price the good sells for and the lowest price the seller is willing to accept for the good: individual producer surplus measures the net gain the seller receives from selling the good. Total producer surplus is the sum of the individual producer surpluses achieved by all the sellers of the good. Total producer surplus is equal to the area above the supply curve but beneath the price.

- The area of producer surplus is a triangle for a smooth supply curve or a series of rectangles for a step-shaped supply curve.

- Holding everything else constant, a decrease in price decreases producer surplus and an increase in price increases producer surplus.

Objective #4. Total surplus is the sum of the consumer and producer surpluses. At the market equilibrium, total surplus is maximized: the market equilibrium allocates the consumption of the good among potential consumers and the sales of the good among potential sellers in order to achieve the maximum possible gains to society. In a well-functioning market, total surplus cannot be increased by reallocating consumption among consumers, by reallocating sales among sellers, or by changing the quantity traded. In fact, each of these actions diminishes the level of total surplus in the market.

- Preventing a sale in a market that would have taken place in equilibrium reduces both consumer and producer surplus, resulting in a loss of total surplus. Increasing sales beyond the equilibrium quantity similarly reduces consumer surplus, producer surplus, and total surplus, since such a sale would represent a situation in which the buyer's willingness to buy must be less than the seller's cost.

Objective #5. Total surplus is maximized at the market equilibrium: (a) the market allocates consumption of the good to those potential consumers who place the highest value on the good; (b) the market allocates sales of the good to those sellers who have the lowest cost of producing the good; (c) the market ensures that any purchase represents a situation in which the buyer values the good more than the seller values the good; and (d) the market ensures that no sales are made in which the seller values the good more than the purchaser does. Markets are efficient when total surplus is maximized.

- Even though the market equilibrium maximizes total surplus, this does not imply that it maximizes the outcome for any individual buyer or seller. Subsequent chapters consider situations of market intervention where individual buyers or sellers are made better off than they would be at the market equilibrium.

Objective #6. Price controls refer to the government's intervention in a market to set the price of the good or service at some level other than the equilibrium price. A price ceiling is the maximum price for a good or service allowed by the government, and a price floor is the minimum price for a good or service allowed by the government.

Objective #7. An effective price ceiling in a competitive market creates a situation of excess quantity demanded. If the price ceiling is set above the equilibrium price in the market, the price ceiling will not be effective and therefore will have no effect on the equilibrium price and the equilibrium quantity in the market.

Objective #8. An effective price ceiling prevents a market from being efficient because the price ceiling prevents transactions from occurring that would make some people better off without making other people worse off. In particular, an effective price ceiling prevents demanders who are willing to pay more for the good from consuming the good, since the good's supply is artificially limited by the imposed price ceiling. Inefficiency arises because the price ceiling:

- reduces the quantity of the good available;

- reduces the value of total surplus;

- misallocates the good or service among consumers;

- wastes resources, as consumers spend resources searching for the good that is artificially scarce due to the price ceiling; and

- reduces the quality of the available units to below the level that would have been supplied in the absence of the price ceiling.

Objective #9. Price ceilings provide incentives for illegal activities. Price ceilings are primarily instituted because they benefit some particular group of demanders.

Objective #10. An effective price floor in a competitive market creates a situation of excess quantity supplied. If the price floor is set below the equilibrium price in the market, the price floor will have no effect on the equilibrium price and the equilibrium quantity in the market.

Objective #11. An effective price floor results in market inefficiency because it prevents transactions from occurring that would make some people better off without making other people worse off. In particular, an effective price floor prevents suppliers who are willing to supply the good from selling the good, since the good's demand is artificially limited by the imposed price floor. Inefficiency arises because the price floor:

- reduces the quantity of the good demanded;

- reduces the value of total surplus;

- misallocates the provision of the good or service by sellers;

- wastes resources, as suppliers search the market for a potential demander of the good; and

- increases the quality of the available units to above the level that would have been demanded in the absence of the price floor.

Objective #12. Price floors provide an incentive for illegal or black market activities, including the bribery and corruption of government officials. Price floors are primarily instituted because they benefit a particular group of sellers.

Objective #13. The government may also implement quantity controls or a quota in a market. In this case, the government sets a limit on the total quantity of the good that can be bought and sold in the market. This quantity is usually limited through the selling of licenses that legally grant the holder of the license the right to supply the good. Quantity controls always set a maximum amount allowed. To be binding in the market, the quota must be set below the equilibrium quantity.

Objective #14. A quota or quantity control creates a wedge between the price consumers are willing to pay for the good and the price at which producers are willing to supply the good. The difference between these two prices is the quota rent, or the income that the license holder receives from his/her ownership of a valuable commodity (the license).

Objective #15. Quantity controls are inefficient because they prevent some mutually beneficial transactions from occurring, since the demand price for a given quantity (the quota amount) is greater than the supply price for that quantity. These missed transactions create an incentive to evade the quota limit, often through illegal activity.

Key Terms

willingness to pay the maximum price a consumer is prepared to pay for a good.

individual consumer surplus the net gain to an individual buyer from the purchase of a good; equal to the difference between the buyer's *willingness to pay* and the price paid.

total consumer surplus the sum of the *individual consumer surpluses* of all the buyers of a good in a market.

consumer surplus a term often used to refer both to *individual consumer surplus* and to *total consumer surplus*.

cost (of seller) the lowest price at which a seller is willing to sell a good.

individual producer surplus the net gain to an individual seller from selling a good; equal to the difference between the price received and the seller's *cost*.

total producer surplus the sum of the *individual producer surpluses* of all the sellers of a good in a market.

producer surplus a term often used to refer both to *individual producer surplus* and to *total producer surplus*.

total surplus the total net gain to consumers and producers from trading in a market; the sum of the *producer surplus* and the *consumer surplus*.

price controls legal restrictions on how high or low a market price may go.

price ceiling a maximum price sellers are allowed to charge for a good or service; a form of *price control*.

price floor a minimum price buyers are required to pay for a good or service; a form of *price control*.

deadweight loss refers to the loss of consumer and producer surplus that occurs when mutually beneficial transactions are prevented from occurring.

inefficient allocation to consumers a form of inefficiency in which people who want the good badly and are willing to pay a high price don't get it, and those who care relatively little about the good and are willing to pay only a low price do get it; often a result of a *price ceiling*.

wasted resources a form of inefficiency in which people expend money, effort, and time to cope with the shortages caused by a *price ceiling*.

inefficiently low quality a form of inefficiency in which sellers offer low-quality goods at a low price even though buyers would prefer a higher quality at a higher price; often a result of a *price ceiling*.

black market a market in which goods or services are bought and sold illegally, either because it is illegal to sell them at all or because the prices charged are legally prohibited by a *price ceiling*.

Key Terms *(continued)*

minimum wage a legal floor on the wage rate. The wage rate is the market price of labor.

inefficient allocation of sales among sellers a form of inefficiency in which sellers who would be willing to sell a good at the lowest price are not always those who actually manage to sell it; often the result of a *price floor*.

inefficiently high quality a form of inefficiency in which sellers offer high-quality goods at a high price even though buyers would prefer a lower quality at a lower price; often the result of a *price floor*.

quantity control an upper limit, set by the government, on the quantity of some good that can be bought or sold; also referred to as a *quota*.

quota an upper limit, set by the government, on the quantity of some good that can be bought or sold; also referred to as a *quantity control*.

quota limit the total amount of a good under a *quota* or *quantity control* that can be legally transacted.

license the right, conferred by the government, to supply a good.

demand price the price of a given quantity at which consumers will demand that quantity.

supply price the price of a given quantity at which producers will supply that quantity.

wedge the difference between the *demand price* of the quantity transacted and the *supply price* of the quantity transacted for a good when the supply of the good is legally restricted. Often created by a *quantity control*, or *quota*.

quota rent the difference between the *demand price* and the *supply price* at the *quota limit*; this difference, the earnings that accrue to the license holder, is equal to the market price of the *license* when the license is traded.

■ AFTER YOU READ THE CHAPTER

Tips

Tip #1. To master the key concepts in this chapter, you must be able to locate the areas of surplus in the graphs of the supply and demand model. You will want to work with the concepts of consumer surplus, producer surplus, and total surplus until you feel confident that you can find these areas in your graphs.

Tip #2. Figure 4.1 illustrates the concept of consumer surplus for a step-shaped demand curve. The area of consumer surplus consists of a series of rectangles that lie under the demand curve but above the market price. Each of these rectangles has been shaded separately in Figure 4.1, but the area of consumer surplus is the entire shaded area. Those consumers whose willingness to pay is equal to or greater than the market price will purchase the good for the market price, and their consumer surplus represents the net gain they receive from purchasing the good.

Figure 4.1

Consumer Surplus for a Step-Shaped Demand Curve

Each rectangle represents the consumer surplus for a particular consumer. The entire shaded area represents total consumer surplus.

Tip #3. Figure 4.2 illustrates the concept of consumer surplus for a smooth demand curve. The area of consumer surplus consists of the area under the demand curve but above the market price. In Figure 4.2, the area of consumer surplus is shaded. The value of consumer surplus can be found by calculating the area of this shaded triangle. The consumer surplus represents the net gain consumers receive from purchasing the good.

Figure 4.2

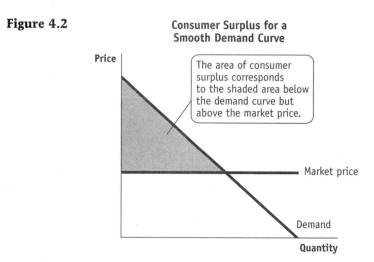

Consumer Surplus for a Smooth Demand Curve

The area of consumer surplus corresponds to the shaded area below the demand curve but above the market price.

Tip #4. Figure 4.3 illustrates the concept of producer surplus for a step-shaped supply curve. The area of producer surplus consists of a series of rectangles that lie above the supply curve but below the market price. Each of these rectangles has been shaded as separate rectangles in Figure 4.3, but the area of producer surplus is the entire shaded area. Those producers whose willingness to sell is equal to or less than the market price will sell the good for the market price, and their producer surplus represents the net gain they receive from selling the good.

Figure 4.3   **Producer Surplus for a**
                                  Step-Shaped Supply Curve

Tip #5. Figure 4.4 illustrates the concept of producer surplus for a smooth supply curve. The area of producer surplus is the shaded region above the supply curve but beneath the market price. The value of producer surplus can be found by calculating the area of this shaded triangle. The producer surplus represents the net gain producers receive from selling the good.

Figure 4.4   **Producer Surplus for a**
                                  Smooth Supply Curve

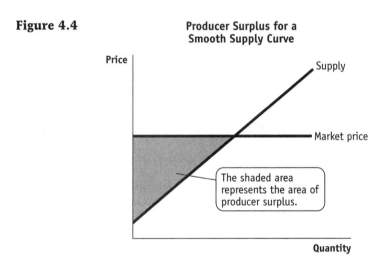

Tip #6. Figures 4.5 and 4.6 illustrate total surplus, which is the sum of consumer surplus and producer surplus. Figure 4.5 illustrates this concept for step-shaped demand and supply curves, and Figure 4.6 illustrates this concept for smooth demand and supply curves.

Figure 4.5

Total Surplus for Step-Shaped Demand and Supply Curves

Total surplus is equal to the entire shaded area. Consumer surplus equals the shaded region above the market price, and producer surplus equals the shaded region below the market price.

Figure 4.6

Total Surplus for Smooth Demand and Supply Curves

Total surplus is represented by the entire shaded area and is composed of consumer surplus and producer surplus.

Tip #7. Students often find it confusing to remember the difference between a price floor and a price ceiling.

- A floor is a surface that you stand on and that is solid. A price floor is the *lowest* price that can be charged for a good. Figure 4.7 illustrates a price floor. To be effective, a price floor must be set at a price that is greater than the equilibrium price. At P_F, Q_1 units will be supplied and Q_2 units will be demanded. An effective price floor always results in a surplus of the good.

Figure 4.7

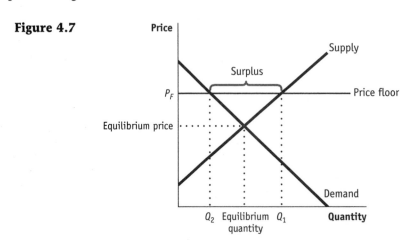

- A ceiling is a surface that you hope is solid and stays above your head. A price ceiling is the *highest* price that can be charged for a good. Figure 4.8 illustrates a price ceiling. To be effective, a price ceiling must be set at a price that is less than the equilibrium price. At P_C, Q_1 units will be supplied and Q_2 units will be demanded. An effective price ceiling always results in a shortage of the good.

Figure 4.8

Tip #8. A quota, or quantity control, is a policy implemented by the government to set a maximum amount of the good or service that can be sold in a market. A quota has no effect if it is set at a level greater than the equilibrium quantity; to be effective a quota must be set at a level lower than the equilibrium quantity. Figure 4.9 illustrates an effective quantity control, or quota, where the maximum allowed quantity is set by the government at Q_1. At Q_1 demanders are willing to pay P_1 for each unit of the good they consume, while suppliers are willing to supply the good at price P_2. This difference, $P_1 - P_2$, is referred to as a wedge. This wedge corresponds to the quota rent the license holder of the good receives when the quantity control is imposed in a market. This quota rent represents the additional compensation the license holder receives from selling the good in a market where the quantity of the good has been artificially restricted.

Figure 4.9

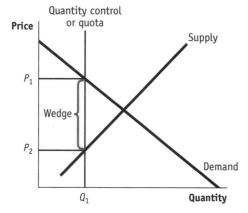

Tip #9. If you are using flash cards, make sure you make up a set with this chapter's new vocabulary and concepts. Review all of your flash cards on a regular basis to make sure you are not forgetting any terms or concepts.

WORKED PROBLEMS

1. Consider a market for cotton in which the market demand curve is given by the equation $Q = 40{,}000 - 200P$ and the market supply curve is given by the equation $Q = 200P$, where Q is bales of cotton and P is the price per bale of cotton. Suppose this market is initially in equilibrium, but then cotton farmers successfully lobby the legislature to impose a price floor of $150 per bale of cotton. After imposition of this price floor, what will be the price of cotton in this market, and how does this price compare to the initial equilibrium price? Identify the number of bales of cotton consumers will purchase once the price floor is implemented. How does this quantity compare to the initial equilibrium quantity in this market? What will the surplus or shortage of cotton equal with the imposition of this price floor? If the government purchases the surplus cotton, what will be the cost of this purchase to the government?

STEP 1: First draw a graph of the market for cotton and find the initial equilibrium price and quantity in this market. Use the two equations to solve for the equilibrium price and quantity. Thus, $40{,}000 - 200P = 200P$, or $P = 100$. If $P = 100$, then the quantity demanded at this price can be found using the demand equation: $Q = 40{,}000 - 200(100)$, or $Q = 20{,}000$. If $P = 100$, then the quantity supplied at this price can be found using the supply equation: $Q = 200(100) = 20{,}000$. Since the market is in equilibrium, the quantity demanded is equal to the quantity supplied when the price is equal to 100.

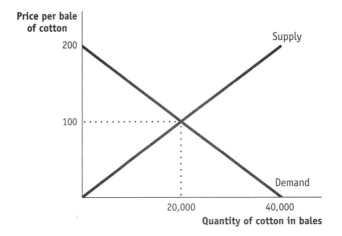

STEP 2: Draw the price floor on your graph and determine if the price floor is an effective one. Once you have determined if the price floor is effective, you will know whether the price in this market is the price floor price of $150 per bale or the equilibrium price of $100 per bale. Identify the number of bales of cotton that consumers demand by using the demand equation to see how many bales of cotton they are willing to demand at the new price for cotton. The effective price floor raises the price of cotton, which causes consumers to purchase fewer units of cotton.

Review the section "Price Floors" on pages 122–127 and Figure 4-11 on page 123.

Since the price floor is greater than the equilibrium price, the price floor is effective in this market. The price of cotton in this market will now be the price floor price of $150 per bale: the price of cotton is now higher than it was before the implementation of the price floor. When the price of cotton is $150 per bale, consumers are willing to purchase 10,000 bales of cotton.

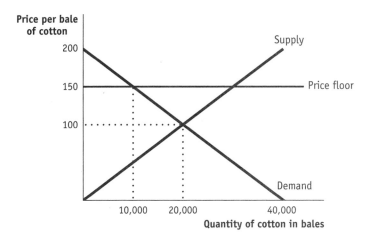

STEP 3: **Identify the surplus of cotton that will be produced in this market when there is a price floor and then determine what the cost of purchasing this surplus will be for the government.**

Review the section "Price Floors" on pages 122–127 and Figure 4-11 on page 123.

To find the surplus with the price floor requires identifying how many units of cotton suppliers are willing to supply at a price of $150, then subtracting out the number of units of cotton demanders are willing to demand at a price of $150. At a price of $150, suppliers are willing to supply 30,000 bales of cotton, but consumers are willing to purchase only 10,000 bales. Thus, the surplus of cotton is equal to 20,000 bales. If the government purchases this amount of cotton at $150 per bale, it will cost the government $4.5 million. The shaded area in the graph below identifies this cost to the government.

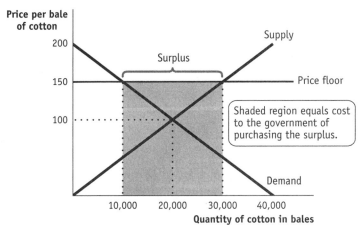

2. Consider the same market for cotton as in problem 1. Suppose this market is initially in equilibrium, but then cotton farmers successfully lobby the legislature to impose a quantity control, or quota, of 10,000 bales of cotton in this market. What will the "wedge" or quota rent be equal to in this market? Calculate the deadweight loss that will occur in this market if this quota is implemented.

STEP 1: **Start by drawing a graph of the market for cotton, identifying the initial equilibrium price and quantity. From your work in problem 1, you already have identified the equilibrium price as $100 per bale of cotton and the equilibrium quantity as 20,000 bales of cotton. After labeling these points on your graph, draw the quantity control or quota on your graph. The quantity control will be a vertical line where the quantity of bales of cotton is 10,000.**

Review the section "Controlling Quantities" on pages 128–133 and Figure 4-14 on page 130.

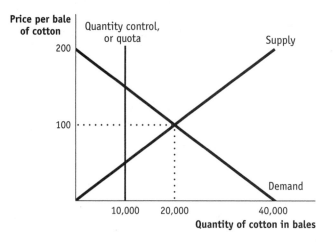

STEP 2: To find the "wedge" or quota rent, you will need to see what price consumers are willing to pay for the quota amount and what price producers must receive in order to provide the quota amount. The difference between the price consumers are willing to pay and the price producers must receive is the "wedge."

Review the section "The Anatomy of Quantity Controls" on pages 128–131, and Figure 4-14 on page 130.

Consumers are willing to pay $150 per bale of cotton when 10,000 bales of cotton are offered in the market. Producers must receive $50 per bale of cotton if they supply 10,000 bales of cotton. The "wedge" is therefore $100, or the difference between these two prices. The following figure illustrates this wedge.

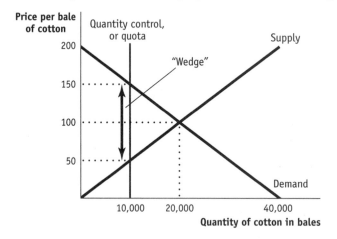

STEP 3: Determine the area of deadweight loss.

Review the section "The Anatomy of Quantity Controls" on pages 128–131, and Figure 4-14 on page 130.

Deadweight loss refers to the loss of consumer and producer surplus that occurs when mutually beneficial transactions are prevented from occurring. The quota rent raises the price of cotton above its equilibrium price, and both consumers and producers find that this quota rent reduces the number of transactions that would have occurred if there had been no intervention in the market. The diagram below indicates the area of deadweight loss: we can calculate the value of the deadweight loss as the area of the shaded triangle, or (1/2)($150 per bale of cotton − $50 per bale of cotton)(20,000 bales of cotton − 10,000 bales of cotton). The deadweight loss is equal to $500,000.

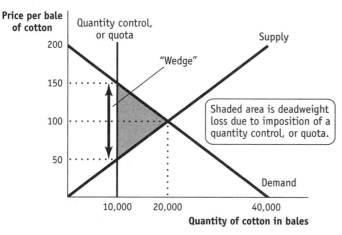

3. The following table describes several interventions in a market. Complete the table.

Situation	This is an example of a (1) price floor, (2) price ceiling, or (3) quantity control or quota	What must be true for this intervention in the market to be effective?
The government decides to limit the number of taxicab licenses in Chicago.		
The minimum price that can be charged for a sports car is set at $75,000 by the government.		
The minimum wage that can be paid to a worker is set at $10 an hour by the government.		
The maximum tuition that can be charged by a public university is set at $5,000 a year by the government.		

STEP 1: To answer this question, you must first have a firm grasp of the differences among a price floor, a price ceiling, and a quantity control or quota. You need to understand what makes each of these interventions effective in the market, which requires that you understand and are comfortable with each type of market intervention.

Review the section "Price Ceilings" on pages 113–121, and Figure 4-7 on page 115. Review the section "Price Floors" on pages 122–127 and Figure 4-11 on page 123. Review the section "Controlling Quantities" on pages 128–133 and Figure 4-14 on page 130.

A price ceiling is a maximum price that can be charged for a good. A price floor is a minimum price that can be charged for a good. A quantity control or quota is a maximum amount of the good that can be provided in the market. This maximum amount is set by the government. To fill in the second column of the table, you will want to consider each situation and determine whether the situation is one in which the government is setting a maximum price, a minimum price, or a maximum quantity.

STEP 2: **For each type of market intervention by the government, you will want to think about what must be true in order for the intervention to have any impact on the market.**

Review the section "Price Ceilings" on pages 113–121 and Figure 4-7 on page 115. Review the section "Price Floors" on pages 122–127 and Figure 4-11 on page 123. Review the section "Controlling Quantities" on pages 128–133 and Figure 4-14 on page 130.

For a price ceiling to be effective, the price ceiling must be set at a price that is less than the market equilibrium amount. For a price floor to be effective, the price floor must be set at a price that is greater than the market equilibrium amount. For a quantity control or quota to have any effect on the market, the quantity control must be set at a quantity that is less than the market equilibrium quantity. The completed table is given below.

Situation	This is an example of a (1) price floor, (2) price ceiling, or (3) quantity control or quota	What must be true for this intervention in the market to be effective?
The government decides to limit the number of taxicab licenses in Chicago	quantity control or quota	Quota amount must be less than the market equilibrium quantity.
The minimum price that can be charged for a sports car is set at $75,000 by the government	price floor	Price floor must be set at a price that is greater than the market equilibrium price.
The minimum wage that can be paid to a worker is set at $10 an hour by the government	price floor	Price floor must be set at a price that is greater than the market equilibrium price.
The maximum tuition that can be charged by a public university is set at $5,000 a year by the government	price ceiling	Price ceiling must be set at a price that is less than the market equilibrium price.

4. Consider the market for bananas in Paradise, a small country that grows all the bananas that are eaten in Paradise. Suppose that the market for bananas in Paradise is described by the demand and supply curves that are given in the graph below. You are asked to identify the equilibrium price and quantity in this market as well as the value of consumer surplus, producer surplus, and total surplus. Paradise is considering implementing a price floor of $20 per box of bananas. How will this price floor affect consumer surplus, producer surplus, and total surplus? Will the price floor create a deadweight loss, and if so, what is the value of this deadweight loss?

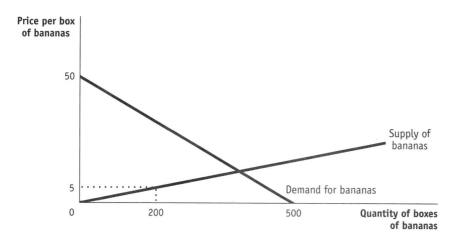

STEP 1: To find the equilibrium price and quantity in this market, you will need both the equation for the demand curve and the equation for the supply curve. The demand curve has a *y*-intercept of 50 and a slope equal to −1/10. The demand curve can be written as $P = 50 − (1/10)Q$, or $Q = 500 − 10P$. The supply curve has a *y*-intercept of 0 and a slope equal to 1/40. The supply curve can be written as $P = (1/40)Q$, or $Q = 40P$. Use these two equations to find the equilibrium price and quantity: the equilibrium price is $10 per box of bananas and the equilibrium quantity is 400 boxes of bananas.

STEP 2: Identify the area of consumer surplus and the area of producer surplus, and then calculate the value of these two areas. Sum these two values to find total surplus.

Review the section "Consumer Surplus and the Demand Curve" on pages 106–108, and Figure 4-2 on page 108. Review the section "Producer Surplus and the Supply Curve" on pages 109–110 and Figure 4-4 on page 111.

First, identify on the graph the areas that correspond to consumer surplus and producer surplus. Then, use the formula for the area of a triangle to calculate the value of these areas. Remember that the area of a triangle is equal to (1/2)(the base of the triangle)(the height of the triangle). The graph below identifies the areas of consumer surplus and producer surplus. Recall that total surplus is just the sum of consumer and producer surplus.

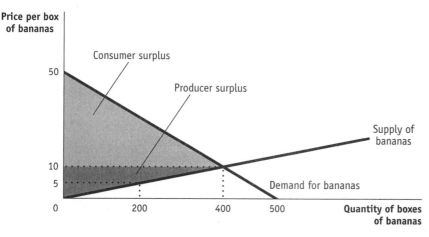

The value of consumer surplus is equal to (1/2)($50 per box of bananas − $10 per box of bananas)(400 boxes of bananas) = $8,000. The value of producer surplus is equal to (1/2)($10 per box of bananas − $0 per box of bananas)(400 boxes of bananas) = $2,000. The value of total surplus is equal to the sum of consumer plus producer surplus, or $10,000.

STEP 3: Analyze the effect of a price floor equal to $20 per box of bananas in Paradise. Determine if the price floor creates a deadweight loss.

Review the section "Price Floors" on pages 122–127, and Figure 4-11 on page 123.

First, check to see if the price floor is effective: recall that a price floor must be set above the equilibrium price in order for it to impact the market. In this example, the equilibrium price in the market is $10 per box of bananas, so the price floor of $20 per box of bananas will be effective. Then, determine how many bananas will be demanded at the price floor price of $20 per box of bananas. To find the number of bananas demanded when the price is $20 per box, use the demand equation. When the price is $20 per box, demanders will demand 300 boxes of bananas. Notice that suppliers need to receive a price of only $7.50 in order to be willing to supply 300 boxes of bananas.

Then, determine the new areas that correspond to consumer and producer surplus. The deadweight loss will be the area that corresponds to the loss in consumer and producer surplus due to the imposition of the price floor. The above graph will help you identify these areas.

The new value for consumer surplus is equal to $4,500. The new value for producer surplus is a bit more difficult to calculate since it is composed of a rectangle and a triangle. Producer surplus will equal (($20 per box of bananas − $7.50 per box of bananas)(300 boxes of bananas) + (1/2)($7.50 per box of bananas − $0 per box of bananas)(300 boxes of bananas)), or $4,875. The area of deadweight loss is equal to (1/2)($20 per box of bananas − $7.50 per box of bananas)(400 boxes of bananas − 300 boxes of bananas), or $625. Notice that the sum of the new consumer surplus, the new producer surplus, and the deadweight loss is equal to the original total surplus prior to the imposition of the price floor in the market for bananas.

Problems and Exercises

1. The following table expresses the amount people are willing to pay to buy a new music-playing device. Use this information to answer this series of questions.

Name of person	Price willing to pay
Joe	$100
Mary	200
Lucinda	150
Pete	50
Mario	300

a. Who places the highest value on this good? Explain your answer.

b. Who places the lowest value on this good? Explain your answer.

c. If the good is offered at a price of $100, who would buy it?

d. If the good is offered at a price of $50, who would buy it?

e. Construct a step-shaped demand curve illustrating the demand for a music-playing device for these five consumers.

Price

Quantity

f. On the graph, shade in the area that represents Mary's consumer surplus if the good sells for $100. Label this area clearly. Calculate the value of Mary's consumer surplus.

g. On the graph, shade in the area that represents Mario's consumer surplus if the good sells for $100. Label this area clearly. Calculate the value of Mario's consumer surplus.

h. Create a new graph that is a duplicate of the one you drew for part (e) and shade in the entire area of consumer surplus if the good sells for a price of $100. Calculate the value of consumer surplus at this price.

2. The following table expresses the amount people are willing to pay to buy a new music-playing device. Use this information to answer this series of questions.

Name of person	Price willing to pay
Joe	$100
Mary	200
Lucinda	150
Pete	50
Mario	300

a. If the market price is $175, who will buy the good and what is the value of total consumer surplus?

b. Suppose the market price is $175, but a decision is made to allocate the two units of the good that are demanded at that price to Mario and Lucinda. What is the value of total consumer surplus in this case?

c. Why does the reallocation of the good in part (b) reduce the value of consumer surplus? What are the implications of the reduction in consumer surplus that occurs when the good is not allocated to those buyers who place the highest value on the good?

3. Demand for widgets in Marksville is given by the equation $P = 100 - Q$.

a. If the market price of widgets in Marksville is $50, what is the value of consumer surplus in this market?

$$50 = 100 - Q$$
$$Q = 50$$

$ 1250

b. If the market price of widgets in Marksville is $40, what is the value of consumer surplus in this market?

$$40 = 100 - Q$$
$$Q = 60$$

1800

c. For a linear downward-sloping demand curve, what happens to consumer surplus when the market price rises?

decreases

d. Suppose the market price of widgets is $30 in Marksville. Will at least 80 widgets be demanded at this price? Explain your answer.

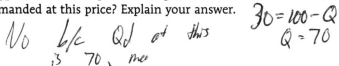

$$30 = 100 - Q$$
$$Q = 70$$

No b/c Qd at this is 70, me

e. Suppose the market price of widgets is $30 in Marksville. Will at least 60 widgets be demanded at this price? Explain your answer.

4. The following table provides a list of sellers of organic apples and the lowest price each seller is willing to accept for a bushel of apples. Assume that each seller will only offer a single bushel of apples for sale. Use this information to answer this series of questions.

Seller	Lowest price seller is willing to accept for a bushel of apples
Ski Top Orchards	$6.00
J. Appleseed's Finest	7.25
Red's Organic	5.80
Pure Apples	8.25
Nature's Medicine	8.00

a. Draw a diagram of this step-shaped supply curve.

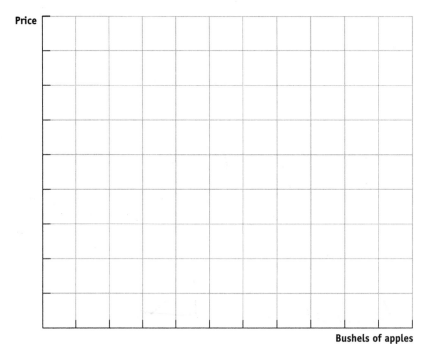

b. If only one bushel of apples is sold, which seller is most likely to make this sale? Explain your answer.

c. If the market price is $7.50, what is the value of the producer surplus received by J. Appleseed's Finest?

d. If the market price is $7.50, what is the value of the producer surplus received by Ski Top Orchards?

e. Redraw your sketch from part (a) and indicate the area of total producer surplus in this market if the market price is $7.50. What is the value of this producer surplus?

Price

Bushels of apples

f. Which sellers will sell a bushel of apples in this market if the market price is $7.50?

5. The following table provides a list of sellers of organic apples and the lowest price each seller is willing to accept for a bushel of apples. Assume that each seller will only offer a single bushel of apples for sale. Use this information to answer this series of questions.

Seller	Lowest price seller is willing to accept for a bushel of apples
Ski Top Orchards	$6.00
J. Appleseed's Finest	7.25
Red's Organic	5.80
Pure Apples	8.25
Nature's Medicine	8.00

a. Suppose the market price of apples is $7.00 a bushel. At this price, which of the above potential sellers will agree to sell a bushel of apples? What is the value of producer surplus when the market price of apples is $7.00 a bushel?

b. Suppose the market price of apples is $7.00 a bushel and that J. Appleseed's Finest is forced to sell a bushel of apples while Ski Top Orchards is forced to *not* sell a bushel of apples. When we reallocate sales according to this plan, what happens to the value of producer surplus in this market?

c. How does reallocation of sales away from the market-provided allocation alter the value of producer surplus? What implications does this result have if your goal is to maximize producer surplus?

6. The supply of widgets in Marksville is given by the equation $P = (1/3)Q$.

a. Draw a sketch of this supply curve and then shade in the area of producer surplus if the market price is $10 per widget.

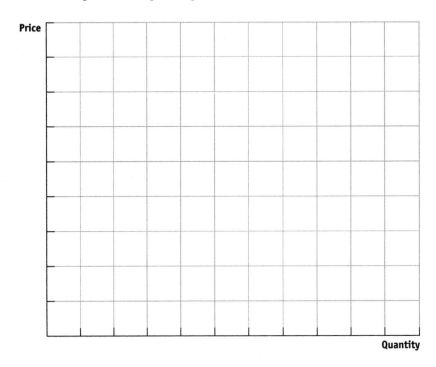

b. If the market price of widgets is $10, what is the value of producer surplus in this market?

c. If the market price of widgets is $20, what is the value of producer surplus in this market?

d. For a linear upward-sloping supply curve, what happens to producer surplus when the market price rises due to an increase in demand?

e. Suppose the market price is $30 per widget in Marksville. Will at least 80 widgets be supplied at this price? Explain your answer.

f. Suppose the market price is $30 per widget in Marksville. Will at least 60 widgets be supplied at this price? Explain your answer.

7. Demand for widgets in Marksville is given by the equation $P = 100 - Q$, while the supply of widgets is given by the equation $P = (1/3)Q$.

   a. Draw a sketch of the demand and supply curves and mark the equilibrium price and the equilibrium quantity. Solve the two equations for the specific equilibrium price and equilibrium quantity.

   b. On the graph identify the areas of producer surplus and consumer surplus. Calculate a numeric value for each of these areas.

   c. What is the value of total surplus in the market for widgets?

d. Suppose that the price of an input in the production of widgets increases so that supply is affected and changes by 60 units. Draw a new graph indicating the changes in the market for widgets due to this input price change. Label the new equilibrium price and equilibrium quantity as well as the initial equilibrium price and quantity.

e. On the graph you drew for part (d), label the areas that correspond to producer and consumer surplus. Calculate a numeric value for consumer surplus and producer surplus. (Hint: When you calculate these values, use the graph you have drawn to guide the math steps you need to take to compute these areas.) Compare your answers in part (e) to your answers in part (b).

f. What happened to total surplus in the market for widgets when input prices increased?

8. George is considering the purchase of some new shirts for work. He is willing to pay $35 for the first shirt, $25 for the second shirt, and $15 for the third. Oxford Clothiers, his favorite shirt manufacturer, currently is selling shirts for $28 a shirt. What is the efficient number of shirts for George to buy? What is George's consumer surplus in this situation? Explain your answers.

9.   Use the graph below to answer the following questions.

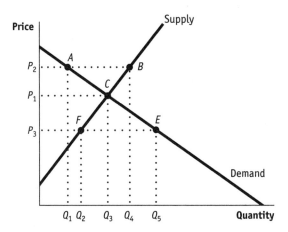

a.   Identify the equilibrium price and the equilibrium quantity.

E Price = P_1

E_Q = Q_3

b.   Suppose a price floor of P_3 is implemented by the government in this market. Describe what will happen to the price and quantity once this price floor is implemented.

Nothing— below eqbrm price   nonbinding

c.   Suppose a price floor of P_2 is implemented by the government in this market. Describe what will happen to the price and quantity once this price floor is implemented.

With a price increase, there will be a surplus as more Qs will be supplied than demand.

d.   What must be true about a price floor in a market for a good or service in order for that price floor to be effective?

Above Eqbrm price

e.   You are told that an effective price floor has been implemented in this market and that the resultant surplus is greater than $Q_4 - Q_1$. What do you know about the level of this price floor?

Above P_2

10. Use the graph below to answer the following questions.

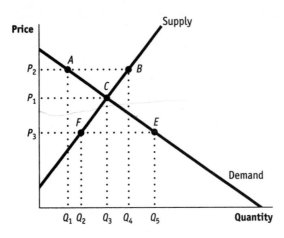

a. Identify the equilibrium price and the equilibrium quantity.

Q₃, P₁

b. Suppose a price ceiling of P_2 is implemented by the government in this market. Describe what will happen to the price and quantity once this price ceiling is implemented.

Nothing

c. Suppose a price ceiling of P_3 is implemented by the government in this market. Describe what will happen to the price and quantity once this price ceiling is implemented.

Price → goes down
Q_s = decr   Q_D = increas
Shortage

d. What must be true about a price ceiling in a market for a good or service in order for that price ceiling to be effective?

lower than E

e. You are told that an effective price ceiling has been implemented in this market and that the resultant shortage is smaller than $Q_5 - Q_2$. What do you know about the level of this price ceiling?

in betw P₁ and P₃

11. Consider the market for housing in Metropolitan City, where all housing units are exactly the same. Currently the equilibrium price of housing is $2,000 a month and local residents consume 1,500 units of housing. The local residents argue that housing is too expensive and that an effective price ceiling should be implemented. Once the price ceiling is implemented by the local government council, only 1,200 units of housing are supplied in this market. Is this an efficient level of housing for Metropolitan City? Explain your answer. To support your answer, provide two sketches: in the first sketch indicate the equilibrium quantity and the equilibrium price; in the second sketch indicate the price ceiling and the quantity provided by the market. Is the price consumers are willing to pay for the last unit equal to the price suppliers must receive in order to be willing to supply the last unit? Explain the significance of your answer to this question.

12. A price ceiling is implemented in the market for housing in Metropolitan City, where all housing units are identical. You know that before the price ceiling is implemented, the demand for housing in Metropolitan City is given by the equation $P = 1,000 - 0.1Q_D$ and the supply of housing is given by the equation $P = 200 + 0.3Q_S$.

   a. Prior to the implementation of the price ceiling, what is the equilibrium price for housing in Metropolitan City and what is the equilibrium quantity of housing?

   b. Fill in the following demand and supply schedules for this market, given the above equations.

Price	Quantity demanded	Quantity supplied
$ 200		
400		
600		
800		
1,000		

c. When the price ceiling is implemented, a housing shortage develops. This shortage is equal to 4,000 housing units. Calculate the price ceiling in this market for housing. (Hint: You may find the table from part (b) helpful in thinking about this problem.)

d. Who benefits from the imposition of the price ceiling in the market for housing in Metropolitan City?

e. Who is hurt by the imposition of a price ceiling in the market for housing in Metropolitan City?

f. Why is this price ceiling apt to result in black market activities in the market for housing? Provide at least two examples of potential black market activities.

g. Does an effective price ceiling in this market result in too many or too few resources being allocated to the market for housing in Metropolitan City? Explain your answer.

13. Farmers in Corntopia successfully lobby their government to enact a price floor for their agricultural commodity. The price floor is set at $10 above the equilibrium price. The initial demand and supply curves for agricultural production in Corntopia are as follows: $P = 100 - Q$ and $P = Q$, where price is per bushel and quantity is measured in bushels.

a. What is the level of the price floor in this market?

$100 - Q = Q$
$EQ = 50 = 7$ Price floor = 60 per bushel

b. How many units of the agricultural product will be demanded and supplied at this price floor level?

$D: P = 100 - Q$ $60 = 100 - Q_p$ $Q_p = 40$
$S: P = Q$ $60 = Q_s$

c. Suppose the government purchases the surplus in this market once the price floor is implemented. What will be the cost to the government of buying this surplus?

20 bushels => $$1200$ money spent

d. Given the price floor, what is the expenditure consumers make when purchasing this commodity? Do not include in your calculation the cost to the government of buying the surplus.

Demand 40 at 60 => $$2400$

e. What is total farm revenue equal to in this market once the price floor is implemented? What is the relationship among total farm revenue, consumer expenditure, and government expenditure on the good, given the price floor? Does total farm revenue increase when the government enacts a price floor? Explain your answer.   *60 . 60 = 3600*

f. Who benefits from the enactment of a price floor in this market?

14. a. Draw a graph of the demand and supply curves given to you in problem 13. Label the equilibrium price and the equilibrium quantity on this graph. Shade in the area that corresponds to total farm revenue in this market and label this area clearly.

Price

Quantity

b. Redraw the graph of the demand and supply curves given to you in problem 13, and draw in a line indicating the price floor. On the graph, indicate the quantity demanded and the quantity supplied using the values you found in problem 13. Shade in and clearly label the areas that correspond to consumer expenditure on the good and government expenditure on the good, given the price floor.

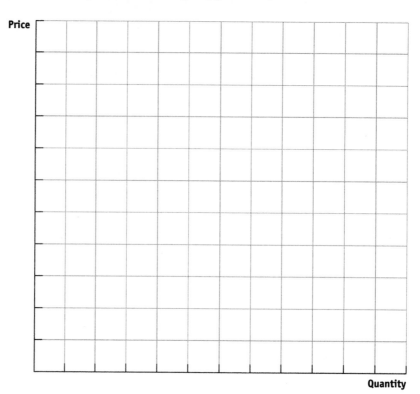

15. Consider the following graph.

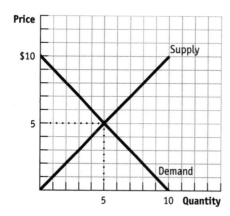

a. What price are consumers willing to pay for this good if 1 unit of the good is produced? What price must sellers receive to be willing to sell 1 unit of the good? Given that resources are scarce, should this first unit of the good be produced? Explain your answer.

b. What price are consumers willing to pay for the second unit of the good if 2 units are produced? What price must sellers receive to be willing to sell this second unit of the good? Given that resources are scarce, should the second unit of this good be produced? Explain your answer.

c. Generalize your findings from parts (a) and (b) of this question. Expressed in terms of the consumers' willingness to pay and the sellers' costs, what is the optimal amount of the good to be produced?

d. If this market produces a total of 4 units of this good, are resources being underallocated or overallocated to this market? Explain your answer.

e. What is the inefficiency cost that occurs if this market produces and sells only 4 units of the good?

16. Consider the following graph.

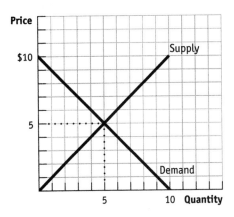

a. What price are consumers willing to pay for this good if 8 units of the good are produced? What price must sellers receive to be willing to provide 8 units of the good? Given that resources are scarce, should this market produce 8 units of the good? Explain your answer.

b. What price are consumers willing to pay if 7 units are produced? What price must sellers receive to be willing to produce 7 units of the good? Given that resources are scarce, should this market produce 7 units of the good? Explain your answer.

c. Given your findings in parts (a) and (b), make a general statement about the optimal amount of the good to produce, expressed in terms of the consumers' willingness to pay and the sellers' costs.

d. If this market produces a total of 9 units of the good, are resources being underallocated or overallocated to this market? Explain your answer.

17. Consider the labor market in Utopia. You are told that the equilibrium wage in this market is $10 per hour and that the equilibrium amount of labor in this market is 1,000 hours of labor. Furthermore, you know that at a wage of $14 per hour, 600 hours of labor are demanded and 1,400 hours of labor are supplied. The workers in Utopia successfully lobby Utopia's government for the implementation of a price floor. This price floor results in 1,200 hours of labor being supplied and 800 hours of labor being demanded.

a. Use the above information to derive the labor demand curve for Utopia. Assume this labor demand curve is linear. In your equation, abbreviate the price of labor, or its hourly wage rate, as W, and the quantity of labor demanded, measured as hours of labor, as L. (Hint: You may find sketching a graph of the above information helpful.)

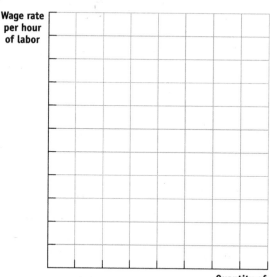

Wage rate per hour of labor

Quantity of hours of labor

b. Use the above information to derive the labor supply curve for Utopia. Assume this labor supply curve is linear. In your equation, abbreviate the hourly wage rate as W and the hours of labor supplied as L.

c. What wage rate did the government set when it implemented the price floor?

d. Describe the effects of this price floor on the labor market in Utopia. Who benefits from the price floor? Who is hurt by the price floor?

18. The market for taxi rides in Metropolia this week is described in the following table. Assume that all taxi rides are the same in Metropolia.

Price of taxi rides	Quantity of taxi rides demanded per week	Quantity of taxi rides supplied per week
$ 1	200	40
2	180	60
3	160	80
4	140	100
5	120	120
6	100	140
7	80	160
8	60	180
9	40	200
10	20	220

a. What is the equilibrium price and the equilibrium quantity of taxi rides in Metropolia per week? $E_p = \$5$ $EQ_D = 120$ $EQ_S = 120$

Suppose the government of Metropolia institutes a medallion system that limits the number of taxi rides available in Metropolia per week to 80 taxi rides.

b. At what price will consumers want to purchase 80 taxi rides per week? $\$7$

c. At what price will suppliers be willing to supply 80 taxi rides per week?

$5

d. What price will a taxi medallion rent for in this market? Explain your answer.

e. Draw a graph of the taxi ride market in Metropolia. On this graph, indicate the quota limit, the demand price, the supply price, and the medallion's rental price.

f. What is the total value of the taxi medallions per week in Metropolia?

BEFORE YOU TAKE THE TEST

Chapter Review Questions

1. To answer this question, use the following table, which expresses the amount people are willing to pay for a dinner tonight at Fast Eddy's Grill.

Name of consumer	Price willing to pay
Matt	$20
Donovan	15
Savannah	8
Gertrude	12
Anna	7

If a dinner at Fast Eddy's tonight sells for $10, what is the value of Donovan's consumer surplus?

a. $20   c. $10
b. $15   d. $5

2. To answer this question, use the following table, which expresses the amount people are willing to pay for a dinner tonight at Fast Eddy's Grill.

Name of consumer	Price willing to pay
Matt	$20
Donovan	15
Savannah	8
Gertrude	12
Anna	7

If a dinner at Fast Eddy's tonight sells for $9, what is the value of the total consumer surplus?

a. $20   c. $10
b. $15   d. $5

3. To answer this question, use the following table, which expresses the amount people are willing to pay for a dinner tonight at Fast Eddy's Grill.

Name of consumer	Price willing to pay
Matt	$20
Donovan	15
Savannah	8
Gertrude	12
Anna	7

If a dinner at Fast Eddy's tonight sells for $11, who will not purchase a dinner at this restaurant?

a. Matt   c. Savannah
b. Donovan   d. Gertrude

4. To answer this question, use the following table, which expresses the amount people are willing to pay for a dinner tonight at Fast Eddy's Grill.

Name of consumer	Price willing to pay
Matt	$20
Donovan	15
Savannah	8
Gertrude	12
Anna	7

If a dinner at Fast Eddy's tonight costs $4, what is the value of the consumer surplus tonight?

a. $80   c. $32
b. $42   d. $12

5. To answer this question, use the following table, which expresses the amount people are willing to pay for a dinner tonight at Fast Eddy's Grill.

Name of consumer	Price willing to pay
Matt	$20
Donovan	15
Savannah	8
Gertrude	12
Anna	7

All five of these consumers want to go out to dinner together at Fast Eddy's tonight. Assuming each consumer pays for his or her own dinner, what is the maximum price that Fast Eddy can charge for each dinner if they all go out?

a. $5   c. $7
b. $6   d. $8

6. The market demand curve for peanuts in Carterville is given by the equation $P = 1 - 0.001Q$, where price is measured in dollars and peanuts are sold by the bag. If the market price is $0.50 per bag, the quantity demanded will equal _____ and the value of consumer surplus will be _____.

a. 5 bags; $125
b. 50 bags; $125
c. 500 bags; $125
d. 5,000 bags; $125

7. The market demand curve for peanuts in Carterville is given by the equation $P = 1 - 0.001Q$, where price is measured in dollars and peanuts are sold by the bag. If the market price is $0.20 per bag, the quantity demanded will equal _____ and the value of consumer surplus will be _____.

a. 80 bags; $640   c. 800 bags; $640
b. 80 bags; $320   d. 800 bags; $320

8. For a given linear demand curve, the value of consumer surplus

a. decreases as the market price decreases.
b. decreases as the market price increases.
c. increases as the market price increases.
d. Answers (a) and (c) are possible.

9. For a given linear demand curve, an increase in consumer surplus must be due to a(n)

a. decrease in the market price.
b. increase in the market price.

10. To answer this question, use the following table, which expresses the number of dinners Fast Eddy's Grill is willing to prepare tonight at different prices.

Total number of dinners prepared	Price per dinner
1	$ 3
2	6
3	10
4	12
5	15

If a dinner at Fast Eddy's tonight sells for $10, what is the value of Fast Eddy's producer surplus?

a. $11
b. $9
c. $16
d. $19

11. To answer this question, use the following table, which expresses the relationship between each dinner and the lowest price Fast Eddy's Grill is willing to accept to prepare that dinner.

	Lowest price Fast Eddy is willing to accept
First dinner	$ 3
Second dinner	6
Third dinner	10
Fourth dinner	12
Fifth dinner	15

If a dinner at Fast Eddy's tonight sells for $13, what is the value of Fast Eddy's producer surplus?

a. $10
b. $17
c. $20
d. $21

12. To answer this question, use the following table, which expresses the relationship between each dinner and the lowest price Fast Eddy's Grill is willing to accept to prepare that dinner.

	Lowest price Fast Eddy is willing to accept
First dinner	$ 3
Second dinner	6
Third dinner	10
Fourth dinner	12
Fifth dinner	15

If the price of a dinner at Fast Eddy's tonight is $9, how many dinners will Fast Eddy sell?

a. 1 dinner
b. 2 dinners
c. 3 dinners
d. 4 dinners

13. To answer this question, use the following table, which expresses the relationship between each dinner and the lowest price Fast Eddy's Grill is willing to accept to prepare that dinner.

	Lowest price Fast Eddy is willing to accept
First dinner	$ 3
Second dinner	6
Third dinner	10
Fourth dinner	12
Fifth dinner	15

If the price of a dinner at Fast Eddy's tonight is $13, how many dinners will Fast Eddy sell?

a. 1 dinner   c. 3 dinners
b. 2 dinners   d. 4 dinners

14. To answer this question, use the following table, which expresses the relationship between each dinner and the lowest price Fast Eddy's Grill is willing to accept to prepare that dinner.

	Lowest price Fast Eddy is willing to accept
First dinner	$ 3
Second dinner	6
Third dinner	10
Fourth dinner	12
Fifth dinner	15

Which of the following dinner prices will lead to Fast Eddy's highest value of producer surplus?

a. $9   c. $11
b. $10   d. $12

15. Use the following graph to answer the question.

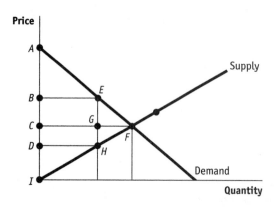

When this market is in equilibrium, consumer surplus is equal to area

a. *AEB.*   c. *ACF.*
b. *EFG.*   d. *CFI.*

16. Use the graph in question 15 to answer this question. When this market is in equilibrium, producer surplus is equal to area

a. *BEGC.*   c. *DHI.*

b. *GFH.*   d. *CFI.*

17. Use the graph in question 15 to answer this question. When this market is in equilibrium, total surplus is equal to area

a. *AFI.*   c. *BEHD.*

b. *BEFHD.*   d. *EFH.*

18. Which of the following statements is(are) true?

   I. In a well-functioning market, each transaction that occurs represents a situation in which the value the buyer places on the good is greater than or equal to the value that the seller of the good places on the good.

   II. In a well-functioning market, all trades are mutually beneficial.

   III. In any well-functioning market situation, it is possible to reallocate sales so as to increase total surplus.

a. Statement I is true.

b. Statement II is true.

c. Statements I and II are true.

d. Statements I, II, and III are true.

19. In a well-functioning market

a. any reallocation of the good or service away from the market equilibrium necessarily increases total surplus.

b. any purchase that does not occur must be because the value the potential consumer places on the good exceeds the value the potential seller places on the good.

c. any purchase that does not occur must be because the value the potential seller places on the good exceeds the value the potential consumer places on the good.

d. consumers who place the lowest value on the good are the first ones able to consume the good.

20. The concept of producer surplus illustrates the idea that the market works to allocate sales to

a. potential sellers who most value the right to sell the good, as indicated by their ability to produce the good at lowest cost.

b. potential consumers who most value the right to consume the good, as indicated by their willingness to purchase the good at the highest price.

21. The implementation of an effective price ceiling

a. decreases the price of the product in the market.

b. increases the price of the product in the market.

22. The implementation of an effective price floor

a. decreases the price of the product in the market.

b. increases the price of the product in the market.

23. When demanders can make a strong moral or political case for lower prices in a market, the government may decide to enact an effective
a. price floor.   b. price ceiling.

24. When suppliers can make a strong moral or political case for higher prices in a market, the government may decide to enact an effective
a. price floor.   b. price ceiling.

25. Consider minimum-wage legislation requiring that all workers receive a wage payment greater than the equilibrium market wage. Which of the following two groups is more likely to have advocated for this legislation?
a. demanders of labor   b. suppliers of labor

26. When the government intervenes in a market to regulate prices, this is an example of a
a. quantity control.   c. price ceiling.
b. price floor.   d. price control.

27. When the government institutes an upper limit on prices, this is referred to as a
a. quantity control.   c. price ceiling.
b. price floor.   d. price control.

28. When the government institutes a lower limit on prices, this is referred to as a
a. quantity control.   c. price ceiling.
b. price floor.   d. price control.

29. Use the information in the following table to answer the question.

Price	Quantity demanded	Quantity supplied
$ 20	200	0
40	150	50
60	100	100
80	50	150
100	0	200

If the government mandates that prices in this market can fall no lower than $50, this results in
a. a situation of excess quantity demanded.
b. a situation of excess quantity supplied.
c. fewer than 100 units being supplied in this market.
d. no effect in this market, since the equilibrium price is greater than $50.

30. Use the information in the following table to answer the question.

Price	Quantity demanded	Quantity supplied
$ 20	200	0
40	150	50
60	100	100
80	50	150
100	0	200

Suppose a price floor of $40 is implemented in this market. This results in

a. an excess demand of 100 units.

b. an excess supply of 100 units.

c. no effect in this market, since the price floor is set below the equilibrium price.

d. no effect in this market, since the price floor is set above the equilibrium price.

31. Use the information in the following table to answer the question.

Price	Quantity demanded	Quantity supplied
$ 20	200	0
40	150	50
60	100	100
80	50	150
100	0	200

Suppose a price ceiling of $40 is implemented in this market. This results in

a. an excess demand of 100 units.

b. an excess supply of 100 units.

c. no effect in this market, since the price ceiling is set below the equilibrium price.

d. a temporary shortage of the good while prices rise, and the quantity demanded and the quantity supplied adjust until they are equal.

32. Use the information in the following table to answer the question.

Price	Quantity demanded	Quantity supplied
$ 20	200	0
40	150	50
60	100	100
80	50	150
100	0	200

If the price ceiling is set at $40 in this market, then

a. too few resources are being allocated to the production of this good.

b. too many resources are being allocated to the production of this good.

33. Which of the following statements is(are) true?

   I. Price ceilings are inefficient because they result in too much of the good being produced in the market.

   II. Price ceilings are inefficient because they result in the production of goods with too low a level of quality.

   III. Price ceilings are inefficient because they lead to wasted resources since they increase the amount of time consumers must search for the price-controlled good.

   a. Statement I is true.

   b. Statement II is true.

   c. Statements I and II are true.

   d. Statements II and III are true.

34. Use the information in the following table to answer the question.

Price	Quantity demanded	Quantity supplied
$ 20	200	0
40	150	50
60	100	100
80	50	150
100	0	200

Suppose a price ceiling of $40 is imposed on this market by the government. The change in consumption due to this price ceiling in comparison to the level of consumption without the price ceiling is

   a. a decrease of 200 units of the good.

   b. a decrease of 100 units of the good.

   c. a decrease of 50 units of the good.

   d. no change in consumption.

35. An effective price ceiling typically causes an inefficient allocation of the good to

   a. consumers of the good.

   b. producers of the good.

36. Black market or illegal activities increase with the imposition of price controls in markets. Black markets result in

   a. improving the situation of all participants in the price-controlled market.

   b. worsening the situation for those people who attempt to obey the rules and restrictions imposed by the government in a price-controlled market.

   c. little or no real impact in price-controlled markets.

   d. the creation of greater respect in society for the need to obey all laws.

37. Use the following graph to answer this question.

An effective price floor is implemented in the market depicted in the graph. This **price floor** generates an excess quantity supplied of 2 units in this market. This **price floor** must be equal to

a. $10.

b. $7.

38. Use the following graph to answer this question.

An effective price floor is enacted in this market, and with this price floor the government promises to purchase any unwanted units produced. If the price floor is set at $10, then the government will spend _____ purchasing the unwanted units of the good.

a. $50

b. $30

c. $21

d. $20

39. Use the following graph to answer this question.

An effective price floor is enacted in this market at a price of $10. With this price floor, consumers' expenditure on this good will equal

a. $50.   c. $21.

b. $30.   d. $20.

40. Which of the following statements is true?

a. An effective price ceiling reduces the quantity of the good available to consumers, while an effective price floor increases the quantity of the good available to consumers.

b. An effective price floor reduces the quantity of the good available to consumers, while an effective price ceiling increases the quantity of the good available to consumers.

c. Government intervention in markets in the form of effective price ceilings or price floors increases the quantity of the good available to consumers.

d. Government intervention in markets in the form of effective price ceilings or price floors decreases the quantity of the good available to consumers.

41. True or false: "An effective price floor always benefits consumers since it effectively places a floor under the price of the good ensuring that consumers pay the fair price for the good."

a. True

b. False

42. When a price is artificially set above the equilibrium price in a market, who determines the quantity of the good bought and sold in the market?

a. demanders

b. suppliers

43. When suppliers determine the quantity of the good bought and sold in a market, this must be due to the imposition of an effective

a. price floor.

b. price ceiling.

44. An effective price floor prevents suppliers from competing for customers through lower prices, so suppliers compete for customers by offering goods with

a. greater quality than consumers desire.

b. lower quality than consumers desire.

45. Which of the following statements is(are) true?

    I. An effective price floor benefits some suppliers.

    II. An effective price floor benefits all demanders.

    III. An effective price floor results in a persistent surplus.

    IV. An effective price floor results in an inefficiently high level of quality in the good offered by suppliers.

    a. Statements I and III are true.

    b. Statements I, III, and IV are true.

    c. Statements III and IV are true.

    d. Statements II, III, and IV are true.

46. A quantity control or quota

    a. limits the price that suppliers can charge for a good or service in the regulated market.

    b. limits the price that demanders must pay for a good or service in the regulated market.

    c. limits the amount of a good or service available in the regulated market.

    d. increases the amount of a good or service available in the regulated market to an amount that exceeds the equilibrium quantity.

47. A quota limit imposed on a market

    a. restricts the amount of a good available in that market.

    b. results in a payment being made by the government to the license holder.

    c. places a lower limit on the amount of a good provided in the regulated market.

    d. places an upper limit on the price of a good provided in the regulated market.

48. Which of the following statements is(are) true?

    I. Quantity controls are inefficient since they prevent mutually beneficial transactions from occurring.

    II. Quantity controls in a market result in too many resources being allocated to that market.

    III. Quantity controls result in a wedge: the price demanders are willing to pay for the last unit is less than the price suppliers must receive to produce this last unit.

    a. Statement I is true.

    b. Statement II is true.

    c. Statements I and III are true.

    d. Statements I, II, and III are true.

49. Quantity controls

    a. provide an incentive to engage in illegal activities.

    b. result in underproduction of the good or service in the market where the quota limit has been imposed.

    c. result in a less efficient outcome than the market outcome.

    d. Answers (a), (b), and (c) are correct.

■ ANSWER KEY

Answers to Problems and Exercises

1. **a.** Mario places the highest value on this good since the price he is willing to pay ($300) is higher than the price any other consumer in this market is willing to pay.

    b. Pete places the lowest value on this good since the price he is willing to pay ($50) is lower than the price any other consumer in this market is willing to pay.

    c. If the good sells for $100, it will be purchased only by those consumers willing to pay $100 or more for the good. At this price Joe, Mary, Lucinda, and Mario will buy the good.

    d. All five consumers would buy the good at this price since their willingness to buy is equal to or greater than $50.

    e.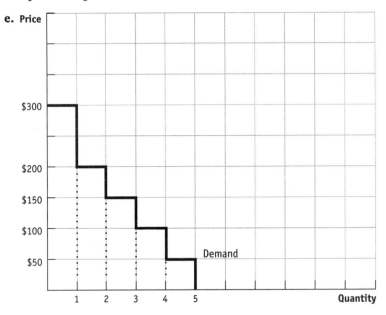

    f. Mary's consumer surplus equals $200 − $100 = $100.

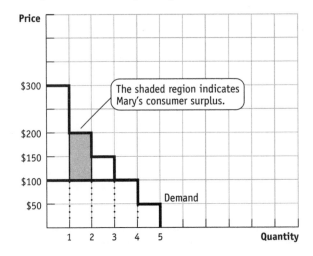

g. Mario's consumer surplus equals $300 − $100 = $200.

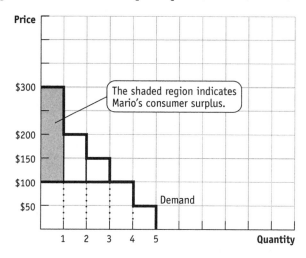

h. Total consumer surplus equals $350.

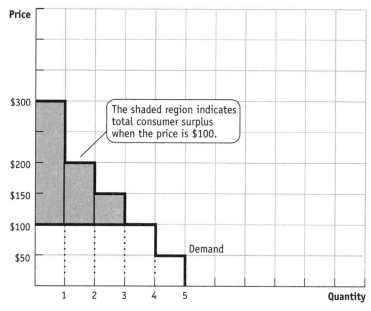

2. a. At a market price of $175, only Mario and Mary will buy the good since they are the only potential consumers who are willing to pay a price that is equal to or greater than the market price. The value of consumer surplus is $150 (Mario receives consumer surplus of $125 while Mary receives consumer surplus of $25).

b. Mario has a consumer surplus of $300 − $175, or $125, while Lucinda's consumer surplus is equal to $150 − $175, or −$25. The total consumer surplus is therefore equal to $100 when the two units are allocated to Mario and Lucinda.

c. Consumer surplus is reduced when the good is reallocated, because the good goes to consumers who place a lower value on the good. This type of reallocation, away from the market's allocation, results in a failure to maximize consumer surplus.

3. a. When the price of widgets is $50, the value of consumer surplus is $1,250. To calculate the value of consumer surplus, you need to find the y-intercept of the demand curve ($100) and the quantity demanded (50 units) when the price is $50. Since the demand curve is smooth and linear, the value of consumer surplus is equal to the area under the demand curve and above the price: $CS = (1/2)(\$100/\text{widget} - \$50/\text{widget})(50 \text{ widgets}) = \$1,250$.

b. Use the process outlined in part (a) but with a price of $40 per widget instead of $50 per widget: $CS = (1/2)(\$100/widget - \$40/widget)(60\ widgets) = \$1,800$.

c. When the market price rises, the consumer surplus decreases.

d. When the market price of widgets is $30, only 70 widgets will be demanded. At this price 80 widgets will not be sold.

e. Yes, when the market price is $30, the demand curve tells us that 70 widgets will be demanded.

4. **a.**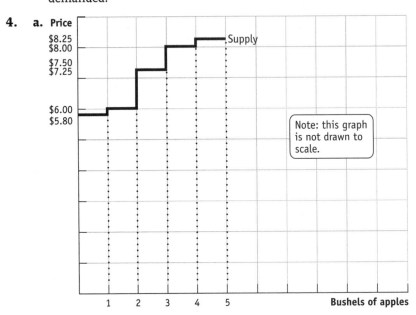

b. Red's Organic is the most likely seller at this quantity since it is willing to accept the lowest price for a bushel of apples.

c. At a price of $7.50 per bushel, the producer surplus for J. Appleseed's Finest is $0.25, or the difference between the market price and the seller's cost.

d. At a price of $7.50 per bushel, the producer surplus for Ski Top Orchards is $1.50, or the difference between the market price and the seller's cost.

e. The value of the producer surplus is $3.45 when the market price is $7.50.

    f. Ski Top Orchards, J. Appleseed's Finest, and Red's Organic will each sell a bushel of apples when the market price is $7.50.

5.   **a.** At a price of $7.00 a bushel, Ski Top Orchards and Red's Organic will be willing to sell apples. The value of producer surplus is equal to $1.00 for Ski Top Orchards and $1.20 for Red's Organic, for a total producer surplus of $2.20.

    b. When the sales in this market are reallocated away from the market-determined allocation, this reduces total producer surplus. Red's Organic's producer surplus is still equal to $1.20, while J. Appleseed's Finest's producer surplus is equal to $7.00 − $7.25, or −$0.25. Thus, total producer surplus under this reallocation plan equals $0.95.

    c. Reallocation of sales away from the market-provided allocation reduces total producer surplus. Producer surplus is maximized when the market allocates sales of the good.

6.   **a.**

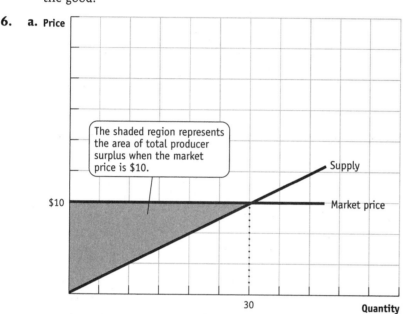

    b. The value of producer surplus is equal to the area under the market price and above the supply curve. When the market price is $10, this area of producer surplus equals $(1/2)(\$10/\text{widget})(30 \text{ widgets}) = \$150$.

    c. When the market price is $20, the value of producer surplus equals $(1/2)(\$20/\text{widget})(60 \text{ widgets}) = \$600$.

    d. Holding everything else constant, for a linear upward-sloping supply curve, the value of producer surplus increases when the market price increases due to an increase in demand.

    e. Yes, at a market price of $30 per widget, 90 widgets will be supplied.

    f. Yes, at a market price of $30 per widget, 90 widgets will be supplied.

7. a.

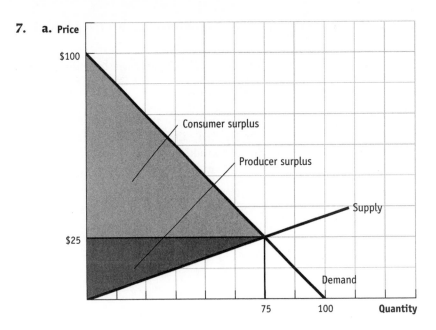

Since demand equals supply in equilibrium, we know $100 - Q = (1/3)Q$. Solving for Q, we find that the equilibrium quantity equals 75 widgets and the equilibrium price is $25.

b. Consumer surplus equals $(1/2)(\$100/\text{widget} - \$25/\text{widget})(75\ \text{widgets}) = \$2,812.50$. Producer surplus equals $(1/2)(\$25/\text{widget} - \$0/\text{widget})(75\ \text{widgets}) = \$937.50$.

c. The value of total surplus in this market equals the sum of the producer and consumer surpluses, or $3,750. Alternatively, you can calculate this area as follows: $TS = (1/2)(\$100/\text{widget} - \$0/\text{widget})(75\ \text{widgets}) = \$3,750$.

d.

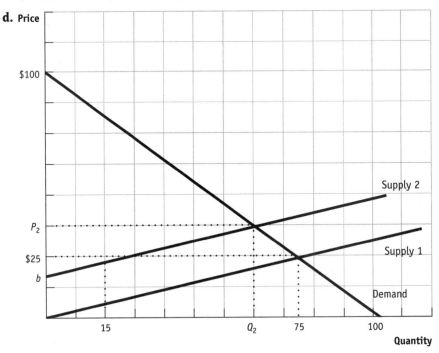

An increase in the price of an input causes the supply curve to shift to the left. In this example, the supply curve shifts to the left by a horizontal distance of 60 units. This tells us that if suppliers initially offered 75 units at a price of $25 per widget, they will now offer 15 widgets at a price of $25 per widget. This leftward shift in the supply curve causes the equilibrium price to rise from $25 to P_2 and the equilibrium quantity to decrease from 75 widgets to Q_2.

e.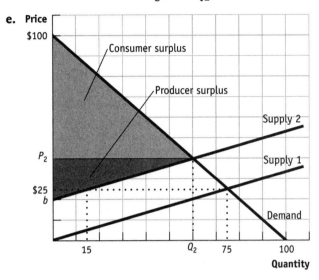

The calculation of consumer surplus and producer surplus is challenging in this problem. You need to write an equation for the new supply curve and then use this new equation with the original demand curve to calculate the numeric values of Q_2 and P_2. The new supply curve has the same slope as the original supply curve, but it has a different y-intercept. We can rewrite the new supply curve as $P = (1/3)Q + b$ and then substitute the coordinates $(15, 25)$ into this equation to find the value of b. When you do this, you find that b, the y-intercept, has a value of 20. Thus, the new supply curve is $P = (1/3)Q + 20$. Using the new supply curve and the original demand curve, we can find Q_2 and P_2: $100 - Q = (1/3)Q + 20$, or $Q_2 = 60$ widgets and $P_2 = 50. To find consumer surplus, we calculate the area of the shaded region marked "consumer surplus" in the above figure: $CS = (1/2)(\$100/\text{widget} - \$40/\text{widget})(60 \text{ widgets}) = \$1,800$. To find producer surplus, we calculate the area of the shaded region marked "producer surplus" in the above figure: $PS = (1/2)(P_2 - b)(Q_2 \text{ widgets}) = (1/2)(\$40/\text{widget} - \$20/\text{widget})(60 \text{ widgets}) = \$600$. Both consumer and producer surplus are decreased when the price of an input increases.

f. Total surplus in the market initially was equal to $3,750. When input prices increased, total surplus decreased to $2,400.

8. George will purchase one shirt since the price he is willing to pay for that shirt ($35) is greater than or equal to the price Oxford Clothiers must receive ($28) to be willing to sell the shirt. George will receive a consumer surplus of $7 when he purchases this shirt. George will not purchase two shirts since the value of the second shirt from George's perspective ($25) is less than the seller's price ($28).

9. a. The equilibrium price is P_1 and the equilibrium quantity is Q_3.

b. This is not an effective price floor since the price floor of P_3 is less than the equilibrium price P_1. Since it is a nonbinding/ineffective price floor, the equilibrium price and quantity will not change.

c. This is an effective price floor, since the price floor of P_2 is greater than the equilibrium price P_1. At P_2, Q_1 units of the good will be demanded and Q_4 units of the good will be supplied. This excess supply of $Q_4 - Q_1$ will not be eliminated by price decreases since the price is artificially set at P_2 by the government and is not allowed to decrease. An effective price floor creates a situation of excess supply, or a surplus, that is not eliminated by changes in the price of the good because the price has been set at a level that is greater than the market-clearing price.

d. For a price floor to have an effect in a market, the price floor must be set at a price that is greater than the equilibrium price.

e. The price floor must be set at a price that is greater than P_2, since we know from part (c) that the surplus in the market at P_2 equals $Q_4 - Q_1$.

10. a. The equilibrium price is P_1 and the equilibrium quantity is Q_3.

b. This is not an effective price ceiling, since the price ceiling of P_2 is greater than the equilibrium price P_1. Since it is a nonbinding/ineffective price ceiling, the equilibrium price and quantity will not change.

c. This is an effective price ceiling, since the price ceiling of P_3 is less than the equilibrium price P_1. At P_3, Q_5 units of the good will be demanded and Q_2 units of the good will be supplied. This excess demand of $Q_5 - Q_2$ will not be eliminated by price increases, since the price is artificially set at P_3 by the government and is not allowed to increase. An effective price ceiling creates a situation of excess demand, or a shortage, that is not eliminated by changes in the price of the good because the price has been set at a level that is less than the market-clearing price.

d. For a price ceiling to have an effect in a market, the price ceiling must be set at a price that is less than the equilibrium price.

e. The price ceiling must be set at a price that is greater than P_3 but still less than the equilibrium price of P_1. We know this because when the price ceiling is set at P_3, the shortage is equal to $Q_5 - Q_2$, and the new price ceiling results in a smaller shortage than the shortage at price P_3.

11. The market is in equilibrium when there are 1,500 units of housing offered at the price of $2,000 per month, so 1,200 is not an efficient level of housing. The price ceiling forces consumers to reduce their consumption of the good from the efficient level. In the first sketch below, the housing market is represented and the equilibrium price and quantity are where the demand and supply curves intersect. In the second sketch, the price ceiling is imposed on the housing market and this results in suppliers' reducing the amount of the good they supply in the market from 1,500 units to 1,200 units. Demanders are willing to pay more for the last unit than suppliers must receive in order to produce this last unit of housing. This indicates that the value to consumers of an additional unit of housing is greater than the cost to producers of providing this additional unit of housing: provision of more housing would lead to greater efficiency.

12. a. The equilibrium price is $800 per unit of housing and the equilibrium quantity of housing is 2,000 units.

b.

Price	Quantity demanded	Quantity supplied
$ 200	8,000	0
400	6,000	666.67
600	4,000	1,333.33
800	2,000	2,000
1,000	0	2,666.67

c. From the table in part (b), you know that a price ceiling of $400 is too low (the shortage is greater than 4,000 units of housing at this price), while a price ceiling of $600 is too high (the shortage at this price is less than 4,000 units of housing). You could try some prices between $400 and $600 or you could solve this problem algebraically. The shortage of 4,000 units is the difference between the quantity demanded and the quantity supplied at the price ceiling, or in other words, $Q_S + 4,000 = Q_D$. Thus, the demand equation can be rewritten as $P_C = 1,000 - 0.1(Q_S + 4,000)$, and the supply equation is equal to $P_C = 200 + 0.3Q_S$, where P_C is the price ceiling level. Solving this set of equations, we find that the quantity supplied is equal to 1,000 units. Thus, the quantity demanded is equal to 5,000 units while the price ceiling level is $500.

d. The people lucky enough to get one of the housing units supplied at the price ceiling price benefit from this government intervention. These individuals pay less than the market-clearing price for their housing unit.

e. Consumers who want housing but who cannot find it due to the price ceiling are hurt by the decision to implement the price ceiling. Additionally, as landlords fail to maintain the housing units in Metropolitan City, the whole community is affected since the general condition of the housing stock deteriorates. And if a black market develops in the housing market, this will erode the general level of lawful behavior in the community.

f. Since the quantity demanded of housing exceeds the quantity supplied of housing at the price ceiling, persistent shortages will exist in this market. Consumers eager to find housing will resort to activities that are illegal, such as subletting housing units at rates higher than the price ceiling rate or making illegal payments to landlords.

g. Too few resources are devoted to the housing market. We know this because the effective price ceiling creates a persistent shortage in the market for housing.

13. a. The level of the price floor in this market is $60 per bushel. To find the price floor level, first solve for the equilibrium price in the market: set demand equal to supply. Thus, $100 - Q = Q$, and thus the equilibrium quantity is 50 bushels of the agricultural commodity. We can then substitute this quantity into either the demand or supply equation to find the equilibrium price. The equilibrium price is $50 per bushel. If the price floor is set $10 above the equilibrium price, we know the price floor must be at $60 per bushel.

b. At $60 per bushel, demanders demand 40 bushels and suppliers supply 60 bushels. There is an excess supply of 20 bushels.

c. If the government buys the surplus 20 bushels at the price floor level of $60 per bushel, it will spend $1,200.

d. Consumers demand 40 bushels at the price of $60 per bushel. The expenditure by consumers on the product will equal $2,400.

e. Total farm revenue equals the total number of bushels supplied times the price floor, or (60 bushels)($60 per bushel), or $3,600. Total farm revenue equals the sum of consumer expenditure on the good plus government expenditure on the good. Total farm revenue without the price floor is equal to the equilibrium price times the equilibrium quantity, or (50 bushels) ($50 per bushel), or $2,500. Total farm revenue increases with the imposition of an effective price floor.

f. The farmers benefit from the imposition of the price floor since it increases total farm revenue.

14. a.

b. Price

15. a. To answer this set of questions, you need the demand and supply equations that correspond to the graph. Using the graph as a reference, we can write the demand equation as $P = 10 - Q$ and the supply equation as $P = Q$. Plugging a quantity value of 1 into both of these equations reveals that demanders are willing to pay $9 for the first unit and suppliers need to receive $1 to produce this first unit. Clearly this first unit should be produced, since the value to the consumer ($9) exceeds the seller's cost of producing it ($1).

b. Using the equations found in part (a), we can substitute a value of 2 for the quantity in both equations to find that demanders are willing to pay $8 for the second unit and suppliers need to receive $2 to produce the second unit. The second unit of the good should be produced since its value to consumers ($8) exceeds the seller's cost of producing it ($2).

c. The optimal amount of the good to produce is the amount at which the consumers' willingness to pay for the last unit exactly equals the producers' cost of producing the last unit. So long as the value consumers place on the good (the price they are willing to pay) exceeds the cost the seller must receive to produce the good, not enough of the good is being produced.

d. Resources are being underallocated to this market since consumers are willing to pay $6 for the last unit produced (the fourth unit), while suppliers are willing to sell this last unit so long as the price is at least equal to $4. When the value the consumers place on the last unit produced is greater than the cost of producing this last unit, not enough of the good is being produced.

e. The inefficiency cost would equal $1. The inefficiency cost is ($\frac{1}{2}$)(the price consumers are willing to pay – the price sellers must receive)(the equilibrium market quantity of the good – the actual level of production), or ($\frac{1}{2}$)($6/unit – $4/unit) (5 units – 4 units), or $1.

16. a. To answer this set of questions, you need the demand and supply equations. Using the graph as a reference, we can write the demand equation as $P = 10 - Q$ and the supply equation as $P = Q$. Plugging a quantity of 8 into both of these equations, we find that consumers are willing to pay a price of $2 for the good, while suppliers need to receive a price of $8 for the good to produce 8 units. Since the value the consumer places on the eighth unit ($2) is less than the cost of producing the eighth unit ($8), the eighth unit should not be produced.

b. Using the same reasoning as outlined in answer (a), we find that consumers are willing to pay $3 per unit if 7 units are produced, while suppliers require a price of $7 per unit to be willing to produce 7 units. Since the value of the seventh unit to the consumer ($3) is less than the cost of producing the seventh unit for the producer ($7), the seventh unit should not be produced.

c. The optimal amount of the good to produce is the amount at which the consumers' willingness to pay for the last unit exactly equals the producers' cost of producing the last unit. So long as the value consumers place on the good (the price they are willing to pay) is less than the cost the seller must receive to produce the good, too much of the good is being produced.

d. Resources are being overallocated to this market: too much of this good is being produced, since the value consumers place on the last unit produced is less than the cost to sellers of producing the last unit.

17. a. The information you are given in this problem can be represented as follows:

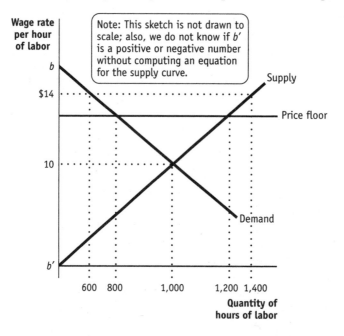

Thus, we know two points of the labor demand curve: (1,000, $10) and (600, $14). Use these two points to compute the slope of the demand curve: slope = rise/run = $(y_1 - y_2)/(x_1 - x_2) = (10 - 14)/(1{,}000 - 600) = -0.01$. The demand equation can be written as $W = b - 0.01L$. Then, use one of the points that you know is on the demand curve—either (1,000, $10) or (600, $14)—with this equation to solve for b. Thus, $W = b - 0.01L$ can be written as $10 = b - 0.01(1{,}000)$, or $b = 20$. The labor demand curve is therefore $W = 20 - 0.01L$.

b. Use a similar procedure to write the supply equation: $W = 0.01L + b'$, where b' is the y-intercept of the labor supply curve. Then use one of the points that you know is on the supply curve—either (1,000, $10) or (1,400, $14)—with this equation to identify the value of b'. Thus, $W = 0.01L + b'$ can be rewritten as $10 = 0.01(1,000) + b'$ and b' therefore equals 0. The labor supply equation is thus $W = 0.01L$.

c. At the price floor, we know that the quantity of labor demanded is 800 units. Substitute this number for L in the labor demand equation: $W = 20 - 0.01(800)$, or $W = \$12$ per hour of labor. To verify that the price floor has been set at a wage of $12 per hour of labor, check your answer with the labor supply equation. At the price floor, we know the quantity of labor supplied is equal to 1,200 units. Using this number for L in the labor supply equation, we find $W = 0.01(1,200)$, or $W = \$12$ per hour of labor.

d. This price floor creates a surplus of labor when the price floor is set at a wage rate of $12 per hour of labor. In a labor market, a surplus of labor implies that there is unemployment: workers who want to work (i.e., they are willing to supply their labor at the prevailing wage rate) cannot find work (i.e., there is insufficient demand for their services at the prevailing wage rate). Workers lucky enough to get a job paying $12 per hour benefit from the price floor, while workers who are unable to find work at that wage rate are harmed by the price floor.

18. a. Equilibrium occurs when the quantity demanded equals the quantity supplied. From the table, we can see that the equilibrium price is $5 and the equilibrium quantity is 120 taxi rides per week.

b. Consumers will demand 80 taxi rides per week at a price of $7.

c. Suppliers are willing to supply 80 taxi rides per week for a price of $3.

d. The medallion will rent for $4 per taxi ride, or the difference between the demand price and the supply price when the quantity of taxi rides is limited to 80 rides per week.

e.

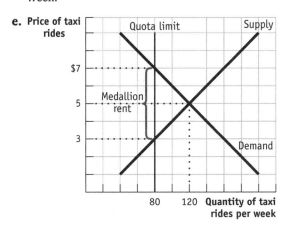

f. The taxi medallions are worth the product of the medallion rent per ride times the number of taxi rides per week. Thus, the taxi medallions' worth per week equals ($4 per taxi ride)(80 taxi rides), or $320.

Answers to Chapter Review Questions

1. **Answer d.** The value of Donovan's consumer surplus is the difference between the price Donovan is willing to pay ($15) and the market price ($10) of the good.

2. **Answer a.** When the price of a dinner is $9, Matt, Donovan, and Gertrude are willing to purchase a dinner, since the price they are willing to pay is greater than the $9 price. Matt's consumer surplus is equal to $20 – $9, or $11; Donovan's consumer surplus is equal to $15 – $9, or $6; and Gertrude's consumer surplus is equal to $12 – $9, or $3. Adding these three numbers together gives a total consumer surplus of $20.

3. **Answer c.** At a price of $11 per dinner, we know that Savannah and Anna are both unwilling to purchase a dinner since the prices they are willing to pay are less than the $11 price.

4. **Answer b.** The value of consumer surplus is the difference between the price each consumer is willing to pay and the market price for all those consumers who are willing to purchase a dinner at the current dinner price. Thus, the total value of consumer surplus is equal to $42.

5. **Answer c.** The maximum price Fast Eddy can charge per dinner is $7, since this is the highest price that Anna is willing to pay for a dinner. Any price greater than $7 would eliminate Anna from purchasing a dinner.

6. **Answer c.** To find the quantity demanded at a price of $0.50 a bag, simply plug $0.50 into the given demand equation for the price and then solve for the quantity. To find the consumer surplus, you need to calculate the area under the demand curve and above the price of $0.50. This area is equal to (1/2)($1 – $0.50)(500 – 0), or $125.

7. **Answer d.** To find the quantity demanded at a price of $0.20 a bag, simply plug $0.20 into the given demand equation for the price and then solve for the quantity. To find the consumer surplus, you need to calculate the area under the demand curve and above the price of $0.20. This area is equal to (1/2)($1 – $0.20)(800 – 0), or $320.

8. **Answer b.** Since the value of consumer surplus is equal to the area under the demand curve and above the given price, this implies that for any given demand curve an increase in the price will decrease the value of consumer surplus.

9. **Answer a.** This follows from the same reasoning as that given in the answer to question 8.

10. **Answer a.** When a dinner sells for $10, Fast Eddy will provide 3 dinners. Eddy would have been willing to sell the first dinner for $3, and thus his producer surplus is equal to $10 – $3, or $7. Fast Eddy would be willing to sell the second dinner for $6, and thus his producer surplus for this dinner is equal to $10 – $6, or $4. Fast Eddy is willing to sell the third dinner for $10, and thus his producer surplus on the third dinner is equal to $0. His total producer surplus is equal to $11.

11. **Answer d.** To answer this question, use the same reasoning as in question 10. The total producer surplus is equal to $21.

12. **Answer b.** Fast Eddy is only willing to sell 2 dinners at a price of $9 per dinner since the third, fourth, and fifth dinners must sell for more than this $9 price.

13. **Answer d.** Fast Eddy is willing to sell 4 dinners at a price of $13. He is unwilling to sell the fifth dinner since he must receive at least $15 to be willing to provide this dinner.

14. **Answer d.** Fast Eddy will have the greatest producer surplus at a dinner price of $12. When the price is $11, his producer surplus is equal to $14, and when the price is $12, his producer surplus is equal to $17.

15. **Answer c.** Consumer surplus is equal to the area under the demand curve and above the equilibrium price. Since the equilibrium price is equal to C in the graph, this implies that the area of consumer surplus is equal to area *ACF*.

16. **Answer d.** Producer surplus is equal to the area above the supply curve and below the equilibrium price, which is area *CFI* in the graph.

17. **Answer a.** Total surplus is the sum of consumer and producer surplus, which is equal to area *AFI*.

18. **Answer c.** In a well-functioning market the equilibrium provides the maximum total surplus, and it is impossible in a well-functioning market to reallocate sales so as to increase total surplus. Statements I and II are fairly transparent, straightforward, and true while statement III is false.

19. **Answer c.** In a well-functioning market, the equilibrium provides the maximum total surplus. Hence, answer (a) is not true. Purchases of a good in a well-functioning market imply that the value the consumer places on the good is greater than or equal to the value that the producer places on the good; hence, answer (b) is not true. Answer (d) is untrue: consumers who place the lowest value on the good are not the first consumers to get the good; the consumers willing to pay the highest price for the good are the first consumers of the good. Answer (c) is true: producers will not sell the good if the value they place on the good is greater than the value consumers have for the good.

20. **Answer a.** Producer surplus measures the difference between the price producers are willing to accept for the good and the market price. Answer (b) is not true because it is focused on consumers.

21. **Answer a.** An effective price ceiling must be set below the equilibrium price in the market; thus, the effective price ceiling reduces the price of the product in the market.

22. **Answer b.** An effective price floor must be set above the equilibrium price in the market; thus, the effective price ceiling increases the price of the product in the market.

23. **Answer b.** Demanders desire lower prices for the good and this can be achieved through the enactment of an effective price ceiling, since it reduces the price below the equilibrium price.

24. **Answer a.** Producers desire higher prices for the good and this can be achieved through the enactment of an effective price floor, since it raises the price above the equilibrium price.

25. **Answer b.** Suppliers of labor will receive this higher wage and therefore benefit from it. Demanders of labor will find that this higher wage increases the cost of hiring labor, and they will not benefit from it.

26. **Answer d.** The government can intervene in a market to regulate prices so that they are lower than the equilibrium level (an effective price ceiling) or higher than the equilibrium level (an effective price floor). Both are examples of price controls.

27. **Answer c.** An upper limit on prices establishes a price level for a product that is less than the equilibrium price and cannot be exceeded. This is an example of an effective price ceiling.

28. **Answer b.** A lower limit on prices establishes a minimum price level for a product that is in excess of the equilibrium price for that product. This is an example of an effective price floor.

29. **Answer d.** Setting a lower limit on prices of $50 in this market is an example of an ineffective price floor, since a price floor of $50 is less than the equilibrium price of $60. This price floor would have no effect on the market.

30. **Answer c.** Setting a price floor of $40 in this market is an example of an ineffective price floor, since a price floor of $40 is less than the equilibrium price of $60. This price floor would have no effect on the market.

31. **Answer a.** A price ceiling of $40 results in 150 units being demanded and 50 units being supplied. This is therefore a situation of excess demand of 100 units.

32. **Answer a.** At a price ceiling of $40, consumers wish to consume 150 units of the good while suppliers are only willing to supply 50 units of the good. This indicates that too few resources are being allocated to this market.

33. **Answer d.** Statement I is incorrect because price ceilings result in too little of the good being produced in the market. Statement II is correct because when price is limited to a level below the equilibrium price, producers have an incentive to reduce the quality of the product they provide to the market. Statement III is correct because an effective price ceiling results in greater costs as demanders seek out the artificially scarce good.

34. **Answer c.** In this market, the equilibrium quantity is 100 units when the market is free to move to its equilibrium. But with the imposition of the price ceiling of $40, suppliers supply 50 units while demanders demand 150 units. The "short" side of the market determines how many units are actually traded in the market; thus, only 50 units of the good are consumed once the price ceiling is imposed. This implies that the change in consumption with the price ceiling is a decrease of 50 units.

35. **Answer a.** An effective price ceiling limits the amount of the good available to consumers in the market by limiting the price to a level that is less than the equilibrium price. Producers produce the amount they are willing to produce at that price, and they do not expand production even though consumers are willing to consume more units of the good.

36. **Answer b.** Answers (a) and (b) are mutually exclusive: if one of these answers is correct, then the other must by necessity be incorrect. Reading answer (b) helps to identify a group that is hurt by black market activities: those individuals who decide not to engage in black market activities are left worse off because of their obedience to the rules imposed by the price-controlled market. Answer (c) is incorrect since price controls do affect markets and do have impacts when they are effective. Answer (d) is also incorrect since price-controlled markets generate black market activities, which are against the law.

37. **Answer a.** An effective price floor is the minimum price that can be charged for a good, and this price must be set above the equilibrium price. At a price of $10, the quantity demanded is 3 units while the quantity supplied is 5 units. At a price floor of $10, there will be an excess supply of 2 units. The price floor must equal $10.

38. **Answer d.** At a price floor of $10, the excess supply is 2 units. If the government purchases these 2 units at $10 each, the cost to the government of this purchase is $20.

39. **Answer b.** With a $10 price floor, consumers in this market will demand 3 units of the good. Their expenditure on the good will equal ($10/unit)(3 units), or $30.

40. **Answer d.** Effective price ceilings and price floors both reduce the quantity of the good available to consumers, so answers (a), (b), and (c) are not true.

41. **Answer b.** A price floor, to be effective, must be set above the equilibrium price level. This means that consumers will now pay more for each unit they purchase, and they will purchase a smaller number of units than they would have without the imposition of the price floor. The price floor does establish a floor beneath which the price is not allowed to fall, but the price floor does not result in a "fair price" that always benefits consumers.

42. **Answer a.** When the price is artificially set above the equilibrium price, demanders determine the quantity demanded in the market since they select the quantity they are willing to demand based on the price of the good.

43. **Answer b.** A price ceiling is set below the equilibrium price. This limits the price that can be charged for a good in the market. Producers take this price and then

determine the number of units of the good they are willing to provide in the market at this price.

44. **Answer a.** When producers cannot compete for customers through prices, they must look for other ways to compete. One way is to offer goods of higher quality, and with an effective price floor producers will compete by offering higher-quality goods.

45. **Answer b.** Statement I is correct because those suppliers who are lucky enough to sell their good at the higher price are benefited. Statement III is also correct since an effective price floor results in excess supply of the good. Statement IV is correct as well because suppliers will compete for customers by offering higher-quality goods since they cannot compete for customers by offering lower prices. Statement II is incorrect: demanders of this good now have to pay a higher price than they would have in a freely functioning market.

46. **Answer c.** A quota control by definition is a limit on the number of units of the good that can be offered in the market. Answers (a) and (b) are both incorrect since they discuss price controls rather than quantity controls. Answer (d) is also incorrect since a quota limit reduces the amount of the good available rather than increasing the amount of the good available.

47. **Answer a.** Answer (a) is the basic definition of a quota limit. Answer (b) is incorrect since there is no assumption that the government will make a payment to the license holder when there is a quota limit. Answer (c) is incorrect since a quota limit represents the maximum amount of the good allowed in a market rather than the minimum amount. Answer (d) is incorrect since it focuses on price controls rather than quantity controls.

48. **Answer a.** Statement I is correct because quantity controls restrict the amount of output to a level that is less than the equilibrium amount of output, and thus are inefficient since they prevent mutually beneficial trades from occurring. Because quantity controls restrict output, this implies that too few resources are devoted to the production of the good, so statement II is incorrect. Quantity controls do result in a wedge being created, but that wedge is the difference between the price consumers are willing to pay and the price producers must receive to provide the good; thus statement III is incorrect.

49. **Answer d.** Quantity controls restrict output, result in too few resources being devoted to the production of the good, and create an incentive for black market activities as consumers seek out alternative methods for getting the scarce good.

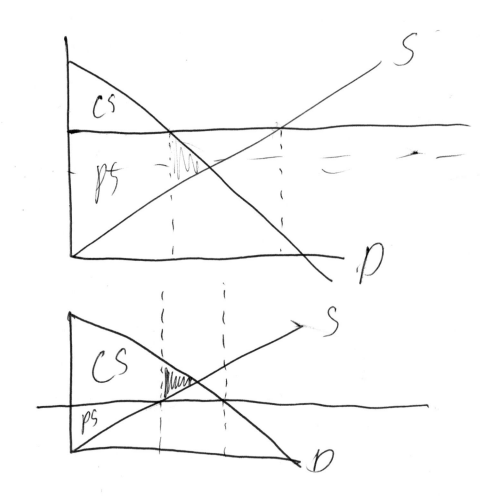

chapter 5

Elasticity and Taxation

▌ BEFORE YOU READ THE CHAPTER

Summary

This chapter develops the concept of elasticity, which provides a numerical measure of the responsiveness of quantity to changes in prices or income. The price elasticity of demand measures the responsiveness of the quantity demanded to changes in the price of the good, while the price elasticity of supply measures the responsiveness of the quantity supplied to changes in the price of the good. Income elasticity of demand measures the responsiveness of the quantity demanded to changes in income. Cross-price elasticity of demand measures the responsiveness of the quantity demanded to changes in the price of another good. This chapter also discusses the factors that influence these elasticities.

This chapter also considers how the price elasticities of supply and demand affect the costs and benefits of taxation. In addition, the chapter examines who pays the economic cost of an excise tax by looking at the loss in consumer surplus and the loss in producer surplus when an excise tax is implemented by the government. The chapter also examines the efficiency cost that arises with taxation.

Chapter Objectives

Objective #1. The price elasticity of demand measures the percentage change in the quantity demanded to the percentage change in the price of the good. Thus, the price elasticity of demand can be written as

$$\text{Price elasticity of demand} = \frac{\%\text{ change in the quantity demanded of good A}}{\%\text{ change in the price of good A}}$$

Since demand curves typically slope downward, a positive change in price (i.e., a price increase) results in a negative change in the quantity demanded (i.e., a decrease in quantity demanded). Thus, the price elasticity of demand is usually a negative number. By convention, economists measure the price elasticity of demand in absolute value terms so that the negative sign is eliminated.

$$\text{Price elasticity of demand} = \left| \frac{\%\text{ change in the quantity demanded of the good}}{\%\text{ change in the price of the good}} \right|$$

a. The calculation of the percentage change in the quantity demanded of good X can be found by using the formula

$$\% \text{ change in quantity demanded} = \frac{\text{change in quantity demanded}}{\text{initial quantity demanded}} \times 100$$

b. The calculation of the percentage change in the price of good X can be found by using the formula

$$\% \text{ change in the price of good X} = \frac{\text{change in price of good X}}{\text{initial price of good X}} \times 100$$

c. To generate consistent measures for price elasticities, regardless of an increase or decrease in price, calculate the percentage changes using the midpoint method. For example, consider two points on a demand curve: (Q_1, P_1) and (Q_2, P_2). The percentage change in quantity demanded using the midpoint method can be expressed as

$$\% \text{ change in quantity demanded} = (Q_2 - Q_1)/[(Q_2 + Q_1)/2]$$

while the percentage change in price is expressed as

$$\% \text{ change in price} = [(P_2 - P_1)/(P_2 + P_1)/2]$$

Using these two formulas, the price elasticity of demand formula using the midpoint method can be written as

$$\text{Price elasticity of demand} = \left| \frac{\dfrac{Q_2 - Q_1}{Q_2 + Q_1}}{\dfrac{P_2 - P_1}{P_2 + P_1}} \right| = \left| \dfrac{\dfrac{Q_2 - Q_1}{Q_2 + Q_1}}{\dfrac{P_2 - P_1}{P_2 + P_1}} \right|$$

Objective #2. Price elasticity of demand can be calculated using the midpoint method. Here is a specific example of this calculation. Suppose the demand curve for good X is given by the equation $P = 100 - Q$ and you are asked to compute the price elasticity of demand when quantity increases from 80 units to 90 units on this demand curve. First you need to calculate the price that demanders are willing to pay when the quantity demanded is equal to 90 units: this price is $10. Then, you need to calculate the price that demanders are willing to pay when the quantity demanded is equal to 80 units: this price is $20. Figure 5.1 below provides a graph of this demand curve with point B on the demand curve corresponding to a price of $10 and a quantity demanded of 90 units and point A on the demand curve corresponding to a price of $20 and a quantity demanded of 80 units.

Figure 5.1

Using this information, you can then calculate the percentage change in the quantity demanded of good X and the percentage change in the price of good X using the midpoint method. Thus,

The percentage change in the quantity demanded of good X =
$[(80 - 90)/2]/[(80 + 90)/2] \times 100 = -5.9$

The percentage change in the price of good X =
$[(20 - 10)/2]/[(20 + 10)/2] \times 100 = 33.3$

To find the price elasticity of demand, take the absolute value of the percentage change in the quantity demanded of good X divided by the percentage change in the price of good X. Thus,

The price elasticity of demand = $5.9/33.3 = 0.18$

Suppose that the price had originally been $10 and that the price had increased to $20. Does the price elasticity of demand change if you move along the demand curve from the point (90, 10) to the point (80, 20)? The midpoint method of calculating the price elasticity of demand ensures that the calculation of elasticity does not depend upon the direction of movement along the demand curve from one point to another. To see this, recalculate the price elasticity of demand moving from point B to point A.

The percentage change in the quantity demanded of good X =
$[(90 - 80)/2]/[(90 + 80)/2] \times 100 = 5.9$

The percentage change in the price of good X =
$[(10 - 20)/2]/[(10 + 20)/2] \times 100 = -33.3$

To find the price elasticity of demand, take the absolute value of the percentage change in the quantity demanded of good X divided by the percentage change in the price of good X. Thus,

The price elasticity of demand = $5.9/33.3 = 0.18$

The midpoint method of calculating the price elasticity of demand results in the price elasticity of demand being the same whether we move from point A to point B or from point B to point A.

Objective #3. A vertical demand curve indicates that the quantity demanded is completely unresponsive to price changes. A vertical demand curve is perfectly inelastic and its measure of price elasticity of demand equals zero.

Objective #4. A horizontal demand curve indicates that the quantity demanded is extremely responsive to price changes: even a small increase in price results in demand dropping to zero units, while a small decrease in price results in an extremely large increase in the quantity demanded. A horizontal demand curve is perfectly elastic and its measure of price elasticity of demand equals infinity.

Objective #5. A large value for the price elasticity of demand indicates that consumers are highly responsive to changes in the price of the good. Referring to the formula for the price elasticity of demand (the general formula given in Objective #1), a price elasticity of demand value that is greater than 1 implies that the percentage change in the quantity demanded in absolute value terms is greater than the percentage change in the price of the good in absolute value terms. When the price elasticity of demand is greater than 1, demand is elastic.

Objective #6. A small value for the price elasticity of demand indicates that consumers are less responsive to changes in the price of the good. A price elasticity of demand value that is less than 1 implies that the percentage change in the quantity demanded in absolute value terms is less than the percentage change in the price of the good in absolute value terms. Thus, when price changes, consumers respond with a relatively small change in the quantity of the good they demand. When the price elasticity of demand is less than 1, demand is inelastic.

Objective #7. When the price elasticity of demand equals 1, the demand is unit elastic. A price elasticity of demand value of 1 implies that the percentage change in the quantity demanded of good X is exactly equal to the percentage change in the price of good X in absolute value terms.

Objective #8. For a straight-line demand curve that intersects both the vertical and horizontal axes, the midpoint of that demand curve is the unit elastic point. Above the midpoint, demand is elastic, while below the midpoint, demand is inelastic. Figure 5.2 illustrates this idea.

Figure 5.2

Objective #9. Total revenue (remember this is price times quantity) is affected by the price elasticity of demand. If demand is inelastic, then an increase in price causes total revenue to increase. If demand is elastic, then an increase in price causes total revenue to decrease. An increase in price that moves symmetrically around the unit elastic point has no effect on total revenue.

Objective #10. A change in price affects total revenue in two ways: first, the price effect is the change in total revenue due to the change in the price of the good, and second, the quantity effect is the change in total revenue due to the change in the number of units of the good sold. The price effect is stronger than the quantity effect when demand is inelastic; the quantity effect is stronger than the price effect when demand is elastic; and the price effect and the quantity effect exactly offset each other when demand is unit elastic.

a. Figure 5.3 illustrates the effect on total revenue of an increase in price when demand is relatively inelastic. Starting at point E, total revenue is initially P_1Q_1, or the sum of areas B and A. When price increases to P_2 (point F), total revenue changes to P_2Q_2, or the sum of areas C and B. In this example, area A represents the quantity effect, while area C represents the price effect. When price increases, the quantity effect on total revenue is negative while the price effect on total revenue is positive, with the price effect dominating the quantity effect and leading to an increase in total revenue.

Figure 5.3

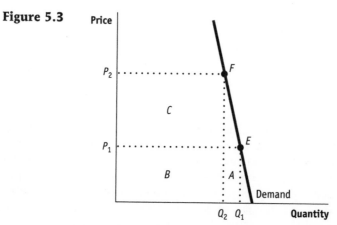

b. Figure 5.4 illustrates the effect on total revenue of an increase in price when demand is relatively elastic. When demand is elastic, the effect on total revenue of the quantity effect (area A) is larger than the price effect (area C).

Figure 5.4

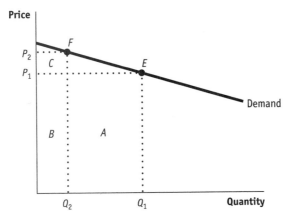

c. The table below summarizes the relationship between the price elasticity of demand and the effect of changes in price on total revenue, the price effect, and the quantity effect.

Demand	Price	Total revenue	Price effect	Quantity effect
Elastic	Increases	Decreases		Dominates
Elastic	Decreases	Increases		Dominates
Inelastic	Increases	Increases	Dominates	
Inelastic	Decreases	Decreases	Dominates	
Unit elastic	Increases	No effect	Exactly offsets quantity effect	Exactly offsets price effect
Unit elastic	Decreases	No effect	Exactly offsets quantity effect	Exactly offsets price effect

Objective #11. Price elasticity of demand is affected by the number of available substitutes, whether the good is a necessity or a luxury, and the time period for adjustment to the price change. Demand is more elastic when there are close substitutes, when the good is a luxury, and/or when there is more time to adjust to the price change. Demand is less elastic when there are no close substitutes, when the good is a necessity, and/or when there is little time to adjust to the price changes.

Objective #12. The cross-price elasticity of demand between goods A and B is equal to the percentage change in the quantity demanded of good A divided by the percentage change in the price of good B. That is,

$$\text{Cross-price elasticity of demand} = \frac{\% \text{ change in the quantity demanded of good A}}{\% \text{ change in the price of good B}}$$

Cross-price elasticity of demand may be a positive or negative number, and the sign of the cross-price elasticity of demand is critical to the interpretation of the meaning of a particular cross-price elasticity value. A positive cross-price elasticity of demand indicates that good A and good B are substitutes: if the price of good B increases, this leads to an increase in the quantity of good A demanded. A negative cross-price elasticity of demand indicates that good A and good B are complements: if the price of good B increases, this leads to a decrease in the quantity of good A demanded.

Objective #13. The income elasticity of demand is equal to the percentage change in the quantity demanded of the good divided by the percentage change in income. That is,

$$\text{Income elasticity of demand} = \frac{\% \text{ change in the quantity demanded of the good}}{\% \text{ change in income}}$$

Income elasticity of demand may have either a positive or negative value. A positive income elasticity of income value indicates that income and the quantity demanded move in the same direction: an increase in income leads to an increase in the quantity demanded, and thus the good is a normal good. A negative income elasticity of demand value indicates an inferior good: as income increases, the quantity of the good demanded decreases.

  a. A good that is income elastic has an income elasticity of demand that is greater than 1. When income increases, demand for income-elastic goods rises faster than income. Luxury goods tend to be income elastic.
  b. Income-inelastic goods have income elasticities of demand that are positive but less than 1. When income increases, demand for income-inelastic goods rises slower than income. Necessities tend to be income inelastic.

Objective #14. The price elasticity of supply is defined as the percentage change in the quantity supplied of good A divided by the percentage change in the price of good A. To get consistent measures of the price elasticity of supply, the percentage changes in quantity supplied and price are both calculated using the midpoint method. Thus, the price elasticity of supply can be expressed as

$$\text{Price elasticity of supply} = \frac{\% \text{ change in the quantity supplied of good A}}{\% \text{ change in the price of good A}}$$

or, for two points (Q_1, P_1) and (Q_2, P_2) on a supply curve,

$$\text{Price elasticity of supply} = \left| \frac{\dfrac{Q_2 - Q_1}{Q_2 + Q_1}}{2} \middle/ \dfrac{\dfrac{P_2 - P_1}{P_2 + P_1}}{2} \right| = \left| \dfrac{\dfrac{Q_2 - Q_1}{Q_2 + Q_1}}{\dfrac{P_2 - P_1}{P_2 + P_1}} \right|$$

  a. A vertical supply curve has a price elasticity of supply equal to zero and is an example of a perfectly inelastic supply curve.
  b. A horizontal supply curve has a price elasticity of supply equal to infinity and is an example of a perfectly elastic supply curve.

Objective #15. The price elasticity of supply is affected by the availability of inputs and the time period for adjustment. Supply is more price elastic the greater the availability of inputs and/or in the long run when full adjustment to price changes has occurred.

Objective #16. Taxes are necessary to provide governments with funds to provide services that the public wants. However, taxes usually have a cost that exceeds the money the government actually receives from the tax, because the imposition of a tax distorts the incentives to engage in mutually beneficial transactions. An efficient tax is one that distorts incentives as little as possible.

Objective #17. A simple tax to consider when analyzing the effects of taxes on consumers and producers is an excise tax, which is a tax that is charged on each unit of a good or service that is sold. An excise tax imposed on producers has the effect of shifting the supply curve to the left by a vertical amount equal to the excise tax. In effect, producers recognize that the excise tax increases their cost of production, since now they must remit to the government an amount equal to the excise tax for every unit of the good they sell. Figure 5.5 illustrates a market in which an excise tax has been levied on producers of the good.

Figure 5.5

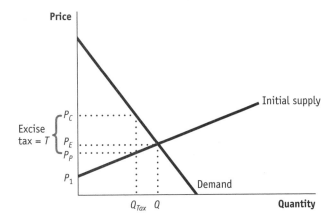

- The imposition of the tax reduces the quantity of the good sold in the market. The tax, because it effectively raises the price of the good, distorts incentives, and this distortion results in missed opportunities for mutually beneficial transactions. In the graph, the reduction in consumption from Q units to Q_{Tax} units is a measure of the missed opportunities for mutually beneficial transactions that arise with the imposition of the tax.

- When the excise tax is imposed, producers sell the good for the price marked P_C. But producers do not get to keep all of this money since they must pay the government the excise tax, which can be measured as the vertical distance between P_C and P_P. Thus, after producers pay the tax, they get to keep the price marked P_P. From the producers' point of view, the effect of the excise tax is that they are now selling fewer units of the good, Q_{Tax} instead of Q, and they are receiving the price P_P for each unit of the good they sell rather than the original price before the imposition of the tax, P_E. The cost of the tax to producers is therefore equal to $(P_E - P_P)(Q_{Tax})$. Figure 5.6 illustrates the area of producer surplus that is lost to the government because of the tax as well as the area of consumer surplus that is lost to the government because of the tax. In this example, the area of lost consumer surplus is greater than the area of lost producer surplus. It is possible for the areas to be equal or for the area of lost producer surplus to be greater than the area of lost consumer surplus. This relationship depends upon the supply and demand curve elasticities.

- From the consumers' point of view, the excise tax raises the price of the good from P_E to P_C while simultaneously reducing the amount of the good transacted in the market—from Q to Q_{Tax}. Thus, the cost of the excise tax to the consumer is equal to $(P_C - P_E)(Q_{Tax})$. Figure 5.6 illustrates the area of consumer surplus that is captured by the government with the imposition of the excise tax.

Figure 5.6

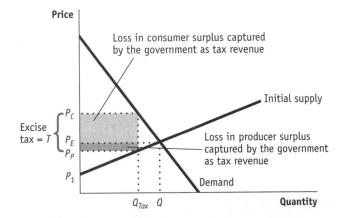

• The incidence of the tax on consumers and producers is dependent on the price elasticity of the demand and supply curves. When demand is relatively price inelastic and supply is relatively price elastic, the economic incidence of the tax falls primarily on consumers. When demand is relatively price elastic and supply is relatively price inelastic, the economic incidence of the tax falls primarily on producers. Figure 5.7 illustrates how these price elasticities can affect whether producers or consumers bear the greater economic burden of the tax.

Figure 5.7

• The tax revenue from an excise tax can be calculated as the product of the tax per unit times the number of units of the good sold. The tax revenue is also equal to the sum of the loss of consumer surplus captured by the government plus the loss of producer surplus captured by the government. The tax revenue is equal to the area of the rectangle whose height is the tax wedge between the supply and demand curves and whose width is the quantity of the good bought and sold when the tax is imposed. The amount of tax revenue raised by an excise tax depends on the tax rate and the price elasticities of supply and demand. For a given tax rate, tax revenue is greater if the price elasticities of supply and demand are both low, since the quantity demanded of the good isn't reduced very much when the tax increases the price of the good. Theoretically it is possible to raise a tax rate to a high enough level that tax revenue falls, or to reduce the tax rate to a level at which tax revenue rises, but in practice politicians take this possibility into account when setting tax rates.

• The excise tax entails the cost that producers and consumers pay to the government, but it also imposes costs over and above the tax revenue collected—costs in the form of inefficiency that arises when the market provides only the Q_{Tax} amount of the good instead of the original Q. This reduction in output due to the tax reflects the mutually beneficial exchanges that the tax prevents. The value to society of these lost exchanges can be measured as the deadweight loss (DWL) associated with the tax.

• All real-world taxes impose some DWL, but a badly designed tax results in a larger DWL than a well-designed tax. Figure 5.8 identifies the area of DWL and tax revenue when an excise tax is imposed. The graphs contrast two different markets and the level of DWL that occurs with the imposition of an excise tax of $\$x$ per unit. Taxes imposed on a good whose price elasticity of demand and/or supply is elastic results in a relatively larger DWL than the same size tax imposed on a good whose price elasticity of demand and/or supply is inelastic. This occurs because the change in the quantity demanded is greater when demand and/or supply is price elastic than when demand and/or supply is price inelastic. Thus, to minimize the inefficiency of a tax, policy makers want to tax goods whose demand and/or supply are relatively inelastic. Conversely, if policy makers wish to discourage a particular activity by taxing it, they will decrease consumption relatively more if demand and/or supply is relatively elastic.

Figure 5.8

- The area of *DWL* is the sum of the consumer surplus and the producer surplus that is lost when the excise tax is imposed. The *DWL* does not include the administrative costs incurred by the government and by taxpayers to pay the tax. The total inefficiency caused by a tax is the sum of the *DWL* and its administrative costs.

Objective #18. There is one other cost that taxes impose on an economy: the administrative costs of the tax. These administrative costs refer to the costs of the resources used by the government to collect the tax and by taxpayers to pay the tax.

Key Terms

price elasticity of demand the ratio of the percent change in the *quantity demanded* to the percent change in the price as we move along the *demand curve* (dropping the minus sign).

midpoint method a technique for calculating the percent change in which changes in a variable are compared with the average, or midpoint, of the starting and final values.

perfectly inelastic demand the case in which the *quantity demanded* does not respond at all to changes in the price; the *demand curve* is a vertical line.

perfectly elastic demand the case in which any price increase will cause the *quantity demanded* to drop to zero; the *demand curve* is a horizontal line.

elastic demand when the *price elasticity of demand* is greater than 1.

inelastic demand when the *price elasticity of demand* is less than 1.

unit-elastic demand the case in which the *price elasticity of demand* is exactly 1.

total revenue the total value of sales of a good or service (the price of the good or service multiplied by the quantity sold).

Notes

Key Terms *(continued)*

cross-price elasticity of demand a measure of the effect of the change in the price of one good on the *quantity demanded* of the other; it is equal to the percent change in the quantity demanded of one good divided by the percent change in the price of another good.

income elasticity of demand the percent change in the quantity of a good demanded when a consumer's income changes divided by the percent change in the consumer's income.

income-elastic demand when the *income elasticity of demand* for a good is greater than 1.

income-inelastic demand when the *income elasticity of demand* for a good is positive but less than 1.

price elasticity of supply a measure of the responsiveness of the quantity of a good supplied to the price of that good; the ratio of the percent change in the *quantity supplied* to the percent change in the price as we move along the *supply curve*.

perfectly inelastic supply the case in which the *price elasticity of supply* is zero, so that changes in the price of the good have no effect on the *quantity supplied;* the perfectly inelastic *supply curve* is a vertical line.

perfectly elastic supply the case in which even a tiny increase or reduction in the price will lead to very large changes in the *quantity supplied*, so that the *price elasticity of supply* is infinite; the perfectly elastic *supply curve* is a horizontal line.

excise tax a tax on sales of a good or service.

tax rate the amount of tax people are required to pay per unit of whatever is being taxed.

administrative costs (of a tax) the *resources* used (which is a cost) by government to collect the tax, and by taxpayers to pay it, over and above the amount of the tax, as well as the resources used to evade it.

▉ AFTER YOU READ THE CHAPTER

Tips

Tip #1. Economists calculate a variety of elasticities because these measures provide important insights into the relationship between two different variables. All elasticities are calculated as the ratio between the percentage changes in quantity (either the quantity demanded or the quantity supplied) to the percentage change in some other related variable. Elasticities are unit-free, making them an ideal measure of sensitivity of one variable to changes in another variable. There are four specific types of elasticity we will calculate in the text. The formula for each type is given below:

$$\text{Elasticity} = \frac{\text{\% change in quantity (either quantity demanded or quantity supplied)}}{\text{\% change in a related variable}}$$

$$\text{Price elasticity of demand} = \left| \frac{\text{\% change in the quantity demanded of good A}}{\text{\% change in the price of good A}} \right|$$

$$\text{Price elasticity of supply} = \frac{\text{\% change in the quantity supplied of good A}}{\text{\% change in the price of good A}}$$

$$\text{Cross-price elasticity of demand} = \frac{\text{\% change in the quantity demanded of good A}}{\text{\% change in the price of good B}}$$

$$\text{Income elasticity of demand} = \frac{\text{\% change in the quantity demanded of good A}}{\text{\% change in income}}$$

Tip #2.   In general, to find the percentage change in a variable requires dividing the change in the variable by its initial value and then multiplying this value by 100. That is,

$$\text{\% change in a variable} = \frac{\text{the change in the variable}}{\text{the initial value of the variable}} \times 100$$

Tip #3.   The midpoint method is used in calculating the price elasticity of demand and the price elasticity of supply. This method modifies the formula given in Tip #2 so that the results of the elasticity calculation provide a measure that is not dependent on which point on the demand or supply curve is designated the initial point. Objective 1c provides the formula for the midpoint method of calculating the price elasticity of demand, and Objective 14 provides the formula for the price elasticity of supply.

Tip #4.   Total revenue is equal to the price per unit times the quantity. Total revenue at any given price is equal to the area of a rectangle whose height is the price and whose width is the quantity demanded at this price. Figure 5.9 illustrates this concept of total revenue for the given demand curve.

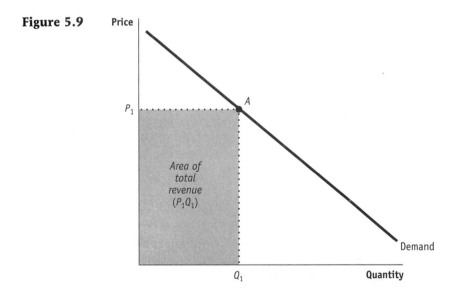

Figure 5.9

At point A, the price is P_1 and the quantity demanded is Q_1. The total revenue for the firm when the price equals P_1 is $P_1 \times Q_1$ (the shaded area in the graph).

Tip #5.   For a given demand curve, a change in price causes total revenue to change because of two effects—the price effect and the quantity effect. Figure 5.10 illustrates these effects.

Figure 5.10

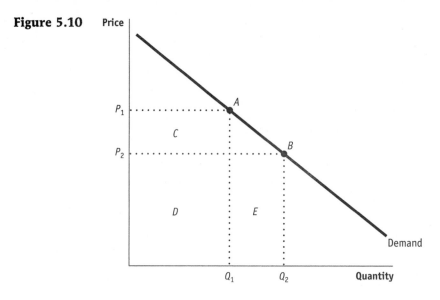

Suppose we are initially at point A with price P_1 and quantity Q_1. Then total revenue equals P_1Q_1, or the sum of areas C and D. If price decreases to P_2, then this causes a movement along the demand curve to point B with price P_2 and quantity Q_2. Total revenue is now equal to P_2Q_2, or the sum of the areas D and E. The price effect on total revenue is measured by area C: it reflects the change in revenue (in this case a loss in revenue) that arises from selling the original quantity Q_1 for the new price of P_2 instead of the initial price of P_1. The quantity effect on total revenue is measured by area E: it reflects the change in total revenue (in this case a gain in revenue) that arises from selling an additional $Q_2 - Q_1$ units of the good at the new price P_2. A similar argument holds for increases in price: you will find it helpful to redo this example starting at point B and moving to point A and thinking about the price and quantity effects.

Tip #6. Students often struggle with finding the new supply curve once an excise tax has been imposed. This is not difficult if you start by recognizing that the new supply curve should be parallel to the old supply curve and you have a y-intercept that is equal to the initial y-intercept plus the amount of the excise tax per unit. If you are working with equations, you should write the supply equation in slope-intercept form and then simply increase the constant in this term by the amount of the excise tax.

Tip #7. The imposition of an excise tax in a market in general reduces both consumer and producer surplus. Let's consider a market in which there is no excise tax and then look at the same market with an excise tax. Figure 5.11 illustrates a market in which there is no excise tax: CS is the area of consumer surplus and PS is the area of producer surplus.

Figure 5.11

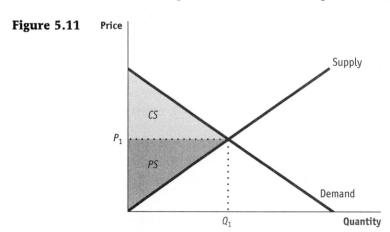

In Figure 5.12, an excise tax is imposed on this market. This excise tax shifts the supply curve to the left by a vertical distance equal to the excise tax. Once the market adjusts to this excise tax, notice that the areas of CS and PS are both decreased. Part of the original area of CS is captured by the government as tax revenue: this area represents the economic burden of the tax on consumers. Part of the original area of PS is captured by the government as tax revenue: this area represents the economic burden of the tax on producers. Part of the original area of CS is now DWL *captured from* CS, *and part of the original area of* PS *is now* DWL *captured from* PS. It is important to see that the excise tax redistributes CS and PS in two ways: some of this surplus goes to the government when it collects tax revenue from the excise tax (the tax revenue is equal to the sum of the areas of producer and consumer tax incidence), and some of this surplus is simply lost because the tax imposes an efficiency cost on this market (the area of DWL). Study this graph carefully.

Figure 5.12

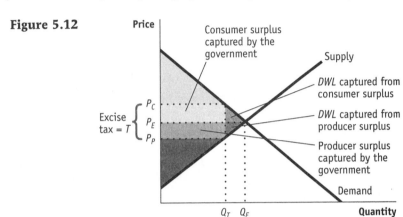

Tip #8.   Students often have trouble with the analysis of the excise tax. The most common error is to think that when an excise tax is imposed on a good, this results in the price of the good increasing by the full amount of the tax. Unless the demand curve is perfectly vertical, the excise tax will cause prices to rise and this causes the quantity demanded of the good to decrease: although the excise tax typically raises the price of the good, the price does not increase by the full amount of the tax.

Tip #9.   There is one final issue about excise taxes that requires some practice and thought: the effect of price elasticity on the effects of the excise tax on the size of consumer surplus; producer surplus; the loss in consumer surplus captured by the government as tax revenue; the loss in producer surplus captured by the government as tax revenue; and the deadweight loss from the tax. Practice drawing some graphs with different price elasticities of demand and the same supply curve to see how the price elasticity of demand affects these different areas. Then practice drawing some graphs with different price elasticities of supply and the same demand curve to see how the price elasticity of supply affects these different areas.

WORKED PROBLEMS

1. George delivers lunchtime sandwiches to a variety of office buildings in his city. Over the ten years he has been in business, he knows that he can sell 2,000 sandwiches a week if he prices each sandwich at $2.00. He is trying to decide whether or not he should raise prices for his sandwiches. In two of his office buildings, he has raised the price of sandwiches to $2.50 and found that this resulted in a 10% decline in the number of sandwiches that he sold in each of the buildings. He is not sure how to make this pricing decision and has sought your advice about how he should go about it. George's prime concern is maximizing his revenue from his sales of sandwiches.

STEP 1: Think about how you can use George's available data to estimate the price elasticity of demand for his lunchtime sandwiches.

Review the section "Calculating the Price Elasticity of Demand" on pages 144–145.

George has some information about how price and quantity relate to each other with regard to his sandwich sales. You will need to put this information together in a way that will help you guide George toward maximizing his revenue from selling sandwiches. First, start by estimating his price elasticity of demand. Price elasticity of demand is equal to the percentage change in the quantity demanded divided by the percentage change in the price. From George's price experiment, you know that the price increase has resulted in a 10% decrease in his sales in two office buildings. Next, calculate the percentage change in price. A simple percentage calculation (we just want to estimate price elasticity of demand) of the percentage change in price can be calculated as [($2.50 − $2.00)/$2.00] × 100, or 25%. The price elasticity of demand is approximated as 10%/25%: since this ratio is less than 1, we know that the price elasticity of demand for George's lunchtime sandwiches is inelastic.

STEP 2: Use your price elasticity of demand calculation to advise George as to his best pricing strategy.

Review the section "Calculating the Price Elasticity of Demand" on pages 144–145.

From George's price experimentation, we can determine that George is selling sandwiches in the inelastic portion of the demand curve. Thus, George can raise his revenue by increasing the price of his sandwiches. You advise him to raise the price to $2.50 at all of his office buildings. George may be able to raise his prices even higher and get even more revenue, but you need more information to fully determine at what price the demand for his product becomes elastic.

2. Hermione is interested in understanding the relationship between the price she receives when she sells one of her artistic creations and the revenue she earns. She estimates that she can sell 50 creations a year at a price of $100 and that her sales decrease by 10 units for every $20 increase in price and that her sales increase by 10 units for every $20 decrease in price. Can you guide her in determining what price and quantity will result in maximum revenue per year?

STEP 1: First, you will need to construct the demand schedule for Hermione's product using the information that you have been given.

From the given information, you know that when price is $100, the quantity demanded is 50 units. You also know that when price increases to $120, the quantity demanded decreases by 10 units to 40 units. You also know that when price decreases to $80, the quantity demanded increases by 10 units to 60 units. Use this constant relationship to create Hermione's demand schedule. The following table provides this demand schedule for a range of prices.

Price	Quantity demanded
$ 20	90
40	80
60	70
80	60
100	50
120	40
140	30
160	20
180	10

STEP 2: From the demand schedule, you can calculate Hermione's revenue at each price.

Review the section "How Elastic Is Elastic?" on pages 148–152, the section "Price Elasticity Along the Demand Curve" on page 152, Table 5-2 on page 152, and Figure 5-5 on page 153.

Recall that total revenue is equal to price times quantity. Using the demand schedule you constructed in step 1, now calculate the total revenue for each pair of price and quantity demanded. The following table provides this information for the demand schedule presented in step 1.

Price	Quantity demanded	Total revenue
$ 20	90	1,800
40	80	3,200
60	70	4,200
80	60	4,800
100	50	5,000
120	40	4,800
140	30	4,200
160	20	3,200
180	10	1,800

STEP 3: Now, you can select that price and quantity that maximizes Hermione's revenue for the year.

Review the section "How Elastic Is Elastic?" on pages 148–152, the section "Price Elasticity Along the Demand Curve" on page 152, Table 5-2 on page 152, and Figure 5-5 on page 153.

From the table, you can see that total revenue is maximized when price is equal to $100 and quantity demanded is equal to 50 units. Hermione is pricing her artistic creations optimally if she wishes to maximize her total revenue.

3. Josie has been provided the following cross-price elasticities of demand.

Goods	Cross-price elasticity of demand
Good A and Good B	−0.3
Good C and Good D	0.5
Good E and Good F	0.2
Good G and Good H	−0.15

Josie has been asked to identify whether each pair are substitutes or complements. She is unsure how to interpret the cross-price elasticity of demand and has sought your help in the matter.

STEP 1: **Review the definition of cross-price elasticity of demand and how its value can determine whether two goods are substitutes or complements.**

Review the section "The Cross-Price Elasticity of Demand" on pages 155–156.

The cross-price elasticity of demand is defined as the percentage change in the quantity demanded of one good divided by the percentage change in the price of the other good.

If two goods are substitutes, this implies that when the price of one of the goods increases, consumers will substitute away from this good and toward the now relatively cheaper good. Thus, if the two goods are substitutes, then an increase in the price of one good will cause an increase in the quantity demanded of the other good. Both the percentage change in the quantity demanded of one good and the percentage change in the price of the other good will therefore move in the same direction: the cross-price elasticity of demand for substitutes is therefore a positive number.

If two goods are complements, this implies that when the price of one of the goods increases, consumers will decrease their consumption of the other, complementary good. Thus, if the two goods are complements, then an increase in the price of one good will cause a decrease in the quantity demanded of the other good. The percentage change in the quantity demanded of one good and the percentage change in the price of the other good will therefore move in the opposite direction: the cross-price elasticity of demand for complements is therefore a negative number.

STEP 2: **For each pair of goods apply the information from step 1 to identify whether the pairs are substitutes or complements.**

Review the section "The Cross-Price Elasticity of Demand" on pages 155–156.

Apply the information you reviewed in step 1 to the table. The following table identifies the relationship between each pair of goods.

Goods	Cross-price elasticity of demand	Relationship between the two goods
Good A and Good B	−0.3	Complements
Good C and Good D	0.5	Substitutes
Good E and Good F	0.2	Substitutes
Good G and Good H	−0.15	Complements

4. Libertyville recently passed a law imposing a $50 per night tax on hotel rooms. During the winter, demand for hotel rooms is relatively inelastic due to the proximity of Libertyville to several excellent ski hills. During the summer, demand for hotel rooms is relatively elastic due to Libertyville's unusually hot and

humid summers. Analyze the impact of this tax on hotel owners and hotel guests as well as the seasonal impact on government tax revenue from this tax. Also, discuss the deadweight loss due to the tax in each season. For simplicity, assume that there are only two real seasons in Libertyville: summer and winter. Assume that the supply of hotel rooms in Libertyville is relatively inelastic, but not perfectly inelastic. Prior to the tax there was a single price charged for hotel rooms no matter what the time of year, and the hotel market was in equilibrium.

STEP 1: First, it is important to recognize that this analysis actually is the analysis of two separate markets—the winter market for hotel accommodation and the summer market for hotel accommodation. You will want to model this situation with two separate graphs, with each graph depicting a different season.

Review the section "The Benefits and Costs of Taxation" on pages 162-170, and Figure 5-11 on page 169.

Start by depicting the two seasons for hotel accommodations in Libertyville. The following graphs represent the winter season and the summer season, respectively.

STEP 2: Depict the effect of a $50 per room tax on the market for hotel rooms in Libertyville on the two graphs you created in step 1.

Review the section "The Benefits and Costs of Taxation" on pages 162-170, Figure 5-9 on page 167, and Figure 5-11 on page 169.

This tax will cause a $50 difference between the price that consumers pay for the room and the price that producers receive for renting the room once they have paid the room tax to the government. The following figure illustrates this room tax for both the

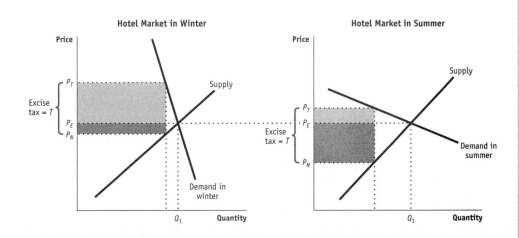

winter and summer season in Libertyville. In your graphs, identify the loss in consumer surplus and producer surplus that is gained as tax revenue by the government.

STEP 3: Analyze the effect of a $50 per room tax on hotel guests, hotel owners, and government revenue. In your analysis consider the effect of the season.

Review the section "The Benefits and Costs of Taxation" on pages 162–170, Figure 5-9 on page 167, and Figure 5-11 on page 169.

In the winter, the hotel room tax results in a relatively large increase in the price of hotel accommodations and a relatively small change in the number of hotel rooms sold. The impact of this when compared to the summer situation is that when the government collects the tax, it captures a large amount of consumer surplus and a smaller amount of producer surplus. Tax revenue from the room tax is relatively large due to the inelasticity of the demand curve: the percentage change in price far outweighs the percentage change in the quantity.

In the summer, the hotel room tax results in a relatively small increase in the price of hotel accommodations and a relatively large change in the number of hotel rooms sold. The impact of this, when compared to the winter situation, is that when the government collects the tax, it captures a smaller amount of consumer surplus and a larger amount of producer surplus. Tax revenue is smaller in the summer season than in the winter season due to the elasticity of the demand curve: the percentage change in price is far smaller than the percentage change in the quantity.

STEP 4: Find the deadweight loss associated with the room tax for both seasons, and then compare the size of these deadweight loss areas.

Review the section "The Benefits and Costs of Taxation" on pages 162–170, Figure 5-9 on page 167, Figure 5-10 on page 167, and Figure 5-11 on page 169.

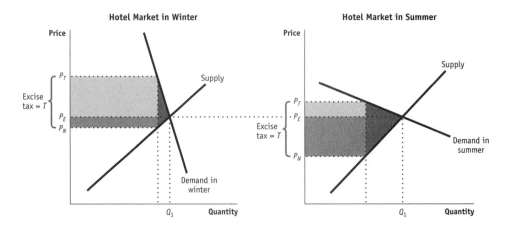

The above graphs depict the deadweight loss areas associated with the implementation of the room tax. During the winter season, in the hotel market the deadweight loss is smaller than it is in the summer season due to the relative inelasticity of the demand curve in winter. The room tax causes the price of a hotel room to rise, but this price increase is larger in winter than in summer: in the winter, quantity is not very price sensitive and that results in a smaller deadweight loss from the tax. In the summer, demand is elastic: quantity is very price-sensitive and this results in a larger deadweight loss from the tax.

Problems and Exercises

1. This problem explores the midpoint method of calculating percentages and why this method is the preferred method when calculating price elasticity of demand or price elasticity of supply. Consider the demand curve in the figure below to answer this question.

a. Suppose the initial price and quantity on the above demand curve is represented by point *A* and then the price and quantity change to point *B*. Calculate the percentage change in price and the percentage change in quantity using the following formula:

$$\text{Percentage change} = \frac{\text{new value} - \text{old value}}{\text{old value}} \times 100$$

Note: We are purposefully *not* using the midpoint method for parts (a) through (e) of this problem so that we can compare these results to the results we would get if we did use the midpoint method.

b. Using the percentage changes you calculated in part (a), calculate the price elasticity of demand from point *A* to point *B*, using the following formula:

$$\text{Price elasticity of demand} = \left| \frac{\% \text{ change in quantity demanded}}{\% \text{ change in price}} \right|$$

c. Redo part (a) starting at point *B* and moving to point *A*. Use the same formula as that given in part (a).

d. Calculate the price elasticity of demand from point *B* to point *A* using the formula given in part (b).

   e. Are your values for the price elasticity of demand the same in parts (b) and (d)?

Now, let's recalculate the price elasticity of demand using the midpoint method.

   f. Suppose you are initially at point *A* and that you move to point *B*. Calculate the percentage change in price and the percentage change in quantity using the following (midpoint method) formula:

$$\% \text{ change} = \frac{\text{new value} - \text{old value}}{\dfrac{\text{old value} + \text{new value}}{2}} \times 100$$

   g. Using the percentage changes you calculated in part (f), calculate the elasticity of demand from point *A* to point *B* using the following formula:

$$\text{Price elasticity of demand} = \left| \frac{\% \text{ change in quantity demanded}}{\% \text{ change in price}} \right|,$$

   where both percentage changes have been calculated using the midpoint method.

   h. Suppose you now start at point *B* and move to point *A*. Calculate the percentage change in price and the percentage change in quantity using the formula given in part (f).

   i. Calculate the price elasticity of demand from point *B* to point *A* using the formula given in part (g).

   j. Are the values you calculated for the price elasticity of demand using the midpoint method the same in parts (g) and (i)? Summarize the significance of the midpoint method when calculating the price elasticity of demand or the price elasticity of supply.

2. Use the figure from problem 1 to answer this question.

   a. Calculate a value for the price elasticity of demand between points *C* and *E* using the midpoint method. Does it matter which point you select as your initial point?

b. Compare the value you calculated in part (a) of this problem with the price elasticity of demand value between points *A* and *B* that you calculated in part (g) of problem 1. Are these two price elasticities of demand the same?

c. Demand is elastic when the absolute value of the percentage change in the quantity demanded exceeds the absolute value of the percentage change in the price. Given the values you compared in part (b), is demand elastic between points *A* and *B* or between points *C* and *E*?

d. Demand is inelastic when the absolute value of the percentage change in the quantity demanded is less than the absolute value of the percentage change in the price. Given the values you compared in part (b), is demand inelastic between points *A* and *B* or between points *C* and *E*?

3.   Use the following figure of a linear demand curve to answer the following set of questions.

5.50.

a. Based on the figure, fill in the following table.

Price	Quantity demanded	Total revenue
$ 0	11	0
1	10	10
2	9	18
3	8	24
4	7	28
5	6	30
6	5	30
7	4	28
8	3	24
9	2	18
10	1	10
11	0	0

b. At what price is total revenue maximized? (Hint: This price may not be in the table and it may not be a whole number.)

c. Suppose the price is initially $6, but it then decreases to $5. Using the midpoint method, calculate the elasticity of demand between these two points on the demand curve.

$$\frac{\frac{5-6}{11/2}}{\frac{6-5}{11/2}} = \frac{-\frac{2}{11}}{\frac{2}{11}} = -1 = |1| = \text{unit elastic}$$

d. Based on your calculations in part (c), describe the relationship between the absolute value of the percentage change in the quantity demanded and the absolute value of the percentage change in price when moving from a price of $6 to a price of $5.

4. For each of the following pairs of goods, identify which good is likely to have the more elastic price elasticity of demand, and then provide an explanation for your choice.

a. Golden delicious apples and all fruit

b. Gasoline and ice cream

c. Leisure travel and business travel $\dfrac{P_2 - P_1}{\left(\dfrac{P_2 + P_1}{2}\right)}$

5. Suppose there are two goods, good A and good B. When the price of good A increases from $10 to $12, the quantity of good B demanded changes from 4 units to 6 units.

   a. Calculate the cross-price elasticity of demand (use the simple formula for percentage changes rather than the midpoint method).

   $$E_{AB} = \frac{\%\,\Delta Q_B}{\%\,\Delta P_A} = \frac{\frac{6-4}{10/2}}{\frac{12-10}{11}} = \frac{\frac{2}{5}}{\frac{2}{11}} = \frac{2}{5} \cdot \frac{11}{2} = \frac{11}{5}$$

   b. What is the relationship between good A and good B? Explain your answer and provide an example of two goods that have this relationship.

   Good A and B are subs. As the price of A increases, the dem. for B increases.

6. Suppose there are two goods, good C and good D. The cross-price elasticity of demand for these two goods is equal to –0.2.

   a. What is the relationship between good C and good D? Explain your answer.

   As the demand for either C/D increases, the price of C/D decreases. Or Q_D C/D decr., the price of C/D incr.

   b. Suppose the price of good C increases from $1 to $2. What do you estimate will be the percentage change in the quantity demanded of good D? (Use the simple formula for percentage changes rather than the midpoint method.)

   $$-.2 = \frac{\frac{2-1}{1.5}}{X} = -.2X =$$

   c. Suppose that when the price of good C is $1, 10 units of good D are demanded. What will be the quantity demanded of good D when the price of good C increases to $2?

   -20%

   8 units

   d. Suppose the cross-price elasticity of demand between two goods is negative and you would like to sell more units of one of these goods. What do you hope will happen to the price of the other good? Explain your answer.

   decrease in price → increase in demand

$\dfrac{Q_2 - Q_1}{\frac{sum}{2}}$

$\dfrac{P_2 - P_1}{\frac{sum}{2}}$

7. Summer Ice, a company that specializes in ice cream treats, wishes to raise its total revenue. It can identify two different groups of buyers: children and adults. Currently its ice cream treats are uniformly priced at $2 per serving. Summer Ice is considering reducing the price of its treats to $1 (a 67% decrease in price using the midpoint method). From its market research, it knows that the two groups of buyers are likely to respond according to the data in the following table.

Price	Quantity demanded by children	Quantity demanded by adults
$2	100	100
1	300	120

a. What is the price elasticity of demand for each of these groups? Use the midpoint method to calculate these price elasticities.

Children: $\dfrac{\frac{300-100}{200}}{\frac{2-1}{\frac{3}{2}}} = \dfrac{1}{\frac{1}{1.5}}$

b. What is Summer Ice's current total revenue if they sell their ice cream treats at a price of $2?

c. What is Summer Ice's total revenue if they sell their ice cream treats at a price of $1?

d. What is Summer Ice's total revenue if they price their treats differently to the two groups, charging the higher price ($2) to adults and the lower price ($1) to children?

e. What is Summer Ice's total revenue if they price their treats differently to the two groups, charging the lower price ($1) to adults and the higher price ($2) to children?

f. What pricing scheme in parts (b) through (e) results in the greatest total revenue for Summer Ice? Using your knowledge of price elasticity of demand, explain why this is the best pricing scheme with regard to maximizing Summer Ice's total revenue in this market.

110

70

8. When Mario's income increases by 10%, his consumption of noodles decreases from 100 units a year to 70 units a year, while his consumption of salmon increases from 20 units a year to 60 units a year.

a. What is Mario's income elasticity of demand for noodles?

b. What is Mario's income elasticity of demand for salmon?

c. Is either of these goods income elastic for Mario?

d. Is either of these goods income inelastic for Mario?

e. From Mario's perspective, is either of these goods a luxury good? Explain your answer.

f. From Mario's perspective, is either of these goods an inferior good? Explain your answer.

9. Government officials in Wonderland are concerned that the economy is entering a recession. They anticipate that this recession will lead to lower levels of production and higher levels of unemployment, thus resulting in many people's experiencing a decrease in their income. Suppose there are two producers in Wonderland: producer A knows that the income elasticity of demand for his product equals −0.6 while producer B knows that the income elasticity of demand for his product equals 0.5. Which producer is likely to view this recession as a more significant problem for his company? Explain your answer.

10. The following table describes a linear supply curve for bicycles in Microland.

Price	Quantity supplied of bicycles
$ 0	0
100	200
200	400
300	600
400	800
500	1,000

a. Graph this supply curve and then write an equation for this supply curve in slope-intercept form.

b. Suppose suppliers initially sell bicycles for $200 but then decrease their price to $100. Using the midpoint method, what is the value of the price elasticity of supply between these two points on the supply curve?

c. Suppose suppliers initially sell bicycles for $400 and then the price increases to $500. Using the midpoint method, what is the value of the price elasticity of supply between these two points on the supply curve?

d. Did your values in part (b) and part (c) of this question differ or were they the same? You might redo this problem with another set of values for a different linear demand curve that goes through the origin. Do you get the same result? Generalize your findings in a simple statement.

11. Let's redo the last example, but for a linear supply curve that does not pass through the origin. The following table describes a supply curve that has these characteristics.

Price	Quantity supplied of bicycles
$100	0
200	200
300	400
400	600
500	800

a. Graph this supply curve and then write an equation for this supply curve in slope-intercept form.

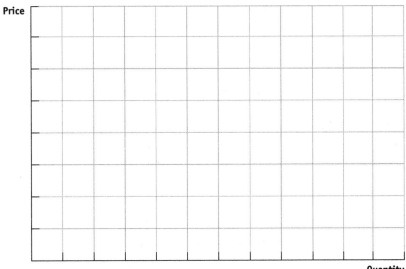

b. Suppose suppliers initially sell bicycles for $200 but then decrease their price to $100. Using the midpoint method, what is the value of the price elasticity of supply between these two points on the supply curve?

c. Suppose suppliers initially sell bicycles for $400 and then the price increases to $500. Using the midpoint method, what is the value of the price elasticity of supply between these two points on the supply curve?

d. Did your values in parts (b) and (c) of this question differ?

12. Briefly describe the factors that influence price elasticity of demand, and then describe the factors that influence price elasticity of supply.

13. The government wishes to limit the quantity of alcoholic beverages sold and therefore is considering the imposition of an excise tax on the market for alcoholic drinks. Suppose the market for alcoholic drinks can be described by the following demand and supply equations:

Demand: $Q = 10{,}000 - 2{,}000P$

Supply: $Q = 2{,}000P$,

where P is the price of an alcoholic drink and Q is the quantity of alcoholic drinks sold and consumed during the time period. The proposed excise tax is $2 per alcoholic drink.

a. Draw a graph representing the initial market for alcoholic drinks. Label the equilibrium price P_1 and the equilibrium quantity Q_1.

b. Compute the numeric value of P_1 and Q_1 in this market.

c. What is the value of consumer and producer surplus (CS and PS) in this market prior to the imposition of the tax? Shade in these two areas on your graph in part (a) and label these areas clearly. What is the value of total surplus before the tax?

d. Suppose the excise tax is implemented and producers are legally responsible for paying the tax. Draw a new graph representing this market now that the excise tax has been implemented. Label the new equilibrium price with the tax (P_T), the new equilibrium quantity with the tax (Q_T), and the net price received by producers after they pay the tax to the government (P_N).

e. Calculate the numeric values of P_T, Q_T, and P_N that you marked on your graph in part (d).

f. On your graph in part (d), label the areas that correspond to consumer surplus with the tax (CS_T), producer surplus with the tax (PS_T), tax revenue, and deadweight loss (DWL).

g. Calculate the values of CS_T, PS_T, tax revenue, and DWL once the tax is implemented. Is the sum of CS_T, PS_T, tax revenue, and DWL equal to the original value of total surplus before the tax was implemented?

h. Suppose the excise tax is raised to $3 per alcoholic drink. What is the effect of this price increase on tax revenue? Provide a qualitative answer as well as a quantitative answer.

14. The textbook emphasizes that the effect of an excise tax depends on the price elasticities of demand and supply. This question and question 15 explore the relationship between elasticity and the excise tax.

   a. Draw two graphs side by side, and draw a demand curve that is the same in both graphs. (Hint: This means that the y-intercept and the x-intercept for these two demand curves are the same in the two graphs.) Label this curve D in both graphs.

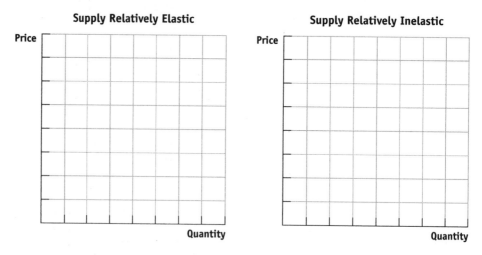

   b. In the first graph, draw a relatively elastic supply curve and label the initial equilibrium price P_E and the initial equilibrium quantity Q_1. In the second graph, mark P_E and Q_1 (the same P_E and Q_1 as in the first graph) and then draw a relatively inelastic supply curve that goes through this equilibrium point. Label the supply curve in both graphs S_1.

   c. In the first graph, draw a second supply curve that shows the effect of an excise tax. This second supply curve should be drawn parallel to the first supply curve. Label the equilibrium price with the tax P_C, the equilibrium quantity with the tax Q_T, and the net price that firms receive after they pay the tax P_P. In addition, on this graph, label consumer surplus with the tax (CS_T), producer surplus with the tax (PS_T), tax revenue, and DWL.

   d. In the second graph, draw a second supply curve that shows the effect of an excise tax that is exactly the same excise tax as in the first graph. (Hint: The y-intercept of the new supply curve for each graph is equal to the y-intercept of the original supply curve plus the excise tax.) Label all the same items for this graph that you labeled in the first graph.

   e. Compare the two graphs and comment on the effect of price elasticity of supply on your results.

15. a. Draw two graphs side by side. In both graphs, draw an identical supply curve. Label this curve S_1.

Demand Relatively Elastic

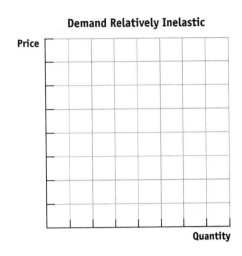

Demand Relatively Inelastic

b. In the first graph, draw a demand curve (D) that is relatively elastic. Label the initial equilibrium price P_E and the initial equilibrium quantity Q_1. In the second graph, mark P_E and Q_1 (the same P_E and Q_1 as in the first graph) and then draw a relatively inelastic demand curve through this equilibrium point. Label this curve D.

c. In both graphs, draw a second supply curve that illustrates an excise tax. The two supply curves should be identical and should be labeled S_T. On both graphs, label the equilibrium price with the tax P_C; the equilibrium quantity with the tax Q_T; and the net price that firms receive after they pay the tax P_P. In addition, on both graphs, label consumer surplus with the tax (CS_T); producer surplus with the tax (PS_T); the loss in consumer surplus captured by the government as tax revenue; the loss in producer surplus captured by the government as tax revenue; and *DWL*.

d. In which graph is the *DWL* greater?

e. In which graph is the loss of consumer surplus captured by the government as tax revenue greater?

f. In which graph is the loss of producer surplus captured by the government as tax revenue greater?

BEFORE YOU TAKE THE TEST

Chapter Review Questions

1. When the absolute value of the percentage change in quantity demanded is greater than the absolute value of the percentage change in price, demand is
   a. inelastic.
   b. elastic.

2. If the price is initially $10 and then increases to $15, the absolute value of the percentage change in price using the midpoint method is
   a. 50%.
   b. 40%.
   c. 5%.
   d. 4%.

3. The midpoint method for calculating price elasticities provides a means of
   a. ensuring that all price elasticities have positive values.
   b. ensuring that all price elasticities have negative values.
   c. generating consistent measures of price elasticities between two points on a demand or supply curve without regard to which point is the initial point.
   d. simplifying the calculation of price elasticities so that all elasticity values are whole numbers.

4. A horizontal demand curve is perfectly
   a. elastic.
   b. inelastic.

5. If the price elasticity of demand between two points on a demand curve is equal to 1.5, then demand between those two points is
   a. price elastic.
   b. price inelastic.

6. If the price elasticity of demand equals infinity, then the demand curve is
   a. horizontal.
   b. vertical.

7. A small value (less than 1) for the price elasticity of demand indicates that consumers are very price
   a. sensitive and that a small percentage change in price will lead to a large percentage change in the quantity demanded when both changes are measured in absolute value terms.
   b. insensitive and that a small percentage change in price will lead to an even smaller percentage change in the quantity demanded when both changes are measured in absolute value terms.

Use the following figure of a linear demand curve to answer the next three questions.

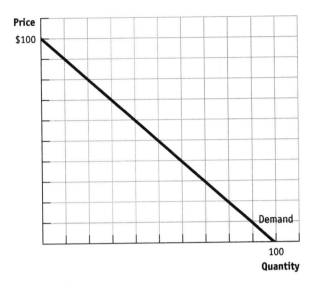

8. Suppose price is initially $60. If price increases to $70, this will cause the quantity demanded to decrease while

a. total revenue increases.

b. total revenue decreases.

c. total revenue does not change.

d. the effect on total revenue depends on consumers' reactions to the price increase.

9. Suppose you are a producer and the demand curve in the graph represents the demand for your product. Furthermore, suppose you are currently selling this product at a price of $30. If you raise the price to $40 and demand remains unchanged, total revenue will _____ because the price effect is _____ than the quantity effect.

a. increase; larger

b. increase; smaller

c. decrease; larger

d. decrease; smaller

10. Suppose you are a producer and the demand curve in the graph represents the demand for your product. To maximize total revenue you should sell the good for _____, resulting in total revenue of _____.

a. $100; $100,000

b. $60; $2,400

c. $40; $2,400

d. $50; $2,500

Use the following figure to answer the next two questions, where point A is the midpoint of the depicted linear demand curve.

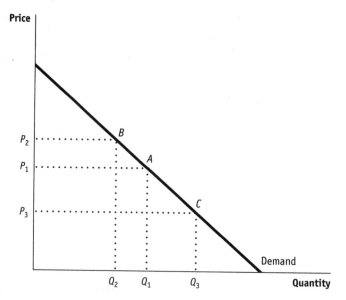

11. At prices greater than P_1, demand is _____; at prices less than P_1, demand is _____, and at price P_1 demand is _____.

    a. elastic; elastic; unit-elastic

    b. inelastic; inelastic; unit-elastic

    c. elastic; inelastic; unit-elastic

    d. inelastic; elastic; unit-elastic

12. Suppose price is initially at P_1. Which of the following statements is true?

    a. If price rises to P_2, then the quantity effect will dominate over the price effect and total revenue will increase.

    b. If price falls to P_3, then the quantity effect will dominate over the price effect and total revenue will increase.

    c. If price rises to P_2, then the price effect will dominate over the quantity effect and total revenue will increase.

    d. If price falls to P_3, then the price effect will dominate over the quantity effect and total revenue will decrease.

13. Which of the following statements is true?

    a. The longer the time period for adjustment to a change in the price of the good, the more elastic the demand for that good.

    b. Goods that have many close substitutes typically have price-elastic demand.

    c. The demand for nonessential goods is more elastic than the demand for goods that are necessities.

    d. All of these statements are true.

14. Tea and coffee are often viewed as substitutes for one another. Which of the following cross-price elasticity values is most likely for tea and coffee?

    a. −0.5

    b. 1.5

15. The price of movie tickets increased 10% this year. Which of the following statements is most likely to be true?

 a. The quantity of popcorn sold at movie theaters decreased this year.

 b. Video movie rentals increased this year.

 c. If the price elasticity of demand for movie tickets is greater than 1, total revenue at the movie theaters decreased.

 d. All of these statements are true.

16. The cross-price elasticity of demand between movie tickets and movie theater popcorn is estimated to equal –0.6. Suppose movie ticket prices increased by 20% this year. The percentage change in the quantity demanded of movie theater popcorn will be a(n)

 a. increase of 1.2%.

 b. increase of 12%.

 c. decrease of 1.2%.

 d. decrease of 12%.

17. This year Joe's income increased by 15%; the quantity of bananas he demanded increased by 8%, and the quantity of orange juice he demanded increased by 6%. Which of the following statements is true for Joe?

 a. Bananas are a normal good and orange juice is an inferior good.

 b. Bananas are an inferior good and orange juice is a normal good.

 c. Bananas and orange juice are both normal goods.

 d. Bananas and orange juice are both inferior goods.

18. Use the data in the following table to answer this question. The table provides information about prices, quantity demanded, and income for Sue for two different years.

Year	Good	Price	Quantity demanded	Income
2004	Pizza	$ 6	10	
2004	Books	9	4	
2004				$200
2005	Pizza	6	7.5	
2005	Books	9	5	
2005				250

Calculate Sue's income elasticity of demand for pizza for this time period. Sue's income elasticity of demand for pizza equals _____ and pizza is a(n) _____ good.

 a. 1; normal

 b. 1; inferior

 c. 1.65; inferior

 d. 1.65; normal

19. Use the information in the following table to answer this question.

Good	Quantity demanded initially	Price initially	Quantity demanded after price change	New price
Pizza	10	$6	8	$6
Books	4	12	5	9

Calculate the cross-price elasticity of demand between the quantity demanded of pizza and the price of books. What is the relationship between pizza and books given this cross-price elasticity of demand value?

a. Pizza and books are complements.

b. Pizza and books are substitutes.

c. Pizza is an inferior good and books are a normal good.

d. Pizza is a normal good and books are an inferior good.

20. Suppose the income elasticity of demand for a good is greater than 1. Which of the following statements is true?

a. The percentage change in the quantity demanded of this good is larger than the percentage change in income.

b. This good is a necessity, since as income increases the quantity demanded of the good increases.

c. This good is an inferior good, since as income increases the quantity demanded of the good increases at a much greater rate than the rate of increase in income.

d. This good could not be a luxury good, since income and the quantity demanded have a positive relationship.

21. Suppose there is an influx of new workers in a community. This will likely result in

a. an increase in the price elasticity of demand for all normal goods.

b. an increase in the price elasticity of supply for goods produced in this community.

c. a decrease in the price elasticity of demand for most goods.

d. little change in any elasticity measure for this community.

22. Acme Manufacturing produces 1,000 widgets when the price of widgets is $20 per widget, and 1,200 widgets when the price of widgets is $22 per widget. Using the midpoint method, what is the value of the price elasticity of supply?

a. 1.9

b. 0.6

c. 0.5

d. 2

23. Acme Manufacturing originally was able to produce 1,000 widgets at a price of $20 per widget, and 1,200 widgets at a price of $22 per widget. Suppose that there is an influx of new workers into the community and Acme now finds it can produce 1,200 widgets at a price of $20 per widget, and 1,600 widgets at a price of $22 per widget. Which statement best describes Acme's situation?

   a. Acme's supply curve is now more price inelastic, which implies that as the price increases Acme can now supply a greater quantity of the good than it could initially.

   b. Acme's supply curve is unaffected by this change in labor: a price increase for widgets simply causes a movement along the supply curve for widgets.

   c. Acme's supply curve is now more price elastic, which implies that as the price increases Acme can now supply a greater quantity of the good than it could initially.

   d. The availability of labor has an unpredictable effect on Acme Manufacturing.

24. The cost of a tax is equal to

   a. the tax revenue raised by the tax.

   b. the tax revenue raised by the tax, plus the deadweight loss associated with the tax, plus whatever administrative costs that compliance with the tax incurs.

   c. the tax revenue raised by the tax plus the deadweight loss associated with the tax.

   d. the deadweight loss associated with the tax and the administrative costs that compliance with the tax entails.

Use the following graph to answer questions 25–31. The graph provides the initial demand and supply curves. In addition, assume that an excise tax on producers equal to $P_5 - P_6$ is implemented. Furthermore, assume that $P_5 - P_6$ is the same distance as $P_2 - P_4$ in the graph. All letters in the diagram refer to areas in the graph.

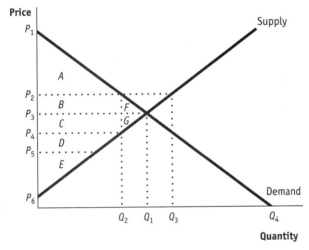

25. The excise tax in the graph is equal to

   a. $P_1 - P_4$.

   b. $P_2 - P_4$.

   c. $P_5 - P_6$.

   d. Answers (a) and (c) both measure the excise tax.

   e. Answers (b) and (c) both measure the excise tax.

26. The consumer surplus before the tax is equal to the sum of areas
    a. A, B, and F.
    b. A and B.
    c. A, B, C, D, E, F, and G.
    d. D, E, F, and I.

27. The producer surplus before the tax is equal to the areas
    a. A, B, C, F, and G.
    b. A and B.
    c. A, B, C, D, E, F, and G.
    d. C, D, E, and G.

28. The tax revenue collected by the government when this excise tax is imposed is equal to
    a. $(P_1 - P_3)(Q_2)$.   c. $(P_2 - P_4)(Q_1)$.
    b. $(P_2 - P_4)(Q_2)$.   d. $(P_2 - P_3)(Q_1)$.

29. The deadweight loss from a consumer's perspective is equal to area(s)
    a. F.   c. F and I.
    b. G.   d. C and G.

30. The efficiency cost of this excise tax can be measured as area(s)
    a. G and C.   c. B and F.
    b. F and G.   d. C, B, and F.

31. A mathematical expression for the deadweight loss caused by this excise tax is
    a. $(P_2 - P_4)(Q_2)$.
    b. $(P_2 - P_4)(Q_2 - Q_1)$.
    c. $(1/2)(P_2 - P_4)(Q_1 - Q_2)$.
    d. $(1/2)(P_2 - P_3)(Q_1 - Q_2)$.

32. An excise tax is imposed on producers of a good. For a given supply curve, the more price elastic the demand for the product, the greater the economic burden of the tax on
    a. consumers.
    b. producers.

33. An excise tax is imposed on producers of a good. For a given demand curve, the more inelastic the supply of the product, the greater the economic burden of the tax on
    a. consumers.
    b. producers.

34. When the price elasticity of demand is low and the price elasticity of supply is high, the burden of an excise tax falls primarily on
    a. sellers of the product.
    b. buyers of the product.

35. When the price elasticity of demand is high and the price elasticity of supply is low, the burden of an excise tax falls primarily on
    a. sellers of the product.
    b. buyers of the product.

36. You are told that the initial supply curve in a market is $P = Q$ and the initial demand curve in the market is $P = 100 - Q$. An excise tax is imposed in this market, and it results in the government's collecting $1,250 in tax revenue. The excise tax in this market is equal to
    a. $10.
    b. $20.
    c. $25.
    d. $50.

37. Excise taxes cause deadweight loss when the excise tax
    a. raises the price of the good being taxed.
    b. decreases the quantity of the good supplied and demanded in the market.
    c. creates an incentive for mutually beneficial exchanges to take place.
    d. Answers (a), (b), and (c) are true.

38. The deadweight loss due to the imposition of an excise tax is lowest when
    a. demand is relatively inelastic and supply is relatively elastic.
    b. demand is relatively inelastic and supply is relatively inelastic.
    c. demand is relatively elastic and supply is relatively elastic.
    d. demand is relatively elastic and supply is relatively inelastic.

39. Policy makers wishing to dramatically decrease the consumption of a good by using an excise tax will find that the success of this policy depends on
    a. the price elasticity of demand.
    b. the price elasticity of supply.
    c. the price elasticities of either demand or supply.
    d. the size of the excise tax. The price elasticities of supply and demand have no impact on how successful the policy is with regard to decreasing the consumption of the good.

■ ANSWER KEY

Answers to Problems and Exercises

1. **a.** % change in price = $[(9 - 10)/10] \times 100 = -10\%$
% change in quantity = $[(2 - 1)/1] \times 100 = 100\%$

b. Price elasticity of demand = $|100\%/-10\%| = 10$

c. % change in price = $[(10 - 9)/9] \times 100 = 11\%$
% change in quantity = $[(1 - 2)/2] \times 100 = -50\%$

d. Price elasticity of demand = $|-50\%/11\%| = 4.5$

e. No, the measures calculated for the price elasticity of demand using the simple percentage formula yield different price elasticities of demand measures when moving from point A to point B or from point B to point A.

f. % change in price = $\dfrac{(9 - 10)}{\dfrac{(10 + 9)}{2}} = -10.5\%$

% change in quantity = $\dfrac{(2 - 1)}{\dfrac{(1 + 2)}{2}} = 66.7\%$

g. Price elasticity of demand = $|66.7\%/-10.5\%| = 6.4$

h. % change in price = $\dfrac{(10 - 9)}{\dfrac{(9 + 10)}{2}} = 10.5\%$

% change in quantity = $\dfrac{(1 - 2)}{\dfrac{(2 + 1)}{2}} = -66.7\%$

i. Price elasticity of demand = $|-66.7\%/10.5\%| = 6.4$

j. Yes, the midpoint method yields the same measure for price elasticity of demand whether you start at point A and move to point B, or move from point B to point A. This consistent measure of price elasticity, whether for the price elasticity of demand or the price elasticity of supply, simplifies the use of elasticity by providing a value that is not dependent on the initial starting point.

2. **a.** Price elasticity of demand = $\left| \dfrac{\% \text{ change in quantity demanded}}{\% \text{ change in price}} \right|$

Price elasticity of demand = $\left| \dfrac{\dfrac{(10 - 9)}{\dfrac{(9 + 10)}{2}}}{\dfrac{(1 - 2)}{\dfrac{(2 + 1)}{2}}} \right| = \left| \dfrac{10.5\%}{-66.7\%} \right| = 0.16$

With the midpoint method for calculating price elasticities, it does not matter which point is the initial point.

b. No, the price elasticity of demand between points A and B equals 6.3, while the price elasticity of demand between points C and E equals 0.16.

c. Demand is elastic between points *A* and *B:* we know that the absolute value of the percentage change in the quantity demanded exceeds the absolute value of the percentage change in price since the ratio has a value greater than 1.

d. Demand is inelastic between points *C* and *E:* we know that the absolute value of the percentage change in the quantity demanded is less than the absolute value of the percentage change in price since the ratio has a value less than 1.

3. a.

Price	Quantity demanded	Total revenue
$ 0	11	$ 0
1	10	10
2	9	18
3	8	24
4	7	28
5	6	30
6	5	30
7	4	28
8	3	24
9	2	18
10	1	10
11	0	0

b. From the table, we can see that total revenue equals $30 when the price is $5 or when the price is $6. At a price of $5.50—the midpoint of the demand curve—we find that total revenue equals $30.25. For a linear demand curve, total revenue is maximized at the midpoint of the demand curve.

c. Price elasticity of demand $= \left| \dfrac{\dfrac{(5-6)}{\dfrac{(6+5)}{2}}}{\dfrac{(5-6)}{\dfrac{(6+5)}{2}}} \right| = 1$

d. When the price elasticity of demand equals 1, the absolute value of the percentage change in the quantity demanded equals the absolute value of the percentage change in the price.

4. a. The price elasticity of demand for golden delicious apples should be far more elastic than the price elasticity of demand for all fruit since there are many possible substitutions for golden delicious apples and far fewer substitute goods for all fruit. Hence, a price increase is likely to result in a significant percentage change in the quantity demanded of golden delicious apples and a far smaller percentage change in the quantity demanded of all fruit.

b. The price elasticity of demand for ice cream should be greater than the price elasticity of demand for gasoline since there are far more available substitutes for ice cream than there are for gasoline.

c. The price elasticity of demand for leisure travel should be greater than the price elasticity of demand for business travel since business travelers must get to their destination within a relatively small window of time, and hence are less sensitive to price than are leisure travelers.

5. a. Cross-price elasticity of demand $= \dfrac{\% \text{ change in the quantity demanded of good B}}{\% \text{ change in the price of good A}}$

% change in the quantity demanded of good B $= (6 - 4)/4 = 0.5$

% change in the price of good A $= (12 - 10)/10 = 0.2$

Cross-price elasticity of demand $= 0.5/0.2 = 2.5$

b. Good A and good B are substitutes because as the price of good A increases, the quantity demanded of good B increases. There are many examples of two goods that are substitutes: coffee and tea, butter and margarine, olive oil and safflower oil, taxi rides and bus rides, tennis and golf.

6. a. A negative cross-price elasticity of demand implies that the percentage change in the quantity demanded of one good moves in the opposite direction to the percentage change in the price of a related good. Thus, if the price of good Y increases, then the quantity demanded of good X decreases. We know that two related goods are either substitutes or complements. In this case, a negative cross-price elasticity of demand indicates that the two goods are complements. (In contrast, a positive cross-price elasticity of demand tells us the two goods are substitutes.)

b. Cross-price elasticity of demand $= -0.2$

$-0.2 = \dfrac{\% \text{ change in the quantity demanded of good D}}{\% \text{ change in the price of good C}}$

$-0.2 = \dfrac{\% \text{ change in the quantity demanded of good D}}{100\%}$

% change in the quantity demanded of good D $= -20\%$

c. With a cross-price elasticity of -0.2, a 100% increase in the price of good C will cause the quantity demanded of good D to fall by 20% (using the simple formula for percentage changes rather than the midpoint method). Thus, if the quantity demanded of good D was initially 10 units, then the quantity demanded of good D will be 8 units after the increase in the price of good C.

d. When the cross-price elasticity of demand is negative, a decrease in the price of one good will lead to an increase in the quantity demanded of the other good.

7. a. The price elasticity of demand for children is equal to 1.5 and the price elasticity of demand for adults is equal to 0.27. Therefore, for the quantities and prices given in this example, the demand for Summer Ice is elastic for children and inelastic for adults.

b. Total revenue $= (\$2/\text{treat})(200) = \$400$

c. Total revenue $= (\$1/\text{treat})(420) = \$420$

d. Total revenue $= (\$2/\text{treat})(100) + (\$1/\text{treat})(300) = \$500$

e. Total revenue $= (\$1/\text{treat})(120) + (\$2/\text{treat})(100) = \$320$

f. Summer Ice will earn the greatest total revenue by charging children $1 per treat and adults $2 per treat: that is, charging a higher price to the group of consumers with inelastic demand and a lower price to those consumers with elastic demand. In effect, this pricing scheme recognizes that the absolute value of the percentage change in the quantity demanded by adults is less than the absolute value of the percentage change in the price of the good, while the absolute value of the percentage change in the quantity demanded by children is greater than the absolute value of the percentage change in the price of the good. Thus, reducing price to the adult group of buyers reduces total revenue, while reducing price to the child group of buyers increases total revenue.

8. a. Income elasticity of demand for noodles $= \dfrac{-30\%}{10\%} = -3$

    b. Income elasticity of demand for salmon $= \dfrac{200\%}{10\%} = 20$

    c. The demand for salmon is income elastic because when his income increases, Mario's quantity of salmon demanded also increases.

    d. Neither good is income inelastic since neither good has an income elasticity of demand value that is positive but is less than 1.

    e. Salmon is a luxury good since the value of the income elasticity of demand for salmon is greater than 1. As Mario's income increases, his demand for salmon increases at an even faster rate.

    f. Noodles are an inferior good, since as Mario's income increases his demand for noodles decreases. A negative value for the income elasticity of demand indicates that the good is an inferior good.

9. Producer B will feel the impact more than producer A since demand for producer B's product will fall as income falls. In contrast, the negative income elasticity of demand value for producer A indicates that as income falls, the quantity demanded of producer A's product will increase.

10. a. $P = (1/2)Q$

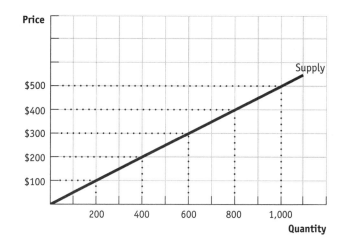

    b. Price elasticity of supply $= \left| \dfrac{\dfrac{200-400}{\dfrac{400+200}{2}}}{\dfrac{100-200}{\dfrac{200+100}{2}}} \right| = 1$

c. Price elasticity of supply = $\left| \dfrac{\dfrac{1,000 - 800}{\dfrac{800 + 1,000}{2}}}{\dfrac{500 - 400}{\dfrac{400 + 500}{2}}} \right| = 1$

d. The values are the same in parts (b) and (c). Redoing the exercise for a different linear demand curve that passes through the origin yields the same value. Thus, as long as the supply curve is linear and passes through the origin, the price elasticity of supply equals 1 for all points on the supply curve.

11. a. $P = (1/2)Q + 100$

b. Price elasticity of supply = $\left| \dfrac{\dfrac{0 - 200}{\dfrac{200 + 0}{2}}}{\dfrac{100 - 200}{\dfrac{200 + 100}{2}}} \right| = 3$

c. Price elasticity of supply = $\left| \dfrac{\dfrac{800 - 600}{\dfrac{600 + 800}{2}}}{\dfrac{500 - 400}{\dfrac{400 + 500}{2}}} \right| = 1.28$

d. The values in parts (b) and (c) differ.

12. The price elasticity of demand depends on the availability of close substitutes, whether the good is a necessity or a luxury, and how much time consumers have to adjust to the price change. The price elasticity of supply depends on the availability of resources to expand production and the amount of time that producers have to adjust to the price change.

13. a.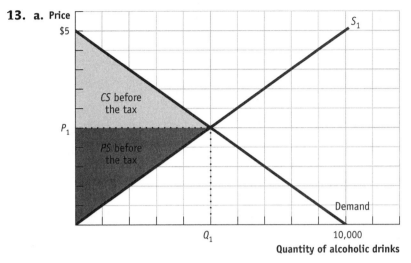

b. To find P_1 and Q_1, use the demand and supply equations: $10{,}000 - 2{,}000P = 2{,}000P$. Solving for P yields an equilibrium price of $2.50. Plug this price into either the demand or the supply equation to find the equilibrium quantity: $Q_1 = 10{,}000 - (2{,}000)(2.50) = 5{,}000$ alcoholic drinks.

c. Consumer surplus (CS) before the imposition of the tax equals the area of a triangle, and can be computed as $(1/2)(\$5/\text{drink} - \$2.50/\text{drink})(5{,}000 \text{ drinks}) = \$6{,}250$. Producer surplus ($PS$) before the imposition of the tax equals the area of a triangle, and can be computed as $(1/2)(\$2.50/\text{drink})(5{,}000 \text{ drinks}) = \$6{,}250$. Total surplus is the sum of CS and PS, or $12,500.

d.

e. The new supply curve with this excise tax is $Q = 2{,}000P - 4{,}000$. To find this new supply curve, it is easiest to rewrite the initial supply curve in slope-intercept form: $P = (1/2{,}000)Q$. Then add the amount of the excise tax to the y-intercept of this equation, since the excise tax shifts the supply curve vertically upward by an amount equal to the tax. Thus, $P = (1/2{,}000)Q + 2$, or $Q = 2{,}000P - 4{,}000$. Combine this new supply equation with the demand equation to find P_T and Q_T. $P_T = \$3.50$ and $Q_T = 3{,}000$ drinks. To find P_P, remember that the price producers receive after they pay the tax is equal to the price with the tax minus the excise tax, or $P_T -$ excise tax. P_P is equal to $1.50.

f. See graph in part (d).

g. CS with the tax = CS_T = $(1/2)(\$5/\text{drink} - \$3.50/\text{drink})(3{,}000 \text{ drinks}) = \$2{,}250$

PS with the tax = PS_T = $(1/2)(\$1.50/\text{drink})(3{,}000 \text{ drinks}) = \$2{,}250$

Tax revenue = $(\$2/\text{drink})(3{,}000 \text{ drinks}) = \$6{,}000$

DWL = $(1/2)(\$2/\text{drink})(5{,}000 \text{ drinks} - 3{,}000 \text{ drinks}) = \$2{,}000$

The sum of $CS_T + PS_T$ + tax revenue + DWL = $\$12{,}500$ and is therefore equal to the original total surplus prior to the imposition of the tax.

h. When the excise tax is raised to $3, we know this causes price to increase and quantity to decrease in this market. Quantity falls to 2,000, which would result in tax revenues of $2{,}000 \times \$3$. Thus, tax revenue remains unchanged at $6,000.

14. a–d.

e. For a given excise tax and demand curve, when supply is relatively inelastic, the excise tax results in a smaller DWL than when supply is relatively elastic. For a given excise tax and demand curve, quantity changes by a larger amount when supply is relatively elastic. Tax revenue depends on the relative elasticities of both the demand and the supply curve.

15. a–c.

d. The *DWL* is greater in the graph in which demand is relatively elastic.

e. The loss in consumer surplus captured by the government is greater in the graph in which demand is relatively inelastic.

f. The loss in producer surplus captured by the government is greater in the graph in which demand is relatively elastic.

Answers to Chapter Review Questions

1. **Answer b.** Demand is price elastic when the absolute value of the percentage change in the quantity demanded is greater than the absolute value of the percentage change in price. This is definitional.

2. **Answer b.** To find this value, you take the absolute value of the following:

$$\left| \frac{15 - 10}{\frac{10 + 15}{2}} \right| \times 100$$

This gives you the absolute value of the percentage change in price, which is equal to 40%.

3. **Answer c.** Price elasticities may have negative values or positive values. For example, for both cross-price elasticity of demand and income elasticity of demand, the values may be positive, negative, or equal to zero. The midpoint method for calculating price elasticities provides a method for getting identical values no matter which point is your initial point when making the calculation. Price elasticities are not always whole numbers.

4. **Answer a.** This is definitional: it is an extreme case of elasticity in which demanders are extremely price sensitive.

5. **Answer a.** Since the value of price elasticity of demand is greater than 1, this implies that the absolute value of the percentage change in the quantity demanded is greater than the absolute value of the percentage change in price, which means that demand is elastic between these two points.

6. **Answer a.** This is definitional: when the demand curve is horizontal, it tells us that consumers are very price sensitive, and at the current price there is infinite demand for the good. When the demand curve is perfectly vertical, it tells us that consumers are not price sensitive, since no matter the price, they will continue to demand the same amount of the good.

7. **Answer b.** When the price elasticity of demand has a value less than 1, this implies that the absolute value of the percentage change in the quantity demanded is less than the absolute value of the percentage change in the price of the good. Consumers are not price sensitive: they will continue to demand a similar amount of the good even though the price has increased.

8. **Answer b.** When price rises from $60 to $70, total revenue changes from $2,400 to $2,100. The price of $60 is above the midpoint on the given demand curve, so an increase in price above $60 implies that price is increasing in the elastic region of the demand curve. As price rises in the elastic portion of the demand curve, there is a decrease in total revenue.

9. **Answer a.** When price rises from $30 to $40, you are moving along the demand curve in the inelastic region. An increase in price in the inelastic region of the demand curve results in an increase in total revenue. In this case, total revenue was initially $2,100, and with the price increase the total revenue is now equal to $2,400.

10. **Answer d.** Total revenue is maximized at the unit-elastic point on the demand curve. For a linear demand curve, this occurs at the midpoint. In this example, the midpoint is at a price of $50 and a quantity of 50 units.

11. **Answer c.** This is definitional: above the midpoint on a linear demand curve, demand is elastic; below the midpoint on a linear demand curve, demand is inelastic; and at the midpoint on a linear demand curve, demand is unit elastic.

12. **Answer d.** When price rises above P_1, the quantity effect is dominant over the price effect and this dominance results in total revenue decreasing. When price falls below P_1, the price effect is dominant over the quantity effect and this dominance results in total revenue decreasing.

13. **Answer d.** All of these statements are true. When there are many substitutes available for a good, demand is more elastic. Demand is also more elastic the longer the time period for adjustment. Goods that are not necessities and therefore do not have to be consumed have more elastic demand than do goods that are necessities.

14. **Answer b.** Two goods are substitutes for one another when the cross-price elasticity of demand between the two goods is positive. This elasticity is positive, since as the price of one of the goods increases there is an increase in the quantity demanded of the other good.

15. **Answer d.** Each of these statements is likely to be true. Popcorn sold at movie theaters is likely to be a complementary good with respect to movie tickets. When movie tickets increase in price, fewer movie tickets are demanded, and this decrease in the quantity demanded results in fewer units of popcorn being sold. Similarly, movie tickets and video rentals are likely to be substitutes with respect to each other: an increase in the price of movie tickets will likely result in increased demand for video rentals. If the price elasticity of demand for movie tickets is greater than 1, this implies that demand is elastic, and an increase in price in the elastic segment of the demand curve causes total revenue to decrease.

16. **Answer d.** To compute this answer, first recall that the cross-price elasticity is the ratio of the percentage change in the quantity demanded of good A divided by the percentage change in the price of good B. The question provides the value for the cross-price elasticity of demand as well as the percentage change in the price of movie tickets. Plugging these values into our equation for cross-price elasticity of demand, we have $-0.6 = x/20\%$, where x is the percentage change in the quantity demanded of movie theater popcorn. Solving this equation, the percentage change in the quantity demanded of movie theater popcorn is a decrease of 12%.

17. **Answer c.** Joe's income increased and so did his consumption of both bananas and orange juice. Therefore they both must be normal goods.

18. **Answer b.** To find the income elasticity of demand, recall that this is the ratio of the percentage change in the quantity demanded of the good divided by the percentage change in income. The percentage change in the quantity demanded of pizza is –25% (using the simple formula for percentage changes given in the Chapter Objectives section of the Study Guide), while the percentage change in income is also 25%. Thus, the income elasticity of demand is equal to –1. Pizza is an inferior good, since as income increases, the quantity demanded decreases.

19. **Answer b.** As the price of books decreases, we see from the table that the quantity of pizzas demanded decreases. This tells us that these two goods are substitutes for one another since as the price of one of the goods decreases this leads consumers to substitute away from the other good and decrease the quantity they demand of the other good at every price.

20. **Answer a.** When income elasticity of demand is greater than 1, this tells us that the good is not an inferior good, since as income increases there is an increase in the quantity demanded of the good. From the definition of income elasticity of demand, a value greater than 1 implies that the percentage change in the quantity demanded of the good is greater than the percentage change in income. When the income elasticity of demand is greater than 1, this implies that the good is a luxury, since the percentage increase in the quantity demanded is increasing at a faster rate than the percentage increase in income.

21. **Answer b.** When there is an influx of new workers into a community, labor becomes more plentiful. Since labor is an input in the production of goods, this likely makes the supply of goods more elastic.

22. **Answer a.** To find the price elasticity of supply, use the midpoint method and calculate the percentage change in the quantity supplied divided by the percentage change in the price of the good. Thus, the price elasticity of supply equals

$$\frac{\dfrac{1,200 - 1,000}{\dfrac{1,000 + 1,200}{2}}}{\dfrac{22 - 20}{\dfrac{20 + 22}{2}}} = 1.9$$

23. **Answer c.** If you sketch out the relationships between price and the quantity supplied, you will notice that the influx of workers results in Acme Manufacturing's supply curve shifting out to the right. This causes the price elasticity of supply to increase, resulting in a more price-elastic supply. Calculation of the new value of the price elasticity of supply would be equal to

$$\frac{\dfrac{1,600 - 1,200}{\dfrac{1,200 + 1,600}{2}}}{\dfrac{22 - 20}{\dfrac{20 + 22}{2}}} = 3$$

Supply is now more price elastic.

24. **Answer b.** When the government imposes a tax, this clearly results in the government receiving tax revenue—which is a cost to the taxpayer—but the imposition of a tax imposes greater costs than just the tax revenue collected. The tax also imposes an efficiency cost (the *DWL*) since the tax causes a distortion in consumer behavior. The tax also imposes an administrative cost associated with complying with the tax.

25. **Answer e.** The excise tax is equal to the vertical distance between the original supply curve and the supply curve with the tax. At quantity Q_2, the vertical distance is equal to $P_2 - P_4$: this is the same distance as $P_5 - P_6$.

26. **Answer a.** The area of consumer surplus is the area above the equilibrium price and below the demand curve. Before the tax is implemented, the equilibrium price is P_3 and thus the area of consumer surplus is equal to the areas *A*, *B*, and *F*.

27. **Answer d.** The area of producer surplus is the area that lies beneath the equilibrium price and above the supply curve. Before the imposition of the tax, the equilibrium price is P_3 and the area of producer surplus is the sum of areas *C*, *D*, *E*, and *G*.

28. **Answer b.** The tax revenue collected by the government is equal to the product of the tax per unit and the number of units of the good sold when the tax is implemented. In this example, the tax per unit is $(P_2 - P_4)$ and the number of units sold is Q_2, so the tax revenue is equal to $(P_2 - P_4)(Q_2)$.

29. **Answer a.** When the excise tax is imposed, the consumer reduces consumption of the good. Some of the consumer's original consumer surplus is captured by the government: the consumer's tax incidence measures the economic burden of the tax borne by consumers. The consumer also loses a part of the original consumer surplus due to the efficiency cost of the tax: in this graph, this is represented as area *F*.

30. **Answer b.** The excise tax imposes an efficiency cost equal to the deadweight loss. This deadweight loss is represented by the areas *F* and *G* in the graph. Prior to the imposition of the excise tax, total surplus is equal to the sum of the consumer and producer surpluses. When the tax is imposed on this market, part of this total surplus is captured by the government as tax revenue, but part of the total surplus is lost to consumers and producers due to the distortion the tax causes with respect to the level of consumption of the good. This distortion is measured by areas *F* and *G*.

31. **Answer c.** The area of deadweight loss can be calculated as an area of a triangle: thus, this area is equal to one-half times the product of the excise tax per unit and the change in quantity due to the imposition of the tax. In this example, the excise tax per unit is equal to $(P_2 - P_4)$ and the change in quantity is $(Q_1 - Q_2)$.

32. **Answer b.** When demand is more price elastic, this implies that consumers are price sensitive and that a small change in price will result in a large change in the quantity demanded. Hence, an excise tax places a greater economic burden on suppliers in this case.

33. **Answer b.** For a given demand curve, an excise tax imposed on the market when supply is inelastic will result in a small increase in the price of the good and a relatively small decrease in the quantity of the good transacted in the market: the incidence of the tax will fall more heavily upon producers of the good rather than consumers of the good. For a given demand curve, an excise tax imposed on the market when supply is elastic will result in a larger increase in the price of the good and a relatively large decrease in the quantity of the good transacted in the market: the incidence of the tax will fall more heavily upon consumers of the good rather than producers of the good. To see this, you might find it helpful to draw two graphs, where both graphs have the same demand curve and the same initial equilibrium but where the first graph features an inelastic supply curve, while the second graph features an elastic supply curve. Then, in each graph, model an excise tax of the same amount and compare the effects of this excise tax on consumer and producer tax incidence.

34. **Answer b.** When price elasticity of demand is low (implying a relatively steep demand curve) while price elasticity of supply is high (implying a relatively flat supply curve), the economic burden of an excise tax falls primarily on consumers since the excise tax causes a relatively large increase in price and a relatively small decrease in the quantity demanded.

35. **Answer a.** When price elasticity of demand is high (implying a relatively flat demand curve) while price elasticity of supply is low (implying a relatively steep supply curve), the economic burden of an excise tax falls primarily on producers since the excise tax causes a relatively small increase in price and a relatively large decrease in the quantity demanded.

36. **Answer d.** One way to solve this problem is to draw a graph with the initial supply and demand curves and then calculate what the tax revenue would equal for each of the excise tax rates. For each level of the excise tax, the supply curve with the tax could be written as $P_S = Q_S +$ (the amount of the excise tax), where P_S is the supply price and Q_S is the quantity supplied at that price. Then, use this equation plus the demand equation and each level of the excise tax to calculate the equilibrium quantity, the equilibrium price with the tax, and then the tax revenue generated by the tax. Thus, if the excise tax is equal to $50 per unit, then the equilibrium quantity in the market once the tax is imposed is 25 units, the equilibrium price with the tax is $75, and the tax revenue is equal to ($50/unit)(25 units) = $1,250.

37. **Answer b.** An excise tax creates a deadweight loss because it discourages mutually beneficial exchanges from taking place. The excise tax creates a deadweight loss by altering the amount of the good supplied and demanded in the market. An increase in price due to the excise tax is not sufficient to create a deadweight loss, because if the demand curve is perfectly inelastic, there is no deadweight loss due to the tax.

38. **Answer b.** The deadweight loss from an excise tax is smallest when both the demand and supply curves are relatively inelastic, since this implies that the percentage increase in the price is relatively greater than the percentage decrease in the quantity supplied and demanded in the market.

39. **Answer c.** A policy to reduce consumption of a good through the imposition of an excise tax is more successful when the activity being discouraged is elastically demanded or supplied.

chapter 6

Behind the Supply Curve: Inputs and Costs

BEFORE YOU READ THE CHAPTER

Summary

This chapter develops the concept of the firm's production function and how the production function relates the level of inputs used by the firm to the level of output the firm produces. The chapter discusses diminishing marginal returns and then develops different measures of a firm's costs, including the firm's total cost of production, average cost of production, and marginal cost of production. The chapter also considers how the firm's costs differ between the short run and the long run. Finally, the chapter develops the idea of returns to scale and then analyzes the relationship between inputs, outputs, and costs in the long run. The chapter also defines and discusses network externalities.

Chapter Objectives

Objective #1. Producers must make a production decision about how much output they should produce. Producers are assumed to select the level of output that will result in the maximization of their economic profits.

Objective #2. Firms combine inputs with technology to produce outputs. The production function for a firm describes the maximum amount of output that can be produced from a general level of inputs and technology.

- In the short run, inputs may be fixed or variable. The level of fixed input used by a firm does not change in the short run as the firm's level of output changes. In contrast, the level of variable input used by a firm does change in the short run as the firm's level of output changes.

- In the long run, all inputs are assumed to be variable since in the long run all desired adjustments to input usage are possible.

Objective #3. In the short run, a firm's ability to produce outputs from its variable inputs depends on the level of fixed input it employs. For a given level of fixed input, as the firm hires additional units of the variable input, the firm will find that its output increases. However, the firm will find that as it hires additional units of the variable input, the marginal product (*MP*) of this variable input declines. That is, as additional units of the variable input are hired, total product (*TP*) increases but it eventually increases at a diminishing rate. This principle of diminishing marginal returns is a short-run concept: in the short run, the marginal product of a variable input diminishes as the level of usage of that variable input increases, holding at least one other input fixed.

- The firm's *TP* curve graphically represents the relationship between a firm's total output and the level of variable input it is using, holding all other inputs constant. The slope of the *TP* curve at any particular level of production is equal to the marginal product of the variable input. Due to diminishing marginal returns, the slope of the *TP* curve flattens as more and more units of the variable input are hired.

- The firm's marginal product of labor is equal to the change in output divided by the change in labor. The marginal product of labor measures the addition to total output from hiring an additional unit of labor while holding all other factors of production constant. Once the firm enters the range of output for which diminishing marginal returns holds, the firm's *MP* of labor curve is downward sloping.

- The firm's *TP* and *MP* curves shift up at every level of usage of the variable input when more of the fixed input is used. For instance, suppose a firm's fixed input is capital and its variable input is labor. When the firm increases the level of its capital from its initial level to a new, higher but constant level of capital, the firm will find that every level of labor usage results in an increased level of production relative to the initial situation because the labor now has more capital resources to work with in producing the product. With more of the fixed input available, the marginal product of the variable input at every level of the variable input is now higher than it was initially.

Objective #4. A firm can construct its cost curves if it combines the information from its production function with information about the prices of inputs. The production function connects the level of input usage to the maximum level of output production possible from these inputs, while input prices allow the firm to then calculate the cost of producing that level of output.

Objective #5. The firm's costs can be described in the short run or in the long run. The short-run costs for a firm include the following:

- Fixed cost (*FC*) is the cost of hiring the fixed input. To calculate the fixed cost, multiply the number of units of the fixed input that the firm is using by the price of a unit of the fixed input. In the short run, fixed cost does not vary as the level of output varies.

- Variable cost (*VC*) is the cost of hiring the variable input. To calculate the variable cost, multiply the number of units of the variable input that the firm is using by the price of a unit of the variable input. Variable cost varies as the level of output varies: the higher the level of output, holding everything else constant, the greater the use of the variable input and, hence, the greater the variable cost.

- Total cost (*TC*) in the short run is equal to the sum of the fixed cost plus the variable cost: thus, $TC = FC + VC$.

The long-run costs for a firm are all variable costs, since in the long run all inputs can be adjusted. Thus, long-run total costs are equivalent to long-run variable costs.

Objective #6.   A firm's total cost depends on the level of output it produces. In the short run, higher levels of output are only possible if more units of the variable input are hired. Further, as additional units of the variable input are hired, the marginal product of the variable input declines (recall the principle of diminishing marginal returns): this implies that as output increases, the variable cost of production rises, as does the total cost of production. Thus, the *TC* curve is upward sloping, and in addition, the *TC* curve gets steeper as the firm's level of output increases due to the diminishing marginal returns to the variable input.

Objective #7.   Marginal cost (*MC*) is the addition to total cost from producing one more unit of output. Marginal cost is the slope of the *TC* curve. As output increases, the *MC* curve is initially downward sloping, but eventually, at higher levels of output, the *MC* curve becomes upward sloping due to diminishing returns. Figure 6.1 illustrates this idea: *MC* decreases as output increases from 0 units to Q_1 units, and then *MC* increases as output increases beyond level Q_1. In the downward-sloping portion of the *MC* curve, the cost of an additional unit of output is falling due to specialization. The firm, in this range of output, experiences increasing returns to scale since its cost of additional output falls.

Figure 6.1

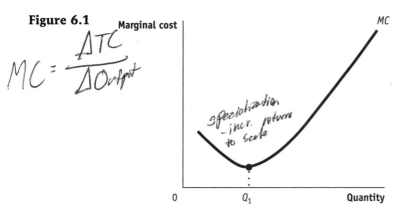

$$MC = \frac{\Delta TC}{\Delta Output}$$

Objective #8.   Average total cost (*ATC*) provides a measure of the cost per unit of output. This measure can be calculated by dividing total cost by the level of output ($ATC = TC/Q$). Average variable cost (*AVC*) is variable cost divided by output ($AVC = VC/Q$). Average fixed cost (*AFC*) is fixed cost divided by output ($AFC = FC/Q$).

- Average total cost is equal to the sum of average variable cost plus average fixed cost. To see this, recall that $TC = VC + FC$. If both sides of this equation are divided by quantity (Q), then $ATC = AVC + AFC$.

- Average total cost provides a measure of the cost per unit of production while marginal cost provides a measure of the cost of producing an additional unit of output.

- The *ATC* and *AVC* curves are U-shaped, and their minimum points intersect the firm's *MC* curve. When *ATC* is decreasing as output increases, this implies that the marginal cost is less than the average total cost: producing an additional unit of output costs less than the current cost per unit, and thus the cost per unit must decrease if that additional unit of output is produced. When *ATC* is increasing as output increases, this implies that the marginal cost is greater than the average total cost: producing an additional unit of output costs more than the current cost per unit, and thus the cost per unit must increase if that additional unit of output is produced. When *ATC* equals *MC*, this implies that the cost of producing an additional unit of output equals the current cost per unit, and thus the cost per unit will not change if that additional unit of output is produced. Figure 6.2 illustrates these relationships.

- Since fixed cost does not vary in the short run for a firm, the *AFC* must decrease as output increases. Figure 6.2 illustrates these relationships.

Figure 6.2

(handwritten notes: "go up once intersect w/ MC", "spreading effect", "min cost output = ATC=MC")

Objective #9. As the firm increases its level of production, the result is two effects on the firm's costs. The diminishing returns effect refers to the increase in the variable cost per unit (the average variable cost) of producing a higher level of output due to the diminishing returns to the variable input that the firm experiences as it increases its level of production. The spreading effect refers to the decrease in the fixed cost per unit (the average fixed cost) of producing a higher level of output due to the spreading of the fixed cost of production over more units of output. At low levels of output, the spreading effect is stronger than the diminishing returns effect, and this causes the ATC to decrease as the level of output increases. At higher levels of output, the diminishing returns effect is stronger than the spreading effect, and this causes the ATC to increase as the level of output increases. When the spreading effect exactly offsets the diminishing returns effect, the ATC curve is at its minimum point.

Objective #10. The minimum-cost output is the level of output at which average total cost is minimized. At this output level, the average total cost is equal to marginal cost. At output levels lower than this minimum-cost output, the marginal cost of producing an additional unit of output is less than the average total cost. At output levels greater than this minimum-cost output, the marginal cost of producing an additional unit of output is greater than the average total cost. Figure 6.3 illustrates this concept: Q_1 is the minimum-cost output; as output increases from 0 units to Q_1, ATC declines, and as output increases beyond Q_1 units, ATC increases.

Figure 6.3

Minimum-cost output is the level of output at which ATC is minimized.

(handwritten notes: "min cost output ATC = minimized")

Objective #11. The long-run average total cost (LRATC) curve illustrates the relationship between output and average total cost when fixed cost has been chosen to minimize the average total cost at every level of output. The LRATC curve is U-shaped: when LRATC is decreasing as output increases, the firm experiences increasing returns to scale; when LRATC is increasing as output increases, the firm experiences decreasing returns to scale; and when LRATC is constant as output increases, the firm experiences constant returns to scale. Figure 6.4 illustrates the LRATC curve and returns to scale: for outputs from 0 units to Q_1, this firm has increasing returns to scale and decreasing costs; for outputs from Q_1 units to Q_2, this firm has constant returns to scale and constant costs; and for outputs greater than Q_2, this firm has decreasing returns to scale and increasing costs.

(handwritten margin notes: "returns to scale? – double inputs = double prices?")

Figure 6.4

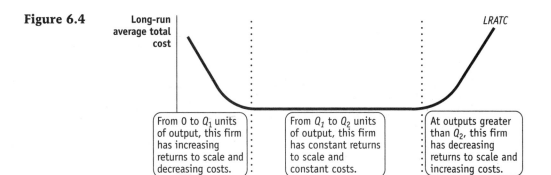

- A firm that has increasing returns to scale in its range of production finds that as its production level increases, its cost of production falls: this firm benefits from getting larger. A firm with increasing returns to scale finds that an equal proportionate increase in all its inputs will result in a greater than proportionate increase in its output: for example, a doubling of all of the firm's inputs causes the firm's output to more than double, and therefore the firm's *ATC* decreases.

- A firm that has decreasing returns to scale in its range of production finds that as its production level increases, its cost of production increases: this firm benefits from staying relatively small. A firm with decreasing returns to scale finds that an equal proportionate increase in all its inputs will result in a less than proportionate increase in its output: for example, a doubling of all of the firm's inputs causes the firm's output to less than double, and therefore the firm's *ATC* increases.

- A firm that has constant returns to scale in its range of production finds that a proportionate increase in all its inputs results in a proportionate increase in its output: for example, if all inputs are doubled, then the firm's output also doubles, and therefore the firm's *ATC* stays constant.

Objective #12. Returns to scale for a firm depend on the firm's production technology. Increasing returns to scale arise because of increasing specialization that is possible at large output levels or because of large initial set-up costs that must be incurred to produce any output or because of network externalities. Decreasing returns to scale arise due to problems of coordination and communication as the level of production increases.

Key Terms

Notes

production function the relationship between the quantity of *inputs* a firm uses and the quantity of output it produces.

fixed input an *input* whose quantity is fixed for a period of time and cannot be varied (for example, land).

variable input an *input* whose quantity the firm can vary at any time (for example, labor).

long run the period in which all *inputs* can be varied.

short run the period in which at least one *input* is fixed.

total product curve a graphical representation of the *production function,* showing how the quantity of output depends on the quantity of the *variable input* for a given quantity of the *fixed input.*

Key Terms *(continued)*

marginal product the additional quantity of output produced by using one more unit of a given *input.*

diminishing returns to an input the effect observed when an increase in the quantity of an *input,* while holding the levels of all other inputs fixed, leads to a decline in the *marginal product* of that input.

fixed cost a cost that does not depend on the quantity of output produced; the cost of a *fixed input.*

variable cost a cost that depends on the quantity of output produced; the cost of a *variable input.*

total cost the sum of the *fixed cost* and the *variable cost* of producing a given quantity of output.

total cost curve a graphical representation of the *total cost,* showing how total cost depends on the quantity of output.

marginal cost the additional cost incurred by producing one more unit of the good or service.

average total cost *total cost* divided by quantity of output produced. Also referred to as *average cost.*

average cost an alternative term for *average total cost;* the *total cost* divided by the quantity of output produced.

U-shaped average total cost curve a distinctive graphical representation of the relationship between output and *average total cost;* the average total cost curve at first falls when output is low and then rises as output increases.

average fixed cost the *fixed cost* per unit of output.

average variable cost the *variable cost* per unit of output.

minimum-cost output the quantity of output at which the *average total cost* is lowest—the bottom of the *U-shaped average total cost curve.*

long-run average total cost curve a graphical representation showing the relationship between output and *average total cost* when *fixed cost* has been chosen to minimize average total cost for each level of output.

increasing returns to scale long-run *average total cost* declines as output increases (also referred to as *economies of scale*).

decreasing returns to scale long-run *average total cost* increases as output increases (also known as *diseconomies of scale*).

constant returns to scale long-run *average total cost* is constant as output increases.

network externalities refers to when the value of a good to an individual is greater when a large number of other people also use that good.

Notes

▌ AFTER YOU READ THE CHAPTER

Tips

Tip #1. The most important tip for this chapter is to learn the new terminology, the abbreviations for this terminology, the graphical representation of these new terms, and how to apply these new terms. Students tend to struggle with these terms and abbreviations because there are so many of them, but understanding the material requires that you become comfortable with all the new vocabulary.

Tip #2. This chapter continues to develop the general concept of *marginal*. In the chapter, the marginal product of an input and the marginal cost of production are introduced. Both of these concepts consider the change in one variable due to a change in another variable: the marginal product of an input looks at the addition to total production when an additional unit of the input is employed, and the marginal cost measures the change in total cost due to the production of an additional unit of output. The marginal concept is a critically important concept for you to understand and be able to use.

Tip #3. It is important that you understand the distinction between the short run and the long run. In the short run at least one input is fixed, while in the long run all inputs are variable. An input is fixed if its level of usage does not change even when the level of production increases. An input is variable when its level of usage varies as the level of production varies. There is no set period of time that determines the boundary between the short run and the long run: the short run is a period of time so short that full adjustment to changes cannot take place, while the long run is a period of time sufficiently long enough to allow full adjustment.

Tip #4. After you have learned the definitions of total cost, variable cost, fixed cost, average total cost, average variable cost, average fixed cost, and marginal cost, and their abbreviations, you should concentrate on learning how these terms are related to one another. Here is a summary of these relationships:

$$TC = FC + VC$$

$$ATC = TC/Q$$

$$AVC = VC/Q$$

$$AFC = FC/Q$$

$$ATC = AFC + AVC$$

$$MC = (\text{the change in } TC)/(\text{the change in } Q)$$

Think about these relationships and their implications. For example, if you know TC and FC, you can calculate VC; or, if you know AVC and ATC, you can calculate AFC.

Tip #5. Once you have learned the definitions and the abbreviations of all the new terms in the chapter, you should work on a thorough understanding of the graphs, particularly the graphs of ATC, AVC, AFC, and MC.

- The graph of AFC is a curve that decreases as output increases because the level of FC is constant in the short run, and as output increases, this implies that AFC must decline ($AFC = FC/Q$, and as Q gets larger and FC stays constant, this means that AFC must get smaller). On a graph of the AFC curve, the fixed cost for a particular level of production can be represented as the area under the curve. Figure 6.5 illustrates the AFC for Q_1 units of output as well as the fixed cost for this level of output.

Figure 6.5

- The AVC curve is a U-shaped curve due to diminishing marginal returns to the variable input. Figure 6.6 represents the AVC curve and indicates the area that corresponds to the variable cost of producing Q_1 units of the good.

Figure 6.6

Average variable cost

The shaded area represents the variable cost of producing Q_1 units, since $AVC_1 * Q_1 = VC$ for Q_1 units of output.

AVC_1

AVC

Q_1 Quantity

- The ATC curve is also U-shaped. Recall from Tip 4 that $ATC = AFC + AVC$. Figure 6.7 illustrates this concept for Q_1 units of production. You should redraw this graph and see if you can locate the AFC, AVC, and ATC curves for a different level of output.

Figure 6.7

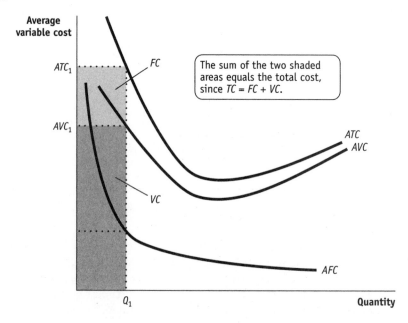

Tip #6. It is important that you understand the distinction between the marginal cost concept and the average cost concept. Marginal cost measures the cost of producing an additional unit of output, while average cost measures the cost per unit. As the firm produces an additional unit of output, it can turn to its marginal cost measure to see how this extra production affects its total cost, and it can also see that if the marginal cost of producing this last unit is less than the average total cost, then producing this additional unit will lower the unit cost of production for the firm. This relationship between marginal and average costs is difficult for many students to grasp, yet it is a relationship that almost all students know and understand in other settings. For example, suppose you form a basketball team with five players. To calculate the average height of your team you would add up the heights of the five players and then divide by 5. Then, if you added another player, this additional player would represent a marginal addition to the height of your team. If this new player were taller than the team's average height, then the team's average height would increase. But, if the player were shorter than the team's average height, then the team's average height would decrease. This basic concept can be applied to a firm's costs: when the marginal cost exceeds the average total cost, the *ATC* must rise; and when the marginal cost is less than the average total cost, the *ATC* must fall. Figure 6.8 illustrates this concept.

Figure 6.8   Marginal cost and average total cost

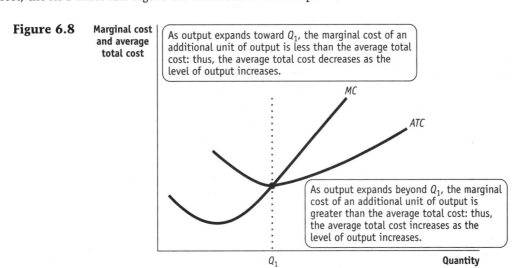

As output expands toward Q_1, the marginal cost of an additional unit of output is less than the average total cost: thus, the average total cost decreases as the level of output increases.

As output expands beyond Q_1, the marginal cost of an additional unit of output is greater than the average total cost: thus, the average total cost increases as the level of output increases.

Tip #7. A firm's returns to scale identifies whether the firm can reduce its costs by increasing its level of production. Firms that have increasing returns to scale benefit from being relatively large, while firms with decreasing returns to scale find that getting larger is detrimental to them since, as their output levels expand, their average costs rise.

- Consider a firm with increasing returns to scale: when this firm doubles its inputs, it doubles its costs. But when inputs are doubled, this firm can produce more than double its original level of output. This implies that its *ATC*, which is equal to *TC/Q*, will decrease since *TC* has doubled while *Q* has more than doubled.

- Consider a firm with decreasing returns to scale: when this firm doubles its inputs, it doubles its costs. But when inputs are doubled, this firm can only produce less than double its original level of output. This implies that its *ATC*, which is equal to *TC/Q*, will increase since *TC* has doubled while *Q* has less than doubled.

Tip #8. Students often mix up the concepts of diminishing marginal returns to an input and returns to scale. Remember that diminishing returns to an input is based on changing the level of one input while holding constant the levels of all other inputs: diminishing returns to scale is a short-run concept since at least one input is being held constant. Returns to scale, in contrast, is a long-run concept based on an equal proportionate increase in all inputs and the effect of this change on the firm's level of output.

WORKED PROBLEMS

1. The following table gives the production function information for Rosie's Gadget Factory, where labor is the variable input and capital is the fixed input.

Quantity of labor	Quantity of output
0	0
1	20
2	38
3	53
4	65
5	70

In a graph, depict this firm's total product curve. How does this total product curve illustrate the idea of diminishing returns to an input? Calculate the marginal product of labor at Rosie's Gadget Factory. How do the numbers you calculated for the marginal product of labor illustrate diminishing returns to labor? Draw a graph of the firm's marginal product of labor curve.

STEP 1: Start by drawing a graph of the total product curve for Rosie's Gadget Factory. In this graph, measure labor along the *x*-axis and output along the *y*-axis.

Review the section "The Production Function" on pages 182–189, and Figure 6-1 on page 183.

STEP 2: Describe what happens to the slope of the production function as more and more units of labor are employed.

Review the section "The Production Function" on pages 182–189, and Figure 6-1 on page 183.

As labor increases, if output increases but at a diminishing rate, this indicates that the production function illustrates diminishing returns to labor: as more and more units of labor are employed, output increases but each successive unit of labor is less productive than the preceding unit of labor. For Rosie's Gadget Factory, we see that output is increasing, but it is increasing at a diminishing rate.

STEP 3: Calculate the firm's marginal product of labor.

Review the section "The Production Function" on pages 182–189, and Figure 6-1 on page 183.

The firm's marginal product of labor is equal to the (change in total product)/(the change in labor). The following table gives the firm's marginal product of labor.

Quantity of labor	Quantity of output	Marginal product of labor
0	0	
		20
1	20	
		18
2	38	
		15
3	53	
		12
4	65	
		5
5	70	

As the amount of labor increases, output increases, but the increase in output diminishes as more and more units of labor are employed: Rosie's Gadget Factory exhibits diminishing returns to labor.

STEP 4: Draw a graph of the firm's marginal product of labor, where labor is measured on the horizontal axis and the marginal product of labor (gadgets per worker) is measured on the vertical axis.

Review the section "The Production Function" on pages 182–189, and Figure 6-1 on page 183.

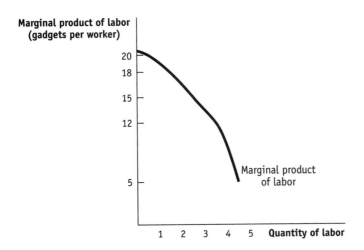

2. Otto's Computers is considering expanding its capital stock. Engineers working for the company have estimated the company's aggregate production function for two levels of capital, and they have provided the company management with the following table of information, where L is units of labor, K_1 is the first level of capital, K_2 is the second, higher level of capital, Q_1 is the quantity of output that Otto's Computers can produce using K_1, and Q_2 is the quantity of output that Otto's Computers can produce using K_2.

L	K_1	Q_1		K_2	Q_2
0	4	0		9	0
1	4	4		9	6
4	4	8		9	12
9	4	12		9	18
16	4	16		9	24
25	4	20		9	30

Provide Otto's Computers with two graphs: one depicting both its total product curve when it employs K_1 units of capital and its total product curve when it employs K_2 units of capital, and the second depicting its marginal product of labor curves for the two different levels of capital. Provide a statement about what happens to labor productivity when Otto's Computers changes its level of capital from K_1 to K_2.

STEP 1: From the table, it is relatively easy to construct a graph representing the total product curves for the two different levels of capital that Otto's Computers is considering.

Review the section "The Production Function" on pages 182–189, and Figures 6-1 on page 183 and 6-3 on page 186.

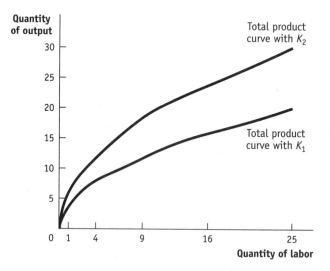

When Otto's Computers uses more capital with a given level of labor, it can produce a higher level of output. This is illustrated by the shifting up of the total product curve when capital is increased.

STEP 2: Depicting the firm's marginal product of labor curves for the two levels of capital is a bit more work, since you must first find the values of the marginal product of labor.

Review the section "The Production Function" on pages 182–189, and Figures 6-1 on page 183 and 6-3 on page 186.

It is important to realize that because labor is not increasing by one unit at a time the calculation of the firm's marginal product of labor will be more complicated. For example, when the firm uses K_1 units of capital and increases its labor usage from 1 to 4 units, the change in output is 4 units, while the change in labor is 3 units. Thus, the firm's marginal product of labor between these two levels of labor usage will be equal to 4/3, or 1.33. The following table summarizes the marginal product of labor for the two different levels of capital.

For K_1:

L	Q_1	MPL_1
0	0	
		4/1
1	4	
		4/3
4	8	
		4/5
9	12	
		4/7
16	16	
		4/9
25	20	

For K_2:

L	Q_2	MPL_2
0	0	
		6/1
1	6	
		6/3
4	12	
		6/5
9	18	
		6/7
16	24	
		6/9
25	30	

Inspection of this table of values indicates that at any given level of labor, the marginal product of labor is greater when the firm uses K_2 units of capital than when it uses K_1 units of capital. In addition, the value of the marginal product of labor gets smaller and smaller as the level of labor usage increases.

STEP 3: Graph the firm's marginal product of labor curves for each level of capital usage.

Review Figures 6-2 on page 185 and 6-3 on page 186.

STEP 4: Assess what happens to labor productivity when Otto's Computers uses a larger amount of labor.

Review Figures 6-2 on page 185 and 6-3 on page 186.

When Otto's Computers uses the larger amount of capital, K_2, its total product curve shifts up, as does its marginal product of labor curve. At each level of labor usage, labor is more productive.

3. Otto's Computers from Worked Problem (2) is interested in calculating its variable costs, fixed costs, total costs, and marginal cost of production for the two possible levels of capital it is considering hiring. Otto's knows that each unit of labor employed costs $10 per unit and each unit of capital costs $5 per unit. Calculate Otto's costs and enter them in the tables that follow.

L	K_1	Q_1	Variable cost	Fixed cost	Total cost	Marginal cost ($ per unit of output)
0	4	0				
1	4	4				
4	4	8				
9	4	12				
16	4	16				
25	4	20				

L	K_2	Q_2	Variable cost	Fixed cost	Total cost	Marginal cost ($ per unit of output)
0	9	0				
1	9	6				
4	9	12				
9	9	18				
16	9	24				
25	9	30				

Then, calculate Otto's average variable cost, average fixed cost, and average total cost for each level of output in the table. Summarize your findings in the following tables.

Production Function and Costs when K equals 4 units:

Q_1	Variable cost	Fixed cost	Total cost	Average variable cost	Average fixed cost	Average total cost
0						
4						
8						
12						
16						
20						

Production function and costs when K equals 9 units:

Q_2	Variable cost	Fixed cost	Total cost	Average variable cost	Average fixed cost	Average total cost
0						
4						
8						
12						
16						
20						

STEP 1: **Start by calculating the variable cost and the fixed cost, then sum these to find the total cost.**

Review the section "Two Key Concepts: Marginal Cost and Average Cost" on pages 189–197, and Figure 6-6 on page 191.

The variable cost of production is the cost of the variable input: in this example, labor is the variable input because it varies as the level of output varies. Since each unit of labor costs $10 per unit, it is a simple matter to calculate the variable cost by multiplying the number of units of labor times $10 per unit.

The fixed cost of production is the cost of the fixed input: in this example, capital is the fixed input. In the first table, capital is fixed at K_1 units of capital, or 4 units of capital, while in the second table capital is fixed at K_2 units of capital, or 9 units of capital. Since each unit of capital costs $5 per unit, the fixed cost can be found by multiplying this price of capital times the number of units of capital.

The total cost of production is equal to the sum of the variable cost plus the fixed cost. The tables following Step 2 summarize this work.

STEP 2: **Calculate the marginal cost for each production function.**

Review the section "Two Key Concepts: Marginal Cost and Average Cost" on pages 189–197, Table 6-1 on page 190, and Figure 6-7 on page 192.

When calculating the marginal cost of production, remember that marginal cost is equal to the change in total cost divided by the change in the quantity of output. Since output is not changing by one unit at a time, you must find both the change in total cost as well as the change in output to calculate marginal cost. For example, to find the marginal cost of going from 4 units of output to 8 units of output using K_1, you must notice that the total cost of producing 4 units of output is $30 and the total cost of producing 8 units of output is $60, or a change in total cost of $30, while the change in output is 4 units since output is changing from 4 units to 8 units. Thus, the marginal cost of going from producing 4 units of output to 8 units of output is equal to $30/4 = $7.50 per unit of output.

The following tables summarize this work.

L	K_1	Q_1	Variable cost	Fixed cost	Total cost	Marginal cost ($ per unit of output)
0	4	0	$0	$20	$20	
1	4	4	10	20	30	10/4 = $2.50
4	4	8	40	20	60	30/4 = 7.50
9	4	12	90	20	110	50/4 = 12.50
16	4	16	160	20	180	70/4 = 17.50
25	4	20	250	20	270	90/4 = 22.50

L	K_2	Q_2	Variable cost	Fixed cost	Total cost	Marginal cost ($ per unit of output)
0	9	0	$0	$45	$45	
1	9	6	10	45	55	10/6 = $1.67
4	9	12	40	45	85	30/6 = 5
9	9	18	90	45	135	50/6 = 8.33
16	9	24	160	45	205	70/6 = 11.67
25	9	30	250	45	295	90/6 = 15

STEP 3: Calculate Otto's average variable cost, average fixed cost, and average total cost and then enter your findings in the given table.

Review the section "Two Key Concepts: Marginal Cost and Average Cost" on pages 189–197, Table 6-1 on page 190, and Figure 6-7 on page 192.

To calculate these average costs, review the formulas for average total cost, average variable cost, and average fixed cost that are given in the text.

Production function and costs when K equals 4 units:

Q_1	Variable cost	Fixed cost	Total cost	Average variable cost	Average fixed cost	Average total cost
0	$0	$20	$20	—	—	—
4	10	20	30	10/4 = $2.50	20/4 = $5	30/4 = $7.50
8	40	20	60	40/8 = 5	20/8 = 2.50	60/8 = 7.50
12	90	20	110	90/12 = 7.50	20/12 = 1.67	110/12 = 9.17
16	160	20	180	160/16 = 10	20/16 = 1.25	180/16 = 11.25
20	250	20	270	250/20 = 12.50	20/20 = 1	270/20 = 13.50

Production function and costs when K equals 9 units:

Q_2	Variable cost	Fixed cost	Total cost	Average variable cost	Average fixed cost	Average total cost
0	$0	$45	$45	—	—	—
6	10	45	55	10/6 = $1.67	45/6 = $7.50	55/6 = $9.17
12	40	45	85	40/12 = 3.33	45/12 = 3.75	85/12 = 7.08
18	90	45	135	90/18 = 5	45/18 = 2.50	135/18 = 7.50
24	160	45	205	160/24 = 6.67	45/24 = 1.88	205/24 = 8.54
30	250	45	295	250/30 = 8.33	45/30 = 1.50	295/30 = 9.83

4. Suppose that Marcy has a choice of producing her product with a set of inputs that is very capital intensive or with a set of inputs that is less capital intensive. Marcy is trying to understand how her choice of production technique will alter her firm's cost curves. She knows that this effect on her costs can be explained by both the spreading effect and the diminishing returns effect, but she is not quite sure how to apply these terms to her situation. You are asked to help out with the explanation.

STEP 1: First, you need to review what the spreading effect and the diminishing returns effect are, and then you will want to think about how to apply these terms to the decision that Marcy is contemplating.

Review the section "Short-Run versus Long-Run Costs" on pages 197–201, and Figure 6-11 on page 198.

Holding everything else constant, when Marcy uses a larger amount of capital, the greater will be her fixed cost of production. For a small level of output, this implies that Marcy's average total cost will be greater since there will be less output to spread the fixed cost over. But at higher levels of output, Marcy's average total cost will be lower since she will be able to spread her fixed cost over a larger amount of output. If Marcy anticipates producing a relatively low amount of output, she will likely want to choose the less capital-intensive production process since she will not be able to reap the full benefits of the spreading effect at low levels of production. If she anticipates producing a relatively large amount of output, she will likely want to choose the more capital-intensive production process since she will be able to take advantage of the spreading effect.

The diminishing returns effect says that as output gets larger, more of the variable input will be needed to produce that level of output, yet as more units of the variable input are employed, each successive unit is less productive and this causes average total cost to rise. Marcy will face the diminishing returns effect no matter which production process she chooses, but this effect will occur at higher levels of variable input usage if she employs the more capital-intensive production process.

STEP 2: Provide some advice or guidance for Marcy as she tries to determine the optimal production process for her business.

Review the section "Short-Run versus Long-Run Costs" on pages 197–201, and Figure 6-11 on page 198.

Marcy's optimal choice of production process ultimately rests on how much of the product she anticipates she will want to produce. If she anticipates that she will want a large quantity of output, she will find that her average costs of production will be lower with the more capital-intensive production process since the spreading effect will dominate the diminishing returns effect only at high levels of output. But if she anticipates that she will want to produce a low level of output, she will find that her average costs of production will be lower with the less capital-intensive production process since the spreading effect will dominate the diminishing returns effect at low levels of output.

Problems and Exercises

1. The following table describes the short-run production function for Harry's company. Harry uses labor and capital to produce can openers.

Quantity of labor (workers)	Quantity of capital (units)	Quantity of output (can openers)
0	10	0
1	10	50
2	10	80
3	10	100
4	10	115
5	10	125
6	10	133
7	10	138

a. How do you know the preceding table represents Harry's short-run production function? How is the short run different from the long run?

There is no change in units. Capital is constant

b. Economists make a distinction between variable inputs and fixed inputs. For the short-run production function in the preceding table, which input is the fixed input and which one is the variable input? Explain your answer.

fixed = capital   variable = labor

c. Draw Harry's total product curve for the production of can openers, holding the level of capital constant. In your graph measure the quantity of labor on the x-axis and the quantity of can openers on the y-axis.

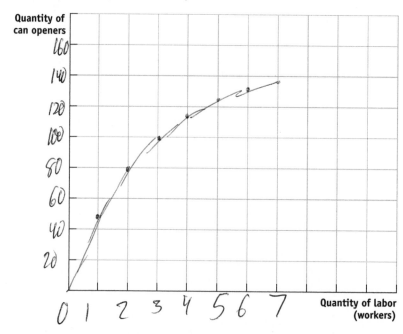

d. Complete the following table using the information given previously in this question and assuming that capital is held constant at 10 units.

Quantity of labor (workers)	Quantity of output (can openers)	Marginal product of labor $MPL = \Delta Q/\Delta L$ (can openers per worker)
0	0	
		50
1	50	
		30
2	80	
		20
3	100	
		15
4	115	
		10
5	125	
		8
6	133	
		5
7	138	

e. Describe the results you found in part (d). What is the relationship between the quantity of labor used and the marginal product of labor at Harry's can opener factory?

f. Graph Harry's marginal product of labor on a graph with the quantity of labor measured on the *x*-axis and the marginal product of labor measured on the *y*-axis. Plot the marginal product values you found in part (d) using the midpoint method. For example, the marginal product of labor from hiring the first unit of labor is equal to 50 can openers per worker: plot this information midway between 0 and 1 unit of labor.

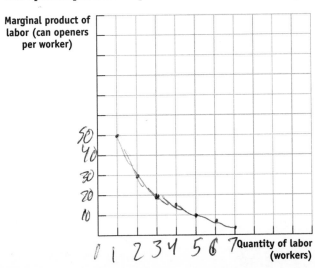

g. What does it mean if the marginal product of labor curve is downward sloping as you hire more units of the variable input?

2. Harry (from problem 1) decides to hire an additional 10 units of capital so that his capital is now fixed at 20 units. He finds that this additional capital doubles his production at every level of labor.

a. Complete the following table, which describes Harry's production function based on his using 20 units of capital.

Quantity of labor (workers)	Quantity of capital (units)	Quantity of output (can openers)
0	20	0
1	20	
2	20	
3	20	
4	20	
5	20	
6	20	
7	20	

b. Draw a graph showing Harry's original production function using 10 units of capital, and his new production function using 20 units of capital. Measure total product along the y-axis and the quantity of labor along the x-axis. Describe the effect of this change in Harry's total product curve.

Quantity of can openers

Quantity of labor (workers)

c. What happens to the marginal product of labor when Harry increases his use of capital? Provide an intuitive explanation for your answer. In your answer, sketch a graph of the original marginal product of labor curve based on 10 units of capital, and the new marginal product of labor curve based on 20 units of capital.

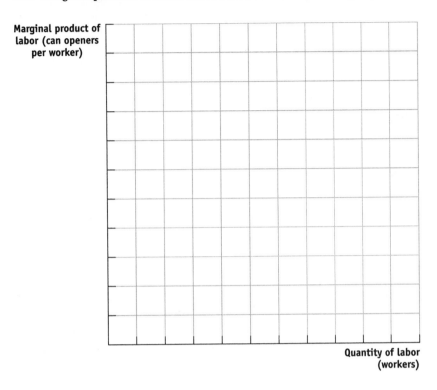

3. In the short run, it is assumed that at least one of a firm's inputs is fixed and cannot be changed. Explain why this assumption is critical for understanding diminishing marginal returns to the variable input.

4. Malthus predicted that as population grew, the economy's diminishing ability to produce food from a given set of resources would necessarily lead to insufficient food. However, population continues to grow and so does food production. What aspect of food production did Malthus fail to anticipate?

5. The following table provides the short-run production function for Sherry's Hair Salon. Sherry uses only two inputs, labor and capital, to produce her output of stylish haircuts. The price of labor is $20 an hour and the price of capital is $50 per unit.

Quantity of capital (units)	Quantity of labor (hours of work)	Quantity of haircuts
10	0	0
10	10	15
10	20	28
10	30	38
10	40	44
10	50	48

a. Complete the following table of Sherry's costs, given the preceding information. Round your calculations to one place past the decimal point.

Quantity of capital (units)	Quantity of labor (hours of work)	Quantity of haircuts	FC ($)	VC ($)	AFC ($ per unit of output)	AVC ($ per unit of output)	ATC ($ per unit of output)	TC ($)	MC ($ per unit of output)
10	0	0	500	0	—	—	—	500	
									13.3
10	10	15	500	200	33.3	13.3	46.6	700	
									$\frac{200}{13}$
10	20	28	500	400	17.9	14.3	32.2	900	
									$\frac{200}{10}$
10	30	38	500	600	13.2	15.8	29	1100	
									$\frac{200}{6}$
10	40	44	500	800	11.4	18.2	29.6	1300	
									$\frac{200}{4}$
10	50	48	500	1000	10.4	20.8	31.2	1500	

b. Does this production function exhibit diminishing marginal returns to labor? Explain your answer.

Yes. As labor increases, the rate that the q haircuts increases is decreasing.

c. Graph the total cost function for Sherry's Hair Salon. Measure total cost on the vertical axis and the quantity of haircuts on the horizontal axis. Describe how increasing the quantity of haircuts affects the slope of the total cost curve.

gets steeper as q ↑,
b/c diminishing returns

d. Graph the marginal cost function for Sherry's Hair Salon using the midpoint method. Measure marginal cost on the vertical axis and the quantity of haircuts on the horizontal axis. Describe the slope of the *MC* curve and then explain why the *MC* is sloped this way.

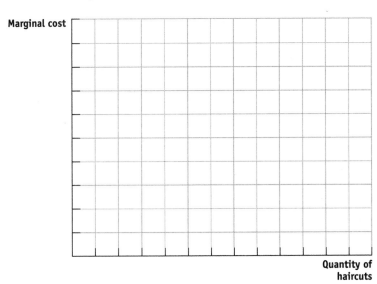

e. In a new graph, draw Sherry's Hair Salon's *AFC* curve. Measure average fixed cost on the vertical axis and the quantity of haircuts on the horizontal axis. On your graph, indicate the area that corresponds to fixed cost if 15 haircuts are currently being produced.

$$AFC = \frac{FC}{Q}$$

$$FC = AFC \cdot Q$$

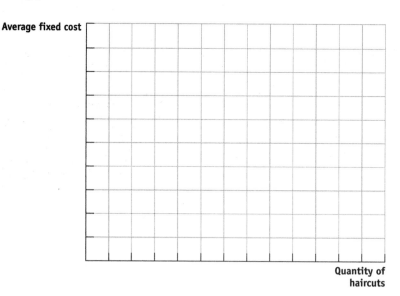

Average fixed cost

Quantity of haircuts

f. In a new graph, sketch Sherry's Hair Salon's *ATC, AVC, AFC,* and *MC* curves. Measure cost per unit on the vertical axis and the quantity of haircuts on the horizontal axis. What must be true about the relationship between the *ATC* and *MC* curves?

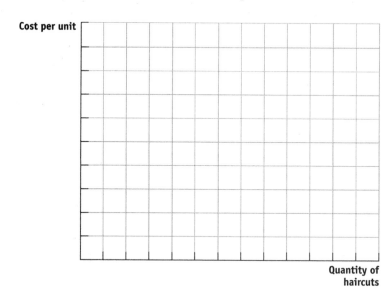

Cost per unit

Quantity of haircuts

6. For each of the following costs, decide whether it is a fixed cost or a variable cost for the firm in the short run. Provide a brief argument for your classification of the cost.

  a. A one-year lease on the building in which the business is located.

  fixed — dsnt change

  b. Annual property taxes that are assessed on the value of the land the business owns.

  fixed

  c. The cost of a necessary metal used in the production of the firm's product.

  variable

  d. A 10-year-old metal stamping machine that has a useful life of 20 years in your business and is sufficient to produce any desired level of output for the firm.

  fixed

  e. Sugar that the firm uses to make the cookies it sells.

  variable

7. Marginal cost and marginal product are both slope measures. Describe the curves that these two slope measures are derived from.

$$MC = \frac{\Delta TC}{\Delta Q}$$

$$MP = \frac{\Delta Q}{\Delta L}$$

MC derived from Avg total cost curve which has a positive, increasing slope

MP derived from total product curve which has a pos., decreasing slope

8. The following table provides some information about Stella's Delight, a business that Stella owns. Stella uses labor and capital as her only inputs in the production of her product.

a. Fill in the table.

VC *FC*

Quantity of labor (units)	Quantity of capital (units)	Quantity of output	VC ($)	FC ($)	AVC ($ per unit of output)	AFC ($ per unit of output)	ATC ($ per unit of output)	TC ($)	MC ($ per unit of output)
0	5	0	0	10	—	—	—		
1	5	10	5	10					
2	5	18	10	10				20	
3	5	24	15	10				25	
4	5	28	20	10					
5	5	30	25	10					
6	5	31	30	10					

b. What is the price of the variable input?

c. What is the price of the fixed input?

d. What is the marginal product of the fifth unit of labor?

e. What is the marginal cost of producing the twenty-fourth unit of output?

25

9. Why is the spreading effect stronger than the diminishing returns effect at low levels of output, while the diminishing returns effect is stronger than the spreading effect at high levels of output?

SE = when high fc, but small var cost

10. Discuss each of the following statements. Decide whether the statement is true or false and then justify your answer.

a. As output increases, if average total cost is decreasing, then marginal cost must be less than average total cost.

True

b. As output increases, if marginal cost is increasing, then marginal cost must be greater than average total cost.

~~True~~ False

c. As output increases, if marginal cost is greater than average fixed cost, then average fixed cost must be increasing.

False

d. As output increases, fixed cost decreases.

~~True~~ False

e. As output increases, variable cost increases.

~~False~~ True

11. Suppose the firm represented in the following table is operating in the long run. This firm produces chairs and uses wood and labor to produce these chairs. Some production information is provided in the table. Assume the price of wood and the price of labor do not change. *fix* *Variable*

Quantity of wood	Quantity of labor	Quantity of chairs
4 units	5 units	20 chairs
8 units	10 units	45 chairs
12 units	15 units	90 chairs
24 units	30 units	150 chairs

$\dfrac{\Delta Q}{\Delta Q} = \dfrac{25}{4}$

a. If this firm is currently using 4 units of wood and 5 units of labor, does it experience increasing, decreasing, or constant returns to scale if it increases its wood use to 8 units and its labor use to 10 units? Explain your answer.

Incr returns to scale b/c as it gets larger, the cost falls b/c the output increases at faster rate then input.

b. Is this firm's *LRATC* curve downward sloping, upward sloping, or constant in the range of production described in part (a)?

downward

c. If this firm is currently using 8 units of wood and 10 units of labor and it increases the use of both inputs by 50%, will the firm experience increasing, decreasing, or constant returns to scale?

~~constant~~ increasing b/c the output increases by 100%.

d. Is this firm's *LRATC* curve downward sloping, upward sloping, or constant in the range of production described in part (c)?

down

e. Suppose this firm is currently using 12 units of wood and 15 units of labor to produce chairs, and then the firm increases its input usage by 100% for both inputs. Will the firm experience increasing, decreasing, or constant returns to scale?

decreasing

f. Is this firm's *LRATC* curve downward sloping, upward sloping, or constant in the range of production described in part (e)?

increasing

■ BEFORE YOU TAKE THE TEST

Chapter Review Questions

1. The process of transforming inputs into output is described by the firm's
   a. cost function.
   b. revenue function.
   c. production function.
   d. marginal product of labor.

2. A firm's ability to produce output depends on
   a. its profitability.
   b. the level of inputs it uses.
   c. its stock price.
   d. its location.

Use the information in the following table about Paul's production function to answer the next five questions. Paul is a surgeon who also maintains an avid interest in economics.

Quantity of labor (hours in surgery)	Quantity of capital (operating rooms)	Total product (number of surgeries)
30	0	0
30	1	15
30	2	25
30	3	32
30	4	35

3. The information in the table about Paul's production function depicts Paul's
   a. short-run production function.
   b. long-run production function.

4. The fixed input in Paul's production function for surgeries is the quantity of
   a. labor.   b. capital.

5. The variable input in Paul's production function for surgeries is the quantity of
   a. labor.   b. capital.

6. Paul's marginal product of capital from hiring a third operating room is
   a. 32 surgeries.
   b. 25 surgeries.
   c. 7 surgeries per operating room.
   d. 3 surgeries per operating room.

7. Paul's production function exhibits diminishing returns to capital because
   a. output increases at a diminishing rate as additional units of capital are hired.
   b. Paul cannot perform competently with more than one operating room.
   c. capital, in the form of operating rooms, is very expensive.
   d. output does not increase at a constant rate as additional units of capital are hired.

Use the following table about the production function for Terry's Widget Shoppe to answer the next four questions. Assume labor is the only variable input Terry uses in the production of widgets.

Quantity of labor hired (workers)	Quantity of widgets per month
0	0
1	100
2	250
3	450
4	600
5	700

8. The marginal product of labor from hiring the third worker is
a. 450 widgets per worker.
b. 200 widgets per worker.
c. 150 widgets per worker.
d. 250 widgets per worker.

9. Diminishing returns to labor begins when Terry hires the
a. second worker.   c. fourth worker.
b. third worker.   d. fifth worker.

10. Terry spends $200 a month to rent a building for his company, $600 a month for the capital he employs to produce widgets, and $10 per hour for every unit of labor he employs. Terry's fixed cost per month equals
a. $200.
b. $600.
c. $800.
d. $810.

11. Terry spends $200 a month to rent a building for his company, $600 a month for the capital he employs to produce widgets, and $10 per hour for every unit of labor he employs. Terry distinguishes between his fixed cost and his variable cost by
a. deciding whether he is producing in the short run or the long run.
b. whether the cost varies as his level of production changes.
c. whether the cost exceeds $500.
d. recognizing that capital is always a fixed cost while rent and labor are variable costs.

12. In the short run, as the level of total production for a firm increases, the firm's total product curve
a. increases but at a decreasing rate.
b. increases at an increasing rate.
c. decreases at a decreasing rate.
d. decreases but at an increasing rate.

Use the information in the following table about the production function for Caroline's Ceramics to answer the following question.

Quantity of variable input (units)	Quantity of output (ceramic vases)
0	0
2	100
4	250
6	500
8	700
10	800

13. Caroline's Ceramics' production experiences diminishing returns to labor when Caroline hires

a. the second unit of labor.

b. the fourth unit of labor.

c. the sixth unit of labor.

d. the eighth unit of labor.

14. Larry's Auto Shop's total cost can be expressed by the equation $TC = 50 + 10Q^2$, where Q is the quantity of repairs made by Larry's Auto Shop. Which of the following statements is true for Larry's Auto Shop?

  I. When Larry's Auto Shop produces 0 repairs, its fixed cost equals its total costs.

  II. Larry's Auto Shop's fixed cost equals $50.

  III. Larry's Auto Shop's fixed cost depends on the level of output that is produced.

a. Statement I is true.

b. Statements I and II are true.

c. Statements I and III are true.

d. Statements I, II, and III are true.

15. Larry's Auto Shop's total cost can be expressed by the equation $TC = 50 + 10Q^2$, where Q is the quantity of repairs made by Larry's Auto Shop. Larry's variable cost equals

a. $10 when 1 unit of output is produced, and $40 when 2 units of output are produced.

b. $60 when 1 unit of output is produced, and $90 when 2 units of output are produced.

16. As the level of output increases, the total cost curve for a firm gets

a. steeper due to diminishing returns to the variable input.

b. flatter due to diminishing returns to the variable input.

Use the information in the following table to answer the next four questions. The table provides production function information for Jimmy's Service Shop. Assume Jimmy hires only labor and capital to produce his services. Furthermore, the price of labor is $100 per worker per week and the price of capital is $10 per unit.

Quantity of labor (workers)	Quantity of capital (units)	Quantity of output produced per week (number of services per week)
0	10	0
1	10	200
2	10	400
3	10	600
4	10	700
5	10	750

17. Jimmy's fixed cost of production equals

a. $0.   c. $110.

b. $100.   d. $500.

18. Jimmy's variable cost of production
    a. is constant and equal to $100, given the available information.
    b. varies with the level of output that is produced.
    c. is always greater than his fixed cost.
    d. decreases as the level of production increases due to diminishing marginal returns.

19. Jimmy's total cost of producing 700 units of output is
    a. equal to the sum of his fixed and variable costs of producing this level of output.
    b. $500.
    c. greater than his total cost of producing 600 units of output.
    d. Answers (a), (b), and (c) are all true.

20. Jimmy's marginal cost of producing the seven-hundredth unit of output is equal to
    a. $500 per unit of output.
    b. $400 per unit of output.
    c. $100 per unit of output.
    d. $1 per unit of output.

21. The marginal cost curve is upward sloping as output increases due to
    a. increasing returns to scale.
    b. decreasing returns to scale.
    c. diminishing marginal returns to the variable input.
    d. increasing marginal returns to the variable input.

22. In the short run, a firm's fixed cost _____ while the firm's average fixed cost _____ .
    a. stays constant as output increases; increases as the firm produces higher levels of output
    b. stays constant as output increases; decreases as the firm produces higher levels of output
    c. increases as the firm produces higher levels of output; stays constant as output increases
    d. decreases as the firm produces higher levels of output; stays constant as output increases

23. The spreading effect refers to the
    a. decrease in *AVC* as the firm produces greater levels of output.
    b. decrease in *AFC* as the firm produces greater levels of output.
    c. combined effect on *AVC* and *AFC* of the firm producing higher levels of output.
    d. combined effect on *AVC*, *AFC*, and *MC* of the firm producing higher levels of output.

24. The diminishing returns effect causes the *AVC* to
    a. decline initially as output increases.
    b. decline at all levels of output.
    c. increase eventually as output increases.
    d. increase at all levels of output.

25. At high levels of output for a firm, the spreading effect is
   a. stronger than the diminishing returns effect.
   b. weaker than the diminishing returns effect.

26. At the minimum-cost output
   a. average variable cost must equal marginal cost.
   b. average fixed cost must equal marginal cost.
   c. average total cost must equal marginal cost.
   d. Answers (a), (b), and (c) are all true.

27. The firm's *LRATC* curve illustrates the relationship between output and
   a. average total cost when fixed cost has been chosen to minimize average total cost for each level of output.
   b. marginal cost when fixed cost has been chosen to minimize average total cost for each level of output.
   c. average total cost when variable cost has been chosen to minimize average total cost for each level of output.
   d. average total cost when marginal cost has been chosen to minimize average total cost for each level of output.

28. When the firm's *LRATC* curve is downward sloping over its range of production, this implies that
   a. when all of the firm's inputs are increased proportionately, the firm's level of production will increase, but by a smaller factor than the increase in the firm's inputs.
   b. when all of the firm's inputs are doubled, the firm's level of production will more than double.
   c. when all of the firm's inputs are tripled, the firm's level of production may or may not increase.
   d. the firm is experiencing decreasing returns to scale over this range of production.

29. A firm finds that past a certain level of production its *LRATC* curve is upward sloping. Which of the following is true?
   a. The firm in this range of production experiences decreasing returns to scale.
   b. Increased specialization allows the firm to operate a larger scale of operation.
   c. The set-up costs of entering this industry must be quite high.
   d. Answers (a), (b), and (c) are all true.

30. Which of the following statements is true?
   I. In the short run, a firm can experience increasing, decreasing, or constant returns to scale.
   II. If a firm doubles all of its inputs with the result that its output doubles, then this firm has constant returns to scale.
   III. Decreasing returns to scale are due to coordination and communication problems.
   a. Statements I and II are true.
   b. Statement II is true.
   c. Statements II and III are true.
   d. Statements I, II, and III are true.

■ ANSWER KEY

Answers to Problems and Exercises

1. **a.** In the short run, at least one input is fixed and does not vary as the level of output varies. From the table, we can see that the level of capital remains constant at 10 units as output increases from 0 units to 138 units. In the long run, all inputs are variable.

    b. The fixed input is the input that is held constant as output changes: in this example, it is the capital input. The variable input is labor since the level of labor used changes as the level of production changes.

    c.

    d.

Quantity of labor (workers)	Quantity of output (can openers)	Marginal product of labor $MPL = \Delta Q / \Delta L$ (can openers per worker)
0	0	
		50
1	50	
		30
2	80	
		20
3	100	
		15
4	115	
		10
5	125	
		8
6	133	
		5
7	138	

e. As Harry uses more labor, his total production of can openers increases, but it increases at a diminishing rate. The marginal product of labor describes the addition to total product from hiring an additional worker: for Harry each additional worker adds to the total production of can openers, but each additional worker adds less to total production than did the previous worker.

f.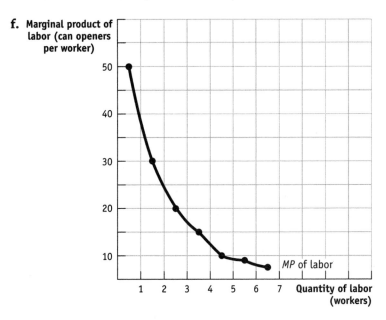

g. When the *MP* of labor curve is downward sloping as you hire additional units of labor, this implies that the production function is subject to diminishing marginal returns to labor.

2. a.

Quantity of labor (workers)	Quantity of capital (units)	Quantity of output (can openers)
0	20	0
1	20	100
2	20	160
3	20	200
4	20	230
5	20	250
6	20	266
7	20	276

b.

An increase in the level of capital causes Harry's total product curve to shift up; at every level of labor used, Harry can now produce a greater amount of output.

c. At every level of labor usage, Harry's marginal product of labor is higher. Each unit of labor now has more capital to work with, which enables each worker to be more productive. Each additional worker can now produce more can openers than was possible with the original level of capital. The following graph illustrates the two *MP* of labor curves based on the different levels of capital.

3. In the short run with at least one input fixed, a firm finds that it can expand its level of production only by hiring additional units of the variable input. But as the firm hires additional units of the variable input, each unit of the variable input has less of the fixed input to work with since the fixed input must be shared. Eventually, the addition to total product produced by the variable input increases at a decreasing rate as more units of the variable input are used. There is no reason to expect diminishing marginal returns if all the inputs can be varied: a firm that can adjust the level of all of its inputs (the long-run situation) may have increasing, decreasing, or constant returns to scale.

4. Malthus did not anticipate the scientific and technological progress in food production that occurred over the past two hundred years. The concept of diminishing marginal returns does not hold in this situation: it is possible, even if the amount of farmland cultivated is unchanged and the amount of labor involved in agricultural production is also unchanged, for production to increase when the available technology improves.

5. a.

Quantity of capital (units)	Quantity of labor (hours of work)	Quantity of haircuts	FC ($)	VC ($)	AFC ($ per unit of output)	AVC ($ per unit of output)	ATC ($ per unit of output)	TC	MC ($ per unit of output)
10	0	0	500	0	—	—	—	500	
									13.3
10	10	15	500	200	33.3	13.3	46.7	700	
									15.4
10	20	28	500	400	17.9	14.3	32.1	900	
									20.0
10	30	38	500	600	13.2	15.8	28.9	1,100	
									33.3
10	40	44	500	800	11.4	18.2	29.5	1,300	
									50.0
10	50	48	500	1,000	10.4	20.8	31.3	1,500	

b. A production function exhibits diminishing marginal returns to labor if, as labor is increased while holding all other inputs constant, the level of total output increases but it increases at a decreasing rate. The marginal product of labor for this production function is summarized in the following table. As you can see from the table, the production function does exhibit diminishing marginal returns to labor.

Quantity of capital (units)	Quantity of labor (hours of work)	Quantity of haircuts	Marginal product of labor (haircuts per hour of work)
10	0	0	
			1.5
10	10	15	
			1.3
10	20	28	
			1
10	30	38	
			0.6
10	40	44	
			0.4
10	50	48	

c.

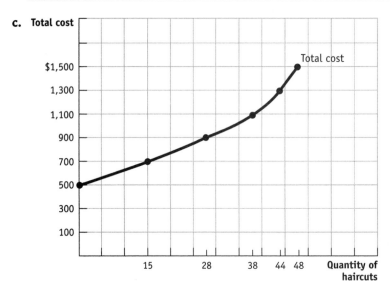

As the quantity of haircuts increases, *TC* increases at an increasing rate due to the diminishing marginal returns to labor.

d. Marginal cost

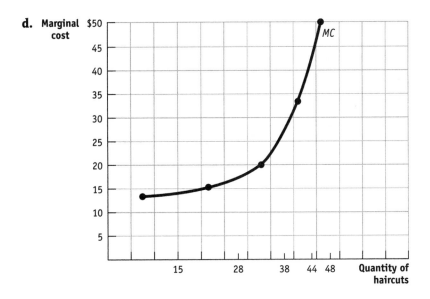

As output gets larger, the effect of diminishing marginal returns to the variable input causes *MC* to increase.

e. Average fixed cost

The shaded area corresponds to the fixed cost of producing 15 haircuts, since *AFC* *Q = FC.*

f.

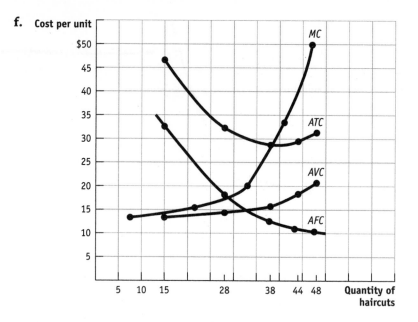

The *ATC* curve intersects the *MC* curve at the minimum point on the *ATC* curve.

6. a. The cost of the one-year lease does not change during the year no matter what level of output the firm produces. This is a fixed cost.

   b. Annual property taxes are set yearly and are not based on the level of production of the firm. This is a fixed cost.

   c. The cost of metal varies as the level of output the firm produces varies. This is a variable cost.

   d. The machine still has a long, useful life and is capable of meeting the production demands of the firm. The cost of this machine does not vary with the level of production. This is a fixed cost.

   e. This is a variable cost since, as the output of cookies increases, the firm finds that it uses more sugar.

7. Marginal cost provides the slope measure of the *TC* curve at a particular level of output: marginal cost at low levels of output may fall as output increases, but eventually as output increases, the marginal cost of producing this output rises. Marginal product is the slope measure of the total product curve at a particular level of variable input usage: marginal product eventually declines as the level of variable input increases due to diminishing marginal returns to the variable input.

8. a.

Quantity of labor (units)	Quantity of capital (units)	Quantity of output	VC ($)	FC ($)	AVC ($ per unit of output)	AFC ($ per unit of output)	ATC ($ per unit of output)	TC ($)	MC ($ per unit of output)
0	5	0	0	10		—	—	10	
									0.50
1	5	10	5	10	0.50	1.00	1.50	15	
									0.63
2	5	18	10	10	0.56	0.56	1.11	20	
									0.83
3	5	24	15	10	0.63	0.42	1.04	25	
									1.25
4	5	28	20	10	0.71	0.36	1.07	30	
									2.50
5	5	30	25	10	0.83	0.33	1.17	35	
									5.00
6	5	31	30	10	0.97	0.32	1.29	40	

b. The price of the variable input is $5 per unit since the variable cost equals $15 when 3 units of labor are hired.

c. The price of the fixed input is $2 per unit since the fixed cost equals $10 when 5 units of capital are hired.

d. The marginal product of the fifth unit of labor equals the change in total output divided by the change in the amount of labor when the firm increases its use of labor from 4 units to 5 units, or (2 units of output)/(1 unit of labor), for a marginal product of 2.

e. The marginal cost of producing the twenty-fourth unit of output is equal to the change in total cost divided by the change in output, or ($5)/(6 units of output), for a marginal cost of $0.83.

9. The spreading effect refers to the ability to spread the fixed cost over all the production of the firm. When the firm produces a few units, the fixed cost is not spread over very many units and the average fixed cost is therefore relatively high; when the firm produces a large number of units, the fixed cost is spread over these units and the average fixed cost is therefore much smaller. This means that the spreading effect is not of great importance when producing a lot of output, but it can have a significant effect at lower levels of production. The diminishing returns effect describes the effect on average variable cost of producing larger amounts of output. To produce larger amounts of output the firm must hire more variable input, but each additional unit of the variable input is less productive than the previous unit, and, therefore, as output increases, average variable cost also increases. The diminishing returns effect gets more pronounced the greater the level of production.

10. a. True. If average total cost is decreasing, this must be because the marginal cost of producing another unit of output is less than the average total cost of producing the current level of output. When an additional unit of output is produced in these circumstances, this causes the average total cost to fall.

   b. False. Marginal cost can be increasing but still be less than average total cost.

c. False. Average fixed cost decreases as output increases, since fixed cost is constant for the firm and does not change as the level of output changes.

d. False. Fixed cost does not change for the firm no matter what level of output they produce.

e. True. As the firm produces more output, it must hire additional units of its variable input, which causes its variable cost to increase.

11. a. In this question, the firm is doubling both inputs (4 units of wood to 8 units of wood, 5 units of labor to 10 units of labor) and the firm finds that this leads to more than double the amount of output (20 chairs to 45 chairs). This firm is experiencing increasing returns to scale, since as the scale or size of operation gets larger, the firm's unit cost of production falls.

b. This firm's *LRATC* curve is downward sloping over this range of output.

c. A 50% increase in the use of inputs would result in the firm using 12 units of wood and 15 units of labor. With a 50% increase in inputs the firm finds that its output increases from 45 chairs to 90 chairs, which is a 100% increase in the level of output. The firm experiences increasing returns to scale over this range of output.

d. This firm's *LRATC* curve is downward sloping over this range of output.

e. The firm changes its wood usage from 12 units of wood to 24 units of wood and its labor usage from 15 units of labor to 30 units of labor. Output changes from 90 chairs to 150 chairs. The increase in output is less than 100%, so this firm experiences decreasing returns to scale over this range of production.

f. This firm's *LRATC* curve is upward sloping over this range of output.

Answers to Chapter Review Questions

1. **Answer c.** This is a definitional statement. Inputs are combined together to produce output, and the production function describes this relationship.

2. **Answer b.** A firm's ability to produce output depends on the level of inputs it uses: this is a definitional statement.

3. **Answer a.** Since one of the inputs is fixed (the quantity of labor), a short-run production function is implied.

4. **Answer a.** The fixed input is the input that does not change in the short run as the level of output changes. Looking at the given table, the quantity of labor is fixed or constant while the quantity of capital varies.

5. **Answer b.** The variable input is the input that varies as the level of output changes. Looking at the given table, the quantity of capital varies.

6. **Answer c.** The marginal product of capital is defined as the change in total output divided by the change in capital, holding all other inputs constant. When Paul increases his number of operating rooms from two to three, his output of surgeries increases from 25 surgeries to 32 surgeries. Paul's marginal product of capital is thus 7 surgeries per operating room.

7. **Answer a.** Diminishing returns to capital occurs when total product increases at a decreasing rate as additional units of capital are hired. Diminishing marginal returns to capital implies that the marginal product of capital declines in value as additional units of capital are hired. Answer (b) is not necessarily correct: Paul finds his 30 hours of labor is more productive when spread across several operating rooms instead of a single operating room. The diminishing marginal returns to capital is due to technology and not the cost of capital—answer (c). Answer (d) is false by virtue of the definition of diminishing marginal returns.

8. **Answer b.** The marginal product of labor is the change in output divided by the change in labor. In this example, labor changes by 1 unit at a time, so we can simply calculate the change in output to find the marginal product of labor. The total product when two workers are hired equals 250 widgets, while the total product when three workers are hired equals 450 widgets; therefore, the marginal product of hiring the third worker is 200 widgets per worker.

9. **Answer c.** Diminishing returns to labor begins when the marginal product of labor falls as the quantity of labor increases. The marginal product of labor for the first worker is 100 widgets per worker; the marginal product of labor for the second worker is 150 widgets per worker; the marginal product of labor for the third worker is 200 widgets per worker; and the marginal product of labor for the fourth worker is 150 widgets per worker. The hiring of the fourth worker increases output, but at a diminishing rate.

10. **Answer c.** Fixed costs are those costs that do not vary as output varies. Terry's fixed costs include his capital costs of $600 a month and his rent of $200 a month: neither of these costs change for Terry no matter what level of output he produces. In contrast, Terry's use of labor varies as he changes his level of production, and when he hires additional labor his variable costs are altered.

11. **Answer b.** There are no fixed costs in the long run, only variable costs; there isn't some dollar amount that exists as a limit to variable costs; and capital or labor can be variable in the short run. What does distinguish variable costs from fixed costs is that variable costs vary as the level of output varies: a firm wishing to produce more of a good in the short run does so by hiring more units of the variable input.

12. **Answer a.** In the short run, the firm has at least one fixed input. To increase its production, it must hire additional units of the variable input, but the addition to total output from hiring an additional unit of the variable input eventually decreases due to the diminishing returns to the variable input. This means that output increases, but at a decreasing rate.

13. **Answer d.** To answer this question, first calculate the marginal product of labor. Recall that the marginal product of labor is the change in total product divided by the change in labor. In this example, labor increases by 2 units at a time, so the change in labor is 2 units of labor. The marginal product of labor of hiring the second unit of labor is thus (100 units of output)/(2 units of labor), or 50 units of output per unit of labor. Once you have calculated the marginal product of labor for each level of labor in the table, you can then determine at what level of labor the marginal product first declines.

14. **Answer b.** Larry's Auto Shop's fixed cost equals his total cost when output is zero, since the firm does not hire any of the variable input if it decides to not produce any output. When Q equals zero, Larry's total cost equals $50, and therefore Larry's fixed cost must equal $50. Fixed cost does not change as the level of output produced by the firm changes.

15. **Answer a.** When output is zero, fixed cost equals total cost and Larry's fixed cost is therefore $50. Larry's variable cost can therefore by expressed as $10Q^2$ since $TC = FC + VC$. When Q equals 1, VC is $10; when Q equals 2, VC is $40.

16. **Answer a.** As the firm produces greater levels of output, its costs increase because it must employ more and more units of the variable input to produce that output. Yet as it employs more of the variable input, it finds that each additional unit of the variable input is less productive than the last unit hired, which therefore leads total cost to increase at an increasing rate.

17. **Answer b.** Jimmy's fixed cost is equal to the number of units of the fixed input he hires times the price of the fixed input. Jimmy hires 10 units of capital, irrespective of his level of production, and so his fixed cost equals $100.

18. **Answer b.** By definition, variable cost for a firm varies as the level of production varies, which eliminates answer (a). Variable cost may or may not be greater than fixed cost. Variable cost increases as the level of output increases due to the diminishing marginal returns to the variable input.

19. **Answer d.** Total cost for producing any level of output can be found by summing variable cost and fixed cost for that level of output. Jimmy's fixed cost equals $100 and his variable cost is $400 when he produces 700 units of output, so Jimmy's total cost of producing 700 units of output is $500. The total cost of producing 600 units of output is

$400. Jimmy's total cost of producing 600 units of output is less than his total cost of producing 700 units of output.

20. **Answer d.** The marginal cost of producing the last unit of output is equal to the change in total cost divided by the change in output. The total cost of producing 700 units is $500 and the total cost of producing 600 units is $400: the change in total cost is $100. The change in output is 100 units. Thus, the marginal cost of producing the seven-hundredth unit of output is $100/(100 units of output), or $1 per unit of output.

21. **Answer c.** As output increases, the marginal cost of producing that level of output also increases because the marginal product of the variable input is falling. This is due to the diminishing marginal returns to the variable input.

22. **Answer b.** FC does not vary as the level of production varies, but average fixed cost declines as output increases since AFC = FC/Q and Q is increasing.

23. **Answer b.** The spreading effect refers to the idea that fixed costs are constant at all short-run levels of output. This implies that the AFC will decline as output increases, since those constant fixed costs will be spread over a larger number of units of output. The spreading effect does not have any impact on the AVC or the MC.

24. **Answer c.** The diminishing returns effect refers to the idea that as the firm increases its production in the short run it must hire additional units of the variable input, but that as the firm's usage of the variable input increases it finds that additional units of the variable input are less productive than the preceding unit. This means that the firm's AVC eventually rises due to the variable cost of production increasing faster than the increase in the level of output.

25. **Answer b.** At high levels of output, the firm's ATC curve increases, indicating that the spreading effect, which causes AFC to fall as output increases, is not as strong as the diminishing returns effect, which causes AVC to rise as output increases.

26. **Answer c.** At the minimum-cost output, average total cost equals marginal cost since the minimum-cost output is the level of output at which average total cost is minimized. At outputs lower than the minimum-cost output, average total cost is falling as output increases, which implies that the marginal cost of producing an additional unit of output is less than the average total cost of producing that output. At outputs greater than the minimum-cost output, average total cost is rising as output increases, which implies that the marginal cost of producing an additional unit of output is greater than the average total cost of producing that output. The average variable cost is not at its minimum point at the minimum-cost output, and the average fixed cost does not have a minimum point since it declines as the level of output increases.

27. **Answer a.** This is the definition of the LRATC curve, which identifies the lowest average total cost of production for every level of output, assuming that the firm has the freedom to set its fixed input at the optimal level for each level of output.

28. **Answer b.** As the firm increases its production the firm's cost rises, but if the LRATC curve is downward sloping this implies that the increase in output must be proportionately greater than the increase in total cost. In this range of output, the firm has increasing returns to scale.

29. **Answer a.** When a firm's LRATC curve is upward sloping this means that increasing the firm's level of production will raise the average total cost of producing the good, and the firm does not benefit from getting larger. In this case the firm has decreasing returns to scale. Decreasing returns to scale arise primarily because of problems of coordination and communication. When a firm has high set-up costs, this implies that the firm is likely to have increasing returns to scale and decreasing average total cost over a large range of outputs. The firm in this example has increasing average total cost.

30. **Answer c.** Statement II is the definition of constant returns to scale, and statement III identifies the primary reasons for the decreasing returns to scale. Returns to scale is a long-run phenomenon and thus statement I, with its focus on the short run, is incorrect.

chapter 7

Perfect Competition and the Supply Curve

Summary

This chapter develops the model of perfect competition and then uses this model to discuss a firm's selection of the profit-maximizing level of output. This model is also used to explore the short-run and long-run production decisions of the firm where these decisions are based on the firm's profitability. The chapter also explores the factors that determine the short-run and long-run industry supply curve for an industry.

Chapter Objectives

Objective #1. A perfectly competitive industry is an industry in which both the producers and consumers in that industry are price-takers. A price-taking producer is one whose actions cannot affect the market price of the good sold. A price-taking firm can sell as many units of the good as it would like at the prevailing market price. A price-taking consumer is a consumer who cannot influence the market price of the good by his or her actions. The market price is therefore unaffected by the actions of either individual producers or individual consumers.

- For an industry to be perfectly competitive there must be many producers in that industry, and no one of these producers can have a large market share of the industry's output.

- For an industry to be perfectly competitive consumers must regard the products produced in that market as being equivalent. The product sold in a perfectly competitive industry is a standardized product or commodity, and consumers must view each producer's product as a perfect substitute for any other producer's product.

- Most perfectly competitive industries also have easy entry of new firms into the industry and exit of existing firms from the industry in the long run. This is referred to as free entry and exit.

Objective #2. A firm's total revenue (*TR*) can be calculated by multiplying the level of production times the market price. The firm can then compare its total revenue with its total cost (*TC*) to find the level of output at which it maximizes profit. The profit-maximizing level of output for the firm is the level of output at which total revenue minus total cost results in the greatest positive number.

[handwritten: profit max when output TR - TC = most]

Objective #3. Marginal revenue (*MR*) is the change in total revenue divided by the change in output from selling another unit of the good. For a perfectly competitive firm, marginal revenue is constant and equals the market price, since the addition to total revenue the firm receives from selling another unit of the good equals the market price the firm receives for the good. Thus, the *MR* curve for a firm can be represented as a horizontal line intersecting the price axis at the market price. Figure 7.1 represents this concept: the firm is depicted in the left-hand graph, and the industry or the entire market for the good is represented in the right-hand graph. The market demand and market supply curves in the right-hand graph determine the market price (*P*) and market quantity (*Q*). The firm accepts this price since it is a price-taking firm. The horizontal line in the left-hand figure represents the marginal revenue the firm receives at any level of output. The firm's *MR* curve is also the firm's demand curve (*d*) since it can sell as many units of the good as it wishes to at the prevailing market price.

[handwritten margin: MR = Price in PC]

Figure 7.1

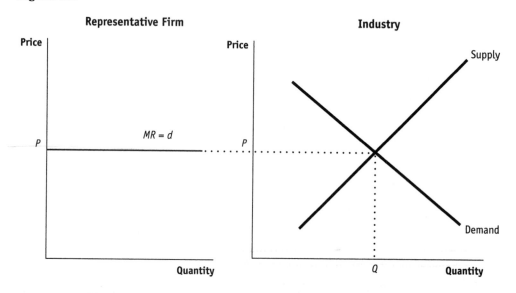

Objective #4. Marginal analysis can be used to compute the profit-maximizing level of output. To do this analysis, marginal revenue and marginal cost must be calculated. Recall that marginal cost (*MC*) is the change in total cost divided by the change in output.

[handwritten margin: MR = MC]

- The profit-maximizing level of output corresponds to that level of output at which marginal revenue equals marginal cost. Marginal revenue measures the addition to total revenue from selling one more unit of the good, while marginal cost measures the addition to total cost from producing one more unit of the good. When marginal revenue is greater than marginal cost the firm's benefit from producing this last unit of output is greater than the cost of producing this last unit: the firm should expand output to include this unit of production. When marginal revenue is less than marginal cost the firm's benefit from producing another unit of output is less than the cost of producing this last unit: the firm should not expand output to include this additional unit of production. It is only when marginal revenue equals marginal cost for the last unit of output produced that the firm earns its highest level of profit.

- The producer's optimal output rule states that profit is maximized by producing that level of output at which marginal revenue equals marginal cost for the last unit produced. That is, the firm should produce that level of output where $MR = MC$. This can be restated as: the firm's profit-maximizing level of output is where $P = MC$, since for the perfectly competitive firm P equals MR. Figure 7.2 illustrates the profit-maximizing level of output (q) for a perfectly competitive firm.

Figure 7.2

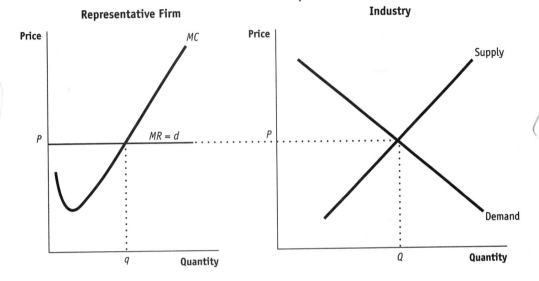

Objective #5. The profit-maximization rule identifies the level of output that results in maximizing the firm's profit, but it does not tell the producer whether they should produce at all. To answer this question, the firm needs to look at whether it is profitable or unprofitable to produce. The decision to produce or not is based on the firm's economic profit and not its accounting profit. The cost curves that the firm uses to make its production decisions are cost curves that include all costs, implicit and explicit. Given the firm's cost curves, whether it is profitable to produce depends on whether the market price of the good is more or less than the firm's average total cost at that level of production.

- The firm makes a profit whenever its total revenue is greater than its total cost. The firm breaks even whenever its total revenue is equal to its total cost. The firm incurs a loss whenever its total revenue is less than its total cost.

- The firm's profitability can also be expressed in terms of averages. Profit = $TR - TC$, and if both sides of this equation are divided by output (Q), this results in profit/Q = TR/Q $- TC/Q$. TR/Q is average revenue, which for a perfectly competitive firm is the market price (P) since the average price for the price-taking firm exactly equals the market-determined price. TC/Q is equal to the average total cost (ATC) of producing the level of output. This equation provides a means for comparing the price of the good to the average total cost at a given level of production; when the price is greater than the average total cost, the firm earns a positive profit; when the price is equal to the average total cost, the firm breaks even; and when the price is less than the average total cost, the firm incurs a loss. Figure 7.3 illustrates three situations: a firm earning a positive economic profit ($P > ATC$), a firm earning zero economic profit ($P = ATC$), and a firm earning negative economic profit ($P < ATC$).

Figure 7.3

find q → go up

Break even P is where MC = ATC

- The firm breaks even, or earns a zero economic profit, if the market price is equal to the minimum of the firm's average total cost; the firm earns a negative profit if the price is less than the minimum of the firm's average total cost; and the firm earns a positive profit if the price is greater than the minimum of the firm's average total cost. Figure 7.3 illustrates these three possibilities and the resultant profit situation for the firm. The minimum point of the average total cost is called the break-even price because it identifies the price at which the firm breaks even (earns a zero economic profit).

Objective #6.   In the short run, a perfectly competitive firm incurs its fixed costs whether or not it produces, while it can reduce its variable costs by deciding not to produce. The firm would therefore want to base its production decision in the short run on whether it can cover its variable cost of production: when the firm's revenues do not cover all of its variable cost of production, then the firm will lose money on its fixed cost as well as some of its variable cost; when the firm's revenues cover all of its variable cost of production, then the firm will lose money only on that part of its fixed cost that the remaining revenue does not cover. In the short run, the firm will be willing to produce only if its revenue is sufficient to cover all of its variable cost of production. This concept can be summarized by the following guidelines:

- In the short run, when the market price is less than the minimum point of the firm's average variable cost (AVC) curve, then the firm should shut down and produce 0 units of output. Its short-run costs will therefore equal its fixed cost and the firm will minimize its losses.

- In the short run, when the market price is greater than or equal to the minimum point of the firm's AVC but is less than the minimum point of the ATC, then the firm should produce the level of output at which P = MC. This level of output will result in negative economic profits in the short run, but these negative profits will be equal to or less than the firm's fixed cost.

- Figure 7.4 illustrates the short-run production decisions for these two possibilities.

Figure 7.4

min AVC = shutdown price
min ATC = break even

> Since *P* is less than the minimum point of *AVC*, this firm should not produce in the short run. Its economic profits in the short run will equal the negative of its fixed costs.

produce where
P = MC

> Since *P* is greater than the minimum point of *AVC*, this firm should produce *q* in the short run, where *P = MC*. This firm will earn negative economic profits (the shaded area), but these negative profits will be less than the firm's fixed costs.

- To summarize, when price is between the minimum point of the *AVC* and the minimum point of the *ATC*, the firm will lose money (earn a negative economic profit) in the short run, but it will lose less money by producing in the short run than it would lose if it decided to shut down in the short run. This decision is similar to the decision to ignore sunk costs: the firm's fixed cost cannot be changed in the short run, so they should be ignored by the firm when the firm makes its short-run production decision.

Objective #7. The firm's short-run supply curve corresponds to the firm's *MC* curve when the market price is equal to or above the shut-down price (the minimum point of the *AVC* curve). The firm's short-run supply curve for market prices less than the shut-down price is the vertical axis: the firm will produce 0 units of output when the market price is less than the shut-down price.

Objective #8. In the long run, a firm can exit the industry or a new firm can enter the industry. Firms will exit the industry if the market price is consistently less than the break-even price, or the minimum point of the firm's *ATC* curve. In other words, firms will exit the industry in the long run if they are consistently making negative economic profit in the short run. Firms will enter the industry if the market price is consistently greater than the break-even price. That is, firms will enter the industry in the long run if existing firms are consistently making positive economic profit in the short run.

Objective #9. The short-run industry supply curve shows the quantity that producers supply at each price, holding the number of producers constant at a given level.

Objective #10. The long-run market equilibrium corresponds to the situation in which the quantity supplied equals the quantity demanded, given that sufficient time has elapsed for producers to either enter or exit the industry. In the long-run market equilibrium, all existing producers and all potential producers have fully adjusted to their optimal long-run choices, and therefore there is no incentive for producers to either exit or enter the industry. Thus, the long-run industry supply curve shows the quantity supplied by the industry at each price, given that producers have had time to enter or exit the industry.

- In an industry that has constant costs across the industry, the long-run industry supply curve is perfectly elastic. The long-run industry supply curve can be drawn as a horizontal line at the break-even price.

- In an industry that has increasing costs across the industry, the long-run industry supply curve is upward sloping. This reflects the fact that some input is in limited supply, and as the industry expands, this results in higher prices for that input and therefore higher costs for the firms producing in that industry.

- Regardless of whether the industry is a constant-cost or increasing-cost industry, the long-run industry supply curve is flatter than the short-run industry supply curve. Entry of new firms in the long run results in greater levels of output and therefore lower prices than in the short run, and the exit of existing firms in the long run results in lower levels of output and therefore higher prices than in the short run.

Objective #11. Perfect competition leads to three conclusions about the cost of production and efficiency.

- When the perfectly competitive industry is in equilibrium, the value of marginal cost is the same for all firms. Since firms produce that output where marginal cost equals the market price, and since all firms are price-takers, this implies that all firms must have the same marginal cost value in equilibrium.

- In the long run, all firms in a perfectly competitive industry earn zero economic profit due to free entry and exit. The existence of positive economic profits in the short run acts as an incentive for new firms to enter the industry. The existence of negative economic profits in the short run acts as an incentive for existing firms to exit the industry. This entry and exit continues until economic profits for all firms in the industry equal zero.

- The long-run market equilibrium in a perfectly competitive industry is efficient because there are no mutually beneficial transactions that are not exploited. In the long-run equilibrium in a perfectly competitive industry, costs are minimized and no resources are wasted.

Key Terms

price-taking producer a producer whose actions have no effect on the market price of the good or service it sells.

price-taking consumer a consumer whose actions have no effect on the market price of the good or service he or she buys.

perfectly competitive market a market in which all participants are price-takers.

perfectly competitive industry an industry in which all producers are price-takers.

Notes

Key Terms *(continued)*

market share the fraction of the total industry output accounted for by a given producer's output.

standardized product output of different producers regarded by consumers as the same good; also referred to as a *commodity*.

commodity output of different producers regarded by consumers as the same good; also referred to as a *standardized product*.

free entry and exit describes an industry that potential producers can easily enter or current producers can leave.

marginal benefit the additional benefit derived from producing one more unit of that good or service.

principle of marginal analysis the optimal amount of an activity is the quantity at which marginal benefit equals marginal cost.

marginal revenue the change in *total revenue* generated by an additional unit of output.

optimal output rule profit is maximized by producing the quantity of output at which the *marginal revenue* of the last unit produced is equal to its *marginal cost*.

price-taking firm's optimal output rule the profit of a price-taking firm is maximized by producing the quantity of output at which the market price is equal to the *marginal cost* of the last unit produced.

marginal revenue curve a graphical representation showing how *marginal revenue* varies as output varies.

economic profit the profit equal to revenue minus the opportunity cost of resources used.

explicit cost a cost that requires an outlay of money.

implicit cost a cost that does not require an outlay of money; it is measured by the value, in dollar terms, of benefits that are forgone.

accounting profit a profit equal to revenue minus explicit costs. It is usually larger than economic profit.

break-even price the market price at which a firm earns zero profits.

shut-down price the price at which a firm ceases production in the short run because the market price has fallen below the minimum *average variable cost*.

short-run individual supply curve a graphical representation that shows how an individual producer's profit-maximizing output quantity depends on the market price, taking *fixed cost* as given.

industry supply curve a graphical representation that shows the relationship between the price of a good and the total output of the industry for that good.

short-run industry supply curve a graphical representation that shows how the *quantity supplied* by an industry depends on the market price, given a fixed number of producers.

Key Terms (continued)

short-run market equilibrium an economic balance that results when the *quantity supplied* equals the *quantity demanded*, taking the number of producers as given.

long-run market equilibrium an economic balance in which, given sufficient time for producers to enter or exit an industry, the *quantity supplied* equals the *quantity demanded*.

long-run industry supply curve a graphical representation that shows how *quantity supplied* responds to price once producers have had time to enter or exit the industry.

■ AFTER YOU READ THE CHAPTER

Tips

Tip #1. This chapter advances the use of cost concepts in analyzing firm behavior. You may find it helpful to work with the graphs depicting the short-run and long-run economic behavior of the perfectly competitive market: these graphs can serve as a roadmap for directing your analyses of how a firm responds to economic events. Students often find that a quick sketch of a representative firm and the industry provides insight into solving a challenging problem.

- Figure 7.5 illustrates an example of this type of quick sketch for a perfectly competitive industry in the short run. In this example, the firm is earning a negative economic profit since the price the good is sold for is less than the average total cost of producing the good. Here's the analysis for this sketch: the industry demand and supply curves determine the equilibrium price (P) in the market and the equilibrium market quantity (Q). Firms are price-takers, so they will sell their output at P and their MR curve is a horizontal line drawn at that price. Firms will select their profit-maximizing level of output (q for the representative firm in our sketch) by producing the quantity at which $MR = MC$, or where $P = MC$. The firm can then calculate its profit by comparing its P to its ATC at the level of production that was chosen. In this example $P < ATC$, so the firm must be making negative economic profit. The shaded area in the graph represents this negative economic profit.

Figure 7.5

- Figure 7.5 could be redrawn to illustrate a short-run equilibrium where the representative firm earns positive economic profit, or it could be redrawn so that the representative firm earns zero economic profit. These three short-run scenarios are important for you to be able to construct and understand: being able to construct the graph and read the graph is vital for your ability to understand this material.

- Figure 7.6 provides a sketch of the long-run equilibrium in a perfectly competitive industry. (This is also the same sketch for a short-run situation where the representative firm earns zero economic profit.) In this example, the firm is earning a zero economic profit because the price the good is sold for is equal to the average total cost of producing the good. Here's the analysis for this sketch: the industry demand and supply curves determine the equilibrium price (P) in the market and the equilibrium market quantity (Q). Firms are price-takers, so they will sell their output at P, and their MR curve is a horizontal line drawn at that price. Firms will select their profit-maximizing level of output (q for the representative firm in our sketch) by producing the quantity at which $MR = MC$, or where $P = MC$. The firm can then calculate its profit by comparing its P to its ATC at the level of production that was chosen. In this example, $P = ATC$, so the firm must be making zero economic profit.

Figure 7.6

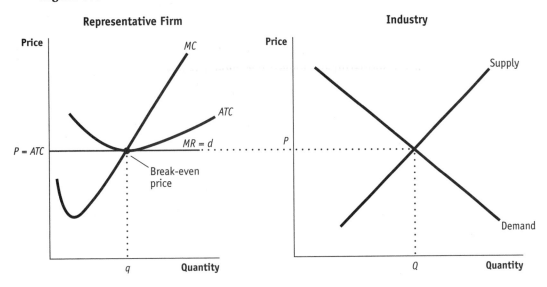

Tip #2. In the short run in a perfectly competitive industry, there is no entry or exit of firms. Thus, positive or negative economic profits can persist in the short run. However, in the long run, there is entry and exit. It is important to understand how this impacts the short-run situation for a perfectly competitive industry.

- Figure 7.7 analyzes the effect of the exit of firms in the long run. Here's the analysis: the representative firm is initially producing q and selling this output at P, resulting in the firm earning negative economic profit in the short run (this is the scenario we had for Figure 7.5). In the long run, some of the existing firms exit the industry due to these negative economic profits, and this causes the market supply curve to shift to the left, which causes the market price to rise to P_2 and the market quantity to fall to Q_2. The representative firm that remains in the industry now faces a higher price for its output and therefore a new MR curve (MR_2). The firm will select its profit-maximizing output by equating MR_2 to MC: the firm will produce q_2 units of the good. The firm will earn zero economic profit, since in the long run the industry will have firms exit until all remaining firms produce at their break-even price. Notice that the firms that remain in the industry produce a higher level of output than they did initially (q_2 versus q), while the overall industry production of the good has fallen (Q_2 versus Q) due to firms exiting the industry. It is important to be able to construct these graphs and make the logical arguments implied by them. Make sure you study and work through these graphs until they are very familiar to you.

Figure 7.7

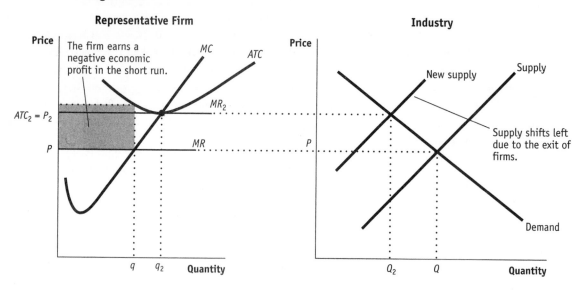

• Figure 7.8 is a graph that represents the long-run equilibrium adjustment when the representative firm earns a positive economic profit in the short run, thereby resulting in the entry of new firms in the long run. Here's the analysis: the representative firm is initially producing q and selling this output at P, resulting in the firm earning positive economic profit in the short run. In the long run, some new firms enter the industry due to these positive economic profits, causing the market supply curve to shift to the right, which causes the market price to fall to P_2 and the market quantity to rise to Q_2. The representative firm in the industry now faces a lower price for its output and therefore a new MR curve (MR_2). The firm will select its profit-maximizing output by equating MR_2 to MC: the firm will produce q_2 units of the good. The firm will earn zero economic profit, since in the long run the industry will have firms enter until all firms in the industry produce at their break-even price. Notice that the firms in the industry produce a lower level of output than they did initially (q_2 versus q), while the overall industry production of the good has risen (Q_2 versus Q) due to firms entering the industry. It is important to be able to construct these graphs and make the logical arguments implied by them. Make sure you study and work through these graphs until they are very familiar to you.

Figure 7.8

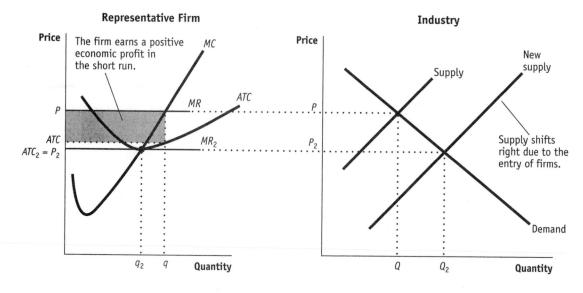

Tip #3. This chapter relies again on marginal analysis, which is used by the firm to determine the profit-maximizing level of output. The firm bases its production decision on the addition to total revenue it gets from selling one more unit of the good (*MR*) versus the addition to total cost of producing one more unit of the good (*MC*). By this point in your study of economics, the concept of marginal analysis should be very familiar to you and something that you naturally consider when analyzing a situation or problem.

Tip #4. The profitability conditions for a perfectly competitive firm can be summarized as follows:

- When *P* > minimum *ATC* or the break-even price, the firm earns a positive economic profit in the short run and firms enter the industry in the long run.

- When *P* = minimum *ATC* or the break-even price, the firm earns zero economic profit in the short run and firms do not enter or exit the industry in the long run.

- When *P* < minimum *ATC* or the break-even price, the firm earns a negative economic profit in the short run and firms exit the industry in the long run.

Tip #5. The production conditions for a perfectly competitive firm can be summarized as follows:

- When *P* > minimum *AVC* or the shut-down price, the firm produces in the short run. If *P* > minimum *ATC*, the firm is covering all of its variable cost as well as its fixed cost of production. If *P* < minimum *ATC* but is still above the minimum *AVC*, the firm is covering all of its variable cost and part of its fixed cost.

- When *P* = minimum *AVC* or the shut-down price, the firm is indifferent between producing in the short run and shutting down in the short run. The firm's revenue is just enough to cover its variable cost of production. The firm's profit is thus equal to the negative of its fixed cost.

- When *P* < minimum *AVC* or the shut-down price, the firm shuts down production in the short run since it cannot cover its variable cost of production. The firm's profit when it produces 0 units of output in the short run is equal to the negative of its fixed cost.

WORKED PROBLEMS

1. Sally and Joe are local businesspeople who supply computer software design services to their community as well as to other customers located throughout the world. Sally and Joe are well aware that their firms are just two of many, many firms that offer similar services. Currently, Sally's and Joe's firms have revenues of $10 million a year and operating costs of $5 million. Sally and Joe both estimate that if they used their time to work for someone else, they could each earn an annual salary of $250,000. Furthermore, Sally and Joe both have $2 million apiece of their own money invested in their firms; if they were to sell their firms, they could invest this money, with each earning 10% profit a year. Sally and Joe want to calculate their accounting profit and their economic profit. They then want to make a prediction about their firms' future prospects with regard to economic profitability. Can you help them out? Assume that Sally's and Joe's firms are identical and assume that depreciation is equal to zero.

STEP 1: Sally and Joe want information about their accounting profit and their economic profit. This requires that you distinguish between explicit costs and implicit costs.

Review the section "Production and Profits" on pages 213–224.

Accounting profits include only explicit costs: recall that explicit costs are those costs that involve the actual laying out of money. Accounting profit is equal to the firm's revenues minus its explicit costs and depreciation. Since this example assumes that depreciation is equal to zero, accounting profits for Sally or Joe will equal $10 million in revenue minus $5 million in operating costs, or an accounting profit of $5 million for the year. Economic profit is equal to the firm's revenues minus its opportunity cost of production. The opportunity cost of production will include the explicit as well as the implicit costs. In this example, Sally could earn $250,000 if she worked for someone else: she foregoes this income when she decides to operate her own company. In addition, she could take her $2 million that is currently invested in the company and, instead of operating her company, invest it and earn $200,000 a year in interest. Thus, Sally's opportunity cost of having her own business is $450,000 a year. Joe has identical opportunity costs. Sally's economic profit from running her business is equal to $10 million – ($5 million + $450,000), or $4,550,000 a year.

STEP 2: Make a prediction about the profitability of Sally's and Joe's firms in the future. This requires you first to determine if their firms are perfectly competitive and then to make a prediction as to whether you expect entry or exit into the computer software industry in the future.

Review the section "Production and Profits" on pages 213–224 and the section "The Industry Supply Curve" on pages 224–230.

Perfect competition requires that no individual producer have a large market share. In the case of Sally and Joe, this is true. Perfect competition also requires that the product being produced in the industry is a standardized product: one could argue that the software produced by Sally and Joe is not a standardized product, but that the actual product that their firms are providing is computer services to generate needed software. There are many firms in the world that can potentially offer this type of service to potential customers. The industry in which Sally and Joe operate seems to meet the criteria necessary to be characterized as a perfectly competitive industry.

Perfectly competitive industries have free entry and exit. This means that new firms can enter the industry easily and that existing firms can exit the industry. When there are positive economic profits in a perfectly competitive industry, new firms will enter the industry and price will fall. Price will continue to fall until economic profits for firms in the industry are equal to zero. Since Sally and Joe are currently earning positive economic profits, new firms will enter the industry and Sally's and Joe's economic profits will fall.

2. The following figure shows three curves, *MC*, *ATC*, and *AVC*: they are for the firm in a perfectly competitive market, where all firms in this industry have identical cost curves. Use the information given in the figure to answer the following questions. Identify what the shut-down price for this firm is in the short run and, if the firm operates at its shut-down price, how many units of output the firm will produce. Identify what the break-even price for this firm is in the short run, and identify the level of output the firm will price if it operates at its break-even price. Identify the market price at which you know with certainty that this firm will exit the industry. If there are no changes in this firm's costs, what is the long-run equilibrium market price in this industry? What must be

true for the firm in order for a particular market price to be the long-run equilibrium price?

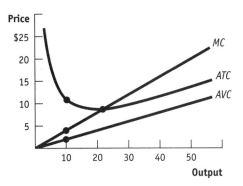

STEP 1: Identify on the preceding graph where the shut-down and the break-even prices are for the firm. At both points identify the level of output that the firm will choose to produce.

Review the section "Production and Profits" on pages 213–224.

The shut-down price corresponds to the minimum point on the firm's average variable cost curve. In this example, the firm's average variable cost is not a U-shaped curve. Its minimum point occurs when output is at zero and average variable cost is equal to $0 per unit of output. The firm will continue to produce in the short run until price is equal to $0 per unit of output since at any other price the firm will receive enough revenue to cover its variable costs of production. As long as price is greater than $0, the firm will choose to produce in the short run: it will choose its level of production by setting the market price (or marginal revenue) equal to its marginal cost curve, and then it will produce the level of output associated with this point.

The break-even price corresponds to the minimum point on the firm's average total cost curve. In this example, the break-even price is when price is equal to $8 per unit and the firm is producing 20 units of output. When the market price is equal to $8, then the firm will equate its marginal revenue (which is equal to the market price, or in this case $8) to its marginal cost: it will produce 20 units and make zero economic profit since its total revenue will exactly equal its total cost of production.

STEP 2: Identify the market price at which you know this firm will exit the industry in the short run.

Review the section "Production and Profits" on pages 213–224, and Figure 7-4 on page 220.

The firm will exit the industry whenever the market price falls to a level at which the firm can no longer earn sufficient revenue to cover all of its variable costs of production. In this example, the firm will have enough revenue to cover its variable costs of production at any price that is greater than zero. So, the firm will not choose to exit the industry unless price falls to zero.

STEP 3: Identify the long-run equilibrium price for this firm and then discuss what must be true for this firm to be at its long-run equilibrium price.

Review the sections "Production and Profits" on pages 213–224 and "The Industry Supply Curve" on pages 224–230, and Figure 7-6 on page 226.

For the firm to be at its long-run equilibrium price, it must be earning revenues that exactly equal its economic costs. This will occur only when it produces that level of output associated with the minimum point of its average total cost curve and then sells that output at the price associated with this point. At this point, its total revenue (price times quantity) will exactly equal its costs (average total cost times quantity), since the market price will be equal to the average total cost of producing that level of output.

3. Suppose that the following graphs illustrate both the market for gadgets and a representative firm's cost curves in this market. Furthermore, suppose this market is a perfectly competitive market with constant costs. From the graphs, identify whether this is a long-run or short-run equilibrium. Then, determine the firm's level of production in the short run and its level of short-run profits. What do you expect will happen to price, market quantity, the representative firm's level of production, and profits in the long run? Explain how this market will adjust in the long run. Finally, draw the short-run equilibrium situation and the long-run equilibrium situation on two different graphs. On these graphs, label the market price, market quantity, firm level of production, and area of profit if there is a profit.

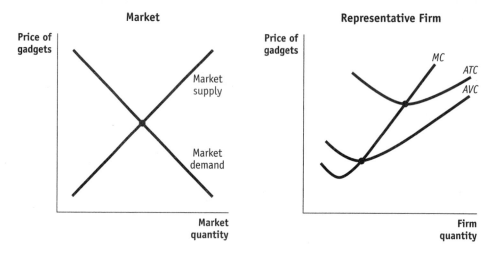

STEP 1: Determine whether the preceding graphs represent a long-run or short-run equilibrium.

Review the sections "Production and Profits" on pages 213–224 and "The Industry Supply Curve" on pages 224–230.

These graphs represent a short-run equilibrium since the market price, P_1, is less than the minimum point of the average cost curve. This indicates that the price per unit is less than the cost per unit: the firm is earning negative economic profits. Since in the long run, perfectly competitive firms earn zero economic profits, we know that these graphs are not depicting a long-run equilibrium in this market.

STEP 2: Determine the firm's level of production and profit in the short run.

Review the section "Production and Profits" on pages 213–224.

In the short run, the firm will produce that quantity at which its marginal revenue curve intersects its marginal cost curve. For the firm, the marginal revenue curve is equal to the market price. The firm will sell the good for the market price and earn total revenue equal to the market price times its level of output. The firm's total cost will be equal to its average total cost of production times its level of production. For this firm, its total cost is greater than its total revenue in the short run: the firm will earn negative economic profit in the short run.

STEP 3: Determine what will happen to price, market quantity, the firm's level of production, and the profits of the firm in the long run.

Review the section "The Industry Supply Curve" on pages 224–230, and Figure 7-7 on page 227.

In the long run, a firm in a perfectly competitive industry will earn zero economic profit. In this case, this will be the result of the exiting of firms from the industry. As firms exit the industry, the market supply curve shifts to the left until the market equilibrium price is just equal to the firm's break-even price. The firm's break-even price is the price that intersects the minimum point on the firm's average total cost curve. Market price will rise, market quantity will decrease, the level of production for the firms remaining in the industry will increase, and profits will equal zero.

STEP 4: Provide an explanation of the long-run equilibrium process.

Review the section "The Industry Supply Curve" on pages 224–230, and Figure 7-7 on page 227.

In the long run, firms will exit the industry due to the presence of short-run negative profits. This exit will shift the market supply curve to the left, resulting in an increase in the equilibrium market price and a decrease in the equilibrium market quantity. This entry will occur until a representative firm in the industry is earning zero profit.

STEP 5: Provide a graph of the short-run equilibrium in this market. In this graph, label the market price, market quantity, firm level of production, and area of profit, if there is a profit.

Review the section "Production and Profits" on pages 213–224, and Figure 7-3 on page 218.

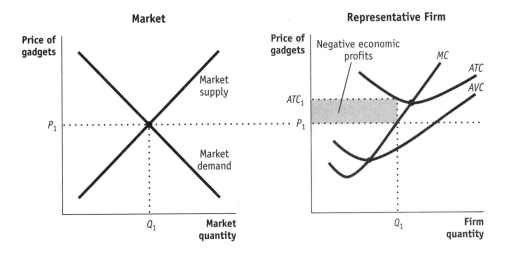

STEP 6: Provide a graph of the long-run equilibrium in this market. In this graph, label the market price, market quantity, firm level of production, and area of profit if there is a profit.

Review the section "The Industry Supply Curve" on pages 224–230, and Figure 7-6 on page 226.

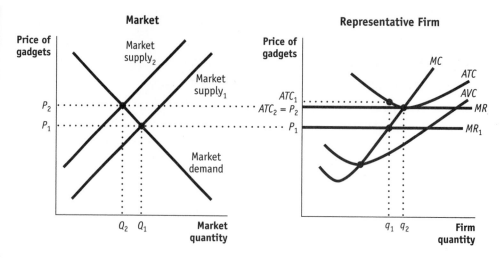

4.   A perfectly competitive market structure is characterized by having many producers, and none of these producers has a large market share. In addition, this
type of market is characterized by its standardized product. Explain why these two
characteristics are necessary for a market to be considered perfectly competitive.

STEP 1: Start by considering the impact on a market when that market has just
a few firms or at least one firm that has significant market share. How would
either of these events affect the market?

Review the section "Production and Profits" on pages 213–224.

If there were just a few firms in a market, then it is likely that each firm would be
very aware of what the other firms were doing in the market. With just a few firms
in the market, it is likely that any action taken by one of the firms would influence
market prices and therefore significantly alter the overall amount of the good supplied in the market. Similarly, if there was a single firm with significant market share
in an industry with many firms, this single firm could still influence market price
and thereby affect the market quantity of the good. In a market with many firms,
none of which has significant market share, all firms will be price-takers: each firm
will sell its output at the market-determined price.

STEP 2: Why is a standardized product a necessary condition for a perfectly
competitive industry?

Review the section "Production and Profits" on pages 213–224.

With a standardized product, consumers view the good as the same no matter which
producer provides the good. Thus, consumers will be willing to pay only the market
price for the good since each producer's product is a perfect substitute for every other
producer's product.

5.   Perfectly competitive firms maximize their profit when they produce that output at which their marginal revenue is equal to their marginal cost. Explain
verbally why firms realize their greatest profit when they produce this particular quantity.

STEP 1: Start by reviewing what marginal revenue means for the firm.

Review the section "Production and Profits" on pages 213–224.

Marginal revenue is the addition to total revenue that a firm earns when it sells an
additional unit of output. Marginal revenue can be calculated by looking at the
change in total revenue that occurs when the firm sells one more unit of the good.

Firms make their production decisions by looking at how producing and selling an additional unit of the good changes their cost and their revenues.

STEP 2: Now, review what marginal cost means for the firm.

Review the section "Production and Profits" on pages 213–224.

Marginal cost is the addition to total cost that a firm incurs when it produces an additional unit of output. Marginal cost can be calculated by looking at the change in total cost that occurs when the firm produces one more unit of the good. Firms make their production decisions by looking at how producing and selling an additional unit of the good changes their cost and their revenues.

STEP 3: Put the two concepts developed in Steps 1 and 2 together to create an explanation for why producing that quantity at which marginal cost equals marginal revenue results in maximum profit for the firm.

Review the section "Production and Profits" on pages 213–224.

By producing that level of output at which marginal cost equals marginal revenue, firms are selecting that level of output at which the addition to total cost from producing one more unit of the good equals the addition to total revenue from selling one more unit of the good. Any other level of output will not maximize profit. To see this, consider what happens if the firm produces that level of output at which marginal revenue is greater than marginal cost: if the firm were to produce an additional unit of the product and sell that unit, it would add more to its total revenue than it would add to its total cost. The firm realizes that, if marginal revenue is greater than marginal cost at its current level of output, then the firm should increase its level of production. If the firm produces that level of output at which marginal cost is greater than marginal revenue, then it is clearly producing too many units of the good. By reducing its level of production, it can enhance its profitability.

Problems and Exercises

1. What does it mean to be a price-taking firm? What does it mean to be a price-taking consumer? What is the relationship between market share and price-taking?

2. The model of perfect competition is based on two necessary conditions and a third condition that is often present as well. Identify each of these conditions and then briefly discuss their importance in the model.

3. The following table provides information about Sarah's Doughnut Shoppe, a small firm operating in a perfectly competitive industry. Use this information to answer this set of questions.

TR = Q · P

Quantity of doughnuts	Total revenue	Total cost	Profit
100	$ 200	$250	−50
200	400	360	40
300	600	530	70
400	800	725	75
500	1,000	950	50

a. What is the market price for a doughnut?

$2

b. Fill in the profit column of the table. At what level of output does Sarah's Doughnut Shoppe maximize its profits?

~~When Output = 200~~   When output = 400

c. Calculate Sarah's Doughnut Shoppe's marginal cost and marginal revenue for each level of output. Use the following table to organize your results.

Quantity of doughnuts	Total revenue	Total cost	Marginal cost ($ per unit of output)	Marginal revenue	Profit
100	$ 200	$250			−50
			$\frac{110}{100}$	2	
200	400	360			40
			$\frac{170}{100}$	2	
300	600	530			70
			$\frac{195}{100}$	2	
400	800	725			75
			$\frac{225}{100}$	2	
500	1,000	950			50

d. What is the relationship between marginal revenue and marginal cost at the profit-maximizing level of output for Sarah's Doughnut Shoppe? Explain the meaning of this relationship and how it relates to profitability.

- Closest where MR = MC, MR = P
- When MR = MC, the profit is maximized
- when MR > MC → produce more
- when MC > MR → produce less

4. Use the graphs that follow of a perfectly competitive market in a constant-cost industry to answer this set of questions.

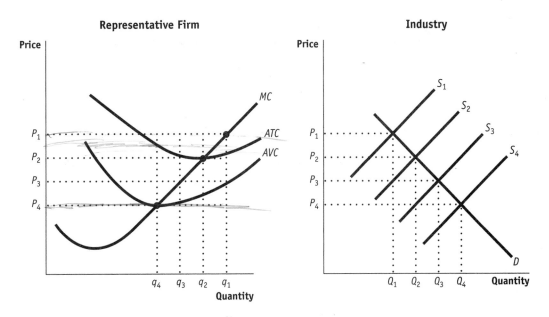

Representative Firm

Industry

a. Suppose in the short run the industry supply curve is given by S_1. Identify the short-run equilibrium market price and quantity, the quantity produced by the representative firm, and whether the firm is making positive, negative, or zero economic profits. Holding everything else constant, what will happen in the long run in this industry? In your answer to this question, identify the long-run equilibrium price and quantity in the industry, the quantity produced by the firm in the long run, and the level of profits for the firm in the long run.

$Sr\ emp = P_1$ (q_1, P_1) q_1

$pos.$ P_4

b. Suppose in the short run the industry supply curve is given by S_4. Identify the short-run equilibrium market price and quantity, the quantity produced by the representative firm, and whether the firm is making positive, negative, or zero economic profits. Do you know with certainty what this firm's profits equal in the short run? Holding everything else constant, what will happen in the long run in this industry? In your answer to this question, identify the long-run equilibrium price and quantity in the industry, the quantity produced by the firm in the long run, and the level of profits for the firm in the long run.

$Sr\ P = P_4$ $q = q_4$, $negative$

c. You are told that this representative firm is currently making negative economic profits in the short run, but that it is covering all of its variable costs of production and some of its fixed costs. Given the price choices in the preceding graph, what is the current price for this good? In the long run will there be entry of new firms into the industry or will existing firms exit the industry? Explain your answer.

5. You are given the following information about the five firms that produce soda in Bigtown. These five firms are the only producers of soda in Bigtown, and all soda consumed in Bigtown comes from these five producers.

Name of company	Quantity of soda sold (cans per month)
Fizzy Water	150
Cool Tonics	200
Carbonated Bliss	100
Mom's Pop	450
Taste of Eden	100

a. Given the preceding information would you characterize the market for soda in Bigtown as perfectly competitive? Explain your answer.

b. Suppose market share is defined as the percentage of total sales represented by a firm's sales of soda over the given period. Calculate the market share of each of the companies producing soda in Bigtown.

No— only 5, not same product, difference in soda sold

c. Is the soda produced in this market likely to be standardized? Explain your answer.

No — diff companies, diff amounts sold

6. The market for books is perfectly competitive and a constant-cost industry. The short-run industry supply curve is given by the equation $P = 4 + Q$, while the industry demand curve is given by the equation $P = 100 - Q$, where P is the market price and Q is the market quantity. The representative firm's MC curve can be written as $MC = 4 + 2q$, and its TC is given by the equation $TC = 36 + 4q + q^2$, where q is the quantity produced by the firm.

a. What is the equilibrium price and the equilibrium market quantity for this good in the short run?

$36 + 4q + q^2 = 4 + 2q$

$32 + 2q + q^2 = 0$

$4 + Q = 100 - Q$
$2Q = 96$
$Q = 48$
$P = 52$

b. Given the market price you calculated in part (a), what is the profit-maximizing quantity, q, for a representative firm to produce in the short run? What rule did you use to calculate this profit-maximizing level of output?

$MC = MR = P$

$4 + 2q = 52$

$2q = 48$

$q = 24$

c. Is this firm making positive, negative, or zero economic profit in the short run? Sketch a diagram of the market and the representative firm. In these diagrams identify the equilibrium price, the market quantity, the firm quantity, the firm's *ATC* curve (a sketch of this is fine), the firm's *MC* curve, and the firm's profits, if there are any.   *Profits = TR − TC*

d. If all the firms are identical in this industry, how many firms are in the industry in the short run?

e. What is the long-run price, the long-run market quantity, the long-run quantity produced by a representative firm, and the long-run number of firms in the industry?

f. Draw a sketch illustrating the long-run equilibrium for this industry and for a representative firm.

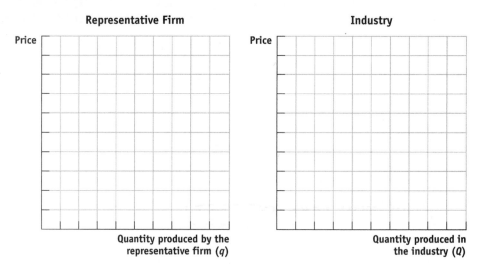

7. Small Town initially has a single firm that serves good coffee and wonderful pastries. This firm is busy every morning with long lines of customers eager to get a hot cup of coffee and a breakfast pastry. The owner of the café is excited that he is earning $50,000 a year as his take-home pay, since in his former job he managed to earn only $30,000.

a. Is this scenario likely to be a long-run equilibrium situation? Explain your answer.

No b/c return is greater than OC. Positive profit will be reduced until he earns no econ. profit

b. What do you anticipate will happen in the long run in Small Town?

c. The owner of the café is interviewed 10 years after the initial story about his success. The reporter finds out that the café owner is no longer in business providing coffee and pastries. Can you think of a possible story to explain this owner's departure from the business? (Hint: The owner did not choose to retire—he simply exited the industry during this 10-year period.)

8. For the most part, our model of perfect competition focuses on constant-cost industries. Is the assumption of constant costs in the long run a plausible assumption for the types of industries that most closely resemble perfect competition? Explain your answer.

9. In the long run, the model of perfect competition predicts that all firms in an industry will earn zero economic profits. Why would firms be willing to continue to produce in the long run if their economic profits are equal to zero?

▮ BEFORE YOU TAKE THE TEST

Chapter Review Questions

1. Perfect competition requires that
   a. producers be able to enter or exit an industry in the short run.
   b. producers be able to distinguish their product from a rival producer's product.
   c. producers have no ability to exert influence over the market price of the product.
   d. consumers compete for the producers' product.

2. In recent years there has been an increased demand for organic produce due to concerns about health issues related to food consumption. Holding everything else constant, in the short run this demand should lead to _____, while in the long run _____.
   a. increases in the price of organic produce; entry of firms into the industry will reduce the price of organic produce
   b. increases in the price of organic produce; exit of firms from the industry will further increase the price of organic produce
   c. decreases in the price of organic produce; entry of firms into the industry will further reduce the price of organic produce
   d. decreases in the price of organic produce; exit of firms from the industry will increase the price of organic produce

3. Which of the following describes a perfectly competitive industry?
   a. Elementary school students are only allowed to attend the school in their attendance area.
   b. Water for household use is sold by the local water utility.
   c. The price of wine is determined by global supply and demand. A small share of the total world production of wine is produced in a local valley by 10 companies.
   d. The price of oil is determined by global supply and demand. A total of five companies produce the world's supply of oil.

4. Marginal revenue is the addition to total
   a. revenue from producing one more unit of the good.
   b. cost from selling one more unit of the good.
   c. revenue from selling one more unit of the good.
   d. profit from producing and selling one more unit of the good.

5. Suppose Jerry calculates that if he produces one more box of pens his total cost will increase by $15, but that he can sell this box of pens for $14. Jerry will

   a. produce the pens and enhance his revenues.

   b. not produce the pens, since the revenue from the additional pens is less than the cost of producing the additional pens.

   c. produce the pens, but wait to sell them until the market price of pens increases.

   d. shut down his pen production, since his addition to revenue from pen production is less than his addition to cost from pen production.

6. Suppose a perfectly competitive firm in the short run sells its product for a price that is less than the minimum point on its *ATC* curve. Which of the following statements is true?

   a. The firm will shut down in the short run since it is not covering all of its costs.

   b. Some firms in this industry will exit the industry in the long run, and the exiting will continue until the market price increases and is equal to the break-even price on the *ATC* curve.

   c. The firm will shut down in the short run only if the price is greater than the shut-down price but less than the break-even price.

   d. Some firms in this industry will exit the industry in the long run, and the exiting will continue until the market price increases and is equal to the shut-down price on the *ATC* curve.

7. Suppose a perfectly competitive industry with constant costs is initially in long-run equilibrium. Demand for the product produced in this industry increases due to a change in tastes and preferences. In the short run this will result in

   a. the product selling for a higher price, each firm producing more of the good, and positive economic profits for the firms in the industry.

   b. the product selling for a higher price; each firm in the industry producing the same level of the good as they did initially, since their capital is fixed; and each firm earning positive economic profit.

   c. the product selling for a higher price initially, but the industry will attract new firms, which will cause the price to fall back to its original level.

   d. the price staying constant, since the firms in this industry are price-takers, and the output of each firm increasing; therefore each firm will earn positive economic profit.

8. Suppose a perfectly competitive industry with constant costs is initially in long-run equilibrium. Demand for the product produced in this industry increases due to a change in tastes and preferences. In the long run this will result in

   a. the industry output of this good increasing, the price staying constant due to the entry of new firms into the industry, and each firm in the industry earning positive economic profits.

   b. the industry output of this good increasing, the price staying constant due to the entry of new firms into the industry, and each firm in the industry earning negative economic profits.

   c. the industry output of this good increasing, the price staying constant due to the entry of new firms into the industry, and each firm in the industry earning zero economic profit.

   d. the industry output of this good increasing, the firm level of output increasing, the price increasing, and each firm in the industry earning zero economic profit.

9. Which of the following statements is true?

   I. The model of supply and demand is a model based upon perfectly competitive market.

   II. In the model of supply and demand, some producers may be able to affect the price of the good.

   III. In the model of supply and demand, some consumers may be able to affect the price of the good.

   a. Statement I is true.

   b. Statements II and III are true.

   c. Statements I, II, and III are true.

   d. None of these statements is true.

10. The optimal output rule for a perfectly competitive firm is to produce that quantity where

   a. $MR = MC$ in the long run, but in the short run to produce that quantity where $MC = ATC$.

   b. $MC = ATC$ in the short run.

   c. $MR = MC$ no matter what the time period, provided that marginal revenue is greater than average variable cost.

   d. $MR = MC$ no matter what the time period, provided that marginal revenue is greater than average total cost.

11. A firm calculates that the cost of producing its tenth unit of output is $0.50, while the revenue from producing this tenth unit is $0.55. This firm

   a. should definitely produce the tenth unit.

   b. should definitely stop producing, since it knows it is profit maximizing and may risk reducing its profit if it produces any more units of the good.

   c. should definitely produce at least five more units if it hopes to profit maximize.

   d. cannot increase its production in the short run since its fixed inputs are constant.

12. A firm in the short run must decide whether it should produce any level of output. This means that the firm must

   a. equate marginal revenue to marginal cost to decide its level of output.

   b. consider whether its revenue is sufficient to cover its total costs of production.

   c. consider whether its revenue is sufficient to cover its average fixed costs of production.

   d. consider whether its revenue is sufficient to cover its variable costs of production.

13. A firm making its short-run decision about whether to produce should ignore its

   a. fixed costs.

   b. variable costs.

   c. average costs.

   d. marginal costs.

14. Production is profitable in the short run whenever price is greater than

   a. average total cost.

   b. marginal cost.

   c. average variable cost.

   d. average fixed cost.

15. Which of the following statements about a perfectly competitive firm is true?
    I. A firm profit maximizes by producing that output where $MR = MC$.
    II. A firm will produce in the short run provided that the price of the good exceeds its average variable cost.
    III. A firm in the long run can make positive economic profits.
    a. Statement I is true.
    b. Statements I and II are true.
    c. Statements I and III are true.
    d. Statements I, II, and III are true.

16. When a perfectly competitive firm earns zero economic profit in the long run, this implies that accounting profits
    a. are also equal to zero.
    b. are positive.
    c. are negative.
    d. may be positive, negative, or equal to zero.

17. A perfectly competitive firm finds that its break-even price occurs at $22 while its shut-down price is at $12. You are told that the market demand curve in this industry is $P = 30 - (1/30)Q$ and the market supply curve is $P = (1/15)Q$. In the short run this firm will
    a. produce, since it is covering its variable costs of production.
    b. produce, since it can earn positive economic profits.
    c. produce, since it is covering its fixed costs of production.
    d. shut down, since it is not covering its fixed costs of production.

18. A perfectly competitive firm's minimum-cost output corresponds to the level of output at which
    a. fixed cost is minimized.
    b. variable cost is minimized.
    c. average total cost is minimized.
    d. total cost is minimized.

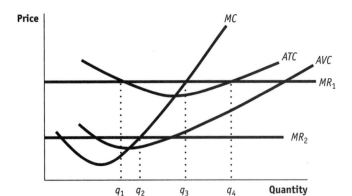

19. Use the preceding graph of a perfectly competitive firm in the short run to answer this question. If the firm's marginal revenue is MR_1, then this firm profit maximizes by producing _____ units of output, and its economic profit will be _____.
    a. q_1; zero
    b. q_2; positive
    c. q_3; positive
    d. q_4; positive

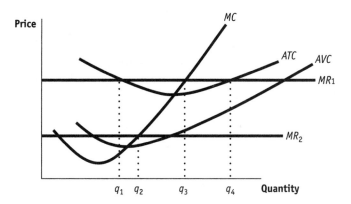

20. Use the preceding graph of a perfectly competitive firm in the short run to answer this question. If the firm's marginal revenue is MR_2, then this firm profit maximizes by producing _____ units of output, and its economic profit will be _____.
   a. q_1; negative
   b. q_2; negative
   c. q_3; zero
   d. q_4; negative

21. For a firm to profit maximize, it must also be true that
   a. the firm is cost minimizing.
   b. the market price is greater than the shut-down price.
   c. the market price is equal to the break-even price.
   d. the firm is earning a positive accounting profit.

22. In the short run, the individual supply curve for a perfectly competitive firm is that firm's
   a. MC curve at or above the shut-down price.
   b. ATC curve above the MC curve.
   c. ATC curve below the MC curve.
   d. MR curve at or above the shut-down price.

23. A perfectly competitive firm will exit the industry in the long run if the
   a. firm's marginal revenue is consistently less than the firm's marginal cost.
   b. market price is consistently less than the break-even price.
   c. firm's fixed cost cannot be eliminated in the long run.
   d. firm's marginal cost is consistently less than the firm's marginal revenue.

24. The short-run industry supply curve for a perfectly competitive market is
   a. perfectly elastic, since buyers can purchase as many units of the good as they desire at the prevailing market price.
   b. equal to the horizontal sum of the supply curves of the individual producers.
   c. equal to the horizontal sum of the individual firms' MC curves at and above the AVC.
   d. Answers (b) and (c) are both true.

25. Suppose there are two firms in a perfectly competitive industry and that each of these two firms have an *MC* curve that can be expressed as *MC* = 2*q*, where *q* is the level of output produced by the firm. Furthermore, suppose that the minimum point of the *AVC* curve occurs at $10. If these two firms comprise the industry (a simplification to make the calculation easier), which of the following equations describes the industry supply curve where *Q* refers to the market quantity and *P* refers to the market price?
    a. *P* = 2*Q* for *Q* ≥ 5
    b. *P* = *Q* for *Q* ≥ 5
    c. *P* = *Q* for *Q* ≥ 10
    d. *P* = 2*Q* for *Q* ≥ 10

26. Which of the following statements for a perfectly competitive industry is true?
    I. In the short run, the number of firms in the industry is fixed.
    II. For a constant-cost industry, the market supply curve in the short run is a horizontal line.
    III. In a short-run market equilibrium, the quantity supplied equals the quantity demanded.
    a. Statement I is true.
    b. Statements I and II are true.
    c. Statements I and III are true.
    d. Statements I, II, and III are true.

27. The long-run market equilibrium in a perfectly competitive industry with identical firms results in all firms
    a. earning zero economic profit.
    b. producing the quantity associated with their break-even price.
    c. producing the profit-maximizing quantity at which *MR* = *MC*.
    d. All of the statements are true.

28. A constant-cost industry in a perfectly competitive market can be identified by its
    a. horizontal long-run market supply curve.
    b. horizontal long-run market demand curve.
    c. upward-sloping long-run market supply curve.
    d. downward-sloping long-run market supply curve.

ANSWER KEY

Answers to Problems and Exercises

1. A price-taking firm is a firm that is so small relative to the entire market that it has no influence on the market price. This firm accepts the price of the good that is determined by the interaction of the market demand and the market supply. A price-taking consumer is a consumer whose purchases in a market are so small relative to the entire market that they can exert no influence on the market price. A price-taking consumer is one who accepts the market-determined price as the price they will pay for the good. Market share refers to the fraction of the total industry output represented by a producer's output: when no producer has significant market share, this implies that no producer is able to influence market prices.

2. The model of perfect competition requires that producers be price-takers and that the good being produced in the market is a standardized product. These two conditions imply that no producer can exert influence on the market price and that any producer who raises their price above the market price will find that they lose all their sales to other producers. A third condition that is often present in a perfectly competitive industry is free entry and exit of firms in the long run. Free entry and exit in the long run ensures that economic profit will equal zero in the long run. Firms enter the industry in the long run if there are positive short-run profits, and they exit the industry in the long run if there are negative short-run profits.

3. **a.** Since total revenue equals the product of price and quantity, we can use this equation to find the price of a doughnut. When $TR = \$200$, $Q = 100$ and price is $2. When $TR = \$400$, $Q = 200$ and price is $2. In a perfectly competitive industry the price the firm sells its product for stays constant and is equal to the market price.

   b. According to the table, Sarah's Doughnut Shoppe maximizes its profits when it produces 400 doughnuts.

Quantity of doughnuts	Total revenue	Total cost	Profit
100	$ 200	$250	−$50
200	400	360	40
300	600	530	70
400	800	725	75
500	1,000	950	50

   c.

Quantity of doughnuts	Total revenue	Total cost	Marginal cost ($ per unit of output)	Marginal revenue	Profit
100	$ 200	$250			−$50
			$1.10	$2	
200	400	360			40
			1.70	2	
300	600	530			70
			1.95	2	
400	800	725			75
			2.25	2	
500	1,000	950			50

d. At the profit-maximizing level of output, $MR = MC$ (or very close to it). Since marginal revenue is also equal to the price of a doughnut, this implies that marginal cost equals the price of a doughnut. When $MR = MC$, the addition to total revenue from selling an additional unit of the good equals the addition to total cost from producing an additional unit of the good. When $MR > MC$, more units of the good should be produced and sold in order to profit maximize; when $MR < MC$, fewer units of the good should be produced and sold in order to profit maximize.

4. a. The equilibrium price is P_1 and the equilibrium quantity is Q_1 in the market. The representative firm produces the quantity at which $MR = MC$, or $P_1 = MC$, since for a perfectly competitive firm $MR = P$. The representative firm produces q_1. The firm earns positive economic profit since $P_1 > ATC$ for q_1 units of output. In the long run, new firms will enter the industry, since the existence of positive economic profits creates an incentive for more competition. As firms enter the industry, the industry supply curve will shift to the right from S_1 to S_2, which will result in a decrease in the market price from P_1 to P_2. The equilibrium output in the industry will increase to Q_2 while the representative firm will decrease its production to q_2. The level of economic profits will equal zero in the long run for the firms in the industry.

b. The equilibrium price is P_4 and the equilibrium quantity is Q_4 in the market. The representative firm finds that the market price goes through its shut-down price at P_4 (the minimum point of the AVC curve), and therefore the firm needs to decide whether or not it wants to produce in the short run. With either choice, the firm will earn negative economic profits equal to the negative of their fixed costs. The firm will produce q_4 units since $MR = MC$ at this level of output. In the long run, firms will exit the industry, causing the industry supply curve to shift to the left to S_2. This will cause the market price to increase to P_2, the market quantity to decrease to Q_2, and the level of production for each firm remaining in the industry to increase to q_2. Economic profits will equal zero in the long run for each firm.

c. Looking at the graph we know that P_4 corresponds to the price that goes through the shut-down price, which implies that the firm covers all of its variable cost, but none of its fixed cost. At P_1, the firm earns a positive economic profit and thus its revenues are greater than the sum of its fixed cost and variable cost. P_2 corresponds to the price that goes through the break-even price: the firm's total revenue is exactly equal to its total cost and therefore the firm is covering all of its variable cost and all of its fixed cost. That leaves P_3, and from the graph we see that P_3 is a price that lies between the break-even price and the shut-down price: the firm will receive enough revenue to cover all of its variable cost and some of its fixed cost. In the long run, firms will exit this industry until the supply curve shifts left from S_3 to S_2. The remaining firms in the industry will earn zero economic profits in the long run.

5. a. No, this market is not perfectly competitive since there are not many producers and at least one of them has substantial market share (Mom's Pop accounts for 45% of total soda sales in Bigtown).

b.

Name of company	Market share
Fizzy Water	15%
Cool Tonics	20
Carbonated Bliss	10
Mom's Pop	45
Taste of Eden	10

c. No, the soda will likely be quite differentiated since customers distinguish between these companies' products (for example, Mom's Pop really outsells every other business in the industry).

6. a. To find the equilibrium price and quantity in the market, use the market demand and supply equations. Solving $100 - Q = 4 + Q$ for Q gives you the equilibrium quantity of 48 units. Substituting this quantity into either the demand or the supply equation gives you the equilibrium price of $52.

b. The profit-maximizing level of output for the firm is found by equating marginal revenue to marginal cost. For the price-taking firm, marginal revenue is equal to the market price. Thus, $52 = 4 + 2q$, or q (the quantity produced by the representative firm) is 24 units.

c. Profit is equal to $TR - TC$. Total revenue for this firm is $(\$52)(24) = \$1,248$, and total cost is equal to $ATC \times q$ or $TC = (36/q + 4 + q)(q) = (36/24 + 4 + 24)(24) = \$708$. This firm makes positive profits equal to $540.

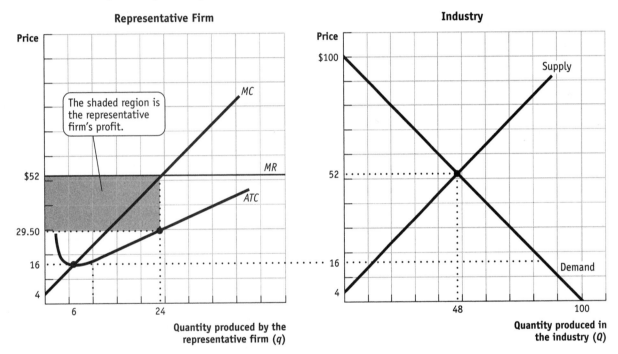

d. The representative firm produces 24 units in the short run when it profit maximizes, while the total market quantity produced is 48 units. This implies that if all firms are identical and produce 24 units of output, then it will take two firms to produce the market quantity (this is a simplified example with just a few firms to make the math easier).

e. In the long run, the representative firm will earn zero economic profits due to the entry of new firms into the industry. For this to be true, the firm must produce at its break-even price where $MC = ATC$. You can find the average total cost by dividing total cost by the firm's quantity, q. Thus, $TC = 36 + 4q + q^2$ gives us $ATC = 36/q + 4 + q$. $MC = 4 + 2q$, so we can set $MC = ATC$ and have $4 + 2q = 36/q + 4 + q$. Solving this equation gives us $36/q = q$ or $q^2 = 36$. The positive quantity that solves this equation is $q = 6$. So, the long-run quantity produced by the representative firm is 6 units. The long-run equilibrium price is the price at which $MC = ATC$ for this firm, so if q equals 6 units, then the long-run price is $4 + 2(6) = \$16$. At a price of $16 the quantity demanded in the market is 84 units. If each firm produces 6 units and a total of 84 units are produced, then there are 14 firms in the industry.

f.

Quantity produced by the
representative firm (*q*)

Quantity produced in
the industry (*Q*)

7. **a.** This is not likely to be a long-run equilibrium since the owner of the café is earning a return that is greater than his opportunity cost. He knows that when working for someone else the best he can do is to earn $30,000, and so the $50,000 he earns running his coffee shop suggests that he is earning positive economic profit and that over the long run this profit should be reduced until he earns zero economic profit, provided that there is free entry into the market for coffee shops.

b. In the long run, entry of new firms should occur, which should reduce the level of profit to zero for all the firms in the industry. This scenario is based on there being no barriers to entry, and in the case of providing coffee and pastries this is a plausible assumption. Entry should continue until all owners of the coffee shops that are in business earn their opportunity cost and until the level of economic profit for the firms equals zero.

c. The model of perfect competition suggests that all firms in the industry in the long run will earn zero economic profit. But some firms may be driven from the industry if they find their costs of production are greater than the cost of production for other firms. It is likely that this owner found that he simply could not compete with the new firms entering the industry and that he was forced to exit the industry in the long run because other firms could provide coffee and pastries at somewhat lower cost than he was able to achieve. This helps us understand the frequent exit of established businesses from an industry: it is not at all unusual for a city to have restaurants or other business enterprises in markets with competition go out of business.

8. The assumption of constant costs for an industry implies that new firms can enter the industry without causing the costs of production for both the existing firms and these new firms to increase. This is an important assumption to consider: implicitly it is saying that it is possible for all these firms to increase their hiring of labor and capital without affecting the price of that labor or that capital. Is this plausible? It is probably not a bad assumption for many productive enterprises in which the amount of labor and capital used is small relative to the total pool of labor and capital used in the economy. It is probably a poor assumption when the amount of labor and capital used in the industry accounts for a large percentage of the total pool of labor and capital used. Perfect competition, with its assumption of price-taking behavior on the part of producers and consumers, is likely to be a modeling situation in which each individual firm's hiring of labor and capital is unlikely to exert upward pressure on the prices of those inputs.

9.   Earning zero economic profits in the long run is not a bad outcome for existing firms in an industry. Rather, this level of profit allows each factor of production (including the owner) to earn a return that is equal to their opportunity cost. Thus, when a firm earns zero economic profit this does not suggest that the firm is performing at a less than ideal level, but that all inputs used by the firm are being compensated at a level equal to their worth as measured by their opportunity costs. In contrast, a firm earning positive economic profit (a possibility in the short run) is receiving a level of compensation that exceeds their opportunity costs: this suggests that an inadequate amount of resources are being devoted to this production since the value placed on the goods being produced exceeds the costs of producing the good. As more resources are devoted to the production of this good through the entry of new firms, the level of economic profit falls until it is at a level where these inputs are valued at their opportunity cost.

Answers to Chapter Review Questions

1.   **Answer c.** Free entry and exit occur in the long run in a perfectly competitive industry. The output produced in a perfectly competitive industry is a standardized commodity: consumers cannot distinguish one producer's output from another producer's output. Consumers are price-takers, and the market price equates the quantity demanded at that price with the quantity supplied at that price. Perfectly competitive industries are characterized by producers being price-takers.

2.   **Answer a.** When the demand for organic produce increases, this causes a rightward shift in the demand curve, which results in the price of organic produce increasing in the short run. In the long run, however, new producers will enter this industry, which will cause the supply curve to shift to the right, thereby lowering the price of organic produce.

3.   **Answer c.** Only answer (c) provides a description of price-taking behavior on both the producer and the consumer side of the model.

4.   **Answer c.** This is a simple definition of marginal revenue, which focuses on measuring the benefit from selling one more unit of the good.

5.   **Answer b.** Jerry is trying to determine the profit-maximizing level of output for his firm. To select this output level he will want to equate marginal revenue to marginal cost. Since the marginal revenue of producing an additional box of pens is less than the marginal cost of producing this box of pens, Jerry knows that this would represent too high a level of production. To determine whether Jerry should shut down his production, we need information about his average costs of production.

6.   **Answer b.** In the short run, if the price is less than average total cost, then firms in this perfectly competitive industry earn negative economic profit. These negative economic profits will lead some firms to exit the industry in the long run until the firms remaining in the industry earn zero economic profits. This implies that price will equal the minimum point of the ATC curve or the break-even price. The shut-down price is not on the ATC curve, as given in answer (d), but is instead on the AVC curve.

7.   **Answer a.** The increased demand for the good will cause the market demand curve to shift to the right, leading to a higher equilibrium level of output in the market and a higher equilibrium price. The firms in this industry are price-takers, and they will take the price they receive from the market and see where this price intersects their MC curve (recall that for a perfectly competitive firm the market price is equal to the marginal revenue) to select the profit-maximizing level of output. The firms will produce a higher level of output relative to their initial level, and they will earn positive economic profit.

8.   **Answer c.** In the long run, this industry will experience the entry of new firms because the increase in tastes and preferences for this good will cause the short-run price of the good to increase, resulting in the existing firms earning positive economic profit. But these profits will act as a signal to potential firms to enter, and this entry will shift the

market supply curve to the right, causing the price to fall back to its initial level. Firms in the long run will produce the same level of output as they did initially, but there will be more firms in the industry, which will lead to an increase in the industry level of output. Firms in the long run will earn zero economic profit.

9. **Answer a.** A basic underlying assumption of the model of supply and demand is that neither consumers nor producers can affect the price of the good. Producers and consumers are price-takers, which eliminates statements II and III.

10. **Answer c.** The profit-maximizing firm, if it produces, always produces that quantity where $MR = MC$. The profit-maximizing firm produces in the short run, provided that the market price is equal to or greater than the firm's average variable cost. The firm makes a positive economic profit if the market price is greater than average total cost, and it earns a negative economic profit if the market price is less than average total cost.

11. **Answer a.** Since the firm's marginal cost of producing the tenth unit of output is less than the marginal revenue from selling the tenth unit of output, the firm should definitely produce this tenth unit. The firm is able to increase its production in the short run, despite fixed inputs, because it can use more of the variable input. Without more information we cannot know with certainty that the firm should produce five more units of output. We do know the firm will profit maximize by producing that level of output where $MR = MC$ for the last unit produced.

12. **Answer d.** In the short run, the firm ignores its fixed cost since it cannot alter these costs. The firm decides whether it should produce in the short run by checking to see if its revenue is sufficient to cover its variable cost. If the revenue will not cover these variable costs, the firm can opt to shut down and incur only the fixed cost of production in the short run.

13. **Answer a.** In the short run, the firm will ignore its fixed cost since in the short run the fixed inputs cannot be altered. In the short run, the firm is able to alter its hiring of the variable input and, hence, its variable cost.

14. **Answer a.** The firm makes positive economic profit whenever the market price is greater than the firm's average total cost, and it makes negative economic profit whenever the market price is less than the firm's average total cost.

15. **Answer b.** Perfectly competitive firms produce that level of output where, for the last unit produced, the addition to total revenue (the marginal revenue) just equals the addition to total cost (the marginal cost). Perfectly competitive firms do not produce in the short run if the market price is less than the shut-down price, or the minimum point of the AVC curve. In the long run, a perfectly competitive firm will earn zero economic profit due to the entry of firms in the event of positive short-run economic profit or the exit of firms in the event of negative short-run economic profit.

16. **Answer b.** Economic profit includes the explicit and the implicit costs of production, while accounting profits exclude implicit costs. When a firm earns zero economic profit, this implies that the firm is earning positive accounting profit.

17. **Answer a.** Solving for the market equilibrium price using the market demand and supply curve yields a price of $20. This price is less than the break-even price and greater than the firm's shut-down price. The firm will produce in the short run since the market price is great enough to cover its variable cost of production (since the price exceeds the shut-down price). But the firm will earn negative profits because the market price is less than its break-even price, and therefore the price is not high enough for the firm to cover all of its variable costs and all of its fixed costs.

18. **Answer c.** The firm's minimum-cost output occurs where the cost per unit (its average total cost) is minimized. The firm's average total cost is minimized at the output level that corresponds to the firm's break-even price.

19. **Answer c.** The perfectly competitive firm sets marginal revenue equal to marginal cost and produces that level of output (q_3). When the firm produces q_3 units, the market price is greater than the average total cost of production for this level of output, and the firm will earn positive economic profit.

20. **Answer b.** The perfectly competitive firm sets marginal revenue equal to marginal cost and produces that quantity of output (q_2). When the firm produces q_2 units of output, the market price is less than the average total cost of production for this level of output, and the firm will earn negative economic profit.

21. **Answer a.** Profit maximization implies that the firm must be minimizing its costs. In addition, profit maximization requires that the firm produce the level of output where $MR = MC$.

22. **Answer a.** The firm decides how much to supply by equating the market price to its MC curve, since the market price is the firm's MR curve. The firm produces in the short run provided that the market price is equal to or greater than its shut-down price, or its AVC. Thus, the firm's short-run supply curve is its MC curve at or above the point of intersection with its AVC curve.

23. **Answer b.** In the long run, a firm can sell its plant and equipment and exit the industry, and it will choose to exit the industry if the market price does not cover its average total cost of production, or in other words, its break-even price.

24. **Answer d.** The supply curves of the individual producers are their MC curves at or above the shut-down price. To find the industry supply curve, simply horizontally sum together these individual supply curves.

25. **Answer c.** The market supply curve is found by horizontally summing the individual supply curves. The firm's supply curve is given by $MC = 2q$, provided that the price is greater than the minimum point of the AVC, or in this case provided that the price is equal to or greater than $10. So at a price of $10, each firm is willing to produce 5 units, for a total of 10 units. At a price of $20, each firm is willing to produce 10 units, for a total of 20 units. Thus, the industry supply curve is $P = Q$ for outputs greater than or equal to 10 units.

26. **Answer c.** In a perfectly competitive industry, the number of firms in the industry is fixed and constant in the short run. Entry of new firms or the exit of existing firms can only occur in the long run. Market equilibrium, whether in the short run or long run, occurs at that price and quantity combination where the quantity demanded equals the quantity supplied. However, in the short run, a constant-cost industry will have an upward-sloping market supply curve because the production of a greater level of output must entail increasing costs due to the diminishing returns to the variable input.

27. **Answer d.** In the long run, entry or exit will occur in the perfectly competitive industry until all firms in the industry earn zero economic profit. Since all firms earn zero economic profit this implies that all firms are producing at the point where price equals average total cost, which can only occur at the break-even price, since firms must also be producing the profit-maximizing quantity where $MR = MC$.

28. **Answer a.** A perfectly competitive industry with constant costs is an industry that can expand its output in the long run without incurring higher or lower costs per unit. This implies that the long-run market supply curve for this industry will be horizontal.

chapter 8

Monopoly, Oligopoly, and Monopolistic Competition

BEFORE YOU READ THE CHAPTER

Summary

This chapter explores monopoly, oligopoly, and monopolistic competition. A monopoly is a situation in which there is a single producer of a good that has no close substitutes. The chapter explores how the monopolist determines its profit-maximizing price and output. The chapter also compares perfect competition and monopoly and then examines how these two different market structures result in different outcomes with respect to social welfare. The chapter also discusses natural monopoly.

Oligopoly is a market structure characterized by a few firms producing a product that may or may not be differentiated. The chapter discusses the incentives for oligopolists to act cooperatively or competitively and the results of these actions on the level of oligopoly profits. The chapter includes a discussion of formal as well as tacit collusion, the formation of cartels, and the reasons why cartels fail. The relationship between oligopolies and antitrust policy is also introduced in this chapter.

Monopolistic competition refers to an industry characterized by many competing firms selling differentiated products with free entry and exit of firms in the long run. The chapter discusses product differentiation and why oligopolistic and monopolistically competitive firms engage in product differentiation. The chapter includes a discussion of the reason for product diversity as well as the cost of this diversity.

Chapter Objectives

Objective #1. There are four principal models of market structure: perfect competition, monopoly, oligopoly, and monopolistic competition. These four types of market structure are distinguished by the number of firms in the market and whether the goods offered in the market are identical or differentiated.

- In a monopoly, a single producer produces a single, undifferentiated product. In oligopoly, a few producers sell products that may or may not be differentiated. In monopolistically competitive markets, many producers sell differentiated products. In perfect competition, many producers produce identical products.

- The number of firms in the market is determined by the long-run conditions that make it difficult for new firms to enter the market: these conditions include government regulations that limit entry, the presence of increasing returns to scale in production, technological superiority that limits potential competition, or the control of necessary resources or inputs. When these conditions are present, the market structure tends to be monopolistic or oligopolistic.

Objective #2.   A monopoly is a market characterized by having a single producer of the good, when the good has no close substitutes. Monopolists, unlike perfectly competitive firms, know that their actions affect the market price, and they take this fact into account when deciding how much to produce.

Objective #3.   In contrast to firms in perfect competition, a monopolist produces a smaller quantity and charges a higher price for its product. The monopolist is able to charge a price that is greater than the competitive price because it has market power: it is the only producer of the good and the good has no close substitutes. By charging a higher price and restricting output, the monopolist is able to increase its profit while maintaining positive profits in the long run.

Objective #4.   Positive economic profits earned by the monopolist continue in the long run because effective barriers to entry prevent new firms from entering the industry. There are four principal barriers to entry: (1) the monopoly controls a scarce resource or input that prevents new firms from being able to compete in the industry; (2) the monopolist enjoys increasing returns to scale and therefore can spread its fixed cost over a larger volume of output, resulting in the monopolist's having lower average total costs than potential competitors; (3) the monopolist enjoys technological superiority over its potential competitors; and (4) the monopolist is protected from competition due to government-created barriers.

- Increasing returns to scale results in lower costs of production as the size of the firm increases. In the case of a monopoly with increasing returns to scale, the single firm finds that its cost of production falls throughout the relevant range of production. Any potential competitor would face higher costs per unit. Natural monopolies are an example of a monopoly that benefits from increasing returns to scale.

- With technological superiority some monopolists also experience network externalities, which is a condition that arises when the value to a consumer of a good increases as the number of people who use the good increases. This advantage may allow the producer to become a monopolist.

- The most important government-created barrier to entry takes the form of patent protection. A similar type of protection afforded producers is the copyright.

Objective #5.   The monopolist's demand curve for its product is the market demand curve, since the monopolist is the only provider of the good in the market. Since the monopolist's demand curve is downward sloping, this implies that the monopolist can sell additional units of the good only by lowering the price on all the units it sells: this results in the monopolist's marginal revenue (MR) curve being beneath the monopolist's demand curve. An increase in production by a monopolist has two opposing effects on revenue: a quantity effect and a price effect.

- When the monopolist sells one more unit of the good, this increases its revenue by the price at which the unit is sold: this is the quantity effect.

- When the monopolist sells one more unit of the good, it must reduce the price on all units sold, which decreases revenue: this is the price effect.

- A firm with market power will find that its MR curve always lies beneath its demand curve due to the price effect.

- At low levels of output, the quantity effect is stronger than the price effect, and the monopolist will find that its total revenue increases as it increases its level of production.

- At high levels of output, the price effect is stronger than the quantity effect, and the monopolist will find that its total revenue decreases as it increases its level of production.

- Figure 8.1 illustrates a linear demand curve for a monopolist as well as the monopolist's MR curve. Notice that the MR curve bisects the distance between the origin and the horizontal intercept of the demand curve. This implies that the slope of the MR curve is twice the slope of the demand curve. Notice also that the y-intercepts for the demand curve and the MR curve are the same.

Figure 8.1

Note that the distance from 0 to $\frac{1}{2}Q_1$ is the same distance as from $\frac{1}{2}Q_1$ to Q_1: the MR curve bisects the distance between the origin and the x-intercept of the demand curve.

Objective #6.   The monopolist maximizes profit by producing the output at which marginal revenue equals marginal cost (MR = MC) for the last unit produced while charging the price consumers are willing to pay for this output. The profit-maximizing price-quantity combination is always a point on the demand curve. Figure 8.2 illustrates this concept.

Figure 8.2

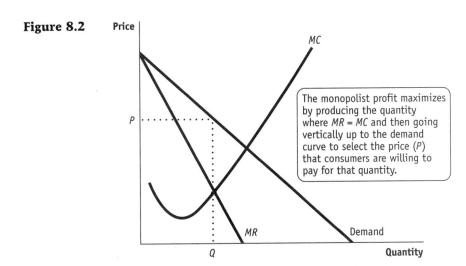

The monopolist profit maximizes by producing the quantity where MR = MC and then going vertically up to the demand curve to select the price (P) that consumers are willing to pay for that quantity.

Objective #7.   Just as with perfect competition, the monopolist's profits are equal to total revenue minus total cost (TR − TC). However, the monopolist can earn profits in the short run as well as the long run since there are effective barriers to entry that protect the monopolist from competition. Figure 8.3 illustrates a monopolist's profit: note that when the price the monopolist charges is greater than its average total cost, then the monopolist earns positive economic profit.

Figure 8.3

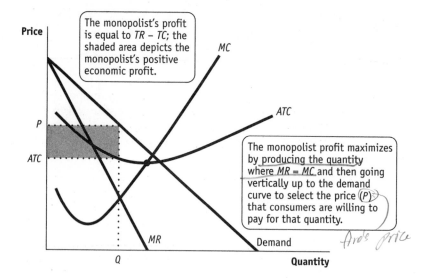

The monopolist's profit is equal to TR – TC; the shaded area depicts the monopolist's positive economic profit.

The monopolist profit maximizes by producing the quantity where MR = MC and then going vertically up to the demand curve to select the price (P) that consumers are willing to pay for that quantity.

Objective #8. In a perfectly competitive industry, each firm equates the marginal cost to the price of the good; in contrast, in a monopoly the price of the good is always greater than the marginal cost at the profit-maximizing level of output. This tells us that the monopolist is not producing the efficient level of output, since the price that consumers are willing to pay for the last unit produced is greater than the cost of producing the last unit. Too few resources are being devoted to the production of the monopolist's product. A monopoly, compared with a perfectly competitive industry, restricts output, charges a higher price for the product, and earns a profit that is not eliminated through the entry of new firms in the long run.

Objective #9. The existence of a monopoly creates a deadweight loss due to the monopolist's restriction of output and its ability to charge a higher price for its product relative to the quantity and price decision made by a perfectly competitive firm. The deadweight loss created by the monopolist occurs because some mutually beneficial transactions do not occur: this is evident when we recall that for the last unit produced by the monopolist, the marginal cost of producing that unit is less than the price consumers are willing to pay for that unit. Because monopoly is inefficient, government policy often is used to offset some of the undesired effects of monopoly. Figure 8.4 indicates for a monopolist the areas that correspond to consumer surplus, producer surplus, and deadweight loss.

Figure 8.4

Note: P^* and Q^* are the profit-maximizing price and quantity for the monopoly.

Objective #10. If an industry is not a natural monopoly, then the best method for avoiding monopoly outcomes is to prevent monopoly from arising or to break up the monopoly if it already exists. Government policies used to prevent or eliminate monopolies are known as antitrust policy.

Objective #11. If an industry is a natural monopoly, then breaking up the monopoly is not a clearly beneficial idea since large-scale producers have lower average total cost than smaller-scale producers. Two policy methods are used for regulating natural monopolies: public ownership and regulation.

- With public ownership, the government establishes a public agency to provide the good and to protect consumers' interests.

- Regulation typically takes the form of price regulation, where the private company is regulated with regard to what prices it can charge for the product. Local utilities are frequently regulated in this way.

Objective #12. Oligopolies are characterized as an industry in which there are a few producers. Each of these individual producers has some market power (like in a monopoly) that enables them to affect market prices, but each of these producers also competes against the other producers in the industry. This competition is different from perfect competition in that each producer is aware of the other firms in the industry and recognizes that each firm's behavior affects the other firms. The key aspect of oligopoly is the tension between cooperation and competition: each firm must decide whether and to what degree it wants to cooperate or compete with the other firms in their industry.

Objective #13. With an oligopolistic industry what matters is not the size of the firm, but rather the number of firms serving the industry. Oligopolies primarily exist because each firm benefits from increasing returns to scale and these returns to scale result in a few producers in the industry rather than many small-scale producers in the industry. Analysis of oligopoly presents several challenging puzzles not encountered in our analysis of perfectly competitive markets or monopolies.

Objective #14. The simplest type of oligopoly to analyze is a duopoly, a situation in which there are only two firms in the industry. These two firms face two strategies: they can decide to cooperate with one another or they can decide to compete with each other by adopting non-cooperative behavior. By cooperating and forming a cartel, these two firms can work together to select the level of output that will maximize their joint profits. Even with an agreement to cooperate, the firms will find that they each have an incentive to cheat on this arrangement. Cartels are inherently unstable because each firm recognizes that it has an incentive to produce more of the good than was agreed. Like a monopolist, each firm in an oligopoly recognizes that selling a greater amount of output creates both a quantity and a price effect; however, the price effect is smaller for the oligopolist than it is for the monopolist, which means that the marginal revenue from selling additional units of the good is higher for the oligopolist than it would be for the monopolist. Ultimately, collusion is more profitable than noncooperative behavior, but collusion is difficult to achieve since formal agreements to collude are illegal in many nations. Some oligopolies find ways to collude without a formal agreement.

Objective #15. The United States legally restricts the behavior of oligopolistic firms and prohibits the creation of monopolies. The Sherman Antitrust Act of 1890 marked the beginning of antitrust policy and the government's commitment to prevent oligopolistic industries from becoming monopolies or behaving like a monopoly.

Objective #16. Although tacit collusion is common, it is hard for firms to push prices up to the monopoly level due to a number of different factors. Monopolistic prices are hard to achieve for at least four reasons: (1) when there are many firms in the industry, firms are less likely to behave cooperatively; (2) when firms produce a variety of products and offer these products at different prices, it is hard to discern when a firm is cheating on the tacit agreement; (3) firms do not always agree on what is fair and in their interests, and this can lead to firms deviating from the tacit agreement; and (4) firms may find that the buyers of their products are large enough relative to the entire market to be able to bargain for lower prices. When tacit collusion breaks down, this is often due to price wars in which each firm reduces the price of its product below the cooperative level. In a worst-case scenario, prices can fall below the non-cooperative level as each seller tries to drive the other sellers out of the business.

Objective #17. A monopolistically competitive industry is composed of many competing firms selling differentiated products with free entry and exit of firms in the long run. The three essential characteristics of monopolistic competition are a large number of producers, differentiated products, and free entry and exit of firms in the long run. Analysis of this market structure reveals that in some ways it resembles perfect competition and in other ways it resembles monopoly.

Objective #18. Because monopolistically competitive firms sell differentiated products, each firm has some degree of market power and therefore faces a downward-sloping demand curve for its product. In fact, product differentiation is the only way monopolistically competitive firms acquire market power. This implies that these firms, like a monopolist, have some power to set the price they charge for their product. However, these firms also face competition, and due to free entry and exit in the long run, they will find that their long-run economic profit is equal to zero. There is no tendency toward collusion in a monopolistically competitive market since all firms recognize that new firms can enter the industry in the long run.

Objective #19. Product differentiation takes three general forms: differentiation by style or type, differentiation by location, and differentiation by quality. Differentiation by style or type creates products that are imperfect substitutes for one another. Differentiation by location offers essentially identical products that are differentiated by their proximity and convenience to the buyer. Differentiation by quality provides a range of products that are of different quality levels to buyers. No matter what type of product differentiation we consider, the monopolistically competitive market structure is characterized by competition among sellers and a more diverse array of products.

Key Terms | Notes

monopolist a firm that is the only producer of a good that has no close substitutes.

monopoly an industry controlled by a *monopolist*.

market power the ability of a producer to raise prices.

barrier to entry something that prevents other firms from entering an industry. Crucial in protecting the profits of a *monopolist*. There are four types of barriers to entry: control over scarce *resources* or *inputs*, increasing returns to scale, technological superiority, and government-created barriers such as *licenses*.

natural monopoly a *monopoly* that exists when *increasing returns to scale* provide a large cost advantage to having all output produced by a single firm.

patent a temporary *monopoly* given by the government to an inventor for the use or sale of an invention.

copyright the exclusive legal right of the creator of a literary or artistic work to profit from that work; like a *patent*, it is a temporary *monopoly*.

oligopoly an industry with only a small number of producers.

Key Terms *(continued)*

oligopolist a firm in an industry with only a small number of producers.

imperfect competition a market structure in which no firm is a *monopolist*, but producers nonetheless have *market power* they can use to affect market prices.

duopoly an *oligopoly* consisting of only two firms.

duopolist one of the two firms in a *duopoly*.

collusion cooperation among oligopolistic producers to limit production and raise prices so as to raise one another's profits.

cartel an agreement among several producers to obey output restrictions in order to increase their joint profits.

noncooperative behavior actions by firms that ignore the effects of those actions on the profits of other firms.

public ownership when goods are supplied by the government or by a firm owned by the government to protect the interests of the consumer in response to *natural monopoly*.

price regulation a limitation on the price that a *monopolist* is allowed to charge.

antitrust policy legislative and regulatory efforts undertaken by the government to prevent oligopolistic industries from becoming or behaving like *monopolies*.

tacit collusion cooperation among producers, without a formal agreement, to limit production and raise prices so as to raise one another's profits.

price war a collapse of prices when *tacit collusion* breaks down.

product differentiation the attempt by firms to convince buyers that their products are different from those of other firms in the industry. If firms can so convince buyers, they can charge a higher price.

monopolistic competition a market structure in which there are many competing producers in an industry, each producer sells a differentiated product, and there is *free entry and exit* into and from the industry in the *long run*.

◼ AFTER YOU READ THE CHAPTER

Tips

Tip #1. It is important that you understand both why the monopolist has a downward-sloping *MR* curve that lies beneath the monopolist's demand curve and also how to find this *MR* curve. When the monopolist thinks about increasing the amount of the good it supplies to the market, it knows that it will increase its revenue when it sells this additional unit of the good. But it also knows that to sell more units of the good it will need to lower the price on all the units of the good it sells, so the decision to sell a larger amount of the good has two effects—one effect adds to the monopolist's revenue, but the second effect decreases the monopolist's revenue. Review this analysis until you understand it and can express it clearly.

Tip #2. To find the monopolist's *MR* curve is a relatively simple matter if the demand curve for the monopolist is linear. For a linear demand curve, the *MR* curve has the same *y*-intercept as the demand curve and twice the slope of the demand curve. For example, if the demand curve is expressed as $P = 1,000 - 2Q$, then the *MR* curve is $MR = 1,000 - 4Q$. Another way of expressing this idea is to realize that the *MR* curve bisects the horizontal distance between the origin and the *x*-intercept of the demand curve. Figure 8.5 illustrates this concept.

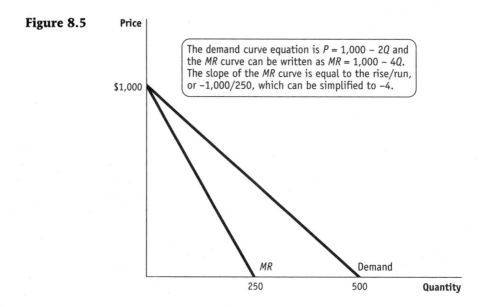

Figure 8.5

The demand curve equation is $P = 1,000 - 2Q$ and the *MR* curve can be written as $MR = 1,000 - 4Q$. The slope of the *MR* curve is equal to the rise/run, or $-1,000/250$, which can be simplified to -4.

Tip #3. Notice the relationship between the elasticity of the linear demand curve and its MR curve. Marginal revenue is positive in the elastic portion of the demand curve, marginal revenue equals 0 at the unit-elastic point (the midpoint) of the demand curve, and marginal revenue is negative in the inelastic portion of the demand curve.

Tip #4. This chapter continues the use of cost curves and marginal analysis. If you are still having trouble with the terminology related to cost curves, or with your understanding and use of these concepts, you should return to Chapter 6 on production and cost, and review this material. To work successfully with this chapter's material, you must have a very strong understanding (and not just memorization) of these underlying concepts.

Tip #5. After you read the chapter and work through the problems, you should have an appreciation for the puzzles presented by the oligopolistic market structure. These puzzles typically reflect the trade-offs between cooperation and competition and the benefits that firms receive from these two strategies.

Tip #6. Monopolistic competition is an odd blend of elements from both the monopoly model and the perfect competition model. Monopolistic competition resembles perfect competition since there are many competing producers and free entry and exit in the long run. Monopolistic competition resembles monopoly since each firm has its own downward-sloping demand curve and marginal revenue curve.

1. Monty's Dry Cleaners is the only dry cleaning establishment in Tuxedoville. Monty knows that the market demand curve for dry cleaning in Tuxedoville is given by the equation $P = 100 - Q$. Furthermore, assume that Monty has no fixed costs and that his marginal costs of production are equal to $10. Monty seeks your advice on what his profit-maximizing price and quantity are. In addition Monty would like to know what his economic profit is in this market. In addition to calculating these values, provide Monty with a calculation of the deadweight loss and the consumer surplus due to his operating as a monopoly.

STEP 1: Start by drawing a graph of Monty's demand curve for his product and his *MC* curve. Then find the marginal revenue curve for Monty's Dry Cleaners.

Review the section "The Monopolist's Demand Curve and Marginal Revenue" on pages 245–248, and Figure 8-5 on page 248.

The following graph gives Monty's demand curve and *MC* curve. Since *MC* = 10, this implies that Monty's *MC* curve is a horizontal line that intersects the vertical axis at $10 per unit. His *MR* curve is also drawn in: to find his *MR* revenue, recall that for a straight-line demand curve, the *MR* curve shares the *y*-intercept with the demand curve and bisects the horizontal axis between the origin and the *x*-intercept of the demand curve. Thus, the *y*-intercept for the demand curve is at $100 per unit, which will also be the *y*-intercept for the *MR* curve. The *x*-intercept for the demand curve is at 100 units and the *x*-intercept for the *MR* curve will be half this number, or 50 units.

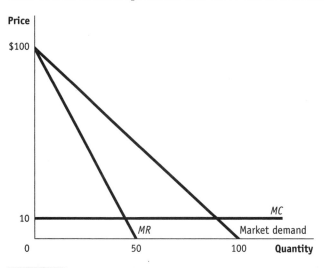

STEP 2: Identify the profit-maximizing quantity, the quantity at which marginal revenue equals marginal cost. Use the demand curve to find the price that Monty should charge for this quantity.

Review the section "The Monopolist's Demand Curve and Marginal Revenue" on pages 245–248, Figure 8-5 on page 248, the section "Monopoly: The General Picture" on page 250, and Figure 8-7 on page 251.

Monty will want to produce that quantity at which $MR = MC$, and then charge the price that demanders are willing to pay for this quantity. The following graph illustrates this profit-maximizing price and quantity. We can solve for the specific price and quantity by first writing an equation for the *MR* curve and then setting this *MR* curve equal to the *MC* curve. Thus, $MR = 100 - 2Q$, and if $MR = MC$, then $Q = 45$. Substituting a quantity of 45 into the demand curve, we get a price of $55. The profit-maximizing quantity is 45 units and the profit-maximizing price is $55. The following graph identifies these profit-maximizing levels.

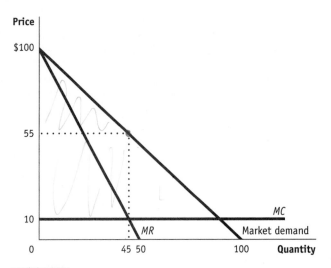

STEP 3: Calculate Monty's total costs and total revenues and then use these figures to calculate the profit he will make.

Review the section "The Monopolist's Profit-Maximizing Output and Price" on page 249, and Figure 8-6 on page 249.

To calculate Monty's total costs, start by recognizing that the cost of each additional unit is $10. Since there are no fixed costs, this implies that producing 45 units will cost Monty $450. (Since *MC* is horizontal and there are no fixed costs, this implies that marginal cost is equal to average total cost.) To calculate Monty's total revenue, multiply the price per unit times the number of units: ($55 per unit)(45 units) = $2,475. Monty's profit is equal to total revenue minus total cost, or $2,475 − $450 = $2,025. In the following figure, the shaded area represents Monty's profit.

STEP 4: Using your graph identify the area that corresponds to deadweight loss and then calculate a value for this area. Also, identify the area that corresponds to consumer surplus and then calculate a value for this area.

Review the section "Welfare Effects of Monopoly" on pages 258–259, and Figure 8-8 on page 258.

Deadweight loss is the area that corresponds to the loss in consumer and producer surplus that results when not all mutually beneficial transactions take place. In this case, the deadweight loss is solely a loss in consumer surplus: if the dry cleaning industry was a perfectly competitive industry, more units of output would be produced and these units would sell for a price equal to *MC*. The following figure represents the deadweight loss due to monopoly. The value of this deadweight loss is equal to (1/2)($55 per unit − $10 per unit)(90 units − 45 units) = $1,012.50.

The consumer surplus in the dry cleaning market will be equal to that area that is beneath the demand curve but above the price consumers pay. In this market, consumers are paying $55 per unit of dry cleaning. The following graph indicates the area that corresponds to consumer surplus. The value of this area is equal to (1/2)($100 per unit − $55 per unit)(45 units) = $1,012.50.

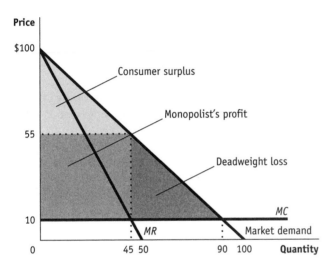

2. Suppose that the dry cleaning market in Tuxedoville is a perfectly competitive industry and not the monopoly described in problem 1. Suppose that the market demand curve for the industry is $P = 100 − Q$ and the *MC* of a representative firm is given by the equation $MC = 10$. How much dry cleaning will be produced in this perfectly competitive industry given this information? What will be the price of dry cleaning if this market is perfectly competitive? What will the individual firm's level of profits be in the long run? What is the deadweight loss equal to in this perfectly competitive industry? Finally, what is the value of consumer surplus if the market is a perfectly competitive one? Compare the outcome in this perfectly competitive market to the outcome when the market is served by the monopolist Monty from problem 1.

STEP 1: Find the profit-maximizing quantity and price for this market, given the above information.

Review the section "Welfare Effects of Monopoly" on pages 258–259, and Figure 8-8 on page 258.

In a perfectly competitive industry, output will be at that level of output at which price is equal to the marginal cost of production. To find this output, equate the demand curve to the *MC* curve: thus, $10 = 100 − Q$, or $Q = 90$. In a perfectly competitive industry, the price charged for the good will be equal to the marginal cost of production: thus, the price for the good will be $10. The following graph illustrates this outcome.

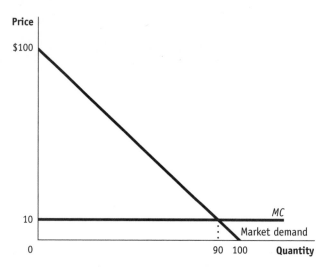

STEP 2: Find the individual firm's level of profit in the long run as well as the deadweight loss in the industry. Calculate the value of consumer surplus when this market is a perfectly competitive market.

Review the section "Welfare Effects of Monopoly" on pages 258–259, and Figure 8-8 on page 258.

In a perfectly competitive industry, firms earn zero economic profit in the long run due to entry and exit of firms. There is no deadweight loss in a perfectly competitive industry since all mutually beneficial transactions are taking place. The value of consumer surplus is equal to the area that is underneath the demand curve and above the price that consumers pay for the product. In this case, that area's value is equal to (1/2)($100 per unit – $10 per unit)(90 units) = $4,050. The following graph indicates the area that corresponds to consumer surplus.

STEP 3: Compare the outcomes when this market is perfectly competitive versus when it is served by a monopolist.

Review the section "Welfare Effects of Monopoly" on pages 258–259, and Figure 8-8 on page 258.

Price is lower and output higher when this industry is perfectly competitive than when it is a monopoly. With perfect competition, the area of consumer surplus is larger and there is no deadweight loss. Thus, monopoly reduces consumer surplus, creates a deadweight loss, prevents mutually beneficial transactions from taking place, and results in higher prices and lower outputs than would be the case if the industry were a perfectly competitive industry. Monopoly does result in positive economic profit for producers.

3. For each of the following situations, fill in the accompanying table. You are asked to determine what type of industry each situation represents and whether the product is differentiated. Choose perfect competition, monopoly, oligopoly, or monopolistic competition for the type of industry and differentiated, undifferentiated, or not applicable for the product differentiation column. If the product is differentiated, describe how the product is differentiated: differentiated by style or type; differentiated by location; or differentiated by quality.

Situation	Type of industry	Is product differentiated, and if so, how is it differentiated
Dress shops for teenagers at malls		
Gasoline stations in a town of 200,000 people		
Meat market in a community of 20 people		
100,000 corn growers in a country		
Gasoline station located on a toll road		
Colleges and universities in a country		

STEP 1: Review the characteristics of each type of industry before filling out the column. Also, review what it means to have a differentiated product.

Review the section "Types of Market Structure" on pages 240–241, Figure 8-1 on page 240, and the section "The Meaning of Monopolistic Competition" on pages 264–267.

STEP 2: Now, fill in the table, recognizing that if there is only one producer in the market, the market structure is a monopoly; that if there are many producers, none of whom has market power, and the good is an identical product, then the market is a perfectly competitive market; that if there are a few producers, the market is an oligopoly; and that if there are many producers producing differentiated products, the market is monopolistically competitive. The completed table follows.

Review the section "Types of Market Structure" on pages 240–241, Figure 8-1 on page 240, and the section "The Meaning of Monopolistic Competition" on pages 264–267.

Situation	Type of industry	Is product differentiated, and if so, how is it differentiated
Dress shops for teenagers at malls	Monopolistic competition	Differentiated by style or type; differentiated by quality
Gasoline stations in a town of 20,000 people	Oligopoly	Differentiated by location
Meat market in a community of 20 people	Monopoly	Not applicable
100,000 corn growers in a country	Perfect competition	Not differentiated
Gasoline station located on a toll road	Monopoly	Not applicable
Colleges and universities in a country	Monopolistic competition	Differentiated by style or type; differentiated by quality; and differentiated by location

4. Suppose there is an industry in which there are just a few producers and each of these producers is aware of the others. Why might it be worthwhile for these producers to cooperate in making decisions to produce the monopoly price and quantity of the good in this market? Why might it be difficult for these producers to be able to adhere to this monopoly-level pricing and production decision?

STEP 1: **Review the benefits of forming a cartel and why it is beneficial in an industry characterized as having just a few firms for those firms to cooperate and produce the monopoly level of its output and price and then divide up this level of production among the different firms.**

Review the section "Oligopoly: The Legal Framework" on pages 260–261, and the section "Tacit Collusion and Price Wars" on pages 262–263.

A successful cartel can restrict output and raise price above the level that would exist without a cartel. That implies that the successful cartel can generate higher joint profits for the firms that are in the cartel.

STEP 2: **List the reasons that undermine the ability of a cartel to collude.**

Review the section "Oligopoly: The Legal Framework" on pages 260–261, and the section "Tacit Collusion and Price Wars" on pages 262–263.

However, it is highly difficult to maintain a cartel agreement among the different firms since each firm faces an incentive to cheat on the cartel arrangement. Cartels find it particularly hard to collude when there are large numbers of firms, complex products or pricing schemes, and differences in interests among the firms in the cartel, as well as when buyers have some degree of bargaining power.

Problems and Exercises

1. Assuming identical costs, what is the monopolist's effect on price and quantity compared to a perfectly competitive industry? Draw two sketches, with one sketch illustrating the perfectly competitive industry and its equilibrium market price and market quantity, and the other sketch illustrating the monopoly and its market price and market quantity. On both sketches, identify the areas that correspond to the consumer surplus, producer surplus, and deadweight loss.

2. For the last unit produced by a monopolist, what is the relationship between the price consumers are willing to pay for this unit and the cost of producing this last unit of the good? What is the implication of this relationship with regard to the allocation of resources to this monopoly?

3. Suppose there is a single firm producing a good for which there are no close substitutes. This firm is currently earning positive economic profit in the short run. Why does this firm care about the existence of barriers to entry in its market? Explain your answer.

4. A firm wishes to increase the price it charges for its product, and it wishes to restrict the level of output available to consumers. What must be true if this firm is to be successful?

5. Briefly review the four general types of barriers to entry and how each of these types effectively restricts the level of competition the monopolist faces.

6.   Suppose the following table describes the market demand schedule for a monopoly.

Price ($)	Quantity demanded (units)
1,000	0
800	200
600	400
400	600
200	800
0	1,000

a.   Draw a graph of this market demand schedule for the monopoly.

b. Compute the firm's total revenue and marginal revenue figures for the following table. For the marginal revenue figures, use the midpoint method.

Price ($)	Quantity demanded (units)	Total revenue ($)	Marginal revenue ($ per unit)
1,000	0		
800	200		
600	400		
400	600		
200	800		
0	1,000		

c. Draw the monopolist's marginal revenue curve on the graph you drew in part (a) of this problem.

d. Write an equation for this monopolist's market demand curve and for its *MR* curve. Compare these two equations. What is true about the *y*-intercept of these two equations? What is the relationship between the slope of the demand curve and the slope of the *MR* curve?

e. If the firm's marginal cost is constant and equal to $200, what is this monopolist's profit-maximizing level of output and what price will this monopolist charge for this good? Label this quantity and this price on your graph.

f. On the graph you drew in part (a), shade in the area that corresponds to the consumer surplus and label it clearly. On this same graph, shade in the area that corresponds to producer surplus and label it clearly. Shade in the area that corresponds to deadweight loss and label it clearly.

g. Calculate the value of consumer surplus, producer surplus, and deadweight loss for this monopoly.

7. Suppose the following table describes the market demand schedule for a monopoly.

Price ($)	Quantity demanded (units)
1,000	0
800	400
600	800
400	1,200
200	1,600
0	2,000

a. Draw a graph of this market demand schedule for the monopoly.

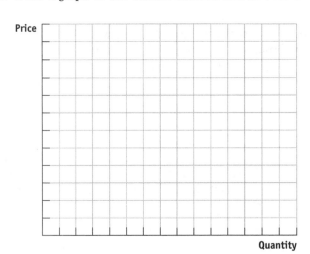

b. Compute the firm's total revenue and marginal revenue figures for the following table. For the marginal revenue figures, use the midpoint method.

Price ($)	Quantity demanded (units)	Total revenue ($)	Marginal revenue ($ per unit)
1,000	0		
800	400		
600	800		
400	1,200		
200	1,600		
0	2,000		

c. Draw the monopolist's marginal revenue curve on the graph you drew in part (a) of this problem.

d. Write an equation for this monopolist's market demand curve and for its *MR* curve. Compare these two equations. What is true about the *y*-intercept of these two equations? What is the relationship between the slope of the demand curve and the slope of the *MR* curve?

e. If the firm's marginal cost is constant and equal to $200, what is this monopolist's profit-maximizing level of output and what price will this monopolist charge for this good? Label this quantity and this price on your graph.

f. On the graph you drew in part (a), shade in the area that corresponds to the consumer surplus and label it clearly. On this same graph, shade in the area that corresponds to producer surplus and label it clearly. Shade in the area that corresponds to deadweight loss and label it clearly.

g. Calculate the value of consumer surplus, producer surplus, and deadweight loss for this monopoly.

8. The following graph represents a monopolist's cost curves and the demand curve for the monopolist's product. Use this graph to answer this set of questions.

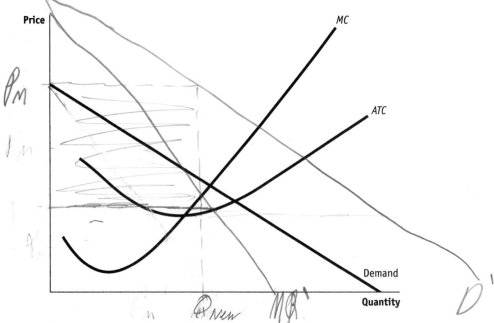

MR=MC

a. On the graph, identify the monopolist's profit-maximizing level of output and label this amount Q_M. (Hint: Don't forget that you will need to first find the monopolist's *MR* curve to answer this question.) On the graph, label the price the monopolist will charge for the good as P_M.

b. Does this monopolist make positive, negative, or zero economic profit in the short run? Identify the area that represents profits in the graph if the firm earns positive or negative profit.

Neg – ATC is higher
Pos ATC < P_M

c. What do you expect will happen to the monopolist in the long run? In your answer, be sure to identify what happens to the firm's profits, level of production, and price.

Profits go up b/c level of production goes up w/ increased returns to scale and price goes down

Continue w/ positive profits b/c there is entry barrier

d. A newspaper runs an article on the benefits of consuming the product this monopolist produces. The result of this article is that demand for this product shifts to the right at every price. Redraw your graph with the old and the new demand curves, and then analyze what happens to output, price, and profits for this firm. Label the new output Q_M' and the new price P_M', and identify the area that represents the firm's profits.

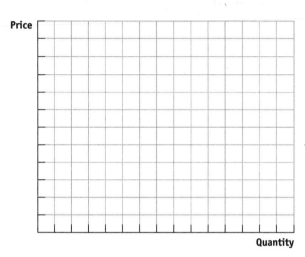

e. Given your answer in part (d), is there an incentive for a monopolist to try to increase the demand for its product?

9. Perfectly competitive firms and monopolies are both assumed to aim to maximize profit. How does the perfectly competitive firm decide on the optimal price and quantity for profit maximization? How does the monopolist decide on the optimal price and quantity for profit maximization? What are the efficiency implications of these two decisions? In your answer to this last question, be sure to comment on the relationship between price and marginal cost for the last unit the firm produces.

10. Suppose a monopolist has a linear market demand curve. At the midpoint of this demand curve, the elasticity of demand is unit-elastic. What do you know about the marginal revenue of the monopolist when the elasticity of demand is equal to 1? If the demand for this monopolist is elastic, what do you know about the marginal revenue for this monopolist? If the demand for this monopolist is inelastic, what do you know about the marginal revenue for this monopolist?

11. A monopolist finds that the demand for its product at the current level of production is elastic. Will this monopolist increase or decrease its revenue if it lowers the price at which it sells its product? Explain your answer, making reference to the quantity effect as well as the price effect. Which of these two effects is dominant in this situation?

12. Use the following graphs to answer this set of questions. The left-hand graph depicts a monopoly with its market demand curve and its MC curve. The right-hand graph depicts a perfectly competitive industry with the same market demand curve and the MC curve for a representative firm. These two graphs are intended to allow you to compare a monopoly to a perfectly competitive industry.

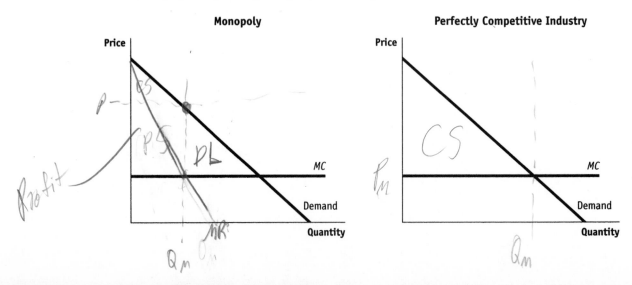

a. On each graph, identify the market level of output. On the first graph, label this output level Q_M, and on the second graph, label this output level Q_{PC}. (Hint: Remember that you must first identify the MR curve before selecting the quantity that will be produced.)

b. On each graph, identify the market price for the good. On the first graph, label this price P_M, and on the second graph, label this price P_{PC}.

c. Compare the level of production and the price of the good in the two markets. Which market outcome is better for consumers? Explain your answer.

d. Is there a deadweight loss in either of the two graphs? If there is a deadweight loss, shade in the relevant area on the graph.

13. Discuss two different government policies for dealing with a natural monopoly. Describe each policy and then discuss any limitations or shortcomings that might arise from the implementation of the policy.

14. An industry has ten producers producing differentiated products, but all the products in the industry are generally viewed by consumers as soft drinks. What kind of market structure does this industry have, and why would you define the market structure in this way?

15. Oligopoly is characterized by having a few firms in the industry. What is the best explanation for why these industries only have a few firms?

16. Suppose there are only two firms in an industry that produces gasoline. To make the analysis simpler, assume that once the companies have incurred the fixed costs of production, the marginal cost of producing another gallon of gasoline is equal to $0. Suppose the demand for gasoline in this market is equal to $Q = 10,000 - 1,000P$.

    a. Draw a graph of the industry demand curve, and draw the *MC* curve for the industry as well.

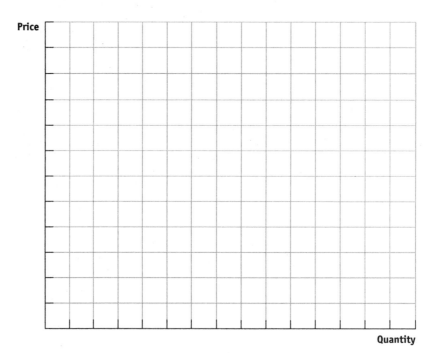

    b. If these two firms acted like perfectly competitive firms, how many units would they produce altogether? What would the total revenue for the two firms equal?

c. Suppose these two firms are able to form a cartel in which they agree to produce the profit-maximizing level of output and then split the market evenly. What is the total amount of output these two firms will produce if they agree to split the market? What is the price of gasoline? What will be the total revenue received by each firm if they agree to split the market and neither firm cheats on this agreement? Are the two firms better off if they agree to this arrangement?

d. On a graph, indicate the market quantity Q^* that these two firms will produce under the arrangement described in part (c). On this same graph, indicate the market price P^* that will be charged for the gasoline.

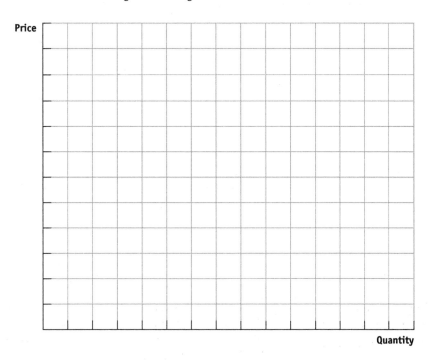

17. Suppose the two firms in problem 16 agree to form a cartel as described in part (c) of that problem, but that one of the firms decides to cheat on the arrangement by producing 3,500 gallons of gasoline instead of the agreed-upon 2,500 gallons of gasoline.

a. What will happen to the total amount of gasoline produced by the two firms?

b. What will happen to the price of gasoline when one firm increases its production to 3,500 gallons while the other firm continues to produce 2,500 gallons?

c. What is the total revenue received by the firm that produces 3,500 gallons of gasoline? What is the total revenue received by the firm that produces 2,500 gallons of gasoline? Is cheating on the cartel arrangement by one firm beneficial to both firms? Explain your answer. When one firm cheats on the cartel, what happens to the level of total profits?

d. Once the second firm realizes what the first firm has done, what do you imagine might be the second firm's response? Why are cartels unstable?

18. Suppose there are two firms in an industry that produces nuclear generators. Furthermore, suppose that each of these firms is able to produce a maximum of twenty generators a year due to its productive capacity. Would you predict that these two firms could successfully collude on price without a formal agreement? Why or why not?

19. What kinds of factors can make it hard for a group of firms in an oligopolistic industry to achieve tacit collusion? Discuss four different factors that make this difficult.

20. Why are fast-food restaurants considered an example of a monopolistically competitive industry? What key attributes need to be present to have a monopolistically competitive industry?

- hard to enter
- moderate long term profit
- differentiated product
- not many sellers, many buyers

21. How are fast-food restaurants similar; that is, why are they all considered to be part of the fast-food industry? How are fast-food restaurants differentiated; that is, why are the meals they sell considered to be differentiated from each other?

22. What aspect of the fast-food restaurant business is competitive? What aspect of the fast-food restaurant business is monopolistic?

23. In Smalltown there are three different gas stations owned by different people. One is located on the west side of town, one is on the east side of town, and one is on the south side of town. They all sell three types of identical gasoline, and their business hours are the same. Are these three firms differentiated?

24. The fast-food industry has many different restaurants selling many different types of food. These restaurants are also located in different places. What types of differentiation are represented by the fast-food industry?

354 CHAPTER 8 MONOPOLY, OLIGOPOLY, AND MONOPOLISTIC COMPETITION

25. Monopolistic competition is particularly noteworthy because of the degree of product differentiation one finds in this type of market structure. Why do firms find it profitable to differentiate their product? Why do consumers like this variety?

different tastes and preferences

26. Some monopolistically competitive firms differentiate their product according to quality. Describe what this means and why a firm might find this a profitable type of differentiation.

different desired levels of quality

■ BEFORE YOU TAKE THE TEST

Chapter Review Questions

1. The demand for the monopolist's product
   a. is downward sloping.
   b. equals the market demand curve.
   c. is equal to the firm's *MR* curve.
   d. All of these statements are true.
   e. Answers (a) and (b) are true.

2. An industry is characterized by having a few firms, each producing a differentiated product. The market structure for this industry is most likely
   a. perfect competition.
   b. monopoly.
   c. oligopoly.
   d. monopolistic competition.

3. Which of the following statements is(are) true?
   I. A monopolistically competitive market structure is composed of many firms producing differentiated products.
   II. A perfectly competitive firm profit maximizes by producing the level of output where $MR = MC$.
   III. A monopolist profit maximizes by charging the price where $MR = MC$.
   a. Statements I and II are true.
   b. Statements I and III are true.
   c. Statements II and III are true.
   d. Statements I, II, and III are true.

4. Monopoly and oligopoly are the typical market structures that occur when there are
   a. no significant entry barriers.
   b. significant entry barriers.

5. In contrast to a firm in perfect competition, a monopolist charges a
   a. higher price and produces a larger quantity.
   b. higher price and produces a smaller quantity.
   c. lower price and produces a larger quantity.
   d. lower price and produces a smaller quantity.

6. A barrier to entry is
   a. always a man-made obstacle to the entry of new firms into a competitive industry.
   b. a term referring to the firm's private property and the firm's right to exclude people from entering this private property.
   c. something that effectively keeps new firms from entering an industry.
   d. only relevant in perfectly competitive industries.

7. A firm that experiences increasing returns to scale
   a. finds that its average total cost of production decreases throughout the relevant region of production.
   b. will find it advantageous to produce a relatively large amount of output rather than a relatively small amount of output.
   c. will benefit from a larger volume of sales.
   d. Answers (a), (b), and (c) are all true.

8. An industry is characterized by having an average total cost that decreases as output increases. In this industry, the output can be produced at the lowest cost if _____ produce(s) the total market output.
   a. many identical firms
   b. a single firm
   c. a large number of firms
   d. a few firms

9. An industry is characterized by having an average total cost that decreases as output increases. This is due to large
   a. variable costs that are more easily borne by a single producer of the good.
   b. fixed costs that are more easily borne by a single producer of the good.
   c. marginal costs that are more easily borne by a single producer of the good.
   d. fluctuations in revenue that create market instability in the industry, which results in many firms exiting the industry and leaving a single firm to produce the good.

10. Patents and copyrights
    a. protect the rights of inventors and writers.
    b. harm consumers of the patented or copyright-protected articles because these articles are more expensive to consumers.
    c. provide an incentive for research and development as well as creative work.
    d. All of these statements are true.

Use the following graph of a monopolist to answer the next four questions.

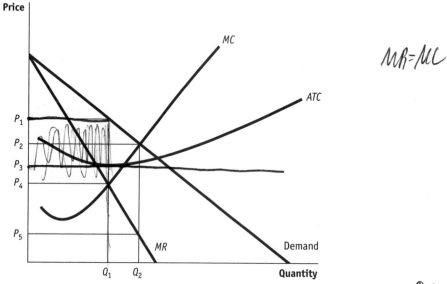

11. This monopolist will produce the profit-maximizing level of output _____ and sell each unit for _____.
    a. Q_1; P_1.
    b. Q_1; P_2.
    c. Q_2; P_2.
    d. Q_1; P_4.

12. If this monopolist were to act as if it were in a perfectly competitive industry, then it would produce _____ units of the good and charge _____ for each unit.
    a. Q_1; P_2
    b. Q_1; P_1
    c. Q_2; P_2
    d. Q_2; P_5

13. The deadweight loss associated with this monopoly can be measured as the area
    a. $(1/2)(P_2/\text{unit} - P_4/\text{unit})(Q_2 \text{ units} - Q_1 \text{ units})$.
    b. $(1/2)(P_1/\text{unit} - P_4/\text{unit})(Q_1 \text{ units})$.
    c. $(1/2)(P_2/\text{unit} - P_4/\text{unit})(Q_1 \text{ units})$.
    d. $(1/2)(P_1/\text{unit} - P_4/\text{unit})(Q_2 \text{ units} - Q_1 \text{ units})$.

$MR = MC$
$MR = MC$

14. This monopolist earns
    a. positive economic profit equal to the area $(P_1/\text{unit} - P_3/\text{unit})(Q_1 \text{ units})$.
    b. positive economic profit equal to the area $(P_1/\text{unit} - P_4/\text{unit})(Q_1 \text{ units})$.
    c. negative economic profit equal to the area $(P_1/\text{unit} - P_3/\text{unit})(Q_1 \text{ units})$.
    d. negative economic profit equal to the area $(P_1/\text{unit} - P_4/\text{unit})(Q_1 \text{ units})$.

Use the following information to answer the next four questions. The demand curve for a monopolist is given by $P = 100 - Q$, while the monopolist's marginal cost is $P = 3Q$. At the profit-maximizing level of output for the monopolist, the average total cost of production is equal to $70.

15. This monopolist's MR curve can be written as
    a. $MR = 100 - Q$.
    b. $MR = 200 - Q$.
    c. $MR = 100 - (1/2)Q$.
    d. $MR = 100 - 2Q$.

16. For this monopolist the profit-maximizing level of output is equal to _____ and the market price for this output is _____.
    a. 20 units; $80   c. 25 units; $75
    b. 20 units; $60   d. 50 units; $50

17. Profits for this monopolist equal
    a. $400.   c. $10.
    b. $200.   d. $20.

18. The deadweight loss associated with this monopoly
    a. cannot be calculated from the information given.
    b. is unimportant, since the monopoly is protected from competition due to the existence of effective barriers to entry.
    c. equals $50.
    d. equals $25.

19. A monopolist is debating whether or not to lower the price it charges for its product. Which of the following statements is(are) true?
    I. When the monopolist lowers its price, the quantity effect always increases the monopolist's total revenue.
    II. When the monopolist lowers its price, the price effect initially causes total revenue to increase, but eventually the price effect causes total revenue to fall.
    III. The monopolist does not need to worry about the quantity or price effect when debating what price to charge for its product, since it is the only producer of the good.
    a. Statement I is true.
    b. Statement II is true.
    c. Statements I and II are true.
    d. Statement III is true.

20. A monopolist estimates that the price elasticity of demand for its product is less than 1. This monopolist knows that an increase in the price of its good will _____ its total revenue.

a. increase

b. decrease

21. A natural monopoly is a monopoly that occurs because of increasing returns to scale. Which of the following statements is(are) true for a natural monopoly?

a. Public ownership, although a policy often used for dealing with natural monopoly, may result in poor service and a failure to minimize the cost of providing the good.

b. Price regulation of a natural monopoly, which limits the price charged for the product, is capable of increasing the total amount of the good available while simultaneously reducing the price of each unit.

c. A natural monopolist that is price-regulated will only be willing to supply the good if the regulated price is equal to or greater than the average total cost of producing its output.

d. Answers (a), (b), and (c) are all true.

Use the following graph of a monopolist to answer the next question.

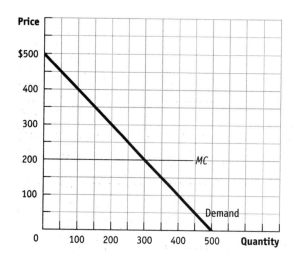

22. If this monopolist profit maximizes, it will produce _____ units of output, charge a price of _____, provide a producer surplus equal to _____, provide a consumer surplus equal to _____, and create a deadweight loss equal to _____.

a. 250; $250; $31,250; $31,250; $0

b. 150; $350; $22,500; $11,250; $11,250

c. 150; $350; $11,250; $22,500; $11,250

d. 300; $200; $0; $45,000; $0

23. An industry characterized by having a few firms, each with some market power, is an example of a(n)

a. monopoly, since the firms have some market power.

b. perfectly competitive industry, since there is more than one firm in the industry.

c. monopolistically competitive industry, since the firms compete with one another while at the same time they have some market power.

d. oligopoly, since the firms have market power and can therefore affect the market price, but there are only a few firms, so each firm recognizes the interdependence between firms.

24. The formation of an oligopoly is primarily due to the
    a. control of an essential input or resource used in the production of the good.
    b. existence of increasing returns to scale in the industry.
    c. effective entry barrier posed by copyrights or patents.
    d. All of these statements are correct.

25. Suppose there is a duopoly and that the two firms in this duopoly collude. The firms have agreed to collude most likely as a means to
    a. stabilize prices.
    b. stabilize quantities.
    c. maximize each firm's profits.
    d. maximize their joint profits.

26. Suppose there is a duopoly and that the two firms in this duopoly have formed a cartel. This cartel will likely be
    a. quite stable, since there are only two firms and they are each aware of the other's actions.
    b. unstable, since both firms have an incentive to cheat on the cartel arrangement.

27. When a monopolist lowers its price, the monopolist experiences both a quantity and a price effect from this action. When a firm in a cartel lowers its price, it also experiences a quantity and a price effect from this action. With respect to the monopolist's experience, the firm in a cartel finds that the
    a. quantity effect is a negative effect on total revenue.
    b. price effect is a larger positive effect on total revenue for the firm in the cartel than it is for the monopolist.
    c. price effect is a smaller negative effect on total revenue for the firm in the cartel than it is for the monopolist.

28. Firms in an oligopoly have a choice of competing with one another or cooperating with one another. Which strategy is typically more profitable to the individual firms in the industry?
    a. compete
    b. cooperate

29. The Sherman Antitrust Act of 1890 was
    a. aimed at preventing the creation of more monopolies.
    b. intended to provide legislation to help break up existing monopolies.
    c. the beginning of antitrust policy in the United States.
    d. Answers (a), (b), and (c) are all true statements.

30. Monopolistic competition is a market structure
    a. that provides greater product diversity than is the case in a perfectly competitive industry.
    b. characterized as having just a few producers of similar, but not identical, products.
    c. in which entry of new firms in the short run is possible.
    d. Answers (a) and (b) are both correct.

31. Monopolistically competitive firms resemble perfectly competitive firms in that
   a. both types of market structure are characterized as having a small number of producers.
   b. entry and exit in the long run are possible for both types of market structure.
   c. firms in both types of market structure always earn positive economic profit in the short run.
   d. firms in both types of market structure compete against other firms offering similar products.

32. Monopolistically competitive firms resemble monopolies in that
   a. producing a differentiated product effectively creates an environment in which there is only one provider of the good in the short run.
   b. producing a differentiated product and earning positive economic profits induce entry of new firms in the long run.
   c. there are effective barriers to entry in the long run that prevent other firms from entering the market to compete against the existing firm(s).
   d. Answers (a) and (c) are both correct.

33. A monopolistically competitive industry is characterized by having
   a. many firms, each producing a differentiated product and operating in an industry with free entry and exit in the short run.
   b. a few firms, each producing a differentiated product but with each firm having market power and the ability to set the price of the good it sells.
   c. a very large number of firms that produce very similar products and that always elect to produce the profit-maximizing amount of output in both the short run and the long run.
   d. None of the answers is true about a monopolistically competitive industry.

34. Monopolistically competitive firms
   a. have no limit as to what price they can charge for the good they produce, since this good is highly differentiated from any other firm's product.
   b. charge the highest price people are willing to pay for the good based on the demand curve for the good.
   c. are price-takers and must accept the market price that is determined in the industry.
   d. do not worry about what price to charge and instead focus the bulk of their attention on deciding what the profit-maximizing level of output is for the firm.

ANSWER KEY

Answers to Problems and Exercises

1. A perfectly competitive industry produces a greater quantity of the good and sells this good at a lower price than does a monopoly with the same cost curves. The figures below contrast the outcomes for these two types of market structure based on the same market demand curve. In the first figure, the perfectly competitive industry sets the market equilibrium price and quantity at the level at which the quantity demanded equals the quantity supplied. This figure also indicates this price and quantity combination and indicates the areas that correspond to consumer and producer surplus.

Market Outcome for a Perfectly Competitive Industry

In contrast, the monopoly selects its output by equating *MR* to *MC* and then setting price by taking this quantity and looking at what price consumers are willing to pay for this quantity. The figure below illustrates the monopoly situation. Note that the monopoly results in a higher price, a lower quantity, and the creation of a deadweight loss.

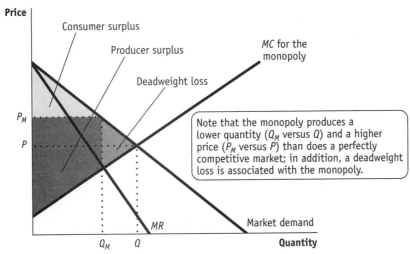

Market Outcome for a Monopoly

Note that the monopoly produces a lower quantity (Q_M versus Q) and a higher price (P_M versus P) than does a perfectly competitive market; in addition, a deadweight loss is associated with the monopoly.

2. For the last unit produced by the monopolist, the price consumers are willing to pay for this unit is greater than the marginal cost of producing this last unit. Refer back to the graph of the monopoly given in the answer to problem 1 to see this. The implication is that the value that consumers place on this last unit, as measured by the price they are willing to pay, is greater than the cost of producing this last unit, as measured by the marginal cost incurred by the firm when it produces this unit. Thus, too few resources are being allocated to the production of this good, since the value to the consumer exceeds the cost to the producer of producing this last unit. This is not surprising, since one of the effects of a monopoly is to restrict output to a level lower than would be produced with perfect competition.

3. This firm is a monopoly in that there is only one producer, and this producer is producing a good for which there are no close substitutes. However, if there are no barriers to entry, then this monopoly will not persist: new firms will be attracted to this industry in the long run due to the existence of positive economic profit. Substantial barriers to entry can prevent the firm from facing competition, and it therefore can continue to sustain its positive economic profit into the long run.

4. A firm can choose to restrict its output and raise its price, but if it competes in an industry where there are many firms and where there are close substitutes for its product, the firm will find that raising price and restricting output is not beneficial to it in terms of its profitability. What makes it possible for a firm to restrict output and raise price is the presence of market power that enables the firm to affect the market outcome.

5. Control of an essential resource or input is a very effective barrier to entry, since new firms will be unable to produce the product if they do not have access to this resource or input. The presence of increasing returns to scale also serves as an effective barrier to entry, since the firm that has a larger volume of sales will find that its average total cost of production is lower than that of a firm with a smaller volume of sales: increasing returns to scale implies that the firm benefits from its large scale of production, which makes it difficult for would-be competitors to enter the industry and compete. Technological superiority can also act an as effective barrier to entry: firms that maintain a consistent technological superiority over potential competitors can establish themselves as monopolists. Lastly, the government may create effective barriers to entry in the form of patents or copyright protections.

6. **a.**

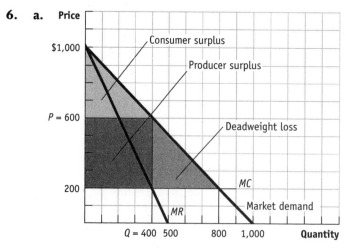

b.

Price ($)	Quantity demanded (units)	Total revenue ($)	Marginal revenue ($ per unit)
1,000	0	0	
			800
800	200	160,000	
			400
600	400	240,000	
			0
400	600	240,000	
			–400
200	800	160,000	
			–800
0	1,000	0	

c. See the graph in part (a).

d. The monopolist's demand curve is $Q = 1{,}000 - P$, or written in slope-intercept form, it is $P = 1{,}000 - Q$. The monopolist's MR curve is $MR = 1{,}000 - 2Q$. The y-intercept for the monopolist's demand curve is the same as the y-intercept for the monopolist's MR curve if the demand curve is linear. The slope of the MR curve is twice the slope of the demand curve, provided that the demand curve is linear.

e. The monopolist profit maximizes by producing the level of output where $MR = MC$ and then moving up to the demand curve to charge the price associated with this level of output. Thus, if $MC = 200$ and $MR = 1{,}000 - 2Q$, then the profit-maximizing quantity is 400 units. To find the monopolist's price, substitute 400 for Q in the demand equation: the monopolist's price is $600.

f. See the graph in part (a).

g. Consumer surplus = (1/2)($400 per unit)(400 units) = $80,000; producer surplus = ($400 per unit)(400 units) = $160,000; deadweight loss = (1/2)($400 per unit) (400 units) = $80,000

7. a.

b.

Price ($)	Quantity demanded (units)	Total revenue ($)	Marginal revenue ($ per unit)
1,000	0	0	
			800
800	400	320,000	
			400
600	800	480,000	
			0
400	1,200	480,000	
			−400
200	1,600	320,000	
			−800
0	2,000	0	

c. See the graph in part (a).

d. The monopolist's demand curve is $Q = 2{,}000 - 2P$, or written in slope-intercept form, it is $P = 1{,}000 - (1/2)Q$. The monopolist's MR curve is $MR = 1{,}000 - Q$. The y-intercept for the monopolist's demand curve is the same as the y-intercept for the monopolist's MR curve if the demand curve is linear. The slope of the MR curve is twice the slope of the demand curve, provided that the demand curve is linear.

e. The monopolist profit maximizes by producing the level of output where $MR = MC$ and then moving up to the demand curve to charge the price associated with this level of output. Thus, if $MC = 200$ and $MR = 1{,}000 - Q$, then the profit-maximizing quantity is 800 units. To find the monopolist's price, substitute 800 for Q in the demand equation: the monopolist's price is $600.

f. See the graph in part (a).

g. Consumer surplus = $(1/2)(\$400$ per unit$)(800$ units$) = \$160{,}000$; producer surplus = $(\$400$ per unit$)(800$ units$) = \$320{,}000$; deadweight loss = $(1/2)(\$400$ per unit$)(800$ units$) = \$160{,}000$

8. a. See the answer to part (d).

b. This monopolist earns positive economic profit since the price it receives on each unit (P_M) is greater than its average total cost (ATC) of production (ATC_M on the graph).

c. This monopolist will continue to earn positive economic profits because there is an effective barrier to entry to this industry that prevents the firm from having to compete with other producers. The firm's profits will continue at the level given in the graph, and the firm's price and quantity decision will remain unchanged.

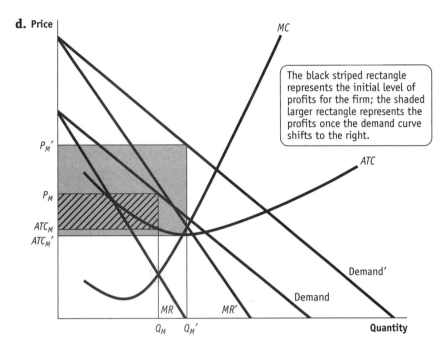

d. Price

The black striped rectangle represents the initial level of profits for the firm; the shaded larger rectangle represents the profits once the demand curve shifts to the right.

e. Holding everything else constant, if the monopolist can increase the demand for its product, it can charge a higher price, produce more units of the good, and increase the level of economic profits it earns.

9. The perfectly competitive firm is a price-taking firm and must charge the market-determined price for its output. It then chooses the profit-maximizing level of output given this price. The profit-maximizing level of output for the perfectly competitive firm is where $MR = MC$, or where $P = MC$, since $P = MR$ for a perfectly competitive firm.

A monopoly can set its own price, subject to market demand for its product. It determines its profit-maximizing level of output by equating marginal cost to marginal revenue, and then charges the price consumers are willing to pay for this level of output. The monopolist finds this price by going vertically up to the demand curve from its selected level of output and charging the price on its demand curve that is associated with this level of output.

A perfectly competitive firm produces an efficient level of output, since $P = MC$ for the last unit of output it produces. This implies that the price consumers are willing to pay for the last unit produced is equal to the cost of producing this last unit: consumers and producers value this last unit equivalently, which tells us that the right amount of resources is being allocated to the production of this good. A monopoly, in contrast, produces an inefficient level of output, since $P > MC$ for the last unit of output it produces. This implies that the price consumers are willing to pay for the last unit produced is greater than the cost of producing this last unit: the value the consumers place on this last unit exceeds the cost of producing this last unit. More resources should be devoted to the production of this good.

10. The *MR* curve for a monopolist with a linear demand curve shares the *y*-intercept with the demand curve and has twice the slope of the demand curve. If you plot this *MR* curve and the demand curve on the same graph, you will find that the *MR* curve intersects the horizontal axis at a quantity that is the quantity found at the midpoint of the demand curve. Thus, when demand is unit-elastic (at its midpoint), marginal revenue equals zero. When demand is elastic, marginal revenue is positive, and when demand is inelastic, marginal revenue is negative.

11. When the demand for the product is elastic, the monopolist can increase its revenue by selling the good for a lower price. When the monopolist lowers its price, it sells more units than it did at a higher price: this quantity effect positively increases the monopolist's revenue. When the monopolist lowers its price, it must cut the price on all units sold: this price effect negatively impacts the monopolist's revenue. When demand is elastic, the quantity effect is dominant over the price effect, resulting in the monopolist's revenues increasing.

12. **a, b.**

c. The perfectly competitive market produces a higher level of output and charges a lower price for this output than does the monopoly. Consumers prefer the outcome of the perfectly competitive industry since it has more output and pays lower prices.

d. The monopoly has a deadweight loss, which is the shaded area in the graph. Notice that the monopoly's level of production occurs where *P* > *MC*. This implies that consumers would like to have more of the good, since they are willing to pay more for another unit of the good than the marginal cost of producing that additional unit of output. Whenever price is not equal to marginal cost for the last unit produced, there is a deadweight loss, since the market is not producing the socially optimal level of output.

13. There are two primary government policies for dealing with natural monopolies: public ownership and price regulation.

   With public ownership, the natural monopoly is operated by a public agency that has a mandate to provide the good while also protecting consumers' interests. A publicly owned natural monopoly can set prices based on efficiency and not profit maximization. However, a publicly owned natural monopoly may fail to keep costs down or to offer high-quality products.

   Price regulation limits the price that natural monopolies can charge for their good. Price regulation takes the form of setting a price ceiling so that the natural monopoly provides more of the regulated good at a lower price than would occur with an unregulated natural monopoly. Price regulation is difficult because the regulators do not have the required information to be able to set price at exactly that point where *P* = *ATC*. In addition, price-regulated natural monopolies have a tendency to inflate their costs to regulators and to provide inferior-quality products.

14. This industry is characterized as having just a few producers, and although the products are differentiated, they are closely related and can be viewed as substitutes for one another. Because of the small number of firms, this industry would be viewed as an oligopoly, although this classification is dependent on the share of market sales that each firm has. If the market is dominated by several of these firms, then the industry is definitely an oligopoly, but if the market is divided evenly among these ten firms, then the industry, despite its small number of firms, would act more like a perfectly competitive industry than like an oligopolistic one.

15. An industry typically has only a few firms because the industry is one in which firms have increasing returns to scale: firms benefit from being relatively large, which implies that the total market is usually easily served by just a few firms rather than many small firms.

16. a.

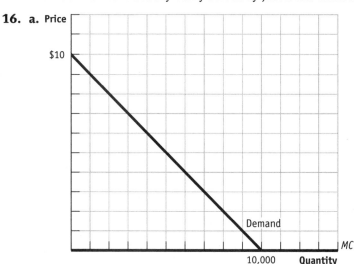

b. If the two firms acted like perfectly competitive firms, they would produce the quantity where the demand curve intersects the MC curve: they would produce a total of 10,000 gallons of gasoline. The price of this gasoline would be $0 since in a perfectly competitive industry $P = MR = MC$ in the market equilibrium. The total revenue for both firms would equal $0.

c. If the two firms collude and split the market, they will produce a total of 5,000 gallons of gasoline (each firm will produce 2,500 gallons of gasoline) since this is the profit-maximizing amount of gasoline. To find this quantity remember that you need to equate the MR curve to the marginal cost. But this time, the two firms act together like a monopolist, so you need to first construct the monopolist's MR curve: $MR = 10 - 0.002Q$. $MR = MC$ at an output of 5,000 gallons. The firms then price this output by going up to the market demand curve and selecting the price on the demand curve that is associated with 5,000 gallons of gasoline. This price will be $5 per gallon of gasoline. The total revenue received by each firm if they split the market evenly is $(1/2)($5 per gallon$)(5,000$ gallons$) = $12,500. Each firm's ATC is equal to the sum of its fixed costs and its variable costs, and since the firm's MC is equal to 0, this implies that the firm's AVC is also equal to 0. Each firm's profit will therefore equal total revenue minus fixed cost. Clearly, colluding leaves both firms better off than they would be under the scenario described in part (b).

d.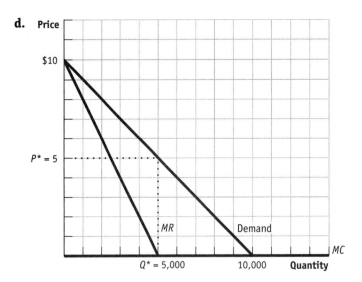

17. a. The total amount produced by the two firms will now be 6,000 gallons of gasoline.

b. When 6,000 gallons of gasoline are produced, the market price decreases to $4 per gallon of gasoline. To see this, remember that the demand curve can be written as $P = 10 - 0.001Q$, and when $Q = 6,000$ gallons, this implies that $P = \$4$ per gallon.

c. The total revenue of the firm that produces 3,500 gallons is now equal to $14,000, while the total revenue of the firm that produces 2,500 gallons is equal to $10,000. The firm that cheats on the cartel benefits since its total revenue increases from $12,500 to $14,000. The firm that maintains the cartel arrangement is hurt when the other firm cheats: its total revenue falls from $12,500 to $10,000. Notice that cheating causes the overall level of joint profits for the cartel to fall from $25,000 to $24,000: the two firms are no longer jointly profit maximizing.

d. The second firm is likely to match the first firm's production decision, which will cause price and therefore total revenue to fall further. The two firms may persist in this price-cutting behavior until they reach the perfectly competitive result where 10,000 gallons of gasoline are produced and the market price is $0. Cartels are inherently unstable due to the incentives both firms face to cheat on the cartel.

18. Since both firms are constrained with regard to their ability to alter the level of output they produce, neither firm needs to worry about the other firm suddenly increasing its level of output and decreasing the price of its product. The two firms should be able to divide the market with relative ease while pricing their product above marginal cost. This will enable both firms to earn a positive economic profit.

19. When there are a large number of firms in the oligopoly, it is harder for the firms to reach an agreement about price and quantity decisions for the industry, and it is harder for firms to ascertain when other firms are cheating on the agreement. In addition, when there are more firms in the oligopoly, this indicates that the barriers to entry are low and that existing firms face the threat of new entry, which acts as a brake on raising price to monopolistic levels.

When the oligopoly produces a number of different products and engages in more than one pricing scheme, this makes it harder for firms to have perfect collusion. It also makes it difficult to know with certainty when firms in the oligopoly are cheating on the tacit agreement.

In addition, firms in an oligopoly may not share the same perspective and reach the same conclusion about what is fair. Some firms may feel that the quantity they are assigned to produce under the tacit agreement is too low, and they may feel they deserve to be able to produce more of the product. This type of disagreement causes the tacit agreement to quickly break down.

Finally, in some oligopolistic markets there are buyers with significant market power that may be able to offset some of the market power held by the oligopoly. This makes it difficult for the oligopoly to maintain prices that are higher than the marginal cost of producing the good.

20. Fast-food restaurants are a good example of a monopolistically competitive industry because there are many firms in the industry, each producing a differentiated product, and there is free entry and exit in the industry in the long run. The key attributes of monopolistically competitive industries are a large number of firms, a differentiated product, and free entry or exit of firms in the long run.

21. Here the answers may vary quite a bit depending on what attributes you have focused on. Fast-food restaurants typically offer relatively cheap meals, in easily accessible locations, at fast speed with little waiting. The food is often easy to eat on the run or to have as carryout. Fast-food restaurants differ from one another in the type of food they serve (e.g., Mexican, hamburgers, Italian). There may also be small price variations that distinguish one restaurant from another.

22. Here again the answers may vary depending on what you focus on in your response. The fast-food restaurant industry is competitive in that there are many firms producing within this industry and each competes to satisfy more or less the same demand—the demand for quick, tasty food. The fast-food restaurant industry is also monopolistic since each firm sells a product that is differentiated from the products of other producers, and this differentiation results in each firm's having some degree of market power.

23. Yes, the type of differentiation these three firms illustrate is differentiation by location. Each of these three firms is located in a different part of the community, which differentiates them even though they sell very similar products.

24. This industry is characterized by having differentiation by style or type as well as differentiation by location.

25. As long as people have different tastes and preferences, firms will find it profitable to offer differentiated products. Variety is appealing to people primarily because people have different tastes and preferences.

26. Differentiation based on quality is the idea that firms can choose to produce a similar product with a range of quality. Some firms find it profitable to produce the product with very high standards of quality, while other firms produce a similar product that has a much lower standard of quality. Consumers can then select the level of quality they desire by selecting the product whose quality most closely resembles the desired level of quality.

Answers to Chapter Review Questions

1. **Answer e.** The monopolist's demand curve is the market demand curve and it is downward sloping. The monopolist's demand curve is not the monopolist's MR curve, however, since for the monopolist the MR curve lies beneath the demand curve.

2. **Answer c.** Oligopolies are characterized by having just a few firms in the industry. These firms may produce differentiated products or they may produce identical products.

3. **Answer a.** The first statement is the definition of monopolistic competition. The second statement correctly states the profit-maximizing rule used by perfectly competitive firms when selecting their optimal output level. The third statement is false: monopolies profit maximize when they produce the level of output where MR = MC and then charge the price on their demand curve that is associated with this level of output.

4. **Answer b.** Entry barriers effectively protect an industry from potential competition from new firms. Entry barriers may be due to government regulation, increasing returns to scale in production, technological superiority, or the control of some essential resource or input.

5.　**Answer b.** Monopolists restrict output and charge consumers higher prices for their product.

6.　**Answer c.** Barriers to entry may be man-made: for example, legislation may grant patents or copyrights to a particular business or individual. But barriers to entry do not act as an obstacle to new firm entry in a competitive industry, since we assume this kind of industry has free entry and exit in the long run; this eliminates answers (a) and (d). Answer (b) is not true: barriers to entry are not about people's rights to trespass at a business site. Answer (c) is a general definition of barriers to entry.

7.　**Answer d.** Increasing returns to scale implies that the average cost of producing the good decreases as the level of production increases: the *ATC* curve is downward sloping throughout the relevant region of production. Thus, firms benefit from producing larger amounts of output (or having larger volumes of sales), since each unit of this output is cheaper on average to produce than would be the case with a smaller level of output.

8.　**Answer b.** This industry is a decreasing-cost industry that is best served by having a single producer supply the good, since a single producer can produce the good at the lowest cost.

9.　**Answer b.** When an industry is characterized as having an average total cost that decreases as output increases, this is due to large fixed costs that result in larger levels of output being produced at a lower cost per unit than smaller levels of output.

10.　**Answer d.** Patents and copyrights are intended to protect the work of inventors and artists. This work is costly in terms of time and resources and would not be undertaken if the inventors and artists did not receive compensation for their creations. However, patents and copyrights create a temporary monopoly and therefore restrict the level of output available while raising the price of the good: both of these effects are harmful to consumers.

11.　**Answer a.** The monopolist profit maximizes when it produces the level of output where $MR = MC$ and then prices this level of output by charging the price on the demand curve that is associated with this level of output. $MR = MC$ at Q_1, and P_1 is the price that is associated with Q_1 on the demand curve.

12.　**Answer c.** If this monopolist were to act as if it were in a perfectly competitive industry, then it would produce the level of output at which marginal cost intersects the demand curve, because this would represent the efficient level of output—the level at which the marginal cost of the last unit produced equals the price from selling the last unit of the good. It would sell these Q_2 units of the good for the price on the demand curve (P_2) that is associated with this level of output.

13.　**Answer d.** The deadweight loss associated with this monopoly is the area that represents the loss in total surplus due to the market's being served by a monopoly instead of by a perfectly competitive industry. This surplus loss is the area $(1/2)(P_1/\text{unit} - P_4/\text{unit})$ $(Q_2 \text{ units} - Q_1 \text{ units})$.

14.　**Answer a.** This monopolist earns positive economic profit since the price it charges for the good (P_1) is greater than the average total cost of producing Q_1 units of the good. To calculate profits you can use the formula $TR - TC = \text{profits}$, or you can calculate the product of the quantity produced times the difference between the price of each unit and the average total cost of producing these units. Using this latter method, the price of each unit is P_1, the average total cost of each unit is P_3, and the number of units produced is Q_1. Thus, profit is $(P_1/\text{unit} - P_3/\text{unit})(Q_1 \text{ units})$.

15.　**Answer d.** For a monopolist with a linear demand curve, the *MR* curve has the same *y*-intercept as the demand curve, and its slope is twice the slope of the demand curve. The *y*-intercept of the demand curve is 100 and the slope of the demand curve is (−1). The *MR* curve has a *y*-intercept of 100 and its slope is (−2). The *MR* curve can be written as $MR = 100 - 2Q$.

16.　**Answer a.** The profit-maximizing monopolist will produce the quantity where $MR = MC$ and then price this level of output by going to its demand curve: $MR = 100 - 2Q$, and

$MC = 3Q$; thus, $Q = 20$ units. Substituting 20 for Q in the demand equation and solving for P gives us the monopolist's market price for this good: $P = \$80$.

17. **Answer b.** Profit can be calculated by multiplying the level of output times the difference between the price of the good and the average total cost of producing the good. Thus, (20 units)($\$80$ per unit – $\$70$ per unit) gives a profit of $\$200$.

18. **Answer c.** There is a deadweight loss due to the monopoly. It is the area that represents the efficiency loss due to the market's not operating as a perfectly competitive market. The efficient level of output in this market is 25 units (where the MC curve intersects the demand curve). The deadweight loss is equal to $(1/2)(\$80$ per unit – $\$60$ per unit)(25 units – 20 units) = $\$50$.

19. **Answer a.** When the monopolist lowers its price, it can sell more units of the good, and these additional units will always make a positive contribution to total revenue. However, when the monopolist lowers its price, it finds that it now has to cut the price on all the units it sells, and this price effect reduces the total revenue from the units that previously would have sold for a higher price. To profit maximize, the monopolist must select the price off the demand curve that corresponds to the quantity where $MR = MC$.

20. **Answer a.** When price elasticity of demand is less than 1, the demand curve is relatively inelastic. An increase in price in the inelastic region of the demand curve results in total revenue increasing.

21. **Answer d.** Public ownership of a natural monopoly does not often work as a solution to the problem because it offers little incentive for the natural monopolist to keep costs down and produce high-quality products. Price regulation of a natural monopolist is a policy that can result in lower prices and greater quantities, provided that the regulated price allows the natural monopolist to at least break even. Provided that the regulated price is equal to or greater than the average total cost of production, the natural monopolist will be able to make zero or positive economic profits and will therefore be willing to produce the good.

22. **Answer b.** The monopolist profit maximizes by producing the quantity where $MR = MC$. The MR curve for this monopolist is $MR = 500 - 2Q$. So the monopolist will produce 150 units, and it will sell these units for a price of $\$350$ (substitute 150 units into the demand curve to find the price the monopolist will charge). The graph below indicates the areas that correspond to consumer surplus, producer surplus, and deadweight loss.

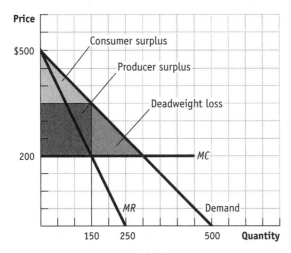

23. **Answer d.** This is just a definitional question. The industry described is not a perfectly competitive industry because there are only a few firms, and these firms all possess some market power: in a perfectly competitive industry there are many firms and none of these firms has market power. The industry is not a monopoly because a monopolistic industry has a single producer of the good. The industry is not monopolistically competitive because there are not enough firms in the market.

24. **Answer b.** Although oligopolies may arise because of an entry barrier based on scarce resources or government protection in the form of copyrights or patents, it is far more likely that the oligopoly arises due to the presence of returns to scale that results in the firms in the industry producing at a large scale relative to the overall market demand for the product.

25. **Answer d.** The two firms collude in order to set price and quantity so that the total amount of profits earned by the two firms is maximized. This does not imply that either firm is necessarily maximizing their own profits, since the market may not be divided evenly between the two firms.

26. **Answer b.** Cartels are inherently unstable because the firms in the cartel have decided to set price and quantity at a level where the marginal revenue from the last unit produced is greater than the marginal cost of producing the last unit. Each firm recognizes that it can expand production and earn more revenue than the costs it generates, so each firm is likely to deviate from the agreed-upon production level.

27. **Answer c.** The price effect is a negative effect on total revenue, since as the firm (whether a monopolist or a firm in a cartel) reduces price on all the units it sells in order to sell more units of the good, this causes total revenue to fall. The quantity effect on total revenue is a positive effect for either type of firm: when the firm reduces price to sell more units of the good, the extra sales increase the firm's total revenue.

28. **Answer b.** Cooperation is the superior strategy because with cooperation the firms can work to maximize the joint profits of the oligopoly. When each firm acts in its own self-interest and adopts a compete strategy, this typically leads to price decreases that erode the general level of profitability in the industry.

29. **Answer d.** All three of these statements are true by definition.

30. **Answer a.** Monopolistic competition is a market structure in which there are many firms, each producing a differentiated product. In this market structure entry and exit are possible in the long run. Answer (b) is incorrect since the products are differentiated and not identical. Answer (c) is incorrect since entry occurs in the long run, not the short run. Answer (a) is correct since perfect competition results in identical products rather than differentiated products.

31. **Answer b.** Answer (a) is incorrect since both types of market structure are characterized as having a large number of producers. Answer (c) is incorrect since it is possible for firms in both types of market structure to earn negative economic profits in the short run. Firms in both types of market structure will produce in the short run provided that their revenues are sufficient to cover their variable costs of production. Answer (d) is incorrect since monopolistically competitive firms offer differentiated products.

32. **Answer a.** In the short run and the long run a monopoly does not face any competition: it is the only provider of the good. In the short run, a monopolistically competitive firm does not face competition for its product since its product is differentiated. In the long run, a monopolistically competitive firm does face competition since there can be entry of new firms into the industry and these new firms will likely offer products that are somewhat similar to the existing firm's product. Answer (b) is incorrect since there is no entry of new firms into a monopoly in the long run due to the existence of barriers to entry. Answer (c) is incorrect because there is entry in the long run in a monopolistically competitive market structure.

33. **Answer d.** Each of the answers (a) through (c) contains some type of error. For example, answer (a) is correct except that entry and exit occur in the long run. Answer (b) is correct except that there are more than a few firms in a monopolistically competitive industry. Answer (c) is incorrect because the firms in a monopolistically competitive industry typically produce highly differentiated products.

34. Answer b. Monopolistically competitive firms first select their profit-maximizing level of output by equating marginal revenue with marginal cost, and then they go to the demand curve to see what price people are willing to pay given this level of output. The firms cannot charge more than the price on the demand curve associated with their level of production because people are not willing to pay more than the price on the demand curve. Monopolistically competitive firms are not price-takers because they have some market power. Monopolistically competitive firms act to maximize profits by producing the right quantity and charging the right price.

chapter **9**

Externalities and Public Goods

Summary

This chapter describes positive and negative externalities and the effects of these externalities in the marketplace. The chapter explores the economic inefficiency that arises when externalities are not accounted for, and it presents several alternative methods for correcting externalities. The chapter makes the case for government intervention in the form of emissions taxes, tradable permits, or Pigouvian subsidies as an efficient means of correcting externalities. The chapter also discusses environmental standards as an inefficient government policy. This chapter also explores two characteristics, the property of rivalness and the property of excludability, that are key to determining whether or not a market can provide the efficient level of the good. The chapter uses these characteristics to explore the problems presented by public goods, common resources, and artificially scarce goods. The chapter also considers the types of government intervention in the production and consumption of these goods that can make society better off, and why it is difficult for the government to determine the right level of intervention when the good is a public good, or when the production or consumption of the good involves the use of common resources. The chapter also discusses cost-benefit analysis.

Chapter Objectives

Objective #1. A principal source of market failure occurs when the market fails to take into account side effects or externalities of consumption or production decisions. A negative externality is a side effect that imposes costs on others, and a positive externality is a side effect that provides benefits to others. When externalities are present, the market fails to produce the optimal amount of the good: in the case of a negative externality, the market produces too much of the good if it does not take into account the externality; in the case of a positive externality, the market produces too little of the good if it does not take into account the externality. When the externality can be directly observed, then it can be regulated through direct controls, taxation, or subsidization. When the externality cannot be directly observed, then the government must implement policies that aim at generating the right amount of the activity that produces the externality. This chapter discusses these two approaches—targeting the side effect versus targeting the original activity—as it reviews different policies available to the government to correct the problem presented by externalities.

Objective #2. Many activities produce pollution as a side effect. One of the problems with pollution is that it inflicts a cost on the entire society, and this cost is typically not borne by the companies or individuals who generate the pollution. The chapter explores how to determine the optimal amount of pollution by developing the concepts of the marginal social cost of pollution and the marginal social benefit of pollution. Pollution generates costs as well as benefits to society.

- The marginal social cost of pollution is the additional cost imposed on society by an additional unit of pollution. The marginal social cost of pollution is an upward-sloping line, since each additional unit of pollution represents a greater cost to society as the environment deteriorates.

- The marginal social benefit of pollution is the additional benefit to society from an additional unit of pollution. Cleaning up pollution requires the use of scarce resources that would otherwise be used to produce goods and services. From a producer's perspective, the benefit from emitting one more unit of pollution is measured by the costs the producer saves from not having to buy and install expensive pollution-control equipment. One can measure the marginal social benefit of an additional unit of pollution by finding out what is the highest willingness to pay for the right to emit this unit of pollution among all the polluters in the society. Polluters know that to avoid polluting requires using scarce resources and that therefore reduction of pollution carries a cost. The marginal social benefit of pollution is a downward-sloping line: when pollution is negligible, then an additional unit of pollution has a high benefit to society; when there is a lot of pollution, then an additional unit of pollution brings little benefit to society.

- The optimal amount of pollution for a society is the level of pollution at which the marginal social cost of pollution is equal to the marginal social benefit of pollution. Figure 9.1 illustrates these concepts.

Figure 9.1

- It is unlikely that the market will generate the optimal amount of pollution, because those who produce the pollution do not have to compensate those who bear the costs of the pollution. The polluting producer can pass along the pollution costs to all members of society, and thus the market, left to its own devices, will result in too much pollution.

- In the absence of government intervention, polluters will pollute up to the point where the marginal social benefit of pollution is equal to zero. The market outcome is represented in Figure 9.2: note that the market level of pollution is greater than the optimal level of pollution, and that the market level of pollution is inefficient since, at this level of pollution, the marginal social cost of pollution is greater than the marginal social benefit of pollution.

Figure 9.2

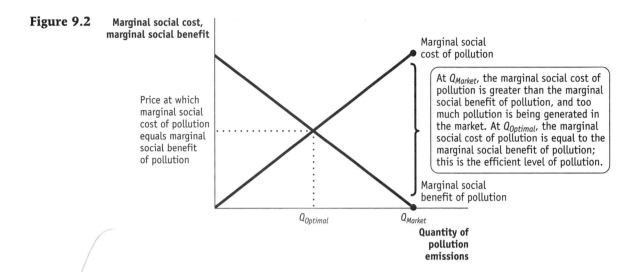

Objective #3. According to the Coase theorem, the private sector can correct externalities and produce the efficient level of the good, provided that transaction costs are sufficiently low. The Coase theorem states that externalities need not lead to inefficiencies since people have an incentive to make mutually beneficial transactions, which leads individuals to take externalities into account when making decisions, provided that the transaction costs are not too great. When individuals take into account externalities when making decisions, this is referred to as internalizing the externality. Internalization of the externality does not occur if the cost of communication between the affected parties is too high, if the cost of making a legally binding agreement is too great, or if there are costly delays in the bargaining. When transaction costs prevent people from internalizing the externality, then the government must intervene to correct the market and its failure to internalize the externality.

Objective #4. The government can reduce the amount of pollution by enforcing environmental standards, which are rules that protect the environment by specifying what actions need to be taken by producers and consumers. Although effective, these standards are not efficient since they do not incorporate the costs of reducing pollution. Economists believe that pollution can be reduced at lower cost through the use of taxes and tradable permits.

- Emissions taxes are taxes that depend on the amount of pollution a firm produces. An emissions tax is more efficient than an environmental standard, since the emissions tax ensures that the marginal benefit of pollution is equal for all sources of pollution while the environmental standard does not consider the marginal benefit of pollution when it is enforced. Figure 9.3 illustrates the differences between these two approaches using two different firms, firm A and firm B, that both produce pollution but have different marginal social benefit of pollution curves. The graph on the left illustrates the environmental-standard approach: pollution for all firms in the society must, by law, be reduced to 450 units. With this standard, however, notice that the marginal social benefit of reducing pollution is different for the two firms: for firm A the marginal social benefit is $225 for the last unit of pollution emissions, while for firm B the marginal social benefit is $450 for the last unit of pollution emissions. The graph on the right illustrates the emissions tax approach using an emissions tax of $300 per unit of pollution: each unit of pollution emitted is taxed, and polluters reduce their pollution by considering the tax versus the benefit of the pollution. Both firm A and firm B select the level of pollution emissions where the emissions tax is equal to their marginal social benefit from pollution: for firm A this corresponds to a reduction in pollution emissions of 600 units, while for firm B this corresponds to a reduction in pollution emissions of 300 units. The total amount of pollution reduction is the same in both programs (900 units), but the emissions tax is efficient since all producers reduce pollution to the point where the marginal social benefit of pollution is exactly equal to the tax.

Figure 9.3

With an environmental standard, both firms are required to reduce their emissions by 450 units each, or a total of 900 units.

With an emissions tax of $300 per unit of pollution, firm A reduces its pollution by 600 units while firm B reduces its pollution by 300 units. Total reduction in pollution is 900 units, but the last unit of pollution produced by each firm has the same marginal social benefit.

- Taxes can be used to reduce any kind of activity that generates a negative externality. This use of taxes to address the problem of negative externality is referred to as a Pigouvian tax. Although effective as a policy, Pigouvian taxes are difficult to implement since government officials do not always know with certainty what level of tax is the efficient level of tax.

- Tradable emissions permits are licenses granted by the government that give the holder of the license permission to emit limited quantities of the pollutant. These tradable emissions permits can be bought and sold by the polluters. In essence, the government determines the legal amount of pollution and then sells permits equal to this amount of pollution. Producers who pollute must own permits granting them the right to generate their level of pollution. Producers can either purchase the right to pollute or they can clean up their production and eliminate the polluting activity. Firms that find the cost of reducing pollution greater than the cost of buying the permits will buy the permits. Firms that find the cost of reducing pollution less than the cost of buying the permits will eliminate their pollution. Since the level of pollution is limited by the number of permits in the market, this results in producers basing their decision about whether or not to pollute on the costs of reducing their pollution. In effect, the government creates a market in the right to pollute by using tradable emissions permits. The greatest challenge for the government when implementing a tradable emissions permit program is determining the optimal number of permits for the economy: issue too many permits, and pollution is not reduced enough; issue too few permits, and pollution is reduced too much.

- Both emissions taxes and tradable emissions permits create an incentive for producers to create and use less-polluting technology.

- Cap-and-trade systems are another name for tradable emissions permits. In this case, the government issues a cap, or a total amount of pollutant that can be emitted, and then the government issues tradable emissions permits and enforces a rule that polluters must hold a number of permits equal to the amount of the pollutant they emit. This policy is effective with pollution that is dispersed, but it is less effective with pollution that is geographically localized. As with any policy, policymakers also face political pressure to set the level of the cap at either too high or too low a level. Finally, these measures to reduce pollution require a high degree of monitoring and compliance if the policy is to be effective.

Objective #5. When an activity generates an external cost, or a cost incurred by someone other than the people directly involved in the transaction, the market produces too much of the good. This situation of an external cost is an example of a negative externality. Figure 9.4 illustrates a negative externality. From the producers' perspective, the market supply curve represents the private costs they incur when they produce the good. However, when this good is produced there are also social costs that the producers do not include in their costs of production. The result is a difference between the market supply curve and the true marginal social costs of production. The market, when it fails to correct for the externality, produces Q_{Market}, which is more than $Q_{Optimal}$. Notice that at Q_{Market} the marginal social benefit of consuming the last unit of the good produced (as measured by the demand curve) is less than the marginal social cost of producing this last unit. Too much of this good is being produced by the market, and therefore too many resources are being devoted to its production. This negative externality can be remedied by applying the appropriate Pigouvian tax, equal to the externality per unit of the good produced, on producers so that $Q_{Optimal}$ is produced by the market. The application of this tax on the market causes the market to internalize the negative externality.

Figure 9.4

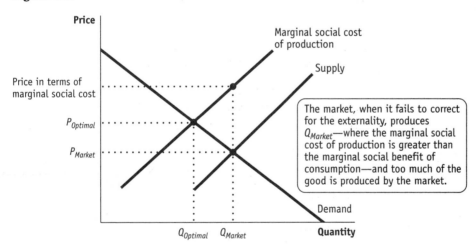

Objective #6. When an activity generates an external benefit, or a benefit received by someone other than the people directly involved in the transaction, the market does not produce enough of the good. This situation of an external benefit is an example of a positive externality. In the case of a positive externality, the government must target the original activity rather than the external benefit because the external benefit can be difficult, or impossible, to measure. For example, the external benefit from people's getting vaccinated is a reduction in the spread of disease among the whole population, but it is impossible to measure how many people benefit from an individual's getting vaccinated. When individuals consider getting vaccinated, they consider only the benefits they directly receive and do not include the external benefits the vaccination provides to other people. This implies that people will consume less than the ideal level of vaccinations because they do not include the external benefits.

- This scenario can be illustrated by thinking about the demand curve that represents the private benefits that individuals receive from the vaccination and the demand curve that includes the private benefits as well as the external benefits. Figure 9.5 illustrates the case of a positive externality: in the graph the quantity produced by the market is Q_{Market}, and the optimal quantity, where the marginal cost of producing the last unit is equal to the marginal social benefit from consuming the last unit, is given by $Q_{Optimal}$. This situation of a positive externality can be corrected by application of the optimal Pigouvian subsidy, a subsidy equal to the positive externality cost per unit of the good. The application of this subsidy in this market causes the market to internalize the externality.

Figure 9.5

Objective #7. The creation of knowledge poses the greatest single source of external benefits in the modern economy. "Technology spillover" is a term that describes the spread of knowledge among individuals and firms: technology spillover measures the external benefit that occurs when new knowledge is discovered in one application and then is used in other applications. Some people advocate for an industrial policy that would support specific industries due to the existence of these technology spillover effects. This industrial policy would amount to subsidization or reductions in competition from foreign producers through the imposition of trade restrictions for specific industries deemed to generate these technology spillovers. Economists are not strong advocates of industrial policy because it is hard to identify with certainty positive externalities, and because these policies may result in the promotion of industries with political power rather than industries that create technology spillovers.

Objective #8. The characteristics of a good determine whether or not the market can provide the good efficiently. When a good is excludable and rival in consumption, the market can provide the good efficiently. A good is excludable when suppliers of the good can prevent people who do not pay for the good from consuming the good. Since the good is excludable, suppliers can charge consumers of the good a price, which gives the producers an incentive to supply the good. A good is rival in consumption when a person's consumption of the good means that no other consumer can consume that same unit of the good. Since the good is rival in consumption, this implies that it is efficient for consumers to pay a positive price equal to the good's marginal cost of production. Private goods are both excludable and rival in consumption, and hence the market provides the efficient quantity of a private good.

Objective #9. A public good is a good that benefits many people whether or not they have paid for it and whose benefits to an individual are not affected by how many other people are consuming the good. Thus, a public good is nonrival, because one consumer's consumption of the good does not change the level of benefits available to other consumers of the good, and it is nonexcludable, since an individual can consume the good once it is produced whether or not they have paid for the good. These two differences result in the market being unable to provide the efficient amount of the good. Because public goods are nonexcludable they suffer from the free-rider problem: this free-rider problem results in firms being unwilling to produce the good since they know it will be possible for consumers to consume the good without paying for it once the good is produced. Because public goods are nonrival in consumption it is inefficient to charge people for consuming these goods, since the marginal cost of another person consuming the good is zero.

Objective #10. A common resource is a good that many people consume whether or not they have paid for the good and whose consumption by each person reduces the amount of the good available to other people. The common resource is thus nonexcludable but rival in consumption since people can consume the good even though they have not paid for it, but their consumption of the good reduces the amount of the good available to others. Common resources are subject to overuse by individuals because individuals will continue to consume units of the good until their marginal benefit from consumption of the common resource is equal to zero. In choosing this level of consumption, individuals ignore the cost their actions inflict on society. Common resources thus present a problem of a negative externality in which individuals consume an inefficiently high amount of the good because they ignore, or fail to internalize, the external costs they impose on other members of society. In the case of a common resource, society must intervene in the market to find a way to get individual users of the resource to take into account the costs they impose on others. This intervention could be in the form of a Pigouvian tax, through a system of tradable licenses for the use of the common resource, or through the assignment of property rights to the common resources. This last intervention, the assignment of property rights, gives the holder of the property rights the ability to limit the use of the common resource and thus prevent the overuse of this resource.

Objective #11. Artificially scarce goods are those goods that are excludable but nonrival in consumption. These are goods that must be paid for in order for the consumer to consume the good but whose consumption does not diminish the ability of other consumers to consume the same unit of the good.

Objective #12. When a good is either nonexcludable or nonrival, the market does not produce the efficient quantity of the good.

- When a good is nonexcludable, this creates a free-rider problem in which consumers are not willing to pay for the good but instead want to free-ride on those who do pay for the good. When consumers free-ride, too little of the good is produced in the market.

- When a good is nonrival in consumption, the cost of providing an additional unit of the good is zero. When consumers are forced to pay a price that is greater than zero, they end up demanding too little of the good and the market therefore produces an inefficient quantity of the good.

Objective #13. A public good may be provided through voluntary contributions or by self-interested individuals or firms who produce the public good with the hope of earning money through some indirect means. For example, broadcast television is produced by firms that earn money through advertisement rather than through payments from consumers who watch the televised programming. A public good may also be provided through social encouragement or social pressure. Many public goods are provided by the government and funded through taxation. This provision of public goods by the government is a crucial role for the government: without government provision, these public goods would either not be provided or would be provided at levels that are inefficiently low.

Objective #14. Governments must decide whether or not to provide the public good and how much of the public good to provide. The optimal level of public good provision is the level

$MSB = MC$

$MSB = \sum_{} indiv. MB$

where the marginal social benefit of the public good is equal to the marginal cost of producing the public good. In the case of a public good, the marginal social benefit from the public good is the sum of the individual marginal benefits that are enjoyed by all consumers of that unit. Since the public good is nonrival, the benefit an individual receives from the consumption of the public good does not diminish the benefit another individual receives from consuming the same unit of the public good. Therefore, the marginal social benefit from consumption of the public good is always greater than the marginal private benefit from the consumption of the public good: individual self-interest does not result in the provision of the efficient quantity of public goods because of this divergence between the marginal public and marginal private benefit from the consumption of the public good. This is similar to the problem presented by positive externalities: the market does not provide the efficient amount of the public good or the efficient amount of a good with a positive externality because the marginal social benefit received by all consumers of another unit of the good is greater than the price the producer would receive from providing that unit of the good. The market produces too little of either type of good.

Objective #15. Governments decide on the optimal amount of the public good to provide by estimating the social benefits and the social costs of providing the public good. This process is known as cost-benefit analysis. Although it is relatively easy to estimate the cost of providing the public good, it is much more difficult to estimate the benefits from the provision of the public good. Individuals have an incentive to not answer truthfully about the benefits they receive from a public good because of the nature of the public good.

Key Terms

marginal social cost of pollution the additional cost imposed on society as a whole by an additional unit of pollution.

marginal social benefit of pollution the additional gain to society as a whole from an additional unit of pollution.

socially optimal quantity of pollution the quantity of pollution that society would choose if all the costs and benefits of pollution were fully accounted for.

external costs uncompensated costs that an individual or firm imposes on others; also known as *negative externalities*.

external benefits uncompensated benefits that an individual or firm confers on others; also known as *positive externalities*.

externalities *external benefits* and *external costs*.

negative externalities *external costs*.

positive externalities *external benefits*.

Coase theorem the proposition that even in the presence of *externalities* an *economy* can always reach an *efficient* solution as long as *transaction costs* are sufficiently low.

transaction costs the costs to individuals of making a deal.

Notes

Key Terms *(continued)*

internalize the externality when individuals take into account *external costs* and *external benefits*.

environmental standards rules established by a government to protect the environment by specifying actions by producers and consumers.

emissions tax a tax that depends on the amount of pollution a firm produces.

Pigouvian taxes taxes designed to reduce *external costs*.

tradable emissions permits *licenses* to emit limited quantities of pollutants that can be bought and sold by polluters.

Pigouvian subsidy a payment designed to encourage activities that yield *external benefits*.

technology spillover an *external benefit* that results when knowledge spreads among individuals and firms.

industrial policy a policy that supports industries believed to yield *positive externalities*.

excludable referring to a good, describes the case in which the supplier can prevent those who do not pay from consuming the good.

rival in consumption referring to a good, describes the case in which one unit cannot be consumed by more than one person at the same time.

private good a good that is both *excludable* and *rival in consumption*.

nonexcludable referring to a good, describes the case in which the supplier cannot prevent those who do not pay from consuming the good.

nonrival in consumption referring to a good, describes the case in which the same unit can be consumed by more than one person at the same time.

free-rider problem when individuals have no *incentive* to pay for their own consumption of a good, they will take a "free ride" on anyone who does pay; a problem with goods that are *nonexcludable*.

public good a good that is both *nonexcludable* and *nonrival in consumption*.

cost-benefit analysis an estimate of the costs and benefits of providing a good. When governments use cost-benefit analysis, they estimate the social costs and social benefits of providing a public good.

Notes

Private – excl, rival
public – non-ex., non rival
club – excluded, non rival
common – non excluded, rival

▉ AFTER YOU READ THE CHAPTER

Tips

Tip #1.   A key concept in this chapter is the idea that markets fail to produce the optimal amount of the good whenever there is a cost or a benefit that the market fails to include in its reckoning when deciding what the optimal quantity of the good will be in the market. A negative externality occurs when there is some kind of cost that is not internalized in the market, and a positive externality occurs when there is some kind of benefit that is not internalized in the market. When there is an externality in the market that is not internalized, the market does not produce the efficient level of output because it is not producing the level of output where the marginal social cost of production is equal to the marginal social benefit of consumption.

Tip #2.   Negative externalities can occur on the production or the consumption side of the model of supply and demand. For example, when a producer produces a good whose production generates substantial pollution and the producer does not take into account the cost of this pollution, then there is a negative externality on the production or cost side of the market. This implies that the producer's supply curve does not represent the true societal costs of producing the good. Alternatively, a consumer can engage in behaviors that inflict a negative benefit on others: for instance, the decision to drink alcoholic beverages and then operate a car has potential negative consequences for others in the community. In this case, the demand curve for the individual does not take into account the negative externality imposed by the individual's consumption decision. In either case (the negative externality on the production side of the model or the negative externality on the consumption side of the model), the market produces too much of the good when the externality is not accounted for in the market. Figure 9.6 illustrates these two examples. Imposition of the appropriate Pigouvian tax will correct the market outcome and result in the market producing the optimal amount of the good, the amount where the marginal social benefit from consuming the last unit of the good is equal to the marginal social cost of producing the last unit of the good.

Figure 9.6

In the following graphs, MSC is the marginal social cost of production, Supply is the marginal private cost of production, MSB is the marginal social benefit of consumption, Demand is the marginal private benefit of comsumption, Q_{MKT} is the quantity produced by the market, Q_{OPT} is the optimal quantity to produce, P_{MKT} is the market-determined price, and $P_{Opt\text{-}subsidy}$ is the optimal price. $P_{Opt\text{-}subsidy}$ includes the Pigouvian subsidy.

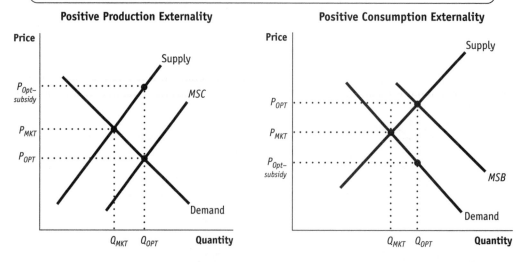

Tip #3. Positive externalities can occur on the production or the consumption side of the model of supply and demand. For example, when a producer produces a good whose production generates technology spillovers and the producer does not take into account the benefit of this technology spillover on the rest of the economy, then there is a positive externality on the production or cost side of the market. This implies that the producer's supply curve does not represent the true societal costs of producing the good. Alternatively, a consumer can engage in behaviors that inflict a positive benefit on others: for instance, the decision to maintain the exterior of one's house results in positive externalities with regard to the property values for neighboring properties. In this case, the demand curve for the individual does not take into account the positive externality created by the individual's consumption decision. In either case (the positive externality on the production side of the model or the positive externality on the consumption side of the model), the market produces too little of the good when the externality is not accounted for in the market. Figure 9.7 illustrates these two examples. Imposition of the appropriate Pigouvian subsidy will correct the market outcome and result in the market producing the optimal amount of the good where the marginal social benefit from consuming the last unit of the good is equal to the marginal social cost of producing the last unit of the good.

Figure 9.7

In the following graphs, MSC is the marginal social cost of production, Supply is the marginal private cost of production, MSB is the marginal social benefit of consumption, Demand is the marginal private benefit of consumption, Q_{MKT} is the quantity produced by the market, Q_{OPT} is the optimal quantity to produce, P_{MKT} is the market-determined price, and $P_{Opt\text{-}tax}$ is the optimal price. $P_{Opt\text{-}tax}$ includes the Pigouvian tax.

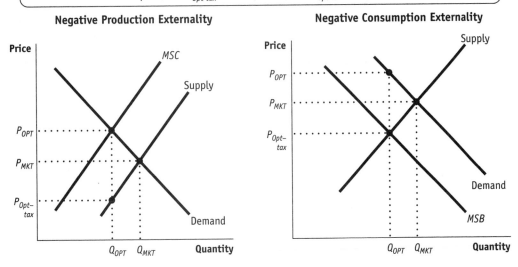

Tip #4. This chapter looks at four types of goods—private goods, public goods, common resources, and artificially scarce goods—from the perspective of whether or not the good is rival in consumption and excludable. To understand this chapter, it is essential that you have a firm grasp on what it means to be rival in consumption versus nonrival in consumption and excludable versus nonexcludable.

- When a good is rival, this means that one person's consumption of the good effectively prevents another consumer from consuming that same unit of the good. Hamburgers and ice cream cones are two examples of goods that are rival: when Sally eats her hamburger or her ice cream cone, this means that Joe cannot eat the same hamburger or the same ice cream cone. Joe and Sally are rivals with regard to the consumption of the hamburger or the ice cream cone.

- When a good is nonrival, this means that one person's consumption of the good does not prevent another consumer from consuming the same unit of the good. Sally and Joe can both enjoy the light from the lighthouse in their community without diminishing the consumption benefits received by the other person from their consumption of the same light. Sally and Joe are not rivals with regard to the consumption of the light from the lighthouse.

- A good is excludable if a supplier can prevent someone from consuming the good if they do not pay for it. Sally can enjoy her fast-food hamburger only if she pays for it. The restaurant will exclude her from the consumption of the hamburger if she cannot first pay for the hamburger. Hamburgers are therefore excludable as well as rival.

- A good is nonexcludable if a supplier cannot prevent someone from consuming the good if they do not pay for it. Residents of a community can benefit from a tornado warning siren even if they do not pay for this siren. It is impossible to exclude the nonpayers from the benefits of consuming this good even though they have not paid for it.

Tip #5. To find the demand curve for a public good requires that you vertically sum the individual demand curves for this public good. In contrast to a private good for which the market demand curve is found by horizontally summing the individual consumer demand curves, the public good requires the vertical summation of the individual consumer demand curves. The private good is rival in consumption, so that when we find the market demand curve we essentially ask how many units demanders want of this good at a particular price. We repeat this process for different prices until we have identified the market demand curve for the private good. The public good, in contrast, is nonrival in consumption. This means that the market demand for the public good at any quantity is equal to the sum of the prices individuals are willing to pay for this particular amount of the public good. This nonrival characteristic of public goods implies that the market demand for public goods is found by considering the sum of what people are willing to pay for each level of public good provision. Figure 9.8 illustrates this idea for a public good when there are two individuals in the market for this good: D_1 represents the first person's demand for the public good, D_2 represents the second person's demand for the public good, and D_3 represents the total demand for the public good.

Figure 9.8

To find the market demand curve for a public good, sum the individual demand curves for the good. To sum the demand curves, hold quantity constant (for example, Q_1) and then see what price each individual is willing to pay for this quantity. Thus, individual 1's marginal benefit from consuming Q_1 units of the public good is P_2, while individual 2's marginal benefit from consuming Q_1 units of the good is P_4. Together the marginal social benefit from Q_1 units is equal to $P_2 + P_4$.

1. Utopia strives to be a perfect society. Recently citizens in Utopia have had a heated debate about pollution in their society. Members of a group called Fresh Air advocate for the elimination of all pollution since this is critical to Utopia's actually being a perfect society. Rivals in an alternative group argue that this is a decision that is economically imperfect, since it would result in the elimination of units of pollution where the marginal benefit of the pollution reduction is less than the marginal cost of that pollution reduction. The two groups have called you in to give a general presentation on the nature of pollution and how they should best determine the optimal amount of pollution for their society. They also want you to advise them on strategies for eliminating pollution to this level, as well as advise them about the optimal strategy for this pollution reduction.

STEP 1: In order to discuss the optimal amount of pollution reduction, you will need to compare the marginal benefit from an additional unit of pollution to the marginal cost of an additional unit of pollution. You will want to identify the market amount of pollution as well as the socially optimal amount of pollution.

Review the section "The Economics of Pollution" on pages 276–281, and Figure 9-1 on page 277.

The marginal social benefit curve of pollution slopes downward: at very low levels of pollution the benefits to society of that pollution are very high, while at high levels of pollution the benefits to society of that pollution are very low. Since it takes scarce resources to reduce pollution, the more pollution that is allowed in an economy, the fewer resources that are diverted to pollution reduction. The marginal social benefit of pollution thus measures how an additional unit of pollution emissions depends on the quantity of pollution emissions.

The marginal social cost of pollution is an upward-sloping line measuring the additional cost to society of an additional unit of pollution. At high levels of pollution, an additional unit of pollution results in a large change in cost to society; at low levels of pollution, an additional unit of pollution results in a small change in cost to society.

The optimal amount of pollution is at that level where the marginal benefit of pollution is just equal to the marginal cost of pollution. When the marginal benefit of pollution is greater than the marginal cost of pollution, this tells us that an additional unit of pollution yields additional benefits that exceed the additional costs of that unit of pollution: in this case, it is optimal for society to allow an additional unit of pollution. When the marginal benefit of pollution is smaller than the marginal cost of pollution, this tells us that an additional unit of pollution yields additional costs that exceed the additional benefits of that unit of pollution: in this case, it is optimal for society to reduce pollution by this additional unit. It is only when the marginal social benefit of pollution is equal to the marginal social cost of pollution that society has produced the optimal amount of pollution.

The market-determined amount of pollution is that amount where the marginal benefit of pollution is equal to zero. That is, the market will provide that amount of pollution where an additional unit of pollution yields zero social benefits: the market will fail to take into account the marginal social cost of this pollution. The following graph illustrates these ideas.

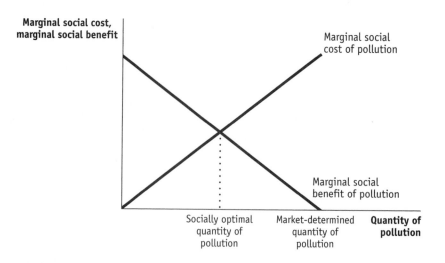

STEP 2: Now that you have identified the optimal amount of pollution, you can turn your attention to policies that can help Utopia reach this goal.

Review the section "Policies Toward Pollution" on pages 282–287, and the section "Economics in Action: Cap and Trade" on page 287.

There are three basic policies that could be utilized to reach the optimal amount of pollution in Utopia: environmental standards, emissions taxes, and tradable emissions permits.

Environmental standards impose rules about what levels of pollution are admissible: although successful at reducing pollution, these standards are less efficient than other methods of pollution abatement since the other methods of pollution abatement allow society to reach the same reduced level of pollution at lower cost to society. This inefficiency occurs because most environmental standards are inflexible and do not allow reductions in pollution to be achieved at minimum cost.

Emissions taxes are taxes that depend on the amount of pollution that a firm produces. When the emissions taxes are set at the level that represents the marginal social cost of pollution, this provides firms with an incentive to internalize the externality imposed by the pollution and to take into account the true costs to society of this pollution. An emissions tax approach is efficient in contrast to an environmental standards approach, since it provides an incentive for firms to produce that level of pollution where the marginal benefit of that pollution is equal for all sources of pollution. Each firm will reduce the amount of pollution they emit until its marginal benefit from that pollution equals the marginal social cost of that pollution as measured by the emissions tax.

Tradable emissions permits are licenses that allow license holders to emit limited quantities of pollutants. These permits can be bought and sold by polluters. In effect, tradable emissions permits create a market for pollution: those who are willing to pay high prices for the right to pollute can enter this market and purchase the right to emit that pollution. This market will enable firms with different costs of reducing pollution to engage in mutually beneficial transactions: those that can reduce pollution cheaply will sell their rights to pollute to firms that find their costs of pollution reduction relatively high. Provided that the government does not issue too many permits or too few permits, a tradable emissions permit policy can efficiently result in pollution being reduced to the socially optimal amount, since it provides an incentive for those who can reduce their pollution most cheaply to do so.

From an efficiency standpoint, emissions taxes or tradable emissions permits are superior to environmental standards.

2. Childhood vaccination benefits the recipient of the vaccination since it reduces or eliminates the possibility that the child will contract a serious childhood disease. Childhood vaccination also generates external benefits: because there are fewer possible transmitters of the disease, childhood vaccination reduces the probability that other people will develop the disease. Suppose that the demand curve for childhood vaccination is given by the equation $Q = 1,000 - 2P$, while the marginal external benefit of childhood vaccination is a constant $100 per vaccination. Suppose also that the supply curve for childhood vaccinations is given by the equation $P = (1/3)Q$. Identify the amount of vaccinations the market will supply as well as the optimal amount of vaccinations. What is the market price for these vaccinations? Finally, suppose the government decided to subsidize consumers of childhood vaccinations. What would be the optimal Pigouvian subsidy per vaccination if the goal of the government was to get the market to provide the socially optimal amount of childhood vaccination? Use a graph to illustrate your answers, but provide numerical answers to each of the questions as well.

STEP 1: Use the demand and supply curve equations to solve for the market equilibrium quantity and market equilibrium price.

Review the section "Positive Externalities" on pages 288–290, and Figure 9-4 on page 289.

Rewrite the supply curve as $Q = 3P$ and then set the quantity supplied equal to the quantity demanded to get $P = 200$. Then use this price to find the market quantity of vaccinations: $Q_{Market} = 600$. Because there is an external benefit in this market, we know that the market-provided quantity and the market-determined price will be too low. Consumers in this market undervalue childhood vaccinations, since they do not take into account the external benefits that these vaccinations generate for society at large.

STEP 2: Sketch a graph of the market for childhood vaccinations, using the numerical values you calculated in Step 1 to guide your sketch. In your graph, indicate the demand curve for vaccinations, the supply curve for vaccinations, and the marginal external benefit of vaccinations.

Review the section "Positive Externalities" on pages 288–290, and Figure 9-4 on page 289.

Start by drawing the demand curve. Close inspection of this demand curve reveals that the x-intercept of the demand curve is 1,000 and the y-intercept of the demand curve is $500. Then, draw in the supply curve: it has a y-intercept of 0. From Step 1, you know the equilibrium price and quantity in the market: mark these levels on your graph. Then, draw in the marginal social benefit curve for childhood vaccinations: since the marginal external benefit of a vaccination is $100 per vaccination, this will result in the marginal social benefit of vaccination curve being parallel to the demand curve with a y-intercept that is $100 greater than the original y-intercept of $500. The following graph illustrates these curves.

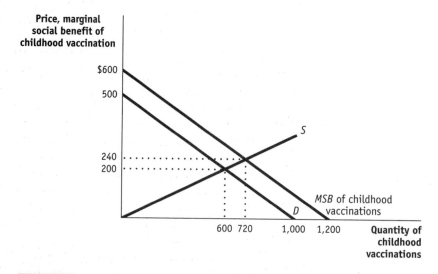

STEP 3: Identify what the optimal Pigouvian subsidy would be if the government intervened by providing a payment designed to encourage vaccinations to the level that would include the external benefits.

Review the section "Positive Externalities" on pages 288–290, and Figure 9-4 on page 289.

From the above graph, we can see that the optimal amount of childhood vaccinations is 720 units when all the external benefits from vaccinations are included. Suppliers are willing to supply this amount of the good if they receive a price of $240. Demanders are only willing to pay a price of $140 for this level of vaccination ($240 minus the external benefit, or alternatively, use the demand curve and the quantity of 720 to find the price that demanders are willing to pay). The government would need to provide a subsidy equal to this price difference ($100) in order for the optimal amount of vaccinations to be provided.

3.   Joe's Garage provides a number of car services, including oil changes. Some of the dirty oil often finds its way into a nearby stream, and this pollution is harmful to the wildlife that frequents the area. Joe does not make any effort to clean up this pollution, since this cleanup would only add to his cost and the pollution does not directly affect him or his business. The demand for Joe's services at this shop is given by $P = 50 - Q$, where Q is a measure of the number of units of car services Joe provides. The supply of services at Joe's shop is given by the equation $P = 4Q$. The pollution cost is estimated to be equal to $5 per unit of car services provided. Recently, a local community group has formed with the intention of identifying polluters and then designing and legislating Pigouvian taxes to correct these situations of negative externalities. You are asked to help this community group first identify the cost of Joe's pollution to the community as well as the deadweight loss from this pollution. (You may need to review an earlier chapter or your notes from former chapters on deadweight loss.) Then, the group would like you to identify the optimal amount of car services and the optimal Pigouvian tax to achieve this level of car services. You may find it helpful to draw a sketch indicating the demand and supply curves for Joe's Garage as well as the marginal social costs of providing these car services. How much revenue will the government receive if it imposes this Pigouvian tax, and how does this amount of revenue compare to the external costs that arise from this production?

STEP 1: Identify the amount of car services and the price of these car services currently provided by Joe's Garage.

Review the section "The Economics of Pollution" on pages 276–281, and the section "Policies Toward Pollution" on pages 282–287.

To find the amount of car services and the price of these car services, use the demand and supply curve to determine at what price the quantity demanded is equal to the quantity supplied. Thus, the price of car services is equal to $40, and the equilibrium quantity of car services in the market is 10 units.

STEP 2: Identify the cost of the pollution to the community that arises from the current production at Joe's Garage.

Review the section "The Economics of Pollution" on pages 276–281, and the section "Policies Toward Pollution" on pages 282–287.

Since each unit of car services generates $5 in pollution costs (the external costs), the cost of the pollution to the community is equal to (10 units)($5/unit), or $50.

STEP 3: Identify the socially optimal amount of car services to provide if the external social costs of providing these services are taken into account.

Review the section "The Economics of Pollution" on pages 276–281, and the section "Policies Toward Pollution" on pages 282–287.

The socially optimal amount of car services to provide is equal to that amount of car services where the quantity demanded is just equal to the marginal social cost of these services. To find this quantity, we must first find the marginal social costs of the car services. Since each car service generates an external social cost of $5 per unit, we can think of these external social costs as simply shifting the initial supply curve upward by this external social cost per unit. Thus, if the initial supply curve is $P = 4Q$, the marginal social cost of providing car services will be given by the equation $P = 5 + 4Q$. Notice that the y-intercept of the marginal social cost curve is simply the original y-intercept of the supply curve plus the external social cost per unit. This will be true provided that the external social cost is a constant amount per unit of the good provided. The optimal amount of car services to provide can be found by using the demand curve and this new marginal social cost curve. The optimal amount of car services to provide is 9 units.

STEP 4: Identify the deadweight loss to society of this pollution.

Review the section "The Economics of Pollution" on pages 276–281, and the section "Policies Toward Pollution" on pages 282–287.

To find the deadweight loss, you will want to think about the area that represents in this case the overproduction of the good by the market. In the following graph, the market quantity (Q_{MKT}) and the socially optimal quantity (Q_{OPT}) are identified along with the market price (P_{MKT}) and the true marginal cost to society of car services (P_{MSC}). The deadweight loss in this graph is shaded: notice that at Q_{MKT}, the true marginal cost to society of car services is greater than the market price: the price people are willing to pay for this last unit of the good is less than the cost to society of producing this last unit of the good. This indicates that too many car services are being provided by the market. This same argument will hold true until the quantity produced is reduced to Q_{OPT}, the quantity at which the true marginal cost of producing the last unit of car services is exactly equal to the price consumers are willing to pay (P_{OPT}). Study this graph carefully.

STEP 5: Identify the optimal Pigouvian tax to apply in this situation in order to have the optimal amount of car services provided by Joe's Garage.

Review the section "The Economics of Pollution" on pages 276–281, and the section "Policies Toward Pollution" on pages 282–287.

The optimal Pigouvian tax will be equal to the external cost of providing the car services, or $5 per unit. Suppliers will charge consumers $41 per unit of car services, send $5 per unit of car services to the government, and then keep $36 per car services. With this tax and pricing arrangement, suppliers will be willing to supply 9 units of car services (the optimal amount), since they will receive the amount ($36 per unit) that they must receive in order to supply this amount. Demanders will demand this amount if they pay $41 (use the demand curve to verify that the price that demanders are willing to pay for 9 units is $41). The price difference, $5 per unit, is the optimal Pigouvian tax.

STEP 6: Identify how much tax revenue the government gets when it implements the optimal Pigouvian tax on this market and then compare this tax revenue to the external costs that occur when these car services are produced.

Review the section "The Economics of Pollution" on pages 276–281, and the section "Policies Toward Pollution" on pages 282–287.

The tax revenue will equal the Pigouvian tax per unit times the number of units provided. Since the Pigouvian tax is equal to $5 per unit and 9 units are provided, the tax revenue is equal to $45, which is equivalent to the amount of external costs generated by this amount of car services. The government has collected enough tax revenue to compensate or remediate the pollution that Joe's Garage generates when it provides car services.

4. Suppose a community is composed of two individuals, Sam and Betty. Furthermore, suppose that in this community there is a recognized need for lighthouse services since the community is located on a rocky seashore. Both Betty and Sam fish daily and would benefit from the lighthouse service. Suppose that Betty's marginal benefit curve for these lighthouse services is given by the equation $P = 10 - Q$ while Sam's marginal benefit curve for these lighthouse services is given by the equation $P = 5 - (1/2)Q$. If the marginal cost of providing lighthouse services is equal to $4, what is the optimal amount of lighthouse services

to provide in this market? In your answer provide the marginal social benefit of lighthouse services to the community. In addition, identify how much Betty and Sam should contribute per unit of lighthouse services if the optimal amount of lighthouse service is provided. You may find a graph depicting Sam's and Betty's marginal benefit curves, as well as the marginal social benefit curve for lighthouse services and the curve for the marginal cost of lighthouse services, to be helpful.

STEP 1: Draw graphs of Betty's and Sam's marginal benefit curves from these lighthouse services.

Review the section "Public Goods" on pages 291–298, and Figure 9-6 on page 296.

When you draw these two graphs you will want to orient them so that one graph is vertically above the other graph. You will want to do this to make it easier to think about vertically summing the two marginal benefit curves to create the marginal social benefit curve. The two marginal benefit curves will be summed vertically, since lighthouse services are a public good: lighthouse services are nonrival and nonexcludable. The following figures give the two marginal benefit curves.

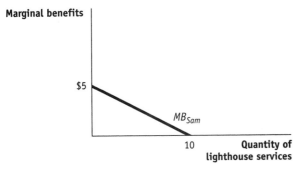

STEP 2: Based on the graphs you drew in Step 1, draw a marginal social benefit curve for lighthouse services in this community.

Review the section "Public Goods" on pages 291–298, and Figure 9-6 on page 296.

To find the marginal social benefit curve, select a quantity and then ask how much Betty is willing to pay for this quantity and how much Sam is willing to pay for this quantity. Sum these two payments together to find the marginal social benefit of this quantity of lighthouse services. The two marginal benefit curves are summed vertically since the good is nonrival: both Betty and Sam can consume the lighthouse services without reducing the amount of these services available to the other. The following figure provides this marginal social benefit curve.

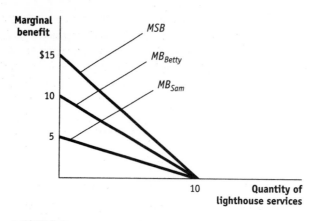

STEP 3: Draw the marginal cost of lighthouse services in the graph you drew in Step 2 and find where the marginal cost of lighthouse services intersects with the marginal social benefit of lighthouse services. Where these two curves intersect will be the optimal amount of lighthouse services to provide to this community.

Review the section "Public Goods" on pages 291–298, and Figure 9-6 on page 296.

Since the marginal costs of lighthouse services are equal to $6, this is a horizontal line. To find where this horizontal line intersects the marginal social benefit from lighthouse services, you will find it helpful to write an equation for the marginal social benefit. This equation is $MSB = 15 - (3/2)Q$. Equate MSC to MSB, or $MSC = 6$ to $MSB = 15 - (3/2)Q$, to find the optimal amount of lighthouse services. Thus, the optimal amount of lighthouse services is equal to 6 units. The following graph illustrates these ideas.

STEP 4: Identify how much Betty and Sam should contribute for each unit of lighthouse services that are provided when the optimal amount of lighthouse services is provided.

Review the section "Public Goods" on pages 291–298, and Figure 9-6 on page 296.

Now that we know the optimal amount of lighthouse services (6 units), we can ask Betty and Sam how much they are each willing to contribute for each unit of lighthouse services. Since Betty's marginal benefit from lighthouse services is given by $P = 10 - Q$, this indicates that when Q is equal to 6 units she is willing to contribute $4 per unit of services provided. Since Sam's marginal benefit from lighthouse services is given by $P = 5 - (1/2)Q$, this indicates that when Q is equal to 6 units he is willing to contribute $2 per unit of services provided. Notice that together they are willing to contribute a total of $6 per unit of lighthouse services, and this is exactly what the marginal cost of providing each unit of lighthouse services is! The following graph identifies the contribution Betty and Sam are willing to make when the optimal amount of lighthouse services is provided.

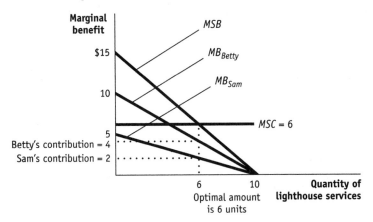

Problems and Exercises

1. Classify each of the following situations as positive or negative externalities, then identify whether the externality occurs on the demand or consumption side of the model, or on the supply or production side of the model.

    a. A manufacturing plant spews toxic gas into the environment as a by-product of its production of furniture.

    b. A group of teenagers gather on Saturday to play loud music and congregate in a downtown park, making it difficult for other people in the town to enjoy the park.

    c. A property owner fills his front yard with trash and old tires.

    d. A company develops a new technology for producing its product, and the new technology can potentially help other companies produce more efficiently.

    e. School-age children in a community do not get immunized prior to attending school.

f. A neighbor decorates the outside of her house with a tasteful holiday display.

g. A neighbor keeps his barking dog outside his house all day and all night.

h. Commercial fishermen catch too many fish and deplete the stock of fish.

2. What is a side effect? What does it mean when a market fails to take into account a side effect? What can you say about the level of production of the good in a market where there are side effects?

3. Suppose the following table provides information about the marginal social benefit of pollution and the marginal social cost of pollution for a society. Assume that both the marginal social benefit of pollution and the marginal social cost of pollution are linear relationships.

Quantity of pollution emissions (tons)	Marginal social benefit of pollution	Marginal social cost of pollution
0	$1,000	$0
2,000	800	133.3
4,000	600	266.7
6,000	400	400
8,000	200	533.3
10,000	0	666.7

a. How would you define the marginal social benefit from emitting pollution?

b. How would you define the marginal social cost of emitting pollution?

c. When 3,000 tons of pollution emissions are emitted, what is the marginal social benefit of this pollution? What is the marginal social cost of this level of pollution emissions? Is this an efficient level of pollution emissions for this society? Explain your answer.

d. When 9,000 tons of pollution emissions are emitted, what is the marginal social benefit of this pollution? What is the marginal social cost of this level of pollution emissions? Is this an efficient level of pollution emissions for this society? Explain your answer.

e. What is the efficient level of pollution emissions for this society?

4. Use the information given in problem 3 to answer this set of questions.

a. Draw a graph of the marginal social benefit (*MSB*) of pollution and the marginal social cost (*MSC*) of pollution; measure *MSB* and *MSC* on the vertical axis and the quantity of pollution emissions on the horizontal axis.

Quantity of pollution emissions (tons)

b. Label the socially optimal amount of pollution emissions in the graph you drew in part (a).

c. Will the socially optimal amount of pollution be produced in this market if there is no government intervention? Explain your answer.

5. Suppose there are just two firms in Smalltown and both of these firms emit pollution as part of their productive process. Firm A's marginal social benefit from pollution is given by the equation $MSB = 100 - Q$, while firm B's marginal social benefit from pollution is given by the equation $MSB = 50 - 0.5Q$, where Q is the quantity of pollution emissions measured in tons.

    a. Draw a graph representing the marginal social benefit of pollution emissions for firm A and firm B.

Marginal social benefit

Quantity of pollution emissions (tons)

    b. Suppose the government in Smalltown decides to impose an emissions standard of 55 tons for every firm producing in Smalltown. How much of a reduction in pollution emissions will occur because of the imposition of this standard? Assume that prior to the emissions standard, firms produced the level of pollution emissions at which their marginal social benefit equaled $0.

    c. What is the marginal social benefit to firm A of the last ton of pollution it emits? What is the marginal social benefit to firm B of the last ton of pollution it emits?

    d. Is this an efficient method for reducing pollution emissions by this amount? Explain your answer.

6. Use the information given in problem 5 to answer this set of questions. Suppose that the government, instead of an emissions standard, imposes a tax on emissions of $30 per ton.

   a. What will be the reduction in pollution emissions by firm A with the imposition of this tax?

   b. What will be the reduction in pollution emissions by firm B with the imposition of this tax?

   c. What will be the total reduction in pollution emissions with this tax?

   d. Is this an efficient method for reducing pollution emissions by this amount? Explain your answer.

   e. Draw a graph illustrating this tax. Identify firm A's and firm B's marginal social benefit from pollution emissions.

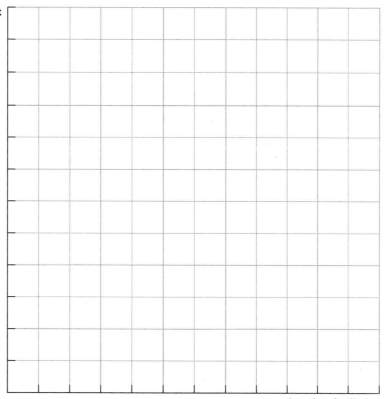

Marginal social benefit

Quantity of pollution emissions (tons)

7. Joan loves dogs and decides that she is going to buy a dog. She analyzes the benefit she will get from owning a dog and values the benefit of owning a dog at $500. Joan's next-door neighbor loathes dogs and is vehemently opposed to dogs being in the neighborhood. This neighbor, Mike, views the cost of an additional dog in the neighborhood as being $800. According to the Coase theorem, is it possible for Joan and Mike to amicably resolve this dilemma about dog ownership? In your answer, identify how this conflict can be resolved provided that the rights to dog ownership are well defined. Also, in your answer consider how it does not matter who owns the rights to dog ownership provided that these rights are well defined.

8. A recent article reports that drunken driving has risen in communities that have imposed smoking bans in their bars and taverns. The gist of the problem is that smokers who also drink are now driving longer distances to get to bars that allow them to smoke while they are drinking. Does the decision to impose a smoking ban on the bars and taverns in the community create an externality? What do you think motivated policy makers to impose this smoking ban?

9. Suppose the consumption of a good generates substantial external benefits due to the presence of side effects. Suppose the government wishes to help the market generate the socially optimal consumption of this good. Will the market by itself generate the socially optimal amount of this good? Explain your answer. What type of policy or policies might the government engage in to meet this goal?

10. Suppose the demand for computer software engineers in Micronesia can be expressed as $Q = 100 - 0.001P$, where Q is the number of computer software engineers demanded and P is the annual salary per computer software engineer. Suppose that the supply of computer software engineers in Micronesia can be expressed as $P = 4,000Q$. Furthermore, suppose that in the market for computer software engineers there are substantial technology spillovers equal to $20,000 per computer software engineer. Currently, the market for computer software engineers does not take into account these technological spillovers.

a. What is the equilibrium quantity of computer software engineers in Micronesia, and what is the annual salary per computer software engineer?

b. Is the quantity of computer software engineers you found in part (a) the socially optimal quantity of computer software engineers for Micronesia? Explain your answer.

c. Draw a graph of the market for computer software engineers. In your graph draw a curve that represents the marginal private benefits (demand), a curve that represents the marginal social benefit (*MSB*), and a curve that represents supply. Identify the market quantity and market price as well as the socially optimal quantity and price.

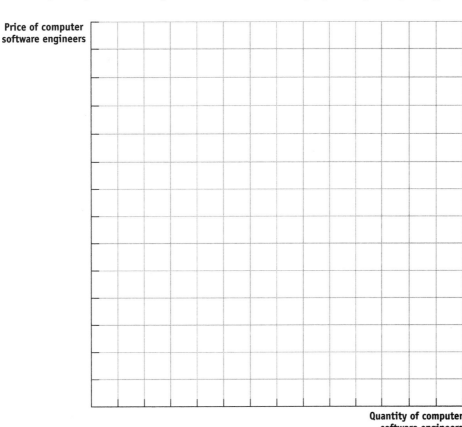

d. What is the optimal quantity of computer software engineers for Micronesia? Explain why you have chosen this quantity as the optimal quantity.

e. What policy could the government enact to enable Micronesia to produce this optimal quantity?

f. Graph the policy you described in part (e) on the following graph and label this graph carefully and completely.

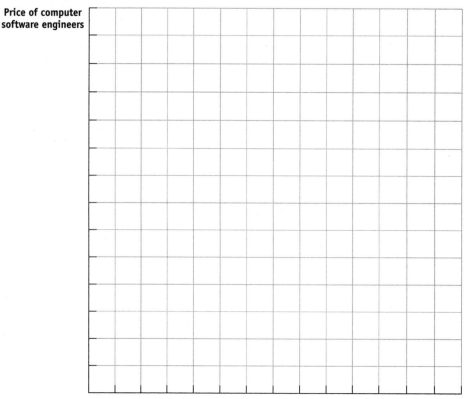

Price of computer software engineers

Quantity of computer software engineers

11. The following table is meant to summarize the market level of production for various situations that might occur due to the presence of externalities. In the table, "*MSC*" refers to the marginal social cost of production, "Supply" refers to the marginal private cost of production, "*MSB*" refers to the marginal social benefit from consuming the good, and "Demand" refers to the marginal private benefit from consuming the good. Read each scenario and then decide whether the market produces the socially optimal amount of the good, too much of the good, or too little of the good. Fill in the second column with the relevant description of the market's production decision.

Situation	Market produces
Demand = *MSB* and Supply = *MSC*	
Demand > *MSB* and Supply = *MSC*	
Demand < *MSB* and Supply = *MSC*	
Demand = *MSB* and Supply < *MSC*	
Demand = *MSB* and Supply > *MSC*	

12. For each of the following situations, determine whether the good in the situation is (1) excludable or nonexcludable, and (2) nonrival in consumption or rival in consumption.

    a. A community erects a lighthouse to guide ships navigating near its rocky shoreline.

    b. A country builds a national defense system of missiles.

    c. A community builds a toll road that has low levels of usage.

    d. A community builds a toll road that has high levels of usage.

    e. A radio station broadcasts the baseball game.

    f. A community builds a non-toll road that has high levels of usage.

    g. Police protection is hired for a community.

    h. The environment of a community is improved.

13. What does it mean when a good is nonexcludable? Explain in your own words what this means.

14. What does it mean when a good is nonrival in consumption? Explain in your own words what this means.

15. Markets provide private goods efficiently since the market price is equal to the marginal cost of producing the good. Why do markets fail to produce the efficient level of public goods?

16. Jimmy and Beth are the only residents of Smalltown. They both think the community would benefit from more parks, but neither Jimmy nor Beth is willing to contribute money to buy land to turn into parks since they both realize that once a park is provided they can enjoy the park even though they have not paid for the park.

    a. Describe Jimmy's and Beth's behavior and why it represents a problem when trying to provide parks in their community.

    b. Suppose Jimmy reveals that his marginal benefit from one park is equal to $50 per park, his marginal benefit from two parks is equal to $25 per park, and his marginal benefit from three parks is equal to $0 per park. Beth reveals that her marginal benefit from one park is equal to $60 per park, her marginal benefit from two parks is equal to $40 per park, and her marginal benefit from three parks is equal to $20 per park. What is the marginal social benefit of two parks equal to in their community? Explain how you found this answer.

    c. Suppose the information in part (b) is still true. Jimmy and Beth analyze the cost of providing parks in their community and they find that the marginal social cost of providing parks is constant and equal to $55. What is the socially optimal amount of parks for this community? Explain how you got this answer.

    d. If Jimmy and Beth are both willing to reveal their preferences with regard to parks (that is, they will tell the truth about the marginal private benefit they receive from the parks), will they both contribute to getting the socially optimal amount of parks for their community?

17. What two characteristics do private goods have that make it possible for markets to efficiently provide the good, and why are these characteristics so important?

18. Big Sports is a television company that has won the rights to broadcast next season's football games in the Big Group college football conference. To watch these televised games, viewers need to subscribe to the Super Cable package that costs an additional $15 per month.

   a. Do Big Sports and its televised games represent a public good, a common resource, or an artificially scarce good? Explain your answer and why you have classified Big Sports in this manner.

   b. What price is the efficient price for consumers to pay for watching these football games? Explain your answer.

   c. Does Big Sports produce the socially optimal, or efficient, level of televised football games for the Big Group college football conference? Explain your answer. If the level of production is not the socially optimal amount, is the amount produced in the market greater than or less than the socially optimal amount? Explain your answer.

19. In which of the following situations is the free-rider problem likely to arise? Explain for each situation that has a free-rider problem why this occurs and what the nature of the free-rider problem is.

   a. The parent-teacher association at your child's elementary school is looking for parent volunteers to direct a fund-raiser to raise money to replace the playground equipment.

   b. Local community organizers are seeking people to serve on a committee to improve the beauty of the community through gardening and landscaping efforts.

   c. The local hamburger joint is testing a new sandwich on its menu.

   d. A local group is organizing a Saturday morning spring cleanup of the lakeshore in their community.

20. For each of the following situations, decide whether the problem is like a positive externality, negative externality, or natural monopoly.

   a. The parent-teacher association at your child's elementary school is looking for parent volunteers to direct a fund-raiser to raise money to replace the playground equipment.

b. Local community organizers are seeking people to serve on a committee to improve the beauty of the community through gardening and landscaping efforts.

c. The number of elephants in Africa is declining due to hunters killing them for their ivory tusks.

d. A local group is organizing a Saturday morning spring cleanup of the lakeshore in their community.

e. The quantity of salmon in the Great Lakes is declining due to too many salmon being caught by sport fishermen.

f. Children at the elementary school, once they are vaccinated for childhood diseases, lower the risk of infection for those who are not vaccinated.

g. The local cable television company charges an additional fee if the customer wants to receive the channel that offers local sports coverage.

■ BEFORE YOU TAKE THE TEST

Chapter Review Questions

1. The optimal amount of pollution is
   a. the amount of pollution where the marginal social benefit of the pollution exceeds the marginal social cost of the pollution.
   b. zero units of pollution, since pollution is harmful to people.
   c. the amount of pollution where the marginal social benefit of the pollution is less than the marginal social cost of the pollution.
   d. the amount of pollution where the marginal social benefit of the pollution equals the marginal social cost of the pollution.

2. The gain to society of an additional unit of pollution is best measured by
   a. an emissions tax.
   b. an emissions standard.
   c. the marginal social benefit of pollution.
   d. the socially optimal quantity of pollution.

Use the following figure to answer the next three questions.

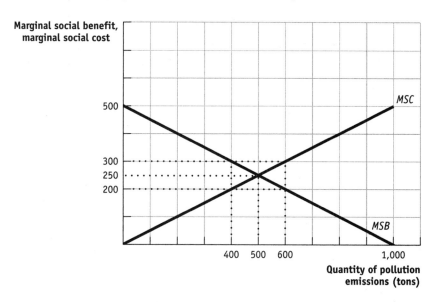

3. The socially optimal amount of pollution emissions in the above graph is
   a. 400 tons.
   b. 500 tons.
   c. 600 tons.

4. When 400 tons of pollution are emitted,
   a. the marginal social cost of pollution is less than the marginal social benefit of pollution.
   b. this economy would be better off producing more pollution emissions.
   c. this economy would be worse off producing more pollution emissions.
   d. Answers (a) and (b) are true.
   e. Answers (a) and (c) are true.

5. What is the appropriate emissions standard for this economy if there is only one producer in the economy, and the goal is to produce the efficient level of pollution emissions?
   a. 400 tons of emissions
   b. 500 tons of emissions
   c. 600 tons of emissions
   d. 0 tons of emissions

6. A government wants to enact a policy that will lead to a reduction in pollution emissions. One policy entails establishing an emissions standard, and another policy entails implementation of an emissions tax. Which of the following statements is(are) true?

    I. An emissions standard and an emissions tax are equally efficient methods for reducing pollution emissions.

    II. An emissions standard ensures that the marginal social benefit of pollution is equal for all sources of pollution.

    III. An emissions tax does not ensure that the marginal social benefit of pollution is equal for all sources of pollution.

    a. Statement I is true.

    b. Statements I and II are true.

    c. Statements I and III are true.

    d. Statements I, II, and III are true.

    e. None of these statements is true.

7. When two firms have a different marginal social benefit of pollution, this implies that

    a. an equal reduction in pollution by both firms is not efficient.

    b. one firm can reduce its level of pollution by a larger amount and still find that its marginal social benefit of pollution is equal to the other firm's marginal social benefit of pollution.

    c. an emissions tax is more efficient than an emissions standard.

    d. All of these statements are true.

8. Taxes that are designed to reduce external costs are known as

    a. excise taxes.   c. Pigouvian taxes.

    b. income taxes.   d. emissions taxes.

9. Suppose a government decides to issue a limited number of tradable pollution permits. Which of the following statements is true?

    a. Firms that can easily and at low cost reduce their level of pollution will find it beneficial to purchase these tradable pollution permits.

    b. When the government issues these tradable pollution permits, it effectively creates a market for the right to pollute.

    c. Firms that sell their tradable pollution permits do not fully understand the costs they will incur when they try to reduce the level of pollution they create.

    d. None of these statements is true.

10. Which of the following tools is likely to encourage firms to find less-polluting technology?

    a. emissions standards

    b. emissions taxes

    c. tradable pollution permits

    d. All of the above will create incentives for firms to find less-polluting technology.

    e. Emissions taxes and tradable pollution permits will create incentives for firms to find less-polluting technology.

11. Which of the following statements is true?

    a. In contrast to the cost of a negative externality like pollution, the benefit from a positive externality is easier to measure, since people like to reveal the amount of positive benefits they receive from different activities.

    b. The benefit from a positive externality is difficult to measure, since these benefits cannot be directly observed.

12. When the consumption of a good generates positive external benefits, the market tends to produce

    a. too much of the good, since there are positive external benefits from the consumption of the good.

    b. too little of the good, since the market does not take into account the positive external benefits from the consumption of the good.

13. Joe really does not enjoy school and is thinking about dropping out this spring. Joe's consumption of formal education is likely to

    a. be the efficient amount of education, since Joe knows best the level of benefit he receives from attending school.

    b. be at too high a level, since Joe has always been an indifferent student and a student who has rarely been engaged in getting an education.

    c. be at too low a level, since Joe only considers his private benefits from getting an education and not the social benefits that society receives when he gets an education.

    d. reflect his family's benefit from his getting an education, and his family thinks they will get a greater benefit if Joe drops out and gets a job. From his family's perspective, this would be an efficient outcome.

Use the following information to answer the next three questions.

Residents of Smalltown recognize that there are private benefits to exercise, and they estimate that the marginal private benefits from exercise can be represented by the demand curve $P = 100 - 0.05Q$, where P measures the marginal private benefit and Q is hours of exercise per year. Exercise also generates positive external benefits for the community because it reduces health care costs, lowers the obesity rate, and results in a more energetic and engaged community. The marginal external benefit from a unit of exercise is estimated to have a value of $10 per hour of exercise. The supply curve for exercise can be represented by the equation $P = 0.05Q$, where P measures the marginal private cost of exercise and Q is hours of exercise per year.

14. The market for exercise will not include the marginal social benefits from exercise without some type of intervention. How many hours of exercise per year will be provided by the market, and what is the price demanders are willing to pay for each unit of exercise consumed?

    a. 0 hours of exercise; $100

    b. 50 hours of exercise; $1,000

    c. 1,000 hours of exercise; $50

    d. 2,000 hours of exercise; $0

15. What is the socially optimal amount of exercise per year for Smalltown?

    a. 0 hours of exercise

    b. 1,000 hours of exercise

    c. 1,100 hours of exercise

    d. 2,000 hours of exercise

16. Smalltown decides it is important for the community to consume the socially optimal amount of exercise. Smalltown therefore decides to enact a policy of

    a. subsidizing everyone who exercises with a payment of $10 per hour of exercise.

    b. taxing everyone who exercises with a tax payment of $10 per hour of exercise.

    c. mandating that everyone exercise an additional 10 hours per year.

    d. reducing the price of each hour of exercise by $20.

17. Policy makers decide they wish to encourage the consumption of an activity that generates positive externalities. Which of the following statements is true?

    I. An excise tax on each unit of the good consumed helps the policy maker achieve the socially optimal amount of consumption of this good.

    II. A subsidy per unit of the good consumed helps the policy maker achieve the socially optimal amount of consumption of this good.

    III. Intervention in this market by the policy maker results in a socially less-optimal outcome for this market, since government intervention in any market results in a deadweight loss.

    a. Statement I is true.

    b. Statement II is true.

    c. Statement III is true.

    d. None of the statements is true, given this situation.

18. Industrial policy is often advocated whenever there are

    a. negative externalities arising from the consumption of a good.

    b. negative externalities arising from the production of a good.

    c. technological spillovers in a market.

    d. national security issues present with regard to the production of a good.

Answer the next two questions based on the following diagram of the market for bottled water that comes from aquifers deep underground. In the production of this product, the level of water in these aquifers is drawn down at a rate faster than the water can be replenished. This action results in a negative externality on the nearby communities that depend on these aquifers for their water, since the producers of the bottled water do not consider the effect of their production on the community's water source. In the following graph, "Supply" represents the marginal private cost of producing the good, "MSC" represents the marginal social cost (the external as well as private cost) of producing the good, and "Demand" represents the marginal social benefit from consuming the good. Assume that the externality per unit of the good produced is a constant amount per unit of bottled water.

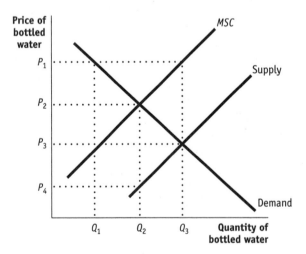

19. What is the socially optimal level of output for this market?

    a. Q_1

    b. Q_2

    c. Q_3

20. At the market-determined level of production in the above market, the deadweight loss due to the negative externality can be expressed as the area
   a. $(1/2)(P_1 - P_3)Q_3$.
   b. $(1/2)(P_2 - P_4)(Q_3 - Q_2)$.
   c. $(1/2)(P_2 - P_4)Q_2$.
   d. $(1/2)P_2(Q_3 - Q_2)$.

21. A public good is a good
   a. that benefits many people whether or not they have paid for it.
   b. whose benefits to any particular individual do not depend on how many other individuals benefit from the good.
   c. that is nonrival in consumption and nonexcludable.
   d. Answers (a), (b), and (c) are all true statements.

22. In the case of a common resource,
   a. one person's consumption of the common resource reduces the amount of the common resource available to other consumers.
   b. one person cannot be excluded from consuming the common resource because it is nonrival in consumption.
   c. one person can exclude others from consuming the common resource if they have not paid for the consumption of the common resource.
   d. it represents the same type of problem found in a market when positive externalities are associated with the good.

23. When the price of a good is greater than its marginal cost of production, the market for this good is producing
   a. the socially optimal amount of the good.
   b. too little of the good.
   c. too much of the good.
   d. as optimal an amount of output as is possible given the circumstances.

24. For a market to efficiently deliver a good, the good must be
   a. rival in consumption.
   b. excludable.
   c. nonrival in consumption.
   d. nonexcludable.
   e. (a) and (b).
   f. (c) and (d).

25. Madison has a number of city parks that are open to the public at no charge. Throughout the year these parks are often crowded, with long lines at the play structures. These public parks represent a good that is
   a. nonrival and nonexcludable.
   b. nonrival and excludable.
   c. rival and nonexcludable.
   d. rival and excludable.

26. Madison is in the middle of tornado country, and because of the imminent danger of tornadoes, it has decided to invest in a siren system. This siren system is an example of a good that is
    a. nonrival in consumption and nonexcludable.
    b. nonrival in consumption and excludable.
    c. rival in consumption and nonexcludable.
    d. rival in consumption and excludable.

27. The Illinois Tollway that connects Rockford to Chicago is constantly congested with traffic jams. Motorists must pay a toll fee to use it. The Tollway is a good that is characterized as
    a. rival in consumption and nonexcludable.
    b. rival in consumption and excludable.
    c. nonrival in consumption and nonexcludable.
    d. rival in consumption and nonexcludable.

28. Mason Street is a quiet residential street that is only three blocks long. There is no toll for driving on Mason Street, and the street gets very little traffic except from the people who live on the street. Mason Street is
    a. nonrival in consumption and nonexcludable.
    b. rival in consumption and excludable.
    c. nonrival in consumption and excludable.
    d. rival in consumption and nonexcludable.

29. Sally and Sue live together in an apartment and neither of them likes to clean the apartment nor do the dishes. After several weeks of living like this, the apartment does get really dirty. Sally often wishes the apartment was clean, but she does not do anything to clean up the apartment because she figures that if she is only patient enough, Sue will clean the apartment. Which of the following statements is true?
    a. Sue free-rides on Sally when it comes to getting the apartment cleaned up.
    b. Sally free-rides on Sue when it comes to getting the apartment cleaned up.
    c. Since there are only two people in the apartment, the free-rider problem is not important because eventually Sally and Sue will clean the apartment.
    d. Free-ridership is a problem that only arises in a society that is trying to provide a public good.

30. Joey's elementary school is organizing a fund-raiser to raise the funds needed to refurbish the library. Each parent has been asked to contribute two hours of their time toward the fund-raiser, but very few parents have come forward to help out. Which of the following statements is true?
    a. The children will benefit from the refurbishment of the library irrespective of whether or not their parents volunteer their time.
    b. If the parents do not volunteer, someone else will, and then they and their children can free-ride on the other parents' work.
    c. The school will suffer from the free-rider problem and will not raise the optimal amount of funds due to the parents' free-riding.
    d. Answers (a), (b), and (c) are all true statements.

31. When a good is nonexcludable, the market produces
   a. too much of the good.
   b. too little of the good.

32. New Glarus has just built and opened a toll road connecting New Glarus to Old Glarus. This toll road is never congested no matter what time of day or what day of the week it is. Since the toll road is both nonrival in consumption and excludable, it is an example of an artificially scarce good. The marginal cost of letting an additional driver use the toll road is equal to
   a. the toll.
   b. zero.
   c. the toll divided by the number of drivers currently using the toll road.
   d. the toll divided by the population of the two communities.

33. New Glarus has just built and opened a toll road connecting New Glarus to Old Glarus. This toll road is never congested no matter what time of day or what day of the week it is. Since the toll road is both nonrival in consumption and excludable, it is an example of an artificially scarce good. Drivers who might benefit from using this toll road will
   a. not use the toll road as much as is socially optimal since the toll is greater than the marginal cost of allowing these drivers to use the road.
   b. use the toll road at the socially optimal level since the toll is sufficient to cover the costs of providing the road.
   c. free-ride on other drivers.

Use the following information to answer the next three questions.

Suppose Joe's marginal private benefit from national defense is given by the equation $P = 100 - Q$, where Q refers to the amount of military goods and P refers to the price Joe is willing to pay for each unit of military goods. Mary's marginal private benefit from national defense is given by the equation $P = 50 - 0.5Q$. Furthermore, suppose the marginal social cost of providing an additional unit of military goods is constant and equal to $60.

34. Which equation represents the marginal social benefit (*MSB*) from military goods if Joe and Mary are the only two individuals in the economy? (Hint: Draw two graphs of the individual demand curves for Joe and Mary, then draw a third graph that adds these two individual demand curves together.)
   a. $MSB = 66.67 - 0.33Q$
   b. $MSB = 150 - 1.5Q$
   c. $MSB = 100 - Q$
   d. $MSB = 50 - 0.5Q$

35. What is the socially optimal amount of national defense for this economy?
   a. 90 units of military goods
   b. 80 units of military goods
   c. 170 units of military goods
   d. 60 units of military goods

36. Suppose both Joe and Mary are truthful about their preferences with regard to national defense and they both fully reveal the marginal benefits they receive from national defense. Furthermore, suppose the socially optimal amount of national defense is produced in this economy. What price per unit of national defense will Joe be willing to pay?

a. $100

b. $60

c. $40

d. $20

37. Which of the following statements about public goods is(are) true?

  I. Public goods can be provided efficiently by the market or by the government.

  II. Public goods can be provided through voluntary contributions or by self-interested individuals or firms.

  III. Some public goods can be provided through social encouragement or pressure.

a. Statement I is true.

b. Statements II and III are true.

c. Statements I, II, and III are true.

d. Statements I and II are true.

e. Statements I and III are true.

Use the following graph of a public good to answer the next three questions. Assume that Joe and Sarah are the only two people who live in their community and that this graph represents Joe's marginal benefit from the public good, Sarah's marginal benefit from the public good, and the total marginal social benefit from the public good. In addition, the marginal cost of producing an additional unit of the public good is constant and equal to P_4.

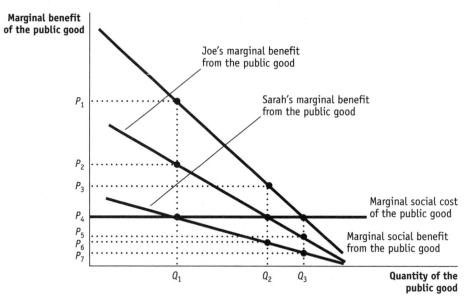

38. At Q_1, the marginal social benefit from this last unit of the public good

a. is equal to P_1 or the sum of $P_2 + P_4$.

b. is greater than the marginal social cost of producing this last unit of the public good.

c. exceeds the marginal social cost of producing another unit of the public good, which tells us that this community is not producing enough of the public good.

d. Answers (a), (b), and (c) are all true statements.

39. What is the socially optimal amount of the good? If both Sarah and Joe contribute to the provision of the public good an amount that equals the marginal benefit they get from the last unit of the good they consume, how much will Joe contribute per unit of the public good?

a. Q_1; P_2 d. Q_3; P_4

b. Q_1; P_4 e. Q_3; P_5

c. Q_2; P_4

40. Given the information in the preceding graph, who places a higher value on the public good represented in the graph?

a. Joe

b. Sarah

41. A community is trying to decide whether or not to install lighting at one of the local city parks. Government officials estimate that the marginal social benefit from installing the lighting will be $100, but that the marginal social cost of installing the lighting will be $105. This community

a. should conduct another study to see if the numbers come out better, since clearly it would be great to have a well-lit park.

b. should not install the lighting at this time, since the marginal benefit from the lighting is less than the marginal cost of installing the lighting.

c. will not install the lighting, since the market will provide the lighting.

d. should install the lighting, because the cost-benefit analysis did not take into account the tendency of individuals to free-ride on the provision of the public good.

42. Fishermen in Oceania report dwindling supplies of their favorite fish. These fishermen fish in open water with no limits placed on who can fish in the sea and how many fish can be taken from the sea. This is an example of a(n)

a. artificially scarce good, since good fisheries management could eliminate the fish scarcity.

b. public good, since no one is paying to fish in the sea and thus no one can be excluded from fishing in that sea water.

c. common resource, since the fishing grounds are nonexcludable but rival in consumption.

d. private good, since each fisherman catches his own fish, and then markets them at the local fish market.

43. A good that is nonexcludable but rival in consumption is a(n)

a. public good.   c. artificially scarce good.

b. positive externality.   d. common resource.

44. In the case of a common resource, the market tends to

a. overconsume the good, since the good is nonexcludable but rival in consumption.

b. underconsume the good, since the good is nonexcludable but rival in consumption.

45. London recently started charging drivers a fee to drive in certain parts of the city during high-traffic times of day. The fee seeks to effectively address the problem of traffic congestion. This fee has successfully reduced traffic congestion in the areas of London where it has been applied. By imposing the fee, government officials have
    a. encouraged consumers to drive less than they otherwise would.
    b. encouraged consumers to drive at times when traffic congestion is less of a problem.
    c. made a common resource excludable: those who pay for the right to drive can drive, and those unwilling to pay must forgo driving.
    d. Answers (a), (b), and (c) are all true.

46. In the case of a common resource, the market does not recognize that
    a. marginal social cost is greater than the private cost of providing the last unit of the good.
    b. marginal social benefit is greater than the marginal benefit individuals receive from consuming the last unit of the good.
    c. marginal social benefit and marginal social cost are both ignored by the market.
    d. the marginal benefits and marginal costs from consumption of the good are ignored.

47. The market can correct the problem posed by common resources by
    a. imposing the appropriate Pigouvian tax on the good.
    b. creating a system of tradable licenses for the right to this common resource.
    c. assigning property rights to this common resource, thereby making the good an excludable good.
    d. Answers (a), (b), and (c) are all feasible corrections to the problem posed by common resources.

48. Economists are excited because they have just discovered a good that is nonrival in consumption but excludable. This good
    a. will be very expensive, since it is such a rare good.
    b. should be free, since the marginal cost of an individual's consumption of this good is equal to zero if this good is to be produced at the socially optimal level of production.
    c. will be overproduced in this market, since the price of the good is less than the marginal cost of providing the good.
    d. will be efficiently produced in this market, since the good is excludable and a price can therefore be assigned to the good by the market.

ANSWER KEY

Answers to Problems and Exercises

1. **a.** This is a negative production externality.

    b. This is a negative consumption externality.

    c. This is a negative consumption externality.

    d. This is a positive production externality.

    e. This is a negative consumption externality.

    f. This is a positive consumption externality.

    g. This is a negative consumption externality.

    h. This is a negative production externality.

2. A side effect is a situation in which the market fails to take into account a cost or a benefit from some action or good. This results in the market failing to produce the right amount of the good, because the market either does not correctly measure the cost to society of producing the good or the benefit to society of consuming the good. When side effects are present in a market, this implies that the market produces either too much of the good (the situation when the side effect is a hidden cost) or too little of the good (the situation when the side effect is a hidden benefit).

3. **a.** The marginal social benefit from emitting pollution is the measure of the additional benefit a society gets from one more ton of pollution. It can be measured in terms of the cost that must be incurred by a society in order to not produce this ton of pollution: to produce less pollution, a society must use some of its scarce resources that could have been used to produce other goods and services. The marginal benefit of emitting pollution is the amount of money a society would save if it were allowed to emit an additional ton of pollution.

    b. The marginal social cost of emitting pollution is equal to the sum of the highest willingness to pay among all members of this society to avoid that ton of pollution. The marginal social cost of emitting pollution measures the true marginal cost of the pollution. Another way of expressing the marginal social cost of pollution is that this measures the additional cost imposed on all of the society of an additional ton of pollution.

    c. Since this level of pollution emissions is not listed in the table, you have to extrapolate from the numbers in the table or write equations for the marginal social benefit of pollution and the marginal social cost of pollution. Extrapolating from the table, you can see that the marginal social benefit of 2,000 tons of pollution is $800 per ton, and the marginal social benefit of 4,000 tons of pollution is $600 per ton: you could infer that the marginal social benefit of 3,000 tons of pollution is therefore $700 per ton. Or you can write the equation for the marginal social benefit of pollution as $MSB = 1,000 - 0.1Q$, where MSB is the marginal social benefit of pollution and Q is the quantity of pollution emissions. Then, substituting 3,000 into the equation for Q, MSB is equal to $700 per ton of pollution emissions. Using a similar technique for the marginal social cost of pollution, $MSC = (1/15)Q$, where MSC is the marginal social cost of pollution emissions. When Q equals 3,000, MSC equals $200 per ton of pollution emissions. This is not an efficient level of pollution emissions since the marginal social benefit is greater than the marginal social cost: too little pollution emissions are being produced at this level, since the marginal social benefit of more pollution emissions is greater than the marginal social cost of pollution emissions.

d. Using the equations found in part (c), the marginal social benefit of 9,000 tons of pollution emissions is equal to $100 per ton of pollution emissions, while the marginal social cost of 9,000 tons of pollution emissions is equal to $600 per ton of pollution emissions. This is not an efficient level of pollution emissions since the marginal social benefit is less than the marginal social cost: too much pollution emissions are occurring in this society.

e. The efficient level of pollution emissions for this society is the level where the marginal social benefit is equal to the marginal social cost. This occurs at 6,000 tons of pollution emissions where the marginal social benefit and the marginal social cost are both $400 per ton of pollution emissions.

4. **a., b.**

c. No, the optimal level of pollution emissions will not be produced in this economy without government intervention since producers do not have any incentive to take into account the costs of pollution that they impose on other people.

5. **a.**

  b. Each firm will reduce its emissions by 45 tons, for a total of 90 tons.

  c. The marginal social benefit for firm A is $45, and the marginal social benefit for firm B is $22.50.

  d. No, this is not efficient since the marginal social benefit of pollution emissions reduction is not equivalent across all the firms in the economy.

6. **a.** Firm A will reduce pollution emissions by 30 units.

  b. Firm B will reduce pollution emissions by 60 units.

  c. The total reduction in pollution emissions will be 90 units (note that this is the same level of pollution reduction achieved with the emissions standard in problem 5).

  d. This is an efficient method for reducing pollution emissions since each firm's marginal social benefit of pollution is the same for the last unit of pollution they emit.

  e.

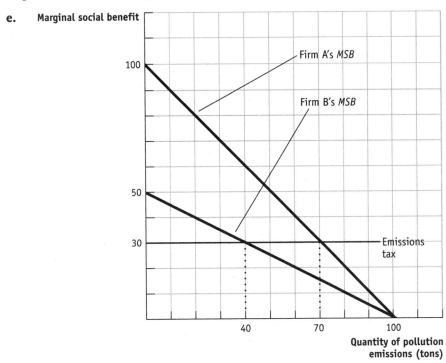

7. To answer this question, we first have to look at the requirements for the Coase theorem: for an externality situation to be resolved by the two transacting parties, the transaction cost must not be too high and the property rights must be well defined. The two neighbors can easily talk to one another, and we can start by assigning the property rights to dog ownership to the potential dog owner. This would mean that Joan has the right to purchase a dog. But Mike could approach Joan and tell her that he is willing to compensate her an amount sufficient to persuade her not to purchase the dog. Mike can offer Joan any amount greater than $500 but less than $800, and both Joan and Mike will be better off. Given Joan's marginal benefit of owning the dog and Mike's marginal cost of another dog in the neighborhood, the two parties, if they are free to discuss this transaction at reasonable cost, will decide that Joan will not purchase the dog and instead will receive compensation for forgoing the consumption of a canine. If the property rights to dog ownership rest with Mike and he therefore gets to decide whether or not a neighbor gets to own a dog, we get the same result. Joan is only willing to pay Mike up to $500 for the right to buy the dog, and since Mike must receive at least $800 to be willing to have a dog in the neighborhood, Joan will not purchase the dog. The thrust of the Coase theorem is that externality issues can be resolved if the parties are well identified, the transaction costs are not high, and the property rights are well defined.

8. This is quite ironic in that the smoking ban was likely motivated by a desire to reduce the negative externality of secondhand smoke in bars and taverns. The policy makers considered the situation of smoking in the bar and identified that this behavior created a cost that was imposed on nonsmokers. By imposing this smoking ban, they would eliminate this side effect. However, in imposing the smoking ban they did not consider how smokers might react. If smokers view smoking as a highly important complement to their bar experience, they may indeed drive longer distances to be able to both smoke and drink. Then, when they get back on the road they impose a side effect, or negative externality, on others in the form of their drunk driving. Which side effect is more costly to society and to the third parties impacted by these drinkers who also smoke is an interesting question!

9. When the consumption of a good generates external benefits, the good is underproduced in the market, since the positive side effects of the consumption of the good are not included in the market's determination of the equilibrium quantity of the good. The government needs to pursue policies that result in higher consumption of the good, which in turn affect the quantity of the side effect produced. The government can achieve this result by targeting the activity, or consumption of the good, by offering subsidies to consumers to encourage a higher level of consumption.

10. a. The equilibrium quantity in the market is where the quantity demanded equals the quantity supplied, or $100{,}000 - 1{,}000Q = 4{,}000Q$. Solving this equation, Q equals 20 computer software engineers. The annual salary for a computer software engineer can be found by using either the demand or the supply curve, and substituting in 20 for the quantity. Thus, the annual salary for a computer software engineer is $80,000.

b. The quantity found in part (a) is not the socially optimal quantity of computer software engineers, since the market does not take into account the side effects of the positive externality that arises from the technology spillover. The market quantity equates demand and supply, instead of equating the marginal social benefit to the marginal social cost.

c.

d. The optimal quantity of computer software engineers is where the marginal social benefit equals the marginal social cost. To find this quantity, first write an equation that expresses the marginal social benefit. This equation is $P = 120{,}000 - 1{,}000Q$ since the marginal social benefit curve has the same slope as the market demand curve but has a y-intercept of 120,000 instead of 100,000. Setting the marginal social benefit curve equal to the supply curve yields the following: $120{,}000 - 1{,}000Q = 4{,}000Q$, or $Q = 24$. When there is an external benefit from the consumption of the good, too few units of the good are consumed in the market: in this case, the optimal quantity of computer software engineers is 24 and not the market-determined quantity of 20 engineers.

e. The government could subsidize the demanders of computer software engineers so that they would effectively view the market demand curve for computer software engineers as being $P = 120{,}000 - 1{,}000Q$. This would entail paying a subsidy of \$20,000 for every computer software engineer demanded. With this subsidy the government would effectively internalize the positive externality.

f.

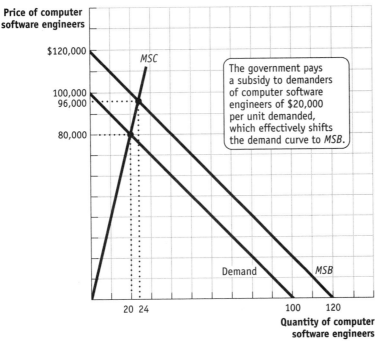

Government Policy of Subsidizing Demanders in the Market for Computer Software Engineers

The government pays a subsidy to demanders of computer software engineers of \$20,000 per unit demanded, which effectively shifts the demand curve to *MSB*.

11.

Situation	Market produces
Demand = *MSB* and Supply = *MSC*	The market produces the socially optimal amount of the good.
Demand > *MSB* and Supply = *MSC*	The market produces too much of the good.
Demand < *MSB* and Supply = *MSC*	The market produces too little of the good.
Demand = *MSB* and Supply < *MSC*	The market produces too much of the good.
Demand = *MSB* and Supply > *MSC*	The market produces too little of the good.

12. a. Nonexcludable and nonrival

b. Nonexcludable and nonrival

c. Excludable and nonrival

d. Excludable and rival

e. Nonexcludable and nonrival

f. Nonexcludable and rival

g. Nonexcludable and rival

h. Nonexcludable and nonrival

13. A good is nonexcludable when once the good is produced, individuals can enjoy the consumption of this good even if they do not pay for the good. Once people realize that a good is nonexcludable, they will free-ride on other people who are willing to pay for the good, knowing that once the good is provided they will be able to consume it even if they have not paid for it.

14. A good is nonrival in consumption if more than one person can consume the same unit of the good without diminishing the other people's benefits of consuming the good. Most of the goods we have discussed thus far in the text are private goods for which one person's consumption of the good means that no one else can consume that unit: this implies that consumers are rivals when they consume private goods. In the case of a good that is nonrival, consumers are not rivals and many people can enjoy the benefits from the same good.

15. A public good is both nonexcludable and nonrival in consumption. This means that consumers can consume the good without paying for the good and that consumers are not rivals with one another in the consumption of the good. This nonrival characteristic of public goods results in the marginal social benefit from the public good being greater than the demand for the public good at all levels of public good provision. This implies that the market does not produce the efficient amount of the public good because it does not equate the marginal cost of producing the good to the marginal social benefit from consuming it. Too few units of the public good are provided by the market.

16. **a.** Both Jimmy and Beth are free-riding on this issue of park provision. They both realize that once the parks are provided they can enjoy the park even if they have not contributed to the creation of the park. When people free-ride, too little or none of the good gets produced. In this case, if neither Jimmy nor Beth is willing to contribute, then the community will end up with no new parks.

   b. The marginal social benefit of two parks is equal to the sum of Jimmy's and Beth's marginal benefits from two parks: Jimmy's marginal social benefit from two parks is equal to $25 per park while Beth's marginal social benefit from two parks is equal to $40 per park, for a total marginal social benefit from two parks of $65 per park.

   c. Since the marginal cost of providing parks is constant and equal to $55 per park, parks should be provided as long as the marginal social benefit from the park is greater than or equal to the marginal cost of providing the park. In this case, two parks will be provided since the marginal social benefit of two parks is equal to $65 per park while the marginal cost of providing two parks is $55 per park. Three parks will not be provided because the marginal social benefit of three parks is only $20 per park while the marginal social cost of three parks is $55 per park.

   d. Yes, if both Jimmy and Beth reveal their preferences they will each contribute, since they each assign a positive marginal benefit to two parks. Jimmy will likely contribute less than Beth because the marginal benefit he receives from two parks is less than the marginal benefit that Beth receives from two parks.

17. Private goods are both rival in consumption and excludable. A good that is rival in consumption is a good whose benefit from consumption can only be enjoyed by the individual consuming it. This quality of being rival in consumption implies that individuals must pay a positive price to consume the good. When a good is excludable, this means that no individual can enjoy the benefits from consuming the good without first paying for the good. These two characteristics allow private goods to be produced efficiently in the market because producers can set a price for these goods that is equal to the marginal cost of producing them.

18. **a.** Since the televised games are available only if the consumer pays for the cable package, these games are an excludable good. But the televised games are nonrival in consumption since one individual's viewing of the game does not diminish the ability of another viewer to watch the game. Thus, Big Sports and its televised games represent an artificially scarce good, since these goods are excludable but nonrival in consumption.

b. The efficient price for consumers would be zero since the marginal cost of delivering the televised games to another consumer is zero. At a price of zero, however, Big Sports has no incentive to provide the games. Big Sports will only provide the games if they can charge consumers a positive price.

c. Big Sports does not produce the optimal amount of the good since the price they charge ($15 per month) is greater than the marginal cost of producing an additional televised game ($0). Since price is greater than marginal cost this indicates that too little of the good is being produced, because the value consumers place on the last unit produced is greater than the cost of producing the last unit.

19. a. There is a free-rider problem in this situation because the final good (the playground equipment) is nonexcludable. Too few parents will come forward to volunteer their time because the parents all realize that once the playground equipment is installed, all the children at the school will be able to use the equipment even if their parents did not help in the fund-raising effort. If the free-rider problem is too severe, the school will not get the new playground equipment.

b. There is a free-rider problem in this situation because the final good (a more beautiful community) is nonexcludable. Too few people will come forward to help with this effort since everyone in the community realizes that if the community is made more beautiful, then everyone in the community can enjoy this beauty even if they did not help in the effort to create that more beautiful community. The community will likely continue to have its blemishes and eyesores and not achieve the socially optimal amount of community beauty.

c. There is no free-rider problem with this situation since the new sandwich is excludable.

d. There is a free-rider problem in this situation because the final good (a cleaner lake and a cleaner lakeshore) is nonexcludable. Too few people will come forward to help clean up the lakeshore because people in the community realize that once the lakeshore is cleaned up, everyone in the community can enjoy this cleaner lakeshore even if they have not contributed to this outcome. The lakeshore will not be cleaned to the socially optimal level.

20. a. Positive externality since the playground equipment will benefit more children than just the children who attend the school.

b. Positive externality since the improved gardening and landscaping in the community will make the community a more attractive place to live. The benefits accrue to more than just the owners of the areas that are improved through gardening and landscaping.

c. Negative externality since the elephant hunters do not take into account the costs of their overhunting of elephants on the rest of the world.

d. Positive externality since a cleaner lakefront will benefit everyone in the community and not just the people who own lakeshore property.

e. Negative externality since the fishermen do not take into account the costs of their overfishing of salmon on the rest of the world.

f. Positive externality since unvaccinated children will benefit from their peers being vaccinated, which thereby reduces the probability that they will be exposed to dangerous childhood diseases.

g. Natural monopoly since there is a single provider of the cable television services.

Answers to Chapter Review Questions

1. **Answer d.** When the marginal social benefit of pollution is greater than the marginal social cost of pollution, too little pollution is being produced. When the marginal social benefit of pollution is less than the marginal social cost of pollution, too much pollution is being produced. It is optimal to produce the amount of pollution where the marginal social benefit of the pollution equals the marginal social cost of the pollution. Zero units of pollution would only be optimal if the marginal social benefit of the pollution is equal to $0.

2. **Answer c.** This is just the definition of the marginal social benefit of pollution.

3. **Answer b.** The socially optimal amount of pollution emissions is the amount of pollution where the marginal social benefit from the pollution equals the marginal social cost of the pollution.

4. **Answer d.** The socially optimal amount of pollution emissions is 500 tons where the marginal social benefit of pollution equals the marginal social cost of pollution. At 400 tons, the marginal social benefit of pollution equals $300 per ton, while the marginal social cost of this pollution equals $200 per ton. This society would be better off producing more pollution emissions.

5. **Answer b.** The socially optimal amount of pollution emissions is 500 tons of emissions.

6. **Answer e.** An emissions standard is not as efficient as an emissions tax because it does not ensure that the marginal social benefit of pollution is equal for all sources of pollution. In contrast, an emissions tax is a tax that results in the marginal benefit of pollution being equal across all sources of pollution.

7. **Answer d.** When two firms have different marginal social benefit of pollution curves, this tells us that the marginal social benefit from reducing pollution by a set amount is different between the two firms. It is therefore more efficient to have the firms reduce pollution by different amounts until the marginal social benefit of pollution is the same for both firms. An emissions standard requires that both firms reduce pollution by an equal amount without regard to their marginal social benefit of pollution.

8. **Answer c.** This is a definitional question. Pigou, an economist, emphasized that the appropriate tax could eliminate the hidden costs imposed by negative externalities.

9. **Answer b.** Firms will sell their permits if it is easy and inexpensive for them to reduce their pollution, since the permits are more valuable to firms that find the cost of reducing their level of pollution high. Firms that sell their pollution permits understand and have analyzed the costs associated with pollution reduction and have determined that they are better off selling the permits than using the permits. The government effectively decides what level of pollution it wants, and then creates a market for the right to pollute within this limit.

10. **Answer e.** Emissions standards are applied uniformly across all producers and therefore do not offer any incentive for producers to find new technology to reduce their pollution levels. In contrast, emissions taxes and tradable pollution permits provide a system of incentives that rewards those firms that find ways to reduce their levels of pollution or find cost-effective methods for pollution reduction.

11. **Answer b.** The positive benefit from the externality cannot be directly observed and measured, while it is possible to measure the external costs due to a negative externality such as pollution.

12. **Answer b.** When a good produces positive external benefits, the market does not include these benefits and therefore tends to undervalue the benefits from the consumption of the good. The market therefore results in too little of the good being produced.

13. **Answer c.** Joe's education reaps benefits not only for Joe and his family, but also for society. Joe will likely be able to better provide for himself with more education; he is likely to be a more productive member of society when he gets more education; and he will likely contribute more to society as a better-educated individual. Joe's education has both private and social benefits, but Joe is likely to consider only the private benefits and therefore select too low a level of education; from an efficiency standpoint the optimal amount of education is where the marginal social benefit of the education is equated to the marginal social cost of the education.

14. **Answer c.** To find the number of hours of exercise consumed in this market, set the demand curve equal to the supply curve: $100 - 0.05Q = 0.05Q$. This results in $Q = 1,000$ hours of exercise with price equal to $50.

15. **Answer c.** The socially optimal amount of exercise is the amount of exercise where MSB = supply (since there are no marginal social costs to include in this problem). Thus, to solve this question you must find the marginal social benefit of exercise, which is equal to the demand curve plus the marginal external benefit. The marginal external benefit is $10 per unit, so this means that the MSB curve can be expressed as $MSB = 110 - 0.05Q$. Setting this equation equal to the supply curve yields $110 - 0.05Q = 0.05Q$. Thus, the socially optimal amount of exercise is 1,100 hours of exercise.

16. **Answer a.** When Smalltown subsidizes the consumption of exercise by an amount equal to the social benefit of the additional hour of exercise, it effectively causes the demand curve for exercise to shift to the right, resulting in more hours of exercise being demanded at every price. With a subsidy of $10 per hour of exercise, the subsidy exactly equals the marginal social benefit of an hour of exercise, and thus this subsidy results in the residents of Smalltown consuming the socially optimal amount of exercise.

17. **Answer b.** When there is a positive externality, the government can encourage the consumption of the good by legislating a subsidy for the consumption of the good. Without the subsidy too little of the good is consumed, so the government intervention in this market can move the market closer to the socially optimal outcome.

18. **Answer c.** Industrial policy refers to pursuing a policy that supports those industries that are deemed to yield positive externalities. Industrial policy takes two general forms: subsidization of the industry, and the creation of barriers to international competition through trade restrictions. Industrial policy is advocated when there are positive externalities arising from the production of the good. In particular, these positive externalities often take the form of technology spillovers, or the external benefits that arise from the creation of knowledge.

19. **Answer b.** The socially optimal level of output for this market is where MSC = Demand for the last unit produced, which occurs when the quantity is Q_2.

20. **Answer b.** The deadweight loss is the area that represents the efficiency loss due to the externality. When the market produces Q_3 units of the good, the marginal social cost of the last unit is greater than the marginal social benefit from the last unit. This difference can be represented by the distance $(P_1 - P_3)$ or by the distance $(P_2 - P_4)$ since the externality per unit of the good produced is assumed to be constant. The market produces Q_3 units instead of the socially optimal Q_2 units, so the deadweight loss can be calculated as $(1/2)(P_2 - P_4)(Q_3 - Q_2)$.

21. **Answer d.** Public goods are nonrival in consumption and nonexcludable. These two characteristics imply that people can benefit from the good even if they did not pay for it (nonexcludable) and that the benefits any individual gets from the good do not depend on whether or not another individual is benefiting from the good (nonrival in consumption).

22. **Answer a.** The common resource is a situation in which the good is rival in consumption but nonexcludable. In the case of the common resource, individuals overuse the common resource, which creates a negative externality on everyone else who would benefit from the use of the common resource.

23. **Answer b.** When the price of the good is greater than its marginal cost this tells us that too little of the good is being produced, since the value consumers place on the good (the price they are willing to pay) is greater than the cost of producing an additional unit of the good. This situation arises with monopoly, oligopoly, public goods, and artificially scarce goods.

24. **Answer e.** Goods that are both rival in consumption and excludable are private goods and can be produced efficiently by the market. Goods that lack one or both of these characteristics are not efficiently provided by the market.

25. **Answer c.** The parks are open to the public at no charge, so they are nonexcludable. But they are often congested with long lines, which implies that the parks are rival in consumption. One child's use of the play structure reduces the available benefits of the play structure for another child.

26. **Answer a.** Once the tornado siren system is in place, everyone living in Madison will be able to benefit from the system even if they did not contribute to its production, so it is nonexcludable. The good is also nonrival in consumption since one person's consumption of the signal from the siren system does not reduce the available benefit to other people from consuming the same signal from the siren system.

27. **Answer b.** The Tollway is rival in consumption, since one person's use of the Tollway reduces the benefit of using the Tollway for other people due to the high level of congestion. The Tollway is also excludable since no one can drive on the Tollway without paying the toll.

28. **Answer a.** Since there is no charge to drive on Mason Street, it is an example of a nonexcludable good: anyone can enjoy driving on the street even though they have not paid for the street. Mason Street is also nonrival in consumption since it is never congested: this means that one person's use of the street does not diminish the level of benefits available to someone else who wishes to use the street.

29. **Answer b.** Sally free-rides: she does not want to contribute to cleaning the apartment, but she enjoys the benefits of a clean apartment once Sue gets everything cleaned. Free-ridership can occur in all sorts of transactions and is not limited to the situation posed by a public good.

30. **Answer d.** These statements are all true. When a good is nonexcludable, people tend to free-ride. Once the library is refurbished, there is no way that the school can prevent those children from using the library whose parents did not help out with the fundraiser. When the good is nonexcludable, too little of the good is provided without intervention in the market because of the free-rider problem.

31. **Answer b.** When a good is nonexcludable, people tend to free-ride and rely on others to provide the good. Because people free-ride, the market undervalues the benefit from the good and therefore too little of the good is produced.

32. **Answer b.** Since the toll road is nonrival in consumption, the marginal cost of letting another driver use the road is equal to zero. When an additional driver on this toll road is forced to pay the toll, this payment is higher than the marginal cost of allowing them to consume the good.

33. **Answer a.** Drivers will not consume as many drives on the toll road as is socially optimal since the price they must pay to use the road (the toll) is greater than the marginal cost of allowing them to use the road (zero). They will not be free-riding since the toll road is excludable and people can free-ride only when the good is nonexcludable.

34. Answer b. To find the *MSB* curve, you need to vertically sum the two individual demand curves for the public good (national defense is a public good since it is nonrival in consumption and nonexcludable). An easy point to find on the *MSB* curve is the *y*-intercept, since it equals the sum of the *y*-intercepts from the two individual demand curves: in this case, the *y*-intercept is equal to 150. Then, given the two individual demand curves, when 100 units of military goods are demanded, neither Joe nor Mary is willing to pay anything for this quantity of military goods. Thus, the *MSB* curve intersects the *x*-axis at 100 units of military goods. The *MSB* curve is therefore $MSB = 150 - 1.5Q$.

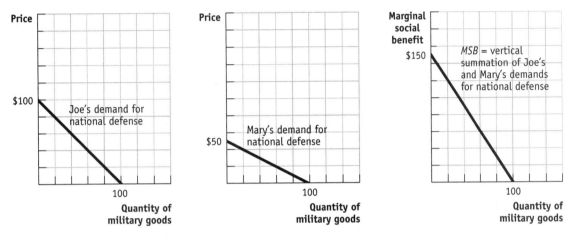

35. Answer d. To find the socially optimal amount of national defense for this economy, you must find where the marginal social benefit equals the marginal social cost. Or, $150 - 1.5Q = 60$, and therefore Q equals 60 units of military goods.

36. Answer c. Since the socially optimal amount of national defense in this problem is 60 units (see question 35), we can find Joe's willingness to pay by substituting this quantity into his demand curve. Thus, Joe's demand for national defense is given by $P = 100 - Q$, and when Q equals 60 units of military goods, Joe is willing to pay a price of $40 per unit of military goods.

37. Answer b. Public goods are not provided for by the market because they are nonrival in consumption and nonexcludable. But public goods may be provided through voluntary contributions, through the self-interested behavior of individuals or firms, or through social encouragement or pressure. For example, some conservation efforts occur through voluntary contributions or through firm activity in which the firm hopes to be able to make money in some indirect way through their efforts to increase conservation. Many people do not litter and actually pick up litter because of social encouragement or pressure. Having less litter is a public good—nonrival in consumption and nonexcludable—and this "good" to some degree is produced by moral suasion.

38. Answer d. It is a relatively easy task to measure the marginal social benefit of producing Q_1 units of the good: you simply need to go vertically up from Q_1 units to the marginal social benefit curve and then read the *y*-intercept value for this level of public good production. The marginal social benefit from the public good curve is constructed by adding the marginal benefit that Joe receives from the public good to the marginal benefit that Sarah receives from the public good: this is equal to $P_2 + P_4$. The marginal social cost of producing an additional unit of the public good is equal to P_4, so the marginal social cost is less than the marginal social benefit. This implies that too little of the public good is being produced.

39. Answer e. The socially optimal amount of the public good is that amount of the public good where the marginal social benefit is equal to the marginal social cost. This is true at Q_3. Joe's marginal benefit from the public good can be found by going vertically up from Q_3 units to Joe's marginal benefit from the public good curve and then reading off the *y*-intercept value for this point.

40. Answer a. Joe's marginal benefit from the public good is greater than Sarah's marginal benefit from the public good: he places a higher value on the public good since the public good yields greater benefits to him.

41. Answer b. When the marginal social benefit is less than the marginal social cost, the good should not be produced. One hopes that the cost-benefit study was well conducted and took into account the tendency for individuals to free-ride on the provision of the public good, since the cost-benefit study would have little value if it was based on poor analysis.

42. Answer c. The fishermen face a problem of a common resource, since all of them use the sea where the fish are located. Since no one owns the fishing rights to the sea and there is no way to limit the amount of fishing in the sea, there is too much fishing. This leads to the quantity of fish available decreasing due to overfishing: a natural outcome of a situation in which the good is nonexcludable but rival. When one fisherman catches a fish, that fish is no longer available for some other fisherman to catch.

43. Answer d. This is the simple definition of a common resource.

44. Answer a. A common resource is overconsumed because individuals cannot be charged for using the good, while at the same time individuals recognize that they are rivals with other individuals for the good. Individuals ignore the cost of their use of the good on the rest of society, which leads them to overuse the good.

45. Answer d. By charging a price for the right to drive in the city during high-traffic hours, London officials have effectively raised the price of driving. This causes individuals to drive less, and it also encourages them to shift their driving to times when the fee is lower (i.e., times when there is less traffic). London officials recognize that traffic congestion is a sign of a common resource problem, and this policy attempts to make a nonexcludable good excludable.

46. Answer a. With a common resource, the marginal cost of consuming an additional unit of the good does not take into account the cost of this consumption on other individuals. This implies that there is a divergence between the marginal social cost of consuming an additional unit of the good and the marginal cost to the individual of consuming an additional unit of the good. The market equates the marginal social benefit of consuming the good with the consumer's marginal cost of consuming the good, rather than equating the marginal social benefit to the marginal social cost.

47. Answer d. Common resources essentially present the same type of problem as those presented by a negative externality. As with a negative externality, the problem of common resources can be eliminated through assigning property rights, or by creating a system of licenses granting the holder the right to use the common resource, or by taxing the users of the common resource.

48. Answer b. When a good is excludable but nonrival in consumption, the market fails to produce the efficient level of the good. The marginal cost of an individual's consumption of this good equals zero since the good is nonrival in consumption: one individual's consumption of the good does not diminish the benefits available to another consumer from consuming the same good. But producers are only willing to produce the good if they can charge for the good: this implies that the price in the market is greater than the marginal cost of the good, and therefore the market-determined quantity of the good is smaller than is socially optimal. To get the socially optimal amount of the good requires that the price of the good be equal to zero.

chapter 10

Macroeconomics:
The Big Picture

■ BEFORE YOU READ THE CHAPTER

Summary

This chapter provides an overview of macroeconomics and discusses how macroeconomics, the study of the economy as a whole, differs from microeconomics. The chapter introduces the concepts of business cycles, the management of business cycles through government policies, long-run growth, inflation, deflation, price stability, and the distinction between open economies, where countries trade with one another, and closed economies, where there is no international trade.

Chapter Objectives

Objective #1. Macroeconomics is the study of the aggregate economy or the economy as a whole. Macroeconomics considers how individual and firm behavior in the aggregate interact to produce a particular level of economic performance in the economy. Central topics in macroeconomics include the determination of the overall level of output, the overall level of prices, and the overall level of employment in the economy. Macroeconomics also considers the impact of the global economy on the behavior of the economy.

- Macroeconomics uses various economic aggregates to study the economy. Economic aggregates are measures of economic variables that summarize data collected from different markets for goods, services, workers, and assets. Examples of economic aggregates include unemployment, aggregate output, investment, and savings.

- Macroeconomics studies long-run economic growth and its causes. Long-run economic growth in the economy is measured as the economy's overall output per person. Long-run growth in an economy raises the level of aggregate income and results in a higher standard of living for people living in that economy. Long-run growth is more important than business cycles in determining a country's standard of living.

- In the short run, the combined effect of individual decisions may have a very different impact on the economy than what any one individual intended. For example, when individual households expect an economic downturn, they reduce their expenditures in order to prepare for this expected recession. This is known as the paradox of thrift since the effect of many households acting in a thrifty manner is to plunge the economy into a deeper recession. The macroeconomic result of individual decisions in the economy often proves to be greater than the sum of these individual decisions.

Objective #2. In the short run, when the economy is in an economic expansion or boom, jobs are plentiful; when the economy is in an economic recession or bust, jobs are difficult to find. A business cycle consists of a period of short-run aggregate economic prosperity and a period of short-run aggregate economic hardship.

- Macroeconomics provides a rationale for government intervention to reduce short-run fluctuations in the economy. John Maynard Keynes argued that a government can help a depressed economy through fiscal and/or monetary policy. Fiscal policy refers to government spending and taxation policy, while monetary policy refers to the control of interest rates and the quantity of money in circulation. Both fiscal and monetary policy are useful tools for offsetting the economic effects of short-run fluctuations (recession or expansion) in the aggregate economy.

Objective #3. Microeconomics focuses on the production and consumption of specific goods and the allocation of scarce resources among competing uses. Microeconomics analyzes how individuals and firms make decisions.

Objective #4. Employment measures the total number of people working in the economy, while unemployment is the total number of people who are actively looking for work but currently not working. The unemployment rate is the most widely used indicator of conditions in the labor market. In a recession, the employment rate decreases while the unemployment rate increases. In an expansion, the employment rate increases while the unemployment rate decreases.

Objective #5. The economy's real output level and unemployment rate move in opposite directions: as output increases, unemployment decreases and as real output decreases, unemployment increases. The economy's real aggregate output is the real value of the total production of final goods and services produced during a given time period and is referred to as real gross domestic product or real GDP.

Objective #6. Long-run growth occurs when aggregate output per person increases. This growth in the economy occurs over several decades and does not refer to the short-run increase in aggregate output that occurs during an expansion. Long-run economic growth is essential in order for wages and the standard of living in an economy to increase.

Objective #7. Inflation refers to a rise in the overall level of prices while deflation refers to a fall in the overall level of prices. In the short run, movements in inflation are closely related to the business cycle. In the long run, movements in inflation are primarily determined by changes in the money supply. Price stability is a desirable macroeconomic goal.

Objective #8. An economy that does not engage in international trade is a closed economy. An economy that participates in international trade is an open economy. Countries engage in trade because this trade is mutually beneficial to them. "Imports" refers to the value of the goods and services a country buys from the rest of the world, and "exports" refers to the value of the goods and services a country sells to the rest of the world.

Objective #9.   An open economy runs a trade deficit when the value of its imports is greater than the value of its exports. An open economy runs a trade surplus when the value of its imports is less than the value of its exports. A country's trade surplus or trade deficit ultimately depends on the saving and investment decisions made by that country.

Key Terms

Notes

self-regulating economy an *economy* in which problems such as *unemployment* are resolved without government intervention, through the working of the *invisible hand*, and in which government attempts to improve the economy's performance would be ineffective at best, and would probably make things worse.

Keynesian economics a school of thought emerging out of the works of John Maynard Keynes; according to Keynesian economics, a depressed *economy* is the result of inadequate spending, and government intervention can help a depressed economy through *monetary policy* and *fiscal policy*.

monetary policy changes in the quantity of money in circulation designed to alter *interest rates* and affect the level of overall spending.

fiscal policy changes in government spending and taxes designed to affect overall spending.

recession a period of economic downturn when output and unemployment are falling; also referred to as a contraction.

expansion period of economic upturn in which output and employment are rising; most economic numbers are following their normal upward trend; also referred to as a recovery.

business cycle the short-run alternation between economic downturns, known as *recessions,* and economic upturns, known as *expansions.*

business-cycle peak the point in time at which the *economy* shifts from *expansion* to *recession.*

business-cycle trough the point in time at which the *economy* shifts from *recession* to *expansion.*

long-run economic growth the sustained rise in the quantity of goods and services the *economy* produces.

inflation a rise in the overall level of prices.

deflation a fall in the overall level of prices.

price stability a situation in which the overall cost of living is changing slowly or not at all.

open economy an *economy* that trades goods and services with other countries.

Key Terms *(continued)*

trade deficit when the value of the goods and services bought from foreigners is more than the value of the goods and services sold to consumers abroad.

trade surplus when the value of goods and services bought from foreigners is less than the value of the goods and services sold to them.

Notes

AFTER YOU READ THE CHAPTER

Tips

Tip #1. Studying economics requires learning both new vocabulary and a new way of thinking. This chapter provides an overview of macroeconomics, the topics covered in the study of macroeconomics, and general definitions of macroeconomic variables. You will need to familiarize yourself with this information and vocabulary. You may find it helpful to make a set of flash cards for all the vocabulary you learn while studying macroeconomics. For each flash card you will find it helpful to write the term on one side of the card and its definition on the other side of the card. You might also find it helpful to identify on the first side of the card the number of the chapter where the term is first introduced. After you make a set of flash cards for the chapter, review these flash cards until you are thoroughly familiar and comfortable with each term.

Tip #2. Macroeconomics focuses on the economic behavior of the overall economy, while microeconomics focuses on the economic behavior of individuals, firms, and specific markets. Macroeconomics studies topics like the determination of the aggregate level of output, the aggregate price level, the level of employment, short-run economic fluctuations, and long-run economic growth. Microeconomics considers topics like supply and demand in particular markets, profit maximization by firms, and utility maximization by individuals.

Tip #3. Aggregation of data is at the heart of macroeconomics. This chapter briefly describes the meaning of aggregation and gives examples of aggregated measures like employment, real GDP, and the overall price level. The concept of aggregation is important to understand as you begin your study of macroeconomics.

Tip #4. In macroeconomics, the aggregate effect is often greater than the sum of the individual effects. In macroeconomics we find that many individual actions accumulate to produce outcomes that are larger than the simple sum of these individual actions. The combined effect of individual decisions can be much different from the intentions that any one individual had. The text provides an example of this with the paradox of thrift.

1. This chapter introduces the concepts of recession, fiscal and monetary policy, business cycles, unemployment, and trade deficits. Since 2007, many of these terms have been widely used in media reporting about the U.S. economy. For each term, think about what has been happening in the U.S. economy since 2007 and relate these real-life events to these terms.

STEP 1: **In order to answer this question you will first want to make sure you know each of the terms and their definitions.**

Review the section "Macroeconomics: Theory and Policy" on pages 309–310, the section "The Business Cycle" on pages 311–316, the section "International Imbalances" on pages 321–322, and Figure 10-3 on page 313.

STEP 2: **Once you have the definitions of these terms clearly in mind, then you will want to review what the economic situation in the United States has been since 2007. Then, apply these terms where appropriate.**

Review the section "Macroeconomics: Theory and Policy" on pages 309–310, the section "The Business Cycle" on pages 311–316, the section "International Imbalances" on pages 321–322, and Figure 10-3 on page 313.

Since 2007, the U.S. economy has experienced a serious recession that has resulted in high levels of unemployment. This recession represents a part of the business cycle, since a business cycle is composed of both periods of economic downturn and periods of economic expansion. At the same time that the U.S. economy experienced this recession, it was also running a large trade deficit: the U.S. economy was importing more goods than it was exporting.

2. The following table includes a number of potential research projects that a group of economists are considering working on during the next few years. Fill in the table to help them identify whether the topic is more likely a microeconomics topic or more likely a macroeconomics topic.

Research topic	Macroeconomic or microeconomic topic?	Explanation for your answer
Impact of Gulf of Mexico oil spill on beach tourism in the Gulf states		
Impact of fiscal stimulus spending programs on employment and production in the United States		
The effect of a government program subsidizing investment on the level of aggregate production and aggregate employment in the economy		
Impact of China's allowing its exchange rates to be market-determined on the demand for Chinese textile goods		
Impact of recent monetary policy on inflation in the U.S. economy		

STEP 1: In order to answer this question, you will obviously need to read the chapter. But you will also find it helpful to think about what topics macroeconomics addresses and then try to relate these topics to the previous table.

Review the section "The Nature of Macroeconomics" on pages 308–311, and Table 10-1 on page 308.

Here is the filled-in table:

Research topic	Macroeconomic or microeconomic topic?	Explanation for your answer
Impact of Gulf of Mexico oil spill on beach tourism in the Gulf states	Micro	This topic looks at the impact of an event on a specific market rather than on the aggregate economy.
Impact of fiscal stimulus spending programs on employment and production in the United States	Macro	This topic looks at the impact of a policy on the entire, or aggregate, economy.
The effect of a government program subsidizing investment on the level of aggregate production and aggregate employment in the economy	Macro	This topic looks at the impact of a policy on the entire, or aggregate, economy.
Impact of China's allowing its exchange rates to be market-determined on the demand for Chinese textile goods	Micro	This topic looks at the impact of an event on a specific market rather than on the aggregate economy.
Impact of recent monetary policy on inflation in the U.S. economy	Macro	This topic looks at the impact of a policy on the entire, or aggregate, economy.

3. On page 317 of your text, the authors present Figure 10-7 as an illustration of long-run economic growth in America. To get a concrete sense of this economic growth, identify three people you can interview: these three people should be of different ages, and if possible, try to find someone who is at least seventy-five. Do a survey of these three people's memories of what items their family possessed and what items they can remember as new and original: for example, most college students today will list portable computers and cell phones, while someone in the fifty-year-old range may recall the family's first color television, while someone who is eighty may be able to remember the first family car. After completing this survey, decide whether or not it convinces you that there has been significant economic growth over the past eighty years.

STEP 1: In order to answer this question, you will first want to think about how you want to collect your data: that is, you will want to think about what questions you will ask the people you have chosen to interview.

Review the section "Long-Run Economic Growth" on pages 316–319, and Figure 10-6 on page 317.

Since you are trying to get a sense of how people lived at different times, you will want to compose a set of questions that is designed to get this information. Thoughtful consideration before you start will help you get more and better information. You will want to make sure that some of your questions are specific, while other questions may be more open-ended.

STEP 2: Identify several people that you think will make good interview subjects. You might want to identify more than three people, since some of the people you have identified may be unavailable to interview. Contact these people to set up a time to come for the interview.

Review the section "Long-Run Economic Growth" on pages 316–319, and Figure 10-6 on page 317.

Make sure you are prepared to take notes on what is said at the interview. As you collect your information, you will want to think about what things you can contrast or compare between the different individuals you are interviewing.

STEP 3: Create a summary statement comparing the information you received. Think about how this information helps support the argument that economic growth has occurred during this period.

Review the section "Long-Run Economic Growth" on pages 316–319, and Figure 10-6 on page 317.

For example, you might decide to present your information in a table or graph. Review Figure 10-6 to see one example of a representation of changes that reflect economic growth over time. Think about and plan a method of presenting your data that makes a strong case in support of your argument.

The answers and presentations with respect to this question will vary with each student: underlying all of the presentations should be a sense of the economic growth and change that have occurred in the last seventy to eighty years.

4. Suppose Jerry's income was $40,000 last year and this year it is $50,000. But over the course of the year, the price of the food that he purchases has risen from $6,000 per year to $10,000 per year, and the price of the gasoline that he purchases has risen from $2,000 per year to $4,000 per year. All other prices that Jerry faces have remained constant over this period. Is Jerry better off now that his salary has increased to $50,000?

STEP 1: To answer this question, you will want to think about what is happening to Jerry's income and what is happening to the prices of gasoline and food. It would be helpful to calculate the percentage change in income, the percentage change in food prices, and the percentage change in gasoline prices in order to see how Jerry is doing.

Review the section "Inflation and Deflation" on pages 319–321.

The percentage change in a variable can be found by calculating [(the new value – the previous value)/(the previous value)] × 100. Thus, the percentage change in Jerry's income is equal to [($50,000 – $40,000)/($40,000)] × 100 = 25%. The percentage change in the price of food and the percentage change in the price of gasoline can be calculated similarly. The percentage change in the price of food is equal to 67%, while the percentage change in the price of gasoline is 100%.

STEP 2: Once you have calculated the percentage changes, you will want to think about what this implies about how Jerry is doing.

Review the section "Inflation and Deflation" on pages 319–321.

Jerry's income has increased, but so have the price of food and the price of gasoline; all other prices that Jerry faces have remained constant. Clearly, Jerry's income cannot purchase as much food or gasoline as it could when his income and the prices were at their initial level: Jerry is worse off than he was in the first year.

Problems and Exercises

1. For each of the following questions identify whether the question is more appropriate for the study of microeconomics or macroeconomics, and why.

   a. What will happen to the wages in our community if Corporation X, an employer of 1,000 people (that's 40% of our workforce), decides to relocate its plant to a different state?

   b. What will happen to the level of overall economic production in our economy if the federal government continues to run record levels of government deficit?

   c. If the government engages in monetary policy and increases the money supply, what will happen to the interest rate in our economy?

   d. How has the recent increase in the price of a barrel of oil affected the prices of bicycles, cars, and airplane fares?

   e. What will the effect of recent tropical storms be on the price of bananas?

2. Suppose that people anticipate an economic recession and decide to increase their rate of saving so they are better prepared financially for the recession. Explain why this response might actually make the recession worse.

3. This chapter distinguishes between an economic expansion as part of the business cycle and long-run economic growth. Concisely explain the difference between these two terms.

4. In the beginning of 2006, suppose the population in Neverland was 2 million people and the level of real GDP, or aggregate output, was $40 million. During 2006, population increased by 2%, while real GDP increased by 5%. During this same period, the aggregate price level was constant. Furthermore, suppose these growth rates continued into 2007 and 2008.

Fill in the following table using the given information. (Make all calculations to two places past the decimal.)

	Beginning of 2006	Beginning of 2007	Beginning of 2008	Beginning of 2009
Real GDP				
Population				
Real GDP/person				

5. In the beginning of 2006, suppose the population in Funland was 2 million people and the level of real GDP, or aggregate output, was $40 million. During 2006, population increased by 3% while real GDP increased by 3%. During 2007, population increased by 4% while real GDP increased by 3%. During 2008, population increased by 5% while real GDP increased by 3%.

a. Fill in the following table using the given information. (Make all calculations to two places past the decimal.)

	Beginning of 2006	Beginning of 2007	Beginning of 2008	Beginning of 2009
Real GDP				
Population				
Real GDP/person				

b. What do you know about this country's standard of living between the beginning of 2006 and the beginning of 2009? Explain your answer.

c. In comparing your answers in problem 4 to your answers in problem 5, what major concept do these problems illustrate?

6. China's economy is growing at a much faster annual rate than the U.S. economy. Does this mean that the standard of living in China is higher than the standard of living in the United States? Explain your answer.

█ BEFORE YOU TAKE THE TEST

Chapter Review Questions

1. Macroeconomics, unlike microeconomics,
   a. considers the behavior of individual firms and markets.
   b. focuses on the production and consumption of particular goods.
   c. tries to explain increases in living standards over time.
   d. finds that the behavior of individuals is more important in determining economic activity than is the aggregate summation of this behavior.

2. Which of the following statements is true?
   a. In macroeconomics, there is no role for government intervention in the economy.
   b. In microeconomics, the prices determined in economic models are aggregate price levels for the economy.
   c. Microeconomics studies business cycle fluctuations in the economy.
   d. Fiscal and monetary policy may be helpful in reducing short-term economic fluctuations in the economy due to adverse economic events.

3. Which of the following is not an aggregate macroeconomic variable?
   a. savings: the sum of household, government, and business savings during a given year
   b. investment: the addition to the economy's supply of productive physical capital
   c. bicycle production: the total number of bicycles manufactured in an economy during a given year
   d. capital account: the total net amount of assets sold to foreigners

4. In a recession,
   a. unemployment increases, aggregate output decreases, and people enjoy higher living standards.
   b. unemployment increases while aggregate output and aggregate income decrease.
   c. aggregate output and aggregate income decrease, eventually leading, in all cases, to an economic depression.
   d. aggregate output must fall for at least three consecutive quarters.

5. Government intervention in the economy is
   a. called fiscal policy if it involves a policy change that alters the interest rate or the level of money in circulation in the economy.
   b. called fiscal policy if it involves changing government spending or taxing in order to offset the economic effects of short-run fluctuations in the macroeconomy.
   c. particularly useful in helping economies in the long run.
   d. only helpful during economic recessions.

6. Economic growth
   a. refers to increases in real GDP per capita over the long run.
   b. refers to short-term fluctuations in real GDP per capita.
   c. is best measured using the employment rate.
   d. is of little importance to economists.

7. Macroeconomics

    a. focuses on how the behavior of individuals and firms in the aggregate economy interact to produce a market price for each good and service offered in the economy.

    b. focuses on how the actions of individuals and firms in the economy interact to produce a particular economy-wide level of economic performance.

    c. considers how specific markets for goods and services determine their equilibrium prices and quantities.

    d. Answers (a), (b), and (c) are all correct.

8. Which of the following statements is true?

    a. An economy in a recession will have a lower unemployment rate than will the same economy operating in an expansion.

    b. In an economic expansion, the unemployment rate decreases while aggregate output increases.

    c. An economy's output level and employment rate move in opposite directions.

    d. Answers (b) and (c) are correct.

9. The paradox of thrift illustrates that

    a. in macroeconomics the combined effect of individual decisions can have effects that are very different from what any one individual intended.

    b. acting virtuously at the microeconomic level by spending less may result in an adverse macroeconomic outcome, since this behavior may result in a lower level of aggregate economic production.

    c. acting in a profligate manner at the microeconomic level by spending more may result in an expansion of the economy.

    d. Answers (a), (b), and (c) are all correct.

10. According to Keynesian economics, a depressed economy is the result of

    a. inadequate spending.

    b. irrational behavior on the part of individuals and firms operating in the economy.

    c. scarce resources.

    d. monetary and fiscal policy.

11. Inflation occurs when

    a. the aggregate level of output increases.

    b. the unemployment rate decreases.

    c. the aggregate price level rises over time.

    d. consumers' purchasing power increases over time.

12. A country that trades goods and services with another country is known as a(n)

    a. open economy.

    b. real economy.

    c. weak economy.

    d. closed economy.

13. Monetary policy refers to the changes in
   a. taxes and government spending designed to change the overall level of spending in an economy.
   b. interest rates and the money supply designed to change the overall level of spending in an economy.

14. The changes in taxes and government spending designed to change the overall level of spending in an economy is called
   a. monetary policy.
   b. fiscal policy.
   c. either monetary or fiscal policy depending upon what is happening to the interest rate.

15. Economic recessions and economic expansions are
   a. long run in nature.
   b. short run in nature.

16. An economic contraction is
   a. another term for an economic recession.
   b. indicates that the economy is experiencing a decrease in the level of employment.
   c. part of the business cycle.
   d. Answers (a), (b), and (c) are all correct.

17. An economic expansion is
   a. another term for an economic recovery.
   b. indicates that the economy is experiencing a decrease in the level of unemployment.
   c. is that part of the business cycle between the business-cycle trough and the business-cycle peak.
   d. Answers (a), (b), and (c) are all correct.
   e. Answers (a) and (c) are both correct.

18. Which of the following statements is true?
   I. The 2007–2009 recession in the United States hit the economy much harder than the 2001 recession did.
   II. The Great Depression in the United States was a 43-month-long economic downturn.
   III. The U.S. recession of 2001 lasted only eight months, while the recession of 2007–2009 lasted more than twice as long.
   a. Statements I, II, and III are all true.
   b. Statements II and III are true.
   c. Statements I and III are true.
   d. Statement II is true.

19. A sustained rise in the quantity of goods and services a country produces is referred to as
   a. an economic expansion or recovery.
   b. a period of employment.
   c. long-run economic growth.
   d. sound fiscal policy.

20. Long-run growth per capita is
  a. the key to higher wages and a rising standard of living.
  b. a situation that occurs when the economy's overall production grows at a faster rate than the economy's population.
  c. a sustained upward trend in output per person.
  d. Answers (a), (b), and (c) are all correct.

21. Deflation occurs when
  a. economic production increases in the aggregate economy.
  b. the overall price level decreases in an economy.
  c. the overall level of employment decreases in the aggregate economy.
  d. both the overall price level and the overall level of employment in an economy decrease.

22. When the economy is in a recession, jobs are
  a. hard to find and the overall level of prices in the economy tends to rise.
  b. easy to find and the overall level of prices in the economy tends to rise.
  c. hard to find and the overall level of prices in the economy tends to fall.
  d. easy to find and the overall level of prices in the economy tends to fall.

23. A country runs a trade deficit when
  a. its level of employment decreases.
  b. its overall price level is falling.
  c. the value of the goods and services it imports exceeds the value of the goods and services it exports.
  d. the value of the goods and services it exports exceeds the value of the goods and services it imports.

24. The value of a country's imports is equal to $1.2 billion this year while the value of the country's exports is equal to $1.3 billion this year. This country is running a
  a. trade surplus this year.
  b. trade deficit this year.

25. Whether a country runs a trade surplus or a trade deficit depends on
  a. what part of the business cycle the country is currently in.
  b. whether or not the country is experiencing deflation or inflation.
  c. whether the country is employing fiscal or monetary policy.
  d. decisions about saving and investment spending in the country.

26. A country's investment spending during the current year is equal to $400 million, while its level of saving for the current year is $350 million. Given this information, this country will likely run a trade
  a. surplus.
  b. deficit.

ANSWER KEY

Answers to Problems and Exercises

1. **a.** Microeconomics: this question is directed at understanding the local effect of this corporation's move instead of its total effect across the aggregate economy.

    b. Macroeconomics: this question focuses on the aggregate performance of the economy.

    c. Macroeconomics: this question considers the impact of monetary policy on the aggregate economy.

    d. Microeconomics: this question addresses the effect of a change in the price of a barrel of oil on specific markets like the market for bicycles, cars, or air travel service.

    e. Microeconomics: this question considers the price of a specific good rather than the overall price level in the economy.

2. Even though the individual's decision is a rational path to follow, the effect of many individuals making this decision is to reduce spending dramatically in the aggregate economy. As spending decreases, producers respond by decreasing their production and reducing their use of labor. This paradox of thrift has the effect of worsening the recessionary tendencies in the economy.

3. An economic expansion is a short-run increase in the level of aggregate output that may not be sustained indefinitely, while long-run economic growth reflects a sustainable increase in an economy's ability to produce more goods and services.

4.

	Beginning of 2006	Beginning of 2007	Beginning of 2008	Beginning of 2009
Real GDP	$40 million	$42 million	$44.1 million	$46.31 million
Population	2 million	2.04 million	2.08 million	2.12 million
Real GDP/person	$20	$20.59	$21.20	$21.84

5. **a.**

	Beginning of 2006	Beginning of 2007	Beginning of 2008	Beginning of 2009
Real GDP	$40 million	$41.20 million	$42.44 million	$43.71 million
Population	2 million	2.06 million	2.14 million	2.25 million
Real GDP/person	$20	$20	$19.31	$19.43

   b. The standard of living in Funland between the beginning of 2006 and the end of 2008 is decreasing, since the rate of population growth exceeds the rate of real GDP growth.

   c. Problems 4 and 5 illustrate the importance of the growth rates of population and real GDP in determining the standard of living. In problem 4, the standard of living increases, since real GDP grows at a faster rate than the rate of population increase, while in problem 5, the standard of living decreases since the population growth rate is greater than the rate of real GDP growth.

6. Although China's economy in recent years has grown at a much faster rate than the U.S. economy, this does not necessarily imply that China's standard of living is higher than the standard of living in the United States. Standard of living depends upon both the level of production in an economy and the population in the economy as well as the initial level of standard of living. Ten years ago the output per person in the United States was much larger than the output per person in China. Over the past ten years, even though China's rate of economic growth has surpassed the U.S. rate of economic growth, it has not been sufficiently long enough for the Chinese standard of living to catch up with the U.S. standard of living.

Answers to Chapter Review Questions

1. **Answer c.** Macroeconomics studies the aggregate economy, not individual action; in studying the aggregate economy, macroeconomics seeks to explain the factors that determine a country's standard of living. In macroeconomics we are reminded that the aggregation of individual behavior often has a larger impact than just the sum of these individual behaviors.

2. **Answer d.** In the aggregate economy, output and employment fluctuate in the short run. Macroeconomic theory analyzes the effect of fiscal and monetary policy on short-run economic fluctuations and provides a rationale for government intervention to lessen the economic impact of business cycles.

3. **Answer c.** Although each of these variables is aggregated to some extent, the bicycle production for the year only aggregates in a market for a single product rather than aggregating over multiple markets.

4. **Answer b.** A recession, by definition, occurs when aggregate output decreases and income decreases. As the economy produces a smaller level of output, employment of labor decreases since less labor is needed to produce the smaller level of output. Not all recessions turn into depressions, and there is no uniform agreement about the length of time aggregate output must decrease for the downturn in economic activity to be viewed as a recession.

5. **Answer b.** Government intervention in the economy is called fiscal policy if it involves a change in government spending and/or taxation implemented to reduce short-run business cycle fluctuation in the economy. Government intervention in the economy is called monetary policy if it involves a change in the interest rate or a change in the amount of money in circulation in the economy implemented in order to reduce short-run business cycle fluctuation in the economy.

6. **Answer a.** Economic growth is measured as an increase in the level of real GDP in the economy. This increase refers to an increase over the long run, rather than a short-run economic expansion.

7. **Answer b.** Macroeconomics is focused on the aggregate economy and its overall performance. Microeconomics focuses on specific markets and how the behavior of firms and individuals interact to determine the prices in those markets as well as the quantities in those markets.

8. **Answer b.** This question centers on the relationship between aggregate output and employment: as aggregate output increases, employment also increases and hence unemployment decreases. An economy can reduce its level of unemployment but cannot eliminate, since there will always be people newly entering the labor force and searching for their first jobs.

9. **Answer d.** The paradox of thrift refers to the situation that occurs when individuals, worried about the possibility of economic hard times, reduce their spending. This prudent behavior on the part of individuals results in less overall spending in the economy and therefore an even greater economic slowdown than would have happened if some of these individuals had not acted so prudently. Conversely, individuals can also elect to spend more when they are optimistic about the economy, and this spending will therefore result in an even greater expansion of the economy than individuals anticipate. Thus, the paradox of thrift is an illustration of how individual decisions can result in effects that are greater than what any one individual intended.

10. **Answer a.** Keynesian economics explains economic downturns as being the result of too little spending, and it suggests that monetary and/or fiscal policy can be used to stimulate the economy. Economics is about the allocation of scarce resources, but this scarcity of resources does not explain why business cycles occur in the economy.

11. **Answer c.** Inflation is defined as the increase in the aggregate price level over time.

12. **Answer a.** A country that engages in international trade is referred to as an open economy, while a country that does not trade is a closed economy.

13. **Answer b.** Monetary policy refers to the changes in interest rates that result from changes in the money supply: these interest rate changes result in a change in the overall level of spending in the economy.

14. **Answer b.** Changes in taxes and/or government spending that are designed to change the overall level of spending in the economy are referred to as fiscal policy. Monetary policy changes the overall level of spending in the economy by altering the level of interest rates in the economy through changes in the money supply.

15. **Answer b.** Business-cycle fluctuations in the economy, whether recessions or expansions, are short-run fluctuations.

16. **Answer d.** An economic contraction or recession is that part of the business cycle where output and employment are falling.

17. **Answer d.** An economic expansion or recovery is that part of the business cycle when output and employment are increasing, and therefore unemployment is decreasing. The economic expansion occurs in that part of the business cycle between the business cycle trough and the business cycle peak, since this is the part of the business cycle when output and employment are increasing.

18. **Answer a.** All of these statements are factual statements that are discussed in this chapter.

19. **Answer c.** When the increase in the production of goods and services is sustained, this implies that the economy is experiencing economic growth; an economic expansion or recovery refers to a short-run increase (not sustained) in the level of production of goods and services in an economy.

20. **Answer d.** For wages and the standard of living to increase in the aggregate in an economy, it is necessary that production increases at a faster rate than the rate of population growth. Answer (b) is just an alternative way of stating long-run growth per capita.

21. **Answer b.** Deflation refers to a decrease in the overall level of prices in an economy and, although deflation may occur at the same time that employment in the economy decreases, the term only refers to the decrease in the overall price level.

22. **Answer c.** In a recession, production is falling, which implies that fewer units of labor will be employed. This, in turn, implies that jobs will be difficult to find. In addition, as the level of production falls in the economy there is less demand for goods and services, which leads to a general decrease in the overall level of prices in the economy.

23. **Answer c.** Answer (c) is the basic definition of a trade deficit.

24. **Answer a.** When the value of a country's exports is greater than the value of its imports for a given time period, then the country is running a trade surplus during that period of time.

25. **Answer d.** The saving and investment spending decisions made in a country ultimately determine whether or not that country will run a trade deficit or a trade surplus. When a country has high investment spending relative to its level of saving, it will run a trade deficit; when a country has low investment spending relative to its level of saving, it will run a trade surplus.

26. **Answer b.** When a country's level of investment spending is high relative to its saving, then the country will run a trade deficit. Since this country's investment spending exceeds its saving for the period under consideration, this implies that the country will run a trade deficit.

chapter 11

GDP and the CPI: Tracking the Macroeconomy

BEFORE YOU READ THE CHAPTER

Summary

This chapter focuses on the measurement of two economic aggregates: gross domestic product (GDP) and the aggregate price level. The chapter discusses three different ways to calculate GDP. It also discusses the difference between nominal and real GDP and how these two measures are related. The chapter defines what is meant by a price index, and then discusses the consumer price index (CPI) as well as the producer price index (PPI). It compares these two price indices to the GDP deflator. The chapter also discusses how a price index can be used to measure the rate of inflation in an economy.

Chapter Objectives

Objective #1. Good macroeconomic policy depends on good measurement of key economic variables that provide information about how the aggregate economy is performing. These key variables include the level of aggregate income and aggregate output, the level of employment and unemployment, and the level and rate of change of prices in the economy.

Objective #2. The national income and product accounts, or the national accounts, provide a set of numbers that indicate the country's state of economic performance. The Bureau of Economic Analysis calculates the national accounts for the United States.

Objective #3. Gross domestic product, or GDP, is the sum of consumer spending on goods and services, investment spending, government spending, and the difference between spending on exports and imports. GDP is the total value of all final goods and services produced in an economy during a given time period. Final goods and services are goods and services sold to the final user. Intermediate goods and services are those items that are used as inputs for the production of final goods and services.

Objective #4.   There are different ways to calculate GDP. One method is to add up the total value of final goods and services produced in an economy during a given time period. This method requires that the value of intermediate goods be excluded from the calculation in order to avoid double counting. An alternative method is to add up total spending on domestically produced final goods and services in an economy during a given time period. A third method of computing GDP is to sum the total value of factor income paid by firms in the economy to households. All three of these methods will yield identical values of GDP for an economy during a given time period.

- In calculating GDP, care must be taken to avoid double counting. For example, in measuring GDP as the value of total spending on final goods and services in an economy, we count only each producer's value added in the calculation. Or, if we calculate GDP as the value of total spending on final goods and services on domestically produced final goods and services, we avoid double counting by counting only the value of sales to final purchasers. When estimating GDP using spending data, we omit sales of inputs from one business to another, unless that spending represents investment spending by firms. Investment spending by firms represents a purchase that will last for a considerable time.

- GDP for an economy can be expressed as an equation: $GDP = C + I + G + X - IM$, where C is consumer spending, I is investment spending, G is government spending, X is spending on domestically produced goods and services by foreigners (the domestic economy's exports), and IM is spending on imports, or the spending on goods and services produced by foreign economies. The difference between exports and imports, or $X - IM$, is referred to as net exports.

- GDP can also be measured as the sum of all the income earned by factors of production in the economy: this is the sum of wages, interest, rent, and profit.

Objective #5.   GDP can change over time because the economy is producing more or because the prices of the goods and services it produces have increased. Real GDP calculates the value of aggregate production during a given time period, using prices from some given base year. In effect, real GDP uses constant prices. In contrast, nominal GDP is the calculation of GDP using current prices. Real GDP measures allow one to compare the growth in aggregate production in an economy over time.

Objective #6.   In comparing GDP across countries or over time, we can eliminate differences in population size by dividing each country's GDP by its population to get GDP per capita, or the average GDP per person. Real GDP per capita is one of many important determinants of human welfare: it measures what a country can do, but it does not address how that country uses that output to affect living standards.

Objective #7.   Economists measure changes in the aggregate price level by tracking changes in the cost of buying a given market basket. A price index measures the cost of purchasing a given market basket in a given year, where that cost is normalized so that it is equal to 100 in the base year. To calculate the cost of the market basket, multiply the quantities of each good in the market basket times its price and then sum these products. Then use this information to calculate a price index by dividing the cost of the market basket for a particular time period by the cost of the market basket in the base year and then multiplying this ratio by 100. The price index for the base year is always equal to 100. An example of a price index is the consumer price index, or the CPI. The producer price index (also known as the wholesale price index), or the PPI, is another price index that measures the cost of a basket of goods typically purchased by producers. The inflation rate between two years can be calculated using this formula: Inflation rate = [(price index in year 2) − (price index in year 1)/(price index in year 1)] × 100.

Objective #8. Many payments are tied or "indexed" to the CPI: that is, many payments are adjusted up or down when the CPI rises or falls. For example, Social Security checks are indexed to the CPI as are income tax brackets and some wage settlements. Due to this indexing there is concern as to whether the CPI accurately reflects changes in the aggregate price level. Some economists believe that the CPI overstates the rate of inflation due to the fact that the CPI calculation uses a fixed market basket and does not allow for the fact that consumers substitute away from relatively more expensive goods and toward relatively cheaper goods when prices change. In addition, the CPI may be biased due to the presence of innovation. Innovation, by widening the range of consumer choice, makes a given amount of money worth more and this is like a fall in consumer prices.

Objective #9. The GDP deflator is not a price index, but it does provide a measure of prices. The GDP deflator is calculated as the ratio of nominal GDP for that year to real GDP for that year times 100: GDP deflator = [(nominal GDP for year n)/(real GDP for year n)] × 100. The value of the GDP deflator for the base year is always equal to 100.

Key Terms

national income and product accounts, or product accounts method of calculating and keeping track of *consumer spending*, sales of producers, business *investment spending*, government purchases, and a variety of other flows of money among different sectors of the *economy*.

final goods and services goods and services sold to the final, or end, user.

intermediate goods and services goods and services, bought from one *firm* by another firm, that are inputs for production of *final goods and services*.

gross domestic product (GDP) the total value of all *final goods and services* produced in the *economy* during a given period, usually a year.

value added (of a producer) the value of a producer's sales minus the value of input purchases.

aggregate output the total quantity of *final goods and services* the *economy* produces for a given time period, usually a year. *Real GDP* is the numerical measure of aggregate output typically used by economists.

real GDP the total value of all *final goods and services* produced in the *economy* during a given year, calculated using the prices of a selected base year.

nominal GDP the value of all *final goods and services* produced in the *economy* during a given year, calculated using the prices current in the year in which the output is produced.

chained dollars method of calculating *real GDP* that splits the difference between growth rates calculated using early base years and the growth rates calculated using late base years.

GDP per capita GDP divided by the size of the population; equivalent to the average GDP per person.

Notes

Key Terms *(continued)*

aggregate price level a single number that represents the overall price level for *final goods and services* in the *economy*.

market basket a hypothetical consumption bundle of consumer purchases of goods and services, used to measure changes in overall price level.

price index a measure of the cost of purchasing a given *market basket* in a given year, where that cost is normalized so that it is equal to 100 in the selected base year; a measure of overall price level.

inflation rate the annual percentage change in a price index—typically the *consumer price index*. The inflation rate is positive when the *aggregate price level* is rising (*inflation*) and negative when the aggregate price level is falling (*deflation*).

consumer price index (CPI) a measure of prices; calculated by surveying market prices for a *market basket* intended to represent the consumption of a typical urban American family of four. The CPI is the most commonly used measure of prices in the United States.

producer price index (PPI) a measure of the cost of a typical basket of goods and services purchased by producers. Because these commodity prices respond quickly to changes in demand, the PPI is often regarded as a leading indicator of changes in the *inflation rate*.

GDP deflator a price measure for a given year that is equal to 100 times the ratio of *nominal GDP* to *real GDP* in that year.

◼ AFTER YOU READ THE CHAPTER

Tips

Tip #1. A primary focus of this chapter is the topic of economic aggregation. Discussion of macroeconomic issues requires the construction and development of different measures that can be used to describe the macroeconomy. Economic aggregation addresses this issue. In this chapter, you need to fully understand the process of economic aggregation and how it relates to the measurement of economic production and the overall price level.

Tip #2. The national income accounts provide measures about the aggregate or overall economy; understanding the concept of economic aggregation is essential in the study of macroeconomics. The national income accounts are data collected and provided by the government about aggregate economic performance. The national income accounts break down the components of total spending so the behavior of households, firms, the government, and the foreign sector can be studied. The national income accounts also break down national income into wages, interest, rent, and other factor payments so that factor income can be analyzed.

Tip #3. There are three methods for calculating GDP, but each method yields the same measure of GDP for a given time period. These three methods of GDP calculation are: (1) the value added by all producers; (2) the value of total expenditure in the domestic economy on final goods and services during a given time period by the sectors of the economy, or in other words, the sum of spending on final goods and services during the time period by households, businesses, government, and the rest of the world; and (3) the value of factor payments in the domestic economy over the given time period. It is important for you to thoroughly understand the concepts underlying each of these approaches.

Tip #4. The distinction between real and nominal variables is important in macroeconomics. Prices are used to measure the relative value of goods and services, but because prices do not stay constant over time in an economy it is important to measure economic variables over time using methods that correct for these price changes. Real economic variables are variables measured using prices from a designated base year. In contrast, nominal economic variables are measured with current prices and therefore are measures that do not correct for price level fluctuations. It is important to realize that if there is inflation, the national income and product accounts may indicate nominal GDP is increasing, even though real GDP may be decreasing, increasing, or staying constant.

WORKED PROBLEMS

1. You are given the following information about an economy that has three firms: Wisconsin Clothing Ltd., which produces clothing; Georgia Fabric Inc., which produces the various fabrics used in clothing production; and Texas Cotton Co., which grows the cotton needed for the production of fabric. From this set of information, you are asked to determine this economy's GDP. In addition, you are asked to identify what information you would need from the table to measure GDP using the factor payments approach. Finally, you are asked to fill in the missing values in the table.

	Wisconsin Clothing Ltd.	Georgia Fabric Inc.	Texas Cotton Co.	Total factor income
Value of sales	$3,200	$2,000	$750	
Intermediate goods	A	B	0	
Wages	500	1,000	400	C
Interest payments	200	25	50	D
Rent	400	150	200	E
Profit	100	75	100	F
Total expenditures by firm	3,200	2,000	750	
Value added per firm	G	H	I	

STEP 1: Start by reviewing the information in the table and thinking about the three ways of measuring GDP. Do you have enough information to measure GDP using one of these methods?

Review the section "Measuring the Macroeconomy" on pages 328–332 and Figure 11-1 on page 329.

There are three ways to measure GDP: (1) survey firms and add up the total value of their production of final goods and services (the value-added approach); (2) add up aggregate spending on domestically produced final goods and services in the economy (the expenditure approach); and (3) sum the total factor income earned by households from firms in the economy (the factor payments approach). Surveying the table, we could measure GDP as the value of the final good being produced: the final good is the clothing that Wisconsin Clothing Ltd. produces. We could also measure GDP using the factor payments approach, since we know the value of payments to households in the form of wages, interest payments, rent, and profits. The value-added approach would take more work, since we would need to calculate the value added at each stage of production.

STEP 2: Provide a measure of this economy's GDP.

Review the section "Measuring the Macroeconomy" on pages 328–332 and Figure 11-1 on page 329.

The value of GDP in this economy is equal to $3,200. We can see that this is the value of sales made by Wisconsin Clothing Ltd. Alternatively, we could sum the wages in this economy ($C = \$1,900$), the interest payments ($D = \$275$), rent ($E = \$750$), and profits ($F = \$275$) to get $3,200, the value of GDP for this economy.

STEP 3: Identify what information you would need in order to measure GDP using the factor payments approach.

Review the section "Measuring the Macroeconomy" on pages 328–332 and Figure 11-1 on page 329.

The factor payments approach to measuring GDP says that the sum of wages, interest payments, rent, and profit is equal to GDP. We would need to have the values for C, D, E, and F in order to do this calculation. These values have already been found in Step 2.

STEP 4: Fill in the missing values in the table.

Review the section "Measuring the Macroeconomy" on pages 328–332 and Figure 11-1 on page 329.

	Wisconsin Clothing Ltd.	Georgia Fabric Inc.	Texas Cotton Co.	Total factor income
Value of sales	$3,200	$2,000	$750	
Intermediate goods	A = 2,000	B = 750	0	
Wages	500	1,000	400	C = $1,900
Interest payments	200	25	50	D = 275
Rent	400	150	200	E = 750
Profit	100	75	100	F = 275
Total expenditures by firm	3,200	2,000	750	
Value added per firm	G = 1,200	H = 1,250	I = 750	

We already know the values for C, D, E, and F from Step 2. The value of B is $750, since this is the value of the cotton that Georgia Fabric Inc. purchases from Texas Cotton Co. The value of A is $2,000, since this is the value of the fabric that Wisconsin Clothing Ltd. purchases from Georgia Fabric Inc. To find the value for I, subtract the value of intermediate goods from the value of sales at Texas Cotton Co. The value of I is thus $750. The value of H is found in the same way: it is the difference between the value of sales and the cost of the intermediate goods at Georgia Fabric Inc. The value of H is $1,250. The value of G is found similarly: it is the difference between the value of sales and the cost of the intermediate goods at Wisconsin Clothing Ltd. The value of G is $1,200. Adding G + H + I together will give us a measure of GDP using the value-added approach: GDP is equal to $3,200, which is exactly the value we found using the other two approaches.

2. You are given the following information about an economy and you are asked to calculate nominal and real GDP for 2010 and 2011 in this economy. When calculating real GDP for this economy you are asked to use 2010 prices. In addition, you are asked to calculate the growth rate in nominal GDP and real GDP during this period. Finally, you are asked to provide guidance as to which growth rate is the more accurate one to use if you are trying to ascertain how much the economy is growing.

	2010	2011
Quantity of bicycles	20	22
Price of bicycle	$100	$110
Quantity of sweaters	10	9
Price of sweater	$20	$30
Quantity of hamburgers	100	140
Price of hamburger	$2	$3

STEP 1: Calculate nominal GDP for these two years.

Review the section "Real GDP: A Measure of Aggregate Output" on pages 332–336, and Table 11-1 and Table 11-2 on page 333.

Nominal GDP is found by multiplying the price of the good in the current year times the quantity of the good in the current year and then summing these products for all the goods produced in the economy. Nominal GDP in 2010 is equal to (20 bicycles)($100 per bicycle) + (10 sweaters) ($20 per sweater) + (100 hamburgers)($2 per hamburger) = $2,400. Nominal GDP in 2011 is equal to (22 bicycles)($110 per bicycle) + (9 sweaters)($30 per sweater) + (140 hamburgers)($3 per hamburger) = $3,110.

STEP 2: Calculate real GDP for these two years.

Review the section "Real GDP: A Measure of Aggregate Output" on pages 332–336, and Table 11-1 and Table 11-2 on page 333.

Real GDP is found by multiplying the price of the good in the base year times the quantity of the good in the current year and then summing these products for all the goods produced in the economy. Real GDP in 2010 is equal to nominal GDP in 2010, since both measures are using prices from 2010 and quantities from 2010. Real GDP in 2011 is equal to the price of the good in 2010 times the quantity of the good in 2011. Real GDP in 2011 is thus calculated as (22 bicycles)($100 per bicycle) + (9 sweaters)($20 per sweater) + (140 hamburgers)($2 per hamburger) = $2,660.

STEP 3: Calculate the growth rate of nominal GDP and real GDP during this period.

Review the section "Real GDP: A Measure of Aggregate Output" on pages 332–336, and Table 11-1 and Table 11-2 on page 333.

To find the growth rate of a variable, use the following formula: [(value of the measure in the current period – value of the measure in the previous period)/(value of the measure in the previous period)] × 100. The rate of change in nominal GDP = [(3,110 – 2,400)/2,400] × 100 = 29.58%. The rate of change in real GDP = [(2,660 – 2,400)/(2,400)] × 100 = 10.83%.

STEP 4: Now, you need to provide guidance as to which growth rate measure is the better one if you are trying to decide how much the economy is growing. You will need to explain your answer.

Review the section "Real GDP: A Measure of Aggregate Output" on pages 332–336, and Table 11-1 and Table 11-2 on page 333.

Given the goal of measuring the growth in the economy, the better measure is the growth rate of real GDP. This is because nominal GDP does not distinguish whether the change in nominal GDP is due to changes in production or changes in prices. In contrast, the growth rate of real GDP removes price fluctuation by holding prices constant and then looks at what is happening to aggregate production.

3. Belgium produces only three goods: chocolate, strawberries, and waffles. The following table gives you information about production and prices for these three goods for 2010 and 2011. You have been asked to calculate real GDP for Belgium using 2010 as the base year. In addition, you have been asked to calculate the growth rate of real GDP during this period and a measure of the GDP deflator for this period.

	Quantity in 2010	Price in 2010	Quantity in 2011	Price in 2011
Units of chocolate	20	$3	30	$4
Units of strawberries	75	4	150	2
Units of waffles	120	5	110	1

STEP 1: Calculate real GDP for 2010 and 2011 using 2010 as the base year.

Review the section "Real GDP: A Measure of Aggregate Output" on pages 332–336, and Table 11-1 and Table 11-2 on page 333.

Since 2010 is the base year, we know that real GDP in 2010 is the same as nominal GDP in 2010. To find this value, multiply the price of the good in 2010 times the quantity of the good, then sum these products together for all the goods produced in Belgium. Thus, real GDP in 2010 = (price of chocolate in 2010)(quantity of chocolate in 2010) + (price of strawberries in 2010)(quantity of strawberries in 2010) + (price of waffles in 2010)(quantity of waffles in 2010) = $960. Real GDP in 2011 = (price of chocolate in 2010)(quantity of chocolate in 2011) + (price of strawberries in 2010)(quantity of strawberries in 2011) + (price of waffles in 2010)(quantity of waffles in 2011) = $1,240.

STEP 2: Calculate the growth rate of real GDP during this period of time.

Review the section "Real GDP: A Measure of Aggregate Output" on pages 332–336, and Table 11-1 and Table 11-2 on page 333.

The growth rate of real GDP during this period = [(real GDP in 2011 − real GDP in 2010)/(real GDP in 2010)] × 100 = 29.17%.

STEP 3: Calculate the value of the GDP deflator for this period.

Review the section "Other Price Measures" on pages 339–340.

The GDP deflator is equal to [(real GDP)/(nominal GDP)] × 100. With 2010 as the base year, this means that in 2010 real GDP is equivalent to nominal GDP and therefore the GDP deflator for 2010 is equal to 100. In 2011, we already know from Step 1 that real GDP is equal to $1,240. To calculate nominal GDP for 2011, multiply the quantities from 2011 by the prices from 2011: thus, nominal GDP in 2011 is equal to $530. Using this information, we can calculate the GDP deflator for 2011 as ($1,240/$530) × 100 = 2.34.

4. In Belgium the market basket is always equal to 4 units of chocolate, 5 units of strawberries, and 2 waffles. Using the information given in Worked Problem 3, calculate the consumer price index in Belgium for 2010 and 2011 using 2010 as your base year. Use this information to calculate the consumer price index for both years and then find the rate of inflation during this period. You are also asked to provide an interpretation of the inflation rate you calculate.

STEP 1: This first step in calculating the consumer price index is to calculate the cost of the market basket for each year.

Review the section "Price Indexes and the Aggregate Price Level" on pages 336–340, the section "Market Baskets and Price Indexes" on pages 336–337, and Table 11-3 on page 337.

The cost of the market basket is equal to the sum of the product of the price of each good in the current year times the market basket quantity of each good. The cost of the market basket in 2010 is equal to (price of chocolates in 2010)(4 units of chocolate)

+ (price of strawberries in 2010)(5 units of strawberries) + (price of waffles in 2010)(2 waffles) = $42. The cost of the market basket in 2011 is equal to (price of chocolates in 2011)(4 units of chocolate) + (price of strawberries in 2011)(5 units of strawberries) + (price of waffles in 2011)(2 waffles) = $28.

STEP 2: Now, use the cost of the market baskets you calculated in Step 1 to create the consumer price index.

Review the section "Price Indexes and the Aggregate Price Level" on pages 336-340, the section "Market Baskets and Price Indexes" on pages 336-337, and Table 11-3 on page 337.

The consumer price index in any year is calculated as [(cost of the market basket in the current year)/(cost of the market basket in the base year)] × 100. Since 2010 is the base year, the cost of the market basket in the current year is equal to the cost of the market basket in the base year: the consumer price index for 2010 has a value of 100. The consumer price index for 2011 is equal to ($28/$42) × 100 = 67.

STEP 3: Use the consumer price index you calculated in Step 2 to find the rate of inflation between 2010 and 2011. Provide an interpretation of the meaning of the inflation rate you calculate.

Review the section "Price Indexes and the Aggregate Price Level" on pages 336-340, the section "Market Baskets and Price Indexes" on pages 336-337, and Table 11-3 on page 337.

The inflation rate is calculated as [(price index in 2011 – price index in 2010)/(price index in 2010)] × 100 = –33%. The negative percentage tells us that using the consumer price index to measure the inflation rate indicates that the aggregate price level has fallen between 2010 and 2011 by 33%.

Problems and Exercises

1. For the following list decide how the item affects the calculation of GDP for Macro States in 2011.

   a. A new house is constructed in Macro States during 2011.

   b. Bruce sells his house in Macro States without the help of a realtor in January 2011.

   c. The government purchases new textbooks for the schools of Macro States during 2011.

   d. Macro States sells 100,000 pounds of beef to Neverlandia during 2011.

e. Judy tutors Ellen's children in exchange for Ellen's driving the children's carpool three days a week throughout 2011.

f. A candlemaker produces 500 candles during 2011 but only sells 200 candles during 2011; the other 300 candles are added to the candlemaker's inventory.

2. Suppose you are told that Finlandia produces three goods: tennis shoes, basketballs, and lawn mowers. The following table provides information about the prices and output for these three goods for the years 2010, 2011, and 2012.

Year	Price of tennis shoes	Quantities of tennis shoes	Price of basketballs	Quantities of basketballs	Price of lawn mowers	Quantities of lawn mowers
2010	$50	100	$10	200	$100	10
2011	52	108	10	205	100	12
2012	54	115	10	212	110	12

a. Using the preceding information, fill in the following table.

Year	Nominal GDP
2010	
2011	
2012	

b. What was the percentage change in nominal GDP from 2010 to 2011?

c. What was the percentage change in nominal GDP from 2011 to 2012?

d. Using 2010 as the base year, fill in the following table.

Year	Real GDP
2010	
2011	
2012	

e. What was the percentage change in real GDP from 2010 to 2011?

f. What was the percentage change in real GDP from 2011 to 2012?

g. Using 2010 as the base year, fill in the following table.

Year	GDP deflator
2010	
2011	
2012	

3. In Macro Space, the price index is based upon a market basket consisting of 10 apples, 2 pizzas, and 5 ice cream cones. You are given prices for these three items for 2010, 2011, and 2012 in the following table.

Year	Price of apples	Price of pizzas	Price of ice cream cones
2010	$0.50 5.00	$4.00 8	$1.00 5.00 =18
2011	0.52 5.20	3.85 7.7	1.10 7.20
2012	0.49 4.90	3.90 7.8	1.30 7.60

a. Fill in the following table using year 2010 as your base year.

Year	Cost of market basket	Price index value
2010	18.00	100
2011	18.40	102.22
2012	19.2	106.67

b. Using the information you computed in part (a), what was the rate of inflation between 2010 and 2011?

2.22 %

c. Using the information you computed in part (a), what was the rate of inflation between 2011 and 2012?

4.35 %

d. Fill in the following table using year 2011 as your base year.

Year	Cost of market basket	Price index value
2010	18	97.83
2011	18.4	100
2012	19.2	105.35

e. Using the information you computed in part (d), what was the rate of inflation between 2010 and 2011?

f. Using the information you computed in part (d), what was the rate of inflation between 2011 and 2012?

g. Compare your answers in parts (b) and (c) to your answers in parts (e) and (f).

4. You are given the following information about the small economy of Hyattville.

   Hyattville's economy is composed of three firms: Hyattville Forest, Inc., which harvests trees, which are used by Hyattville Lumber Products, Inc., to manufacture various lumber products, which are used by Hyattville Houses, Inc., to produce houses. Assume lumber is the only raw material used to produce the houses in Hyattville.

	Hyattville Forest, Inc.	Hyattville Lumber Products, Inc.	Hyattville Houses, Inc.	Total Factor Income
Value of sales	$15,000	A	$100,000	
Intermediate goods	B	$15,000	40,000	
Wages	6,000	15,000	35,000	G
Interest payments	1,000	3,000	6,000	H
Rent	3,000	D	3,000	I
Profit	5,000	4,000	F	J
Total expenditures by firm	15,000	40,000	100,000	
Value added per firm	C	E	60,000	

a. Fill in the missing entries [A–J] in the table, recalling that GDP can be calculated in three different ways: (1) by measuring GDP as the value of the production of final goods and services in an economy as measured by the value added by each firm; (2) by measuring GDP as the sum of aggregate spending on domestically produced final goods and services in an economy; and (3) by measuring GDP as the sum of factor income earned from firms in the economy.

b. Using the value added approach, what is the value of GDP? Explain how you found this answer, using the table as a reference.

c. Using the factor income approach, what is the value of GDP? Explain how you found this answer using the table as a reference.

d. Using the aggregate spending on domestically produced final goods and services approach, what is the value of GDP? Explain how you found this answer, using the table as a reference.

5. The chapter discusses the distinction between nominal and real GDP. Briefly explain these two terms in your own words, and then explain why real GDP instead of nominal GDP is used to measure economic growth over time.

6. Use the following information to answer this next set of questions. The table that follows provides you with economic data about two economies: Chimex and Ameritime. Round all answers to the nearest whole number or percent.

	Nominal GDP in 2012	Nominal GDP in 2013	Real GDP in 2012	Real GDP in 2013	Population in 2012	Population in 2013
Chimex	$10m	$12m	$10.8m	$12m	1 million	1.2 million
Ameritime	$5m	$5.5m	$5.2m	$5.5m	200 thousand	220 thousand

a. You are told that the base year for the preceding data is either 2012 or 2013. Given the data, which year is the base year? Explain your answer.

2013 b/c real + nominal are the same, for 2013

b. Using the preceding data, calculate the percentage change in nominal GDP between 2012 and 2013 for both countries. Based upon nominal GDP, which country grew faster during this time period?

Chi → 20%   (Chi)

Amer → 10%

c. Using the preceding data, calculate the percentage change in real GDP between 2012 and 2013 for both countries. Based upon real GDP, which country grew faster during this time period?

Chi - 11.11%

Amer - 5.77%

d. Using the preceding data, calculate nominal GDP per capita. Then, calculate the percentage change in nominal GDP per capita between 2012 and 2013 for both countries.

	2012	2013
Chi	*10*	*10*
Amer	*25*	*25*

e. Using the preceding data, calculate real GDP per capita. Then, calculate the percentage change in real GDP per capita between 2012 and 2013 for both countries.

[handwritten: Chi - 2012 - 10.8, 2013 - 10, -7.4%] [Amor - 2012 - 26, 2013 - 25 = GDP - 3.85%]

f. Compare these two economies. Which economy has the higher standard of living? Explain your answer.

[handwritten: Amor b/c their GDP per capita is 25, meaning $25 is contrib. to each]

BEFORE YOU TAKE THE TEST

Chapter Review Questions

Use the information and the following table to answer the next three questions. The table represents data about an economy's performance during a year. Suppose in the economy represented in the table there are only three firms: American Racquet Co., which produces tennis racquets; American Metal Co., which produces the various metals that go into racquet production; and American Ore Co., which mines the ores needed for the manufacture of the metal. This economy produces 100 racquets that sell for $50 each.

	American Racquet Co.	American Metal Co.	American Ore Co.	Total factor income
Value of sales	$5,000	$3,000	$500	
Intermediate goods	A	B		
Wages	2,000	1,000	100	C
Interest payments	100	50	20	D
Rent	500	100	50	E
Profit	200	750	130	F
Total expenditures by firm	5,800	2,400	300	
Value added per firm	G	H	I	

1. GDP for this hypothetical economy is equal to
   a. $5,000 or the value of sales for American Racquet Co.
   b. $8,500 or the sum of the value added for the three firms.
   c. $3,500 or the value of the intermediate goods used by the American Racquet Co.
   d. $980 or the sum of the profits for the three firms.

2. GDP can be measured using different methods. If you were using the factor payments approach, which entries would you combine to get a measure of GDP?
   a. G, H and I
   b. A and B
   c. A, B, C, and D
   d. C, D, E, and F

3. GDP can be measured using the value added method. Using this method, which of the following values are correct for the missing entries in the table?
   a. $A = \$3,000$, $B = \$3,000$, $G = \$2,000$, $H = \$0$, $I = \$500$
   b. $A = \$3,000$, $B = \$500$, $G = \$2,000$, $H = \$2,500$, $I = \$500$
   c. $A = \$3,000$, $B = \$3,000$, $G = \$0$, $H = \$4,500$, $I = \$500$
   d. $A = \$3,000$, $B = \$500$, $G = \$0$, $H = \$4,500$, $I = \$500$

4. Double counting is
   a. the inclusion of the value of goods and services more than once when calculating GDP.
   b. the failure to include the value of intermediate goods in the final calculation of an economy's GDP.
   c. a process that artificially lowers the value of GDP.
   d. avoided if we do not use the value added method in calculating GDP.

Use the information in the following table to answer the next three questions.

	Price in 2011	Price in 2012
Oranges	$0.50	$0.40
Apples	0.25	0.40
Bananas	0.40	0.50

Suppose 2011 is the base year and the market basket for purposes of constructing a price index consists of 200 oranges, 100 apples, and 100 bananas.

5. What is the value of the price index in 2011?
   a. 1.15
   b. 100
   c. 165
   d. 190

6. What is the value of the price index in 2012, using 2011 as the base year?
   a. 0.97
   b. 1
   c. 100
   d. 103

7. What is the rate of inflation between 2011 and 2012 in this economy?
   a. 0%
   b. 3%
   c. 103%
   d. 67%, since two of the three prices increased between 2011 and 2012

8. In Macroland the GDP deflator for 2012 is 105, with 2011 the base year. Real GDP in 2012 equals $210 billion; therefore, nominal GDP in 2012 equals _____, while nominal GDP in 2011 equals _____.
   a. $220.5 billion; $200 billion
   b. $220.5 billion; $210 billion
   c. $200 billion; $210 billion
   d. $200 billion; $220.5 billion

9. $C + I + G + X - IM$ is
   a. equal to an economy's GDP for a given period of time.
   b. a measure of the overall market value of the goods and services the economy produces during a given period of time.
   c. the value of all final goods and services produced in an economy during a given time period.
   d. Answers (a), (b), and (c) are all correct.
   e. Answers (a) and (c) are both correct.
   f. Answers (a) and (b) are both correct.

10. Which of the following is NOT included in the calculation of GDP?
   a. Joey's Electronics manufactures CD players that individuals install in cars that do not have CD players.
   b. Susy's Leather Goods manufactures leather pieces that are sold to manufacturers that produce handbags and wallets from these leather pieces.
   c. Harry's Ice Cream Shoppe sells ice cream cones at the beach.
   d. Monica's Hair Salon sells haircuts and manicures to the residents of Marco Island.

11. To avoid double counting when computing GDP for an economy, it is important to
   a. count the total value of each producer's sales in an economy.
   b. only count each producer's value added in the calculation.
   c. include the cost of all inputs at each stage of production.
   d. exclude the cost of all inputs at each stage of production.

12. Income spent on imported goods
   a. represents income that has "leaked" across national borders.
   b. must be subtracted from spending data in order to calculate an accurate value for domestic production.
   c. is income that is not spent on domestically produced goods and services.
   d. Answers (a), (b), and (c) are all correct.

Use the information in the following table to answer the next three questions.

Smallville produces tractors and pizzas. You are given the following information about Smallville's production of these two goods and their prices for three years.

	Year 2010	Year 2011	Year 2012
Quantity of tractors	5	5	5
Price of tractors	$10,000	$12,000	$15,000
Quantity of pizzas	100	80	100
Price of pizzas	$10	$20	$20

13. Nominal GDP in 2011
   a. is greater than nominal GDP in 2010.
   b. is less than nominal GDP in 2012.
   c cannot be calculated until a base year is specified.
   d. Answers (a) and (b) are both correct.

14. Suppose the base year is 2010. Real GDP in 2011 using 2010 as the base year
   a. is greater than nominal GDP in 2011.
   b. is less than nominal GDP in 2011.
   c. is equal to nominal GDP in 2011.
   d. may be greater than, less than, or equal to nominal GDP in 2011.

15. Using 2011 as the base year, real GDP is greatest in
   a. 2010.
   b. 2011.
   c. 2012.
   d. 2010 and 2012 since real GDP using 2011 as the base year is the same for these two years.

Answer the next two questions based on the following information.

Littleville is a small economy whose current GDP in 2011 is $10,000 and whose population is 10 people.

16. GDP per capita in Littleville in 2011 is
   a. $10,000 per person.
   b. $1,000 per person.
   c. $100 per person.
   d. $100,000 per person.

17. Suppose GDP in Littleville in 2012 increases to $20,000 while the population increases by 50%. Then, GDP per capita in Littleville in 2012
   a. increases, since the percentage change in GDP is greater than the percentage change in population.
   b. equals approximately $1,333 per person.
   c. decreases due to the very large percentage increase in population.
   d. Answers (a) and (b) are correct.

◼ ANSWER KEY

Answers to Problems and Exercises

1. **a.** New home construction is included in GDP as investment spending.

    b. This is not included in GDP, since the value of the house was counted in GDP the year the house was built.

    c. Textbook purchases by the government are included in GDP as government spending.

    d. Macro States exports beef and the value of these exports are included in the GDP of Macro States.

    e. Although there is production occurring, Ellen and Judy do not exchange money, therefore this transaction does not get included in GDP.

    f. The value of 200 candles sold is included in GDP as part of consumption. The increase in inventory of 300 candles is included in GDP as part of investment, since it represents new production in the economy of Macro States.

2. **a.**

Year	Nominal GDP
2010	$8,000
2011	8,866
2012	9,650

    To calculate nominal GDP, multiply the price of each good times the quantity produced of that good and then sum together these products. For example, nominal GDP in 2010 = (price of tennis shoes)(quantity of tennis shoes) + (price of basketballs)(quantity of basketballs) + (price of lawn mowers)(quantity of lawn mowers) = $8,000.

    b. The percentage change in nominal GDP from 2010 to 2011 was 10.83%: [(8,866 − 8,000)/8,000] × 100 = 10.83%.

    c. The percentage change in nominal GDP from 2011 to 2012 was 8.84%: [(9,650 − 8,866)/8,866] × 100 = 8.84%.

    d.

Year	Real GDP
2010	$8,000
2011	8,650
2012	9,070

    To calculate real GDP, multiply the price of each good in the base year (2010) times the quantity produced of that good in a given year and then sum together these products. The value of real GDP will equal nominal GDP in the base year. In 2011, real GDP can be calculated as the following sum: ($50 per pair of tennis shoes)(108 pairs) + ($10 per basketball)(205 basketballs) + ($100 per lawn mower)(12 lawn mowers).

    e. The percentage change in real GDP from 2010 to 2011 was 8.13%: [(8,650 − 8,000)/8,000] × 100.

    f. The percentage change in real GDP from 2011 to 2012 was 4.86%: [(9,070 − 8,650)/8,650] × 100.

g.

Year	GDP deflator
2010	(8,000/8,000) × 100 = 100
2011	(8,866/8,650) × 100 = 102.50
2012	(9,650/9,070) × 100 = 106.39

3. a.

Year	Cost of market basket	Price index value
2010	(10)(0.5) + (2)(4) + (5)(1) = $18	(18/18) × 100 = 100
2011	(10)(0.52) + (2)(3.85) + (5)(1.1) = $18.4	(18.4/18) × 100 = 102.22
2012	(10)(0.49) + (2)(3.9) + (5)(1.3) = $19.2	(19.2/18) × 100 = 106.67

b. The rate of inflation between 2010 and 2011 was 2.22%: [(102.22 − 100)/100] × 100 = 2.22%.

c. The rate of inflation between 2011 and 2012 was 4.35%: [(106.67 − 102.22)/102.22] × 100 = 4.35%.

d.

Year	Cost of market basket	Price index value
2010	(10)(0.5) + (2)(4) + (5)(1) = $18	(18/18.4) × 100 = 97.83
2011	(10)(0.52) + (2)(3.85) + (5)(1.1) = 18.4	(18.4/18.4) × 100 = 100
2012	(10)(0.49) + (2)(3.9) + (5)(1.3) = $19.2	(19.2/18.4) × 100 = 104.35

e. The rate of inflation between 2010 and 2011 was 2.22%: [(100 − 97.83)/97.83] × 100 = 2.22%.

f. The rate of inflation between 2011 and 2012 was 4.35%: [(104.35 − 100)/100] × 100 = 4.35%.

g. Answers (b) and (c) are the same as answers (e) and (f). This is not surprising since the choice of a base year will generate different values for the price index, but the rate of change in prices between years should be equivalent no matter what year is chosen as the base year.

4. a.

	Hyattville Forest, Inc.	Hyattville Lumber Products, Inc.	Hyattville Houses, Inc.	Total factor income
Value of sales	$15,000	$40,000	$100,000	
Intermediate goods	0	15,000	40,000	
Wages	6,000	15,000	35,000	$56,000
Interest payments	1,000	3,000	6,000	10,000
Rent	3,000	3,000	3,000	9,000
Profit	5,000	4,000	16,000	25,000
Total expenditures by firm	15,000	40,000	100,000	
Value added per firm	15,000	25,000	60,000	

b. To find GDP using the value added approach requires summing the horizontal entries that are found in the row labeled "Value added per firm" in the above table. From your answer in part (a), the sum of these entries is equal to $15,000 + $25,000 + $60,000, or $100,000.

c. To find GDP using the factor income approach requires first summing horizontally the entries of the amount of wages paid, the amount of interest payments, the amount of rent, and the amount of profit, which corresponds to finding the values of *G, H, I,* and *J* in the table. Then, once these amounts have been calculated, these four values must be summed to find the total factor income in the economy; thus, from part (a) of this question we have $56,000 (the amount of total wages paid in the economy) + $10,000 (the total amount of interest payments in the economy) + $9,000 (the total amount of rent payments in this economy) + $25,000 (the total amount of profits in this economy) for a total of $100,000 (GDP using the factor payments approach).

d. To find GDP using the aggregate spending on domestically produced final goods and services approach, first recognize that Hyattville only produces one type of final good or service: houses. The value of the houses produced in Hyattville is equal to $100,000.

5. Nominal GDP is the value of the final goods and services produced in an economy during a specified time period using current dollars to measure that value, while real GDP is the value of the final goods and services produced in an economy during a specified time period using constant dollars. Comparison of nominal GDP over time has, therefore, a crucial problem in that each measure of nominal GDP uses a different "yardstick": the purchasing power of a dollar in year X is unlikely to be the same as the purchasing power of a dollar in year Y. Comparison of nominal values of GDP cannot accurately tell you if an economy is growing, since the increase or decrease in nominal GDP may reflect changes in the price level rather than changes in production. Real GDP, in contrast, uses a constant dollar to value the level of output over time. Thus, if real GDP changes over time, this reflects a change in the production and not just a change in the value of the dollar measure used to value this production.

6. **a.** The real value is equal to the nominal value in the base year. Examining the data, real GDP in 2012 is not equal to nominal GDP in 2012 for either country. However, real GDP in 2013 is equal to nominal GDP in 2013 for both countries. The base year is 2013.

b. To find the percentage change in nominal GDP between 2012 and 2013, use the following formula: Percentage change in nominal GDP between 2012 and 2013 = [(Nominal GDP in 2013 − Nominal GDP in 2012)/(Nominal GDP in 2012)] × 100.

Thus, for Chimex, the percentage change in nominal GDP between 2012 and 2013 = [(12 − 10)/10] × 100 = 20%.

For Ameritime, the percentage change in nominal GDP between 2012 and 2013 = [(5.5 − 5)/5] × 100 = 10%.

Using the nominal values, Chimex grew at a faster rate than Ameritime during the period 2012 to 2013.

c. To find the percentage change in real GDP between 2012 and 2013, use the following formula: Percentage change in real GDP between 2012 and 2013 = [(Real GDP in 2013 − Real GDP in 2012)/(Real GDP in 2012)] × 100.

Thus, for Chimex, the percentage change in real GDP between 2012 and 2013 = [(12 − 10.8)/10.8] × 100 = 11%.

For Ameritime, the percentage change in real GDP between 2012 and 2013 = [(5.5 − 5.2)/5.2] × 100 = 6%.

Using the real values, Chimex grew at a faster rate than Ameritime during the period 2012 to 2013.

d. To find nominal GDP per capita for a particular year, use the following formula:

Nominal GDP per capita for year n = (Nominal GDP for year n)/(Population for year n).

Thus, in Chimex, the nominal GDP per capita for 2012 is equal to $10 million/ 1 million people or $10 per person. In Chimex, the nominal GDP per capita for 2013 is equal to $12 million/1.2 million people, or $10 per person. Note that the nominal GDP per capita does not change between 2012 and 2013 because both nominal GDP and population grow at the same rate.

In Ameritime, the nominal GDP per capita for 2012 is equal to $5 million/200 thousand people or $25 per person. In Ameritime, the nominal GDP per capita for 2013 is equal to $5.5 million/220 thousand people, or $25 per person. Note that the nominal GDP per capita does not change between 2012 and 2013 because both nominal GDP and population grow at the same rate.

The percentage change in nominal GDP per capita in Chimex for this period is equal to 0%, since the nominal GDP per capita does not change over this period. The percentage change in nominal GDP per capita in Ameritime for this period is also equal to 0%, since there is no change in nominal GDP per capita during this period.

e. To find real GDP per capita for a particular year, use the following formula:

Real GDP per capita for year n = (Real GDP for year n)/(Population for year n).

Thus, in Chimex, the real GDP per capita for 2012 is equal to $10.8 million/ 1 million people or $10.80 per person. In Chimex, the real GDP per capita for 2013 is equal to $12 million/1.2 million people or $10 per person.

In Ameritime, the real GDP per capita for 2012 is equal to $5.2 million/200 thousand people or $26 per person. In Ameritime, the real GDP per capita for 2013 is equal to $5.5 million/220 thousand people or $25 per person.

The percentage change in real GDP per capita in Chimex for this period is equal to [(10 − 10.8)/10.8)] × 100, or approximately 7%. The percentage change in real GDP per capita in Ameritime for this period is equal to [(25 − 26)/26] × 100, or approximately −4%.

f. Even though real GDP per capita is falling in Ameritime, it still has the higher standard of living. Note that when comparing two economies one needs not only to consider the value of the output that is produced in the economy but also the population. A country with a larger population has more resources for production than a country with a smaller population, and it has more consumers. Thus, to compare two economies' standard of living we should compare the real GDP per capita in the two countries.

Answers to Chapter Review Questions

1. **Answer a.** Since GDP is equal to the value of all final goods and services produced in an economy during a given time period, GDP for this economy can be found by multiplying the number of racquets produced during the given time period times their price. This yields $5,000. Alternatively, one could add up the total payments to factors of production: wages, interest payments, rent, and profit sum to $5,000.

2. **Answer d.** To get the value of GDP using the factor payments approach, you would need to add up the sum of factor payments: this would be the sum of wages, interest payments, rent, and profit, or cells C, D, E, and F.

3. **Answer b.** The cost of intermediate goods in entry A is equal to the value of metal sales from American Metal Co., or $3,000. The cost of intermediate goods in entry B is equal to the value of ore sales from American Ore Co., or $500. The value added by American Racquet Co., or entry G, is equal to the value of sales by this company minus the value of intermediate goods used by this company ($5,000 − $3,000, or $2,000). The value added by American Metal Co., or entry H, is equal to the value of sales by this company minus

the value of intermediate goods used by this company ($3,000 – $500, or $2,500); the value added by American Ore Co., or entry I, is equal to the value of sales by this company minus the value of intermediate goods used by this company ($500 – $0 or $500).

4. **Answer a.** Double counting is when you count the production of an item more than once when calculating the value of GDP. This can arise because the good is used as an intermediate good in the production of a final good. For this reason, intermediate goods are not counted as part of GDP because this would result in an overstatement of the level of production that has occurred in an economy.

5. **Answer b.** The value of a price index in the base year is always equal to 100. To calculate a price index in general, you need to calculate the ratio of the cost of the market basket in the current year to the cost of the market basket in the base year and then multiply this ratio by 100. In this question, the ratio is equal to 1 since the cost of the two market baskets is the same and thus the price index equals 100.

6. **Answer d.** Calculate the value of the market basket in the base year: (200 oranges) ($0.50/orange) + (100 apples)($0.25/apple) + (100 bananas)($0.40/banana) = 165. Calculate the value of the market basket in 2011: (200 oranges)($0.40/orange) + (100 apples)($0.40/apple) + (100 bananas)($0.50/banana) = 170. Then put these two values into the following formula:

Price index = [(cost of market basket in current year)/(cost of market basket in base year)] × 100

Price index = [(170)/(165)] × 100 = 103

Note that the market basket stays fixed when calculating a price index.

7. **Answer b.** To calculate the inflation rate between two time periods, you need the price index for each time period. Then, use the following formula:

Inflation rate = [(price index in period 2 – price index in period 1)/(price index in period 1)] × 100

In this case,

Inflation rate = [(103 – 100)/100] × 100 = 3%

8. **Answer a.** To answer this question, it is helpful to first organize the information you are given into a table.

Year	GDP deflator	Nominal GDP	Real GDP
2011	100		
2012	105		$210 billion

We know that in the base year nominal GDP equals real GDP, but we still need to calculate this value. We can calculate this value using the formula:

Price index in 2012 = [(real GDP in 2012)/(real GDP in base year)] × 100

Or, in this case

105 = [($210 billion)/(real GDP in base year)] × 100

or

Real GDP in base year = $200 billion

To calculate nominal GDP in 2012, we use the formula for the GDP deflator:

Price index in 2012 = [(nominal GDP in 2012)/(real GDP in 2012)] × 100

Rearranging the formula we have

Real GDP in 2012 = [(nominal GDP in 2012)/(price index in 2012)] × 100

or

$210 billion = [(nominal GDP in 2012)/105] × 100

or

Nominal GDP in 2012 = $220.5 billion

Our completed table is

Year	GDP deflator	Nominal GDP	Real GDP
2011	100	$200 billion	$200 billion
2012	105	220.5 billion	210 billion

9. **Answer d.** The sum of consumer spending, investment spending, government spending, and net exports is equal to GDP. GDP provides a measure of the market value of the goods and services produced in an economy: this is the value of all final goods and services produced in the economy.

10. **Answer b.** Answers (a), (c), and (d) are all included in GDP, since they each represent a final good or service. Answer (b) is not included in GDP, since the leather pieces are intermediate goods that are used to manufacture the final goods—handbags and wallets—that are included in GDP.

11. **Answer b.** To avoid double counting when calculating GDP, it is important to only count each producer's value added to GDP; alternatively, we can think about avoiding the double counting problem by subtracting out the cost of inputs—the intermediate goods—at each stage of production in order to arrive at the value added at that stage. Then, if the value added at each stage is summed, this will yield the economy's GDP without any double counting.

12. **Answer d.** Income spent on imported goods is by definition income that is not being spent on domestically produced goods and services; this income is leaking out of the domestic economy, since it is being spent in a foreign economy. In order to accurately calculate domestic production from spending data, it is necessary to subtract all the spending that occurs on foreign-produced final goods and services.

13. **Answer d.** To answer this question, it is helpful to calculate the nominal GDP for each of these years. Nominal GDP in 2010 equals the sum of the product of the prices of the goods produced times the quantity of the goods produced or ($10,000/tractor)(5 tractors) + ($10/pizza)(100 pizzas), or $51,000. Using the same process, nominal GDP in 2011 equals $61,600 and nominal GDP in 2012 equals $77,000. Thus, nominal GDP in 2011 is greater than nominal GDP in 2010 and less than nominal GDP in 2012.

14. **Answer b.** To answer this question, first calculate real GDP in 2011 using 2010 as the base year. Real GDP in 2011 equals the sum of the product of the quantities produced in 2011 times the price of the product in the base year. Thus, real GDP in 2011 using 2010 as the base year equals ($10,000/tractor)(5 tractors) + ($10/pizza)(80 pizzas), or $50,800. Nominal GDP in 2011 equals $61,600 (see previous question), so real GDP in 2011 using 2010 as the base year is less than nominal GDP in 2011.

15. **Answer d.** To answer this question, first compute real GDP for each year using 2011 as the base year. Real GDP in 2011 will equal nominal GDP in 2011 since 2011 has been designated the base year. Thus, real GDP in 2011 equals $61,600. Real GDP in 2010 using 2011 as the base year equals ($12,000/tractor)(5 tractors) + ($20/pizza)(100 pizzas), or

$62,000. Real GDP in 2012 using 2011 as the base year equals ($12,000/tractor)(5 tractors) + ($20/pizza)(100 pizzas), or $62,000.

16. **Answer b.** To find GDP per capita, divide the economy's GDP by its population. For Littleville, GDP per capita in 2011 is equal to ($10,000)/(10 people), or $1,000 per person.

17. **Answer d.** Littleville's GDP in 2012 increases by $10,000 (a 100% increase) from its GDP in 2011, while its population increases by 50%. Since the percentage increase in GDP is greater than the percentage increase in population, this implies that GDP per capita has risen in Littleville. To find GDP per person in 2012, we need to first find the level of population in 2012. Since population in 2012 is 50% larger than the population in 2011, this implies population in Littleville is now 15 people. GDP per capita in 2012 in Littleville is thus equal to ($20,000)/(15 people), or approximately $1,333 per person.

chapter 12

Unemployment and Inflation

▉ BEFORE YOU READ THE CHAPTER

Summary

This chapter discusses how unemployment is measured and why the unemployment rate in an economy is significant. The chapter also explores the relationship between the unemployment rate and economic growth. The chapter develops the concept of the natural rate of unemployment. In addition, the chapter considers the costs of inflation and deflation and how inflation and deflation create winners and losers. Finally, the chapter discusses why policy makers want to avoid temporary rises in inflation.

Chapter Objectives

Objective #1. A person is considered to be employed if he or she has a job. To be considered unemployed, an individual must currently not have a job and, in addition, must have actively sought employment during the past four weeks. Individuals who are disabled or retired are not included in the number of unemployed in an economy. The economy's labor force is equal to the sum of the employed and the unemployed in that economy.

- The labor force participation rate is the percentage of the population over 16 years of age that is either employed or unemployed. The labor force participation rate is equal to [(labor force)/(population age 16 and older)] × 100.

- The unemployment rate is equal to [(number of unemployed workers)/(number of unemployed workers + number of employed workers)] × 100.

- Since the number of unemployed workers plus the number of employed workers is equal to the labor force, the unemployment rate is equal to [(number of unemployed workers)/(labor force)] × 100.

Objective #2.   The unemployment rate provides a good indicator of current conditions in the labor market, but it is not a perfect measure.

- The unemployment rate overstates the difficulty of finding a job since it includes those individuals who are looking for a job and are confident that they will be employed once they identify a suitable position.

- The unemployment rate understates the difficulty of finding a job since it does not include discouraged workers, those jobless individuals who have given up searching for a job because there are no jobs available where they live. The unemployment rate also does not include the marginally attached workers, a group of individuals who are out of work and have recently looked for work, but who are currently not seeking employment. Lastly, the unemployment rate does not include those individuals who are currently working part-time jobs but who want to work full-time; these underemployed workers are counted as employed rather than unemployed even though they are unable to find jobs that are full-time.

- The unemployment rate varies among demographic groups: younger workers and older workers typically experience higher rates of unemployment than do workers between the ages of 25 and 54.

Objective #3.   The unemployment rate rises during economic recession and generally falls during economic expansion. Economic data generally indicates that there is a negative relationship between economic growth and the rate of unemployment: when real GDP grows at a high rate, the unemployment rate falls; and when real GDP grows at a low or negative rate, the unemployment rate rises. A falling level of real GDP is always associated with increases in the unemployment rate and its resultant hardship on families.

Objective #4.   The unemployment rate never falls to zero. This is due to several reasons. First, jobs are constantly being created and eliminated. Jobs are created and eliminated due to structural changes in the economy: these changes reflect new technologies as well as changes in consumers' tastes. In addition, the process of locating a job or the job search can take time. *Frictional unemployment* is the term that describes unemployment that is due to job search, whether this job search is due to the process of job creation and job destruction or the fact that new workers are constantly entering the labor force.

Objective #5.   *Structural unemployment* refers to unemployment that occurs when there are more people seeking jobs in a labor market than there are jobs. Structural unemployment may reflect a situation where there are more workers with a particular skill than there are available jobs using that skill, or where there are more workers in a particular geographic area than there are jobs in that area.

Objective #6.   In a labor market, the demand for labor indicates the amount of labor employers demand at different wage rates, while the supply of labor indicates the amount of labor that individuals are willing to supply at different wage rates. The demand for labor is downward sloping: as the wage rate falls, firms demand more labor. The supply of labor is typically upward sloping: as the wage rate falls, individuals supply less labor. The equilibrium wage rate is that wage rate where the quantity demanded of labor is equal to the quantity supplied of labor. However, at that equilibrium wage rate there is still frictional unemployment, since there will always be some workers who are searching for a job even if the number of available jobs equals the number of available workers. But, at the equilibrium wage rate, structural unemployment is equal to zero. Whenever the wage rate exceeds the equilibrium wage rate, there is structural unemployment: the primary causes of this structural unemployment are the minimum wage, labor unions, efficiency wages, and the side effects of government policies.

- A minimum wage is a government-imposed floor on the price of labor and, when binding, the minimum wage can lead to structural unemployment since it artificially raises the wage rate above the equilibrium wage rate in the labor market. Although an effective minimum wage helps those who secure employment, it may also eliminate the opportunity to work for some workers who would have been willing to work for lower wages.

- Effective labor unions may also result in structural unemployment if the unions are successful in bargaining for wage contracts that are higher than the equilibrium market wage rate. Through successful collective bargaining, labor unions may raise the wage rate to a level at which the number of people willing to work is greater than the number of jobs available at that wage rate.

- Firms that pay efficiency wages as an incentive for better worker performance may also create structural unemployment: the efficiency wage is a wage rate greater than the equilibrium wage rate.

- Public policy may generate unintended side effects that result in structural unemployment. For example, generous unemployment benefits may reduce the incentive of the unemployed to find new jobs.

Objective #7. The natural rate of unemployment is that rate of unemployment that the actual unemployment fluctuates around. This natural rate of unemployment takes into account frictional rate unemployment as well as structural rate unemployment. In contrast, cyclical unemployment is the difference between the actual rate of unemployment and the natural rate of unemployment: cyclical unemployment rate measures the amount of unemployment due to the business cycle fluctuations. Thus,

natural v. cyclical

Natural unemployment = frictional unemployment + structural unemployment

Actual unemployment = natural unemployment + cyclical unemployment

Objective #8. The natural rate of unemployment is not constant over time and may be affected by economic policies. It changes with changes in the characteristics of the labor force, changes in labor market institutions, changes in government policies, and changes in productivity.

- When the labor force has many inexperienced workers, this results in higher rates of frictional unemployment since these workers are apt to stay in a particular job for a shorter period of time than are experienced workers. In addition, older workers often have family responsibilities that provide a stronger incentive to find and keep jobs.

- Economies with strong labor unions tend to have higher rates of natural unemployment, since the labor unions may contribute to higher rates of structural unemployment. Temporary employment agencies and Internet Web sites listing jobs may reduce the level of frictional employment and therefore the natural rate of unemployment by helping match unemployed workers to jobs.

- Government policies such as a high minimum wage or generous unemployment benefits can cause structural unemployment and, thus, lead to a higher rate of natural unemployment. Government policies may also reduce the natural rate of unemployment. For example, job training works to provide unemployed workers with skills that will enable them to widen the range of jobs they can do, while employment subsidies provide payments to either workers or firms to create an incentive for these groups to accept or offer jobs.

Objective #9. The level of prices in an economy does not determine how well off people are, but the percentage increase in the overall level of prices per year, or the inflation rate, does matter since a high rate of inflation imposes significant economic costs. The inflation rate for a given year (for example, year 2) can be calculated using the following formula:

$$\text{Inflation rate for year 2} = \{[(\text{price index in year 2}) - (\text{price index in year 1})]/(\text{price index in year 1})\} \times 100$$

High rates of inflation result in shoe-leather costs, menu costs, and unit-of-account costs.

- Shoe-leather costs refer to the effort people expend to reduce their holdings of money during periods of high inflation. The high rate of inflation reduces the purchasing power of money and makes holding money less desirable since the money does not hold its value. The high rate of inflation significantly increases transactions costs, as individuals expend valuable resources to reduce their money holdings.

- Menu costs refer to the cost of changing the list price of items that are offered for sale. In periods of high inflation, firms are forced to alter prices often and this results in higher costs for the economy as a whole.

- Unit-of-account costs of inflation refer to the way inflation makes money a less reliable unit of measurement; in particular, in periods of high inflation, contracts that are stated in monetary terms are harder to evaluate due to the changing value of the monetary unit. Tax systems are subject to unit-of-account costs if these tax systems are not adjusted for inflation, since the inflation can distort the measures of income on which taxes are collected.

Objective #10. In addition to the three overall costs on the economy (shoe-leather costs, menu costs, and unit-of-account costs), inflation also produces winners and losers within the economy. This distributional effect of inflation primarily arises because many economic transactions involve contracts that extend over a period of time, and these contracts are normally specified in nominal, rather than real, terms. To understand this issue requires understanding the distinction between nominal and real interest rates: the nominal interest rate is the interest rate in dollar terms, while the real interest rate is the nominal interest rate minus the rate of inflation. When the actual inflation rate is greater than the expected inflation rate, borrowers gain at the expense of lenders: borrowers will repay their loans with funds that have a lower real value than had been expected. When the actual inflation rate is lower than the expected inflation rate, lenders gain at the expense of borrowers: borrowers will repay their loans with funds that have a higher real value than had been expected.

- Long-term contracts are adversely affected by uncertainty about the future inflation rate, since this uncertainty discourages people from entering into long-term contracts with one another. Thus, high rates of inflation and high levels of uncertainty about future rates of inflation reduce long-term investment in an economy.

- Deflation, an unexpected fall in the price level, also produces winners and losers. In periods of deflation, borrowers see a sharp increase in the real value of their debt: deflation redistributes wealth from borrowers to lenders.

Objective #11. Reducing the level of inflation in an economy, a process called disinflation, is difficult and costly once a high rate of inflation is established. To eliminate established inflation in an economy requires policies that temporarily depress the economy—and these policies lead to high levels of unemployment.

Key Terms

employment the total number of people currently employed for pay in the *economy*, either full-time or part-time.

unemployment the total number of people who are actively looking for work but aren't currently employed.

labor force the sum of *employment* and *unemployment*; that is, the number of people who are currently working plus the number of people who are currently looking for work.

labor force participation rate the percentage of the population age 16 or older who are in the *labor force*.

unemployment rate the percentage of the total number of people in the *labor force* who are unemployed, calculated as *unemployment/ (unemployment + employment)*.

discouraged workers individuals who want to work but who have stated to government researchers that they aren't currently searching for a job because they see little prospect of finding one given the state of the job market.

marginally attached workers nonworking individuals who say they would like a job and have looked for work in the recent past but are not currently looking for work.

underemployment the number of people who work part-time because they cannot find full-time jobs.

jobless recovery refers to a period of time in which the growth rate of real GDP is positive but the unemployment rate is still rising.

job search when workers spend time looking for *employment*.

frictional unemployment *unemployment* due to time workers spend in *job search*.

structural unemployment *unemployment* that results when there are more people seeking jobs in a labor market than there are jobs available at the current wage rate.

efficiency wages wages that employers set above the *equilibrium* wage rate as an incentive for workers to deliver better performance.

natural rate of unemployment the normal *unemployment rate* around which the actual unemployment rate fluctuates; the unemployment rate that arises from the effects of *frictional* and *structural unemployment*.

cyclical unemployment the difference between the actual rate of *unemployment* and the *natural rate of unemployment*.

real wage the wage rate divided by the price level.

real income income divided by the price level.

shoe-leather costs (of inflation) the increased costs of transactions caused by *inflation*.

Key Terms *(continued)*

menu costs the real cost of changing a listed price.

unit-of-account costs (of inflation) costs arising from the way *inflation* makes money a less reliable unit of measurement.

interest rate on a loan is the price, calculated as a percentage of the amount borrowed, that a lender charges a borrower for the use of their savings for one year.

nominal interest rate the *interest rate* in dollar terms.

real interest rate the *nominal interest rate* minus the *inflation rate*.

disinflation the process of bringing down *inflation* that has become embedded in expectations.

▮ AFTER YOU READ THE CHAPTER

Tips

Tip #1. The distinction among frictional, structural, and cyclical unemployment is important. All economies experience frictional unemployment. Jobs are created and destroyed and new workers are constantly entering the labor market: these events make some unemployment inevitable. Structural unemployment occurs because there is a mismatch between the supply of labor and the demand for labor: this mismatch is the result of the current wage exceeding the wage rate that would equate the supply of labor to the demand for labor. Cyclical unemployment is the unemployment that occurs due to fluctuations in economic production due to the business cycle.

Tip #2. This chapter introduces new vocabulary and, as usual, you will want to make sure you learn and understand these new terms. In particular, you will want to be able to define and distinguish between real and nominal interest rates, and deflation and disinflation. The nominal interest rate is the interest rate expressed in money terms, while the real interest rate is the interest rate adjusted for inflation. The real interest rate is equal to the nominal interest rate minus the inflation rate. Deflation refers to a fall in the aggregate price level, and disinflation refers to a decrease in the inflation rate reflecting policy makers' decisions that the economy has built-in inflationary expectations that need to be reduced.

Tip #3. Students often find the concept of the natural rate of unemployment challenging. It is not possible for an economy to achieve and maintain zero unemployment due to the ongoing creation and destruction of jobs as well as the entry of new labor market participants. The natural rate of unemployment is that level of unemployment that the economy can achieve when it is producing with no cyclical unemployment: it is the rate of unemployment achieved when the economy produces at its potential output level.

1. Consider an economy that has 100,000 people who are 16 years old or older. Of this group, 2,000 are currently in the military, 1,000 are homemakers, 10,000 are retired, and 14,000 are full-time students who are not employed. Further, 10,000 people are currently not working and are actively seeking jobs, 5,000 people are temporarily laid off and anticipate that their jobs will resume within the next two months, and 5,000 people are currently not working and are not actively seeking jobs because they live in a community with a severely depressed economy (like Detroit today). All other adults in this economy can be assumed to be working: in this group, 80% are fully employed and 20% are underemployed. You are asked to identify what the civilian labor force is in this economy, what the number of unemployed people is in this economy, and what the number of employed people is in this economy. You are also asked to calculate the unemployment rate and the civilian labor force participation rate for this economy. The government of this economy is considering changing its definition of unemployed so that it includes discouraged workers. If this new policy is implemented, what will the new unemployment rate equal? Suppose the government changes its classification of discouraged workers and, in addition, decides to treat underemployed workers as unemployed workers since this group is not fully utilizing their labor resources. If both of these policy changes are implemented, what will happen to the unemployment rate?

STEP 1: Start by identifying all those individuals who would not be in the civilian labor force. Then identify all those who are considered employed and all those who are considered unemployed. Remember that the number of the employed plus the unemployed must sum to the civilian labor force. (Hint: Your text refers to the labor force, but this is just the civilian labor force—in this example, we are emphasizing this since we want to make sure you do not include the military in your calculations of the employed and the unemployed.)

Review the section "The Unemployment Rate" on pages 348–354.

The intent of the unemployment rate is to measure that fraction of the labor force that is not employed. The government does not want to include in this measurement individuals who are clearly not interested in working, individuals who clearly cannot work, or individuals who are not part of the adult population. The government also does not want to include military personnel since they are employed by the military. Thus, in this example, the civilian labor force excludes all those under 16, the military, homemakers who are not currently seeking work, the retired, and full-time students who are not currently seeking work. The civilian labor force is equal to 68,000. To find the civilian labor force, start with the initial population of 100,000 and then subtract out those in the military (2,000), full-time students (14,000), those not working and not looking for work (10,000), those that are discouraged workers (5,000), and those who are homemakers (1,000). The 5,000 who are laid off but who expect to be called back are treated as unemployed workers, since they are currently not working. The civilian labor force is equal to the sum of the employed plus the unemployed. We can find the number of unemployed workers: it is the sum of the unemployed plus the laid-off workers, or 10,000 plus 5,000, for a total of 15,000. To find the number of employed people, subtract the unemployed from the civilian labor force: 68,000 − 15,000 = 53,000.

STEP 2: Calculate the unemployment rate and the civilian labor force participation rate for this economy.

Review the section "The Unemployment Rate" on pages 348–354.

The unemployment rate is equal to [(number of unemployed)/(civilian labor force)] × 100. Recall that the civilian labor force is just the sum of the unemployed plus the employed. In this example, the civilian labor force is equal to 68,000. The unemployment rate is [(15,000)/(68,000)] × 100, or 22%.

The civilian labor force participation rate is equal to [(civilian labor force)/(civilian population age 16 or older)] × 100 = [(68,000)/(98,000)] × 100, or 69.4%.

STEP 3: Recalculate the unemployment rate, but this time treat discouraged workers as part of the group of unemployed workers.

Review the section "The Unemployment Rate" on pages 348–354.

This change in policy will change the number of unemployed from 15,000 to 20,000 and the number of the civilian labor force from 68,000 to 73,000. The new unemployment rate can be calculated as [(20,000)/(73,000)] × 100 = 27.4%. Notice that the treatment of discouraged workers can have a significant impact on the unemployment statistics. Current treatment makes the unemployment rate lower than it would be if discouraged workers were treated as unemployed workers.

STEP 4: Recalculate the unemployment rate, but this time treat both discouraged workers and underemployed workers as part of the group of unemployed workers.

Review the section "The Unemployment Rate" on pages 348–354.

Initially, there are 53,000 employed people in this economy. Of that 53,000, we are told that 80% are fully employed and 20% are underemployed. The number of employed people is equal to 0.8(53,000), or 42,400, and the number of underemployed people is equal to 0.2(53,000), or 10,600. If the government changes its policy to include discouraged workers and underemployed workers in the category of unemployed workers, this means that the number of unemployed workers will increase from 15,000 to 30,600. In addition, the civilian labor force will now equal 73,000: the 30,600 who are unemployed and the 42,400 who are employed. To calculate the number of employed people, recall that initially there were 53,000 employed people but that this number included the underemployed. If we categorize the underemployed as unemployed, this will cause the unemployed number to increase by 10,600 and the employed number to decrease by 10,600. The new unemployment rate with these changes in policy will equal [(30,600)/(73,000)] × 100, or 41.92%. Notice that the treatment of discouraged workers and underemployed workers can have a significant impact on the unemployment statistics. Current treatment makes the unemployment rate lower than it would be if discouraged workers and underemployed workers were treated as unemployed workers.

2. In the library, you read the following newspaper headline from the 2008 archives: "Sharp rise in unemployment rate as global financial crisis hits jobs market." Based on this reading, what do you know about frictional, structural, and cyclical unemployment in this economy? What do you know about the relationship between this economy's current unemployment rate and its natural rate of unemployment?

STEP 1: Review the definitions of frictional, structural, and cyclical unemployment and then apply these definitions to this situation.

Review the section "The Natural Rate of Unemployment" on pages 354–362.

The headline about the global financial crisis and the rise in unemployment suggests that the world economy is experiencing a deviation from the natural rate of unemployment, the level of unemployment that is the normal unemployment rate around which the actual unemployment rate fluctuates. This deviation is referred to as cyclical unemployment. So, in this economy not only is there frictional and structural unemployment, the kinds of unemployment that occur normally in an economy, but there is also the additional kind of unemployment that refers to the departure of the economy from its normal unemployment rate.

STEP 2: Review the definition of the natural unemployment rate and then consider how this economy's current unemployment rate differs from its natural unemployment rate.

Review the section "The Natural Rate of Unemployment" on pages 354–362.

This economy is experiencing frictional, structural, and cyclical unemployment: this implies that its current unemployment rate is greater than its natural unemployment rate.

3. The following data on the labor market have been provided to you by the U.S. Bureau of Labor Statistics. You are asked to provide the overall unemployment rate for this economy, the unemployment rate for males, and the unemployment rate for females. Furthermore, you are asked to compute the labor force participation rate for this economy as well as the female labor force participation rate and the male labor force participation rate.

Adult Population	% Female
400	52%
Labor Force	% Female
310	40%
Employed	% Female
260	45%

STEP 1: It would be helpful to know the number of men and women in each of the above categories rather than just the percentages that have been provided.

Review the section "The Unemployment Rate" on pages 348–354.

Take the time to construct a table that provides these data in a straightforward, easy-to-access manner. The following table provides this information.

Variable	Male	Female
Adult Population	192	208
Labor Force	186	124
Employed	143	117

STEP 2: Find the unemployment rate in general and then find the unemployment rate for men and the unemployment rate for women.

Review the section "The Unemployment Rate" on pages 348–354.

Recall that the unemployment rate = [(number of unemployed)/(number of unemployed + number of employed)] × 100. To find the number of unemployed, you need to remember that the labor force is the sum of employed plus unemployed. Since the labor force is equal to 310 and the number of employed is equal to 260, the number of unemployed is equal to 50. The unemployment rate is [(50)/(310)] × 100, or approximately 16%.

To find the unemployment rate for males, you will need to find the number of unemployed men and the number of men in the labor force. From the preceding table, we know that there are 186 men in the labor force and 143 of them are employed. That implies that 43 are unemployed. The male unemployment rate is [(43)/(186)] × 100, or approximately 23%.

To find the unemployment rate for females, you will need to find the number of unemployed women and the number of women in the labor force. From the preceding table, we know that there are 124 women in the labor force and 117 of them are employed. That implies that 7 are unemployed. The female unemployment rate is [(7)/(124)] × 100, or approximately 5.6%.

STEP 3: Compute the labor force participation rate for the entire economy and then compute the labor force participation rate for men and the labor force participation rate for women.

Review the section "The Unemployment Rate" on pages 348–354.

Recall that the labor force participation rate = [(labor force)/(population)] × 100. From the table, we know both the labor force and the population: the labor force participation rate is [(310)/(400)] × 100, or approximately 77.5%.

To find the labor force participation rate for men, you will need to know how many men there are in the labor force and how many men there are in the population. This information is in the table you created in Step 1. The labor force participation rate for men = [(number of men in the labor force)/(number of men in the population)] × 100. The labor force participation rate for men is [(186)/(192)] × 100, or approximately 97%.

To find the labor force participation rate for women, you will need to know how many women there are in the labor force and how many women there are in the population. This information is in the table you created in Step 1. The labor force participation rate for women = [(number of women in the labor force)/(number of women in the population)] × 100. The labor force participation rate for women is [(124)/(208)] × 100, or approximately 60%.

4.   Answer the following set of questions using this CPI information for an economy.

Year	CPI with base year 2005
2008	100
2009	105
2010	110
2011	115

a. Joe's nominal income in 2009 is $100,000. What must his nominal income be in 2011 in order for his real income to be unchanged?

STEP 1: **Examine the given data and determine what the base year is from the information that you are given.**

Review the section "Inflation and Deflation" on pages 362–368. (Hint: You may find it helpful to return to Chapter 11 and review the sections on the consumer price index in that chapter.)

Examination of the data indicates that 2008 is the base year, since the value of the consumer price index in the base year is always equal to 100.

STEP 2: **Now calculate the rate of inflation between each year.**

Review the section "Inflation and Deflation" on pages 362–368.

The rate of inflation can be calculated from the CPI numbers that you are given. Thus, the rate of inflation between 2008 and 2009 is equal to {[(price index for 2009) − (price index for 2008)]/(price index for 2008)} × 100, or 5%. The rate of inflation for the other years can similarly be calculated. The following table provides the inflation rates.

Year	CPI with base year 2005	Rate of yearly inflation
2008	100	
2009	105	5%
2010	110	4.76%
2011	115	4.55%

STEP 3: **Calculate how much Joe's nominal income needs to change each year in order for him to have the same real purchasing power that he did in 2009.**

Review the section "Inflation and Deflation" on pages 362–368.

If Joe earns $100,000 in 2009, then he will need to earn $100,000(1.0476) in 2010 to maintain the same purchasing power. Thus, in 2010, he needs to earn $104,760. If he earns $104,760 in 2010, then he will need to earn $104,760(1.0455) in 2011 to maintain the same purchasing power. Thus, in 2011, he needs to earn $109,526.

STEP 4: **Here's an alternative method for figuring out what nominal income Joe must earn in 2011 in order to maintain the same purchasing power that he had in 2009.**

Review the section "Inflation and Deflation" on pages 362–368. (Hint: You might find it helpful to review the section on the GDP deflator in Chapter 11.)

Use the following formula to calculate what nominal income Joe must receive in 2011 in order to have the same purchasing power as he had in 2009: the real value of the variable = [(nominal value of the variable)/(price index)] × 100. In this example, the price index is the CPI. So, in 2009, the nominal value of Joe's income is $100,000 and the CPI is 105. We can find the real value of this income for Joe measured in the base year in 2008 dollars as follows: the real value of Joe's income measured in 2008 dollars = [($100,000)/(105)] × 100, or $95,238.

In 2011, Joe wants his real income to have the same purchasing power that he had in 2009. From our calculation, we know that this real income measured in 2008 dollars was equal to $95,238. So, let's use this information and our CPI information to solve for the nominal income Joe must get in 2011 in order to have the same command over goods and services. Thus, (real income in 2008 measured in 2008 dollars) = [(nominal income in 2011)/(CPI for 2011)] × 100, or $95,238 = [(nominal income in 2011)/(115)] × 100. Solving this equation, we get that Joe's nominal income in 2011 must equal $109,524. If you compare this nominal income with the nominal income you found in Step 3, you will see that they are very close to each other: the difference is due to rounding error.

b. Mike borrows $1,000 in 2008 and repays this loan in 2009. Mike pays the lender $1,060 in 2009. What is the real value of this payment in 2009 using 2008 as the base year? What nominal interest rate is Mike paying for this loan? What real interest rate is Mike paying for the loan?

STEP 1: Start by calculating the nominal interest rate that Mike is paying for the loan.

Review the section "Inflation and Deflation" on pages 362–368.

The nominal interest rate refers to the payment that a borrower makes in excess of the amount of the loan or principal that he or she borrowed. In this example, Mike borrowed $1,000, so he needs to repay this loan amount, or the principal amount. He also needs to compensate his lender for the use of the lender's money. So, when Mike pays the lender $1,060 a year after the loan, he is in effect making two payments: a payment of $1,000 representing the amount he borrowed, and a payment of $60 that represents the interest payment he is making. To find the nominal interest rate, you need to calculate what percentage of the loan amount the interest payment is: thus, the nominal interest rate is equal to [(the amount of money paid back – the principal)/(the principal)] × 100. The nominal interest rate is therefore equal to [(1,060 – 1,000)/1,000] × 100, or 6%.

STEP 2: Calculate what the real value of Mike's payment of $1,060 is, given the information you have about the CPI.

Review the section "Inflation and Deflation" on pages 362–368.

Mike's payment of $1,060 is a nominal payment. To convert this payment to a real payment, you need to use the following formula: real payment = [(nominal payment)/(CPI)] × 100. Or, real payment = ($1,060/105) × 100 = $1,009.52.

STEP 3: Calculate the real interest rate that Mike is paying for the loan.

Review the section "Inflation and Deflation" on pages 362–368.

The real interest rate is equal to [(the real payment made – the principal)/(the principal)] × 100. In this example, the real interest rate is equal to [(1,009.52 – 1,000)/1,000] × 100, or 0.952%. Alternatively, we can approximate the real interest rate by recalling that the real interest rate is equal to the nominal interest rate minus the rate of inflation. In this case, the rate of inflation is 5%, the nominal interest rate is 6%, and therefore the real interest rate is 1%. If you compare these two answers, you see that the approximation method provides a good estimate of the real interest rate.

Problems and Exercises

1. Use the following graph to answer this question.

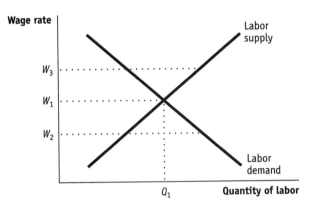

a. What is the equilibrium wage and quantity of labor in this labor market?

b. At the equilibrium wage rate, what is the structural unemployment rate? Explain your answer.   *0*

c. If the structural unemployment rate is a positive number, what do you know must be true about the current wage in this labor market? Explain your answer.
    It is not at eqbrm

d. Suppose the government passes minimum wage legislation setting the minimum wage at W_2, where W_2 is less than W_1. Explain the effect of this legislation on this labor market.
    No effet

e. Suppose the government passes minimum wage legislation setting the minimum wage at W_3, where W_3 is greater than W_1. Explain the effect of this legislation on this labor market.

2. Economists believe that the natural rate of unemployment is greater than zero. Assuming structural unemployment and cyclical unemployment are both zero, how do you explain this insistence that the natural rate of unemployment must still be a positive number? Explain your answer fully.

3. The text considers the effect of minimum wage legislation and union power on the workings of the labor market. Compare and contrast the effects of minimum wage legislation and union power on the labor market, noting how they are similar in their impact on the labor market as well as how they differ in their impact on that market.

4. Suppose there are 12,000 people living in Macroland. Of these 12,000 people, 1,000 are either too old to work or too young to work. Of the remaining individuals, 5,000 are employed with full-time jobs; 3,000 are employed part-time, but wish to work full time; 1,000 are underemployed, but working full-time jobs; 1,000 are currently not working, but are looking for work; and the remainder are discouraged workers.

   a. What is the size of the labor force in Macroland?

   b. What is the employment rate in Macroland?

   c. What is the unemployment rate in Macroland?

d. What percentage of the population are discouraged workers?

e. Suppose you are told that 100 people find jobs for every $10,000 increase in the level of aggregate output in Macroland. If you wanted the unemployment rate to equal 8%, what would the change in output need to be? Assume no changes in the number of young and old in the population or in the number of discouraged workers.

f. Suppose the government department in Macroland responsible for compiling unemployment statistics redefines the employed as including only those with full-time jobs. How does this change the unemployment rate, given the initial information?

5. Suppose that there are 10,000 adults in Finlandia and that 5,000 of these adults are employed, 2,000 are unemployed, 500 are discouraged workers, and the rest are not currently working and/or not seeking employment.

   a. What is the labor force equal to in Finlandia?

   50%

   b. What is the unemployment rate in Finlandia?

   20%

   c. What would the unemployment rate equal in Finlandia if discouraged workers were counted as unemployed workers?

   25%

   d. Currently the Bureau of Labor Statistics does not count discouraged workers as unemployed workers. How does this decision affect the calculated value of the unemployment rate? *It lowers the rate, in this case by 5%.*

e. Suppose that for every $10,000 increase in GDP in Finlandia, unemployment decreases by 100 people. If GDP increases by $20,000, what will Finlandia's unemployment rate equal? Assume there is no change in the number of discouraged workers and that discouraged workers are not counted as unemployed workers.

$$2000 \quad -200 = \frac{1800}{10,000} = 18\%$$

f. What is the relationship between GDP and unemployment?

6. Macroland decides to join the Central Union, which is a group of countries that have negotiated a trade zone. All members of the Central Union must adopt the CU dollar, the currency of the Central Union. Currently a Macroland dollar purchases 3 CU dollars.

a. Suppose you live in Macroland and have lent someone 50,000 Macroland dollars. Once Macroland joins the Central Union, how many CU dollars is your loan worth? Has the value of your loan changed with the change from Macroland dollars to CU dollars?

b. You have agreed to lend a friend of yours 10,000 Macroland dollars. Once Macroland joins the Central Union, how many CU dollars will your friend owe you?

c. When you made the loan described in part (b), you negotiated that you would be paid 10% of the value of the loan this year as compensation for the use of your funds. If this payment is made in Macroland dollars, how many Macroland dollars will you receive? If this payment is made in CU dollars, how many CU dollars will you receive? Are you better off being paid in Macroland dollars or CU dollars? Explain your answer.

7. Sarah currently works for a firm in which her union has negotiated a cost-of-living adjustment that automatically adjusts her income to whatever the annual rate of inflation is for her community. Bob works for a firm that routinely grants its employees a 5% annual income increase. Milt is retired and receives two payments: a pension payment from his former employer that is fixed at $2,000 per month and a government-provided retirement payment whose real value is equal to $1,000 per month in the base year. The government-provided retirement payment is indexed to the inflation rate in the community.

   a. Suppose the rate of inflation is 8% this year. Describe the effect of this inflation rate on Sarah, Bob, and Milt in terms of their real purchasing power. Who is left in worse shape with this inflation? Does anyone end up better off despite this inflation rate? Explain your answer.

   Bob - ~~good~~ ~~more~~ not good b/c 5% doesn't keep up w/ 8%
   Milt - bad - his income is fixed, so increase in costs don't affect income
   Sarah - doesn't change b/c adjusted for inflation

   b. Suppose the rate of inflation is 20% this year. Describe the effect of this inflation rate on Sarah, Bob, and Milt.

▌ BEFORE YOU TAKE THE TEST

Chapter Review Questions

1. Which of the following statements is true?
   a. The natural rate of unemployment equals a country's unemployment rate during a recession.
   b. The natural rate of unemployment equals a country's unemployment rate during an expansion.
   c. The natural rate of unemployment is the sum of frictional and structural unemployment.
   d. The natural rate of unemployment is the sum of frictional and cyclical unemployment.

2. Job creation and job destruction are
   a. a natural occurrence in a labor market.
   b. only a problem during an economic expansion.
   c. a primary reason for why there is unemployment even when the economy is at full employment.
   d. Answers (a), (b), and (c) are all correct.
   e. Answers (a) and (c) are both correct.

3. Which of the following statements is true?
   a. Even small amounts of structural unemployment are harmful to an economy.
   b. There is always frictional unemployment since there are always new workers entering the job market.
   c. Even small amounts of frictional unemployment are harmful to an economy.
   d. Answers (a), (b), and (c) are all correct.
   e. Answers (a) and (b) are both correct.
   f. Answers (b) and (c) are both correct.

4. Which of the following statements is true?
   a. Structural unemployment refers to the unemployment that occurs when there are more employers demanding labor than there are employees supplying labor.
   b. Structural unemployment refers to a situation when the market wage rate is lower than the equilibrium wage rate.
   c. Structural unemployment occurs when there is a surplus of labor at the current wage rate.
   d. When there is structural unemployment, frictional unemployment equals zero.

5. In order to be binding, a minimum wage must be
   a. equal to or less than the equilibrium wage rate.
   b. greater than the equilibrium wage rate.
   c. set so that there is a persistent surplus in the labor market.
   d. set so that there is a persistent shortage in the labor market.
   e. Answers (a) and (d) are both correct.
   f. Answers (b) and (c) are both correct.

6. Which of the following statements is true?
   a. Strong labor unions and an effective minimum wage reduce the level of structural unemployment in an economy.
   b. Strong labor unions and an effective minimum wage benefit all workers equally.
   c. Workers acting collectively through a union may find that they have more power than if they act individually.
   d. Answers (a), (b), and (c) are all correct.
   e. Answers (b) and (c) are both correct.

7. Efficiency wages
   a. are wages negotiated by unions.
   b. are always less than the minimum wage.
   c. are wages paid by employers that exceed the equilibrium wage rate and that are offered as an incentive for better performance.
   d. are a means for employers to retain employees while providing incentives for greater work effort.
   e. Answers (b), (c), and (d) are all correct.
   f. Answers (c) and (d) are both correct.

8. The natural rate of unemployment is
   a. equal to 0% in every economy, since this is the level of unemployment that every economy should naturally want to achieve.
   b. the sum of frictional and cyclical unemployment.
   c. equal to cyclical unemployment when the economy is producing at the full employment level of aggregate output.
   d. Answers (b) and (c) are correct.
   e. None of the answers is correct.

9. The natural rate of unemployment
   a. is constant and does not change over time.
   b. changes when there are changes in labor force characteristics.
   c. may change due to changes in labor market institutions like unions, temporary employment agencies, and technological change.
   d. increases with increases in the minimum wage level.
   e. Answers (a), (b), (c), and (d) are all correct.
   f. Answers (b), (c), and (d) are correct.
   g. Answers (b) and (d) are both correct.

10. Which of the following statements is true?
   a. Most contracts that extend over a period of time are expressed in real terms so that borrowers and lenders can fully understand the consequences of their economic agreement.
   b. The nominal interest rate is equal to the real interest rate minus the inflation rate.
   c. When the actual inflation rate equals the anticipated inflation rate, borrowers are better off.
   d. Anticipated inflation can inflict real costs on the economy.

11. Mary expects the inflation rate to be 5%, and she is willing to pay a real interest rate of 3%. Joe expects the inflation rate to be 5%, and he is willing to lend money if he receives a real interest rate of 3%. If the actual inflation rate is 6% and the loan contract specifies a nominal interest rate of 8%, then
   a. Joe is glad he lent out funds even though his real interest rate has fallen.
   b. Joe is sorry he lent out funds since his real interest rate is now 9%.
   c. Mary is glad she borrowed the funds because her real interest rate has fallen.
   d. Mary is sorry she borrowed funds since her real interest rate is now 9%.

12. Disinflation in an economy, which has grown to expect inflation, is
   a. easy to achieve and does not affect actual output.
   b. difficult to accomplish and invariably results in an increase in the natural rate of unemployment.
   c. possible only if policy makers are willing to accept higher rates of unemployment and a lower level of aggregate output.
   d. Answers (a) and (c) are both correct.
   e. Answers (b) and (c) are both correct.

13. In a period of unexpected deflation,

a. borrowers find that it is easier for them to make their loan payments, since prices are falling.

b. lenders benefit, since there are more people eager to borrow money during a period of deflation.

c. lenders benefit, since they are repaid dollars with greater real value than they anticipated when signing the loan contract.

d. Answers (a), (b), and (c) are all correct.

Use the following information to answer the next two questions.

Suppose the adult population of Macronesia is 100,000 people. Of these 100,000 people, 20,000 are not in the labor force. Of the remaining 80,000 people, 16,000 have given up searching for a job and are not actively seeking work; 4,000 are unemployed and actively seeking work; 14,000 work part-time; and the remainder are fully employed.

14. What is the unemployment rate in Macronesia?

a. 5%

b. 6.25%

c. 8.5%

d. 10%

15. What would happen to Macronesia's unemployment rate, relative to your answer in the last question, if discouraged workers were counted as unemployed workers?

a. The unemployment rate would be unchanged.

b. The unemployment rate would decrease.

c. The unemployment rate would increase.

d. The unemployment rate could increase, decrease, or remain the same.

16. Which of the following statements is true?

I. The two principal goals of macroeconomic policy are price stability and low frictional unemployment.

II. The primary goals of macroeconomic policy are price stability and low unemployment.

III. In order to achieve the two primary goals of macroeconomic policy of price stability and low unemployment, it is necessary for policy makers to reduce the level of frictional unemployment.

a. Statements I, II, and III are all true.

b. Statements I and II are true.

c. Statements II and III are true.

d. Statement I is true.

e. Statement II is true.

f. Statement III is true.

Answer the next three questions based on the following information about a small economy.

An economy is composed of five people: George, Sarah, Mason, Abbot, and Jin. George works for Plastics, Inc., 40 hours a week. Sarah works for Baker's United for 20 hours a week and would like to move from part-time work to full-time work. Mason has been looking for work for the past six months after he finished completing his high school education. Abbot worked for Baker's United for the first six months of the year before he was fired; for the next four months Abbot sought work, but finally gave up looking for work when he realized that it was unlikely he would be able to find work in this economy. Jin is 70 years old and enjoys reading, needlepoint, and watching movies.

17. In this economy, the employed include
   a. George, Sarah, and Mason.
   b. George and Sarah.
   c. George since he is the only person in this economy who is fully employed.
   d. George, Sarah, Mason, and Jin. (Jin is fully employed with a variety of activities that occupy all her waking moments.)

18. What is the labor force participation rate in this economy?
   a. 40%
   b. 60%
   c. 80%
   d. 100%

19. What is the unemployment rate in this economy?
   a. 20%
   b. 33%
   c. 40%
   d. 50%

20. Which of the following statements is true?
   I. To be considered unemployed, one must simply not have a job.
   II. To be considered unemployed, one must not have a job and must also not be looking for a job.
   III. To be considered unemployed, one must not have a job and must also be looking for a job.
   a. Statement I is true.
   b. Statement II is true.
   c. Statement III is true.
   d. Statements I, II, and III are all false.

21. When the unemployment rate is high, this usually implies that it is
   a. easy to find a job.
   b. difficult to find a job.

22. The Bureau of Labor Statistics' treatment of discouraged workers results in the unemployment rate
   a. overstating the true level of unemployment.
   b. understating the true level of unemployment.

23. Underemployed workers, those workers currently working part-time jobs but wishing to work full-time jobs, are

a. not included in the calculation of the employment rate.

b. included in the calculation of the employment rate.

24. Different age groups and different ethnic groups in the economy typically experience

a. the same unemployment rate.

b. different unemployment rates.

25. During an economic expansion, the unemployment rate typically

a. increases.

b. decreases.

26. Historically the relationship between the change in unemployment and the annual growth rate of real GDP is a

a. positive relationship.

b. negative relationship.

27. Job search refers to the time that workers spend looking for employment. Job search results in

a. cyclical unemployment.

b. structural unemployment.

c. frictional unemployment.

d. both structural and frictional unemployment.

28. Suppose the demand for labor is given by the equation $W = 15 - (1/200)L$ and the supply of labor is given by the equation $W = 5 + (1/200)L$, where W is the wage rate and L is the quantity of labor. What is the equilibrium wage and quantity of labor in this market?

a. The equilibrium wage is \$15 while the equilibrium quantity of labor is 200 workers.

b. The equilibrium wage is \$5 while the equilibrium quantity of labor is 100 workers.

c. The equilibrium wage is \$10 while the equilibrium quantity of labor is 1,000 workers.

d. The equilibrium wage is \$10 while the equilibrium quantity of labor is 200 workers.

29. Suppose the demand for labor is given by the equation $W = 15 - (1/200)L$ and the supply of labor is given by the equation $W = 5 + (1/200)L$, where W is the wage rate and L is the quantity of labor. Suppose the government imposes a minimum wage of \$12 in this market. What will be the effect of this minimum wage in this market?

a. The minimum wage will not be binding since it is set below the equilibrium wage.

b. The minimum wage will create a situation of excess demand for labor since it is a binding minimum wage.

c. The minimum wage will create a situation of excess supply of labor since it is a binding minimum wage.

d. This minimum wage will benefit all workers in this labor market.

30. Binding minimum wages generally lead to

a. cyclical unemployment, since not everyone can find a job at the minimum wage rate.

b. frictional unemployment, since the binding minimum wage results in longer job search.

c. structural unemployment, since more people want to work than can find jobs at the minimum wage.

d. Answers (a), (b), and (c) are all correct.

31. Which of the following statements is true?

    I. An employer can encourage its workers to work hard by paying an efficiency wage.

    II. An efficiency wage is equal to the market wage rate.

    III. When many firms pay efficiency wages, this creates structural unemployment.

  a. Statement I is true.

  b. Statement II is true.

  c. Statement III is true.

  d. Statements I and II are true.

  e. Statements II and III are true.

  f. Statements I and III are true.

  g. Statements I, II, and III are all true.

32. Utopia has recently experienced a high rate of inflation and proposes changing its currency from the Utopian dollar to the Utopian mark at an exchange rate of 5.0 Utopian dollars per Utopian mark. Suppose Joe currently has a debt of 100,000 Utopian dollars. Which of the following statements is true?

  a. The switch to Utopian marks will make Joe better off since the Utopian mark is replacing the Utopian dollar, whose purchasing power has fallen due to the presence of inflation in Utopia.

  b. The switch to Utopian marks will reduce the real value of Joe's debt.

  c. Joe's debt will now equal 20,000 Utopian marks.

  d. Joe's debt will now equal 500,000 Utopian marks.

33. The extra time and effort expended to make transactions during times of high rates of inflation impose

  a. shoe-leather costs.

  b. menu costs.

  c. unit-of-account costs.

ANSWER KEY

Answers to Problems and Exercises

1. **a.** The equilibrium wage rate is W_1 and the equilibrium quantity of labor is Q_1, where the quantity of labor supplied is equal to the quantity of labor demanded.

   b. At the equilibrium wage rate, the structural unemployment rate equals zero since the number of people seeking jobs in the labor market equals the number of jobs available at that equilibrium, or current, wage rate.

   c. If the structural unemployment rate is a positive number, then the wage rate must be greater than the equilibrium wage rate and the quantity supplied of labor must exceed the quantity demanded for labor, resulting in a surplus of labor.

   d. For a minimum wage to have any impact on the market, it must be set above the equilibrium wage rate. The minimum wage rate is just a specific example of a price floor, and price floors only impact markets when they are set above the equilibrium price.

   e. When the government sets the minimum wage above the equilibrium wage rate, it affects the market by preventing the wage rate from adjusting to that point where the quantity demanded of labor equals the quantity supplied of labor. Thus, an effective minimum wage will create a surplus of labor and, hence, a positive structural unemployment rate.

2. Even when the economy produces at its potential output and the unemployment rate equals the natural rate, there will be people entering the job market as well as workers moving between jobs. This frictional unemployment is a natural part of the working of the labor market; hence, even when the economy is at its natural rate of unemployment, there will still be positive frictional unemployment.

3. Labor unions and effective minimum wage legislation both affect the labor market by working to raise the current wage above the equilibrium wage rate and by creating barriers to prevent the wage from adjusting back to the equilibrium level. Both labor unions and minimum wage legislation have the potential to create structural unemployment through their ability to create a situation where the quantity supplied of labor is greater than the quantity demanded of labor. Labor unions, through collective bargaining, often result in workers securing higher wages than the market would have provided if workers bargained individually. Labor unions often negotiate for long-term contracts, and these contracts may lead to structural unemployment due to the wage rigidity they introduce into the labor market.

4. **a.** The labor force is defined as the number of employed workers plus the number of unemployed workers. The number of employed workers equals the sum of full-time workers, part-time workers, and underemployed workers, or, in this example, 9,000 workers. The number of unemployed workers is equal to the 1,000 workers who are currently not working, but who are actively looking for work. Thus, the labor force equals 10,000 workers.

   b. Employment rate = [employed/labor force] × 100 = (9,000/1,000) × 100 = 90%

   c. Unemployment rate = [unemployed/labor force] × 100 = (1,000/10,000) × 100 = 10%

   d. Percentage of discouraged workers in population = [(discouraged workers)/population] × 100 = (1,000/12,000) × 100 = 8.33%

   e. The current unemployment rate is 10%. To reduce the unemployment rate to 8% requires that 200 of the currently unemployed workers find jobs. If output increases by $10,000 for every 100 people who find jobs, then output must increase by $20,000 for 200 people to find employment.

    f. Using the new definition of employment, the number of employed now equals 6,000, and the unemployed would increase by 3,000 for a total of 4,000 unemployed. This change in definition results in a much higher unemployment rate (40%) and a much lower employment rate (60%). The definitions underlying calculations do matter.

5. **a.** The labor force is equal to the sum of employed plus unemployed workers. In this case, the labor force is equal to 5,000 + 2,000, or 7,000.

    b. To find the unemployment rate, use the formula: Unemployment rate = (unemployed/ labor force) × 100. In this case, the unemployment rate equals (2,000/7,000) × 100, or 28.57%.

    c. If discouraged workers were counted as unemployed workers, the formula for calculating the unemployment rate would change to: Unemployment rate = [(unemployed + discouraged workers)/(labor force)] × 100. The unemployment rate would equal (2,500/7,000) × 100, or 33%.

    d. The decision by the Bureau of Labor Statistics to exclude discouraged workers from the calculation of the unemployment rate results in an understatement of the unemployment rate in the economy.

    e. Since GDP increases by $20,000, we know that unemployment decreases by 200 people (2,000 − 200 = 1,800). Thus, the unemployment rate is now equal to (1,800/ 7,000) × 100, or 25.71%.

    f. As GDP increases, unemployment decreases.

6. **a.** With the change to CU dollars, your loan will now be valued at 150,000 CU dollars. But, since 3 CU dollars trade for 1 Macroland dollar, the value of the loan has not changed with the switch to the new currency.

    b. As in part (a), the change to CU dollars will make your loan value three times larger: your loan value will be 30,000 CU dollars. But, since 3 CU dollars trade for 1 Macroland dollar, the value of the loan has not changed with the switch to the new currency.

    c. When the loan is 10,000 Macroland dollars, the interest payment the first year is equal to (0.1)(10,000 Macroland dollars) or 1,000 Macroland dollars. When the loan is denominated in CU dollars, the interest payment the first year is equal to (0.1)(30,000 CU dollars) or 3,000 CU dollars, which has the same value as 1,000 Macroland dollars when 1 Macroland dollar is exchanged for 3 CU dollars. The two payments are equivalent: the switch to the new currency does not change the value of the interest payment or the loan value.

7. **a.** With an inflation rate of 8% for the year, Sarah finds that her income is automatically adjusted upward by that 8%: Sarah's real income has not changed since prices rose by 8%, the same as her income. Bob's income will rise by 5% even though the inflation rate was 8%: Bob is worse off since his nominal income rose, but by an amount smaller than the amount needed to stay even with the inflation rate. Bob has less purchasing power than he did initially. Milt's situation is complicated: his pension from his former employer is fixed and does not adjust with the inflation rate: this implies that Milt will now have less purchasing power from his fixed pension of $2,000 per month than he did initially. Milt's government-provided retirement payment maintains its real value since it is adjusted with changes in the rate of inflation. Overall, Milt has less purchasing power than he did initially. No one in this example ends up better off despite this inflation rate.

    b. Again, Sarah's purchasing power is not affected since her nominal income is adjusted each year based on the rate of inflation. Bob is much worse off this year, since the overall price level rose 20% while his nominal income only rose 5%. Milt's fixed pension sees an even bigger erosion in its purchasing power than in part (a), while his government-provided retirement payment maintains its real value.

Answers to Chapter Review Questions

1. **Answer c.** The natural unemployment rate is defined as the sum of frictional and structural unemployment. It is the unemployment rate that occurs when there is no cyclical unemployment, which is the unemployment directly tied to economic business cycles.

2. **Answer e.** Job creation and job destruction naturally occur in an economy, and it is this natural process that leads to economies always having some unemployment even if the economy is producing at full employment. We can think about how there are always people in the economy who are entering the labor force and looking for work, and there are always people whose jobs are ending and are in need of finding new work. This process occurs during both economic expansions and recessions.

3. **Answer b.** All economies will experience some frictional and structural unemployment as a natural functioning of their labor market. Frictional unemployment occurs because of job creation and job destruction, and because there are always new workers entering the job market. Frictional unemployment can be beneficial to an economy, since the economy may be more productive if workers take the time to find jobs that are well matched to their skills. Structural unemployment occurs because of such factors as minimum wages, unions, efficiency wages, and government policies that are designed to help laid-off workers.

4. **Answer c.** Structural unemployment occurs when there is an excess supply of labor in a labor market. This occurs when the wage rate is greater than the equilibrium wage rate in the market. Every economy has frictional unemployment due to job creation and job destruction as well as the entry of new workers into the economy.

5. **Answer f.** To be effective and therefore binding, a minimum wage must be set at a level in excess of the equilibrium wage rate. This will result in the quantity supplied of labor exceeding the quantity demanded for labor and thus a surplus of labor.

6. **Answer c.** Strong labor unions and an effective minimum wage act to increase the level of structural unemployment in an economy, since they both tend to create a surplus of labor in the labor market. It is true, though, that workers acting collectively may possess greater negotiating power in an industry than would those workers acting individually. Strong unions and an effective minimum wage benefit those people who continue to work, but hurt those who become unemployed when the wage rate rises above the equilibrium wage rate in the labor market.

7. **Answer f.** Efficiency wages are those paid by employers in excess of the equilibrium wage rate. They are offered to improve employee work effort while also providing an incentive for workers to stay with their current employer. Efficiency wages may be equal to or greater than the minimum wage.

8. **Answer e.** The natural rate of unemployment is equal to the sum of the frictional unemployment rate plus structural unemployment. It will always be greater than zero, since there will always be new workers entering the job market and workers moving from one job to another. The cyclical unemployment rate is equal to zero when the economy produces at the full employment level of aggregate output, but at this level of output there is still frictional unemployment.

9. **Answer f.** The natural rate of unemployment is affected by changes in labor force characteristics and by changes in labor market institutions. In addition, the natural rate of unemployment will increase whenever the government mandates more generous benefits for workers (for example, an increase in the minimum wage rate).

10. **Answer d.** Most contracts that extend over time are expressed in nominal terms and not real terms. The nominal interest rate equals the real interest rate plus the inflation rate. When the actual inflation rate equals the anticipated inflation rate, the inflation rate does not create winners or losers in loan contracts, since both parties to the contract

have used accurate expectations of inflation to anticipate the inflation rate, and they have both agreed to the real rate they actually receive when the contract is honored. Anticipated inflation diverts resources from productive uses to less productive uses: resources are used to avoid the inflation tax.

11. **Answer c.** Both Mary and Joe would like to negotiate a contract where the real interest rate is 3%, and they both anticipate the expected inflation rate will be 5%. Thus, the nominal rate in the contract will equal the desired real rate of interest plus the expected inflation rate, or 8%. When the actual rate of inflation is 6%, this means that the dollars paid back have less purchasing power than anticipated: Mary will find this beneficial to her as the borrower, while Joe will find this hurts him since the dollars he receives in payment for the loan have less purchasing power than the dollars he loaned out.

12. **Answer c.** Disinflation in an economy where inflationary expectations are embedded is possible only if policy makers are willing to push the economy into a recession and thereby reduce inflationary expectations. This will necessarily result in an increase in the unemployment rate and a decrease in the level of aggregate output the economy produces. This policy does not affect the natural rate of unemployment.

13. **Answer c.** In a period of unexpected deflation, borrowers will find that the real value of the loan payments they make have risen in value, so borrowers will be hurt by the unexpected deflation. Lenders will benefit because the loan payments they receive will have greater real value due to the deflation. Borrowers, due to the increased economic burden of their debt, will typically reduce their overall spending and will choose, therefore, to borrow less during a period of deflation.

14. **Answer b.** Calculate the unemployment rate using this formula: Unemployment rate = [(number of unemployed)/(labor force)] × 100, where the labor force is equal to the number of employed workers plus the number of unemployed workers. In this case, the unemployment rate = [(4,000)/(64,000)] × 100 = 6.25%. Note that the labor force does not include discouraged workers (16,000) or the 20,000 people who are not currently in the labor force.

15. **Answer c.** The unemployment rate now equals [(20,000)/(80,000)] × 100, or 25%. The unemployment rate increases when discouraged workers are counted as unemployed workers.

16. **Answer e.** The two primary macroeconomic policy goals are low unemployment and price stability. In order to achieve low unemployment, the economy must produce at or near its potential output level: low unemployment necessitates reducing the level of cyclical unemployment. Economies always have some amount of frictional unemployment and although policy makers can adopt policies that will lower the level of frictional unemployment, they cannot eliminate it.

17. **Answer b.** To be considered employed, an individual must have a part-time or full-time job. Only George and Sarah satisfy this requirement in the described economy.

18. **Answer b.** The labor force participation rate is equal to the product of 100 times the sum of the employed plus the unemployed divided by the population over 16 years of age. In this example, the employed is equal to 2 (George and Sarah), the unemployed is equal to 1 (Mason), and the population over 16 years of age is equal to 5. Thus, (3/5) × 100 = 60%.

19. **Answer b.** The unemployment rate is equal to the product of 100 times the number of unemployed divided by the labor force. There is one unemployed person (Mason) and two employed people (George and Sarah); therefore, the labor force is equal to 3 while the number of unemployed is equal to 1. The unemployment rate equals (1/3) × 100 or 33%.

20. **Answer c.** To be considered unemployed, a person must not have a job and must, in addition, be actively seeking a job. For example, the retired neither have jobs nor are they seeking employment: they are not part of the unemployed and they are not part of the labor

force, since they do not intend to work. The discouraged worker, although not working, is not considered unemployed, since he or she has given up looking for a job.

21. **Answer b.** The unemployment rate is a good indicator of how easy or difficult it is to find a job in the economy. When the economy's unemployment rate is high, this implies that many people are out of work and it will therefore be difficult to find employment. When the economy's unemployment rate is low, this implies that it will be relatively easy to find a job.

22. **Answer b.** Currently the Bureau of Labor Statistics does not include discouraged workers in the number of unemployed even though these workers are currently not working. This exclusion results in a lower rate of unemployment than would be the case if these discouraged workers were included in the number of unemployed.

23. **Answer b.** Underemployed workers are included in the number of employed workers even though these workers would like to attain full-time employment.

24. **Answer b.** Unemployment rates in an economy vary widely depending upon the age group and ethnic group; for example, teenagers have much higher rates of unemployment than do adults between the ages of 25 and 54, while African Americans experience higher unemployment rates than the national average.

25. **Answer b.** When the economy is in an economic expansion, the unemployment rate usually falls as an increase in the level of aggregate output usually requires an increase in the level of aggregate employment in the economy.

26. **Answer b.** If the relationship between the change in unemployment and the annual growth rate of real GDP is graphed as a scatter diagram, these points indicate a negative relationship between these two measures.

27. **Answer c.** Frictional unemployment is unemployment due to the time workers spend in job search. Structural unemployment is the unemployment due to the number of people seeking work exceeding the number of available jobs at the current wage rate. Cyclical unemployment is unemployment due to economic recession; cyclical unemployment is a result of business cycle fluctuations.

28. **Answer c.** To find the equilibrium quantity of labor, set the demand equation equal to the supply equation and solve for L. L will equal 1,000 workers. Using either the demand equation or the supply equation, substitute 1,000 into the equation for L and then solve for W: the equilibrium wage will equal $10.

29. **Answer c.** To find out if $12 is a binding minimum wage requires first solving for the equilibrium wage in this market. From the previous question we know that the equilibrium wage is equal to $10, so $12 is a binding minimum wage. A binding minimum wage will create a situation of excess labor supply, since the wage is artificially raised above that level where the quantity demanded of labor equals the quantity supplied of labor. The minimum wage, when binding, does not benefit all workers since some workers would like to work at this higher minimum wage but cannot find jobs.

30. **Answer c.** A binding minimum wage results in the quantity supplied of labor exceeding the quantity demanded of labor; thus, more people want to work at the minimum wage rate than can find jobs. Thus, the binding minimum wage results in structural unemployment.

31. **Answer f.** An efficiency wage is one that is greater than the equilibrium wage rate in the labor market. A firm will pay an efficiency wage for a variety of reasons, including the hope that a wage exceeding the equilibrium wage rate will encourage its employees to put forth greater work effort, since the workers do not want to risk losing their relatively high paying jobs. Payment of an efficiency wage results in excess supply of labor and, therefore, structural unemployment.

32. **Answer c.** To find Joe's debt measured in Utopian marks, multiply Joe's debt in Utopian dollars times the ratio (1 Utopian mark)/(5 Utopian dollars) or (100,000 Utopian dollars)(1 Utopian mark)/(5 Utopian dollars) to get 20,000 Utopian marks. Joe is not better off, since he is only changing the unit of measurement of his debt but not his real debt level.

33. **Answer a.** The transactions costs associated with high rates of inflation are referred to as shoe-leather costs. Menu costs refer to the cost associated with printing new menu and price lists due to the presence of inflation. Unit-of-account costs refer to the costs inflation imposes because of its effects on contracts that are stated in monetary, instead of real, terms.

chapter 13

Long-Run Economic Growth

BEFORE YOU READ THE CHAPTER

Summary

This chapter focuses on long-run economic growth and its sources. Long-run economic growth can be measured as the change in real GDP per capita over time. Comparison of real GDP per capita for different countries reveals different economic growth experiences: some countries have experienced rapid economic growth over time, while other countries have been much less fortunate. Long-run economic growth depends on productivity, which depends on physical capital, human capital, and technological progress. This chapter also discusses the convergence hypothesis: this theory states that relatively poor countries should have higher rates of growth of real GDP per capita than relatively rich countries. The chapter also discusses sustainability and the challenges to economic growth arising from natural resource scarcity and environmental damage.

Chapter Objectives

Objective #1.   Real GDP per capita provides a measure of economic growth. This measure calculates the value in constant dollars of final goods and services produced in an economy in a given time period divided by the population of that economy.

Objective #2.   When computing how long it takes real GDP per capita, or any other variable that grows slowly over time, to double, the rule of ⟨70⟩ is useful. This rule states that the number of years it takes a variable to double is approximately equal to 70 divided by the annual growth rate of the variable.

rule of 70

$$\# \text{ years} = \frac{70}{\text{annual growth rate}}$$

Objective #3.   Long-run economic growth depends almost exclusively on increases in output per worker, or <u>labor productivity.</u> For the aggregate economy, we can measure labor productivity as real GDP divided by the number of people working. Increases in labor productivity are due to increases in physical capital, human capital, or changes in technology.

- Physical capital refers to man-made resources such as buildings and machines.

- Human capital refers to the improvement in labor created by education and knowledge.

- Technology refers to the technical means of producing goods and services.

Objective #4.   The aggregate production function is a mathematical equation describing the relationship between the level of output per worker (productivity) and the amount of human capital per worker, physical capital per worker, and the state of technology. The aggregate production function exhibits diminishing returns to physical capital: holding the level of human capital per worker and the state of technology constant, increases in physical capital per worker eventually increase output per worker by smaller and smaller amounts. That is, as the quantity of physical capital per worker increases, holding everything else constant, the growth rate of productivity will fall but remain positive. Figure 13.1 illustrates an aggregate production function. This function is drawn with a given amount of labor, human capital per worker, and technology, and it shows the relationship between physical capital per worker and real GDP per worker.

Figure 13.1

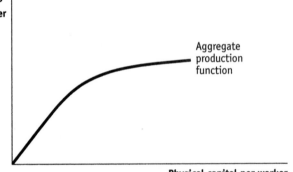

Notice that real GDP per worker eventually increases at a decreasing rate as physical capital per worker is increased. An increase in technology, the amount of labor, or the level of human capital will cause the aggregate production function to shift upward. Figure 13.2 illustrates the shift that occurs if there is an increase in one of these variables. The aggregate production function shifts upward whenever productivity is raised. This may be due to an increase in technology or an increase in human capital per worker.

tech, labor,
human capital
cause production
to shift up

Figure 13.2

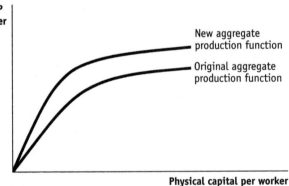

Objective #5.   Growth accounting estimates the contribution of each major factor—physical capital per worker, human capital per worker, and the state of technology—to economic growth. Total factor productivity is the amount of output that can be produced from a given set of factor inputs. When total factor productivity increases, the economy can produce a higher level of output from a given amount of physical capital, human capital, and labor. Technological change results in increases in total factor productivity: technological change is crucial for economic growth.

Objective #6.   Growth rates differ across countries and across periods of time. Countries with rapid growth rates tend to be countries that increase their physical capital, human capital, and/or technology. Countries that pursue policies of and support institutions that enhance these three factors experience greater economic growth.

- An economy increases its physical capital through investment spending. Investment spending can be funded by domestic savings or by borrowing funds from foreigners.

- A well-functioning banking system is very important for economic growth because this system is a primary means for directing savings into productive business investment. Financial regulation is necessary to ensure a well-functioning banking system.

- A government can adversely affect economic growth if there is political instability, poor enforcement of property rights, government corruption, or excessive government intervention.

- A country's human capital is primarily enhanced through government spending on education. The quality of education in a country has a significant impact on a country's economic growth rate.

- A country's infrastructure, or that part of its physical capital that serves as a foundation of economic activity, is critical. Inadequate infrastructure slows the rate of economic growth. Government plays a critical role in building both physical capital and human capital infrastructure. For example, the government plays a vital role in ensuring clean water and disease control.

Objective #7.   Technological improvement is a key force behind economic growth. Technological improvement depends upon scientific advances. Spending on research and development (R&D) enhances the development of new technologies and the practical uses of new technologies.

Objective #8.   The convergence hypothesis says that economic differences between countries, measured as real GDP per capita, tend to narrow over time. That is, the convergence hypothesis suggests that differences in living standards between countries should narrow over time. Countries with relatively low real GDP per capita will tend to have higher growth rates than countries with relatively high real GDP per capita.

Objective #9.   Conditional convergence states that countries with relatively low real GDP per capita will tend to have higher rates of growth than countries with relatively high real GDP per capita provided other things are equal. When there are differences in education, infrastructure, and political stability among countries, there is no clear tendency toward convergence in the world economy as a whole.

Objective #10. There is debate about the sustainability of economic growth due to the scarcity of natural resources and the impact of economic growth on the environment. Economists are optimistic about the ability of economies to continue to grow despite resource scarcity because they posit that increases in the price of these scarce resources will provide strong incentives to conserve these resources as well as find alternatives to them. Economists recognize that economic growth may be threatened by environmental damage and that the problem of addressing environmental damage is a difficult one, since it requires effective political action.

- Environmental damage from production often represents a negative externality, a situation where there are costs that individuals or firms impose on others without offering compensation for these costs. Without government intervention, these negative externalities will continue. Effective government intervention is necessary to eliminate or reduce such externalities.

- In the case of climate change, the government can implement a set of market-based incentives, like a "carbon tax" or a "cap and trade" system in order to provide incentives for firms to reduce the amount of greenhouse gases they emit into the environment.

Key Terms

rule of 70 a mathematical formula that states that the time it takes *real GDP* per capita, or any other variable that grows gradually over time, to double is approximately 70 divided by that variable's annual growth rate.

labor productivity output per worker; also referred to as simply *productivity*. Increases in labor productivity are the only source of *long-run economic growth*.

productivity output per worker; a shortened form of the term *labor productivity*.

physical capital manufactured resources, such as buildings and machines.

human capital the improvement in labor created by the education and knowledge embodied in the workforce.

technological progress an advance in the technical means of the production of goods and services.

aggregate production function a hypothetical function that shows how productivity (*real GDP* per worker) depends on the quantities of *physical capital* per worker and *human capital* per worker as well as the state of technology.

diminishing returns to physical capital in an *aggregate production function* when the amount of *human capital* per worker and the state of technology are held fixed, each successive increase in the amount of *physical capital* per worker leads to a smaller increase in productivity.

growth accounting estimates the contribution of each of the major factors (physical and human capital, labor, and technology) in the *aggregate production function*.

total factor productivity the amount of output that can be produced with a given amount of factor inputs.

research and development (R&D) spending to create new technologies and prepare them for practical use.

infrastructure *physical capital*, such as roads, power lines, ports, information networks, and other parts of an *economy*, that provides the underpinnings, or foundation, for economic activity.

Notes

Key Terms *(continued)*

convergence hypothesis a principle of economic growth that holds that international differences in *real GDP* per capita tend to narrow over time because countries that start with lower real GDP per capita tend to have higher growth rates.

sustainable long-run economic growth long-run growth that can continue in the face of the limited supply of natural resources and the impact of growth on the environment.

■ AFTER YOU READ THE CHAPTER

Tips

Tip #1. Real GDP per capita is a key statistic for measuring economic growth. Real GDP and not nominal GDP is used to measure economic growth, since real GDP focuses on the increase in the quantity of goods and services being produced and not on the effects of an increase in the aggregate price level. Real GDP per capita provides a measure of the average standard of living in a country.

Tip #2. Familiarize yourself with the rule of 70 and how to apply it. The rule of 70 provides a simple mathematical formula for estimating the amount of time it takes a variable that grows gradually over time to double. The rule of 70 states that the number of years it takes for a variable to approximately double is equal to 70 divided by the annual growth rate of the variable.

Tip #3. It is important to understand and know the sources of long-run economic growth. Economic growth arises because of increases in productivity, or output per worker. This increase in productivity is due to increases in human capital per worker, physical capital per worker, and/or technological advances. Economic growth is enhanced by high levels of saving and investment spending, a strong educational system, adequate infrastructure, well-supported research and development, political stability, and appropriate levels of government intervention in the economy.

Tip #4. Productivity increases when physical capital per worker, human capital per worker, or technology increases. Increases in productivity are the primary source of economic growth over time. It is important to understand what productivity is and how an economy's productivity can be improved. You should make sure you understand what an aggregate production function is and how it illustrates the relationship between productivity and the variables that determine productivity.

Tip #5. The concept of diminishing returns to physical capital is important. Holding everything else constant, an increase in physical capital per worker will eventually lead to smaller increases in productivity. Adding additional physical capital to a fixed level of labor and technology initially increases output at an increasing rate, but eventually each successive addition to physical capital per worker produces a smaller increase in output per worker.

Tip #6. Investment spending determines the level of physical capital available to workers. Investment spending plays a vital role in determining an economy's rate of economic growth. Investment spending can be funded through domestic saving or through the borrowing of foreign saving.

WORKED PROBLEMS

1. Suppose that a country in 2010 has a real GDP per capita that is equal to $20,000. Furthermore, suppose that real GDP grows by 10% a year and that population holds steady at its current level. Using the rule of 70, in what year will this economy's real GDP per capita quadruple? If the country's real GDP grew by 5% a year, in what year would this economy's real GDP quadruple? Does the growth rate of an economy's real GDP matter?

STEP 1: Start by reviewing the rule of 70.

Review the section "Growth Rates" on pages 380–382.

The rule of 70 states that the number of years it takes a variable to double is approximately equal to 70 divided by the annual growth rate of the variable. If the growth rate is 10% a year, then it will take approximately 7 years for the variable to double and 14 years for the variable to quadruple. Therefore, real GDP per capita in this economy will be approximately $40,000 in 2017 and real GDP per capita will be approximately $80,000 in 2024.

STEP 2: Complete a similar calculation, but this time assume that the growth rate of real GDP per year is 5%.

Review the section "Growth Rates" on pages 380–382.

When real GDP grows by 5% a year, the rule of 70 predicts that it will take approximately 14 years for real GDP to double. Thus, real GDP per capita in this economy will be approximately $40,000 in 2024 and real GDP per capita in this economy will be approximately $80,000 in 2038.

STEP 3: Discuss why the growth rate of real GDP in an economy matters.

Review the section "Comparing Economies Across Time and Space" on pages 378–382, and the section "Growth Rates" on pages 380–382.

An economy's growth rate of real GDP, considered along with its population growth rate, determines the rate of growth in real GDP per capita. Holding everything else constant, when an economy grows at a faster rate, this implies that real GDP per capita will increase by a faster rate: on average, living standards will improve.

2. The following graph depicts the aggregate production function for Macroland. This aggregate production function has been drawn holding the level of physical capital and technology in Macroland fixed. Currently, Macroland employs 200 units of labor per year. The graph indicates this level of labor usage and the level of real GDP that can be produced when 200 units of labor are employed. Holding everything else constant, what will happen to real GDP in Macroland if 400 units of labor are employed? What will happen to labor productivity when labor usage increases? Suppose that at the same time that Macroland increases its use of

labor to 400 units, it simultaneously experiences a technological advance. How will this alter the following graph, and how will it affect the level of real GDP produced in Macroland and labor productivity?

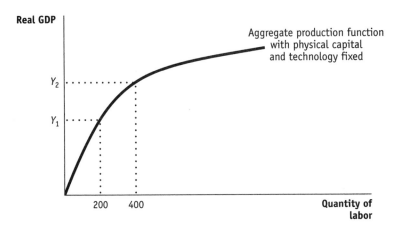

STEP 1: First describe the effect on real GDP of increasing the use of labor from 200 units to 400 units.

Review the section "The Sources of Long-Run Growth" on pages 382–389.

When this economy increases its employment of labor from 200 units to 400 units, this leads to an increase in real GDP from Y_1 to Y_2. With more labor employed, the economy can produce more goods and services than it could when it employed a smaller amount of labor.

STEP 2: Now think about what happens to labor productivity as the level of labor usage increases, holding everything else constant.

Review the section "The Sources of Long-Run Growth" on pages 382–389.

Labor productivity is defined as output per worker. In the graph, we can see that as labor usage increases from 200 units to 400 units, output increases. But from the graph, we can also see that although as labor usage increases, output increases, it does so at a diminishing rate. This is due to the fact that capital and technology are being held constant: as more and more units of labor are employed, each additional unit of labor will be less productive due to the growing scarcity of capital for labor to use (since capital is fixed, the amount of capital available is not increasing as the amount of labor is increased). Thus, although both output and labor increase, output increases by a smaller proportion than does labor: labor productivity decreases.

STEP 3: Consider the effect of a change in technology holding the use of labor constant at 200 units and the effect of this change on real GDP and labor productivity. Now think about the effect of this change in technology on real GDP and labor productivity if labor simultaneously increases to 400 units.

Review the section "The Sources of Long-Run Growth" on pages 382–389.

If technology increases, this will cause the aggregate production function to shift upward at every level of labor usage, since this improvement in technology will allow the economy to produce a larger amount of goods and services (real GDP increases) from the available labor and capital. If technology changes and labor and capital are held constant, this will cause labor productivity to rise since each unit of labor can now produce more than it could before the technological change.

If technology improves and the amount of labor employed simultaneously increases to 400 units, real GDP will increase, but the effect of these two changes on labor productivity is impossible to calculate without quantitative information about the size of the shift in the aggregate production function due to the change in technology. Labor productivity may increase, decrease, or remain the same depending upon whether real GDP increases by a greater proportionate amount than does labor, real GDP increases by a smaller proportionate amount than does labor, or real GDP increases by the same proportionate amount as does labor.

STEP 4: **Illustrate the changes in the preceding graph of this increase in technology and labor usage. Discuss the effect of these two changes on real GDP and labor productivity.**

Review the section "The Sources of Long-Run Growth" on pages 382–389.

From Step 3 we know that an increase in technology will shift the aggregate production function upward. We also know from Step 3 that when technology improves and there is an increase in the amount of labor used, this leads to a situation where labor productivity may increase, decrease, or remain the same. The two graphs that follow depict two possible scenarios: the first graph illustrates the case of increasing labor productivity, while the second graph illustrates the case of decreasing labor productivity.

3. You recently went to a lecture on economic growth where the speaker, a noted expert, stressed the importance of increases in human capital, as well as increases in physical capital. The speaker then asserted that the most important factor determining the rate of economic growth is technological improvement. Comment on how changes in each of these factors improve an economy's ability to produce goods and services. With regard to growth accounting, order these three factors from the most important determinant of economic growth to the least important determinant.

STEP 1: **Discuss what improvements in human capital mean and how an improvement in human capital affects an economy's growth rate.**

Review the section "Explaining Growth in Productivity" on pages 383–384.

Improvements in human capital refer to changes in the labor force that reflect education and knowledge. The more educated and knowledgeable the workforce is, the greater the ability of this workforce to produce goods and services from a given amount of resources. As human capital increases, labor becomes more productive and real GDP increases.

STEP 2: **Discuss what improvements in physical capital mean and how an improvement in physical capital affects an economy's growth rate.**

Review the section "Explaining Growth in Productivity" on pages 383–384.

Improvements in physical capital refer to increases in manufactured resources such as buildings and machines. When there are improvements in physical capital, workers are more productive, and this enables a given amount of labor to produce a greater amount of output. As physical capital increases, this increases the rate of economic growth possible in an economy.

STEP 3: **Discuss what improvements in technology mean and how an improvement in technology affects an economy's growth rate.**

Review the section "Explaining Growth in Productivity" on pages 383–384.

Improvement in technology is broadly defined as improvement in the technical means for the production of goods and services. When technology improves, this implies that labor is more productive and that the economic growth rate in an economy increases.

STEP 4: **Based on growth accounting, order improvements in human capital, physical capital, and technology in order of their importance in determining the rate of growth in an economy.**

Review the section "Explaining Growth in Productivity" on pages 383–384.

According to growth accounting, technology is the primary driver of economic growth. This is followed by improvements in human capital and finally by increases in physical capital.

4. You are given the following information about Productiva and Macrostan. You are asked to compute and then compare labor productivity for both countries as well as real GDP per capita for both countries.

Country	Population	Employment	Output (Real GDP)
Productiva	80 million	40 million	$300 billion
Macrostan	60 million	30 million	200 billion

STEP 1: Compute labor productivity for both countries.

Review the section "Comparing Economies Across Time and Space" on pages 378–382 and the section "The Sources of Long-Run Growth" on pages 382–389

Labor productivity is defined as output per worker. For this example, output is measured as real GDP and the number of workers is given by the employment figures. Thus, labor productivity in Productiva is equal to ($300 billion)/(40 million workers), or $7,500 per worker. Labor productivity in Macrostan is equal to ($200 billion)/(30 million workers), or $6,667 per worker.

STEP 2: Compute real GDP per capita for both countries.

Review the section "Comparing Economies Across Time and Space" on pages 378–382 and the section "The Sources of Long-Run Growth" on pages 382–389.

Real GDP per capita in a country is equal to the country's real GDP divided by the country's population. Thus, real GDP per capita in Productiva is equal to ($300 billion)/(80 million people), or $3,750 per person. Real GDP per capita in Macrostan is equal to ($200 billion)/(60 million people), or $3,333 per person.

STEP 3: Compare the labor productivity and real GDP per capita for these two countries.

Review the section "Comparing Economies Across Time and Space" on pages 378–382 and the section "The Sources of Long-Run Growth" on pages 382–389.

Productiva has higher labor productivity and higher real GDP per capita than does Macrostan.

Problems and Exercises

1. You are given the following information about the country of Macronesia.

Year	Nominal GDP	CPI	Real GDP	Population
2009	$10 billion	100		1.0 million
2010	10.5 billion	105		1.05 million
2011	11.0 billion	108		1.08 million

a. What is the base year for the economy represented in the table? How did you identify the base year?

b. Calculate the missing values in the table. Calculate the missing value and then round to the nearest thousand million: e.g., 14,829,000,000 would be rounded to 14.8 billion.

c. Use the completed table from part (b) to calculate the missing values in the following table. You will find it helpful to define real GDP in millions (for example, 14.8 billion is 14,800 million), since population is expressed in millions.

Year	Real GDP per capita
2009	
2010	
2011	

d. Let's compare the percentage changes in some of the variables we are working with in this problem. Use the following table to organize your calculations.

Year	Percentage change in nominal GDP	Percentage change in real GDP	Percentage change in population	Percentage change in real GDP per capita
2009				
2010				
2011				

e. In order for real GDP per capita to increase over time, what must be true about the relationship between the percentage change in real GDP and the percentage change in population?

f. Why do we focus on computing real GDP per capita instead of nominal GDP per capita?

2. Suppose real GDP per capita in Fun Land is $10,000 in 2009. Economists in Fun Land predict steady increases in real GDP in Fun Land of 7% a year for the foreseeable future.

   a. According to the rule of 70, how many years will it take for Fun Land's real GDP per capita to double?

b. To verify your answer in part (a), compute the values for real GDP per capita in the following table.

Year	Real GDP per capita
2009	$10,000
2010	
2011	
2012	
2013	
2014	
2015	
2016	
2017	
2018	
2019	

c. Is your value for real GDP per capita for 2019 equal to $20,000? If it differs, does this surprise you? Explain your answer.

3. The economy of Macro States estimates its aggregate production function as

$$Y/L = 50(K/L)^{1/2}$$

when technology and human capital per worker are held constant. In the equation, Y is real GDP, L is the number of workers, and K is the quantity of physical capital. Macro States has 500 workers.

a. Calculate real GDP per worker (Y/L) and physical capital per worker (K/L) for the given levels of physical capital in the following table. Round both (K/L) and (Y/L) to the nearest hundredth.

K	K/L	Y/L
0		
20		
40		
60		
80		
100		
200		
400		

b. Plot Macro States' aggregate production function on the following graph, where physical capital per worker is measured on the x-axis and real GDP per worker is measured on the y-axis.

c. As physical capital per worker increases, what happens to real GDP per worker?

4. Suppose that Macro States increases its level of technology and human capital per worker relative to its economic condition in problem 3. Now, Macro States' economists estimate that the aggregate production function for Macro States is given by the equation

$$Y/L = 60(K/L)^{1/2}$$

a. Relative to the aggregate production function you plotted in problem 3b, what do you anticipate will happen to Macro States' aggregate production function because of this increase in human capital per worker and technology?

b. Compare productivity in Macro States in the initial situation to its new situation, assuming that Macro States has $100 worth of physical capital.

c. Why are increases in productivity important?

5. Suppose there are two countries, Macroland and Pacifica, that currently have real GDP per capita of $10,000 and $15,000, respectively. Furthermore, suppose Macroland's economy has an average annual growth rate of 2%, while Pacifica has an average annual growth rate of 1.4%.

a. Compute real GDP per capita for both Macroland and Pacifica 50 years from now.

b. Compute real GDP per capita for both Macroland and Pacifica 100 years from now.

c. Initially, Macroland's real GDP per capita is 67% of Pacifica's real GDP per capita. After 50 years, what will be the relationship of Macroland's real GDP per capita to Pacifica's real GDP per capita in percentage terms? What is this relationship after 100 years?

6. Many people worry that the world may run out of important resources like oil and that this depletion of a vital resource will bring an end to economic growth. Why do many economists *not* believe in this particular perspective?

7. Economists argue that the problems presented by widespread climate destruction can only be resolved through government intervention as well as cooperation among different governments. Why do they hold this view?

8. Paul Romer in his "new growth theory" emphasizes the importance of providing incentives in order to encourage research and development that will lead to technological innovation. Discuss how the presence of monopolies through patents or copyrights may encourage expenditures on research and development that can lead to technological innovation.

BEFORE YOU TAKE THE TEST

Chapter Review Questions

1. Real GDP per capita is
    a. the value of real GDP divided by the number of units of capital in an economy in a given time period.
    b. always increasing over time for any given economy.
    c. the value of real GDP divided by population for a given country.
    d. Answers (b) and (c) are both correct.

2. Suppose real GDP for Macronesia is $200 million in 2010. Furthermore, suppose population in Macronesia is 100,000 in 2010. If population increases to 105,000 in 2011 while GDP increases by 5%, then it must be true that real GDP per capita in Macronesia in 2011
    a. increased.
    b. decreased.
    c. stayed constant.
    d. may have increased, decreased, or remained constant.

3. Which of the following statements is true?
    a. Other things being equal, an increase in population raises the average standard of living in an economy.
    b. In 1900, the U.S. economy produced only 13% as much per person as it did in 2010.
    c. The median American household income in the United States in 2010 was approximately $50,000.
    d. Answers (a), (b), and (c) are all true.
    e. Answers (b) and (c) are both true.

4. Suppose that real GDP per capita grows at 2% per year. How many years will it take for real GDP per capita to approximately double? It will take:
    a. 70 years because of the rule of 70.
    b. 140 years, because the rule of 70 states that a variable will double in 70 years if the variable has an annual growth rate of 1%; therefore, a variable growing at 2% will take twice as long to double.
    c. 35 years, because the rule of 70 states that the number of years it takes for a variable to double is equal to 70 divided by the annual growth rate of the variable.
    d. 50 years, since at 2% per year it takes 50 years to reach 100% more than the initial real GDP per capita.

5. Which of the following has been most important in driving long-run economic growth?
    a. rising labor productivity or output per worker
    b. putting more people to work
    c. being a relatively rich country initially
    d. the availability of abundant natural resources

6. Productivity increases can be attributed to
   a. increases in physical capital or the amount of machinery and office space available to workers.
   b. increases in human capital or the level of workers' education.
   c. technological advances.
   d. Answers (a), (b), and (c) are all correct.

7. Which of the following statements is true?
   a. An aggregate production function indicates how output per worker depends on the level of physical capital per worker, human capital per worker, and the state of technology.
   b. Holding everything else constant, an increase in human capital per worker reduces the level of output per worker.
   c. Holding everything else constant, a decrease in physical capital per worker increases the level of output per worker.
   d. Answers (a), (b), and (c) are all true.

8. Suppose the amount of human capital per worker and the state of technology are held constant. As physical capital per worker increases, each additional increase in physical capital per worker leads to
   a. greater increases in output per worker.
   b. greater decreases in output per worker.
   c. smaller increases in output per worker.
   d. smaller decreases in output per worker.

9. Economists often use the other things equal expression. This expression indicates that
   a. a group of variables is held constant while we examine how changing one variable affects our economic model.
   b. an individual views two possible outcomes as being equivalent in their impact.
   c. the distribution of income is equal among all members of an economy.
   d. equal amounts of all factors of production are used in the economy under study.

Use the following information to answer the next two questions.

An economy initially has 100 units of physical capital per worker. Each year it increases the amount of physical capital by 5%. According to the aggregate production function for this economy, each 1% increase in physical capital per worker, holding human capital and technology constant, increases output per worker by 1/5th of 1%, or 0.20%.

10. In two years time, what is the level of physical capital per worker in this economy?
    a. 110 units of physical capital per worker
    b. 105 units of physical capital per worker
    c. 110.25 units of physical capital per worker
    d. 210 units of physical capital per worker

11. Suppose output per worker is initially $1,000. After one year, what does estimated output per worker equal? Assume there is no inflation in this economy: real GDP equals nominal GDP.

    a. $1,000

    b. $1,001

    c. $1,010

    d. $1,100

12. An economy increases its level of physical capital per worker by increasing the level of investment spending. This can be achieved by

    a. having domestic residents spend more of their income on consumption spending.

    b. having domestic residents spend less of their income on consumption spending while increasing their domestic savings.

    c. borrowing foreign savings from residents of other countries.

    d. Answers (a) and (c) are both correct.

    e. Answers (b) and (c) are both correct.

13. Which of the following statements is true?

    a. Between 1900 and 2010, U.S. real GDP per capita increased by approximately 658%.

    b. Despite rapid economic growth in China and India over the past 30 years, China has only recently exceeded the standard of living that the United States enjoyed in the early twentieth century, and India is still poorer than the United States was at that time.

    c. Today, about 50% of the world's population lives in countries that are poorer than the United States was a hundred years ago.

    d. Answers (a), (b), and (c) are all true.

14. Suppose real GDP in Macroland was $400 billion in 2010 and $450 billion in 2011. Then the growth rate of real GDP in Macroland between 2010 and 2011 was

    a. 50%.

    b. 5%.

    c. 125%.

    d. 12.5%.

15. Which of the following statements is true?

    a. Countries with low levels of infrastructure typically experience low rates of economic growth.

    b. Infrastructure is primarily provided by private companies.

    c. Basic public health measures, like clean water, are not considered part of an economy's infrastructure.

    d. Answers (a), (b), and (c) are all true.

16. Long-run economic growth requires

    a. the imposition of bureaucratic restrictions on business and household activity.

    b. political stability and respect for property rights.

    c. extensive government intervention in markets in the form of import restrictions, government subsidies, and protection of firms from competitive economic pressures.

    d. Answers (a), (b), and (c) are all correct.

17. Economic growth can be especially fast
  a. for countries playing catch-up with countries that already have high real GDP per capita.
  b. for relatively poorer countries, if the convergence hypothesis holds true.
  c. if the country is able to benefit from adopting the technological advances already utilized in advanced countries.
  d. Answers (a), (b), and (c) are all true.

18. Suppose that real GDP per capita in an economy doubles in 10 years. Using the rule of 70, the average growth rate of real GDP for this economy is approximately
  a. 70%.
  b. 0.7%.
  c. 7%.
  d. 1.43%.

19. Which of the following statements is true?
  a. Today there is approximately $150,000 worth of physical capital per average U.S. private-sector worker.
  b. The American population today is more highly educated than it was 50 years ago.
  c. Modest innovations can result in large technological gains for an economy.
  d. Answers (a), (b), and (c) are all true.
  e. Answers (a) and (b) are both true.

20. Holding human capital per worker, the number of workers, and the level of technology constant, suppose an economy increases the amount of physical capital per worker. In this economy, output per worker will
  a. initially increase at a diminishing rate but will eventually increase at an increasing rate as the economy uses greater amounts of physical capital per worker.
  b. eventually lead to output per worker increasing at a diminishing rate.
  c. eventually lead to output per worker increasing at an increasing rate.
  d. eventually lead to output per worker staying constant at the potential output level for the economy.

21. Growth accounting estimates the
  a. effect of a change in physical capital per worker on real GDP per worker.
  b. effect of a change in human capital per worker on real GDP per worker.
  c. effect of a change in the growth rate of real GDP per worker on a country's average standard of living.
  d. contribution of each major factor in the aggregate production function to economic growth.

22. Suppose that the amount of human capital per worker grows by 6% a year in Myland. Furthermore, suppose that estimates of the aggregate production function in Myland show that for each 1% increase in human capital per worker, holding physical capital per worker and technology constant, output per worker increases by 0.5 of 1%. What is your estimate of the effect of this growing human capital per worker on the productivity growth per year in Myland? The growth in human capital per worker in Myland accounts for approximately

    a. 6% of productivity growth per year.

    b. 0.5% of productivity growth per year.

    c. 3% of productivity growth per year.

    d. 30% of productivity growth per year.

23. When total factor productivity increases, this implies that

    a. the economy can produce the same amount of output with a greater quantity of physical capital, human capital, and labor.

    b. the economy can produce the same amount of output with a smaller quantity of physical capital, human capital, and labor.

    c. the economy can produce a greater amount of output with a greater quantity of physical capital, human capital, and labor.

    d. each factor's productivity increases by the same amount.

24. Natural resources in the modern world are

    a. less important in determining productivity than human or physical capital for the majority of countries.

    b. more important in determining productivity than human or physical capital for the majority of countries.

25. Sometimes the development of a new technology does not immediately translate into a large increase in productivity because

    a. the new technology provides a new means of producing the good, but the new means may not necessarily enable greater production from a given set of resources.

    b. it may take time for firms to learn how to effectively use the new technology.

26. Fast-growing economies typically spend a

    a. very small share of their GDP on investment goods.

    b. large share of their GDP on government-provided goods and services.

    c. very large share of their GDP on investment goods.

    d. very large share of their GDP on consumer goods.

27. Which of the following statements is true?

    I. Since 1980, real GDP per capita in India has more than tripled.

    II. Between 1978 and 2004, the economy in China grew faster than the economy in India.

    III. More than half the growth in labor productivity in the United States between 1948 and 2010 is explained by technological progress.

  a. Statement I is true.

  b. Statement II is true.

  c. Statement III is true.

  d. Statements I and II are true.

  e. Statements II and III are true.

  f. Statements I and III are true.

  g. Statements I, II, and III are all true.

28. Resource scarcity

  a. is inevitable and will lead to reduced economic growth.

  b. will result in price increases for those scarce resources, and these price increases will provide incentives to conserve scarce resources and to find alternatives to these scarce resources.

29. Environmental damage from economic growth

  a. is of no great consequence and can easily be remedied through market forces.

  b. may lead to climate change, and this environmental damage can only be reduced by concerted government intervention to provide incentives for businesses and individuals to reduce environmentally degrading activities.

  c. can be remedied through the appropriate use of "carbon taxes" or "cap and trade" systems for carbon emissions.

  d. Answers (b) and (c) are both correct.

30. Which of the following statements is true about "new growth theory"?

  a. This theory recognizes that spending on research and development by businesses is different than spending on equipment and factories.

  b. This theory recognizes that spending on research and development may result in improvements in our knowledge of how to work with our available resources.

  c. This theory recognizes that once new knowledge has been discovered, it can be used by other people at no or very low cost.

  d. This theory recognizes the importance of innovators' ability to establish monopolies in order to provide an incentive for engaging in research and development.

  e. Answers (a), (b), (c), (d), and (e) are all correct answers.

ANSWER KEY

Answers to Problems and Exercises

1. **a.** 2009. The base year is that year with the CPI value of 100.

    b.

Year	Nominal GDP	CPI	Real GDP	Population
2009	$10 billion	100	$10 billion	1.0 million
2010	10.5 billion	105	10 billion	1.05 million
2011	11 billion	108	10.19 billion	1.08 million

    c.

Year	Real GDP per capita
2009	$10,000
2010	9,524
2011	9,435

    d.

Year	Percentage change in nominal GDP	Percentage change in real GDP	Percentage change in population	Percentage change in real GDP per capita
2009	—	—	—	—
2010	5%	0%	5%	−4.8%
2011	4.8	1.9	2.9	−0.93

    e. The percentage change in real GDP must be greater than the percentage change in population for real GDP per capita to increase over time.

    f. Real GDP per capita allows us to track the increase in the quantity of goods and services available in our economy rather than just the effects of a rising price level.

2. a. Ten years, since the rule of 70 says the number of years it takes for a variable to double is approximately equal to 70 divided by the annual growth rate of the variable.

b.

Year	Real GDP per capita
2009	$10,000
2010	10,700
2011	11,449
2012	12,250
2013	13,108
2014	14,026
2015	15,007
2016	16,058
2017	17,182
2018	18,385
2019	19,672

c. The value of real GDP per capita for 2019 is $19,672, which is less than the estimated $20,000. This is not surprising, since the rule of 70 is an estimation of the number of years it takes a variable to double rather than a numerically precise calculation.

3. a.

K	K/L	Y/L
0	0	0
20	0.04	10.00
40	0.08	14.14
60	0.12	17.32
80	0.16	20.00
100	0.20	22.36
200	0.40	31.62
400	0.80	44.72

b.

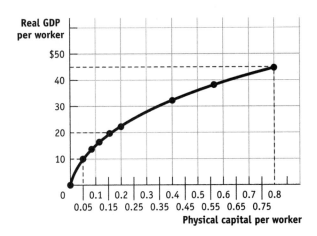

c. Real GDP per worker increases as physical capital per worker increases, but it increases at a diminishing rate. For example, if we hold the number of workers and all other variables constant, real GDP per worker increases by $4.14 when physical capital increases from $20 to $40, but real GDP per worker increases by $3.18 when physical capital increases from $40 to $60.

4. a. Macro States' aggregate production function will shift up relative to its initial position for every level of physical capital per worker. We can see this by recalculating output per worker given the new aggregate production function.

K	K/L	Y/L
0	0	0
20	0.04	12.00
40	0.08	16.97
60	0.12	20.78
80	0.16	24.00
100	0.20	26.83

b. Productivity is defined as output per worker. When physical capital equals $100, output per worker is initially $22.50, while, after the increase in human capital per worker and technology, output per worker increases to $26.83.

c. Increases in productivity are important because they indicate that each worker on average is now producing a greater level of output. This, in turn, makes it possible for people on average to experience higher standards of living.

5. a. Real GDP per capita in Macroland in 50 years will equal ($10,000)$(1 + 0.02)^{50}$, or $26,916. Real GDP per capita in Pacifica in 50 years will equal ($15,000)$(1 + 0.014)^{50}$, or $30,060.

b. Real GDP per capita in Macroland in 100 years will equal ($10,000)$(1 + 0.02)^{100}$, or $72,446. Real GDP per capita in Pacifica in 100 years will equal ($15,000)$(1 + 0.014)^{100}$, or $60,240.

c. In 50 years, Macroland's real GDP per capita to Pacifica's real GDP per capita in percentage terms will be 89.5%, while in 100 years it will be 120.3%.

6. Economists argue that vital resources, as they grow scarce, will command increasingly higher prices and that these high prices will cause people to conserve these resources and, in addition, spur the development of alternatives to replace the scarce, but vital, resources.

7. Climate destruction arises from widespread economic growth, and this destruction is an example of a negative externality. Negative externalities arise when a market fails to include all the costs of producing a good in the calculation of the good's price. Many goods produced today also produce significant pollution, and the market does not internalize these costs of pollution. Without government intervention, firms and individuals do not have any incentive to reduce negative externalities. Reducing pollution and the climate destruction that accompany this pollution will require the cooperation of governments in imposing some form of market-based incentives: for example, a "carbon tax" or a "cap and trade" system both would reduce the amount of carbon emitted into the air.

8. Paul Romer, in his research on economic growth, notes the importance of technological innovation that basically results in a "new set of instructions" for how to use resources. However, he also notes that this kind of technological innovation, once discovered, can be copied at either no cost or very low cost by competitors. Businesses will have little incentive to engage in this kind of research and development if their ideas can be quickly copied by those who have not invested in the research. Government, by providing monopoly power to the business that creates this information via patents or copyrights, effectively creates an incentive for businesses to engage in research and development that may lead to technological innovation.

Answers to Chapter Review Questions

1. **Answer c.** Real GDP per capita is defined as the value of real GDP in a country divided by that country's population. Real GDP per capita may increase, decrease, or remain steady over time.

2. **Answer c.** In 2012, the population in Macronesia increased by 5% as did real GDP. Since both population and real GDP increased by the same percentage amount, real GDP per capita is unaffected.

3. **Answer e.** Answers (b) and (c) are factual statements that are in the chapter text. Answer (a) is not true: an increase in population, other things equal, will reduce the average standard of living since the average standard of living is calculated as real GDP per capita. The increase in population increases the size of the denominator in this ratio, while the numerator, or real GDP, stays constant.

4. **Answer c.** This is a straightforward use of the definition of the rule of 70: this rule states that an estimation of the number of years it takes for a variable to double is equal to 70 divided by the annual growth rate of the variable.

5. **Answer a.** Sustained economic growth occurs only when an economy steadily increases the amount of output each worker produces; in other words, long-run economic growth depends upon rising labor productivity. Putting more people to work can increase output in the short run, but it does not result in sustained economic growth. Long-run economic growth is possible in relatively poor countries (for example, South Korea before 1970) and in countries endowed with low levels of resources (for example, Japan).

6. **Answer d.** Each of these reasons—physical capital, human capital, and technological advances—contributes to increases in productivity, or the ability to produce more output per worker.

7. **Answer a.** Answer (a) provides a definition of the aggregate production function. In answers (b) and (c), we know there is a relationship between output per worker and the amount of human capital per worker or physical capital per worker: in both cases, an increase in either human or physical capital, holding everything else constant, will lead to an increase in output per worker.

8. **Answer c.** This question focuses on the concept of diminishing returns to physical capital: given an aggregate production function with a constant level of human capital per worker and state of technology, an increase in the quantity of physical capital per worker will lead the rate of productivity to fall while remaining positive. Thus, output per worker will increase but by smaller and smaller amounts.

9. **Answer a.** The other-things-equal expression is used when economists want to single out the effect of a change in one variable on their economic model. To see this effect, all other variables that might affect the model are held constant, or equal to their initial value, while the single variable is allowed to change.

10. **Answer c.** Physical capital per worker in the first year increases by 5%, or $(100)(1.05) =$ 105 units. In the second year, physical capital per worker increases another 5%, or $(105)(1.05) = 110.25$ units.

11. **Answer c.** Using growth accounting, we can estimate output per worker as being equal to the percentage change in physical capital per worker times the impact on output per worker. In this case, a 5% increase in physical capital per worker will lead to a 1% increase in output per worker. Since output is initially $1,000, a 1% increase in output will equal $1,010.

12. **Answer e.** Investment spending depends upon the availability of savings. An increase in investment spending is possible either by increasing the level of domestic savings or by borrowing foreign savings.

13. **Answer d.** All of these statements are factual statements found in the text of the chapter.

14. **Answer d.** To find the growth rate of real GDP in Macroland between 2010 and 2011, use the following formula:

    Growth rate of real GDP between 2010 and 2011 = {[(real GDP in 2011) − (real GDP in 2010)]/(real GDP in 2010)} × 100 = [(450 − 400)/(400)] × 100 = 12.5%

15. **Answer a.** Infrastructure includes roads, power lines, ports, information networks, and basic public health measures. Countries lacking this infrastructure find it hard to maintain high rates of economic growth. Infrastructure is primarily provided by government, not private enterprise.

16. **Answer b.** Long-run economic growth requires political stability and well-defined property rights. Long-run economic growth is hindered by bureaucratic restrictions and excessive government intervention in markets.

17. **Answer d.** The convergence hypothesis says that differences in real GDP per capita among countries tend to narrow over time because countries that start with lower GDP per capita tend to grow at faster rates than countries that start with higher GDP per capita. Answers (a) and (b) express comparable ideas. Relatively poor countries may experience fast economic growth if they implement existing technological advances.

18. **Answer c.** The rule of 70 says that the number of years for a variable to double is approximately equal to 70 divided by the annual growth rate of that variable. Hence, if the real GDP per capita in an economy doubles in 10 years, then the annual growth rate of that variable must equal 70/10, or 7%.

19. **Answer d.** All of the statements are true: answers (a) and (b) are in the text. Answer (c) refers to the idea that technological innovation can result from relatively modest innovations and not just major innovations: the text provides the examples of flat-bottomed paper bags and Post-it® notes.

20. **Answer b.** With fixed technology, labor, and human capital, an increase in physical capital per worker will eventually result in output per worker increasing at a decreasing rate due to diminishing returns to physical capital. The economy, despite its increased physical capital per worker, finds that each additional unit of this physical capital per worker results in smaller and smaller increases to output per worker, since the fixed amount of labor cannot fully utilize the increases in physical capital per worker.

21. **Answer d.** This answer is the definition of growth accounting. Growth accounting seeks to assign the contribution of each major factor—physical capital per worker, human capital per worker, and technology—in the aggregate production function to economic growth.

22. **Answer c.** To find the productivity growth per year from this growth in human capital per worker, multiply the growth rate of human capital per worker times the effect of a 1 percent change in the human capital per worker on output per worker, or 6%(0.5). The growth in human capital per worker is responsible for 3 percentage points of productivity growth per year.

23. **Answer b.** When total factor productivity increases, this enables an economy to produce more output from a given set of resources or to produce the same amount of output from fewer resources.

24. **Answer a.** In the world today, human and physical capital are far more important in determining a country's productivity than are natural resources.

25. **Answer b.** New technology takes time to fully incorporate at the firm level: the new technology may require reconfiguring the physical setup of the firm, or the training of labor in the new technology. In addition, it may take time for firms to learn how to best use the new technology.

26. **Answer c.** Fast-growing economies grow fast because their capital stock is increasing rapidly. This increase in capital stock can only occur if there is a high level of investment spending. Thus, the share of GDP that reflects investment goods tends to be very large in comparison to countries that have lower economic growth rates.

27. **Answer g.** All of these statements are true. See the text for coverage of these statements.

28. **Answer b.** Economists believe that resource scarcity will lead to higher prices for those resources. As the prices of these resources rise, people will move to conserve the scarce resources and, in addition, new alternatives to replace these scarce resources will be developed.

29. **Answer d.** Environmental damage from economic growth and, in particular, the use of fossil fuels contributes to climate change and can be remedied by the government imposing "carbon taxes" or "cap and trade" systems for carbon emissions. Government intervention is necessary, since the negative externality of the pollution created by firms and individuals will not be eliminated without government intervention to limit these activities through the appropriate incentive systems.

30. **Answer e.** All of these statements are true. "New growth theory" recognizes that technological innovation, which consists of new knowledge, provides information on how to better use existent resources. Once this knowledge has been discovered, it can be used by many people at no or very low additional cost. However, if everyone can use this knowledge once it has been discovered, then there is little incentive for businesses to engage in activities to find this knowledge. Paul Romer discusses the need to provide innovators with monopoly power, at least initially, so that the innovators who discover new knowledge can profit from their effort before the information is made available to other producers.

chapter **14**

Aggregate Demand and Aggregate Supply

■ BEFORE YOU READ THE CHAPTER

Summary

This chapter develops the basic model of aggregate supply (*AS*) and aggregate demand (*AD*) that describes the relationship between the level of aggregate output and the aggregate price level. A distinction is made between the short-run *AS* curve, where the aggregate price level is positively related to the aggregate output level, and the long-run *AS* curve, a vertical curve where aggregate output is at the economy's potential output and independent of the aggregate price level. This model enables us to find both the short-run and the long-run macroeconomic equilibrium. The chapter further explores the economic changes that result in the *AD* or *AS* curve shifting and the effect of these shifts on economic fluctuations. The chapter also explores how monetary and fiscal policies can stabilize the economy.

Chapter Objectives

Objective #1. Deflation refers to the fall in the aggregate price level, while inflation refers to an increase in the aggregate price level. Stagflation refers to the combination of inflation coupled with a decrease in the level of aggregate output and an increase in unemployment.

Objective #2. The model of aggregate supply (*AS*) and aggregate demand (*AD*) can help us understand economic fluctuations and the use of macroeconomic policy to reduce these fluctuations.

Objective #3.   The *AD* curve depicts the inverse relationship between the aggregate price level (*P*) and the total quantity of aggregate output demanded by households, businesses, government, and the foreign sector. A higher aggregate price level, other things equal, reduces the quantity of aggregate output demanded; a lower aggregate price level, other things equal, increases the quantity of aggregate output demanded.

- A movement up or down the *AD* curve is due to changes in the prices of all final goods and services. In contrast, a movement up and down the demand curve for any individual good is due to a change in the price of that good while all other prices are held constant.

- *AD* curves are downward sloping because of the wealth effect and the interest rate effect.

  - When the aggregate price level changes, this affects the purchasing power of consumers' assets and hence consumers' wealth. This effect on purchasing power is called the wealth effect. For example, a decrease in the aggregate price level increases the purchasing power of many assets and therefore leads to an increase in the quantity of aggregate output demanded.

  - When the aggregate price level changes, this affects the purchasing power of a given amount of money; for example, as the price level increases, people find they need more money to purchase the same basket of goods and services. Consumers bid up interest rates with their increased demand for money. As interest rates increase, this results in less investment spending and therefore a reduction in the quantity of aggregate output demanded. This effect is referred to as the interest rate effect.

Objective #4.   The *AD* curve shifts, holding everything else constant, when there are changes in expectations, wealth, or physical capital, or when there are changes in government fiscal or monetary policy.

- When consumers and firms become more optimistic, spending increases and the *AD* curve shifts to the right. A negative change in consumer or firm expectations shifts the *AD* curve to the left.

- When the value of household assets increases, consumer spending increases. *AD* shifts to the right with an increase in household wealth and to the left with a decrease in household wealth, other things held constant.

- Firms' incentives to engage in investment spending depend on many things, including how much physical capital they already have. If firms already have a high level of physical capital, the incentive to engage in investment spending is low: *AD*, holding everything else constant, shifts to the left when firms experience higher levels of physical capital. If firms have a low level of physical capital, the incentive to engage in investment spending is high: *AD*, holding everything else constant, shifts to the right when firms experience low levels of physical capital.

- Fiscal policy, or government spending and taxing policy, can cause the *AD* curve to shift to the right or to the left. An increase in government spending or a decrease in taxes, holding everything else constant, shifts *AD* to the right. A decrease in government spending or an increase in taxes, holding everything else constant, shifts *AD* to the left.

- An increase in the money supply reduces interest rates and increases investment spending. Thus, an increase in money shifts the *AD* curve to the right, while a decrease in money shifts the *AD* curve to the left.

Objective #5.   The aggregate supply (*AS*) curve illustrates the relationship between the aggregate price level and the total quantity of final goods and services, or aggregate output, producers are willing to supply. In the short run there is a positive relationship between the amount of aggregate output or real GDP producers are willing to supply and the aggregate price level. That is, holding everything else constant, in the short run as the aggregate price level increases, the level of aggregate production increases. Figure 14.1 illustrates a short-run *AS* curve (*SRAS*): notice the positive relationship between the aggregate price level and the level of aggregate output or real GDP.

Figure 14.1

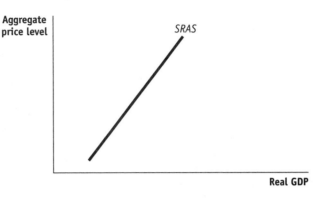

- In the short run, producers decide on their level of production by comparing the price they receive from selling a unit of output to their costs of producing that unit of output. Since some production costs are fixed in the short run, an increase in the aggregate price level increases profit per unit and therefore leads producers to increase their level of production. Hence, the short-run *AS* curve is upward sloping.

- In the short run, nominal wages are sticky due to the existence of both formal and informal agreements. This means that nominal wages decrease slowly even in the presence of high unemployment and increase slowly in the presence of low unemployment. In the long run, nominal wages are completely flexible.

- The short-run *AS* curve shifts due to changes in commodity prices, nominal wages, and productivity. An increase in commodity prices or nominal wages results in a shift to the left of the short-run *AS* curve, while a decrease in commodity prices or nominal wages results in a shift to the right of the short-run *AS* curve. An increase in productivity shifts the short-run *AS* curve to the right. There will be a movement along the *AS* curve with a change in the aggregate price level.

Objective #6.   In the long run, nominal wages and prices are flexible and therefore in the long run, the aggregate price level has no effect on the quantity of aggregate output supplied. The *AS* curve in the long run is vertical, where the level of aggregate output equals potential output, or the level of real GDP the economy would produce if all prices and wages were completely flexible. Figure 14.2 illustrates a long-run *AS* curve (*LRAS*): notice that this curve is vertical and that no matter what the aggregate price level, the level of real GDP is constant and equal to potential GDP.

Figure 14.2

- Over time if the level of potential output for an economy increases, then this implies that the long-run AS curve is shifting to the right. These shifts represent economic growth and are due to increases in the labor force and increases in the productivity of labor.

Objective #7.   The economy is always in only one of two states with respect to the short-run and long-run AS curves: (1) it can be on both curves simultaneously by being at a point where the two curves cross; or (2) it can be on the short-run AS curve but not on the long-run AS curve. Figure 14.3 illustrates these two possibilities. In the graph on the left, the SRAS and the LRAS curves intersect at the potential output level Y_P and the aggregate price level P. In the graph on the right, the economy is producing at Y_1 with the aggregate price level P: this level of production is not equal to potential output. In the short run, the economy can produce at a level of aggregate output that is less than potential output (as illustrated in the right graph in Figure 14.3), or it can produce at a level of aggregate output that is greater than potential output (you might want to practice drawing this situation).

Figure 14.3

- When the level of aggregate production is less than potential output, this implies that unemployment is high. Jobs are scarce and workers are abundant, which causes nominal wages to fall over time; the short-run AS curve will shift to the right, moving the short-run level of aggregate production closer to potential output. Figure 14.4 illustrates this situation.

Figure 14.4

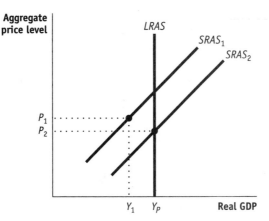

- When the level of aggregate production is greater than potential output, this implies that unemployment is low. Jobs are abundant and workers are scarce, which causes nominal wages to rise over time; the short-run *AS* curve will shift to the left, moving the short-run level of aggregate production closer to potential output. Figure 14.5 illustrates this situation.

Figure 14.5

Objective #8. The *AD–AS* model is the basic model we use to understand economic fluctuations. In the *AD–AS* model there are two states of equilibrium the economy can be in: (1) the economy can be in short-run equilibrium where *AD* equals short-run *AS*; or (2) the economy can be in long-run equilibrium where *AD* equals long-run *AS* (as well as short-run *AS*) and aggregate output equals potential output. If the economy is in the first state, over time the short-run *AS* curve will shift eventually, bringing the economy into long-run equilibrium.

- In short-run equilibrium, aggregate output may be less than, equal to, or greater than potential output. If aggregate output is less than potential output, this implies unemployment is relatively high: since jobs are scarce and workers are abundant, nominal wages will respond by falling over time, and this will shift the short-run *AS* to the right, leading output to expand toward the level of potential output. Figure 14.6 illustrates this situation. The economy moves from the short-run equilibrium where real GDP equals Y_1 and the aggregate price level equals P_1, to the long-run equilibrium where real GDP equals Y_2 or the potential output level Y_P and the aggregate price level equals P_2.

Figure 14.6

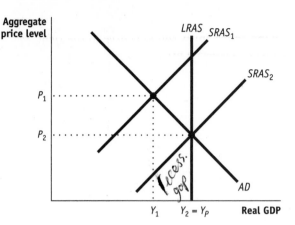

- If aggregate output is greater than potential output, this implies unemployment is relatively low. Since jobs are plentiful and workers are scarce, nominal wages will respond by rising over time and this will shift the short-run *AS* to the left, leading output to contract toward the level of potential output. Figure 14.7 illustrates this situation. The economy moves from the short-run equilibrium where real GDP equals Y_1 and the aggregate price level equals P_1, to the long-run equilibrium where real GDP equals Y_2 or the potential output level Y_p and the aggregate price level equals P_2.

Figure 14.7

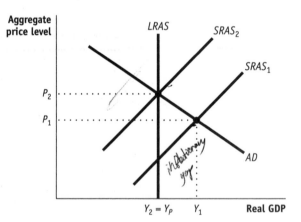

Objective #9. In the *AD-AS* model the short-run macroeconomic equilibrium occurs at the intersection of the *AD* curve with the short-run *AS* curve.

- An event that shifts the short-run *AS* curve is called a supply shock. Negative supply shocks shift the short-run *AS* curve to the left, while positive supply shocks shift the short-run *AS* curve to the right.

  - A negative supply shock leads to stagflation, where falling aggregate output and rising unemployment combine with an increasing price level.

  - A positive supply shock leads to rising aggregate output, falling unemployment, and a decrease in the aggregate price level.

  - Supply shocks cause aggregate output and the aggregate price level to move in opposite directions.

- An event that shifts the *AD* curve is called a demand shock.

    - A positive demand shock shifts the *AD* curve to the right, resulting in higher aggregate output and a higher aggregate price level.

    - A negative demand shock shifts the *AD* curve to the left, resulting in lower aggregate output and a lower aggregate price level.

    - Demand shocks cause aggregate output and the aggregate price level to move in the same direction.

- Short-run macroeconomic equilibrium aggregate output may be less than, equal to, or greater than potential output. Thus, the short-run macroeconomic equilibrium can represent an economy in an economic recession or an economy in an economic expansion.

Objective #10. Long-run macroeconomic equilibrium occurs when the short-run macroeconomic equilibrium is also a point on the long-run *AS* curve. Long-run macroeconomic equilibrium aggregate output is always equal to potential output.

- A recessionary gap occurs when the short-run macroeconomic equilibrium is below potential output. Recessionary gaps are hurtful due to the high levels of unemployment and low levels of production associated with them. Eventually, high unemployment causes nominal wages to fall and this shifts the short-run *AS* to the right, leading to higher levels of production and lower unemployment as the economy reaches long-run macroeconomic equilibrium. Figure 14.6 represents a recessionary gap since the equilibrium level of short-run production (Y_1) is less than the long-run equilibrium level of production (Y_2 or Y_P): the recessionary gap is the difference between potential output and actual short-run output, or $Y_P - Y_1$.

- An inflationary gap occurs when the short-run macroeconomic equilibrium is above potential output. In an inflationary gap, unemployment is low and this leads to increases in nominal wages that shift the short-run AS to the left, leading to lower levels of production and higher unemployment as the economy reaches long-run macroeconomic equilibrium. Figure 14.7 represents an inflationary gap since the equilibrium level of short-run production (Y_1) is greater than the long-run equilibrium level of production (Y_2 or Y_P): the inflationary gap is the difference between actual short-run output and potential output, or $Y_1 - Y_P$.

- In both the recessionary gap and inflationary gap, the economy is self-correcting: given enough time the economy will adjust to economic shocks so that these shocks affect aggregate output in the short run but have no effect on aggregate output in the long run, provided the government does not intervene with activist policy.

Objective #11. Active stabilization policy by the government can be used to offset demand shocks to the economy: active stabilization policy can reduce the severity of recessions that are due to negative demand shocks.

- Figure 14.8 illustrates a negative demand shock and the use of active stabilization policy to reduce the severity of the recession created by the demand shock. Initially the economy is in long-run equilibrium where *LRAS* intersects *SRAS* and AD_1: the economy produces $Y_1 = Y_P$ and the aggregate price level is P_1. Then there is a negative demand shock that shifts the *AD* curve from AD_1 to AD_2. The new short-run equilibrium is where *SRAS* and AD_2 intersect and the level of aggregate output is Y_2 and the aggregate price level is P_2: the economy operates with a recessionary gap equal to $Y_P - Y_2$. If the government engages in active stabilization policy, by either increasing the money supply, increasing the level of government spending, or decreasing taxes, this will cause the *AD* curve to shift from AD_2 to AD_3 (the same as AD_1): the economy will return to its initial long-run equilibrium aggregate output level Y_P and its initial aggregate price level P_1.

Figure 14.8

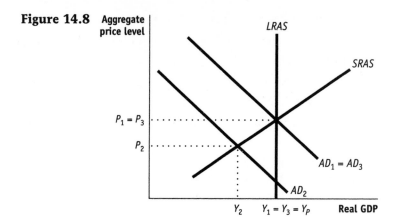

- Figure 14.9 illustrates a positive demand shock and the use of active stabilization policy to reduce the economic expansion created by the demand shock. Initially the economy is in long-run equilibrium where *LRAS* intersects *SRAS* and AD_1: the economy produces $Y_1 = Y_P$ and the aggregate price level is P_1. Then there is a positive demand shock that shifts the *AD* curve from AD_1 to AD_2. The new short-run equilibrium is where *SRAS* and AD_2 intersect and the level of aggregate output is Y_2 and the aggregate price level is P_2: the economy operates with an inflationary gap equal to $Y_2 - Y_P$. If the government engages in active stabilization policy, by either decreasing the money supply, decreasing the level of government spending, or increasing taxes, this will cause the *AD* curve to shift from AD_2 to AD_3 (the same as AD_1): the economy will return to its initial long-run equilibrium aggregate output level Y_P and its initial aggregate price level P_1.

Figure 14.9

Objective #12. There are no easy stabilization policies available to offset negative supply shocks. When policy makers try to offset negative supply shocks, they face a difficult trade-off: one can increase aggregate output only by increasing the aggregate price level, or one can decrease the aggregate price level only by decreasing aggregate output.

- Figure 14.10 illustrates a negative supply shock. The economy is initially in long-run equilibrium with aggregate output equal to Y_P and the aggregate price level equal to P_1. Then the *SRAS* shifts to the left due to a negative supply shock: the aggregate output level falls to Y_2 and the aggregate price level rises to P_2. If the government engages in active stabilization policy, it can either (1) shift *AD* to the right through increases in the money supply, increases in government spending, or decreases in taxes; or it can (2) shift *AD* to the left through decreases in the money supply, decreases in government spending, or increases in taxes. With the first option, the equilibrium level of aggregate output will increase as will the aggregate price level; with the second option, the equilibrium level of aggregate output will decrease as will the aggregate price level. In the case of active stabilization policy for a negative supply shock, it is not possible to simultaneously increase the level of aggregate output while decreasing the aggregate price level.

Figure 14.10

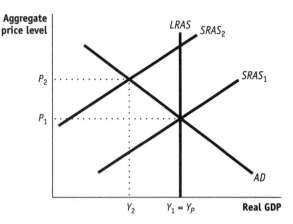

Key Terms

aggregate demand curve a graphical representation that shows the relationship between the *aggregate price level* and the quantity of *aggregate output* demanded by *households, firms,* the government, and the rest of the world. The aggregate demand curve has a negative slope due to the *wealth effect of a change in the aggregate price level* and the *interest rate effect of a change in the aggregate price level*.

wealth effect of a change in the aggregate price level the effect on *consumer spending* caused by the change in the purchasing power of consumers' assets when the *aggregate price level* changes. A rise in the aggregate price level decreases the purchasing power of consumers' assets, so consumers decrease their consumption; a fall in the aggregate price level increases the purchasing power of consumers' assets, so consumers increase their consumption.

interest rate effect of a change in the aggregate price level the effect on *consumer spending* and *investment spending* caused by a change in the purchasing power of consumers' money holdings when the *aggregate price level* changes. A rise (fall) in the aggregate price level decreases (increases) the purchasing power of consumers' money holdings. In response, consumers try to increase (decrease) their money holdings, which drives up (down) interest rates, thereby decreasing (increasing) consumption and investment.

aggregate supply curve a graphical representation that shows the relationship between the *aggregate price level* and the total quantity of *aggregate output* supplied.

nominal wage the dollar amount of any given wage paid.

sticky wages *nominal wages* that are slow to fall even in the face of high *unemployment* and slow to rise even in the face of labor shortages.

Notes

Key Terms *(continued)*

short-run aggregate supply curve a graphical representation that shows the positive relationship between the *aggregate price level* and the quantity of *aggregate output* supplied that exists in the short run, the time period when many production costs, particularly *nominal wages*, can be taken as fixed. The short-run aggregate supply curve has a positive slope because a rise in the aggregate price level leads to a rise in profits, and therefore output, when production costs are fixed.

long-run aggregate supply curve a graphical representation that shows the relationship between the *aggregate price level* and the quantity of *aggregate output* supplied that would exist if all prices, including *nominal wages*, were fully flexible. The long-run aggregate supply curve is vertical because the aggregate price level has no effect on aggregate output in the long run; in the long run, aggregate output is determined by the *economy's potential output*.

potential output the level of *real GDP* the *economy* would produce if all prices, including *nominal wages*, were fully flexible.

AD–AS model the basic model used to understand fluctuations in *aggregate output* and the *aggregate price level*. It uses the *aggregate supply curve* and the *aggregate demand curve* together to analyze the behavior of the *economy* in response to shocks or government policy.

short-run macroeconomic equilibrium the point at which the quantity of *aggregate output* supplied is equal to the *quantity demanded*.

short-run equilibrium aggregate price level the *aggregate price level* in *short-run macroeconomic equilibrium*.

short-run equilibrium aggregate output the quantity of *aggregate output* produced in *short-run macroeconomic equilibrium*.

demand shock an event that shifts the *aggregate demand curve*. A positive demand shock is associated with higher demand for *aggregate output* at any price level and shifts the curve to the right. A negative demand shock is associated with lower demand for aggregate output at any price level and shifts the curve to the left.

supply shock an event that shifts the *short-run aggregate supply curve*. A negative supply shock raises production costs and reduces the *quantity supplied* at any *aggregate price level*, shifting the curve leftward. A positive supply shock decreases production costs and increases the quantity supplied at any aggregate price level, shifting the curve rightward.

stagflation the combination of *inflation* and falling *aggregate output*.

long-run macroeconomic equilibrium the point at which the *short-run macroeconomic equilibrium* is on the *long-run aggregate supply curve*; so *short-run equilibrium aggregate output* is equal to *potential output*.

recessionary gap exists when *aggregate output* is below *potential output*.

Key Terms *(continued)*

inflationary gap exists when *aggregate output* is above *potential output*.

output gap the percentage difference between the actual level of *real GDP* and *potential output*.

self-correcting describes an *economy* in which shocks to aggregate demand affect *aggregate output* in the short run but not in the long run.

stabilization policy the use of government policy to reduce the severity of *recessions* and to rein in excessively strong *expansions*. There are two main tools of stabilization policy: *monetary policy* and *fiscal policy*.

▮ AFTER YOU READ THE CHAPTER

Tips

Tip #1. It is important to distinguish between short-run and long-run *AS*. In the short run, wages are sticky: this stickiness results in a short-run *AS* curve (*SRAS*) that is upward sloping. In the long run, wages are fully flexible, leading the economy to always produce its long-run equilibrium at the potential output level of real GDP. This is the output level the economy produces when all wages and prices are fully flexible. In Figure 14.11, the short-run aggregate supply curve is *SRAS*, the aggregate demand curve is *AD*, the long-run aggregate supply curve is *LRAS*, and the potential output level, which represents the long-run equilibrium level of output, is Y_P. The economy in the short run may produce an aggregate output level that is greater than or less than the potential level of output Y_P. Figure 14.11 represents an economy where the short-run level of aggregate output Y_1 is less than the long-run level of output, labeled Y_P.

Figure 14.11

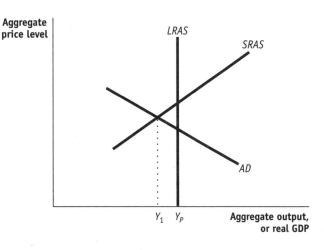

Tip #2. It is important to distinguish between a movement along the *AD* or *SRAS* curve and a shift of the *AD* or *SRAS* curve. A change in the aggregate price level causes a movement along either curve (see Figures 14.12a and 14.12b), while a change in commodity prices, nominal wages, or productivity shifts the *SRAS* curve, and a change in expectations, wealth, physical capital, fiscal policy, or monetary policy shifts the *AD* curve (see Figures 14.12c and 14.12d).

Figure 14.12a

Figure 14.12b

Figure 14.12c

Figure 14.12d

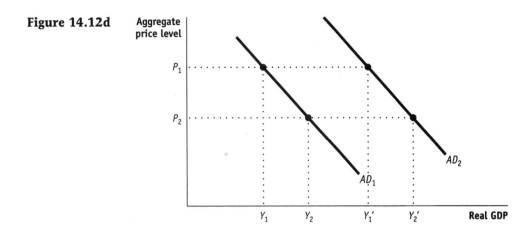

Tip #3. It is important to know the variables that shift *SRAS* and *AD* curves. The text provides a list and an explanation for the variables that cause either the *SRAS* or the *AD* curves to shift. It is crucial that you know these variables and that you understand the direction the curves shift with changes in these variables. (See the previous tip for a quick review of these variables.)

Tip #4. Changes in commodity prices have large impacts on production costs. Understanding the impact of commodity prices on the *SRAS* curve will enhance your understanding of the impact of supply shocks on the *AD-AS* model.

Tip #5. The long-run *AS* curve (*LRAS*) is vertical, and its position represents the economy's potential output when all resources are fully employed. It is important to understand why the *LRAS* curve is vertical as well as the relevance of its position on the horizontal axis. Over time if an economy experiences economic growth, the *LRAS* curve shifts to the right, indicating that the economy's potential output has increased.

Tip #6. It is important to understand why the *AD* curve is downward sloping. Note that the inverse relationship between the aggregate price level and aggregate output are explained by the wealth and interest rate effects.

Tip #7. It is important to understand the difference between short-run and long-run macroeconomic equilibria and the relationship between these equilibria. In long-run macroeconomic equilibrium, aggregate output equals potential output and the economy's *AD* equals both its short-run and long-run *AS* (see Figure 14.13a). In short-run macroeconomic equilibrium aggregate, output need not equal potential output, but the economy's *AD* must equal the short-run *AS*. Figure 14.13b illustrates a short-run equilibrium for an economy that is operating with an inflationary gap. Figure 14.13c illustrates a short-run equilibrium for an economy that is operating with a recessionary gap.

Figure 14.13a

Figure 14.13b

Figure 14.13c

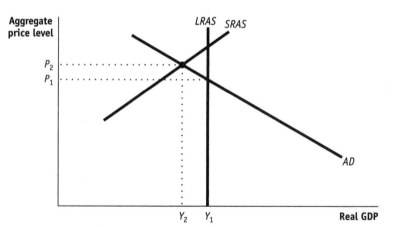

1. For each of the following changes, determine the effect on the aggregate demand curve and the short-run aggregate supply curve, as well as the effect on the aggregate price level and aggregate level of output.

Description of change	Effect on aggregate demand	Effect on short-run aggregate supply	Effect on the aggregate price level	Effect on the aggregate level of production
World oil prices increase				
The central bank increases the money supply				
The government reduces taxes				
The government reduces taxes at the same time that nominal wages increase				
The country goes to war at the same time that world oil prices increase				
People's real wealth decreases				

STEP 1: Review the factors that shift the aggregate demand curve and the aggregate supply curve. In addition, think about sketching a graph that will help guide your answer to this question.

Review the section "Shifts of the Aggregate Demand Curve" on pages 414–416, the section "Shifts of the Short-Run Aggregate Supply Curve" on pages 421–423, Table 14-1 on page 415, and Table 14-2 on page 423.

Before you can begin to answer this question, you must have a firm grasp of the factors that shift the aggregate demand curve and the factors that shift the short-run aggregate supply curve. Then, for each description determine which curve or curves are shifting and sketch a diagram to guide your thinking.

STEP 2: There is a challenge in this question when both the aggregate demand curve and the short-run aggregate supply curve shift simultaneously.

Review the section "Shifts of the Aggregate Demand Curve" on pages 414–416, the section "Shifts of the Short-Run Aggregate Supply Curve" on pages 421–423, Table 14-1 on page 415, and Table 14-2 on page 423.

When both curves shift and there is no quantitative information about the size of the shift, this results in either the change in the equilibrium aggregate price level or the change in the equilibrium aggregate output level being ambiguous. Be particularly careful in your analysis when you see that both curves are shifting.

STEP 3: Fill in the table.

Review the section "Shifts of the Aggregate Demand Curve" on pages 414–416, the section "Shifts of the Short-Run Aggregate Supply Curve" on pages 421–423, Table 14-1 on page 415, and Table 14-2 on page 423.

Description of change	Effect on aggregate demand	Effect on short-run aggregate supply	Effect on the aggregate price level	Effect on the aggregate level of production
World oil prices increase	This event causes a movement along the *AD* curve.	This event causes the *SRAS* curve to shift to the left.	The aggregate price level increases.	The aggregate level of production decreases.
The central bank increases the money supply	This event causes the *AD* curve to shift to the right.	This event causes a movement along the *SRAS* curve.	The aggregate price level increases.	The aggregate level of production increases.
The government reduces taxes	This event causes the *AD* curve to shift to the right.	This event causes a movement along the *SRAS* curve.	The aggregate price level increases.	The aggregate level of production increases.
The government reduces taxes at the same time that nominal wages increase	The reduction in taxes causes the *AD* curve to shift to the right.	The increase in nominal wages causes the *SRAS* curve to shift to the left.	The aggregate price level will increase.	The aggregate level of production may increase, decrease, or remain the same.
The country goes to war at the same time that world oil prices increase	The country's entry into war causes the *AD* curve to shift to the right.	The rise in world oil prices causes the *SRAS* curve to shift to the left.	The aggregate price level will increase.	The aggregate level of production may increase, decrease, or remain the same.
People's real wealth decreases	This event causes the *AD* curve to shift to the left.	This event causes a movement along the *SRAS* curve.	The aggregate price level will decrease.	The aggregate level of production will decrease.

2. Today on a radio talk show you heard the commentator say that aggregate demand expresses an inverse relationship between the level of aggregate production and the aggregate price level. The commentator said this was due to the wealth effect and the interest rate effect. A friend listening to the show with you doesn't understand what this means, and she has asked you to explain the ideas behind these two effects and how they are related to the inverse relationship between the aggregate price level and the aggregate level of production.

STEP 1: Review the definitions of the wealth effect and the interest rate effect.

Review the section "Why Is the Aggregate Demand Curve Downward Sloping?" on pages 413–414.

The wealth effect focuses on the effect of a change in the aggregate price level on the purchasing power or real income of consumers. When the aggregate price level increases, this reduces the real income that consumers have: for any given level of nominal income, a rise in the aggregate price level will lower consumers' ability to purchase goods and services. As the aggregate price level rises, consumption spending will therefore fall. Thus, as the aggregate price level increases, the level of aggregate output demanded will fall.

The interest rate effect focuses on the effect of a change in the aggregate price level on the interest rate in the economy. When the aggregate price level increases, people will demand more money since they will need more money in order to purchase the same basket of goods and services. As the demand for money increases, this causes the interest rate to rise, and this rise in interest rates means that it will cost more for businesses to borrow to finance their investment spending. Thus, as the interest rate rises, investment spending falls. This fall in investment spending results in a decrease in aggregate demand as the aggregate price level rises.

STEP 2: Explain why these two effects suggest that there is an inverse relationship between the aggregate price level and the aggregate level of production.

Review the section "Why Is the Aggregate Demand Curve Downward Sloping?" on pages 413–414.

Both effects, the wealth effect and the interest rate effect, indicate that when the aggregate price level rises, this will cause aggregate demand to decrease. The aggregate demand curve is downward sloping: there is an inverse relationship between the level of real GDP and the aggregate price level.

3. Suppose that you know the following information about an economy.

Long-run aggregate supply:	$Y = 8$
Short-run aggregate supply:	$P = 100Y$
Aggregate demand:	$P = 1,000 - 100Y$

As shown here, P refers to aggregate prices and Y refers to the aggregate level of production. You are asked to determine the short-run equilibrium aggregate price level and aggregate output level. You are also asked to identify if there is a short-run recessionary gap or a short-run inflationary gap. Comment on the implications of this gap on the level of unemployment in this economy in the short run. In addition, you are asked to provide a graph that depicts this short-run equilibrium as well as the long-run aggregate supply curve for this economy. Finally, you are asked to propose several policy options for the government of this country if it wishes to return to the long-run equilibrium. You are also asked to discuss the implications of not implementing any active policy to return the economy to long-run equilibrium.

STEP 1: Use the short-run aggregate supply curve and aggregate demand curve to determine the short-run equilibrium level of aggregate prices and the short-run equilibrium level of aggregate output.

Review the section "The AD-AS Model" on pages 428–436, the section "Macroeconomic Policy" on pages 436–439, and Figure 14-13 on page 433.

Since you are given equations for the three curves, you can solve for the equilibrium values of P and Y. To find the short-run equilibrium aggregate price level and the short-run equilibrium aggregate output level, use the short-run aggregate supply curve and the aggregate demand curve. Thus, $100Y = 1,000 - 100Y$, and therefore $P = 500$ and $Y = 5$.

STEP 2: Determine whether there is a recessionary gap or an inflationary gap by comparing the short-run equilibrium level of aggregate output to the long-run level of aggregate output. Then consider the implications of this gap on this economy's unemployment rate.

Review the section "The AD-AS Model" on pages 428–436, the section "Macroeconomic Policy" on pages 436–439, and Figure 14-13 on page 433.

A recessionary gap occurs when the short-run level of aggregate output is less than the long-run level of aggregate output. An inflationary gap occurs when the short-run level of aggregate output is greater than the long-run level of aggregate output. In this case, the short-run level of aggregate output is equal to 5 and the long-run level of aggregate output is equal to 8: this economy has a recessionary gap. It is currently producing a level of aggregate output that is lower than its potential or long-run level of output: the economy is in a recession and unemployment is relatively high.

STEP 3: Draw a graph that depicts the short-run aggregate supply curve, the long-run aggregate supply curve, and the aggregate demand curve. On your graph, mark the short-run equilibrium aggregate price level and the short-run equilibrium level of aggregate output. Also, mark the long-run level of aggregate output.

Review the section "The AD-AS Model" on pages 428–436, the section "Macroeconomic Policy" on pages 436–439, and Figure 14-13 on page 433.

Here is the graph of this economy's short-run equilibrium as well as its long-run level of aggregate output.

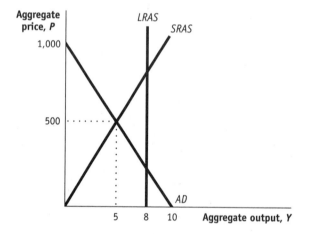

STEP 4: Determine what type of activist policy, monetary or fiscal, will move this economy to the long-run level of aggregate output.

Review the section "The AD-AS Model" on pages 428–436, the section "Macroeconomic Policy" on pages 436–439, and Figure 14-13 on page 433.

Since short-run aggregate output is less than long-run aggregate output, activist policy should stimulate the economy. The government could implement activist fiscal policy: this could involve an increase in government spending, a decrease in taxes, or a combination of these two policies. The effect of this government intervention in the economy would be to shift the aggregate demand curve to the right, restoring the economy to its long-run equilibrium level of aggregate output. This policy would also raise the aggregate price level.

Alternatively, the government could pursue activist monetary policy: the central bank could increase the money supply in order to shift the aggregate demand curve to the right. As with fiscal policy, activist monetary policy in this example will cause aggregate output to increase to the long-run level while also causing the aggregate price level to rise.

STEP 5: Discuss what would happen in this economy if no activist policy is implemented.

Review the section "The AD-AS Model" on pages 428–436, the section "Macroeconomic Policy" on pages 436–439, and Figure 14-13 on page 433.

If there is no activist policy implemented, this economy will return to the long-run level of aggregate output eventually. With the recessionary gap, the economy finds that its unemployment rate is relatively high and over time this will cause nominal wages to decrease. As nominal wages decrease, this will cause the short-run aggregate supply curve to shift to the right. The short-run aggregate supply curve will shift to the right until the economy's production returns to the potential or long-run level of aggregate output. Notice that this adjustment to the long-run equilibrium results in a higher level of aggregate output than was present in the short run and a lower aggregate price level than the short-run aggregate price level.

4. For this question, continue with the information you were given in Worked Problem 3 about the economy's short-run aggregate supply curve, the economy's long-run aggregate supply curve, and the economy's aggregate demand curve. You are told that simultaneously this economy experiences three shocks. These three shocks are as follows:

    • The price of every unit produced in this economy increases by $100 due to a change in the price of inputs. This shock only affects the short-run aggregate supply curve.

    • There is an increase in the wealth of individuals that increases the y-intercept of the aggregate demand curve by 30%. This change in wealth does not alter the slope of the aggregate demand curve.

    • A hurricane destroys a significant amount of capital in this economy, and the long-run aggregate supply curve is now $Y = 5$.

Given these three shocks to the economy you are asked to determine the short-run equilibrium aggregate price level and the short-run equilibrium level of aggregate output. You are also asked to identify if there is a short-run recessionary gap or a short-run inflationary gap. Comment on the implications of this gap on the level of unemployment in this economy in the short run. In addition, you are asked to provide a graph that depicts this short-run equilibrium as well as the long-run aggregate supply curve for this economy. Finally, you are asked to propose several policy options for the government of this country if it wishes to return to the long-run equilibrium. You are also asked to discuss the implications of not implementing any active policy to return the economy to long-run equilibrium.

STEP 1: **Determine what the new short-run aggregate supply curve is, given the above information. Then determine what the aggregate demand curve is, given this information. Finally, determine what the long-run aggregate supply curve is, given the above information.**

Review the section "The AD–AS Model" on pages 428–436, the section "Macroeconomic Policy" on pages 436–439, Figure 14-13 on page 433, and Figure 14-14 on page 435.

To answer this set of questions, you will first need to determine how these three shocks affect the three equations that you have been given.

We know that the short-run aggregate supply curve has shifted to the left due to the increase in the price of inputs. The y-intercept of the short-run aggregate supply curve has shifted up by $100. We can write this as $P = 100 + 100Y$.

The aggregate demand curve has shifted to the right due to the increase in wealth. The y-intercept of the aggregate demand curve is initially 1,000 and now it will be 30% greater. 30% of 1,000 is 300, so the new y-intercept for the aggregate demand curve is 1,300. Since the slope of the aggregate demand curve is unaffected, we can write the new aggregate demand curve as $P = 1,300 - 100Y$.

The long-run aggregate supply curve has shifted to the left due to the loss in the capital stock. The new long-run aggregate supply curve can be written as $Y = 5$.

STEP 2: Use the short-run aggregate supply curve and aggregate demand curve to determine the short-run equilibrium level of aggregate prices and the short-run equilibrium level of aggregate output.

Review the section "The AD–AS Model" on pages 428–436, the section "Macroeconomic Policy" on pages 436–439, Figure 14-13 on page 433, and Figure 14-14 on page 435.

From the short-run aggregate supply, we have $P = 100 + 100Y$ and from the aggregate demand, we have $P = 1{,}300 - 100Y$. Setting these two equations equal to one another, we find that $Y = 6$ and that $P = 700$.

STEP 3: Determine whether there is a recessionary gap or an inflationary gap by comparing the short-run equilibrium level of aggregate output to the long-run level of aggregate output. Then consider the implications of this gap on this economy's unemployment rate.

Review the section "The AD–AS Model" on pages 428–436, the section "Macroeconomic Policy" on pages 436–439, Figure 14-13 on page 433, and Figure 14-14 on page 435.

A recessionary gap occurs when the short-run level of aggregate output is less than the long-run level of aggregate output. An inflationary gap occurs when the short-run level of aggregate output is greater than the long-run level of aggregate output. In this case, the short-run level of aggregate output is equal to 6 and the long-run level of aggregate output is equal to 5: this economy has an inflationary gap. It is currently producing a level of aggregate output that is greater than its potential or long-run level of output: the economy currently has an unemployment rate that is lower than its natural rate of unemployment.

STEP 4: Draw a graph that depicts the short-run aggregate supply curve, the long-run aggregate supply curve, and the aggregate demand curve. On your graph, mark the short-run equilibrium aggregate price level and the short-run equilibrium level of aggregate output. Also, mark the long-run level of aggregate output.

Review the section "The AD–AS Model" on pages 428–436, the section "Macroeconomic Policy" on pages 436–439, Figure 14-13 on page 433, and Figure 14-14 on page 435.

Here is the graph of this economy's short-run equilibrium as well as its long-run level of aggregate output.

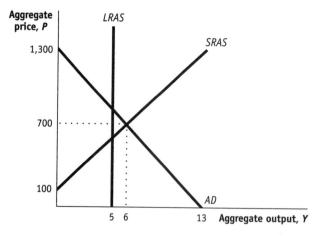

STEP 5: Determine what type of activist policy, monetary or fiscal, will move this economy to the long-run level of aggregate output.

Review the section "The AD–AS Model" on pages 428–436, the section "Macroeconomic Policy" on pages 436–439, Figure 14-13 on page 433, and Figure 14-14 on page 435.

Since short-run aggregate output is greater than long-run aggregate output, activist policy should contract the economy. The government could implement activist fiscal policy: this could involve a decrease in government spending, an increase in taxes, or a combination of these two policies. The effect of this government intervention in the economy would be to shift the aggregate demand curve to the left, restoring the economy to its long-run equilibrium level of aggregate output. This policy would also decrease the aggregate price level.

Alternatively, the government could pursue activist monetary policy: the central bank could decrease the money supply in order to shift the aggregate demand curve to the left. As with fiscal policy, activist monetary policy in this example will cause aggregate output to decrease to the long-run level while causing the aggregate price level to fall.

STEP 6: Discuss what will happen in this economy if no activist policy is implemented.

Review the section "The AD–AS Model" on pages 428–436, the section "Macroeconomic Policy" on pages 436–439, Figure 14-13 on page 433, and Figure 14-14 on page 435.

If no activist policy is implemented, this economy will eventually return to the long-run level of aggregate output. With the inflationary gap, the economy finds that its unemployment rate is relatively low, and over time this will cause nominal wages to increase. As nominal wages increase, this will cause the short-run aggregate supply curve to shift to the left. The short-run aggregate supply curve will shift to the left until the economy's production returns to the potential or long-run level of aggregate output. Notice that this adjustment to the long-run equilibrium results in a lower level of aggregate output than was present in the short run and a higher aggregate price level than the short-run aggregate price level.

5. Suppose that an economy is initially in long-run equilibrium and is producing a level of aggregate output that is equal to its potential output level. What will the short-run consequences be in this economy if there is an increase in the price of oil? Make sure that your answer addresses the effect of this price increase on both the level of aggregate output and the aggregate price level. In the short run, will this economy experience an inflationary gap or a recessionary gap?

STEP 1: Analyze the short-run effect of a change in the price of oil on the short-run aggregate supply curve and the aggregate demand curve.

Review the section "The AD–AS Model" on pages 428–436, the section "Macroeconomic Policy" on pages 436–439, and Figure 14-13 on page 433.

When the price of oil rises, this is a change in a commodity price or an input price, which will cause the short-run aggregate supply curve to shift to the left. The change in the oil price will not cause a shift in the aggregate demand curve.

STEP 2: Having determined in Step 1 what the impact of this change in the price of oil was on the short-run curves in the aggregate demand and aggregate supply model, now predict the impact of this change on the aggregate price level and the aggregate output level.

Review the section "The AD-AS Model" on pages 428–436, the section "Macroeconomic Policy" on pages 436–439, and Figure 14-13 on page 433.

If the short-run aggregate supply curve shifts to the left, this will cause a movement along the aggregate demand curve: the aggregate price level will increase while the aggregate output level will decrease.

STEP 3: **Determine whether this economy experiences an inflationary gap or a recessionary gap in the short run.**

Review the section "The AD-AS Model" on pages 428–436, the section "Macroeconomic Policy" on pages 436–439, and Figure 14-13 on page 433.

Since the level of aggregate output has decreased, which implies that the economy is now producing at a level of output that is lower than the potential or full employment level of output, the economy is experiencing a recessionary gap. Notice that this economy has both higher prices and lower output: this is an example of stagflation.

Problems and Exercises

1. Consider an economy that is initially in long-run equilibrium as drawn in the following graph, where *LRAS* is the long-run *AS* curve, AD_1 is the aggregate demand curve, $SRAS_1$ is the short-run *AS* curve, Y_1 is potential output, and P_1 is the equilibrium aggregate price level.

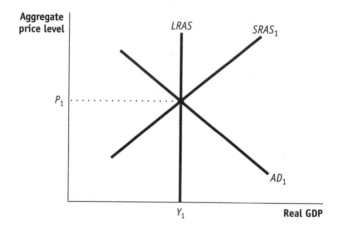

a. Draw a graph using the *AD-AS* model to illustrate the effect of each of the following separate changes to the model in the short run.
(1) The economy's central bank decreases the money supply.

Aggregate price level

Real GDP

(2) Productivity decreases in the economy.

Aggregate price level

Real GDP

(3) Consumer confidence in the economy increases.

Aggregate price level

Real GDP

(4) Commodity prices fall dramatically.

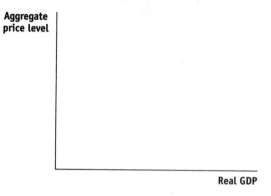

b. Identify verbally what happens to aggregate output and the aggregate price level relative to the initial long-run equilibrium for each of the scenarios.

c. For each of the scenarios determine whether the economy faces a short-run recessionary gap or an inflationary gap.

d. For each of the scenarios determine if there is an active stabilization policy that will offset the particular shock. If so, discuss what this active stabilization policy is. You may find it helpful to draw a graph illustrating the effects of your active policy prescription on the aggregate economy.

e. For each of the scenarios identify what happens in the long run to the aggregate price level and the aggregate output level if there is no active stabilization policy.

2. Consider an economy operating with an inflationary gap in the short run. Briefly describe what this short-run equilibrium looks like, making specific reference to potential output and then describe the process by which this economy moves from short-run to long-run macroeconomic equilibrium. Use a graph to illustrate your description.

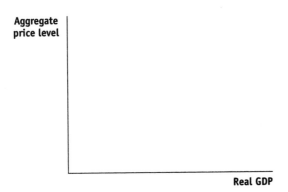

3. Consider an economy operating with a recessionary gap in the short run.

   a. Why does this represent a problem for this economy? Draw a graph illustrating your answer.

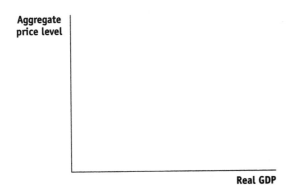

   b. What policies are available to policy makers to address this problem? Draw a graph illustrating possible policies.

c. If policy makers do nothing, describe the mechanism by which this economy will return to long-run macroeconomic equilibrium. Draw a graph illustrating this long-run adjustment.

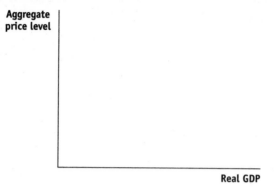

4. The *AD–AS* model is said to have a self-correcting mechanism. Explain what this means and how this self-correcting mechanism works. Use a graph to illustrate your answer.

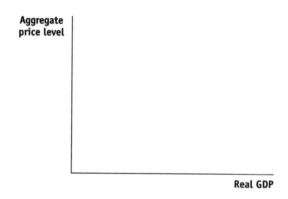

5. Use a graph of the *AD–AS* model to illustrate long-run economic growth in an economy. Explain your graph and how it illustrates economic growth. Assume in your answer that *AD* does *not* change over time.

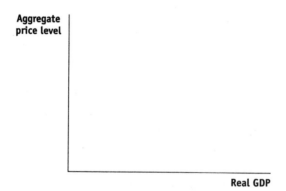

6. Macroland is a small, closed economy that is currently operating at the long-run equilibrium level of output. It is therefore producing Y_P where Y_P is potential output. Its aggregate price level is P_1.

a. Draw a graph of this long-run equilibrium for Macroland depicting the AD curve, the $SRAS$ curve, and the $LRAS$ curve. Label both axes and identify Y_P and P_1 on your graph.

b. Suppose that Macroland experiences a negative demand shock. Draw a new graph depicting the short-run changes in the original equilibrium that will occur because of this demand shock. On your graph identify the new short-run equilibrium level of output Y_2 and the new short-run equilibrium aggregate price level P_2. Label any shifts in AD or AS clearly.

Aggregate price level

Real GDP

c. Given the change in part (b), draw a third graph illustrating the long-run adjustment to the negative demand shock. Label any shifting curves clearly and identify the new long-run equilibrium level of aggregate output Y_3 and the new long-run aggregate price level P_3.

d. Given the change in part (b), suppose the government wishes to engage in activist monetary policy in order to restore the economy to its initial equilibrium. What monetary policy would you advise in order to reach this goal?

e. Given the change in part (b), suppose the government wishes to engage in activist fiscal policy in order to restore the economy to its initial equilibrium. Provide two policy approaches that would enable this economy to return to its initial equilibrium.

7. For each of the following scenarios, describe the effect on the *AD* curve, the *SRAS* curve, and the *LRAS* curve. Identify whether the effect causes a shift of the curve or a movement along the curve, and identify the direction of the shift or the movement.

a. An increase in the money supply causes interest rates to fall.

b. The price of commodities increases by 10% this year.

c. The price of oil falls.

d. Labor unions successfully negotiate an increase in nominal wages for their workers.

e. The supply of unsold houses in an economy increases by 20%.

f. There is an increase in labor productivity due to increases in human capital.

g. The government increases spending in order to finance the war against terrorists.

▌BEFORE YOU TAKE THE TEST

Chapter Review Questions

1.   In the short run, a situation where the aggregate price level increases while the aggregate output level decreases is
a. best explained as the result of a positive demand shock.
b. stagflation.
c. best explained as the result of a negative demand shock.
d. Answers (a) and (b) are both correct.
e. Answers (b) and (c) are both correct.

2.   In the short run, an increase in the aggregate price level due to a shift in *AD* first results in
a. a rightward shift in the *SRAS* curve.
b. a movement along the *SRAS* curve.
c. no change in the level of aggregate production.
d. a leftward shift in the *SRAS* curve.

3.   Suppose the *AD-AS* model is initially in long-run equilibrium. Suppose there is an increase in wealth, holding everything else constant. Then, in the short run,
a. there will be a movement along the *AD* curve.
b. the economy will produce at its potential level of output.
c. there will be a rightward shift in the *AD* curve.
d. the aggregate level of production will increase while the aggregate price level will fall.

4.   Nominal wages
a. are often determined by contracts that were signed at some previous point in time.
b. are slow to decrease in times of high unemployment, since employers may be reluctant to alter wages as a response to economic conditions.
c. are fully flexible in both the short run and the long run.
d. Answers (a) and (b) are both correct.
e. Answers (a), (b), (c), and (d) are all correct.

5. Which of the following statements is true? In the short run, holding everything else constant,
   a. as production costs increase, profit per unit decreases, and this causes suppliers to increase their production.
   b. as production costs increase, profit per unit decreases, and this causes suppliers to reduce their production.
   c. as production costs decrease, profit per unit increases, and this causes suppliers to reduce their production.
   d. the *AS* curve is unaffected by changes in production costs.

6. Suppose there is an increase in the price of a commodity, holding everything else constant. In the short run,
   a. the producer will increase production since commodity prices have risen.
   b. the producer's profit per unit of output will decrease.
   c. the producer's price per unit of output will decrease.
   d. there will be a movement along the *AS* curve.
   e. Answers (a) and (b) are both correct.

7. Which of the following will *not* make the *AS* curve shift to the left?
   a. an increase in the aggregate price level
   b. a decrease in commodity prices
   c. an increase in nominal wages
   d. None of the above causes the *AS* curve to shift to the left.
   e. Answers (a) and (b) are both correct.
   f. Answers (b) and (c) are both correct.

8. In comparing the short run with the long run, which of the following statements is true?
   a. In both the short run and the long run, the aggregate price level and the aggregate output level are positively related.
   b. In the short run, the economy never produces at the potential output level, while in the long run, the economy always produces at the potential output level.
   c. In the short run, nominal wages are slow to fully adjust to economic changes, while in the long run, nominal wages are completely flexible and make full adjustment to economic changes.
   d. Answers (a), (b), and (c) are all correct.
   e. Answers (a) and (c) are both true.
   f. Answers (b) and (c) are both true.

9. In the long run, the aggregate price level increases. This
   a. is due to the short-run *AS* curve shifting to the right and the economy producing a level of aggregate output that is not equal to its potential output.
   b. is due to the *AD* curve shifting to the right.
   c. has no effect on the level of aggregate production in the economy.
   d. results in the economy moving to the level of production where aggregate output exceeds potential output.
   e. Answers (a) and (c) are both correct.
   f. Answers (b) and (c) are both correct.
   g. Answers (c) and (d) are both correct.

10. Suppose the economy is in short-run equilibrium and the level of aggregate output is less than potential output. Then, it must be true that
    a. unemployment in this economy is relatively low.
    b. over time the short-run *AS* curve will shift to the left.
    c. over time nominal wages will fall.
    d. the economy is also in long-run equilibrium.

11. *AD*
    a. depicts the relationship between the aggregate price level and the quantity of aggregate output demanded.
    b. is a positive relationship between the aggregate price level and the quantity of aggregate output demanded.
    c. is always equal to potential output, no matter what the aggregate price level is.
    d. increases, other things equal, as the aggregate price level increases.

12. As the aggregate price level increases, holding everything else constant,
    a. this reduces the purchasing power of many assets.
    b. this reduces the purchasing power of a given amount of money.
    c. the wealth and interest rate effects lead to a reduction in the quantity of aggregate output demanded.
    d. Answers (a), (b), and (c) are all correct.

13. Holding everything else constant, the *AD* curve will shift to the right when
    a. the central bank decreases the money supply.
    b. household wealth increases.
    c. the government increases taxes paid by households.
    d. Answers (a), (b), and (c) are all correct.
    e. Answers (a) and (b) are both correct.
    f. Answers (b) and (c) are both correct.

14. Which of the following statements is true?
    a. Stagflation refers to the economic situation where aggregate output is falling and the aggregate price level is rising.
    b. Stagflation is most easily explained as the economic outcome that occurs due to a negative supply shock.
    c. Stagflation is most easily explained as the economic outcome that occurs due to a negative demand shock.
    d. Stagflation is most easily explained as the economic outcome that occurs due to either a negative supply shock or a negative demand shock.
    e. Statements (a) and (b) are both true.
    f. Statements (a) and (c) are both true.
    g. Statements (a) and (d) are both true.

15. The economic slump of the 1970s was largely due to events in the Middle East that caused oil prices to
    a. increase and led to a leftward shift in aggregate demand.
    b. decrease and led to a rightward shift in short-run aggregate supply.
    c. increase and led to a rightward shift in aggregate demand.
    d. increase and led to a leftward shift in short-run aggregate supply.

Answer the next two questions using the following information:

Suppose Macroland is initially in long-run equilibrium. Then, suppose the central bank of Macroland increases the money supply.

16. In the short run, we know that this policy action
   a. will reduce interest rates and therefore stimulate investment spending.
   b. will lead to a reduction in unemployment and an increase in aggregate production.
   c. will lead to the short-run *AS* curve shifting to the right.
   d. Answers (a), (b), and (c) are all correct.
   e. Answers (a) and (b) are both correct.
   f. Answers (b) and (c) are both correct.
   g. Answers (a) and (c) are both correct.

17. In the long run, Macroland will produce at
   a. the potential output level.
   b. a level of aggregate output greater than potential output.
   c. a level of aggregate output less than potential output.
   d. the same level of aggregate output as it did initially before the central bank increased the money supply, but with a lower aggregate price level than its initial level.

18. Which of the following statements is true?
   a. In a recessionary gap, aggregate output exceeds potential output.
   b. In an inflationary gap, aggregate output exceeds potential output.
   c. A recessionary gap is a long-run phenomenon that requires government policy action to eliminate.
   d. Recessionary gaps and inflationary gaps, if they exist, will be eliminated in the short run by the natural workings of the economy.

19. Suppose Funland is initially in long-run macroeconomic equilibrium. Then, there is a supply shock due to a severe increase in commodity prices. If Funland's policy makers use active stabilization policy to offset this supply shock,
   a. they can effectively eliminate the economic effects of the supply shock.
   b. they can either reduce the aggregate price level down to its initial equilibrium level, or they can increase aggregate output to its initial level.
   c. they can either increase the aggregate price level to its initial equilibrium level, or they can decrease aggregate output to its initial level.
   d. this will greatly reduce the economic fluctuations Funland experiences from this supply shock.

20. Which of the following statements is true?

    I. One reason the aggregate demand curve slopes downward is the wealth effect, which states that as the aggregate price level increases, holding everything else constant, the purchasing power of people's assets decline, leading people to decrease the quantity of aggregate production they demand at every price.

    II. One reason the aggregate demand curve slopes downward is the interest rate effect, which states that as the aggregate price level increases, holding everything else constant, people demand more money and this causes interest rates to rise. This increase in interest rates causes the level of investment spending in the economy to decline.

    III. One reason the aggregate demand curve slopes downward is that as the aggregate price level decreases, people decide to buy more units of relatively inexpensive goods and fewer units of relatively expensive goods.

    a. Statements (I), (II), and (III) are all true.

    b. Statements (I) and (II) are both true.

    c. Statements (I) and (III) are both true.

    d. Statements (II) and (III) are both true.

21. An increase in the interest rate, holding everything else constant,

    a. reduces investment spending since the cost of borrowing is now higher.

    b. reduces consumer spending since households will respond to the higher interest rate by saving more.

    c. leads to a reduction in the level of aggregate demand for final goods and services.

    d. Answers (a), (b), and (c) are all correct.

22. Which of the following will *not* cause a shift in the *AD* curve?

    a. an increase in the level of wealth in the economy

    b. a reduction in government spending

    c. the decision by the central bank in an economy to expand the money supply

    d. the increase in the price of a commodity

23. Suppose the aggregate price level in the economy falls. Holding everything else constant, this will result in the wealth effect,

    a. which will cause the *AD* curve to shift to the right.

    b. because the fall in the aggregate price level increases consumers' purchasing power, and this increase in purchasing power will result in a downward movement along the *AD* curve.

    c. which will cause the *AD* curve to shift to the left.

    d. because the fall in the aggregate price level increases consumers' purchasing power, and this increase in purchasing power will result in an upward movement along the *AD* curve.

24. Which of the following policies will shift the *AD* curve to the right?

    a. The government increases its level of taxation in the economy.

    b. The government decreases the money supply in the economy.

    c. The government decreases its level of taxation in the economy.

    d. The government decreases its level of spending in the economy.

    e. Answers (a) and (d) will both shift the *AD* curve to the right.

    f. Answers (c) and (d) will both shift the *AD* curve to the right.

25. An increase in the aggregate price level, holding everything else constant, causes
    a. movement along the *AS* curve.
    b. a shift to the right of the *AD* curve due to the wealth effect and the interest rate effect.
    c. a shift to the left of the *AD* curve due to the wealth effect and the interest rate effect.
    d. a shift to the right of the *AS* curve, since producers will be willing to supply more goods and services at every price than they were initially.
    e. a shift to the left of the *AS* curve, since producers will supply fewer goods and services at every price than they did initially.

26. Suppose an economy is currently in short-run equilibrium where the level of real GDP is less than potential output. Which of the following statements is true?
    a. In the long run, nominal wages will fall and the *SRAS* curve will shift to the left, restoring the economy to potential output.
    b. In the long run, nominal wages will fall and the *SRAS* curve will shift to the right, restoring the economy to potential output.
    c. In the long run, nominal wages will fall and the *AD* curve will shift to the left, restoring the economy to potential output.
    d. In the long run, nominal wages will fall and the *AD* curve will shift to the right, restoring the economy to potential output.

27. In the *AD-AS* model, a key feature that distinguishes the long run from the short run is wages and prices are sticky in the
    a. long run.   b. short run.

28. Suppose that short-run equilibrium real GDP for an economy is currently greater than potential output. This implies that
    a. nominal wages will need to adjust upward as the economy moves from the short run to the long run.
    b. the level of unemployment is very low for this economy.
    c. jobs are plentiful in this economy.
    d. to reach long-run equilibrium, the *SRAS* curve will shift to the left, resulting in a higher aggregate price level.
    e. Answers (a), (b), (c), and (d) are all correct.
    f. Answers (a), (b), and (c) are correct.
    g. Answers (a) and (d) are both correct.

29. A positive demand shock shifts *AD* to the
    a. right and results in a higher aggregate price level and a higher level of real GDP in the short run, holding everything else constant.
    b. left and results in a higher aggregate price level and a higher level of real GDP in the short run, holding everything else constant.

30. Suppose an economy is initially in long-run equilibrium. Then, holding everything else constant, there is an increase in people's wealth in this economy. If the government wishes to maintain the same aggregate price level and aggregate level of real GDP as it had initially, it should increase
    a. government spending.
    b. the money supply.
    c. the level of investment spending.
    d. the level of taxes.

ANSWER KEY

Answers to Problems and Exercises

1. a.

(1)

(2)

(3)

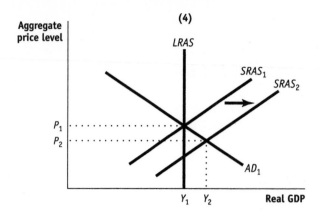

b. In scenario (1), the aggregate price level and the aggregate level of output both decrease relative to their initial levels. In scenario (2), the aggregate price level increases, while the aggregate level of output decreases relative to their initial levels. In scenario (3), the aggregate price level and the aggregate level of output both increase relative to their initial levels. In scenario (4), the aggregate price level falls, while the aggregate level of output increases relative to their initial levels.

c. A short-run recessionary gap is defined as a situation where the economy produces at a level of output that is less than potential output: scenarios (1) and (2) illustrate this situation. Scenarios (3) and (4) represent inflationary gaps since the level of aggregate output is greater than potential output.

d. For scenario (1), active stabilization policy can be used to bring the economy back to its initial aggregate price level and aggregate output level. This policy would need to shift AD to the right (back to its initial position) and could be accomplished by increasing government spending, decreasing taxes, or increasing the money supply.

For scenario (2), active stabilization policy cannot restore the economy to its initial equilibrium. A policy that shifts AD to the right would result in an increase in the aggregate price level relative to its initial level (P_3 versus P_1), and a return to the initial level of production, Y_1, for aggregate output. The following graph illustrates the implementation of an active stabilization policy that shifts AD to the right.

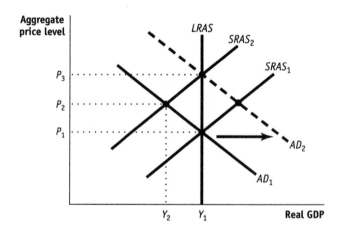

A policy that shifts AD to the left would result in a return to the initial aggregate price level of P_1, and a decrease in the level of aggregate output relative to its initial position (Y_3 versus Y_1). The following graph illustrates this.

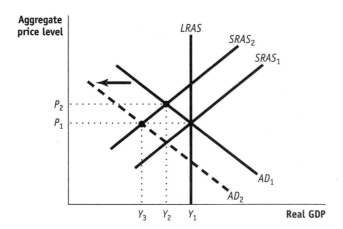

In scenario (3), active stabilization policy can be used to bring the economy back to its initial equilibrium. This policy would shift AD to the left and could be accomplished by decreasing government spending, increasing taxes, or decreasing the money supply.

In scenario (4), active stabilization policy cannot restore the economy to its initial equilibrium: shifting AD to the right restores the original price level to P_1, but increases the level of output above the initial level (Y_3 versus Y_1), thus creating an inflationary gap. The following graph illustrates this.

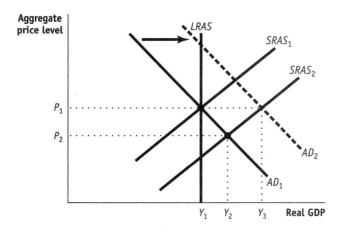

Shifting AD to the left restores output to its initial level Y_1, but the aggregate price level falls relative to its initial level (P_3 versus P_1). The following graph illustrates this.

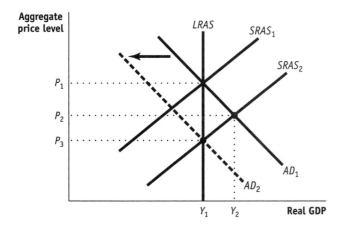

e. If there is no active stabilization policy implemented, then in scenario (1) the short-run *AS* curve will shift to the right as the nominal wage decreases in response to the recessionary gap. As the short-run *AS* curve shifts out, the economy will eventually reach long-run equilibrium where the aggregate output level returns to potential output, Y_1, while the aggregate price level falls to a lower long-run aggregate price level than the initial long-run P_1. In scenario (2), if there is no active stabilization policy implemented, the short-run *AS* curve will shift to the right, returning the economy back to its initial long-run macroeconomic equilibrium. In scenario (3), if there is no active stabilization policy implemented, the short-run *AS* curve will shift to the left, restoring the economy to the original level of aggregate output but a higher aggregate price level than the initial long-run P_1. In scenario (4), if there is no active stabilization policy implemented, the short-run *AS* curve will shift to the left, returning the economy to its initial equilibrium position.

2. An economy operating in the short run with an inflationary gap is producing a level of aggregate output, Y_1, that is greater than potential output, Y. This is illustrated in the following diagram.

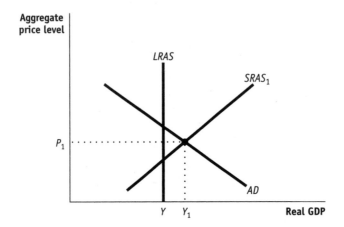

This implies that unemployment is relatively low and, therefore, workers are scarce and jobs are abundant. Over time this situation puts pressure on nominal wages to rise and this causes the short-run *AS* curve to shift to the left. As short-run *AS* shifts to the left ($SRAS_2$), the level of aggregate production in the economy falls and this brings aggregate output closer to potential output. The nominal wage will continue to adjust until the short-run *AS* curve intersects the *AD* curve and the long-run *AS* curve at the same point. Then the economy will be in long-run macroeconomic equilibrium, where aggregate output equals potential output while the aggregate price level has risen to P_2 from P_1. This is illustrated in the following graph.

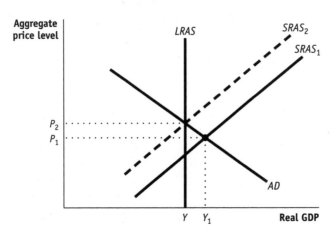

3. **a.** A recessionary gap for an economy is problematic, since it indicates that the economy is producing a lower level of aggregate output (Y_1) than its potential (Y): this lower output also signals that the economy faces higher unemployment than necessary. This is illustrated in the following graph.

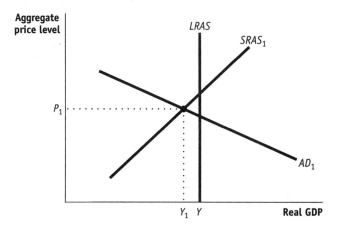

b. To offset a recessionary gap, active stabilization policy can be implemented that will return the economy to potential output. A recessionary gap caused by a leftward shift in *AD* is easily offset by using fiscal policy or monetary policy to shift *AD* to the right and returning the aggregate output to the level of potential output (Y). A recessionary gap caused by a leftward shift in short-run *AS* is a more difficult problem: active stabilization policy that shifts *AD* to the right can bring the aggregate level of production back to potential output but only by raising the aggregate price level to a higher level (P_2 versus P_0). This is illustrated in the following graph.

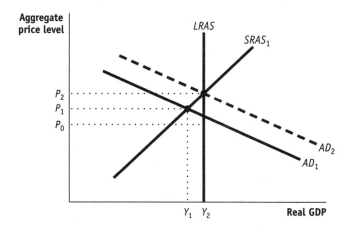

c. If policy makers do nothing, the economy will return to a long-run macroeconomic equilibrium over time through changes in the nominal wage and accompanying shifts in the short-run *AS* curve. If the recessionary gap is due to a leftward shift in *AD*, over time we can expect short-run *AS* to shift to the right, bringing the economy back to potential output and a lower aggregate price level than experienced during the recessionary gap. If the recessionary gap is due to a leftward shift in short-run *AS*, over time we can expect short-run *AS* to shift back to the right, returning the economy to its potential output and a lower aggregate price level than it experienced during the recessionary gap. Both of these possibilities are illustrated in the following graph.

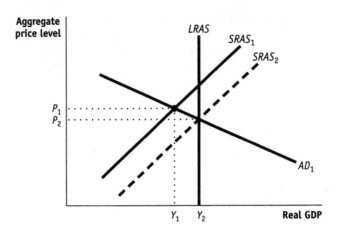

4. The *AD–AS* model is self-correcting, since it will always return to long-run macroeconomic equilibrium if given a sufficient amount of time for the short-run *AS* curve to adjust to economic changes through changes in the nominal wage. This adjustment process has been reviewed in several earlier problems: essentially, it is the idea that the short-run *AS* curve shifts due to changes in the nominal wage until that point where *AD* intersects both the short-run and the long-run *AS* curves at potential output. If this is still unclear to you, review problems 1 and 2 and the diagrams illustrating their answers.

5. Long-run economic growth is depicted in the *AD–AS* model as the long-run *AS* shifting to the right. Thus, your graph should depict several vertical *AS* curves, with each one farther to the right on the horizontal axis, representing the ability of the economy to reach even higher levels of potential output. For a given *AD* curve, the level of aggregate output increases as the *LRAS* curve shifts to the right. The following graph illustrates this idea.

6. a.

b.

c.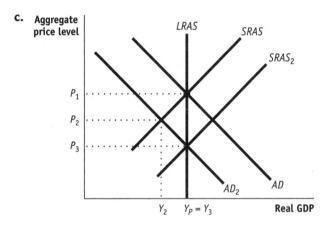

d. To offset a negative demand shock, the government needs to shift the *AD* curve to the right. Monetary policy that increases the money supply will shift the *AD* curve to the right and return the economy to P_1 and Y_P.

e. To offset a negative demand shock, the government needs to shift the *AD* curve to the right. Fiscal policy offers two approaches to shifting the *AD* curve to the right: the government can increase the level of government spending or it can decrease the level of taxes.

7. a. An increase in the money supply is an example of monetary policy: the *AD* curve will shift to the right and there will be a movement upward along the *SRAS* curve. There will be no change in the *LRAS* curve.

b. When the price of commodities increases, this causes the *SRAS* curve to shift to the left. There will be a movement upward along the *AD* curve and no change in the *LRAS* curve.

c. When the price of oil decreases, this causes the *SRAS* curve to shift to the right and results in a downward movement along the *AD* curve. There is no change in the *LRAS* curve.

d. The result of the successful labor union negotiation is higher wages, which leads to a leftward shift in the *SRAS* curve and an upward movement along the *AD* curve. There is no change in the *LRAS* curve.

e. When the inventory of unsold houses increases in an economy, this implies that the level of investment is high and there is therefore less incentive for firms to invest in this economy. As investment spending falls, this causes the *AD* curve to shift to the left, resulting in a downward movement along the *SRAS* curve. There is no change in the *LRAS* curve.

f. When labor productivity increases, this causes the *SRAS* curve to shift to the right, but it also causes the *LRAS* curve to shift to the right since the economy can now produce at a higher potential output level. There is a downward movement along the *AD* curve.

g. When the government increases spending to finance a war, this causes the *AD* curve to shift to the right, resulting in a movement upward along the *SRAS* curve. There is no change in the *LRAS* curve.

Answers to Chapter Review Questions

1. **Answer b.** Stagflation refers to the combination of rising inflation and decreasing aggregate production. When the *SRAS* curve shifts to the left (a negative supply shock), this causes the aggregate price level to increase and the aggregate level of output to decrease.

2. **Answer b.** A change in the aggregate price level due to a shift in *AD* results in a movement along the *SRAS* curve. In the short run the *SRAS* curve is upward sloping, so an increase in the aggregate price level results in a higher level of aggregate production.

3. **Answer c.** The economy produces at its potential level of output if it is at a long-run equilibrium. The increase in wealth will cause the *AD* curve to shift to the right, causing a movement along the *SRAS* curve, and an increase in aggregate production and the aggregate price level.

4. **Answer d.** In the short run, nominal wages are sticky and take time to adjust to changes in economic conditions due to pre-existing contracts and employer reluctance to frequently alter wages. In the long run, nominal wages are fully flexible.

5. **Answer b.** Production costs affect the level of aggregate production: as production costs increase, holding everything else constant, profit per unit decreases. Producers respond to this decrease in profit per unit by decreasing the quantity of goods and services they are willing to supply.

6. **Answer b.** An increase in the price of a commodity, holding everything else constant, will cause the *AS* curve to shift to the left as aggregate production decreases at any given aggregate price level. Aggregate production decreases due to the decrease in producers' profit per unit, arising from the higher commodity price they must now pay.

7. **Answer e.** An increase in the aggregate price level results in a movement along the *AS* curve and not a shift of the curve. A decrease in commodity prices results in a rightward shift of the *AS* curve. An increase in nominal wages causes the *AS* curve to shift to the left.

8. **Answer c.** In the long run, the *AS* is vertical and not upward sloping as it is in the short run. It is possible for an economy to be in both long-run and short-run equilibrium simultaneously so that the economy is producing its potential level of output. In the short run, we assume nominal wages are constrained from full adjustment and are therefore sticky, while in the long run, nominal wages are assumed to be fully flexible.

9. **Answer f.** In the long run, the economy by definition is already producing at the level of aggregate output we refer to as potential output. An increase in the aggregate price level in the long run can only be explained by a shift in the *AD* curve, and this shift will not affect aggregate output since the long-run *AS* curve is vertical.

10. **Answer c.** Since the economy is producing at a level of aggregate output smaller than the level of potential output, the economy cannot be in long-run equilibrium. And since output is below potential output, we know that not all workers are being fully utilized: if all workers were fully employed this would result in higher levels of production. Therefore, unemployment must be relatively high, and this will lead to decreases in the nominal wage over time since jobs are scarce and workers are abundant.

11. **Answer a.** The aggregate price level and the quantity of aggregate output demanded is the relationship captured by the *AD* curve. It is an inverse relationship: as the aggregate price level increases, other things equal, there is a decrease in the quantity of aggregate output demanded.

12. **Answer d.** An increase in the aggregate price level, holding everything else constant, leads to a decrease in aggregate demand for goods and services. This is due to the wealth effect and the interest rate effect. Answer (a) expresses how an increase in the aggregate price level affects people's wealth, while answer (b) expresses how this price change affects their purchasing power (via the interest rate effect).

13. **Answer b.** The *AD* curve will shift to the left if the central bank decreases the money supply, since this policy action will increase interest rates, reduce investment spending, and therefore lead to a reduction in the quantity of aggregate goods and services demanded at every aggregate price level. An increase in taxes reduces the disposable income that households have and will therefore lead to a reduction in the quantity of aggregate goods and services demanded at every aggregate price level (the *AD* curve will shift left). An increase in household wealth will shift the *AD* curve to the right, since households will increase their spending due to their increased wealth.

14. **Answer e.** Stagflation refers to a falling aggregate output level accompanied by a rising aggregate price level. In the *AD–AS* model this is most easily explained as a negative supply shock since this shift in the short-run *AS* curve causes economic output to fall while the aggregate price level increases.

15. **Answer d.** During the 1970s, events in the Middle East caused oil prices to rise. This increase in commodity prices caused the short-run aggregate supply curve to shift to the left, resulting in lower levels of aggregate output and a higher aggregate price level.

16. **Answer e.** Since the economy is initially in long-run macroeconomic equilibrium, we know aggregate output is initially equal to potential output. The central bank's policy action will cause interest rates to fall and investment spending to increase. This will cause the *AD* curve to shift to the right, resulting in short-run aggregate output exceeding potential output. This increase in output will result in a decrease in unemployment. Over time this will lead nominal wages to increase, which will result in the short-run *AS* curve shifting to the left.

17. **Answer a.** In the long run, macroeconomic equilibrium requires that the economy produce at that point where *AD* equals long-run *AS* as well as short-run *AS*. Short-run *AS* adjusts through changes in nominal wages to bring the equilibrium to this long-run equilibrium. When the central bank increases the money supply, this shifts the *AD* curve to the right. For a given long-run *AS* curve and this central bank action, it is possible to return to long-run macroeconomic equilibrium only if the short-run *AS* curve shifts to the left, resulting in a higher aggregate price level.

18. **Answer b.** A recessionary gap is a situation in the short run where aggregate output is less than potential output. A recessionary gap is eliminated in the long run as the short-run *AS* curve adjusts to return the economy to potential output and long-run equilibrium. An inflationary gap is a situation in the short run where aggregate output is greater than potential output. As the economy moves to a long-run equilibrium, this inflationary gap will be eliminated and aggregate output will return to potential output.

19. **Answer b.** Policy makers face a difficult trade-off when they try to offset a supply shock. In this case, the supply shock reduces aggregate output and increases the aggregate price level. Active stabilization policy can shift *AD* to the right or to the left: if *AD* shifts to the right, this will stimulate aggregate output while simultaneously increasing the aggregate price level to even higher levels; and if *AD* shifts to the left, this will reduce the aggregate price level while simultaneously decreasing the aggregate output level to even lower levels.

20. **Answer b.** The aggregate demand curve slopes downward due to the wealth and interest rate effects. Answer (c) is true for the demand for a particular good or service, but is not true for the aggregate demand for all final goods and services.

21. **Answer d.** When the interest rate rises, this makes borrowing more expensive for firms and leads firms to reduce their level of investment spending. At the same time, a higher interest rate will provide households with an incentive to save more. Both of these effects will lead to the quantity of aggregate output demanded to fall when there is a rise in the interest rate: this is referred to as the interest rate effect on aggregate demand.

22. **Answer d.** An increase in the price of a commodity will shift the *AS* curve to the left, which will result in a movement along the *AD* curve. Changes in wealth, the level of government spending, or the money supply will shift the *AD* curve.

23. **Answer b.** A fall in the aggregate price level changes the purchasing power of consumers' existing wealth and this wealth effect, due to the fall in the aggregate price level, will result in a movement down the *AD* curve. At the new lower aggregate price level, the quantity of aggregate output demanded for the economy increases.

24. **Answer c.** When the *AD* curve shifts to the right, this implies that the level of aggregate output demanded is greater at any given aggregate price level than it was initially. When the government increases government spending, decreases taxes, or increases the money supply, this results in greater aggregate output demanded at every price level. When the government decreases government spending, increases taxes, or decreases the money supply, this results in less aggregate output demanded at every price level.

25. **Answer a.** A change in the aggregate price level, holding everything else constant, causes a movement along the *AS* curve. It is important to realize that a change in the aggregate price level, holding everything else constant, causes a movement along the *AD* and the *AS* curves. For instance, suppose the aggregate price level is currently greater than the equilibrium aggregate price level: in the *AD–AS* model this will result in a situation of excess aggregate supply, and over time as the aggregate price level falls the level of aggregate output demanded will increase while the level of aggregate output supplied will decrease until the aggregate price level falls to that level where the *AD* cuts the *AS*.

26. **Answer b.** In the short run this economy is producing a level of real GDP that is less than potential GDP. This implies that jobs are scarce and unemployment high: over time workers will accept lower nominal wages in order to find employment. As the level of nominal wages falls, this causes the *SRAS* curve to shift to the right causing the level of real GDP to increase toward the potential output level.

27. **Answer b.** In the short run, wages and prices are not perfectly flexible because of informal and formal agreements that limit the short-run flexibility of wages and prices. Ultimately, formal contracts and informal agreements can be renegotiated to take into account changed economic circumstances. In the long run, wages and prices are fully flexible.

28. **Answer e.** When the economy in the short run produces a level of real GDP that is greater than potential output, this implies that unemployment is very low (since output is greater than the long-run potential level of output) and jobs very plentiful. In order to reach long-run equilibrium at the potential output, this economy's *SRAS* curve must shift to the left, which will cause the aggregate price level to rise. This shift of the *SRAS* curve will be due to the increase in nominal wages that occurs over time due to the tension between very low levels of unemployment and the abundance of jobs.

29. **Answer a.** A positive demand shock implies that the quantity of goods and services demanded at any given aggregate price level has increased: *AD* shifts to the right. As *AD* shifts to the right for a given *SRAS* curve, the aggregate price level and the aggregate level of real GDP increases.

30. **Answer d.** An increase in wealth causes the *AD* curve to shift to the right, resulting in a higher aggregate price level and a higher level of real GDP. If the government wishes to restore the economy to the original aggregate price level and aggregate output level, it can accomplish this goal by reducing government spending, raising taxes, or decreasing the money supply.

chapter 15

Fiscal Policy

BEFORE YOU READ THE CHAPTER

Summary

This chapter focuses on fiscal policy—government spending and taxation—and its use as an economic tool for managing economic fluctuations. The chapter discusses expansionary fiscal policy, or the use of government spending and/or taxation policy to stimulate the economy, as well as contractionary fiscal policy, or the use of government spending and/or taxation policy to slow down the economy. In addition, the chapter explores the multiplier effect of fiscal policy as well as the effect of automatic stabilizers on the size of the multiplier. The chapter continues with the development of the budget balance and how economic fluctuations affect this budget balance. The chapter also discusses the long-run consequences of public debt and the significance of the government's implicit liabilities.

Chapter Objectives

Objective #1. Discretionary fiscal policy refers to the use of government spending or tax policy to manage aggregate demand *(AD)*. Discretionary fiscal policy may be used to stimulate or contract *AD*.

Objective #2. Government collects funds in the form of taxes and government borrowing and then uses these funds to make government purchases of goods and services and government transfers to individuals. Total government spending includes government expenditure on goods and services as well as government expenditure on transfer payments.

- The three most expensive transfer programs in the United States are Social Security, Medicare, and Medicaid.

- Social insurance refers to government programs aimed at protecting families against economic hardship.

Objective #3. The basic equation of national income accounting, $GDP = C + I + G + X - IM$, reminds us that government purchases of goods and services (G) has a direct impact on total spending in the economy. The government also affects C through changes in taxes and transfers, and it may affect I through government policy.

- Increases in taxes, holding everything else constant, reduce disposable income and consumer spending. Decreases in taxes, holding everything else constant, increase disposable income and consumer spending.

- Increases in government transfer payments, holding everything else constant, increase disposable income and consumer spending. Decreases in government transfer payments, holding everything else constant, decrease disposable income and consumer spending.

- Government can impact the incentives to engage in investment spending through changes in tax policy.

- The government can use changes in taxes or government spending to shift the *AD* curve. Holding everything else constant, *AD* shifts to the right with increases in government spending, decreases in taxes, or increases in government transfers; *AD* shifts to the left with decreases in government spending, increases in taxes, or decreases in government transfers.

- When the country faces a recessionary gap, aggregate output is less than potential output: use of expansionary fiscal policy will shift *AD* to the right to help eliminate the gap between actual and potential GDP.

- When an economy faces an inflationary gap, aggregate output is greater than potential output: use of contractionary fiscal policy will shift *AD* to the left to help eliminate the gap between actual and potential GDP.

Objective #4. Important lags exist in the use of fiscal or monetary policy. These lags include the time necessary for the government to realize the need for policy intervention, the time necessary for the government to develop policy, and the time necessary for the government to implement the policy and have the policy take effect. The existence of lags makes the use of fiscal policy and monetary policy to correct economic fluctuations more challenging than our simple analysis suggests.

Objective #5. A change in government spending is an example of an autonomous change in aggregate spending. Holding the price level constant, this change in autonomous aggregate spending will change GDP by an amount equal to the multiplier times the change in autonomous aggregate spending. Recall that the multiplier in our simple model equals $1/(1 - MPC)$.

Objective #6. A change in taxes or government transfers of a given size shifts the *AD* curve by less than an equal-sized change in government purchases. A decrease in taxes or increase in transfers will increase GDP by $MPC/(1 - MPC)$ times the change in taxes (measured in absolute value terms) or the change in transfers; an increase in taxes or a decrease in transfers will decrease GDP by $MPC/(1 - MPC)$ times the change in taxes or the change in transfers (measured in absolute value terms).

Objective #7. Holding everything else constant, when GDP increases, government tax revenue automatically increases. The effect of this automatic increase in government tax revenue when GDP rises is to reduce the size of the multiplier.

- When the economy slows down and GDP falls, the automatic fall in government tax revenue acts like an automatic expansionary fiscal policy implemented in the face of the recession.

- When the economy expands, the automatic increase in government tax revenue acts like an automatic contractionary fiscal policy implemented in the face of the expansion.

- Government spending and taxation rules that cause fiscal policy to be automatically expansionary when the economy contracts and automatically contractionary when the economy expands are referred to as automatic stabilizers since they act to automatically stabilize the economy.

- Examples of automatic stabilizers include taxes, unemployment insurance benefits, Medicaid, and food stamps. Transfer programs as well as taxes can act as automatic stabilizers.

Objective #8. Discretionary fiscal policy refers to fiscal policy that is the direct result of policy action by policymakers. It does not refer to automatic adjustment in the economy that occurs because of automatic stabilizers.

Objective #9. Recall that the budget balance equals tax revenue minus government spending on both goods and services as well as government transfers. We can write the budget balance, $S_{Government}$, symbolically as $S_{Government} = T - G - TR$.

[handwritten note: Budget balance = T - G - TR, taxes, spending, transfers]

- A positive budget balance indicates a budget surplus, while a negative budget balance indicates a budget deficit.

- Holding everything else constant, discretionary expansionary fiscal policy reduces the budget balance, while discretionary contractionary policy increases the budget balance.

- Equal-sized changes in government spending or taxes impact the budget balance equally, but have very different impacts on *AD* due to the multiplier effect of a change in government spending being greater than the multiplier effect of an equal-sized change in government taxes or transfers.

- Changes in the budget balance often are the result of economic fluctuations.

Objective #10. The cyclically adjusted budget balance estimates the size of the budget balance if real GDP was exactly equal to potential output. It effectively eliminates the impact of recessionary or inflationary gaps on tax revenue and government transfers.

Objective #11. Most economists do not endorse legislation requiring that the government maintain a balanced budget, since this type of rule would undermine the role of taxes and transfers as automatic stabilizers.

Objective #12. When governments spend more than their tax revenue, they usually borrow the extra funds needed. Governments that run persistent deficits find that they have a rising government debt.

- A government deficit is the difference between the amount of money a government spends and the amount of money the government receives in taxes over a given period of time.

- A government debt is the sum of money a government owes at a particular point in time.

- The public debt refers to the government debt held by individuals and institutions outside the government at a particular point in time.

- When the government runs persistent budget deficits, it competes with firms that plan to borrow funds for investment spending. The government borrowing may crowd out private investment spending and lead to a reduction in the economy's long-run growth rate.

- When the government runs persistent budget deficits, this leads to financial pressure on future budgets due to the increasing size of the interest payments on the accumulated debt. Holding everything else constant, a government that owes large amounts in interest must raise more revenue from taxes or spend less.

- Governments that print money to pay their bills find that this leads to inflation.
- The long-run effects of persistent budget deficits suggest that governments should run a budget that is approximately balanced over time.

Objective #13. In the United States, government budget totals are kept for the fiscal year that starts on October 1 and runs through September 30. For example, fiscal 2010 began on October 1, 2009, and ended on September 30, 2010.

Objective #14. The debt–GDP ratio is a measure used to assess the ability of governments to pay their debt. The debt–GDP ratio measures government debt as a percentage of GDP. This measure recognizes that the size of the economy as a whole, as measured by GDP, provides information about the amount of potential taxes a government can collect. When GDP grows at a faster rate than the rate of growth of the government's debt, then the burden of paying the debt is falling relative to the government's ability to collect tax revenue.

- The debt–GDP ratio can fall even when debt is rising provided that GDP grows faster than debt.
- The debt–GDP ratio will rise when debt is rising if GDP grows more slowly than debt.

Objective #15. Implicit liabilities are promises made by governments that represent debt not included in the government's debt statistics. In the United States, the largest implicit liabilities are Social Security, Medicare, and Medicaid.

- Spending on Social Security is projected to rise dramatically over the next few decades due to demographic issues related to the retirement of the baby boomer generation.
- Spending on Medicare and Medicaid is also projected to rise dramatically primarily because long-run health care spending increases faster than overall spending.
- Both Social Security and Medicare are funded from dedicated taxes, a special tax levied on wages. At the time of this writing, there is a surplus of tax revenue from these dedicated taxes. For example, the surplus funds of Social Security are held in a Social Security Trust Fund. The funds in these trust funds are owed to the Social Security system and other trust funds by another part of the government; this debt is referred to as the United States government debt held by Social Security and other trust funds. The gross debt for the U.S. government thus consists of two parts: first, the public debt, and second, the United States government debt held by Social Security and other trust funds.

Key Terms

social insurance government programs—like Social Security, Medicare, unemployment insurance, and food stamps—intended to protect families against economic hardship.

expansionary fiscal policy *fiscal policy* that increases aggregate demand by increasing government purchases, decreasing taxes, or increasing transfers.

contractionary fiscal policy *fiscal policy* that reduces aggregate demand by decreasing government purchases, increasing taxes, or decreasing transfers.

autonomous changes in aggregate spending an initial change in the desired level of spending by firms, households, or government at a given level of real GDP.

Notes

Key Terms *(continued)*

multiplier the ratio of the total change in real GDP caused by an autonomous change in aggregate spending to the size of that autonomous change.

Notes

$$\frac{1}{1 - MPC}$$

marginal propensity to consume, or MPC the increase in consumer spending when disposable income increases by $1.

lump-sum taxes taxes that don't depend on the taxpayer's income.

automatic stabilizers government spending and taxation rules that cause *fiscal policy* to be automatically expansionary when the *economy* contracts and automatically contractionary when the economy expands without requiring any deliberate actions by policy makers. Taxes that depend on *disposable income* are the most important example of automatic stabilizers.

Taxes - income

discretionary fiscal policy *fiscal policy* that is the direct result of deliberate actions by policy makers rather than rules.

impl. by politicians

cyclically adjusted budget balance an estimate of what the *budget balance* would be if *real GDP* were exactly equal to *potential output*.

fiscal year the time period used for much of government accounting, running from October 1 to September 30. Fiscal years are labeled by the calendar year in which they end.

10/1 - 9/30

public debt government debt held by individuals and institutions outside the government.

debt–GDP ratio government debt as a percentage of GDP, frequently used as a measure of a government's ability to pay its debts.

implicit liabilities spending promises made by governments that are effectively a debt despite the fact that they are not included in the usual debt statistics. In the United States, the largest implicit liabilities arise from Social Security and Medicare, which promise transfer payments to current and future retirees (Social Security) and to the elderly (Medicare).

▮ AFTER YOU READ THE CHAPTER

Tips

Tip #1. This chapter contains some new vocabulary. You need to be familiar with these concepts, including the government deficit, government debt, implicit liabilities, and the debt–GDP ratio. As in the other chapters it is essential that you learn and understand any new terms that are introduced. Many of the terms in this chapter represent complicated concepts or relationships.

Tip #2. Two multipliers are presented and used in this chapter: the multiplier for a change in government spending and the multiplier for a change in taxes. The multiplier for a change in government spending equals $1/(1 - MPC)$, while the multiplier for a change in taxes equals $[-MPC/(1 - MPC)]$. For example, if the MPC equals 0.8, then the multiplier for a change in government spending is equal to 5, while the multiplier for a change in taxes is equal to -4. A \$1 increase in government spending will increase aggregate output by \$5, holding everything else constant, while a \$1 increase in taxes will decrease aggregate output by \$4, holding everything else constant. Make sure you work some problems using these multipliers and that you understand why they do not have equivalent values. Also, spend time thinking about why the multiplier for government spending is positive while the multiplier for a change in taxes is negative. An increase in government spending represents an increase in the level of spending in the economy and will stimulate aggregate production, while an increase in taxes reduces the level of spending in the economy and will therefore contract aggregate production.

Tip #3. Review the distinction between fiscal policy that is discretionary versus fiscal policy that reflects the impact of automatic stabilizers.

Tip #4. The use of the multiplier thus far in our models presumes a horizontal $SRAS$. If the $SRAS$ is upward sloping, then the impact on aggregate output will be smaller than that predicted by the multiplier. Essentially this tip should remind you that a horizontal $SRAS$ implies a fixed price level, while an upward-sloping $SRAS$ implies that the aggregate price level is not fixed. A shift in AD due to a change in autonomous spending or taxes will cause a larger change in aggregate output (and a change equal to the amount predicted by the multiplier effect) if the aggregate price level is constant than if the aggregate price level is allowed to change. Let's look at a diagram of this represented in Figure 15.1.

Figure 15.1

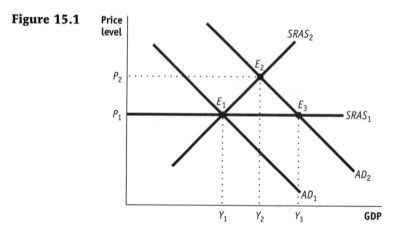

AD_1 is our initial AD curve; $SRAS_1$ is the short-run aggregate supply curve if the aggregate price level is held constant, and $SRAS_2$ is the short-run aggregate supply curve if the aggregate price level is allowed to vary in the short run. Initially the economy is at point E_1, producing Y_1 at an aggregate price level P_1. When autonomous aggregate spending increases, this shifts AD_1 to AD_2, and the horizontal distance Y_1 to Y_3 measures the multiplier effect on aggregate output (moving from the initial equilibrium E_1 to the new equilibrium E_3). However, given $SRAS_2$ a rightward shift in AD from AD_1 to AD_2 increases output from Y_1 to Y_2 while simultaneously increasing the aggregate price level from P_1 to P_2 (moving from the initial equilibrium E_1 to the new equilibrium E_2).

Tip #5. You will want to understand what the cyclically adjusted budget balance is and how it relates to the budget balance and to potential GDP. The cyclically adjusted budget balance is an estimate of what the budget balance would be if real GDP were exactly equal to potential GDP. This measure takes into account the extra tax revenue the government would receive and the smaller level of transfer payments the government would make if the recessionary gap were eliminated, or the tax revenue the government would lose and the extra transfer payments the government would make if the inflationary gap were eliminated. The cyclically adjusted budget balance fluctuates less than the actual budget deficit, because years with a large budget deficit are typically associated with large recessionary gaps.

WORKED PROBLEMS

1. Suppose you are an economic advisor for a country with a closed economy. You estimate that this country's potential level of output is $1,000 in year 1 and that this level of potential output will grow 10% a year for the next four years. Your government employers ask you to complete the following table for them based on this information.

Year	Potential output
Year 1	$1,000
Year 2	
Year 3	
Year 4	
Year 5	

You are also given the following information (all numbers in the table are in dollars) about projected spending over the next five years and are asked to provide the government with an equation that expresses this country's consumption function based on the information you have received. In the table, T is net taxes, YD is disposable income, C is consumption spending, I is investment spending, and G is government spending. Besides providing an equation for the country's consumption function, you are also asked to fill in the missing information in the table.

Year	Potential output	Actual output	T	YD	C	I	G
Year 1	$1,000		$50	$950	$770	$200	$30
Year 2		$1,200	50			200	110
Year 3		1,300	50			200	150
Year 4			50	1,100		200	90
Year 5			50	1,200	920	200	80

You are also asked to provide this country with guidance about the projected state of its economy in each of the next five years. From your previous work, fill in the following table for this economy.

Year	Recessionary gap	Inflationary gap	Actual output equals potential output
Year 1			
Year 2			
Year 3			
Year 4			
Year 5			

Finally, suppose this economy wishes to pursue fiscal policy that will ensure that actual output equals potential output every year. For each year, describe whether the government should pursue contractionary fiscal policy, expansionary fiscal policy, or no fiscal policy. Summarize your findings in the following table.

Year	Discretionary fiscal policy
Year 1	
Year 2	
Year 3	
Year 4	
Year 5	

STEP 1: Start by calculating potential output, or GDP, based on an annual growth rate of 10%.

Review the section "Fiscal Policy: The Basics" on pages 450–457 and the section "Fiscal Policy and the Multiplier" on pages 457–461.

You will want to enter your calculations in the summary table. To find year 2's potential GDP, multiply year 1's GDP by 1.10 since year 2's GDP will be 10% greater than year 1's GDP. Continue the same calculation for the next three years.

Year	Potential output
Year 1	$1,000
Year 2	1,100
Year 3	1,210
Year 4	1,331
Year 5	1,464

STEP 2: From the information that you have been given, find this economy's consumption equation.

Review the section "Fiscal Policy: The Basics" on pages 450-457 and the section "Fiscal Policy and the Multiplier" on pages 457-461.

Inspecting the table, you see that there are two rows that provide you with information about consumption and disposable income: in year 1, when disposable income is $950, consumption is $770; and in year 5, when disposable income is $1,200, consumption is $920. You know that in general the relationship between consumption and disposable income can be written as $C = a + b(Y - T)$, where a is autonomous consumption, b is the marginal propensity to consume, and $(Y - T)$ is disposable income. From the information in the table, you can write two consumption relationships: $770 = a + b(950)$ and $920 = a + b(1,200)$. Use these two equations to find the values for autonomous consumption and the marginal propensity to consume. The consumption equation for this economy can be written as $C = 200 + 0.6(Y - T)$.

Now, you are ready to complete the table. Recall that actual output is equal to the sum of spending in the economy: thus, actual output = $C + I + G$. In year 1, actual output = $770 + 200 + 30 = 1,000$. In year 2 and year 3, you need first to calculate disposable income and then to use this disposable income and the consumption equation to find consumption. In year 4 and year 5, you are given disposable income and net taxes, and with this information you can find actual output.

The following table summarizes this work.

Year	Potential output	Actual output	T	YD	C	I	G
Year 1	$1,000	$1,000	$50	$ 950	$770	$200	$30
Year 2	1,100	1,200	50	1,150	890	200	110
Year 3	1,210	1,300	50	1,250	950	200	150
Year 4	1,331	1,150	50	1,100	860	200	90
Year 5	1,464	1,250	50	1,200	920	200	80

STEP 3: From the information you are given and the work you did in Steps 1 and 3, determine whether this economy is projected to operate with a recessionary gap, an inflationary gap, or at potential output for each of the five years.

Review the section "Fiscal Policy: The Basics" on pages 450-457 and the section "Fiscal Policy and the Multiplier" on pages 457-461.

Remember that when actual output is less than potential output, the economy is operating with a recessionary gap; when actual output is greater than potential output, the economy is operating with an inflationary gap. Use this information and the table you completed in Step 2 to ascertain the projected state of the economy for the next five years. The following table summarizes this work.

Year	Recessionary gap	Inflationary gap	Actual output equals potential output
Year 1	No	No	Yes
Year 2	No	Yes	No
Year 3	No	Yes	No
Year 4	Yes	No	No
Year 5	Yes	No	No

STEP 4: Determine the type of activist fiscal policy the government of this economy will need to implement in each of the five years if the economy is going to produce at the level of aggregate output at which actual output equals potential output. Base your advice on the projections you have calculated in the previous steps of this problem.

Review the section "Fiscal Policy: The Basics" on pages 450–457 and the section "Fiscal Policy and the Multiplier" on pages 457–461.

Expansionary fiscal policy acts to increase the level of actual output: activist expansionary fiscal policy is the appropriate fiscal policy response if the desire of the government is to increase the level of actual output. Contractionary fiscal policy acts to decrease the level of actual output: activist contractionary fiscal policy can slow the economy and bring actual output down to the level of potential output.

Year	Fiscal policy
Year 1	None needed since actual output equals potential output
Year 2	Contractionary fiscal policy needed since actual output exceeds potential output
Year 3	Contractionary fiscal policy needed since actual output exceeds potential output
Year 4	Discretionary fiscal policy needed since actual output is less than potential output
Year 5	Discretionary fiscal policy needed since actual output is less than potential output

2. The current short-run economic situation in Urbana is depicted in the following graph: *SRAS* is the short-run aggregate supply curve, *LRAS* is the long-run aggregate supply curve, and *AD* is the aggregate demand curve. You are asked to describe the current short-run economic situation with regard to the relationship between current production and potential production. In addition, you are asked to compare the current level of unemployment to the natural rate of unemployment. Is Urbana operating with a recessionary gap or an inflationary gap? Finally, you are asked to comment on the effect of three possible government policies on both the short-run and the long-run economy in Urbana. The first government policy is a policy that would provide incentives to increase private investment spending. The second government policy is a decision to attack a neighboring country and engage in a large-scale war effort. The third government policy is a decision to increase the level of taxes in this economy. Consider each of these policy choices as independent of one another: that is, assume the government in Urbana will only implement one of these policies at a time.

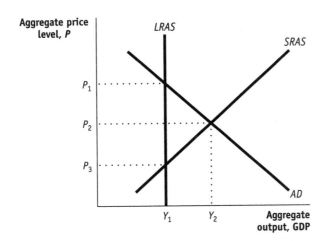

STEP 1: Describe the current state of the economy in Urbana, making sure to identify whether the economy is operating with a recessionary gap or an inflationary gap. In your description, describe the state of the labor market as well as the relationship between actual output and potential output.

Review the section "Fiscal Policy: The Basics" on pages 450–457, the section "Fiscal Policy and the Multiplier" on pages 457–461, and Figure 15-4 on page 453.

In the previous graph, you can see that the long-run level of aggregate output, or the potential output level, is at Y_1. Since the economy is currently operating at the short-run equilibrium where *SRAS* intersects *AD*, we know that actual output is at Y_2. Thus, actual output is greater than potential output, and therefore this economy is operating with an inflationary gap. Since actual output exceeds potential output, this tells us that unemployment is relatively low and is below the natural rate of unemployment.

STEP 2: Evaluate the short-run and long-run implications of the government of Urbana implementing a policy to encourage greater private investment spending.

Review the section "Fiscal Policy: The Basics" on pages 450–457, the section "Fiscal Policy and the Multiplier" on pages 457–461, and Figure 15-4 on page 453.

If the government implements a policy that encourages increased private investment spending, this will cause the aggregate demand curve to shift to the right. Holding everything else constant, in the short run this will cause the level of actual output to increase to an even higher level and the aggregate price level to increase as well. In the long run, the low unemployment rate will cause nominal wages to increase, and this will shift the *SRAS* curve to the left. In the long-run equilibrium, aggregate output will return to potential output, while the aggregate price level may increase, decrease, or remain unchanged. To see why the aggregate price level in the long run is ambiguous, consider the effect of increased private investment spending on the level of capital in this economy. Increases in private investment spending will increase the capital stock in this economy, leading to greater economic growth. This, in turn, will shift the long-run aggregate supply curve to the right. Since we do not know how big this shift is, we cannot with certainty predict what will happen to the aggregate price level in the long run.

STEP 3: Evaluate the short-run and long-run implications of the government of Urbana implementing a policy to go to war.

Review the section "Fiscal Policy: The Basics" on pages 450–457, the section "Fiscal Policy and the Multiplier" on pages 457–461, and Figure 15-4 on page 453.

A decision to go to war will shift the aggregate demand curve to the right, as the government increases its spending in order to fight the war. In the short run, this will cause the level of aggregate output to increase, which will lead to an even greater inflationary gap. In the short run, there will be an increase in the aggregate price level as well. In the long run, the very low levels of unemployment will cause nominal wages to rise. As these nominal wages rise, the short-run aggregate supply curve will shift back to the left, returning the economy to potential output but at a higher level of aggregate prices.

STEP 4: Evaluate the short-run and long-run implications of the government of Urbana increasing the level of taxes in the economy.

Review the section "Fiscal Policy: The Basics" on pages 450–457, the section "Fiscal Policy and the Multiplier" on pages 457–461, and Figure 15-4 on page 453.

A decision to increase the level of taxes will shift the aggregate demand curve to the left, since the increase in taxes will reduce disposable income and therefore lead to decreases in consumption spending. In the short run, this will cause the level of aggregate output to fall relative to its initial short-run level. The aggregate price level will also fall. In the long run, the economy will return to potential output as the short-run aggregate supply curve adjusts. Since we do not know the magnitude of the tax increase, it is impossible to tell whether the short-run aggregate supply curve will need to shift to the left or to the right to bring the economy back to the natural level of output.

3. Grandview is a closed economy where the level of planned investment spending is constant and equal to $50. In Grandview, people always spend 80% of any increase in disposable income and their autonomous consumption is equal to $10. Grandview currently has a zero budget balance and the level of net taxes is equal to $20. Grandview also is assumed to have fixed prices in the short run. Long-run potential output in Grandview is equal to $400. You are asked to find the short-run level of production in Grandview and determine whether Grandview is currently operating with a recessionary gap or an inflationary gap. In addition, you are asked to provide three possible fiscal policies for returning Grandview to its long-run potential output: a tax policy using lump-sum taxes, a government spending policy, and a tax and government-spending policy that requires that the government budget balance remain zero (continue to assume that the tax change is a change in lump-sum taxes). For each of these three policies, you are asked to provide numerical values for the size of the policy to be implemented. In addition, you should calculate what happens to the government budget balance if there are no other changes.

STEP 1: Before you can find the short-run equilibrium level of output in Grandview, you will first need to find the consumption function for this economy.

Review the section "Fiscal Policy: The Basics" on pages 450–457, the section "Fiscal Policy and the Multiplier" on pages 457–461, and the section "The Budget Balance" on pages 461–466.

Recall that the consumption function is written as $C = a + b(Y - T)$, where a is autonomous consumption and b is the marginal propensity to consume. In the provided information, we are told the value of autonomous consumption, and we are also told that consumers spend 80% of any increase in disposable income. The marginal propensity to consume is defined as the change in consumption divided by the change in disposable income: in this example, the marginal propensity to consume would equal 0.8. Thus, the consumption function is $C = 10 + 0.8(Y - T)$.

STEP 2: Recall that actual output is equal to the sum of expenditure in the economy. Use this information to find the short-run equilibrium level of output in Grandview.

Review the section "Fiscal Policy: The Basics" on pages 450–457, the section "Fiscal Policy and the Multiplier" on pages 457–461, and the section "The Budget Balance" on pages 461–466.

Since Grandview is a closed economy, spending will only come from three sectors: households, businesses, and the government. We can find total expenditure by summing $C + I + G$. In equilibrium, total expenditure will equal production, Y. Thus, $Y = C + I + G$. By substituting the consumption function into this equation along with the given values for I and G, we can solve for the short-run equilibrium level of output. $Y = 10 + 0.8(Y - T) + 50 + 20$, or the short-run equilibrium level of output, Y, is equal to $320.

STEP 3: Compare the short-run equilibrium level of output with the long-run potential level of output to decide whether Grandview is currently operating with a recessionary gap or an inflationary gap.

Review the section "Fiscal Policy: The Basics" on pages 450–457, the section "Fiscal Policy and the Multiplier" on pages 457–461, and the section "The Budget Balance" on pages 461–466.

The short-run equilibrium level of output is $320, which is smaller than the long-run or potential level of output. Grandview is currently operating with a recessionary gap since its actual level of output is less than its potential level of output.

STEP 4: Grandview wishes to use activist fiscal policy to restore the economy to the potential level of aggregate output. Calculate the change in lump-sum taxes that would be necessary for Grandview to achieve this goal by changing current tax policy. Once you have calculated the change in lump-sum taxes, then calculate the change in the government budget balance.

Review the section "Fiscal Policy: The Basics" on pages 450–457, the section "Fiscal Policy and the Multiplier" on pages 457–461, and the section "The Budget Balance" on pages 461–466.

The government of Grandview wishes to stimulate the economy through a change in lump-sum taxes so that output in the economy increases from $320 to $400. The tax expenditure multiplier is equal to $[(-b)/(1 - b)]$, and in this case the value of this multiplier is -4. In order to increase output by $80, lump-sum taxes will need to be reduced by $20 since $(-4)(-20)$ is equal to $80, the desired increase in aggregate production. If government spending is constant at $20 and taxes decrease by $20, then the government budget balance will become negative since the government will be spending more than the amount of tax revenue that it is collecting.

STEP 5: Grandview wishes to use activist fiscal policy to restore the economy to the potential level of aggregate output. Calculate the change in government spending that would be necessary for Grandview to achieve this goal by changing current government spending. Once you have calculated the change in government spending, then calculate the change in the government budget balance.

Review the section "Fiscal Policy: The Basics" on pages 450–457, the section "Fiscal Policy and the Multiplier" on pages 457–461, and the section "The Budget Balance" on pages 461–466.

The government of Grandview wishes to stimulate the economy through a change in government spending so that output in the economy increases from $320 to $400. The multiplier for a change in government spending is equal to $[1/(1 - b)]$, and in this case the value of the multiplier is 5. In order to increase output by $80, government spending would need to be increased by $16 since $(5)(16)$ is equal to $80, the desired increase in aggregate production. If taxes are constant and equal to $20, then this increase in government spending will result in total government spending of $36. The government budget balance will be negative and equal to −$16, since the government is spending more than it is collecting in tax revenue.

STEP 6: Grandview wishes to use activist fiscal policy to restore the economy to the potential level of aggregate output while at the same time maintaining a government budget balance of zero. Calculate what the change in government spending and lump-sum taxes must be to achieve this goal.

Review the section "Fiscal Policy: The Basics" on pages 450–457, the section "Fiscal Policy and the Multiplier" on pages 457–461, and the section "The Budget Balance" on pages 461–466.

We know that the desired increase in aggregate output is $80, and the government of Grandview would like to achieve this level of output by increasing government spending and lump-sum taxes by an equivalent amount so that the government budget balance will remain equal to zero. This implies that the change in government spending should be exactly equal to the change in lump-sum taxes. The change in output will equal the government spending multiplier times the change in government spending, plus the tax expenditure multiplier times the change in lump-sum taxes. Symbolically we can write this as $\Delta Y = [1/(1 - b)]\Delta G + [(-b)/(1 - b)]\Delta T$. Since $\Delta G = \Delta T$, we can rewrite this equation as $\Delta Y = [1/(1 - b)]\Delta G + [(-b)/(1 - b)]\Delta G$, or $\Delta Y = \Delta G$. This means that if the government of Grandview wishes to increase output by $80 while maintaining a budget balance of zero, it will need to increase government spending and lump-sum taxes by $80.

4. Zinfindel is a closed economy that is concerned about its debt–GDP ratio and the projections about this ratio for the next five years. The government of Zinfindel anticipates that real GDP will grow by 10% a year over the next five years, while the level of government deficit is expected to grow by 5% a year over the next five years. The following table provides information about Zinfindel this year. You are asked to complete the table, giving Zinfindel some projections about what it can expect over the next five years. For this problem assume that government debt in the next year is equal to the debt from the year before plus the deficit for that year: for example, in year 2, the debt would be equal to $25 million plus the additional $10 million in deficit spending, for a total debt of $35 million. Round all numbers to the nearest hundredth.

Year	Real GDP (millions of dollars)	Debt (millions of dollars)	Budget deficit (millions of dollars)	Debt (percentage of real GDP)	Budget deficit (percentage of real GDP)
Year 1	$100	$25	$10	25%	10%
Year 2					
Year 3					
Year 4					
Year 5					

STEP 1: Start by calculating the value of real GDP for each of the next four years given the assumption that real GDP is growing by 10% a year.

Review the section "The Budget Balance" on pages 461–466 and the section "Long-Run Implications of Fiscal Policy" on pages 466–474.

To find real GDP for year 2, you will multiply real GDP in year 1 by 1.1. To find real GDP for year 3, you will multiply real GDP in year 2 by 1.1. The results of these calculations are provided in the table at the end of this problem.

STEP 2: Calculate the value of the government deficit for each year given the assumption that this deficit will grow by 5% a year.

Review the section "The Budget Balance" on pages 461–466 and the section "Long-Run Implications of Fiscal Policy" on pages 466–474.

To find the government deficit for year 2, you will multiply the government deficit for year 1 by 1.05. To find the government deficit for year 3, you will multiply the government deficit for year 2 by 1.05. The results of these calculations are provided in the table at the end of this problem.

STEP 3: Calculate the value of the debt using the budget deficit figures that you calculated in step 2.

Review the section "The Budget Balance" on pages 461–466 and the section "Long-Run Implications of Fiscal Policy" on pages 466–474.

Remember that the value of the debt in a particular year is equal to the sum of the debt and the budget deficit from the previous year. The results of these calculations are provided in the table at the end of this problem.

STEP 4: Calculate the debt as a percentage of GDP and the budget deficit as a percentage of GDP.

Review the section "The Budget Balance" on pages 461–466 and the section "Long-Run Implications of Fiscal Policy" on pages 466–474.

To find the debt as a percentage of GDP, divide the debt by real GDP and then multiply your answer by 100 to make it a percentage.

To find the budget deficit as a percentage of GDP, divide the budget deficit by real GDP and then multiply your answer by 100 to make it a percentage. The results of these calculations are provided in the table at the end of this problem.

Year	Real GDP (millions of dollars)	Debt (millions of dollars)	Budget deficit (millions of dollars)	Debt (percentage of real GDP)	Budget deficit (percentage of real GDP)
Year 1	$100	$25	$10	25%	10%
Year 2	110	35	10.5	31.82	9.55
Year 3	121	45.5	11.03	37.60	9.12
Year 4	133.1	56.53	11.58	42.47	8.70
Year 5	146.41	68.10	12.16	46.51	8.31

Problems and Exercises

1. For each of the following situations identify whether it is an example of expansionary discretionary fiscal policy, contractionary discretionary fiscal policy, or fiscal policy in the form of an automatic stabilizer.

   a. During 2009, tax revenue for Macrovia falls as the economy enters a recession.

   b. During 2009, in light of projected deficiencies in *AD*, Macrovia's legislature authorizes an expenditure of $200 million in order to build a new hydroelectric dam.

   c. In 2012, fearing a too rapidly expanding economy, Macrovia adopts a budget that calls for 10% spending cuts in all government departments for the following fiscal year.

   d. In 2011, unemployment benefits rise 5% in response to rising unemployment in Macrovia.

2. The following graph depicts the economy of Macroland's short-run aggregate supply curve (*SRAS*), its long-run aggregate supply curve (*LRAS*), and its aggregate demand curve (*AD*). Macroland is currently producing at point *E*.

   a. Is potential GDP for Macroland equal to Y_1 or Y_2? Describe Macroland's current production relative to its potential production.

    b. Does Macroland have a recessionary gap or an inflationary gap? Explain your answer.

    c. Suppose Macroland wishes to produce at its potential output level. Holding everything else constant, identify which of the following policy initiatives might help it reach this goal and how these policy initiatives would help.

       i. The government initiates policies that encourage private investment spending.

      ii. The government increases the amount of money it borrows in the loanable funds market in order to increase its level of government spending in the economy.

     iii. The government increases taxes on consumers and corporations.

     iv. The government authorizes new spending programs.

    d. What is the current price level in Macroland? If Macroland successfully engages in expansionary fiscal policy so that *AD* shifts and actual output equals potential output, what will happen to the price level?

3. Funlandia's economists estimate that its potential level of output is $100 in year 1 and this level of potential output grows 5% per year. Assume Funlandia is a closed economy.

    a. Fill in the following table for Funlandia given the information.

Year	Potential output
Year 1	$100
Year 2	
Year 3	
Year 4	

Suppose Funlandia's economists provide you with the following table of data. (All numbers in the table are in dollars.)

Year	Potential output	Actual output	T	YD	C	I	G
Year 1	$100		$10	$ 90	$55	$30	$15
Year 2		$104	10			30	17
Year 3		115	10			30	22.5
Year 4			10	108	64	30	24

b. What is the consumption function for this economy?

c. Fill in the missing values for the same table using the information you have been given or that you computed in parts (a) and (b).

d. Fill in the following table for Funlandia.

Year	Recessionary gap	Inflationary gap	Actual output equals potential output
Year 1	No	No	Yes
Year 2			
Year 3			
Year 4			

e. Suppose Funlandia maintains a policy of using discretionary fiscal policy to ensure that actual output equals potential output. Summarize the recommended discretionary fiscal policy necessary to achieve this goal in the following table.

Year	Discretionary fiscal policy
Year 1	
Year 2	
Year 3	
Year 4	

4. Suppose Uplandia is a closed economy where the level of planned investment spending equals $100 and is unaffected by the level of aggregate spending. Furthermore, suppose consumers consume 60% of any increase in their disposable income and autonomous consumer spending equals $20. Uplandia currently has a zero budget balance, with taxes equal to $50, transfers equal to $0, and government spending on goods and services equal to $50. Furthermore, assume the price level is fixed in Uplandia in the short run.

a. What is Uplandia's consumption function?

b. What is the income–expenditure equilibrium for Uplandia?

c. Suppose Uplandia wants output to equal $400, the potential level of output. Does Uplandia have an inflationary gap or a recessionary gap? Explain your answer.

d. What is the change in government spending needed to enable this economy to reach its potential output, holding everything else constant?

e. Instead of a change in government spending, Uplandia decides to pursue a change in taxes in order to reach its potential output. Holding everything else constant, what is the change in taxes needed to enable this economy to reach its potential output?

f. Suppose the government decides it wants to maintain a zero budget balance. This implies that any increase in government spending, G, must be accompanied by an equivalent increase in taxes, T. Suppose Uplandia chooses to reach its potential output level while maintaining a zero budget balance. What will the change in G and T need to be in order to accomplish this goal?

g. In your answers to parts (d), (e) and (f), you use different multipliers to reach potential output in Uplandia. If your only criterion for choosing policy is getting the most "bang for the buck" or, in other words, getting the largest change in aggregate output for a given dollar change in government spending or taxation, which is the best policy? Explain your answer.

h. Relate your answer in part (g) to the debate over the wisdom of a balanced-budget rule for the federal government.

5. Uplandia is concerned about its debt–GDP ratio and the projections about this ratio over the next five years. The following table gives data about Uplandia's real GDP for this year (year 1) and its projected real GDP for the next five years. Real GDP is projected to grow 3% per year over the next five years as is the government deficit.

a. Fill in the missing cells in the table.

Year	Real GDP (millions of dollars)	Debt (millions of dollars)	Budget deficit (millions of dollars)	Debt (percentage of real GDP)	Budget deficit (percentage of real GDP)
Year 1	$800	$200	$20	25%	2.5%
Year 2					
Year 3					
Year 4					
Year 5					
Year 6					

b. Describe in words what is happening to the government's debt–GDP ratio and deficit–GDP ratio when real GDP and the government deficit grow at the same rate.

Suppose Uplandia decides to reduce government spending over the next five years. This results in the government deficit growing 1% per year over the next five years while real GDP continues to grow 3% per year.

c. Fill in the table based on these projections.

Year	Real GDP (millions of dollars)	Debt (millions of dollars)	Budget deficit (millions of dollars)	Debt (percentage of real GDP)	Budget deficit (percentage of real GDP)
Year 1	$800	$200	$20	25%	2.5%
Year 2					
Year 3					
Year 4					
Year 5					
Year 6					

d. Describe in words what is happening to the government's debt–GDP ratio and deficit–GDP ratio when real GDP grows at 3% per year while the deficit grows at 1% per year.

Suppose Uplandia, buoyed by its projected real GDP growth rate, passes legislation reducing its taxes while simultaneously deciding to go to war. Its economists project real GDP will continue to grow at 3% per year but now, due to these policy decisions, the government deficit is projected to grow at 10% per year. The results of these changes is shown in the following table.

Year	Real GDP (millions of dollars)	Debt (millions of dollars)	Budget deficit (millions of dollars)	Debt (percentage of real GDP)	Budget deficit (percentage of real GDP)
Year 1	$800	$200	$20	25%	2.5%
Year 2	824	222	22	26.94	2.67
Year 3	848.72	246.2	24.2	29.01	2.85
Year 4	874.18	272.82	26.62	31.21	3.05
Year 5	900.41	302.10	29.38	33.55	3.25
Year 6	927.42	334.30	32.2	36.05	3.47

e. Describe in words what is happening to the government's debt–GDP ratio and deficit–GDP ratio when real GDP grows at 3% per year while the deficit grows at 10% per year.

f. Can you generalize your findings from this exercise? What general principles does this exercise present?

6. Explain why automatic stabilizers reduce the size of the multiplier. Provide several examples of automatic stabilizers and their effect on the economy during economic fluctuations.

7. Suppose that the government currently operates with a deficit and that this deficit grows by 4% a year. Furthermore, suppose that this economy initially had zero debt until the government started operating with a deficit. The economy's annual economic growth rate is 5% a year. What will happen to this economy's debt–GDP ratio over time given this information? Explain your answer fully.

▮ BEFORE YOU TAKE THE TEST

Chapter Review Questions

1. Which of the following statements is true?
   a. Personal income taxes, corporate profits taxes, and social insurance taxes are the primary taxes at the federal level of government in the United States.
   b. State and local governments in the United States rely on sales taxes, property taxes, income taxes, and fees for their sources of revenues.
   c. In 2007, 48% of government revenue in the United States came from taxes on personal income and corporate profits.
   d. All of the above statements are true statements.
   e. Statements (a) and (b) are both true.
   f. Statements (b) and (c) are both true.

2. Total government spending differs from government expenditure because it
   a. refers to the purchase of goods and services and does not include transfers since this represents a transfer of income from one individual to another.
   b. refers to the purchase of goods and services as well as expenditures on transfers.
   c. includes, in the United States, transfers such as spending on Social Security, Medicare, and Medicaid.
   d. Answers (a) and (c) are both correct.
   e. Answers (b) and (c) are both correct.

3. Contractionary fiscal policy
   a. is most helpful for restoring an economy to the potential output level of production when there is a recessionary gap.
   b. shifts the *AD* curve to the right, restoring the equilibrium level of output to the potential output level for the economy.
   c. often causes inflation or an increase in the aggregate price level.
   d. if effective, shifts *AD* to the left, resulting in a reduction in the aggregate output and the aggregate price level for a given short-run aggregate supply curve (*SRAS*).

4. Which of the following statements is true? Holding everything else constant,
   a. an economy can eliminate an inflationary gap by increasing government spending.
   b. expansionary fiscal policy refers to an increase in taxes.
   c. when potential output is greater than actual aggregate output, the economy faces a recessionary gap.
   d. when *SRAS* intersects *AD* to the right of the long-run aggregate supply (*LRAS*) curve, the economy faces a recessionary gap.

5. Monetary and fiscal policy
   a. affect the economy in predictable ways and with relatively short time lags.
   b. involve significant time lags with regard to their implementation and effect on the economy.
   c. take so long to implement in the economy that they prove to be useless policies.
   d. when implemented always worsen economic fluctuations because of the lags involved in their implementation.

6. The Social Security program in the United States

    a. is a "pay-as-you-go" system in which current workers pay payroll taxes that fund the benefits of current retirees.

    b. had 34 retirees receiving benefits for every 100 workers in 2010, while projections suggest that in 2030 there will be 46 retirees receiving benefits for every 100 workers.

    c. had accumulated a Social Security trust fund of $3 trillion at the end of fiscal 2012.

    d. Answers (a), (b) and (c) are all correct.

7. Holding everything else constant, the multiplier effect for taxes or transfers

    a. is the same as the multiplier effect for changes in autonomous aggregate spending.

    b. is smaller than the multiplier effect for changes in autonomous aggregate spending.

    c. is larger than the multiplier effect for changes in autonomous aggregate spending.

    d. may be smaller than, larger than, or equal to the multiplier effect for changes in autonomous aggregate spending.

8. Which of the following statements is true?

    a. Automatic stabilizers act like automatic expansionary fiscal policy when the economy is in a recession.

    b. Automatic stabilizers refer to government spending and taxation rules that cause fiscal policy to be expansionary when the economy expands and contractionary when the economy contracts.

    c. Automatic stabilizers reduce the size of the multiplier.

    d. Statements (a), (b), and (c) are all true.

    e. Statements (a) and (c) are both true.

9. Discretionary fiscal policy refers to

    a. the effect of automatic stabilizers on the economy.

    b. a situation in which citizens can choose to participate or not participate in government programs.

    c. fiscal policy that is the direct result of deliberate decisions made by policy makers.

    d. fiscal policy that is either the direct result of deliberate decisions made by policy makers or the result of the impact of automatic stabilizers on the economy.

10. Holding everything else constant, the government's budget balance

    a. tends to increase during a recession.

    b. tends to increase during an expansion.

    c. will increase if the government pursues expansionary fiscal policy.

    d. Answers (a) and (c) are both correct.

    e. Answers (b) and (c) are both correct.

11. Which of the following statements is true?

    a. Two different changes in fiscal policy that have equal effects on the budget balance will always have equal effects on *AD*.

    b. A change in taxes or transfers will have a larger effect on *AD* than an equal-sized change in government purchases of goods and services.

    c. The budget deficit almost always falls when unemployment rises.

    d. The cyclically adjusted budget balance provides an estimate of the budget balance, assuming real GDP is equal to potential output.

12. When a government decides to spend more than it collects in tax revenue,
   a. it usually borrows the necessary funds.
   b. the budget balance increases.
   c. it runs a budget deficit but reduces its overall level of government debt.
   d. it is forced to sell valuable assets to finance its spending.

13. Which of the following statements is true?
   a. The fiscal year 2001 runs from October 1, 2001 through September 30, 2002.
   b. Public debt is that amount of government debt held by individuals and institutions outside the government.
   c. The government's total debt includes the public debt as well as the debt owed by one part of the government to another part of the government (for example, the Social Security trust funds).
   d. Statements (a), (b), and (c) are all true.
   e. Statements (b) and (c) are both true.

14. In the United States, at the end of the fiscal year 2012, the
   a. total government debt equaled 37% of GDP.
   b. government's public debt at the federal level equaled 72% of GDP.
   c. government's public debt equaled $7.4 trillion.
   d. level of government debt measured by the public debt–GDP ratio was far higher than that of comparable economies.

15. The government debt is
   a. an alternative but equivalent term for the government deficit.
   b. the difference between the amount of money government spends and the amount of tax revenue the government collects during a given period of time.
   c. the amount of money the government owes at a particular point in time.
   d. best measured over a given period of time.

16. Suppose the government of Macroland repeatedly finds itself running a deficit. This may
   a. result in less private investment spending as government borrowing crowds out this spending.
   b. result in lower long-run economic growth if the deficit reduces private investment spending.
   c. cause the government of Macroland to have less budgetary flexibility in the future due to the diversion of tax revenue to pay interest on the debt.
   d. Answers (a), (b), and (c) are all possible effects of repeatedly running a deficit.

17. The debt–GDP ratio
   a. provides a measure of government debt as a percentage of GDP.
   b. provides a measure of government debt relative to the potential ability of the government to collect taxes to cover that debt.
   c. can fall, even if the level of government debt is rising, provided that GDP grows faster than the debt.
   d. Answers (a), (b), and (c) are all correct.

18. Implicit liabilities

    a. are not included in the calculation of the debt–GDP ratio in the United States.

    b. are promises made by the government that represent a debt that must be paid by the government at some future point in time.

    c. are usually included in debt statistics.

    d. Answers (a), (b), and (c) are all correct.

    e. Answers (a) and (b) are both correct.

19. Which of the following statements is true?

    a. The demographic issues underlying Social Security will lessen with the passage of time in the United States as the baby boom generation moves into retirement.

    b. Health costs tend to rise at approximately the same rate as other costs in wealthy economies like the United States.

    c. Social Security and Medicare are funded by dedicated taxes: any excess funds collected from these dedicated taxes accumulate in trust funds that other parts of the government may borrow from to fund other spending. When this type of borrowing occurs an implicit liability is created.

    d. The sum of public debt and the United States government debt held by Social Security and other trust funds overstates the seriousness of the government's fiscal health.

20. When an economy is operating with a recessionary gap, the decision to increase government spending in order to stimulate the economy is an example of

    a. discretionary fiscal policy.

    b. monetary policy, since it will lead to everyone having more money than they did prior to the increase in government spending.

    c. automatic stabilizers acting to stabilize the economy.

    d. Answers (a) and (c) are both correct.

21. Revenue for the operation of state and local governments comes primarily from

    a. personal income taxes.

    b. corporate taxes.

    c. a mix of sales taxes, property taxes, income taxes, and fees of various kinds.

    d. payroll taxes.

22. Government transfers are payments from the government

    a. to households as compensation for taxes that the household has paid.

    b. to households for which no good or service is provided in return.

    c. that redistribute purchasing power from one group of households to another group of households.

    d. Answers (a) and (c) are both correct.

    e. Answers (b) and (c) are both correct.

23. Government programs that are designed to protect individuals or families from economic hardship are described as

    a. fiscal policy.

    b. discretionary fiscal policy.

    c. monetary policy.

    d. social insurance.

24. Which of the following will cause the *AD* curve to shift to the left?

   a. Government increases the amount of transfer payments it makes.

   b. Government increases the amount of taxes it collects from households.

   c. Government increases its level of defense spending after declaring war on a nearby country.

   d. Government institutes an investment tax credit that effectively reduces the cost of investment purchases made by firms.

25. Suppose an economy currently is operating with an inflationary gap. If the government wishes to return the economy to potential output, which of the following initiatives is most likely to achieve this goal?

   a. The government implements an investment tax credit.

   b. The government passes more generous social insurance programs for the retired and disabled in the economy.

   c. The government increases taxes.

   d. The government increases spending on national defense.

26. Which of the following situations describes the use of contractionary fiscal policy?

   a. Recovery Rebate and Stimulus for the American People Act of 2008

   b. Investment Tax Credit of 2002

   c. Argentina's reductions in government spending and increases in taxes during the period 1997 to 2001

   d. President Lyndon Johnson's surcharge on income taxes in 1968

   e. Answers (c) and (d) are both examples of contractionary fiscal policy.

27. Economists caution that

   a. recessionary gaps are so threatening that the government ought to be always ready to enact discretionary fiscal policy to counteract the recessionary gap.

   b. there are important time lags in the use of fiscal policy, and that discretionary fiscal policy must be carefully employed if it is to result in less economic fluctuation rather than more economic fluctuation.

   c. recessionary gaps are often over before discretionary fiscal policy has any impact and, thus, the discretionary policy has no impact on the economy.

   d. the existence of lags makes the implementation of fiscal policy easier than it would be without the lags.

28. Assume an economy is initially in long-run income–expenditure equilibrium. In addition, assume that this economy's short-run aggregate supply curve is upward sloping. Holding everything else constant, an increase in government spending causes the *AD* curve to shift to the

   a. right, the aggregate price level to increase, and the total change in output to equal the multiplier effect.

   b. left, the aggregate price level to increase, and the total change in output to be less than the amount calculated as the multiplier effect.

   c. right, the aggregate price level to increase, and the total change in output to be less than the amount calculated as the multiplier effect.

29. The government is considering two proposals: one would increase government spending by $100 while the other would decrease the level of taxes collected by the government by $100. Suppose the government's goal is to stimulate the economy as much as possible for a given level of expenditure. Which of the following statements is true?

a. The government will stimulate the economy more when it increases government spending.

b. The government will stimulate the economy more when it decreases taxes.

c. The stimulus to the economy from these two proposals is the same: it does not matter which proposal the government implements.

30. Which of the following statements is true?

  I. The *MPC* for unemployed people is usually higher than the *MPC* for people who own stocks.

  II. The macroeconomic effects of an increase in unemployment benefits will be greater than the macroeconomic effects of a decrease in taxes on profits distributed as dividends to shareholders.

  III. Automatic stabilizers reduce the size of the multiplier.

a. Statement I is true.

b. Statement II is true.

c. Statement III is true.

d. Statements I and II are both true.

e. Statements I and III are both true.

f. Statements II and III are both true.

g. Statements I, II, and III are all true.

31. Suppose the government spends $500 billion during the fiscal year 2007 on goods and services. In addition, the government collects tax revenues of $480 billion and makes transfer payments equal to $150 billion. Assume the economy is producing at the potential output level. The budget balance for this economy is equal to _____ and the government is running a _____.

a. $170 billion; surplus

b. −$170 billion; deficit

c. $130 billion; surplus

d. −$130 billion; deficit

32. Economists generally do not believe that the government should balance its budget every year. Instead, economists advocate that governments run a surplus during economic

a. recessions and a deficit during economic expansions.

b. expansions and a deficit during economic recessions.

33. When a government runs a deficit persistently year after year, this may

a. place financial pressure on future budgets.

b. result in higher taxes over time since the government will need to collect tax revenue to cover its interest payments on the government debt.

c. reduce the level of private investment spending as the government's borrowing crowds out over investment spending.

d. Answers (a), (b), and (c) are all correct.

e. Answers (a) and (b) are both correct.

ANSWER KEY

Answers to Problems and Exercises

1. **a.** This is an example of an automatic stabilizer: as GDP in Macrovia falls, this leads automatically to smaller tax collections for a given tax rate.

   b. This is an example of expansionary discretionary fiscal policy: the additional government expenditure will stimulate AD.

   c. This is an example of contractionary discretionary fiscal policy: Macrovia moves to cut government spending, which will reduce AD and slow down the economic expansion.

   d. This is an example of an automatic stabilizer: as unemployment rises, this leads to less AD. But the payment of unemployment benefits lessens this fall in aggregate spending and results in a smaller overall impact on AD.

2. **a.** The potential output level for Macroland is Y_2 where LRAS equals SRAS equals AD. Currently, Macroland is producing Y_1 at price level P_2: this represents a recessionary situation, or a recessionary gap, since Macroland has the potential to produce a higher level of output than it is currently producing.

   b. Macroland has a recessionary gap since their current level of production, Y_1, is less than their potential level of production, Y_2.

   c. Any policy initiative that shifts AD to the right will help Macroland move toward its potential output level. Items (i) and (iv) will both shift AD to the right: government policies that stimulate private investment spending lead to higher levels of aggregate spending and a rightward shift in AD; and new spending by government will also lead to higher levels of aggregate spending and a rightward shift in AD. Item (ii) will cause the AD to shift to the right unless the increase in government borrowing crowds out private investment to that point where private investment decreases by an amount equal to the increase in government spending. In that case item (ii) would result in no shift in the AD curve. Item (iii) will reduce disposable income and lead to lower levels of aggregate spending: AD may shift to the left if the decrease in spending is greater than the increase in government spending, or AD may shift to the right if the increase in government spending is greater than the decrease in spending.

   d. The current price level in Macroland is P_2. If the government engages in fiscal policy that results in the economy's returning to the potential level of output, this will lead to increases in the price level from P_2 to P_3.

3. **a.**

Year	Potential output
Year 1	$100
Year 2	105
Year 3	110.25
Year 4	115.76

   b. The consumption function can be written as $C = A + MPC(Y - T)$. From the table we can compute the MPC as the change in consumption divided by the change in disposable income, or 9/18, which equals 0.5. To find A, we need to use one of the consumption and disposable income combinations from the table. For example, when disposable income equals 90, consumption equals 55. So, $C = A + 0.5 (Y - T)$ can be rewritten as $55 = A + 0.5(90)$ and solving for A, we find A equals 10. Thus, the consumption function for this economy is $C = 10 + 0.5 (Y - T)$.

c.

Year	Potential output	Actual output	T	YD	C	I	G
Year 1	100	100	10	90	55	30	15
Year 2	105	104	10	94	57	30	17
Year 3	110.25	115	10	105	62.5	30	22.5
Year 4	115.76	118	10	108	64	30	24

d.

Year	Recessionary gap	Inflationary gap	Actual output equals potential output
Year 1	No	No	Yes
Year 2	Yes	No	No
Year 3	No	Yes	No
Year 4	No	Yes	No

e.

Year	Discretionary fiscal policy
Year 1	No policy necessary
Year 2	Increase government spending or decrease taxation
Year 3	Decrease government spending or increase taxation
Year 4	Decrease government spending or increase taxation

4. a. To find the consumption function first recall the general form: $C = A + MPC(Y - T)$. From the given information we know A equals \$20 and the MPC equals 0.6. Thus, $C = 20 + 0.6(Y - T)$.

b. To find the income–expenditure equilibrium, solve the equation $Y = C + I + G$. We know C can be written as $20 + 0.6(Y - T)$; I equals \$100; and G equals \$50. We also know T, taxes, equals \$50. So, $Y = 20 + 0.6(Y - 50) + 100 + 50$, or Y equals \$350.

c. Uplandia is currently producing with a recessionary gap, since its current output of \$350 is less than its potential output of \$400.

d. The multiplier for a change in aggregate spending equals $1/(1 - MPC)$. We know that the change in aggregate production equals the multiplier times the change (in this case) in government spending. In this problem, we want output to increase by \$50, our multiplier value is 2.5, and thus government spending must increase by \$20 in order for this economy to produce its potential output of \$400.

e. The multiplier for a change in taxes equals $-MPC/(1 - MPC)$, or in this case -1.5, since the MPC equals 0.6. Recall that the change in aggregate output equals the multiplier times the change in the level of taxes. We want output to increase by \$50, the multiplier's value is -1.5, and, thus, taxes must decrease by \$33.33. Here you need to remember that aggregate output increases as taxes fall, holding everything else constant, and aggregate output decreases as taxes increase, holding everything else constant.

f. We can find our answer by recognizing that we have two multiplier effects occurring simultaneously if the government chooses to maintain a zero budget balance. We could write this as the change in aggregate output equals the multiplier effect from the change in government spending plus the multiplier effect from the change in taxes. Note, though, that the change in government spending equals the change in taxes. Thus, the change in aggregate output equals $1/(1 - MPC)$ times the change in government spending plus $[-MPC/(1 - MPC)]$ times the change in government spending. Since the desired change in aggregate output equals $50, we can solve this equation and find that the change in government spending and in taxes must both equal $50.

g. The most "bang for the buck" comes from a change in government spending since the multiplier has a value of 2.5. A change in taxes is multiplied by the smaller (in absolute value) multiplier of 1.5 and the balanced budget scenario has an even smaller multiplier value of 1.

h. A balanced budget rule for the federal government would restrict the government's ability to engage in discretionary fiscal policy in times of economic need. It would also prove costly, since for any given change in aggregate output, a balanced-budget rule forces the federal government to spend more than it would if the government were free to pursue discretionary fiscal policy without regard to its budgetary consequences.

5.   a.

Year	Real GDP (millions of dollars)	Debt (millions of dollars)	Budget deficit (millions of dollars)	Debt (percentage of real GDP)	Budget deficit (percentage of real GDP)
Year 1	$800.00	$200.00	$20.00	25%	2.5%
Year 2	824.00	220.60	20.60	26.77	2.5
Year 3	848.72	241.82	21.22	28.49	2.5
Year 4	874.18	263.68	21.85	30.16	2.5
Year 5	900.41	286.18	22.51	31.79	2.5
Year 6	927.42	309.37	23.19	33.36	2.5

b. When the real GDP and the government deficit grow at the same rate, the deficit–GDP ratio stays constant at 2.5%, while the debt–GDP ratio increases from 25% to 33.36% in five years.

c.

Year	Real GDP (millions of dollars)	Debt (millions of dollars)	Budget deficit (millions of dollars)	Debt (percentage of real GDP)	Budget deficit (percentage of real GDP)
Year 1	$800.00	$200.00	$20.00	25%	2.5%
Year 2	824.00	220.20	20.20	26.72	2.45
Year 3	848.72	240.60	20.40	28.35	2.40
Year 4	874.18	261.21	20.61	29.88	2.36
Year 5	900.41	282.02	20.81	31.32	2.31
Year 6	927.42	303.04	21.02	32.67	2.27

d. When the real GDP grows at 3% per year and the government deficit grows at 1% per year, the deficit–GDP ratio falls from 2.5% to 2.27% in five years, while the debt–GDP ratio increases from 25% to 32.68% in five years.

e. When real GDP grows at 3% per year and the deficit grows at 10% per year, the deficit–GDP ratio increases from 2.5% to 3.47% over five years while the debt–GDP ratio increases from 25% to 36.05% over five years.

f. The rate of growth of both real GDP and the deficit each year are important when considering what happens to the debt–GDP ratio and the deficit–GDP ratio. If GDP grows at a faster rate than the deficit, the deficit–GDP ratio will decline while the debt–GDP ratio may continue to increase, but at a slower rate than would occur if the deficit and GDP grew at the same rate.

6. Automatic stabilizers act to moderate the effects of economic recessions or economic expansions. In the case of economic recessions, the automatic stabilizers provide a source of additional spending that occurs as the economy goes into the recession. For example, as production and spending slow in the economy, the amount of taxes people pay naturally decrease as their income levels decrease, and this moderates the fall in consumer spending. Or, as unemployment rates increase, the number of people receiving unemployment compensation rises, and this enables people to spend more than they would otherwise be able to spend. In the case of economic expansions, the automatic stabilizers slow down spending: as people's incomes rise, their taxes also rise, reducing the overall increase in consumer income, and this moderates the economic expansion. (Students may provide different examples of automatic stabilizers.)

7. The government will operate with a deficit each year and, therefore, the government debt will grow over time. But, because the economy is growing at a faster rate than the growth rate of the deficit, this means that the debt–GDP ratio will fall over time.

Answers to Chapter Review Questions

1. **Answer d.** This question is a review of facts presented in the chapter. Each statement is factual.

2. **Answer e.** Total government spending includes the government's purchases of goods and services as well as the expenditures the government makes in the form of transfer payments. The three primary transfer programs in terms of dollar cost in the United States are Social Security, Medicare, and Medicaid.

3. **Answer d.** Contractionary fiscal policy is a reduction in government spending or an increase in taxes aimed at shifting *AD* to the left. For a given *SRAS,* this leftward shift in *AD* will lead to a lower level of equilibrium aggregate output and a reduction in the aggregate price level. Contractionary fiscal policy is implemented when the economy produces a level of output in excess of potential output: contractionary fiscal policy is used to offset an inflationary gap.

4. **Answer c.** When *SRAS* intersects *AD* to the right of *LRAS,* the economy faces an inflationary gap. This inflationary gap can be eliminated through a decrease in government spending or an increase in taxes, since either policy will cause *AD* to shift to the left holding everything else equal. A decrease in government spending and an increase in taxes are examples of contractionary fiscal policy. By definition, when potential output is greater than actual aggregate output, the economy is operating with a recessionary gap.

5. **Answer b.** There are significant lags involved in the implementation of fiscal and monetary policy. These lags can result in a situation where the implemented policy actually worsens the economic situation (for example, using expansionary fiscal policy to counteract a recessionary gap that has turned into an inflationary gap by the time the fiscal policy takes effect).

6. **Answer d.** Answers (a), (b), and (c) are all factual statements about the Social Security program in the United States. These statements are all discussed in the text.

7. **Answer b.** In our simple model, the multiplier effect for changes in taxes or transfers equals (in absolute value) $MPC/(1 - MPC)$, while the multiplier effect for changes in autonomous aggregate spending equals $1/(1 - MPC)$. The multiplier effect of changes in taxes and transfers is smaller than the multiplier effect of changes in autonomous aggregate spending.

8. **Answer e.** Automatic stabilizers act to automatically lessen the economic consequences of recessions and expansions. They do this by providing an automatic fiscal policy response that stimulates a contractionary economy and slows down, or contracts, an expansionary economy. This activity effectively lessens the multiplier process and therefore reduces the size of the multiplier.

9. **Answer c.** Discretionary fiscal policy refers to fiscal policy that is implemented at the discretion of policy makers. It is therefore the direct result of deliberate actions taken by policy makers.

10. **Answer b.** The budget balance, $S_{Government}$, is defined by the equation $S_{Government} = T - G - TR$. In an expansion, tax revenue increases and transfers decrease (both of these changes are the result of automatic stabilizers): for a given level of government spending, the budget balance increases. If the government pursues expansionary fiscal policy while holding everything else constant, this will decrease the budget balance.

11. **Answer d.** Answers (a), (b), and (c) are all incorrect. The multiplier effect from a change in taxes and transfers is smaller than the multiplier effect from a change in government spending, and therefore the effect of a change in taxes and transfers on *AD* will be smaller than an equal change in government spending. When unemployment rises, this leads to lower tax revenue (as income falls in the economy, tax revenue also decreases) and higher expenditures on transfer programs like unemployment compensation: thus, the budget deficit almost always rises when unemployment rises. Answer (d) provides a straightforward definition of the cyclically adjusted budget balance.

12. **Answer a.** When the government spends more than it collects in tax revenue, the government runs a deficit and must acquire additional funds: typically it does this by borrowing the necessary funds. When the government's deficit increases, this adds to the value of the government debt. It is unusual for governments to sell valuable assets to finance their spending programs. When the government spends more than it collects in tax revenue, this causes the budget balance to decrease (recall that the budget balance is defined in equation form as $S_{Government} = T - G - TR$).

13. **Answer e.** The fiscal year runs from October 1 through September 30th: so, for example, if the fiscal year runs from October 1, 2001 through September 30, 2002, it is considered fiscal year 2002 (and *not* fiscal year 2001). Public debt is defined as given in answer (b), and the total government debt includes not only the public debt but also the debt that one part of government owes to another part of government.

14. **Answer b.** At the end of fiscal year 2012, the U.S. total government debt equaled $16.1 trillion. The public debt for fiscal year 2012 equaled $11.3 trillion, which represented 72% of GDP. The public debt–GDP ratio for the United States and other wealthy countries was more or less the same.

15. **Answer c.** The government debt is not the same as the government deficit. The government deficit is the difference between the amount of money a government spends and the amount of money it collects in tax revenue during a given period of time. The government debt, in contrast, is the total amount of money a government owes at a particular point in time.

16. **Answer d.** Answers (a), (b), and (c) are all possibilities. When the government runs a deficit, it will typically borrow funds. When the government borrows funds, it competes

with firms in the financial markets for those funds. This competition may crowd out private investment spending and therefore lead to lower long-run rates of economic growth. In addition, as the deficits persist the government will find that increasing amounts of its tax revenue must be dedicated to paying the interest expense of the debt, and this means the government must either reduce its spending in other areas or raise more revenue from taxes.

17. **Answer d.** The debt–GDP ratio provides a measure of the size of the government debt relative to the size of the economy: this is a helpful comparison, since the size of the economy provides a measure of the potential tax revenue that can be raised by the government. If the government debt is increasing at the same time that GDP is also increasing, it is possible that the debt–GDP ratio is actually falling, provided that GDP is growing at a faster rate than debt.

18. **Answer e.** Implicit liabilities are promises made by governments that represent future payments that must be made by the governments. Examples in the United States would include transfer programs like Social Security and Medicare. Implicit liabilities are not included in debt statistics typically, nor are they included in the calculation of the debt–GDP ratio.

19. **Answer c.** The demographic issues of the retirement of the baby boom generation will only worsen as this group reaches retirement age and begins drawing on Social Security and Medicare. In addition to these demographic issues related to an aging population, we also need to recognize that health care costs rise faster than other costs in wealthy economies: this will place additional financial pressures on the cost of Medicare and Medicaid. Social Security and Medicare are funded by dedicated taxes: when the taxes generated exceed the level of spending, the excess funds are set aside in trust funds. These funds may then be borrowed by other parts of the government: this borrowing creates an implicit liability where the borrowing by one part of the government reflects a responsibility to repay these dollars back to the trust funds where they originated. Often the focus is just on the United States debt owed to the public; such a focus understates the true nature of the government debt, since it does not include the implicit liabilities that represent borrowing within the government. Including both public debt and the United States government debt held by trust funds gives a full accounting of the level of debt the government faces.

20. **Answer a.** A change in government spending is an example of fiscal policy. An increase in government spending, holding everything else constant, will stimulate the economy in the short run while a decrease in government spending, holding everything else constant, will contract the economy in the short run.

21. **Answer c.** State and local governments rely on revenue that comes from sales taxes, property taxes, income taxes, and various fees.

22. **Answer e.** Government transfers are payments that the government makes to households even though the government has not received a good or a service from the household. These transfer payments effectively redistribute purchasing power in the economy: the household receiving the transfer payment can now command more goods and services than they could before the transfer.

23. **Answer d.** This is just a definitional question. See the text for a description of these programs. For example, social insurance programs include Social Security, Medicare, and Medicaid.

24. **Answer b.** When the government increases the amount of taxes it collects from households, this reduces disposable income and leads households to reduce their level of consumption spending. This decrease in consumption spending leads to further reductions in spending in the economy due to the multiplier effect: the *AD* curve shifts to the left. Answers (a), (c), and (d) would all shift the *AD* curve to the right.

25. **Answer c.** If the economy is currently operating with an inflationary gap, that implies that the level of actual output in this economy is greater than potential output. To return the economy to its potential output level, the government will need to shift the *AD* curve to the left. Only answer (c) causes a leftward shift in *AD;* the other answers all cause the *AD* curve to shift to the right.

26. **Answer e.** Argentina's reduction in government spending and increase in taxes in the period 1997–2001 were designed to contract the economy as was the Lyndon Johnson surcharge on income taxes enacted in 1968. This was a temporary increase of 10% on income taxes designed to reduce consumer spending and thereby contract the economy. Answers (a) and (b) are both examples of expansionary fiscal policy; in each example, the policy was enacted with the hope that it would spur greater spending and hence higher levels of aggregate output.

27. **Answer b.** Discretionary fiscal policy is difficult to use due to significant time lags: there is the lag in recognizing that there is an economic problem, there is a legislative lag, and there is an implementation lag. These lags result in a situation where the discretionary fiscal policy may not actually be felt in an economy until after the recessionary gap is eliminated; in this case, the discretionary fiscal policy may cause economic fluctuations to be greater than they would have been absent the discretionary fiscal policy.

28. **Answer c.** With an upward-sloping aggregate supply curve, an increase in government spending will cause the *AD* curve to shift to the right while causing a movement along the short-run aggregate supply curve. In the short run the level of real GDP will increase in this economy but by an amount less than that predicted by the multiplier, while the aggregate price level increases.

29. **Answer a.** The multiplier effect for a change in government spending is greater than the multiplier effect for a change in taxes: the government will stimulate the economy more if it increases government spending.

30. **Answer g.** Unemployed people tend to be less wealthy than people who own stocks: this leads them to spend more of their disposable income. Since unemployed people tend to have a higher *MPC* than people who own stocks, this leads to a larger multiplier effect on the level of aggregate output from an increase in unemployment benefits than from a decrease in taxes on profits. The effect of automatic stabilizers is to reduce economic fluctuations. For example, when income increases, this causes tax revenue to increase automatically, and this increase in tax revenue results in the increase in aggregate output being less than it would have been had there been no taxes. Thus, automatic stabilizers reduce the size of the multiplier.

31. **Answer b.** To find the budget balance, recall that this is the same as government saving, or $S_{Government}$, which can be written as $S_{Government} = T - G - TR$. In this example, the budget balance is therefore equal to –$170 billion. When the budget balance is negative, this indicates that the government is running a deficit, since the sum of spending plus transfer payments exceeds the value of tax revenue.

32. **Answer b.** The government should run a deficit during a recession: in a recession there is too little spending and the government can augment the level of spending by operating with a deficit during the recession. The government should run a surplus during an expansion: in an expansion there is the potential for too much spending and the government can moderate this tendency toward overspending by operating with a surplus during the expansion.

33. **Answer d.** All of the answers are correct. See the text for the discussion of how persistent deficit spending can place financial pressure on future budgets, crowd out investment spending due to government borrowing, and result in the need for higher taxes in order to pay the interest payments on the government debt

chapter 16

Money, Banking, and the Federal Reserve System

BEFORE YOU READ THE CHAPTER

Summary

This chapter explores the topic of money. It considers the role of money and different forms of money in an economy, the impact of private banks and the Federal Reserve on the money supply, and the use of open-market operations by the Federal Reserve to change the monetary base.

Chapter Objectives

Objective #1. Money is an asset that can easily be used to make purchases of goods and services. Money includes cash, which is liquid, plus other assets that are highly liquid.

- Currency in circulation consists of cash in the hands of the public. Checkable bank deposits are bank accounts that provide check-writing privileges to the owners of these accounts.

- The money supply is the total value of financial assets in the economy that are considered money. There are multiple definitions of the money supply based on the degree of liquidity of the assets included in the particular measure of the money supply.

- Debit cards automatically transfer funds from the buyer's bank account, while credit cards access funds that can be borrowed by the user of the credit card. Debit cards allow the user to access part of the money supply while credit cards create a liability for the user and therefore are not part of the money supply.

Objective #2. Money enhances gains from trade by making indirect exchange possible. In a barter economy, exchange can only occur when there is a double coincidence of wants: you must want the good or service I offer and I must want the good or service you offer. Money, by increasing gains from trade, increases welfare.

Objective #3. Money acts as a medium of exchange, a store of value, and a unit of account.

- An asset that is used to make purchases of goods and services serves as a medium of exchange. Over time many different kinds of assets have served in this role.

- Provided there is little inflation, money acts as a store of value due to its ability to maintain its purchasing power over time.

- Money is a measure people use to set prices and make economic calculations. We refer to this role for money as the unit of account.

Objective #4. The types of money fall into three broad categories.

- Commodity money refers to the use of an asset as a medium of exchange that has useful value independent of its role as a medium of exchange.

- Commodity-backed money refers to items used as mediums of exchange that have no intrinsic value (for example, paper currency) but whose ultimate value rests on the promise that they could be exchanged for valuable goods.

- Fiat money refers to money whose value derives strictly from the government's decree that it be accepted as a means of payment.

Objective #5. The Federal Reserve (the Fed) provides two measures of the money supply. These monetary aggregates—M1 and M2—measure the money supply using different definitions. M1 defines money most narrowly as the sum of currency in circulation, traveler's checks, and checkable bank deposits. M2 is comprised of M1 plus other near-monies, which are financial assets that are easily converted into cash or checkable bank deposits. M1 measures the money supply from a liquidity perspective: all items included in M1 are highly liquid. M2 includes the liquid assets of M1 as well as a group of less liquid assets.

Objective #6. A T-account is a type of financial spreadsheet that displays an institution's financial position. On the left-hand side of the T-account, the institution's assets and their values are listed; on the right-hand side of the T-account, the institution's liabilities and their values are listed. Banks hold reserves in order to meet the demand for funds from their depositors. Bank reserves are composed of the currency in the banks' vaults and the bank deposits held by the Fed in each bank's own account. The reserve ratio is the fraction of bank deposits a bank holds as reserves: in the United States the reserve ratio is regulated by the Fed.

Objective #7. Banks receive deposits of funds from their customers and then use these funds to make interest-earning financial transactions. For example, banks make loans to customers and purchase Treasury bills: both financial transactions provide income in the form of interest to the bank.

Objective #8. Bank runs occur when many depositors at a bank, fearing a bank failure, simultaneously decide to withdraw their funds. Banks can find themselves in a situation where they lack the liquidity to satisfy these depositor demands since many of the deposited funds are used to finance relatively illiquid bank loans.

Objective #9. Bank regulation reduces the probability of bank runs.

- The Federal Deposit Insurance Corporation (FDIC) provides deposit insurance, a guarantee by the federal government that depositors will be paid up to a designated maximum amount per account (currently $250,000 per depositor at any given bank) even if the bank fails. When there is deposit insurance depositors have no incentive to remove their funds from a bank, even if there are rumors that the bank is in financial trouble.

- The existence of deposit insurance creates an incentive problem: banks, knowing they are insured, are apt to engage in overly risky behavior while depositors, knowing they are insured, are not inclined to monitor bank behavior. Capital requirements address this incentive problem by requiring owners of banks to hold more assets than the value of their bank deposits. Should some loans prove bad, the bank will still have assets larger than their deposits: the bank owners, rather than the government, can absorb the loss from the bad loans.

- Bank runs are also prevented by requiring banks to hold a higher reserve ratio than the banks would otherwise choose to hold.

- Banks that are in financial trouble can borrow money from the Fed through an arrangement referred to as the discount window. This enables banks to get funds instead of being forced to sell their assets at prices below their value when confronted by a sudden demand for funds from depositors.

Objective #10. Banks affect the money supply in two ways. First, they remove some money out of circulation by holding currency in their bank vaults and in their reserve accounts at the Fed. Second, banks create money when they accept deposits and make loans.

Objective #11. Excess reserves are those reserves held by a bank that exceed the level of reserves required by the Fed.

- In a simplified model, where banks lend out all their excess reserves and borrowers hold their loans as bank deposits and not currency, the increase in bank deposits from lending out the excess reserves equals the excess reserves divided by the required reserve ratio. We can write this money multiplier as $1/rr$, where rr is the required reserve ratio.

- In the real world, the money multiplier is smaller than the money multiplier in our simplified model. The monetary base equals the sum of currency in circulation and reserves held by the bank. The monetary base is controlled by the monetary authorities. The money supply equals currency in circulation plus bank deposits. The money multiplier is the ratio of the money supply to the monetary base. The actual money multiplier is smaller than our simple model predicted because a dollar of currency in circulation, unlike a dollar in reserves, does not support multiple dollars of the money supply.

Objective #12. Central banks oversee and regulate the banking system and they control the monetary base. In the United States the central bank is the Federal Reserve. The Federal Reserve consists of a Board of Governors and 12 regional Federal Reserve Banks. The Board of Governors has seven members including the Chairman of the Federal Reserve.

- The Federal Reserve Bank of New York carries out open-market operations in which the Fed buys or sells some of the existing stock of U.S. Treasury bills.

- Monetary policy decisions are made by the Federal Open Market Committee (FOMC), whose members include the Board of Governors and five of the regional bank presidents. The president of the Federal Reserve Bank of New York is always a member of the FOMC while the other 11 presidents rotate on and off the FOMC.

- The Fed's organizational structure creates an organization that is accountable to the voting public while simultaneously insulated from short-term political pressures.

Objective #13. The Fed possesses three monetary policy tools: the reserve requirement, the discount rate, and open-market operations.

- The reserve requirement sets the minimum level of reserves each bank must hold. Penalties are assessed on banks that fail to meet the required reserve ratio on average over a two-week period. The Fed seldom changes the required reserve ratio.

- The discount rate is the interest rate banks must pay the Fed if they borrow additional reserves from the Fed. Banks that are in need of additional reserves usually borrow these reserves from other banks in the federal funds market. The federal funds market interest rate, the federal funds rate, is determined by supply and demand. The Fed typically sets the discount rate above the federal funds rate to discourage bank borrowing from the Fed. Normally the discount rate is set one percentage point above the federal funds rate, but starting in the fall of 2007 the Fed, in response to the financial crisis, reduced the spread between the discount rate and the federal funds rate.

- Open-market operations are the Fed's most important monetary policy tool. The Fed possesses both assets and liabilities: its liabilities consist of bank reserves, both deposited at the Fed and in bank vaults, and currency in circulation. In other words, the Fed's liabilities are equal to the monetary base.

  - When the FOMC directs the Federal Reserve Bank of New York to purchase Treasury bills, it effectively increases the amount of reserves in the banking system by crediting the commercial banks that sell the Treasury bills with additional reserves. These additional reserves start the money multiplier process, which leads these additional reserves to support a higher level of bank deposits. The money supply increases.

  - When the FOMC directs the Federal Reserve Bank of New York to sell Treasury bills, it effectively decreases the amount of reserves in the banking system: commercial banks that purchase these Treasury bills pay for them when the Fed debits their reserve accounts at the Fed. This reduction in reserves starts the money multiplier process, which results in these reduced reserves supporting a lower level of bank deposits. The money supply decreases.

  - The Fed can create the funds it needs to purchase Treasury bills. Thus, the Fed can create monetary base at its own discretion. In addition, the Fed earns interest from the Treasury bills its holds: this interest is returned to the Treasury and provides a source of revenue to the Treasury.

Objective #14. There are many different central banks in the world today. The European Central Bank is the central bank for the members of the European Union. Like the Federal Reserve its organization is answerable to voters while protected from short-term political pressures.

Objective #15. Financial crises over the course of U.S. history have resulted in legislation as well as awareness of policy issues with regard to financial markets and institutions.

- After the financial crisis of 1907, legislation was passed creating the Federal Reserve. The Fed was given responsibility for centralizing the holding of reserves, inspecting banks, and providing a sufficiently elastic money supply in response to changing economic conditions.

- During the Great Depression in the early 1930s, bank runs were a problem and legislation was passed creating federal deposit insurance to help eliminate these bank runs. In addition, during this time period the federal government recapitalized banks by lending to them and purchasing shares of banks. In 1933, banks were separated into two classes of banks: commercial banks and investment banks.

- In the 1980s, the S&L Crisis revealed tendencies for banking institutions to engage in overly speculative transactions and pointed out the need not only for federal deposit insurance, but also regulation with regard to capital requirements and reserve requirements.

- In the 1990s, some firms—using huge amounts of leverage—speculated in global markets, and this speculation led to financial crises in Asia and Russia. During these crises there were particular problems associated with deleveraging where large firms (in particular LTCM) sold their assets to cover their losses, and this selling of assets created balance sheet problems for other firms around the world. These problems led to the failure of various credit markets and required intervention by the New York Fed to get these world credit markets functioning.

- In the mid-2000s, the housing bubble in the United States—accompanied by the securitization of subprime lending—led to massive losses by banks and other nonbank financial institutions once the housing bubble burst. This financial crisis required intervention by the U.S. government to expand its lending to bank and nonbank institutions as well as the provision of bank capital through government purchase of bank shares. By 2008, it was clear that this latest financial crisis would result in the creation of a wider safety net and broader regulation of the financial sector.

Key Terms

Notes

money any asset that can easily be used to purchase goods and services.

liquid an asset is liquid if it can be quickly converted into cash without much loss of value.

currency in circulation actual cash held by the public.

checkable bank deposits *bank* accounts on which people can write checks.

money supply the total value of *financial assets* in the *economy* that are considered *money*.

medium of exchange an asset that individuals acquire for the purpose of trading for goods and services rather than for their own consumption.

store of value an asset that is a means of holding purchasing power over time.

unit of account a measure used to set prices and make economic calculations.

commodity money a *medium of exchange* that is a good, normally gold or silver, that has intrinsic value in other uses.

commodity-backed money a *medium of exchange* that has no intrinsic value whose ultimate value is guaranteed by a promise that it can be converted into valuable goods on demand.

fiat money a *medium of exchange* whose value derives entirely from its official status as a means of payment.

monetary aggregate an overall measure of the *money supply*. The most common monetary aggregates in the United States are M1, which includes *currency in circulation*, traveler's checks, and *checkable bank deposits*, and M2, which includes M1 as well as *near-monies*.

near-money a *financial asset* that cannot be directly used as a *medium of exchange* but can be readily converted into cash or *checkable bank deposits*.

Key Terms *(continued)*

bank reserves currency held by *banks* in their vaults plus their deposits at the Federal Reserve.

T-account a simple tool that summarizes a business's financial position by showing, in a single table, the business's assets and liabilities, with assets on the left and liabilities on the right.

reserve ratio the fraction of *bank deposits* that a *bank* holds as reserves. In the United States, the minimum required reserve ratio is set by the Federal Reserve.

bank run a phenomenon in which many of a *bank*'s depositors try to withdraw their funds due to fears of a bank failure.

deposit insurance a guarantee that a *bank*'s depositors will be paid even if the bank can't come up with the funds, up to a maximum amount per account.

reserve requirements rules set by the Federal Reserve that set the minimum *reserve ratio* for banks. For *checkable bank deposits* in the United States, the minimum reserve ratio is set at 10%.

discount window a protection against *bank runs* in which the Federal Reserve stands ready to lend money to *banks* in trouble.

excess reserves a *bank*'s *reserves* over and above the reserves required by law or regulation.

monetary base the sum of *currency in circulation* and *bank reserves*.

money multiplier the ratio of the *money supply* to the *monetary base*.

central bank an institution that oversees and regulates the banking system and controls the *monetary base*.

federal funds market the *financial market* that allows *banks* that fall short of *reserve requirements* to borrow funds from banks with *excess reserves*.

federal funds rate the *interest rate* at which funds are borrowed and lent in the *federal funds market*.

discount rate the rate of interest the Federal Reserve charges on loans to *banks* that fall short of *reserve requirements*.

open-market operation a purchase or sale of U.S. Treasury bills by the Federal Reserve, normally through a transaction with a *commercial bank*.

commercial bank a *bank* that accepts deposits and is covered by *deposit insurance*.

investment bank a *bank* that trades in *financial assets* and is not covered by *deposit insurance*.

Notes

$1/(1-mpc)$

$\dfrac{1}{rr}$

Key Terms *(continued)*

Notes

savings and loans (thrifts) deposit-taking *banks*, usually specialized in issuing home loans.

leverage the degree to which a financial institution is financing its investments with borrowed funds.

balance sheet effects the reduction in a firm's net worth from falling asset prices.

vicious cycle of deleveraging the sequence of events that takes place when a *firm's* asset sales to cover losses produce negative *balance sheet effects* on other firms and force creditors to call in their *loans*, forcing sales of more assets and causing further declines in asset prices.

subprime lending lending to home buyers who don't meet the usual criteria for borrowing.

securitization the pooling of loans and mortgages made by a financial institution and the sale of shares in such a pool to other investors.

AFTER YOU READ THE CHAPTER

Tips

Tip #1. It is important to understand the definition and the distinction between the monetary base, the money supply, and reserves. The money supply is the value of financial assets in the economy that are considered money: this would include cash in the hands of the public, checkable bank deposits, and traveler's checks, using the narrow definition of the money supply given by the monetary aggregate M1. Bank reserves are composed of the currency that banks hold in their vaults plus their deposits at the Federal Reserve. The monetary base is the sum of currency in circulation and bank reserves. The monetary base is not equal to the money supply: the money supply is larger than the monetary base.

Tip #2. It is important to understand the distinction between assets and liabilities. Make sure you clearly understand what an asset and a liability are and then recognize that any financial instrument represents both an asset and a liability. For example, a mortgage represents a liability for the borrower and an asset for the lender; a checking account deposit represents a liability for the bank providing the check service and an asset to the individual depositing the funds.

Tip #3. For any T-account, clearly identify whose perspective is represented in the T-account. T-accounts represent the assets and liabilities of an institution or an individual. When making a T-account, consider whose T-account it represents: this will help you more clearly identify whether the financial instruments you include are assets or liabilities. For example, bank reserves are a liability in the Fed's T-account and an asset in a bank's T-account.

Tip #4. Each T-account must always balance: that is, total assets must equal total liabilities where total liabilities include capital. If your T-account does not balance, check your entries to find your error.

Tip #5. Remember that when the Fed purchases Treasury bills it injects reserves into the banking system and this increases the money supply. When the Fed sells Treasury bills, it removes reserves from the banking system and this decreases the money supply.

WORKED PROBLEMS

1. Your professor instructs you to create a T-account of your financial situation. In this T-account, you should list your assets and your liabilities and then you should compute your net worth. Your professor explains that net worth is simply total assets minus total liabilities. Your professor also instructs you to interview someone who is at least 20 years older than you are and create a T-account that lists this person's assets, liabilities, and net worth. How might your T-account differ from the T-account of this older person? Why do you anticipate this difference?

STEP 1: Review the definition of a T-account as well as the definitions of assets, liabilities, and net worth. Create a T-account form that you will be able to use both for yourself and when you interview the other person.

Review the section "The Monetary Role of Banks" on pages 488–492, and Figure 16-2 on page 488.

A T-account provides a summary of the financial position of an individual or firm. On the left side, assets are listed: these are all the items that the individual or firm owns that are valuable. The value of these assets is listed along with the name of the asset. On the right side, liabilities are listed: these are all the items that the individual or firm owes. The value of these liabilities is listed along with the name of the liability. Net worth, the difference between assets and liabilities, is listed on the right side of the T-account: the sum of the value of total liabilities and net worth always equals the value of total assets.

Here is a T-account form that you can use when constructing your own T-account or the T-account of the individual you have chosen to interview.

Assets	Liabilities
	Net worth
Value of total assets	Value of total liabilities + net worth

STEP 2: Make a list of all of those items, both physical and financial, that you own that are valuable. Make a list of all of those items, both physical and financial, that you owe to others or that represent a debt.

Review the section "The Monetary Role of Banks" on pages 488–492, and Figure 16-2 on page 488.

Enter the items that you own on the left side of your T-account along with their value. Sum the values together to get the value of total assets.

Enter the items that you owe, or the debt that you have, on the right-hand side of your T-account along with their value. Sum the values together to get the value of total liabilities.

Now compare the value of your total assets to the value of your total liabilities to get a measure of your net worth. It is possible that you have a negative net worth: if you have not had a chance to work full-time and you have taken out student loans, your liabilities may well exceed your assets.

Here is an example of a possible T-account for a mythical student, Joe. Joe is 20 years old and is a full-time student. He owns a car that is worth $2,000, he has $500 in a checking account, and he has student loans equal to $10,000. This is his T-account:

Assets		Liabilities	
Car	$2,000	Student loan	$10,000
Checking account	$500		
		Net worth	−$7,500
Total value of assets	$2,500	Total liabilities + net worth	$2,500

STEP 3: **Find a person to interview who will be comfortable discussing his or her financial position.**

Review the section "The Monetary Role of Banks" on pages 488–492, and Figure 16-2 on page 488.

Make a list of the person's assets and liabilities and the dollar value of each item. Construct the person's T-account and calculate his or her net worth.

Answers in Step 3 will vary for each person since each person's financial situation is unique to him or her.

STEP 4: **Compare and contrast the two T-accounts.**

Review the section "The Monetary Role of Banks" on pages 488–492, and Figure 16-2 on page 488.

It is likely that the older individual has a positive and greater net worth than does the student. This is due to the fact that older people have had more time to accumulate assets, have likely saved for retirement, have had a full-time job for a longer period of time than the student, and have likely had time to pay off some of their debt, particularly educational debt.

2. Suppose that there is only one bank, First National Bank, in your economy. First National Bank maintains its required reserves but never holds excess reserves. The required reserve ratio in this economy is 10% of checkable deposits. Furthermore, suppose that everyone in this community banks at this bank and that all of their transactions are made using checks or their debit cards. No one carries currency in this economy. The following tables provide the initial T-accounts of the central bank of this economy as well as of First National Bank. Suppose that the central bank in this economy purchases $50,000 worth of Treasury bills from First National Bank. How will this affect the money supply in this economy? Make sure you indicate what the initial money supply is before the central bank makes this purchase and what the final money supply is once all adjustments to this purchase have occurred. What is the value of the money multiplier in this economy? For this example, assume that the difference between First National Bank's assets and its liabilities stays constant.

Initial situation at the central bank:

Assets		Liabilities	
Treasury bills	$20,000	Reserves of First National Bank	$20,000

Initial situation at First National Bank:

Assets		Liabilities	
Reserves at the central bank	$20,000	Checkable deposits	$200,000
Treasury bills and other loans	$180,000		

STEP 1: Start by thinking about how the T-accounts for the central bank and First National Bank will change when the central bank purchases $50,000 worth of Treasury bills. Do not try to analyze more than just the initial change in the T-accounts.

Review the section "The Monetary Role of Banks" on pages 488–492, the section "Open-Market Operations" on pages 499–501, and Figure 16-8 on page 500.

When the central bank purchases Treasury bills, its assets will increase. But the central bank must pay for these new assets, and the simplest way to do this is for the central bank to simply credit the reserve account of First National Bank with the value of the purchase. The central bank's T-account looks like the following:

Assets		Liabilities	
Treasury bills	$70,000	Reserves of First National Bank	$70,000

Notice that the central bank's purchase of Treasury bills alters both the asset and the liability entries for its T-account.

First National Bank's T-account is also altered by this transaction. First National Bank has $50,000 less in Treasury bills but $50,000 more in its reserve account. The T-account for First National bank follows.

Assets		Liabilities	
Reserves at the central bank	$70,000	Checkable deposits	$200,000
Treasury bills and other loans	$130,000		

Notice that First National Bank now has excess reserves. First National Bank has $70,000 in reserves, but it needs only $20,000 to meet its required reserve. First National Bank will want to lend out these excess reserves in order to earn interest.

STEP 2: Calculate the level of checkable deposits that First National Bank can support if it holds $70,000 in reserves. Once you have calculated this, provide a new T-account showing First National Bank's financial position once all adjustments to the central bank's purchase have occurred.

Review the section "The Monetary Role of Banks" on pages 488–492, the section "Open-Market Operations" on pages 499–501, and Figure 16-8 on page 500.

A simple way to think about this is to realize that required reserves equal the product of the required reserve ratio and the level of checkable deposits. In this example, you know the level of reserves and the required reserve ratio, but you do not know the level of checkable deposits. Thus, $70,000 = (0.10)(\text{checkable deposits})$, or checkable deposits equal $700,000.

Assets		Liabilities	
Reserves at the central bank	$70,000	Checkable deposits	$700,000
Treasury bills and other loans	$630,000		

STEP 3: Compare the level of the initial money supply to the level of the money supply after all adjustments to the central bank's purchase of $50,000 in Treasury bills have occurred.

Review the section "The Monetary Role of Banks" on pages 488–492, the section "Open-Market Operations" on pages 499–501, and Figure 16-8 on page 500.

The money supply is defined as currency in circulation plus checkable deposits. In this example, there is no currency in circulation since all transactions are made with checks or with debit cards. The money supply initially is $200,000, and the money supply after the full adjustment to the central bank's purchase is $700,000. The money supply increases by $500,000.

STEP 4: Calculate the value of the money multiplier in this example.

Review the section "The Monetary Role of Banks" on pages 488–492, the section "Open-Market Operations" on pages 499–501, and Figure 16-8 on page 500.

The money multiplier is equal to $[1/(\text{required reserve ratio})]$, or in this example, $1/0.1$, which is equal to 10. In this example, the central bank increased the amount of reserves in the banking system by $50,000 when it purchased the Treasury bills. This led to the money supply increasing by $500,000: the change in the money supply equals the product of the money multiplier and the change in reserves. That is, $500,000 = (10)($50,000)$.

3. The government's provision of deposit insurance for checkable deposits is often cited as an example of government intervention that helps stabilize the financial system by eliminating or at least vastly reducing the probability of bank runs. Is there any incentive problem associated with the provision of deposit insurance? Discuss how deposit insurance reduces the risk of bank runs but creates a different kind of problem. How does regulation address the incentive problem created by deposit insurance?

STEP 1: Discuss what a bank run is and why provision of deposit insurance by the government eliminates bank runs.

Review the section "The Problem of Bank Runs" on pages 489-490 and the section "Bank Regulation" on pages 490-492.

A bank run is when bank depositors try to withdraw their funds due to fears that the bank may fail. If a sufficient number of depositors seek their funds, the bank will fail since the bank will not have adequate funds on hand to meet all of these demands. In addition, the failure of one bank may lead to other banks failing as depositors at these other banks lose faith in their own bank's solvency.

When the government provides deposit insurance this means that even if the bank fails, the depositor will not lose his or her deposit. Deposit insurance thus protects the banking system from bank runs.

STEP 2: Discuss the incentive problem that is created by banks once deposit insurance is in effect. In your answer, provide one method used by regulators to deal with this incentive problem.

Review the section "The Problem of Bank Runs" on pages 489-490 and the section "Bank Regulation" on pages 490-492.

Deposit insurance creates an incentive problem, since once people's deposits are insured, they have little incentive to actually monitor what their bank does. Banks will often take riskier positions than would be considered optimal from the perspective of the taxpayers who will have to cover the deposits should the bank fail. One way to reduce this incentive problem is to require banks to provide a minimum level of capital that provides a buffer against bad loans.

4. The Federal Reserve has three monetary policy tools: the required reserve ratio, the discount rate, and open-market operations. Briefly describe each of these tools and then comment on each tool's usefulness in controlling the money supply in the economy.

STEP 1: Review what the required reserve ratio is and how it can affect the money supply. Then explain why the Federal Reserve does not rely on this monetary policy tool to change the money supply.

Review the section "What the Fed Does: Reserve Requirements and the Discount Rate" on pages 498-499 and the section "Open-Market Operations" on pages 499-501.

The required reserve ratio refers to the percentage of checkable deposits that a bank must hold in its reserve account. The higher the required reserve ratio, the smaller will be the money multiplier. If the Federal Reserve wanted to alter the money supply using the required reserve ratio, it could either raise this ratio to reduce the money supply or lower this ratio to increase the money supply. However, changing the required reserve ratio is administratively costly to banks because they must adjust their balance sheets to meet the new required reserve levels. The Federal Reserve rarely changes the required reserve ratio.

STEP 2: Review what the discount rate is and how it can affect the money supply. Then explain why the Federal Reserve does not rely on this monetary policy tool to change the money supply.

Review the section "What the Fed Does: Reserve Requirements and the Discount Rate" on pages 498-499 and the section "Open-Market Operations" on pages 499-501.

The discount rate refers to the interest rate that the Federal Reserve charges banks that borrow funds from the Federal Reserve. Typically the Federal Reserve sets the discount rate above the federal funds rate: banks will find it cheaper to borrow funds from other banks than to borrow funds from the Federal Reserve at the discount window. If the Federal Reserve wanted to change the money supply via the discount rate, it could lower the spread between the discount rate and the federal funds rate: this would effectively reduce the cost of being short on reserves, and banks would therefore increase their borrowing. This action by banks to the reduced spread will cause the money supply to increase. In contrast, an increase in the spread between the discount rate and the federal funds rate will cause the money supply to decrease. The Federal Reserve does not try to manage the level of the money supply via the discount rate, however, because this method is not very flexible, nor is it easy to fine-tune this method to ensure that the appropriate level of the money supply is achieved.

STEP 3: **Review what open-market operations are and how they can affect the money supply. Then explain why the Federal Reserve relies on this monetary policy tool to change the money supply.**

Review the section "What the Fed Does: Reserve Requirements and the Discount Rate" on pages 498–499 and the section "Open-Market Operations" on pages 499–501.

Open-market operations refer to the buying and selling of Treasury bills by the Federal Reserve in the open market. This is the Federal Reserve's primary monetary policy tool because it is flexible, can easily be fine-tuned to get precisely the effect the Federal Reserve desires, and can be implemented at relatively low administrative cost. When the Federal Reserve purchases Treasury bills it injects new reserves into the financial system, and via the money multiplier process these new reserves lead to a higher level of the money supply. When the Federal Reserve sells Treasury bills it removes reserves from the financial system, and via the money multiplier process this reduction in reserves leads to an even greater reduction in the money supply.

Problems and Exercises

1. Consider the following three lists of assets.

List A	List B	List C
$50 in cash	A car	A boat
A six-month CD worth $50,000, redeemable without penalty six months from today's date	A checking account deposit	The coins you collect in a jar
	A Treasury bond issued by the government of the United States	A savings account deposit
A share of stock		
A savings account deposit		

   a. Rank each of these lists of assets from the most liquid asset to the least liquid asset.

    b. For each list, identify any item that is included in M1.

    c. For each list, identify any item that is included in M2.

    d. Why is money *not* equivalent to wealth?

2. Suppose Fantasia has a single bank that initially has $10,000 of deposits, reserves of $2,000, and loans of $8,000. To simplify our example, we will assume that bank capital equals zero. Furthermore, Fantasia's central bank has a required reserve of 10% of deposits. All monetary transactions are made by check: no one in Fantasia uses currency.

    a. Construct a T-account depicting the initial situation in Fantasia. In your T-account, make sure you differentiate between required and excess reserves and that your T-account's assets equal its liabilities.

    b. Explain how you calculated the level of excess reserves in Fantasia.

    c. Suppose the bank in Fantasia lends these excess reserves [the amount of excess reserves you calculated in part (b)] until it reaches the point where its excess reserves equal zero. How does this change the T-account?

    d. Did the money supply in Fantasia change when the bank loaned out the excess reserves? Explain your answer.

    e. What is the value of the money multiplier in Fantasia? Using the money multiplier, compute the change in deposits.

3. You are provided the following T-accounts for the central bank of Economia and the only commercial bank in Economia. In Economia, all financial transactions occur within the banking system: no one holds currency. The required reserve ratio imposed by the central bank is 20% of deposits.

Central bank of Economia

Assets		Liabilities	
Treasury bills	$20,000	Reserves	$20,000
Total assets	$20,000	Total liabilities	$20,000

Commercial bank of Economia

Assets		Liabilities	
Required reserves	$20,000	Deposits	$100,000
		Capital	$20,000
Loans	$70,000		
Treasury bills	$30,000		
Total assets	$120,000	Total liabilities and capital	$120,000

Suppose the central bank in Economia purchases $2,000 of Treasury bills from the commercial bank.

a. Provide a T-account for both the central bank and the commercial bank showing the immediate effect of this transaction. Be sure to differentiate between required and excess reserves for the commercial bank.

b. Provide a T-account for the commercial bank once the commercial bank lends out its excess reserves and all adjustments have been made through the money multiplier process.

c. What happens to the money supply when the central bank purchases $2,000 of Treasury bills from the commercial bank?

d. Relate the change in the money supply to the money multiplier.

e. What was the monetary base initially?

f. What is the monetary base after all adjustments to the central bank's monetary policy have taken effect?

4. The following T-accounts are for the central bank of Macropedia and its sole commercial bank. In Macropedia, citizens always hold $1,000 in currency and the reserve requirement equals 10%. The commercial bank adheres to a strict policy of always lending out its excess reserves.

Central bank of Macropedia				Commercial bank of Macropedia			
Assets		**Liabilities**		**Assets**		**Liabilities**	
Treasury bills	$11,000	Reserves	$10,000	Reserves	$10,000	Deposits	$100,000
		Currency in circulation	$1,000	Loans	$80,000	Capital	$0
				Treasury bills	$10,000		
Total assets	$11,000	Total liabilities	$11,000	Total assets	$100,000	Total liabilities and capital	$100,000

a. Does the commercial bank initially satisfy the required reserve? Explain your answer.

Suppose the central bank sells $5,000 in Treasury bills to the commercial bank.

b. Provide T-accounts for both the central bank and the commercial bank showing the immediate effect of this transaction.

c. Given your answer in part (b), describe the commercial bank's problem. Be specific in your answer and identify what options the commercial bank has for resolving its problem.

d. Provide a T-account for the commercial bank after it fully adjusts to the central bank's selling of $5,000 in Treasury bills.

e. What happens to the monetary base in this problem?

f. What happens to the money supply?

5. Use the following information about Macroland to answer this question.

Bank deposits at the central bank	$100 million
Currency in bank vaults	$ 50 million
Currency held by the public	75 million
Checkable deposits	600 million
Traveler's checks	5 million

a. What are bank reserves equal to in Macroland?

b. Suppose banks hold no excess reserves in Macroland. What is the required reserve ratio given the information in this table?

c. If the public does not change its currency holdings, what will happen to the level of checkable deposits in Macroland, relative to their initial level, if the central bank of Macroland purchases $10 million worth of Treasury bills in the open market? Explain your answer and provide a numerical answer.

d. If the public does not change its currency holdings, what will happen to the level of checkable deposits in Macroland, relative to their initial level, if the central bank of Macroland sells $5 million in Treasury bills in the open market? Explain your answer and provide a numerical answer.

6. Explain how the use of money increases the gains from trade.

7. For each of the following situations, determine what kind of money—commodity money, commodity-backed money, or fiat money—is being described.

    a. Prisoners of war use cigarettes as the monetary unit.

    b. When they babysit for other families, young families in Anytown receive paper coupons that can be redeemed for babysitting services. These coupons serve as a monetary unit for these transactions.

    c. Two tribes use corn as the monetary unit when trading with one another.

    d. In Midtown, the central bank issues paper currency that is fully redeemable in gold or silver.

    e. In Uptown, the central bank issues paper currency that the government of Uptown accepts as payment for taxes.

8. Currently in the United States, the money supply is large enough that people on average hold over $3,000 in their wallets. Yet, clearly most individuals do not carry that large an amount of money in their wallets. Explain how the money supply could be so large and yet we do not on average hold this amount of dollars per person.

9. Bank deposit insurance provides insurance for depositors so that they do not have to worry about losing money they have deposited into insured banks. This seems like a really good protection to have. Is there a downside to this protection? Explain your answer fully.

10. How does a requirement that banks hold more assets than liabilities help to reduce the banks' tendency to engage in riskier investment behavior than is optimal from the government's point of view?

11. Financial panics have been a relatively common occurrence in U.S. history. Based upon the information provided in the text on financial crises, answer the following questions.

   a. During the panic of 1907, why did the failure of Knickerbocker Trust lead to bank runs among other trusts?

   b. As a result of the panic of 1907, the Federal Reserve Act was passed in 1913 creating the Federal Reserve. What did the legislature hope to accomplish with the creation of the Federal Reserve?

c. Why were there more bank runs during the Great Depression?

d. The text includes a discussion of the S&L Crisis of the 1980s and, in this discussion, the text mentions "new freedom did not bring with it increased oversight." Explain what the text meant by this statement and then explain how this statement helps us understand the S&L Crisis of the 1980s.

e. How was the financial crisis of 2008 similar to other financial crises experienced in the United States?

BEFORE YOU TAKE THE TEST

Chapter Review Questions

1. Which of the following statements is true?
   a. The definition of money includes all forms of wealth.
   b. Money is an asset that can be easily used to purchase goods and services.
   c. Money consists of cash, which is liquid, plus other assets that are relatively illiquid.
   d. All of the above are true.
   e. Statements (a) and (b) are both true.
   f. Statements (b) and (c) are both true.

2. Credit cards
   a. are just another name for debit cards that allow users to access funds in their bank account.
   b. create an asset for users since the use of credit cards enables people to purchase goods and services.
   c. provide a means of borrowing funds, thus creating a liability, in order to make purchases of goods and services.
   d. Answers (a) and (b) are both correct.
   e. Answers (a) and (c) are both correct.

3. Money

    a. increases welfare since it increases gains from trade.

    b. eliminates the need for a "double coincidence of wants" between trading partners.

    c. includes currency in circulation plus checkable deposits.

    d. Answers (a), (b), and (c) are all correct.

    e. Answers (b) and (c) are both correct.

4. Use the following statements to answer the question.

    I. The price of bananas is quoted in dollars rather than in units of apples, and the price of apples is quoted in dollars rather than in units of bananas.

    II. The $100 Sue saved this year will have $100 worth of purchasing power five years from now, provided there is no inflation.

    III. The building contractor said the new roof for our house would cost $6,000.

    Money has three roles in an economy. Statement _____ illustrates the use of money as a medium of exchange; statement _____ illustrates the use of money as a unit of account; and statement _____ illustrates the use of money as a store of value.

    a. III; I; II   c. III; II; I

    b. I; III; II   d. II; III; I

5. Which of the following statements is true?

    a. Fiat money is paper currency issued by the government and redeemable in a valuable asset like gold.

    b. Fiat money is money issued by a ruler and thus is found only in countries with a monarchy.

    c. Commodity money is a poor type of money, since it cannot be used in trade even though it is a valuable commodity.

    d. None of these statements is true.

6. M1 includes currency in circulation,

    a. savings account deposits, and checkable bank deposits.

    b. traveler's checks, other near-monies, and checkable bank deposits.

    c. traveler's checks, and checkable bank deposits.

    d. traveler's checks, checkable bank deposits, and savings account deposits.

7. In a bank's T-account,

    a. Joe's checking account deposit is treated as an asset.

    b. Ellen's car loan is counted as a liability.

    c. bank deposits at the Fed are an asset for the bank.

    d. assets exactly equal liabilities when there are positive capital requirements.

Use the following T-account for a bank to answer the next three questions. T-bill refers to Treasury bills.

Assets		Liabilities	
Required reserves	$100	Deposits	$1,000
Loans	$400		
Treasury bills	$800		

8. Given this T-account and assuming the bank holds no excess reserves, what is the required reserve ratio?
   a. 10%   c. 80%
   b. 40%   d. 1%

9. Given this T-account, how much capital does this bank currently hold?
   a. zero
   b. $300
   c. $400
   d. $500
   e. $1,300

10. Suppose this is the only bank in the banking system. Furthermore, suppose all money is held in this bank and the bank holds no excess reserves. If the Fed makes an open-market sale of $50 worth of T-bills to this bank, what will happen to the money supply after all adjustments are made?
    a. The money supply will increase by $50.
    b. The money supply will decrease by $50.
    c. The money supply will increase by $500.
    d. The money supply will decrease by $500.

11. Bank runs
    a. can be reduced by providing deposit insurance, requiring banks to hold significant amounts of capital, and mandating required reserves.
    b. are often caused by rumor and the fear that other people will withdraw their funds.
    c. when rumored, may significantly impact the prices banks receive when they sell assets to increase their liquidity.
    d. Answers (a), (b), and (c) are all correct.

12. Banks affect the money supply
    a. when they take deposited currency out of circulation and deposit it into their bank vaults.
    b. when they lend their excess reserves to their customers.
    c. when a customer from one bank writes a check to a customer of another bank who deposits that check into his or her checking account.
    d. All of the above are true.
    e. Answers (a) and (b) are correct.

13. The monetary base consists of
  a. currency in circulation plus bank deposits.
  b. bank deposits plus bank reserves.
  c. bank deposits, bank reserves, and currency in circulation.
  d. currency in circulation plus bank reserves.

14. In a simple banking system, where banks hold no excess reserves and all funds are kept as bank deposits, then
  a. the money multiplier equals 1 divided by the required reserve ratio.
  b. total deposits will equal reserves multiplied by the reciprocal of the required reserve ratio.
  c. $1 increase in excess reserves will increase deposits by an amount equal to 1 divided by the required reserve ratio.
  d. Answers (a), (b), and (c) are all correct.

15. Holding everything else constant, in the simple banking model presented in the text, the greater the numeric value of the required reserve ratio the
  a. higher the discount rate the Federal Reserve Bank charges for loans from the Federal Reserve Bank.
  b. greater the money multiplier.
  c. smaller the money multiplier.
  d. Answers (a) and (b) are both correct.
  e. Answers (a) and (c) are both correct.

16. Suppose the required reserve ratio initially is 10% of bank deposits but is increased by the Fed to 20% of bank deposits. Holding everything else constant, this will
  a. reduce the size of the money multiplier.
  b. cause the banking system to contract the level of bank deposits in the banking system.
  c. change the value of the money multiplier from 10 to 5.
  d. Answers (a), (b), and (c) are all correct.

17. Which of the following statements is true?
  a. Americans increased their holdings of currency between 1929 and 1933.
  b. As Americans withdrew currency from the banking system between 1929 and 1933, this led to increases in bank deposits as banks lent funds to customers who lacked adequate funding.
  c. M1 fell sharply between 1929 and 1933, as the decline in currency holding by the public was much greater than the decline in bank deposits.
  d. All of the above are true.
  e. Statements (a) and (b) are both true.
  f. Statements (a) and (c) are both true.

18. Which of the following statements is true?
  I. Provided that no one knows that counterfeit dollars are being used, the use of these counterfeit dollars does not hurt anyone in an economy.
  II. The use of counterfeit dollars in an economy reduces the revenues available to pay for the operations of that economy's government.
  III. Counterfeit money is not an issue when the government uses fiat money and not commodity-backed money.
  a. Statement I is true.
  b. Statement II is true.
  c. Statement III is true.
  d. Statements I, II, and III are all true.
  e. Statements II and III are both true.

19. To be included in the measure of M1, the asset must be
  a. a near-money.
  b. highly liquid.
  c. money.
  d. either money or some other form of wealth.

20. Commodity-backed money
  a. restricts the use of fewer resources than does commodity money.
  b. is money that has no intrinsic value but whose value is guaranteed by a promise that the commodity-backed money can be converted into valuable goods on demand.
  c. is a way for society to provide the functions of money without tying up valuable resources.
  d. Answers (a), (b), and (c) are all correct.

21. Stocks and bonds are
  a. part of M1.
  b. part of M2, but not M1.
  c. not part of M1 or M2 because they are not sufficiently liquid.

22. Bank reserves include
  a. the currency banks hold in their vaults.
  b. bank deposits held at the Federal Reserve.
  c. outstanding loans that the bank has made to borrowers.
  d. the bank capital that the owners of the bank provide.
  e. Answers (a), (b), (c), and (d) are all correct.
  f. Answers (a) and (b) are both correct.
  g. Answers (a), (b), and (d) are correct.

23. Bank regulation is helpful in reducing bank runs since bank regulation typically

   a. requires banks to keep a minimum required reserve ratio.

   b. provides deposit insurance so that depositors have little incentive to remove their money from a bank even when there are rumors about the bank's soundness.

   c. sets capital requirements to help align the incentive problem for banks so that they will have a lower tendency to engage in overly risky investment behavior.

   d. Answers (a), (b), and (c) are all correct.

   e. Answers (a) and (b) are both correct.

   f. Answers (a) and (c) are both correct.

   g. Answers (b) and (c) are both correct.

24. When banks find that they must borrow money, and they can only borrow from the Federal Reserve, this is referred to as using

   a. open-market operations.

   b. the discount window.

   c. the FDIC.

   d. the required reserve ratio.

25. Which of the following statements is true?

   I. Banks decrease the money supply because they remove some currency from circulation when they place currency in their bank vaults or deposit currency at the Federal Reserve.

   II. Banks increase the money supply when they accept deposits and then make loans with some of the money that has been deposited.

   a. Statement I is true.   c. Statements I and II are true.

   b. Statement II is true.   d. Neither statement I nor II is true.

26. The three primary policy tools available to the Federal Reserve include

   a. reserve requirements, the ability to tax banks, and the discount rate.

   b. reserve requirements, the discount rate, and open-market operations.

   c. reserve requirements, the ability to tax banks, and open-market operations.

   d. the ability to tax banks, the discount rate, and open-market operations.

27. When banks borrow from one another, the rate of interest they pay for this loan is called the

   a. discount rate.

   b. federal funds rate.

28. Suppose a hypothetical economy that uses a checkable-deposits-only monetary system has a required reserve ratio of 20%. When the central bank in this economy purchases $100 million worth of Treasury bills, this will increase the money supply by

   a. 20%.

   b. $100 million.

   c. $500 million.

   d. $5 million.

29. Suppose a hypothetical economy that uses a checkable-deposits-only monetary system has a required reserve ratio of 10%. When the central bank in this economy sells $10 million worth of Treasury bills, this will decrease the money supply by

a. 10%.

b. $10 million.

c. $100 million.

d. $1 million.

30. Which of the following statements is true?

    I. Regarding the United States and its economic history, the financial crisis of 2008 is an event that is unlike any other event in U.S. history.

    II. The U.S. economy is never subject to financial crisis.

    III. Financial crisis in a country usually results in legislation providing for greater financial regulation.

a. Statement I is true.

b. Statement II is true.

c. Statement III is true.

d. Statements I and II are true.

31. The financial crisis of 2008 can be characterized as a financial crisis with

a. excessive speculation particularly in the housing market.

b. a failure to regulate some of the involved institutions.

c. inadequate intervention by the government when the crisis first appeared.

d. excessive amounts of leverage in use by some of the involved firms.

e. Answers (a), (b), (c), and (d) are all correct.

■ ANSWER KEY

Answers to Problems and Exercises

1. **a.** List A: $50 in cash, a savings account deposit, a share of stock, a six-month CD redeemable without penalty six months from today's date

    List B: The checking account deposit, a Treasury bond issued by the government of the United States, a car

    List C: The coins you collect in a jar, a savings account deposit, a boat

    b. In List A, the $50 in cash is included in M1; in List B, the checking account deposit is included in M1; and in List C, the coins in a jar are included in M1.

    c. M2 includes any item in M1 plus the savings account deposit (List A) and (List C), and the six-month CD (List A).

    d. Wealth includes all assets, physical or financial, that an individual owns at a particular point in time. Although these assets may be quite valuable, they may not all possess the characteristic of liquidity. Money possesses this characteristic, and thus includes only those items that can easily be used to purchase goods and services. In this question, the bonds, stock, car, and boat are assets and therefore part of the owner's wealth, but they are not considered money.

2. **a.**

Assets		Liabilities	
Required reserves	$1,000	Deposits	$10,000
Excess reserves	$1,000		
Loans	$8,000		
Total assets	$10,000	Total liabilities	$10,000

    b. Excess reserves are equal to total reserves minus required reserves, or $1,000. To find required reserves, multiply deposits by the required reserve ratio [($10,000)(0.1) = $1,000].

    c.

Assets		Liabilities	
Required reserves	$2,000	Deposits	$20,000
Excess reserves	$0		
Loans	$18,000		
Total assets	$20,000	Total liabilities	$20,000

    d. Yes, since the money supply is defined as bank deposits plus currency in circulation. Since Fantasia has no currency in circulation, we need only consider what happens to bank deposits. Initially, bank deposits equaled $10,000 and after the lending out of all the excess reserves, bank deposits equal $20,000. Thus, the money supply increased by $10,000.

e. The money multiplier equals $1/rr$, or 10 in this example, since no one holds currency and the bank does not hold excess reserves. The change in deposits equals the money multiplier times the change in reserves or, in this case, the change in deposits equals $(1/0.1)(\$1,000)$ or $10,000.

3. a.

Central bank of Economia				Commercial bank of Economia			
Assets		**Liabilities**		**Assets**		**Liabilities**	
Treasury bills	$22,000	Reserves	$22,000	Required reserves	$20,000	Deposits	$100,000
				Excess reserves	$2,000	Capital	$20,000
				Loans	$70,000		
				Treasury bills	$28,000		
Total assets	$22,000	Total liabilities	$22,000	Total assets	$120,000	Total liabilities and capital	$120,000

b.

Commercial bank of Economia			
Assets		**Liabilities**	
Required reserves	$22,000	Deposits	$110,000
Loans	$80,000	Capital	$20,000
Treasury bills	$28,000		
Total assets	$130,000	Total liabilities and capital	$130,000

c. The money supply increases from $100,000 to $110,000. Recall that the money supply equals checkable deposits plus currency in circulation: since Economia has no currency in circulation, the money supply equals the level of deposits.

d. The change in the money supply equals the money multiplier times the change in the monetary base. In this problem, the money multiplier equals 5, and the change in the monetary base is the $2,000 increase in reserves that occurs when the central bank purchases the Treasury bills.

e. The monetary base equals reserves plus currency in circulation. In Economia, currency in circulation equals zero, so the monetary base is equivalent to reserves. Initially the monetary base is $20,000.

f. The monetary base increases to $22,000.

4. a. Yes, the commercial bank has reserves of $10,000 and deposits of $100,000: reserves equal 10% of deposits, which satisfies the required reserve ratio.

b.

Central bank of Macropedia				Commercial bank of Macropedia			
Assets		**Liabilities**		**Assets**		**Liabilities**	
Treasury bills	$6,000	Reserves	$5,000	Reserves	$5,000	Deposits	$100,000
		Currency in circulation	$1,000	Loans	$80,000	Capital	$0
				Treasury bills	$15,000		
Total assets	$6,000	Total liabilities	$6,000	Total assets	$100,000	Total liabilities	$100,000

c. The commercial bank has insufficient reserves to meet the required reserve ratio: when its deposits equal $100,000, it needs $10,000 in required reserves. With reserves of $5,000, it can only support $50,000 of deposits. In the short term, it can borrow reserves from the central bank of Macropedia. Because there is only one commercial bank in Macropedia, it cannot borrow from the federal funds market since there is no federal funds market. Over time the commercial bank will find it needs to decrease its outstanding loans, and therefore deposits, until its reserves are sufficient to meet the required reserve ratio.

d.

Commercial bank of Macropedia			
Assets		**Liabilities**	
Reserves	$5,000	Deposits	$50,000
Loans	$30,000	Capital	$0
Treasury bills	$15,000		
Total assets	$50,000	Total liabilities	$50,000

e. The monetary base is initially equal to $11,000 ($10,000 in reserves plus $1,000 in currency in circulation). After the central bank's activity, the monetary base is $6,000 ($5,000 in reserves plus $1,000 in currency in circulation).

f. The money supply is initially $101,000 ($100,000 in checkable bank deposits plus $1,000 in currency in circulation). After the central bank's actions and full adjustment, the money supply is $51,000 ($50,000 in checkable bank deposits plus $1,000 in currency in circulation). The money supply decreases by $50,000, or the amount predicted by the money multiplier process.

5. a. Bank reserves equal currency in bank vaults plus bank deposits at the central bank, or $150 million.

b. We can calculate the required reserve ratio, *rr*, as the ratio of required reserves to checkable deposits. Since there are no excess reserves in Macroland, the bank reserves calculated in part (a) equal the required reserves: thus, $150 million/$600 million equals a required reserve ratio of 0.25.

c. When the central bank of Macroland purchases $10 million in Treasury bills, this increases the level of reserves in the banking system by $10 million. This increase in reserves starts the multiplier process: the change in the money supply is calculated as the increase in reserves times the money multiplier or ($10 million)(4) = $40 million. Thus, the money supply increases by $40 million when the central bank purchases Treasury bills on the open market.

d. Using the concept explained in part (c), this sale of Treasury bills by the central bank will decrease the money supply by $20 million. We can see this by recalling that the change in the money supply equals the change in reserves times the money multiplier or (−$5 million)(4), or −$20 million.

6. Money makes indirect exchange possible, which enhances the possible gains from trade since it eliminates the need for a double coincidence of wants between two trading individuals. Money enables people to trade for what they have to offer and then use the money they receive from selling these goods and services to then purchase the goods and services they want.

7. **a.** Cigarettes are an example of commodity money since the unit of exchange is a commodity that has intrinsic value in other uses.

    b. The paper coupons are an example of commodity-backed money since these paper coupons can be redeemed for a particular commodity: a certain number of hours of babysitting.

    c. Corn is an example of commodity money since the unit of exchange is a commodity that has intrinsic value in other uses.

    d. This is an example of commodity-backed money since the paper currency can be exchanged for a commodity: gold or silver.

    e. This is an example of fiat money since it is not backed by anything other than the government's guarantee: if the government were no longer willing to accept this currency in payment for taxes, it would lose its value as a monetary unit.

8. Although the money supply divided by the U.S. population suggests that individuals on average hold a very high level of dollars, the reality is that most people carry a considerably smaller amount of dollars. The other dollars are held in business cash registers and by people not living in the United States since dollars are used by many foreigners, particularly in places where the stability of the national currency is questionable over time.

9. Although deposit insurance protects individual depositors so that they do not have to fear losing the dollars they deposit in insured institutions, it does create a moral hazard problem. Depositors, once they are insured, do not need to monitor the actions their banking institution engages in, which may lead to a situation where the institutions engage in riskier investment activities than is optimal. The banks have an incentive to engage in risky investments since the owners of the bank will benefit if the investment proves profitable and can pass on the loss to the government if the investment proves unprofitable.

10. When a bank holds more assets than liabilities, this means that the bank faces a potential loss for any investment that proves unprofitable. Another way of thinking about this is to realize that if some of the banks' loans prove to be bad and the banks take a loss, the banks will still have assets larger than their deposits. This reduces the probability that the government will need to step in and provide funds to cover depositors' funds.

11. **a.** The failure of Knickerbocker Trust led to bank runs among other trusts because of rumors about these other institutions. Trusts during this period were less regulated and, in addition, opted not to join the New York Clearinghouse. Over time the trusts speculated in real estate and the stock market until 1907 when Knickerbocker Trust was the first trust to suffer massive losses in unsuccessful stock market speculation.

    b. The Federal Reserve was meant to create a financial system where all deposit-taking institutions would be forced to hold adequate reserves. In addition, the legislative act made provision for all deposit-taking institutions covered by the Federal Reserve to undergo inspection by regulators.

    c. Even with the creation of the Federal Reserve, there were still problems with bank runs since it was possible for banks to hold fewer reserves than the value of their total deposits. The Glass-Steagall Act of 1932 created federal deposit insurance and increased the ability of banks to borrow from the Federal Reserve. The creation of federal deposit insurance effectively ended the problem of bank runs since depositors no longer had to fear losing their deposits.

d. Prior to the S&L Crisis of the 1980s, the S&Ls were covered by federal deposit insurance and tightly regulated. During the 1970s, high inflation meant that S&Ls found it increasingly difficult to maintain the level of deposits they needed in order to make long-term mortgages. In addition, the high inflation rates eroded the value of the S&L assets. Congress passed legislation designed to help S&Ls respond to the problem of insufficient deposits and eroding asset values: this legislation enabled S&Ls to undertake riskier investments. Unfortunately, the legislation gave the S&Ls greater investment freedom but failed to consider what the appropriate level of oversight would be for this increased freedom. This meant that some S&Ls engaged in riskier investment than was optimal from the government's point of view since the government ultimately had to cover any losses to depositors.

e. The financial crisis of 2008 shared many commonalities with other financial crises from other periods of time. Like the Panic of 1907, the financial crisis of 2008 involved excessive speculation as well as institutions that were not as strictly regulated as depository institutions. As in the Great Depression, the financial crisis of 2008 involved a federal government that was reluctant to take action until the level of financial loss was very large.

Answers to Chapter Review Questions

1. **Answer b.** Answer (b) provides a straightforward definition of money. Money includes cash plus other assets that are highly liquid like checking accounts. Money does not include all forms of wealth since some forms of wealth are highly illiquid.

2. **Answer c.** Credit cards and debit cards are not equivalent: credit cards allow the user to borrow funds, and this borrowing represents a liability for the user since the funds must be repaid.

3. **Answer d.** Answers (a), (b), and (c) are factual statements about money that are all discussed in the text.

4. **Answer a.** Statement I is an example of money used as a unit of account since it provides a standard measure for the prices of all goods and services in an economy. Statement II is an example of money's role as a store of value: we value money because of its ability to represent purchasing power over time. Statement III provides an example of money as a medium of exchange: the building contractor gives us a price for a particular item.

5. **Answer d.** Each of these statements is incorrect. Fiat money is money whose value derives entirely from its official status as a means of exchange: this is not limited to countries with monarchies. Fiat money is not redeemable in some other commodity. Commodity money is a more limited form of money than commodity-backed money or fiat money, since it ties up more of an economy's resources to facilitate making transactions rather than using those resources for more productive uses.

6. **Answer c.** M1 is the narrowest definition of money and includes only currency in circulation, traveler's checks, and checkable bank deposits.

7. **Answer c.** Joe's checking account balance is an asset from Joe's perspective but a liability from the bank's perspective since the bank is liable, or owes money, to Joe. Ellen's car loan is a liability for Ellen since it represents something she owes to someone else, while it represents an asset to the bank since it represents a promise to pay the bank a certain amount of money. When the bank deposits funds at the Federal Reserve, this deposit is an asset for the bank and a liability for the Federal Reserve. If there are positive capital requirements, then assets are greater than liabilities.

8. **Answer a.** The required reserve ratio is equal to required reserves divided by checkable deposits: in this example, this bank holds 10% of its checkable deposits as required reserves.

9. **Answer b.** The bank's capital is the difference between its total assets and total liabilities. In this case, the bank's assets sum to $1,300 while the liabilities total $1,000. The difference, $300, is the bank's capital.

10. **Answer d.** When the Fed sells $50 worth of T-bills, it debits the reserve account of the bank that sells the T-bills to the Fed. This results in the bank having insufficient reserves to support their current level of deposits. The bank will contract the loans it holds until the deposits in the bank are the amount that can be supported by the new level of reserves. The new reserves in this problem equal $50 (the initial $100 minus the $50 spent on the T-bills): $50 in reserves can support $500 in deposits when the required reserve ratio equals 10. So the money supply will decrease from $1,000 to $500, or a decrease of $500.

11. **Answer d.** Even the rumor of a potential bank run can result in dramatic decreases in the value of a bank's assets. Rumor and fear can combine to create a self-fulfilling prophecy: depositors fear that the behavior of other depositors will drive even a financially stable bank into instability. The potential for bank runs can be eliminated through effective regulation that provides deposit insurance while requiring bank capital and a designated reserve ratio.

12. **Answer e.** Banks affect the money supply, or the sum of currency in circulation plus bank deposits, when they hold currency in their bank vaults, thus reducing the total amount of currency in circulation. Banks also affect the money supply when they lend out their excess reserves and create additional bank deposits. Check writing and check cashing do not affect the money supply since they do not change the overall level of currency in circulation plus bank deposits.

13. **Answer d.** The monetary base consists of currency in circulation and bank reserves, while the money supply equals currency in circulation plus bank deposits.

14. **Answer d.** All of the statements restate the relationship between excess reserves and the required reserve ratio and their impact on the level of bank deposits. We can write this relationship as: the change in bank deposits equals excess reserves times ($1/rr$). Recall that $1/rr$ is simply the reciprocal of the required reserve ratio.

15. **Answer c.** Since the money multiplier is defined as $1/rr$, when the required reserve ratio increases, the money multiplier decreases, holding everything else constant. The required reserve ratio has no impact on the discount rate, the interest rate that the Federal Reserve charges banks that borrow funds from the Federal Reserve.

16. **Answer d.** When the required reserve ratio increases, the money multiplier, defined as $1/rr$, must necessarily decrease. If the required reserve ratio equals 10%, the money multiplier equals 10; and if the required reserve ratio equals 20%, the money multiplier equals 5. When the reserve requirement increases, banks find that their reserves' ability to support bank deposits decreases, and this leads banks to contract the level of bank deposits in the banking system.

17. **Answer a.** As banks failed in the period 1929 to 1933, many Americans withdrew their bank deposits from the banking system due to their fear that more banks would fail. As bank deposits were withdrawn, this led to lower bank reserves, which reduced the capacity of the banking system to support bank deposits: bank deposits fell sharply. M1 did fall during this period due to the decrease in bank deposits being much greater than the increase in currency in circulation.

18. **Answer b.** The use of counterfeit money in an economy hurts the ability of that economy's government to generate revenues to pay for government services even if no one in the economy recognizes that counterfeit dollars are being used to make exchanges. Governments cover a small amount of their expenses by issuing new currency to meet the growing demand for this currency. Counterfeit money exacts this cost of the government no matter if the government endorses fiat money or commodity-backed money.

19. **Answer b.** To be included in the measure of M1, the asset must be highly liquid since M1 is defined very narrowly to include only currency in circulation, traveler's checks, and checkable bank deposits. M2, a broader defined monetary aggregate, includes near-monies. Wealth is not the same as money and may include assets that are highly illiquid.

20. **Answer d.** Commodity-backed money is something that is used as a medium of exchange that has no intrinsic worth itself (e.g., paper money) but that can be converted into a valuable good on demand. Commodity-backed money reduces the amount of resources used to provide the functions of money since it does not require the circulation and direct use of the commodity in order to serve its various monetary roles. So, for example, if the commodity-backed money is backed by gold and silver, only enough gold and silver must be kept on hand in order to satisfy the demands for those individuals wishing to redeem their commodity-backed money.

21. **Answer c.** M1 is just checkable deposits, traveler's checks, and currency in circulation. M2 includes all of M1 plus other near-monies. Near-monies do not include stocks or bonds because neither of these two types of financial assets are sufficiently liquid.

22. **Answer f.** Bank reserves are composed of the currency in bank vaults and the bank deposits held at the Federal Reserve. Bank reserves are not part of currency in circulation.

23. **Answer d.** The text provides a description of these three components of bank regulation: deposit insurance, capital requirements, and reserve requirements. All three of these aspects of bank regulation help to reduce the probability of a bank run.

24. **Answer b.** When banks borrow from the Federal Reserve, this is referred to as using the discount window. The FDIC is the Federal Deposit Insurance Corporation, and it refers to the group that provides and oversees deposit insurance for the banking industry. Open market operations refers to the buying and selling of Treasury bills by the Federal Open Market Committee (FOMC). The required reserve ratio is set by the Federal Reserve and is the percentage of deposits that the Fed requires banks to hold either in their vaults or in their account at the Federal Reserve.

25. **Answer c.** Both of these statements are true. On the one hand, banks decrease the money supply when they remove currency from circulation and place that currency in their vaults or deposit it at the Federal Reserve; on the other hand, banks increase the money supply by accepting deposits and then lending out a portion of these deposited dollars to borrowers.

26. **Answer b.** The Federal Reserve can affect the money supply by engaging in open market operations in which the Federal Reserve either purchases Treasury bills or sells Treasury bills. The Fed can also affect the money supply by changing the reserve requirements: when the reserve requirement increases, this reduces the money supply, and when the Fed reduces the reserve requirement, this increases the money supply. Finally, the Fed can affect the money supply by changing the discount rate. When the discount rate falls relative to the federal funds rate, this means that it is now relatively cheaper to borrow from the Fed, which leads to increases in the money supply.

27. **Answer b.** The interest rate charged for loans from one bank to another is called the federal funds rate. The interest rate charged for a loan to a bank from the Fed is called the discount rate.

28. **Answer c.** In a checkable-deposits-only monetary system, the money multiplier is equal to $1/rr$, where rr is the required reserve ratio. Thus, for this economy the money multiplier is equal to 5 and a $100 million purchase of Treasury bills by the central bank will result in an increase in the money supply of $500 million.

29. **Answer c.** When the required reserve ratio is 10%, this implies that the money multiplier is equal to 10 in a checkable-deposits-only monetary system. Thus, an open market sale of $10 million worth of Treasury bills will result in a $100 million decrease in the money supply.

30. **Answer c.** Over the course of its history, the United States has experienced numerous financial crises, with each crisis typically resulting in a mandate for greater regulation of the financial market.

31. **Answer e.** All of these statements are true, and they are discussed in the text. As you read this section, notice the similarities and comparisons that the authors make among various financial crises.

chapter 17

Monetary Policy

Summary

This chapter explains money demand and then uses this concept to develop the liquidity preference model of short-run interest rate determination. The chapter considers the Fed's ability to move interest rates and explores the effect of monetary policy on short-run economic performance. The chapter also explores why monetary policy is the primary tool used by the central bank to stabilize the economy. The chapter also discusses monetary neutrality, or the idea that monetary policy in the long run does not affect real aggregate output but does affect the price level.

Chapter Objectives

Objective #1. Money is held by individuals and firms in order to facilitate making transactions. There is an opportunity cost to holding money: money normally yields a lower rate of return than nonmonetary assets. The opportunity cost of holding money is the difference between the interest rate on assets that are not money and the interest rate on assets that are money. The higher the short-term interest rate, the higher the opportunity cost of holding money: people reduce their holding of money as the short-term interest rate increases. This implies that the demand curve for money slopes downward: as the interest rate decreases, the quantity of money demanded increases. Figure 17.1 illustrates the relationship between the quantity of money demanded and the interest rate.

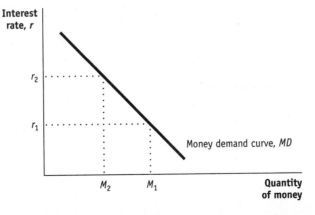

Figure 17.1

643

- Short-term interest rates are interest rates on financial assets that mature in less than a year. Short-term interest rates tend to move together since they are in effect competing for the same business. A short-term asset that offers a lower-than-average interest rate will be sold by investors. When these assets are sold, this forces the interest rate on these assets to increase since new buyers must be rewarded with a higher rate in order to be willing to buy the asset. This reasoning implies that short-term interest rates will tend to equalize across the financial assets found in the short-term interest rate market.

- Long-term interest rates are interest rates paid on financial assets that mature a number of years into the future. Long-term interest rates may differ from short-term interest rates. In this chapter's discussion of interest rates, we will simplify our discussion and assume that there is only one interest rate.

Objective #2. The money demand curve illustrates the relationship between the nominal quantity of money demanded and the interest rate. It is a downward-sloping curve. For a given interest rate, an increase in the aggregate price level causes the demand curve for money to shift to the right, while a decrease in the aggregate price level causes the demand curve for money to shift to the left. Figure 17.2 illustrates the effect of a change in the aggregate price level on the demand for money.

Figure 17.2

- There are a number of factors that shift the real money demand curve, including changes in the level of real aggregate spending, changes in banking technology, and changes in banking institutions that alter people's real demand for money.

  - Holding everything else constant, an increase in real aggregate spending will shift the real money demand curve to the right, while a decrease in real aggregate spending will shift the real money demand curve to the left.

  - Holding everything else constant, advances in information technology tend to shift the real money demand curve to the left since these advances make it easier for the public to make transactions while holding smaller amounts of money.

  - Changes in institutions can increase or decrease the demand for money by changing the opportunity cost of holding money.

Objective #3. In the United States, the Federal Open Market Committee (FOMC) sets a target interest rate for the federal funds rate and then uses open-market operations to achieve that target interest rate.

- The liquidity preference model of the interest rate illustrates how the Fed can control the interest rate through its open-market operations. The liquidity preference model says that the interest rate is determined by the intersection of the supply and demand for money in the market for money.

- In the liquidity preference model, the money supply is a vertical line whose location is controlled by the Fed through its open-market operations. The intersection of this vertical money supply curve with the downward-sloping money demand curve determines the equilibrium interest rate. Figure 17.3 illustrates this relationship.

Figure 17.3

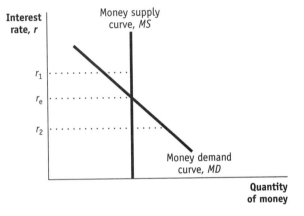

- If the nominal interest rate is lower than the equilibrium level, then the quantity of money demanded will be greater than the quantity of money supplied. People will want to increase their money holdings, and they will sell other financial assets to achieve this goal: in order to sell these financial assets, they will have to offer a higher interest rate to attract buyers. This will lead the nominal interest rate in the market for money to increase, bringing about equilibrium between the demand and supply of money.

- If the nominal interest rate is higher than the equilibrium level, then the quantity of money demanded will be less than the quantity of money supplied. People will want to decrease their money holdings and they will do so by buying other financial assets. Due to the increased demand for these interest-bearing financial assets, sellers of these assets will find that they can offer them at a lower nominal interest rate and still find willing buyers. Thus, the nominal interest rate will decrease, thereby restoring the money market to equilibrium, where the supply of money equals the demand for money.

- When the Fed purchases Treasury bills in the open market, this increases the money supply, causing the money supply curve to shift to the right. For a given money demand curve, this increase in the supply of money will result in interest rates decreasing. Thus, if the FOMC sets a target interest rate lower than the prevailing interest rate, it can reach this target by engaging in open-market purchases. Figure 17.4 illustrates an open-market purchase by the Fed.

Figure 17.4

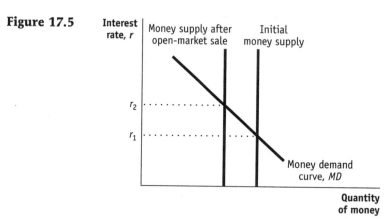

- When the Fed sells Treasury bills in the open market, this decreases the money supply, causing the money supply curve to shift to the left. For a given money demand curve, this decrease in the supply of money will result in interest rates increasing. Thus, if the FOMC sets a target interest rate higher than the prevailing interest rate, it can reach this target by engaging in open-market sales. Figure 17.5 illustrates an open-market sale.

Figure 17.5

Objective #4. Changes in the money supply cause the short-run level of real GDP to change.

- Monetary expansion in the short run reduces the interest rate and leads to higher investment spending and higher consumer spending, holding everything else constant. This higher investment spending results in higher GDP through the multiplier process. Thus, an increase in the money supply causes the *AD* curve to shift to the right and is referred to as expansionary monetary policy. The Federal Reserve and other central banks tend to engage in expansionary monetary policy when real GDP is below potential real GDP.

- Monetary contraction in the short run increases the interest rate and leads to lower investment spending and lower consumer spending, holding everything else constant. This lower investment spending results in lower GDP through the multiplier process. Thus, a decrease in the money supply causes the *AD* curve to shift to the left and is referred to as contractionary monetary policy. The Federal Reserve and other central banks tend to engage in contractionary monetary policy when real GDP is above potential real GDP.

- The Taylor rule for monetary policy is a rule for setting the federal funds rate that takes into account both the inflation rate and the output gap. The Taylor rule for the period from 1988 to 2008 can be summarized as: Federal funds rate = 2.07 + (1.28 × inflation) − (1.95 × unemployment gap).

Objective #5. The Federal Reserve bank does not set an explicit inflation target, but pursues monetary policy that will keep inflation low but positive. Other central banks do set inflation targets: central banks with inflation targets announce the inflation rate that they are trying to achieve and then set policies in an attempt to hit the stated target. Inflation targeting is based on forecasts of future inflation while the Taylor rule adjusts monetary policy in response to past inflation: the former is forward looking while the latter is backward looking.

- Inflation-targeting proponents argue that this type of policy is both transparent and accountable.

- Inflation-targeting opponents argue that this type of policy is too restrictive.

Objective #6. Monetary expansion in the short run can increase aggregate output beyond the potential output level, but in the long run this monetary expansion does not result in an increase in aggregate output, since aggregate output in the long run always equals potential output due to adjustments in the level of nominal wages. Thus, a monetary expansion in the long run raises the aggregate price level while having no effect on real GDP.

- A change in the money supply leads to a proportional change in the aggregate price level in the long run. That is, if an economy is initially in long-run equilibrium and the nominal money supply increases, long-run equilibrium can only be restored when all real values return to their original levels. Since the nominal money supply increased, the real money supply can only return to its initial level with a proportionate increase in the aggregate price level.

- Money neutrality refers to the idea that changes in the money supply have no real effects on the economy. An increase in the money supply results in the money supply curve shifting to the right. It also results in the money demand curve shifting to the right. In the long run, these two shifts result in the interest rate returning to its initial level and the money supply increasing from its initial level. Monetary policy, in the long run, has no effect on the interest rate.

- Monetary policy does have powerful real effects in the short run and can be used to ward off recessions or slow an expanding economy.

Key Terms

short-term interest rate the *interest rate* on *financial assets* that mature within less than a year.

long-term interest rate the *interest rate* on *financial assets* that mature a number of years into the future.

money demand curve a graphical representation of the relationship between the *interest rate* and the quantity of money demanded. The money demand curve slopes downward because, other things equal, a higher interest rate increases the *opportunity cost* of holding money.

liquidity preference model of the interest rate a model of the market for money in which the *interest rate* is determined by the supply and demand for money.

money supply curve a graphical representation of the relationship between the quantity of money supplied by the Federal Reserve and the *interest rate*.

Notes

Key Terms *(continued)*

target federal funds rate the Federal Reserve's desired level for the *federal funds rate*. The Federal Reserve adjusts the *money supply* through the purchase and sale of Treasury bills until the actual rate equals the desired rate.

expansionary monetary policy *monetary policy* that, through the lowering of the *interest rate*, increases aggregate demand and therefore output.

contractionary monetary policy *monetary policy* that, through the raising of the *interest rate*, reduces aggregate demand and therefore output.

Taylor rule for monetary policy a rule for setting the *federal funds rate* that takes into account both the *inflation rate* and the *output gap*.

inflation targeting an approach to *monetary policy* that requires the *central bank* to try to keep the *inflation rate* near a predetermined target rate.

zero lower bound for interest rates the fact that interest rates cannot fall below zero.

monetary neutrality the concept that changes in the *money supply* have no real effects on the *economy* in the long run and only result in a proportional change in the price level.

AFTER YOU READ THE CHAPTER

Tips

Tip #1. The interest rate is the price of money, because the interest rate provides a measure of the opportunity cost of holding money. As the interest rate increases, the quantity of money demanded decreases since the opportunity cost of holding money rises with increases in the interest rate. This relationship implies that the demand for money is downward sloping: the quantity of money demanded is inversely related to the interest rate. This relationship is illustrated in Figure 17.6: when the interest rate is r_1, the quantity of money demanded is M_1; when the interest rate rises to r_2, the quantity of money demanded decreases to M_2.

Figure 17.6

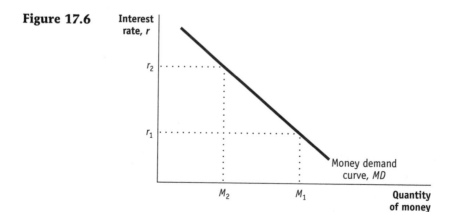

Tip #2. It is important to understand what causes a movement along the money demand curve and what factors cause a shift in the money demand curve. As with other demand curves, a change in the price of money—the interest rate—causes a movement along the demand curve (see Figure 17.6). A change in the aggregate price level shifts the nominal money demand curve: when the aggregate price level increases, the nominal money demand curve shifts to the right since people will now demand a greater amount of nominal money at every interest rate due to the higher aggregate price level; when the aggregate price level decreases, the nominal money demand curve shifts to the left since people will now demand a smaller amount of nominal money at every interest rate due to the lower aggregate price level. Money demand (real or nominal) also shifts with changes in real aggregate spending, changes in banking technology, and changes in banking institutions. We can summarize these changes in the following table.

Change	Effect on money demand
Increase in interest rate	Movement along money demand curve and decrease in quantity of money demanded
Decrease in interest rate	Movement along money demand curve and increase in quantity of money demanded
Increase in aggregate price level	Money demand shifts to the right
Decrease in aggregate price level	Money demand shifts to the left
Increase in real aggregate spending	Money demand shifts to the right
Decrease in real aggregate spending	Money demand shifts to the left
Advances in bank technology	Money demand shifts to the left
Changes in institutions	Money demand shifts to the left or right, depending on the institutional change

Tip #3. Equilibrium in the money market equates the quantity of money demanded with the quantity of money supplied at the equilibrium interest rate. Figure 17.7 illustrates the money market.

Figure 17.7

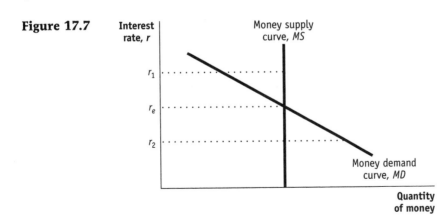

If the interest rate (r_1 in Figure 17.7) is greater than the equilibrium interest rate (r_e), the quantity of money supplied is greater than the quantity of money demanded at that interest rate. Investors will drive the interest rate down to the equilibrium level r_e by shifting their assets out of money holdings and into nonmonetary interest-bearing financial assets. This will cause the interest rate to decrease toward r_e.

If the interest rate (r_2 in Figure 17.7) is less than the equilibrium interest rate (r_e), the quantity of money supplied is less than the quantity of money demanded at that interest rate. Investors will drive the interest rate up to the equilibrium level r_e by shifting their assets out of nonmonetary interest-bearing financial assets and into money holdings. This will cause the interest rate to increase toward r_e.

Tip #4. It is important to understand how the Federal Open Market Committee (FOMC) through its open-market operations effectively controls interest rates in the economy. Figure 17.8 illustrates the effect of an open-market purchase on the interest rate. When the FOMC purchases Treasury bills in the open market, this injects new reserves into the banking system and leads to an expansion in the money supply from MS_1 to MS_2. For a given money demand curve, MD, this results in a decrease in the interest rate from r_1 to r_2.

Figure 17.8

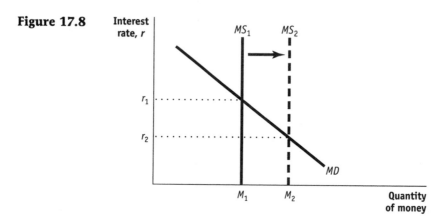

When the FOMC sells Treasury bills in the open market, this removes reserves from the banking system and effectively shifts the money supply curve to the left. For a given money demand curve, this action by the FOMC results in an increase in the interest rate.

Tip #5. It is important to distinguish between the short-run and long-run effects of monetary policy. In the short run, monetary policy can be used to stimulate AD and shift it to the right, resulting in an increase in aggregate real output, or monetary policy can be used to contract AD, thereby shifting it to the left and leading to a decrease in the level of aggregate real output. In the long run, monetary policy has no effect on aggregate real output since aggregate real output in the long run will always equal potential output. Economists refer to this as monetary neutrality: money is neutral in its effect on aggregate real output in the long run, since it cannot affect the level of aggregate real output.

1. The following table provides different situations. For each situation, determine whether the money demand curve or the money supply curve shifts and, if so, the direction of the shift. Then, determine what happens to the equilibrium interest rate and the equilibrium quantity of money.

Situation	Shift in the demand for money (provide direction of shift)	Shift in the supply of money (provide direction of shift)	Effect on the equilibrium interest rate	Effect on the equilibrium quantity of money
The information technology for making transactions improves				
The Federal Reserve makes an open-market purchase of Treasury bills				
Real GDP increases in the economy				
Real GDP decreases in the economy, and the Federal Reserve makes an open-market purchase of Treasury bills				
The aggregate price level increases				

STEP 1: Before you fill out the table, you will want to review the factors that shift the money demand curve. You may also find it helpful to review the effect of open-market operations by the Federal Reserve on the money supply curve.

Review the section "Shifts of the Money Demand Curve" on pages 521–522 and the section "Expansionary and Contractionary Monetary Policy" on pages 528–529.

The money demand curve will shift to the right with increases in the aggregate price level and increases in real income. The money demand curve will also shift with changes in institutions (the shift may be to the right or the left depending upon the nature of the change) or changes in technology (again, the shift can be to the right or the left depending upon the nature of the change).

The money supply curve will shift to the right when the Federal Reserve makes an open-market purchase of bonds, since the Federal Reserve will be injecting new reserves into the banking system with this purchase. The money supply curve will shift to the left when the Federal Reserve makes an open-market sale of bonds, since the Federal Reserve will be removing reserves from the banking system when it makes this sale.

STEP 2: Now that you have reviewed the factors that shift the two curves, you are ready to fill in the table.

Review the section "Shifts of the Money Demand Curve" on pages 521–522 and the section "Expansionary and Contractionary Monetary Policy" on pages 528–529.

Here is the completed table.

Situation	Shift in the demand for money (provide direction of shift)	Shift in the supply of money (provide direction of shift)	Effect on the equilibrium interest rate	Effect on the equilibrium quantity of money
The information technology for making transactions improves	Demand for money shifts left, since at every interest rate people will wish to hold less money	There is a movement along the supply of money curve due to the shift in the demand for money	The equilibrium interest rate will decrease	The equilibrium quantity of money will be unchanged
The Federal Reserve makes an open-market purchase of Treasury bills	There is a movement along the demand for money curve due to the shift in the supply of money	Supply of money will shift to the right, as the Federal Reserve injects new reserves into the banking system	The equilibrium interest rate will decrease	The equilibrium quantity of money will increase
Real GDP increases in the economy	Demand for money will shift to the right when real GDP increases	There is a movement along the supply of money curve due to the shift in the demand for money	The equilibrium interest rate will increase	The equilibrium quantity of money will be unchanged
Real GDP decreases in the economy, and the Federal Reserve makes an open-market purchase of Treasury bills	Demand for money will shift to the left when real GDP decreases	Supply of money will shift to the right when the Federal Reserve makes an open-market purchase	The equilibrium interest rate will decrease	The equilibrium quantity of money will increase
The aggregate price level increases	Demand for money shifts to the right when the aggregate price level increases	There will be a movement along the supply of money curve due to the shift in the demand for money	The equilibrium interest rate will increase	The equilibrium quantity of money will be unchanged

2. Suppose there are two kinds of assets that an individual can choose between as a means of holding wealth: money, which does not provide any interest payment, and bonds, which provide the owner of the bond with an interest payment. Suppose that the money market is currently not in equilibrium and that the interest rate is lower than the equilibrium interest rate. First, describe the money market and whether there is a shortage or a surplus of money. Then, using these two types of assets, explain how the money market adjusts in order to ensure that the quantity of money demanded is equal to the quantity of money supplied.

STEP 1: Determine whether there is a shortage or a surplus of money when the interest rate is lower than the equilibrium interest rate in the market for money.

Review the section "The Equilibrium Interest Rate" on pages 524–525, and Figure 17-3 on page 524.

In general when price is lower than the equilibrium price this results in a situation of excess demand for the good. This is no different in the market for money: when the interest rate, the price of money, is lower than the equilibrium level, then we know that the quantity of money demanded will be greater than the quantity of money supplied.

STEP 2: Explain how the money market returns to equilibrium when the quantity of money demanded is greater than the quantity of money supplied.

Review the section "The Equilibrium Interest Rate" on pages 524–525, and Figure 17-3 on page 524.

When the quantity of money demanded exceeds the quantity of money supplied this means that people want to shift some of their wealth out of interest-bearing assets and into money. When there is excess quantity of money demanded this implies that there is excess supply of interest-bearing assets like bonds: to induce people to purchase bonds, the owners of these bonds will have to offer higher interest rates. Interest rates will rise until the bond market clears and the money market clears: when the interest rate rises sufficiently, then the quantity of money demanded will equal the quantity of money supplied.

3. Suppose there are two kinds of assets that an individual can choose between as a way of holding wealth: money, which does not provide any interest payment, and bonds, which provides the owner of the bond with an interest payment. Suppose that the money market is currently not in equilibrium and that the interest rate is higher than the equilibrium interest rate. First, describe the money market and whether there is a shortage or a surplus of money. Then, using these two types of assets, explain how the money market adjusts in order to ensure that the quantity of money demanded is equal to the quantity of money supplied.

STEP 1: Determine whether there is a shortage or a surplus of money when the interest rate is higher than the equilibrium interest rate in the market for money.

Review the section "The Equilibrium Interest Rate" on pages 524–525, and Figure 17-3 on page 524.

In general when price is higher than the equilibrium price this results in a situation of excess supply of the good. This is no different in the market for money: when the interest rate, the price of money, is higher than the equilibrium level, then we know that the quantity of money demanded will be less than the quantity of money supplied.

STEP 2: Explain how the money market returns to equilibrium when the quantity of money demanded is less than the quantity of money supplied.

Review the section "The Equilibrium Interest Rate" on pages 524–525, and Figure 17-3 on page 524.

When the quantity of money demanded is less than the quantity of money supplied this means that people want to shift some of their wealth into interest-bearing assets and out of money. When there is excess quantity of money supplied this implies that there is excess demand for interest-bearing assets like bonds: people desire bonds and the interest rate on bonds can fall since there is excess demand for these bonds. Interest rates will fall until the bond market clears and the money market clears: when the interest rate falls sufficiently, then the quantity of money demanded will equal the quantity of money supplied.

4. Suppose the economy in the short run is currently operating with an inflationary gap in which actual output is greater than potential output. If the government wishes to address this issue with activist monetary policy in order to restore the economy to potential output, what monetary policy should the central bank pursue? How will the implementation of this monetary policy work to return the economy to potential output?

STEP 1: First think about the implications of operating in the short run with an inflationary gap.

Review your notes on inflationary gaps and consult the preceding chapter on this topic if you need further review.

It is important that you can visualize this economic situation in terms of the *AD–AS* model. The following graph depicts the initial situation for this economy.

This economy is producing Y_1 in the short run: it is operating with an inflationary gap since actual output exceeds potential output. This implies that the economy has very low unemployment.

STEP 2: Consider the effect of a change in the money supply and how this will impact the level of aggregate production. Make a decision about the optimal activist monetary policy to pursue.

Review the section "Monetary Policy and Aggregate Demand" on pages 528–533, and Figure 17-7 on page 529.

When the Federal Reserve engages in an open-market purchase, this increases the level of reserves in the banking system, expands the money supply through the money multiplier process, and reduces interest rates. These in turn cause aggregate demand to shift to the right at every aggregate price level.

When the Federal Reserve engages in open-market sales, this decreases the level of reserves in the banking system, reduces the money supply through the money multiplier process, and increases interest rates. These in turn cause aggregate demand to shift to the left at every aggregate price level.

If you examine the preceding graph, you can see that to return to the potential output level using an aggregate demand curve shift, the aggregate demand curve must shift to the left. The Federal Reserve will need to make open-market sales in order to shift the aggregate demand curve to the left.

STEP 3: Discuss how this activist monetary policy returns this economy to potential output.

Review the section "Monetary Policy and Aggregate Demand" on pages 528–533, and Figure 17-7 on page 529.

When the Fed contracts the money supply this leads to a higher interest rate. The higher interest rate leads investment spending to fall, and therefore the level of aggregate expenditure will fall. As aggregate expenditure falls, this results in a decrease in real GDP. With the fall in the total quantity of goods and services demanded, the *AD* curve shifts to the left, restoring the economy to potential output Y.

5. Suppose the economy is initially in long-run equilibrium as depicted in the *AD-AS* model. Suppose politicians view the current level of output as too low, and they encourage the central bank to engage in expansionary monetary policy. Describe the effects of this expansionary monetary policy on this economy in the short run, and then discuss what will happen in this economy in the long run if there are no further shocks to the economy. How does this example illustrate monetary neutrality?

STEP 1: Start by drawing a graph of this economy in long-run equilibrium using the *AD–AS* model.

Review the section "Money, Output, and Prices in the Long Run" on pages 533–537, and Figure 17-11 on page 534.

In the *AD-AS* model, long-run equilibrium occurs at that output level at which *SRAS*, *AD*, and *LRAS* all intersect. This will occur at the potential output level of real GDP. The following figure illustrates this long-run equilibrium.

STEP 2: Alter your graph to illustrate the short-run effects of the expansionary monetary policy on this economy, making sure to note what happens to real GDP in the short run.

Review the section "Money, Output, and Prices in the Long Run" on pages 533–537, and Figure 17-11 on page 534.

When the Fed engages in expansionary monetary policy this means that the Fed is purchasing Treasury bills in the open market. This will cause *AD* to shift to the right. The following graph illustrates the short-run effects of this policy: notice that real GDP increases to Y_2 and the aggregate price level increases to P_2. Y_2 is greater than potential output, which indicates that the economy is operating with an inflationary gap and that unemployment is unusually low.

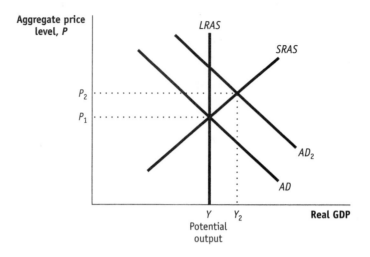

STEP 3: Discuss the adjustment process in this economy to the long-run equilibrium, making sure to note what happens to real GDP in the long run.

Review the section "Money, Output, and Prices in the Long Run" on pages 533-537, and Figure 17-11 on page 534.

Since unemployment is unusually low, this indicates that over time there will be pressure for nominal wages to increase. As nominal wages increase, this will cause the *SRAS* curve to shift to the left. This curve will continue to shift until it intersects AD_2 at the potential output level. The following figure represents this shift. Notice that the economy returns to a real GDP level that is equal to potential output and that the aggregate price level has increased to P_3.

STEP 4: Discuss monetary neutrality and how it relates to your findings in Step 3.

Review the section "Money, Output, and Prices in the Long Run" on pages 533-537, and Figure 17-11 on page 534.

In the preceding graph, we see the economy return to long-run equilibrium after the full adjustment to the expansionary monetary policy. Although the expansionary monetary policy altered real GDP in the short run to Y_2, in the long run this expansionary monetary policy had no effect on real GDP. The expansionary monetary policy does have a long-run impact on our model: this policy causes the aggregate price level to increase.

This idea that changes in the money supply have no long-run impact on the level of real GDP is an illustration of the concept of monetary neutrality. Money is neutral in the long run since it does not impact the level of real GDP; the impact of money in the long run is to alter the aggregate price level.

Problems and Exercises

1. The following figure illustrates the relationship between the nominal quantity of money demanded, M, and the interest rate, r.

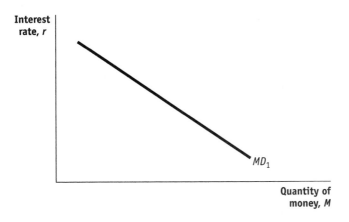

For each of the following situations, use the graph provided for reference.

   a. Holding everything else constant, the interest rate increases from r_1 to r_2. Graph this in the following figure.

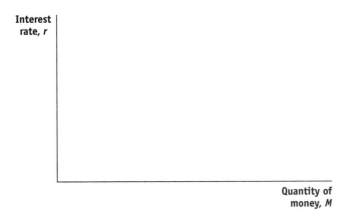

b. Holding everything else constant, the level of aggregate real income decreases. Graph this in the following figure.

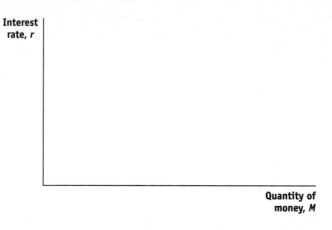

c. Holding everything else constant, there is an increase in the aggregate price level. Graph this in the following figure.

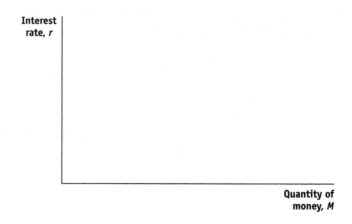

d. Holding everything else constant, individuals in a community are now able to use Internet banking for their money and financial assets accounts. Graph this in the following figure.

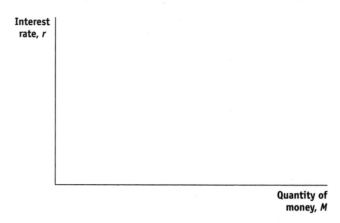

2. Consider two assets: both Asset A and Asset B are one-month bonds issued by different companies that have the same amount of risk. Asset A initially earns a higher interest rate for its holder than does Asset B. Explain why you would expect this interest rate differential to disappear. Explain the process that leads Assets A and B to have approximately the same interest rate.

3. Use the following table to answer this question.

Change	Effect on nominal money demand	Effect on real money demand
Decrease in aggregate price level		
Increase in interest rate		
Change in regulation so that interest is now allowed on checking accounts		

a. In the table, enter how each scenario will affect nominal money demand and real money demand.

b. Explain why a change in the aggregate price level affects the nominal demand curve differently than it does the real money demand curve.

4. Use the following figure of the money demand and money supply curves to answer this question. Assume this market is initially in equilibrium with the quantity of money equal to M_1 and the interest rate equal to r_1.

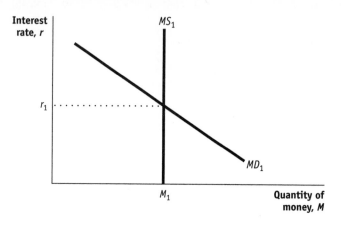

a. Suppose the FOMC engages in an open-market purchase of Treasury bills. Holding everything else constant, what happens to the equilibrium quantity of money and the equilibrium interest rate? Sketch a graph illustrating these changes.

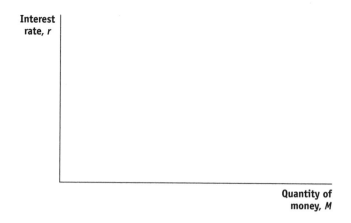

b. Suppose the FOMC engages in an open-market sale of Treasury bills. Holding everything else constant, what happens to the equilibrium quantity of money and the equilibrium interest rate? Sketch a graph illustrating these changes.

c. Suppose the aggregate price level increases. Holding everything else constant, what happens to the equilibrium quantity of money and the equilibrium interest rate? Sketch a graph illustrating these changes.

Interest
rate, *r*

Quantity of
money, *M*

5. Use the *AD–AS* model to answer this question.
   (i) Scenario I

   The economy of Macroland is initially in long-run equilibrium. Then the FOMC of Macroland decides to reduce interest rates through an open-market operation.

   a. Draw a graph representing the initial situation in Macroland. In your graph, be sure to include the short-run aggregate supply curve (*SRAS*), the long-run aggregate supply curve (*LRAS*), and the aggregate demand curve (*AD*). On your graph mark the equilibrium aggregate price level and the aggregate output level as well as potential output.

Aggregate
price
level, *P*

Real GDP

b. Draw a graph of the money market depicting Macroland's initial situation before the FOMC engages in expansionary monetary policy as well as the effect of the FOMC's monetary policy actions. Be sure to indicate the initial equilibrium as well as the equilibrium after the monetary policy action.

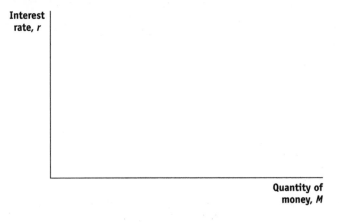

c. How does this monetary policy action affect the aggregate economy in the short run? Explain your answer verbally while also including a graph of the *AD–AS* model to illustrate your answer.

d. How does this monetary policy action affect the aggregate economy in the long run?

(ii) Scenario II

Econoland is currently operating with a recessionary gap.

e. Draw a graph representing Econoland's economic situation using an *AD-AS* model. Be sure to indicate in your graph *SRAS, LRAS, AD*, the short-run equilibrium aggregate price level (P_1), the short-run equilibrium aggregate output level (Y_1), and the potential output level (Y_E).

Real GDP

f. What monetary policy would you suggest the FOMC of Econoland pursue if its only goal is to restore production in Econoland to the potential output level? Explain how this monetary policy would achieve this goal.

g. Is there a potential drawback to the implementation of this particular monetary policy? Explain your answer.

(iii) Scenario III

Upland is currently operating with an inflationary gap.

h. Draw a graph representing Upland's economic situation using an *AD–AS* model. Be sure to indicate in your graph *SRAS, LRAS, AD*, the short-run equilibrium aggregate price level (P_1), the short-run equilibrium aggregate output level (Y_1), and the potential output level (Y_E).

Real GDP

    i. What monetary policy would you suggest the FOMC of Upland pursue if its only goal is to restore production in Upland to the potential output level? Explain how this monetary policy would achieve this goal.

    j. Is there a potential drawback to the implementation of this particular monetary policy? Explain your answer.

6. Suppose that when the FOMC reduces the interest rate by 1 percentage point it increases the level of investment spending by $500 million in Macroland. If the marginal propensity to save equals 0.25, what will be the total rise in real GDP, assuming the aggregate price level is held constant? Explain your answer.

7. In your own words, explain how the Fed's actions can affect the economy. Be sure to include an explanation about how the Fed can affect the economy when the economy is in recession or when the economy is producing at an aggregate output level that is greater than the potential output level.

8. Why is the quantity of money people want to hold inversely related to the interest rate? Explain your answer fully.

9. Suppose the aggregate price level increases by 25%. What does this increase imply about the percentage increase in the quantity of money demanded in the long run? Explain your answer fully.

10. For each of the following situations, determine the appropriate central bank monetary response.

   a. The central bank adopts an interest rate target of 5%. Currently the interest rate in the economy is at 8%.

   b. The central bank adopts an inflation target of 3%. Currently the inflation rate is 4%.

   c. The central bank adopts an inflation target of 4%. Current inflation is 4%. However, this quarter the central bank expects data to reveal that the economy is entering a recession and has a projected negative output gap.

   d. Current unemployment is greater than the natural rate of unemployment.

▆ BEFORE YOU TAKE THE TEST

Chapter Review Questions

1. People choose to hold money because
   a. it has little or no opportunity cost since money does not earn interest.
   b. it facilitates making transactions.
   c. it yields a lower rate of return than nonmonetary assets.
   d. Answers (b) and (c) are both correct.

2. The opportunity cost of holding money is
   a. always greater than the short-term interest rate.
   b. equal to the difference between the interest rate on assets that are not money and the interest rate on assets that are money.
   c. equal to the long-term interest rate.
   d. always equal to zero since it costs you nothing to hold money.

3. Which of the following statements is true?
   a. The nominal demand for money is proportional to the real demand for money.
   b. All short-term interest rates tend to move together.
   c. The higher the short-term interest rate, the lower the opportunity cost of holding money.
   d. The quantity of money demanded is positively related to the interest rate.

4. Which of the following statements is true?
   a. The real quantity of money is equal to the nominal amount of money divided by the aggregate price level.
   b. The real quantity of money measures the purchasing power of the nominal quantity of money.
   c. The real quantity of money is proportional to the nominal quantity of money for any given interest rate.
   d. All of these statements are true.
   e. Statements (a) and (b) are both true.
   f. Statements (a) and (c) are both true.
   g. Statements (b) and (c) are both true.

5. If the price level doubles, holding everything else constant, we know that
   a. the nominal quantity of money demanded also doubled.
   b. the real quantity of money demanded also doubled.
   c. the interest rate also doubled.
   d. Answers (a) and (b) are both correct.

6. For a given interest rate, when the quantity of money demanded is greater than the quantity of money supplied, then
    a. interest rates will increase.
    b. interest rates will decrease.
    c. people will sell nonmonetary assets.
    d. people will buy nonmonetary assets.
    e. Answers (a) and (c) are both correct.
    f. Answers (b) and (d) are both correct.
    g. Answers (a) and (d) are both correct.

7. The Federal Open Market Committee sets a target interest rate and can achieve that interest rate through
    a. open-market purchases, if the federal funds rate is initially less than the target rate.
    b. open-market sales, if the federal funds rate is initially less than the target rate.
    c. legislative action by Congress that decrees the level of the discount rate and thus the federal funds rate.
    d. stimulating the demand for money, if the initial interest rate is less than the target rate.

8. The liquidity preference model of interest rate determination states that
    a. interest rates are determined solely by the Federal Open Market Committee.
    b. interest rates are determined by the supply of and demand for money.
    c. people always prefer liquidity and do not consider the opportunity cost of holding money when they decide how much money they wish to hold at any given point in time.
    d. interest rates are determined in the market for nonmonetary assets and not the market for money.

9. The money supply curve in the liquidity preference model is drawn as a vertical line, since
    a. there is only one level of money supply that will enable an economy to produce at the full employment level of output and the appropriate aggregate price level.
    b. Congress sets by law the level of the money supply in the economy.
    c. the Fed can control the level of the money supply through its open-market operations.
    d. the money supply curve is unimportant in determining the equilibrium level of interest rates in the liquidity preference model.

10. When people offering to sell nonmonetary financial assets find that they must increase the interest rate these assets pay in order to sell them, this tells us that
    a. the quantity of money demanded is less than the quantity of money supplied.
    b. the quantity of money supplied equals the quantity of money demanded.
    c. the quantity of money demanded is greater than the quantity of money supplied.
    d. we cannot know anything about the relationship between the quantity of money demanded and the quantity of money supplied from this information.

11. Which of the following statements is true?

    a. Short-term interest rates tend to move independently of one another.

    b. Long-term interest rates tend to move together, and they tend to mimic short-term interest rates.

    c. Open-market purchases by the FOMC result in the interest rate decreasing.

    d. Open-market sales by the FOMC increase the money supply and cause a movement along the money demand curve.

Use the following graph to answer the next two questions.

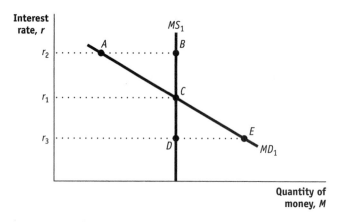

12. The economy is currently operating at its potential output level. Which point in the graph is most likely to represent this long-run situation in the money market? Point

    a. *A,* since high interest rates encourage people to save more, leading to higher levels of investment

    b. *B,* since the FOMC controls the money supply, we know we must be on the money supply curve in the long run

    c. *C,* since at this point the money market is in equilibrium

    d. *D,* since low interest rates encourage business investment, which leads to higher economic growth

    e. *E,* since low interest rates reduce inflationary pressures in the economy

13. In the graph, which point *most* likely represents a possible new short-run equilibrium if the FOMC conducts an open-market sale? Point

    a. *A*

    b. *B*

    c. *C*

    d. *D*

    e. *E*

14. Which of the following statements is true?

    a. In the long run, an increase in the nominal money supply increases the potential output level.

    b. In the long run, an increase in the nominal money supply will have no effect on real variables, including the aggregate price level.

    c. In the long run, an increase in the nominal money supply will lead to a proportionate increase in the aggregate price level.

    d. Answers (a) and (b) are both true.

    e. Answers (a), (b), and (c) are all true.

15. Suppose that an economy experiences an increase in the aggregate output level. Assuming that the central bank does not engage in monetary policy, which of the following statements is true?

    a. The interest rate in this economy will increase.

    b. The interest rate in this economy will decrease.

    c. The interest rate in this economy will be unaffected by this change in aggregate output.

    d. This change in aggregate output will cause a movement along the money demand curve.

16. The money supply curve shifts to the left. The most likely cause for this shift is the FOMC's open-market

    a. purchase of Treasury bills.

    b. sale of Treasury bills.

17. The money demand curve shifts to the right. The most likely cause for this shift among the following explanations is

    a. an increase in the interest rate.

    b. a decrease in the interest rate.

    c. a change in bank institutions that allows banks to pay even higher rates of interest on checking account funds.

    d. Answers (b) and (c) are both correct.

18. When the quantity of money demanded is greater than the quantity of money supplied, this implies that the interest rate is too low and people will decide to

    a. sell interest-bearing assets, resulting in the price of these assets falling while the interest rate paid on these assets rises.

    b. buy interest-bearing assets, resulting in the price of these assets rising while the interest rate paid on these assets rises.

19. When the Fed targets the federal funds rate, this means that the FOMC changes the money supply through open-market operations until the

    a. rate of inflation in the economy matches their target.

    b. actual federal funds rate equals the target rate.

20. Expansionary monetary policy will, holding everything else constant,

    a. lower the interest rate and cause *AD* to shift to the right.

    b. lower the interest rate and cause *AD* to shift to the left.

    c. raise the interest rate and cause *AD* to shift to the right.

    d. raise the interest rate and cause *AD* to shift to the left.

21. Suppose in the short run the level of aggregate output in an economy decreases at the same time the aggregate price level decreases. This is most likely due to a

    a. leftward shift in the short-run aggregate supply curve, holding everything else constant.

    b. rightward shift in the short-run aggregate supply curve, holding everything else constant.

    c. leftward shift in the aggregate demand curve, holding everything else constant.

    d. rightward shift in the aggregate demand curve, holding everything else constant.

22. When the economy is currently producing at a short-run level of aggregate output that is less than potential output, it is most likely that the Fed will engage in open-market
    a. purchases of Treasury bills.
    b. sales of Treasury bills.

23. The Taylor rule for monetary policy for the period from 1988 through 2008 provided guidance for setting the federal funds rate and stated that this rate should be set by considering
    a. both the inflation rate and the output gap.
    b. both the inflation rate and the level of unemployment.
    c. both the output gap and the level of unemployment.
    d. the inflation rate, the output gap, and the level of unemployment.

24. Inflation targeting means that
    a. the central bank adheres to maintaining a very strict interest rate target.
    b. the central bank announces the inflation rate that it is trying to achieve and then uses monetary policy to achieve this inflation rate.
    c. there may be a range of acceptable inflation rates or a specific inflation rate that the central bank hopes to achieve through monetary policy.
    d. Answers (a), (b), and (c) are all correct.
    e. Answers (b) and (c) are both correct.

25. Suppose the aggregate economy in the short run is operating at an aggregate output level that is greater than the potential output level. Holding everything else constant, what do you anticipate will happen to nominal wages in the long run given this information?
    a. Nominal wages will decrease.
    b. Nominal wages will remain constant.
    c. Nominal wages will increase.

26. In the short run, money is
    a. neutral since it can have no effect on real aggregate output.
    b. not neutral since changes in the money supply can cause real aggregate output to change.

27. After 2008, the Taylor rule
    a. resulted in a negative interest rate due to the combination of high unemployment and low inflation.
    b. did not predict Federal Reserve policy well since it is impossible to have a negative interest rate.

28. The zero lower bound refers to
    a. an upper limit for the interest rate where no matter what happens in the economy the interest rate cannot rise above this limit.
    b. the idea that interest rates cannot be less than zero since no one would be willing to accept a negative interest rate as the interest rate they would receive for lending out funds.

29. When an economy faces a zero lower bound, this implies that the central bank in this economy will be able to stimulate the economy

    a. by engaging in open market purchases.

    b. by engaging in open market sales.

    c. at very low cost since the interest rate is so low.

    d. In this economy, the central bank will find it difficult to stimulate the economy through open market purchases, since the interest rate cannot fall below zero.

30. The Federal Reserve Bank engaged in "quantitative easing" in November of 2010 because

    a. the Fed no longer believed, no matter what the situation, in open market operations as a monetary policy tool.

    b. the Fed recognized the zero lower bound problem and thought that "quantitative easing" might be a method of stimulating the economy given that open market purchases were ineffective.

    c. the Fed hoped this would drive interest rates on long-term debt down and that this would lead to economic expansion.

    d. Answers (a), (b), and (c) are all correct.

    e. Answers (b) and (c) are both correct.

    f. Answers (a) and (c) are both correct.

ANSWER KEY

Answers to Problems and Exercises

1. **a.** An increase in the interest rate causes a movement along the money demand curve as illustrated in the following figure.

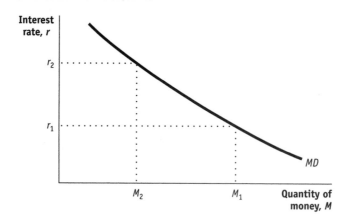

b. As the level of aggregate real income decreases, this causes the money demand curve to shift to the left as individuals demand less money at every interest rate. This is illustrated in the following figure.

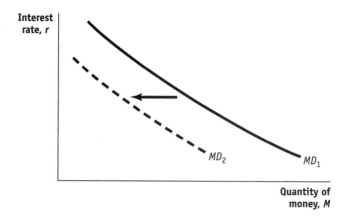

c. An increase in the aggregate price level causes the money demand curve to shift to the right, as individuals demand more money at every interest rate to facilitate making their transactions at the new higher price levels. This is illustrated in the following figure.

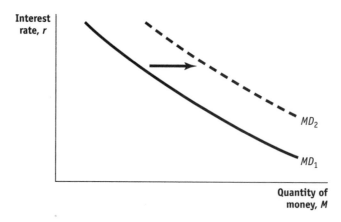

d. With new technology for managing money and financial assets, people will decrease their demand for money at every interest rate. This will cause money demand to shift to the left, as illustrated in the figure from part (b) of this answer.

2. Since both Asset A and Asset B are short-term financial assets, we anticipate that the interest rate paid on both assets should be roughly equivalent. If the returns differ, investors will sell the asset offering the lower return: to find a buyer for this asset, they must offer a higher rate on it. This buying and selling of assets will lead the returns on these short-term financial assets to move toward approximately the same return.

3. **a.**

Change	Effect on nominal money demand	Effect on real money demand
Decrease in aggregate price level	Shifts the nominal money demand curve to the left	Has no effect
Increase in interest rate	Causes a movement along the nominal money demand curve	Causes a movement along the real money demand curve
Change in regulation so that interest is now allowed on checking accounts	Shifts the nominal money demand curve to the right	Shifts the real money demand curve to the right

b. When the aggregate price level changes, the nominal money demand curve does not automatically take into account the effect of this change in prices on the nominal demand for money. For example, as the aggregate price level rises, people will find that, due to the increase in the aggregate price level, they need to hold greater amounts of money in order to make their transactions. This causes the nominal money demand curve to shift to the right: people demand a greater quantity of nominal money at every interest rate. In contrast, the real money demand curve automatically takes into account any change in the aggregate price level: a change in the aggregate price level requires a proportionately equal change in the nominal quantity of money in order that the real quantity of money is unchanged.

4. **a.** When the Fed increases the money supply through an open-market purchase of Treasury bills, this shifts the money supply curve from MS_1 to MS_2 and results in a decrease in the equilibrium interest rate from r_1 to r_2 and an increase in the equilibrium quantity of money from M_1 to M_2. The following figure illustrates these changes.

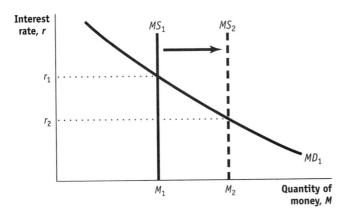

b. When the FOMC decreases the money supply through an open-market sale of Treasury bills, the money supply curve shifts from MS_1 to MS_2. This causes the equilibrium interest rate to increase from r_1 to r_2, while the equilibrium quantity of money decreases from M_1 to M_2. These changes are illustrated in the following figure.

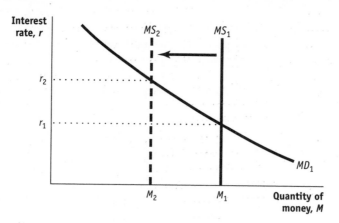

c. An increase in the aggregate price level shifts the money demand curve to the right from MD_1 to MD_2. This causes the equilibrium interest rate to increase from r_1 to r_2, while the equilibrium quantity of money is unchanged. The following figure illustrates this situation.

5. a.

b.

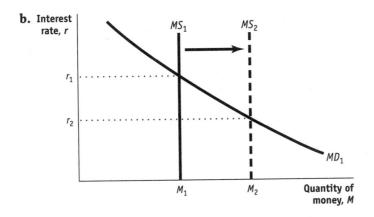

c. When the FOMC reduces interest rates through an open-market purchase of Treasury bills, this increases aggregate demand and causes the *AD* curve to shift to the right to AD_2. In the short run, this causes aggregate real output to increase to Y_2 and the aggregate price level to increase to P_2. This is illustrated in the following figure.

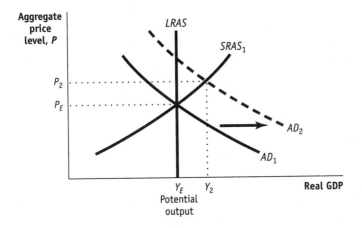

d. In the long run, the economy must return to producing its potential output, Y_E. This economic adjustment will occur as the *SRAS* curve shifts to the left as nominal wages rise. As the *SRAS* curve shifts back to $SRAS_3$, this will eliminate the inflationary gap, restore the economy to its potential output level, and lead to an even higher aggregate price level, P_3. The following figure illustrates this long-run adjustment.

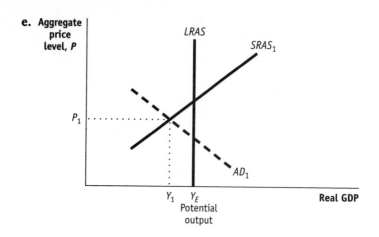

f. If the FOMC expands the money supply through open-market purchases, this will reduce interest rates and stimulate investment spending and, therefore, aggregate demand. As AD shifts to the right from AD_1 to AD_2, this will cause real GDP to increase to Y_E and prices to rise to P_2. The following figure illustrates this situation.

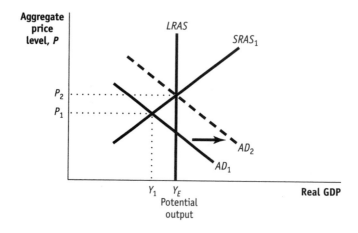

g. If the FOMC engages in activist monetary policy, this will cause the aggregate price level to increase. Alternatively, policymakers could do nothing and wait for the $SRAS$ to shift to the right as nominal wages fall. In the long run, aggregate output would return to Y_E and the aggregate price level would fall below its initial level of P_1.

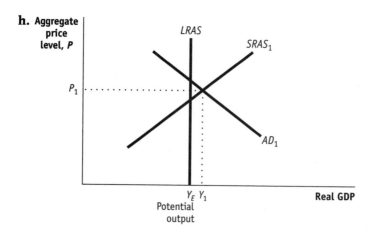

i. The FOMC should decrease the money supply and thereby increase the interest rate through open-market sales of Treasury bills. This action by the FOMC will cause the *AD* to shift to the left, restoring the economy to its potential output level at a lower aggregate price level than P_1.

j. No, this policy restores the economy to its long-run position without raising the aggregate price level.

6. The action by the FOMC effectively creates a change in autonomous investment spending of $500 million. This change in autonomous investment spending will cause real GDP to increase by a larger, multiplied amount due to the multiplier process. Since the multiplier equals $1/(1 - MPC)$ or, in this case, 4, we can compute the total change in real GDP as 4($500 million), or $2 billion.

7. The Fed can affect the economy through its open-market operations. When the Fed expands the money supply by purchasing Treasury bills, this causes the interest rate to fall, holding everything else constant. As the interest rate declines, this acts as a stimulus to investment and consumer spending and, therefore, as a stimulus to aggregate demand. Thus, open-market purchases typically are used to stimulate the economy: when the economy is producing below the potential output level (i.e., the economy is in a recession), the Fed has the potential to alter this output level via active monetary policy. Conversely, when the economy is producing at a level greater than the potential output level, the Fed can engage in open-market sales that will effectively lead to higher interest rates and lower investment and consumer spending, thereby causing the level of aggregate demand to fall, holding everything else constant.

8. Holding money has an opportunity cost since the money could have been used to purchase a financial item that could have yielded the holder an interest return. Thus, when the interest rate increases, this implies that the opportunity cost of holding money has risen: people will want to hold less money as the opportunity cost of holding that money increases. Thus, the interest rate and the quantity of money that people want to hold (that is, the quantity of money they demand) are inversely related to one another.

9. When the aggregate price level increases by 25%, this means that on average prices in the economy have risen by 25%. This in turn implies that people will need 25% more money to make the same purchases; thus, the demand for money at any given interest rate will need to shift to the right and by an amount that is 25% greater than the original money demand. The idea here is that the demand for money will be proportional to the price level in the long run.

10. a. The central bank will want to decrease the interest rate. It can accomplish this goal by engaging in open-market purchases of Treasury bills.

b. The central bank wants to reduce the inflation rate. It can do this by increasing the interest rate since this will slow the economy and result in a smaller output gap, which will help to pull the interest rate and, therefore, the rate of inflation down in the economy. The central bank should engage in open-market sales of Treasury bills.

c. Since the central bank anticipates a slowdown in the economy, they also anticipate that there will be downward pressure on the aggregate price level as the level of spending in the economy falls. The central bank can stabilize the aggregate price level by engaging in expansionary monetary policy: the central bank should engage in open-market purchases of Treasury bills.

d. Since the current rate of unemployment is greater than the potential rate of unemployment, the economy is in a recession. The central bank will want to engage in expansionary monetary policy unless it is actively seeking to reduce the targeted rate of inflation and the actual rate of inflation in the economy.

Answers to Chapter Review Questions

1. **Answer b.** Although money typically does yield a lower rate of return than nonmonetary assets, this is not the reason people choose to hold money. Rather, they choose to hold money because money facilitates making transactions. There is an opportunity cost of holding money: when you hold money you forego the higher rate of return you could earn by holding nonmonetary assets.

2. **Answer b.** The opportunity cost of holding money is measured by what is lost when holding money: this is calculated as the difference between the rate of return you could earn by holding nonmonetary assets minus the rate of return on monetary assets.

3. **Answer b.** The nominal demand for money is proportional to the aggregate price level. The higher the short-term interest rate, the greater the opportunity cost of holding money since you could be earning this higher short-term interest rate if you chose to hold nonmonetary assets. The quantity of money demanded is inversely, or negatively, related to the interest rate: as the interest rate increases, the quantity of money demanded decreases. Short-term interest rates do move together since if there is a difference in the rate of return on short-term financial assets, there will be movement toward the asset that pays the higher return and away from the asset that pays the lower return. As the market adjusts to this movement, there will be a tendency for the rate of returns for both assets to move toward one another: short-term interest rates will therefore tend to move together.

4. **Answer e.** The first two statements are factual statements that are true by definition. The real quantity of money is not proportional to the nominal quantity of money. However, the nominal quantity of money demanded is proportional to the aggregate price level.

5. **Answer a.** To maintain the same level of purchasing power as was initially had, when the aggregate price level doubles, the nominal quantity of money demanded will also double. However, a doubling of prices will have no effect on the real quantity of money demanded since this real money demand is, by definition, the amount of money that holds purchasing power constant. Holding everything else constant, assumes that a doubling of the price level will have no impact on the interest rate.

6. **Answer e.** When the quantity of money demanded is greater than the quantity of money supplied, people wish to increase their money holdings. This will cause them to sell their nonmonetary assets: as the supply of these nonmonetary assets increases, people will find they must offer higher interest rates on these assets in order to sell them. Thus, interest rates will increase.

7. **Answer b.** If the target interest rate is greater than the federal funds rate, then the Fed needs to engage in monetary policy that will shift the money supply curve to the left, resulting in an increase in interest rates for a given money demand curve. The FOMC, therefore, will engage in open-market sales of Treasury bills. Congress does not set the discount rate, and the Fed's monetary policy affects the money supply curve and not the money demand curve.

8. **Answer b.** The liquidity preference model uses the interaction between the quantity of money demanded and the quantity of money supplied to analyze the determination of interest rates. Interest rates are impacted by Federal Reserve policy and its effect on the money supply curve. People consider the opportunity cost of holding money when making their decisions about the level of money they wish to hold. One can model interest rate determination in either the framework of money demand and supply or the framework of demand and supply of loanable funds.

9. **Answer c.** The Fed controls the money supply through open-market operations. We know that the determination of interest rates depends not only on the quantity of money demanded but also on the quantity of money supplied. Congress does not have the authority to determine the country's money supply. Different levels of money supply are compatible with the full-employment level of output, since interest rate determination depends on both the money supply and the money demand.

10. **Answer c.** When interest rates must rise, this implies they are initially too low: in the money market, this would imply that the interest rate is initially below the equilibrium interest rate or where the quantity of money demanded is greater than the quantity of money supplied.

11. **Answer c.** Short-term interest rates tend to move together, while long-term interest rates may or may not mimic short-term interest rates. When the FOMC makes an open-market purchase, this increases the level of reserves in the banking system, which leads to an expansion in the money supply and a decrease in the interest rate.

12. **Answer c.** In the long run, the economy is in equilibrium, including the money market where the quantity of money demanded must equal the quantity of money supplied. This is only true at point C in the graph.

13. **Answer a.** When the FOMC conducts an open-market sale, this causes the money supply to shift to the left and, for a given demand curve, results in the interest rate increasing. Only point A illustrates this scenario.

14. **Answer c.** In the long run, the economy will operate at the potential output level: any increase in the money supply will not affect the real value of aggregate output, but will lead to a proportionate increase in the aggregate price level.

15. **Answer a.** When aggregate real output increases in an economy, this causes the demand for money to shift to the right. For a given money supply curve (remember the central bank is not engaging in monetary policy), this will cause the interest rate to increase.

16. **Answer b.** When the FOMC engages in open-market sales of Treasury bills, it sells Treasury bills to the public and receives dollars for those Treasury bills. The FOMC effectively removes reserves from the banking system with the sale of Treasury bills, which reduces the quantity of money supplied at every interest rate: the supply of money curve shifts to the left.

17. **Answer c.** A change in the interest rate, whether an increase or a decrease, causes a movement along the money demand curve. An increase in the amount of interest banks can pay on checking account funds reduces the opportunity cost of holding funds in a checking account rather than in an interest-bearing asset: people will increase the quantity of money they demand at every interest rate with this change, which will result in the money demand curve shifting to the right.

18. **Answer a.** When quantity of money demanded is greater than quantity of money supplied, this implies that the interest rate is too low: the opportunity cost of holding money is relatively low and, therefore, people choose to hold more money. This causes people to sell interest-bearing assets (like bonds) and as the supply of these interest-bearing assets increases, this leads to a decrease in the price of these interest-bearing assets. As the price of these assets decreases, this implies that the interest rate paid on these assets is increasing.

19. **Answer b.** Targeting the federal funds rate means that the Fed is using open-market operations to alter the interest rate banks charge one another for loans (the federal funds rate) so that it reaches a desired, or targeted, level.

20. **Answer a.** Expansionary monetary policy is an increase in the money supply: when the money supply increases, this means that the supply of money curve shifts to the right, causing the interest rate to fall. A fall in the interest rate results in higher investment spending and consumption spending: this causes the AD curve to shift to the right.

21. **Answer c.** If there is only one shift in either the short-run AS curve or the AD curve, then a fall in both the aggregate output level and the aggregate price level is only possible with a leftward shift of the AD curve.

22. **Answer a.** When the current level of aggregate output is less than potential output, the Fed will likely engage in expansionary monetary policy to stimulate the economy to return to the potential output level. Expansionary monetary policy implies that the Fed is increasing the money supply; hence, the Fed is purchasing Treasury bills in the open market.

23. **Answer b.** The original Taylor rule for setting the Federal funds rate for the period 1988 through 2008 is given by the following equation: Federal funds rate = 2.07 + 1.28 × inflation − 1.95 × unemployment gap. Although there is a relationship between the level of output and the unemployment rate, the Taylor rule for this time period does not explicitly include the output gap.

24. **Answer e.** Inflation targeting involves having the central bank announce the inflation rate or range for the inflation rate it is trying to achieve and then use its monetary policy to achieve this announced goal. Monetary policy to achieve a stated inflation goal will necessarily imply the loss of interest rate control since the interest rate will need to vary in order for the central bank to achieve its inflation target.

25. **Answer c.** When the economy operates in the short run at an aggregate output level greater than the potential level of output, this implies that unemployment is below the natural rate of unemployment. As the economy moves to the long run, nominal wages will increase due to labor market pressures arising from this lower-than-natural level of unemployment. The nominal wage will continue to increase until the short-run *AS* curve shifts far enough to the left to return this economy to its potential output level.

26. **Answer b.** Money in the short run is not neutral: when the central bank changes the money supply, this causes the *AD* curve to shift and in the short run this shift will cause the economy to either contract or expand. In the long run, the short-run aggregate supply curve shifts, returning the aggregate economy to its potential output level: in the long run, money is neutral since it cannot alter the level of aggregate real output.

27. **Answer b.** Application of the Taylor rule after 2008 predicted that interest rates would be negative. But it is impossible for interest rates to be negative, so the Taylor rule was not very insightful after 2008 due to the combination of high unemployment and low inflation creating a prediction that simply could not come true.

28. **Answer b.** Interest rates must be positive or equal to zero because no one would willingly accept a negative return since they can always earn an interest rate of zero if they choose to hold cash. The zero lower bound refers to the idea that interest rates cannot fall below zero.

29. **Answer d.** Open-market purchases are used by central banks to stimulate the economy because these open-market purchases typically result in the interest rate decreasing when the money supply increases. When an economy is operating at its zero lower bound, this implies that interest rates in the economy are as low as they can go and that any open-market purchase will have little impact since the interest rate will not drop any further.

30. **Answer e.** In November 2010, the Fed wanted to pursue an expansionary economic policy due to the state of the economy. However, the interest rate at that time was at or near zero and open-market purchases would have been ineffective since the interest rate could not be lowered any further. The Fed engaged in "quantitative easing" so that it would lead to lower interest rates on long-term debt, which, the Fed hoped, would lead to an expansionary effect on the economy.

chapter **18**

Crises and Consequences

Summary

This chapter discusses the difference between depository banks and shadow banks and how both types of banks are subject to bank runs. The chapter also discusses what happens during financial panics and bank crises and why these types of economic disruption result in severe and long-lasting impacts on the economy. The chapter also discusses the role of regulatory loopholes and the rise of shadow banking in the banking crisis of 2008 and how regulatory frameworks seek to avoid another banking crisis.

Chapter Objectives

Objective #1. People face a trade-off between liquidity and the rate of return. Without banks people would be forced to hold large amounts of cash to meet their liquidity needs; as holdings of cash increase, the rate of return decreases. Banks allow depositors to have immediate access to their funds (addressing their liquidity needs) while simultaneously providing depositors interest on these deposited funds (addressing their desire for a return on their idle cash). Banks are able to do this through maturity transformation, where they transform short-term liabilities into long-term assets.

Objective #2. Shadow banks have grown since 1980. Shadow banks provide a higher rate of return to savers than depository banks. Like depository banks, shadow banks engage in maturity transformation: they use short-term borrowing to finance their investments in long-term assets. Shadow banks until recently faced little regulation, but due to their similarity to depository banks they were vulnerable to bank runs.

Objective #3. Banking crises occur primarily due to two reasons: shared mistakes and financial contagion. Shared mistakes refer to financial institutions making the same mistake of investing in an asset bubble. Financial contagion spreads through bank runs or a vicious circle of deleveraging. Unregulated banking institutions, like the shadow bank sector, are highly vulnerable to contagion. The most recent financial crisis in the United States was a result of a real estate bubble, the rise of a very large shadow banking sector, and a vicious circle of deleveraging.

Objective #4.   Banking crises are a frequent occurrence throughout the world. After a banking crisis or financial panic, there is usually a severe downturn in the economy. Bank crises typically result in bank reform that aims to reduce the frequency of future bank crises or financial panic.

Objective #5.   Financial crisis typically results in a prolonged and severe drop in economic activity in an economy primarily because of the credit crunch, the debt overhang, and the ineffectiveness of monetary policy. The credit crunch refers to the increased difficulty that consumers and businesses have in getting needed credit: credit markets freeze up in the wake of financial crisis and do not operate properly. The debt overhang arises out of the vicious circle of deleveraging in which the value of assets falls, leaving individuals and businesses with greater debt but diminished assets. Monetary policy is ineffective during a banking crisis as a means to fight negative demand shocks caused by a fall in consumer and investment spending.

Objective #6.   During a bank crisis, the government tries to limit the damage from the bank crisis by serving as a lender of last resort and by guaranteeing bank liabilities. The government may need to nationalize banks and then later reprivatize them in order to slow or halt the spread of the bank crisis.

Objective #7.   The development of shadow banking eroded the bank regulatory system that was put into place in the 1930s. Particularly the repo market, a primary feature of shadow banking that provides very short-term loans, was not regulated at the time of the financial crisis of 2008. The shadow bank sector was subject to bank runs due to the use of the repo, the lack of regulation, and the fact that this sector was not part of the lender of last resort system.

Objective #8.   The financial crisis of 2008 started with a real estate bubble. This crisis was the most severe crisis since the Great Depression. Persistently high unemployment is likely to endure for many years as a result of this financial crisis.

Objective #9.   The Dodd-Frank bill was passed by the United States Congress in hopes of preventing another financial crisis like that of 2008. This reform bill provides for consumer protection, greater regulation of derivatives, regulation of shadow banking, and resolution authority for a variety of financial institutions.

Key Terms

maturity transformation the conversion of short-term liabilities into long-term assets.

shadow bank a nondepository financial institution that engages in maturity transformation.

banking crisis occurs when a large part of the depository banking sector or the shadow banking sector fails or threatens to fail.

Notes

Key Terms *(continued)*

asset bubble when the price of an asset is pushed to an unreasonably high level due to expectations of further price gains.

financial contagion a vicious downward spiral among depository banks as well as shadow banks: each institution's failure increases the likelihood that another will fail.

financial panic a sudden and widespread disruption of the financial markets that occurs when people lose faith in the liquidity of financial institutions and markets.

credit crunch when potential borrowers either cannot get credit at all or must pay very high interest rates.

debt overhang occurs when a vicious circle of deleveraging leaves a borrower with high debt by diminished assets.

liquidity trap when conventional monetary policy is ineffective, because nominal interest rates are up against the zero bound.

lender of last resort an institution, usually a country's central bank, that provides funds to financial institutions when they are unable to borrow from the private credit markets.

█ AFTER YOU READ THE CHAPTER

Tips

Tip #1. This chapter introduces new terms that you will want to spend time learning. These terms often are challenging for students, since they are terms related to the financial industry, and this industry may not be familiar to you. Mastery of these terms is important.

Tip #2. This chapter discusses the vicious circle of deleveraging, and it is this concept that is essential for understanding why bank crises and financial panics can have such large and long-lasting impacts on the economy. A vicious circle of deleveraging begins when financial institutions find that they need to reduce debt and raise cash. This need may force these institutions into selling their assets quickly, and this often means that these assets must sell at deeply discounted (lower) prices. As the institutions sell these assets at reduced prices, other financial institutions' positions are hurt as well. Thus, creditors may stop lending to more and more institutions. The vicious circle of deleveraging leads to a downward spiral of asset prices, and this results in major impacts on consumer and business spending in the economy.

Tip #3. Students are used to thinking about the term *banking* as referring to financial institutions that provide checking and saving accounts. This chapter introduces and develops the idea of the shadow banking system. It is critical that students understand the concept of shadow banking: shadow banking and commercial banks are both in the business of maturity transformation, but the shadow bank—unlike commercial banks—does not take deposits. Instead, the shadow bank uses short-term borrowing in markets, like the repo market, to finance its lending. Shadow banking has grown in both its size and its impact on the financial system in recent years. Prior to the financial crisis of 2008, shadow banking was not regulated.

Tip #4. There is a tendency to think financial crises are rare and unusual events. This chapter provides historical evidence suggesting that these crises are not that rare, and that they do cause major economic disturbances, particularly with regard to unemployment and production. Recognizing that financial crises do occur and have some common causes can help policymakers design better policies aimed at reducing both the frequency and severity of financial crises.

Tip #5. It is important to understand the three reasons for why banking crises typically lead to recessions: (1) a credit crunch occurs, which reduces the availability of credit, (2) financial distress caused by a debt overhang occurs, and (3) there is a loss of monetary policy effectiveness. The loss of monetary policy effectiveness provides the primary explanation for why banking-crises recessions are so severe and why they last so long.

Tip #6. It is important for students to realize that financial regulation is a long-standing policy in most economies. However, financial regulation periodically lags financial innovation, and for financial regulation to be effective it must be continually updated in order to maintain pace with a changing world.

WORKED PROBLEMS

1. Prime Bank has 500 customers who have each deposited $50,000. Prime Bank has kept 20% of these deposits as reserves to meet depositor demand for funds. The other 80% of Prime Bank's deposits have been used to make mortgage loans to individuals who have not deposited funds at Prime Bank. Each mortgage loan has a value of $200,000. To make this problem simpler, we will assume that each mortgage represents a loan made to a customer to finance the purchase of a residence that is initially selling for $210,000. Suppose that there is a real estate bubble in the economy, and home prices fall by 10%. Prime Bank asks that you help it understand the effect of this drop in prices on the value of its assets relative to the value of its deposits. In your answer, provide an analysis of the total level of deposits at the bank, the total reserves, the total amount of funds the bank has loaned out as mortgages, and the new market value of these loans, given the fall in home prices should Prime Bank decide to sell some of these mortgages. Analyze the impact of this real estate price decrease on the assets and liabilities of Prime Bank. As a simplifying assumption, assume that there are no costs to running the bank.

    STEP 1: Start by first calculating the level of deposits at First Bank, and use this information to then calculate the level of reserves and the dollar amount of mortgages financed at Prime Bank. Calculate how many mortgages Prime Bank will be able to make from this information.

    Review the section "Banking: Benefits and Dangers" on pages 544–548.

    This is a mathematical exercise: since there are 500 customers who each deposit $50,000 at the bank, this implies that total deposits at the bank are equal to 500($50,000), or $25,000,000. Since Prime Bank holds 20% of its deposits as reserves, this means that reserves at the bank are equal to $5,000,000. The remaining $20,000,000 is used by Prime Bank to finance mortgages. If each mortgage is worth $200,000, then the bank has funds to support 100 mortgages.

STEP 2: Analyze the effect of the fall in real estate prices on the value of the mortgages held by Prime Bank.

Review the section "Banking: Benefits and Dangers" on pages 544-548.

The homes that have been purchased with the mortgages issued by Prime Bank were initially valued at $210,000. So, at the time of purchase each home buyer provided $10,000 of the funds needed to buy the house, and the bank had loaned the home buyer the remaining balance of $200,000. Now that home prices have fallen by 10%, the value of the home can be computed as $210,000 − .1($210,000), or $189,000. Since Prime Bank holds 100 mortgages, this implies that the value of the mortgages according to the price that these homes are now selling for is equal to $18,900,000 instead of the original $20,000,000.

STEP 3: Analyze the effect of this real estate price decrease on the value of the assets and liabilities of Prime Bank.

Review the section "Banking: Benefits and Dangers" on pages 544-548.

Before the real estate price decrease the value of assets at Prime Bank was equal to the sum of reserves plus loans or $25,000,000, while the value of liabilities at Prime Bank was equal to the value of deposits at the bank, or $25,000,000. After the real estate price decrease, the value of assets at Prime Bank is now equal to the sum of reserves plus the value of the mortgage loans following the price decrease, or $5,000,000 plus $18,900,000 for a total of $23,900,000. The value of liabilities at Prime Bank is still equal to $25,000,000. The effect of the real estate price decrease on Prime Bank is to make its liabilities greater than its assets: Prime Bank is no longer solvent.

2. The opening story details the demise of Lehman Brothers. Discuss how this story illustrates the vicious circle of deleveraging and how this vicious circle of deleveraging can be destabilizing to otherwise financially sound institutions.

STEP 1: Review what the term the *vicious circle of deleveraging* means before analyzing the Lehman Brothers story.

Review the section "Banking Crises and Financial Panics" on pages 548-552.

The vicious circle of deleveraging refers to a phenomenon that occurs when a financial institution is under pressure to reduce debt and raise cash. Under these circumstances, the institution may be forced to sell assets quickly and at steeply discounted prices. This results in financial contagion, since other financial institutions that own similar assets will find that the values of these assets are negatively impacted by the decline in asset prices. As creditors reduce the amount of credit they are willing to provide, more financial institutions are forced to sell assets, reinforcing the downward spiral of asset prices.

STEP 2: Discuss Lehman's situation in September 2008, paying close attention to the assets it held and why these assets represented a potential problem for the firm.

Review the opening story "From Purveyor of Dry Goods to Destroyer of Worlds" on pages 543-544.

In September of 2008, Lehman Brothers held a large number of subprime mortgages. These were mortgages made to individuals who had too little income or too few assets to qualify for prime, or standard, mortgages. During the summer and heading into the fall of 2008, the real estate market in the United States saw housing prices decline. This decrease in price lessened the value of the investments that Lehman Brothers had in the housing industry. Lehman Brothers was rumored to have heavy exposure to housing price volatility, and this led to the firm having trouble getting short-term credit to finance its operations and trading. On September 15, 2008, Lehman Brothers declared bankruptcy. It was the largest bankruptcy in United States history.

STEP 3: **Discuss the impact of Lehman's bankruptcy on the financial system.**

Review the opening story "From Purveyor of Dry Goods to Destroyer of Worlds" on pages 543-544.

Lehman's bankruptcy came as a big surprise to the financial system because the firm had hidden the magnitude of the problem it faced. Other financial firms holding securitized mortgages realized that their holdings of real estate loans were quickly falling in value, particularly as the default rates on these loans increased. In light of these troubles, credit markets froze as those with funds decided it was better to hold onto their funds rather than lend them, given the state of both the financial markets and the real estate market. This created a global credit crunch, and this inability to get credit resulted in dramatic declines in stock markets around the world. Lehman's collapse had triggered a financial panic and resulted in a severe recession.

3. For each of the following scenarios determine whether the scenario represents the concept of shared mistake, a credit crunch, financial contagion, debt overhang, or the ineffectiveness of monetary policy. Explain your answers.

   a. Sarah and her husband Mario in the early 2000s built several houses as speculation houses. They would borrow funds to build a house, then sell the house once the construction was finished. The real estate market was strong at the time, and they earned substantial returns on their investments. They continued to build these houses because they thought house prices would continue to rise. However, in 2007, they built a house and by the time it was finished they found that housing prices had fallen, and they were unable to sell the house for what they had put into building it. They also noticed that there were many similar houses on the market in similar subdivisions in their community.

   b. In the 1990s, tech stocks became very popular, and their prices rose dramatically. At the end of the 1990s, tech stock prices fell dramatically.

   c. First State Bank finds that it has too much debt and needs cash. It is forced to sell some of its assets at a dramatic discount. This causes other firms holding similar assets to find the values of their assets falling, and as the value of these assets fall, these firms find that they need to reduce their debt and raise cash quickly. This puts even greater downward pressure on the price of these assets.

   d. Rumor is circulating that Second Street Bank has substantial exposure in an asset that is losing value in the market. Second Street Bank needs short-term credit to insure its own operations and lending, and it finds that its creditors are no longer willing to lend funds. Second Street Bank is not the only financial institution facing this problem; in fact, it appears to be endemic to the entire banking system.

   e. Lucinda bought a house for $200,000 in 2005. She financed this purchase with a mortgage for 90% of the value of the house. However, house prices have fallen since 2005 by 25%. Lucinda is now substantially poorer than she was when she first bought the house.

f. Since the financial crisis of 2008, the unemployment rate has been very high and the level of production has been low in the United States. In the period immediately after the financial crisis of 2008, the Federal Reserve pursued a policy of very low interest rates. But the economy at that time continued to have a high unemployment rate and aggregate production levels below the potential level of production.

STEP 1: Before characterizing each of the preceding scenarios, review the definitions of each of the given terms.

Review the sections "Banking Crises and Financial Panics" on pages 548-552 and "The Consequences of Banking Crises" on pages 552-557.

Shared mistake refers to the idea of many institutions (or individuals) making the same mistake of investing in an asset bubble. A *credit crunch* refers to a disruption in the availability of credit due to the disruption in the banking system. *Financial contagion* refers to a vicious downward spiral where each institution's failure increases the odds that another institution will fail. Financial contagion is usually accompanied by a vicious circle of *deleveraging,* in which institutions are under pressure to reduce debt and raise cash: this pressure results in assets being sold at a deep discount, and this discounting of asset values has an adverse impact on other institutions holding similar assets. *Debt overhang* refers to the situation where a vicious circle of deleveraging leaves a borrower with high debt but diminished assets. *Ineffective monetary policy* refers to a situation where monetary policy is not effective at fighting negative demand shocks: ineffective monetary policy often occurs during banking-crisis recessions.

STEP 2: Consider each of the scenarios and decide which of the preceding terms describes the scenario best.

Review the sections "Banking Crises and Financial Panics" on pages 548-552 and "The Consequences of Banking Crises" on pages 552-557.

a. The house construction business of Sarah and Mario illustrates the idea of shared mistakes: they erroneously believed that housing prices could only continue to increase, and when housing prices fell they lost money on their houses built for speculation. The fact that there were many houses for sale in the subdivisions illustrates that they were not the only ones to believe that housing prices could only move in one direction.

b. Tech stock prices were bid up beyond their worth in the tech stock bubble. This is another illustration of shared mistakes, whereby many people made the same mistake of investing in tech stocks, leading to a tech stock bubble.

c. This scenario illustrates a vicious circle of deleveraging, which is one of the identifying characteristics of a financial contagion. One firm's need to reduce debt and raise cash quickly results in many firms having problems with falling asset prices and an inability to secure needed credit.

d. Second Street Bank is suffering from a credit crunch. The bank is not able to get the needed credit, and as the credit situation tightens, more and more banks will need to reduce their lending. This will lead businesses and consumers to cut back on their spending, causing the economy to go into a recession.

e. Lucinda's situation illustrates the concept of debt overhang, where a vicious circle of deleveraging leaves a borrower with high debt but diminished assets. Lucinda still owes most of her mortgage, but the value of the house has fallen. This has increased her level of debt even though the value of her house is lower.

f. A key feature of banking-crisis recessions is that monetary policy is not very effective. Despite a very low interest rate, the monetary policy was not particularly effective in the aftermath of the financial crisis of 2008. Monetary policy tends to break down after a banking crisis due to a lack of confidence on the part of banking institutions and an unwillingness on the part of consumers and businesses to borrow.

4. Your neighbor Sanjay exclaimed to you the other night, "I have lived through a number of recessions, but this recession is the worst I have ever seen!" Sanjay was speaking of the recession following the financial crisis of 2008. Sanjay knows that you have been studying macroeconomics this term, and he would like you to help him understand why the recession following this crisis was so severe and why it has lasted so long.

STEP 1: Show how the financial crisis of 2008 illustrates shared mistakes as well as financial contagion.

Review the sections "Banking Crises and Financial Panics" on pages 548–552 and the section "Regulation in the Wake of the Crisis" on pages 561–563.

The financial crisis of 2008 was preceded by a real estate bubble, in which real estate prices rose by more than 60% in the period after 2000 before they fell back down to levels more in keeping with their historical levels. As real estate prices fell, many homeowners found that the value of their homes had fallen below their mortgage amounts: these homeowners were underwater, owing more money than the value of the assets—their homes—were worth. Many of these homeowners went into default on their mortgages, and many homes were in foreclosure. Many of the loans to homeowners were subprime mortgages that were subsequently securitized with other mortgage loans. Shares in these securitized loans were sold to other investors who were highly exposed to losses from the bursting of the housing bubble. This led to financial contagion due to a vicious downward spiral of deleveraging, which worsened the recession and hindered economic recovery.

STEP 2: Identify the three main reasons that banking and financial crises lead to severe recessions.

Review the section "The Consequences of Banking Crises" on pages 552–557.

There are three main reasons a banking and financial crisis can lead to a severe recession: (1) A credit crunch, whereby potential borrowers find they either cannot get credit or, if they can get credit, the borrowers must pay very high rates of interest for this credit; (2) debt overhang, whereby borrowers find that the pushing down of asset prices results in their having additional financial stress due to their continuing to have high amounts of debt, while the assets the borrowers hold have diminished in value; and (3) in the aftermath of a financial crisis, loss of monetary policy effectiveness as a means of restoring consumer and investment spending.

STEP 3: Discuss how the financial crisis of 2008 created a credit crunch.

Review the sections "The Consequences of Banking Crises" on pages 552–557 and the section "Regulation in the Wake of the Crisis" on pages 561–563.

When the real estate bubble burst, it left many homeowners with mortgages that were greater than the value of their homes. As the homeowners went into default and foreclosure, the financial institutions holding these mortgages found that they were highly exposed to losses from the bursting of the housing bubble. Financial institutions became concerned about the solvency of other financial institutions, and that led to a freezing up of the credit markets. This situation was a classic illustration of a credit crunch.

STEP 4: Discuss how the financial crisis of 2008 created a debt overhang.

Review the sections "The Consequences of Banking Crises" on pages 552-557 and the section "Regulation in the Wake of the Crisis" on pages 561-563.

After the housing bubble burst, many homeowners found that the amount they owed on their mortgages was greater than the value of their homes. These homeowners were "underwater," and their plight illustrated the debt overhang concept. Recall that debt overhang refers to a situation where the individual or institution has high levels of debt but diminished assets. As housing prices fell, this diminished the value of the homes (the assets), while leaving the debt owed (the mortgages) at the same level.

STEP 5: Discuss how the financial crisis of 2008 created a scenario where monetary policy was largely ineffective.

Review the sections "The Consequences of Banking Crises" on pages 561-563 and the section "Regulation in the Wake of the Crisis" on pages 561-563.

Even though the Federal Reserve kept interest rates at very low levels after the bursting of the housing bubble, this did little to stimulate the economy. Many households facing high debt levels and decreases in the value of their assets were not in a position to increase their spending levels. In addition, many households had been adversely affected by the recession and the accompanying loss of jobs in the economy. Businesses were equally reluctant to increase their spending despite very low interest rates: household demand was not strong, and there was excess capacity in the economy. Thus, monetary policy implemented to increase consumer and investment spending proved to be ineffective.

Problems and Exercises

1. Suppose First Bank has 1,000 customers who have each deposited $10,000 at the bank. First Bank has kept 20% of these deposits as reserves to meet depositor demand for funds. The other 80% of First Bank's deposits have been used to make mortgage loans to individuals who have not deposited funds at First Bank. Each mortgage loan has a value of $100,000. For simplicity sake, let's assume that each mortgage represents a loan made to a customer to finance the purchase of a residence that is initially selling for $120,000.

   a. What is the total amount of deposits at First Bank, given the information provided?

   b. What is the total amount of reserves at First Bank, given the information provided?

   c. What is the total number of mortgages issued by First Bank, given the information provided?

Suppose a rumor circulates that First Bank may be unable to meet its financial obligations, and 50% of First Bank depositors demand their funds.

d. Given its initial level of reserves, will First Bank have sufficient funds on hand to meet the demand by these depositors for their funds? Explain your answer and provide a numerical value of the surplus or shortage of funds that First Bank will have, given this scenario.

e. To meet the demand for funds, First Bank decides to sell some of the mortgages it holds. Since First Bank needs funds immediately, it must sell these mortgages for less than their face value. Suppose that it sells each $100,000 mortgage for $75,000 to raise the necessary funds to meet depositor demands. How many mortgages will First Bank need to sell to raise the needed funds?

f. Consider First Bank's financial position after the sale of the mortgages in part (e). First Bank has sold mortgages to cover the demand for depositor funds. How many deposits (liabilities for First Bank) are still in the bank? Suppose that the remaining mortgages held by First Bank are now also valued at $75,000, the price First Bank has been able to sell mortgages for in the market. What is the value of the mortgages still owned by First Bank? Finally, what do reserves at First Bank equal?

g. Given your answers in part (f), is First Bank solvent (that is, do the value of assets exceed the value of liabilities) after it meets the demand for depositor funds that arises from the rumor?

2. A bank accepts deposits and uses these deposits to finance 30-year mortgages. How do these transactions represent maturity transformation?

3. What is shadow banking and how is it similar to the banking represented by depository institutions? How is shadow banking different from the banking represented by depository institutions? Discuss how shadow banking can be subject to bank runs.

4. Consider a bank run that becomes a financial contagion. Who loses when this happens? Explain your answer.

5. What kinds of bank regulation can policy makers impose to reduce the likelihood of banking and financial crises?

6. Briefly discuss the four major elements of the Wall Street Reform and Consumer Protection Act, otherwise known as the Dodd-Frank bill. In your explanation, discuss why each of these elements is important.

▌ BEFORE YOU TAKE THE TEST

Chapter Review Questions

1. Which of the following statements is true?
   a. Commercial banks and investment banks refer to identical financial institutions.
   b. Commercial banks accept deposits from customers, while investment banks trade in financial assets but do not accept deposits from customers.
   c. Investment banks accept deposits from customers, while commercial banks trade in financial assets but do not accept deposits from customers.
   d. Commercial banks and investment banks both accept deposits from customers, but only investment banks trade in financial assets.

2. A subprime mortgage is

  a. a mortgage issued to a homebuyer who does not have sufficient income to qualify for a standard or prime mortgage.

  b. a mortgage issued to a homebuyer who does have sufficient assets to qualify for a standard or prime mortgage.

  c. less risky for the lender than a prime mortgage.

  d. Answers (a) and (c) are both correct.

  e. Answers (b) and (c) are both correct.

3. A global credit crunch occurs when

  a. borrowers cannot find credit or they must pay very high interest rates for credit.

  b. lenders cannot loan money or they receive very low interest rates for any loans they do make.

  c. lenders are willing to loan money to borrowers, but borrowers refuse to take out loans.

  d. borrowers are willing to borrow money, but lenders do not have any money they can lend to borrowers.

4. Shadow banking refers to

  a. commercial banks that accept deposits and make loans.

  b. a wide variety of types of financial firms including investment banks, hedge funds, and money market funds.

  c. financial firms that, prior to the banking crisis of 2008, were not closely watched or effectively regulated.

  d. Answers (a), (b) and (c) are all correct.

  e. Answers (b) and (c) are both correct.

5. The existence of banks reduces the need to

  a. hold cash in the event of an unexpected financial need.

  b. balance the need for liquidity against the rate of return one can earn from interest-earning assets.

  c. have regulation of the financial industry.

  d. hold cash rather than using these funds to help pay for productive investment spending.

  e. Answers (a), (b), (c), and (d) are all correct.

  f. Answers (a), (b), and (d) are all correct.

6. Depository banks

  a. borrow on a short-term basis from their depositors and lend these funds on a long-term basis to others.

  b. borrow on a long-term basis from their depositors and lend these funds on a short-term basis to others.

7. Maturity transformation is done by

  a. depository institutions when they borrow on a short-term basis and lend on a long-term basis.

  b. shadow bank institutions even though these institutions do not take deposits.

  c. Answers (a) and (b) are both correct.

8. Prior to the financial crisis of 2008, shadow banks were
   a. not regulated and therefore did not need to meet capital requirements or reserve requirements.
   b. not regulated and could therefore offer their customers a higher rate of return on their funds.
   c. about 1.5 times larger in the United States, in terms of dollars, than the formal, deposit-taking banking sector.
   d. Answers (a), (b), and (c) are all correct.

9. A shadow bank is subject to a bank run if
   a. the shadow bank's lenders decide it is no longer safe to lend funds to the shadow bank, and the shadow bank finds it is unable to fund its operations.
   b. bank regulators fail to adequately evaluate the safety and soundness of the shadow bank.
   c. the government issues a warning that shadow banks are inherently unstable.
   d. Answers (a), (b) and (c) are all correct.

10. When many banking institutions get into trouble at the same time this is due to
    a. government regulations that prevent banking institutions from pursuing profitable business opportunities.
    b. these institutions making similar mistakes that are often due to the existence of an asset bubble.
    c. these institutions suffering from financial contagion in which the problems and difficulties of one institution spread to and create trouble for other institutions.
    d. Both answers (b) and (c) are reasons for banking crises.
    e. Answers (a), (b) and (c) all provide reasons for banking crises.

11. Which of the following statements is true?
    a. A "vicious circle of deleveraging" refers to the quick selling of assets that result in these assets being sold at a deep discount. This selling off of assets creates financial contagion, since other institutions holding similar assets will find that these assets have lost value.
    b. The shadow banking system is not prone to financial contagion.
    c. The shadow banking system, prior to 2008, was highly regulated.
    d. Lehman's was not affected by a "vicious circle of deleveraging."

12. A financial panic
    a. is a sudden and widespread disruption of financial markets that arises when people lose faith in the liquidity of financial institutions and markets.
    b. is typically accompanied by a banking crisis.
    c. could be the result of an asset bubble and a vicious circle of deleveraging.
    d. Answers (a), (b), and (c) are all correct.
    e. Answers (a) and (b) are both correct.
    f. Answers (a) and (c) are both correct.

13. From after the Civil War to the Great Depression,
    a. the United States rarely had bank crises.
    b. frequently had bank crises due primarily to the lack of regulation in the banking system.
    c. frequently had bank crises despite regulation of the banking system.
    d. had bank crises primarily because of the existence of a system of guarantees for depositors.

14. The banking crises of the early 1930s
    a. were milder than earlier periods of bank crises.
    b. resulted in about 40% of banks in the United States failing.
    c. were due to President Franklin Roosevelt proclaiming a bank holiday.
    d. resulted in GDP falling by a third and prices falling as well.
    e. Answers (b) and (d) are both correct.
    f. Answers (b), (c), and (d) are all correct.

15. Which of the following statements is true?
    a. From 1970 to 2007, there were only 10 "systemic banking crises" in the world.
    b. From 1970 to 2007, there were many "systemic banking crises" in the world, but most of these crises were in small, poor countries and most were not as severe as the U.S. Panic of 1873 or 1893.
    c. At the beginning of the 1990s, Finland, Sweden, and Japan all experienced major banking crises that were the result of real estate lending.
    d. Statements (a), (b) and (c) are all correct.
    e. Statements (a) and (c) are both correct.
    f. Statements (b) and (c) are both correct.

16. The "Celtic Tiger" refers to
    a. Portugal.
    b. India.
    c. Ireland.
    d. South Korea.

17. Banking crises are
    a. commonly associated with recessions.
    b. do not affect the overall health of the economy.
    c. typically not associated with long-running impacts on the aggregate economy.
    d. easily resolved within days of becoming apparent.

18. A severe banking crisis is characterized as
    a. a situation in which a large fraction of the banking system goes bankrupt or suffers a major loss of confidence.
    b. a situation requiring government intervention to bail out the banking system.
    c. a situation that always leads to deep recession followed by a slow economic recovery.
    d. Answers (a), (b) and (c) are all correct.
    e. Answers (a) and (b) are both correct.

19. Banking crises typically result in prolonged recessions because of
   a. the credit crunch that leads to a reduction in available credit due to the disruption of the banking system.
   b. the debt overhang that arises as a result of falling asset prices that lead to a vicious circle of deleveraging; as this circle progresses, it leads to even greater decreases in asset prices. As asset prices fall, consumers and businesses cut back on their spending in order to reduce their debt and rebuild their assets.
   c. the loss of monetary effectiveness as a means to stimulate aggregate spending in the economy.
   d. Answers (a), (b), and (c) are all correct.

20. After a banking crisis, when the central bank expands the money supply in order to reduce interest rates and stimulate the level of aggregate spending,
   a. banks tend to hold onto excess reserves rather than loaning out these reserves because the banks are worried about bank runs and/or a loss of confidence by their investors.
   b. consumers and businesses are unwilling to borrow because of the financial difficulties caused by a loss in the price of the financial assets they hold.
   c. even a very low interest rate may not be sufficient to encourage expanded economic activity.
   d. Answers (a), (b), and (c) are all correct.

21. When financial institutions find they are unable to borrow from private credit markets,
   a. the country's central bank may step in as a lender of last resort.
   b. they may have to sell their assets at steeply reduced prices unless the central bank steps in and provides credit to them.
   c. this may start a vicious circle of deleveraging.
   d. the government may step in to guarantee the liabilities of these financial institutions.
   e. All of the answers are correct.

22. Bank regulation was first recommended in
   a. the 1930s, after the financial crash of 1929 that precipitated the Great Depression.
   b. *The Wealth of Nations* (1776) by Adam Smith, when Smith compared the need for bank regulation to the need for fire standards in the building code.
   c. 1980, when Ronald Reagan became President of the United States.
   d. 1976, when Jimmy Carter became President of the United States.

23. From the 1930s until the crisis of 2008, banking regulation addressed three primary elements:
   a. deposit insurance, capital requirements, and interest rate ceilings.
   b. deposit insurance, interest rate ceilings, and excess reserve requirements.
   c. deposit insurance, capital requirements, and reserve requirements.
   d. interest rate ceilings, capital requirements, and limitations of the types of assets that banks could hold.

24. When the government guarantees bank deposits via deposit insurance, this results in
    a. the risk that bank owners will engage in reckless behavior with these bank funds, since any loss is insured by the government.
    b. bank owners acting with greater caution, since they know that any adverse outcome of their decisions will cost taxpayers money due to the existence of deposit insurance.

25. Financial regulation broke down prior to the crisis of 2008 primarily because of the
    a. rise of shadow banking.
    b. expansion of the commercial banking system.
    c. rise of the shadow banking system as well as the expansion of the commercial banking system.

26. A repo is
    a. a very long-term loan.
    b. a very short-term loan.
    c. a loan where the seller agrees to repurchase the asset from the borrower at a higher price.
    d. Answers (a) and (c) are both correct.
    e. Answers (b) and (c) are both correct.

27. The repo market prior to the crisis of 2008
    a. paid a higher rate of return than traditional depository institutions did on their deposits.
    b. was used as a way for shadow banks to finance their speculative investments, since the shadow banks could borrow funds in the repo market, use these funds to purchase mortgage-backed securities, and then use these mortgage-backed securities as collateral for another repo trade.
    c. by 2008, the repo and other forms of shadow banking had grown larger than traditional depository banking.
    d. Answers (a) and (b) are both correct.
    e. Answers (a), (b), and (c) are all correct.

28. The shadow banking system in the 2000s
    a. had little safety net in the form of deposit insurance.
    b. did have capital requirements but these requirements were minimal compared to the capital requirements that conventional depository institutions had to meet.
    c. had no lender of last resort to turn to in the event of a bank run.
    d. Answers (a), (b), and (c) are all true statements.

29. When a homeowner is "underwater," this means that the
    a. value of the house is less than the amount owed on the homeowner's mortgage.
    b. value of the mortgage is less than the value of the house.
    c. institution providing the mortgage for the homeowner is insolvent; thus, the homeowner must find a new lender.
    d. homeowner has defaulted on their mortgage.
    e. home is in foreclosure in which the lending institution is in the process of reclaiming the house as the collateral on a loan that is not being paid back to the institution.

30. A subprime mortgage is a loan
    a. to people who would not qualify for a traditional, or "prime" mortgage.
    b. at a lower interest rate than a traditional, or "prime" mortgage.

31. After the banking crisis of 2008
    a. it was recognized that financial regulation was a continuing process that could require regulations to change over time to keep up with financial innovations.
    b. it was clear that the traditional scope of banking regulation was too wide and there was need to constrict the expansion of bank regulation.
    c. it was evident that shadow banking did not need to be regulated.
    d. Answers (a), (b), and (c) are all correct.
    e. Answers (a) and (b) are both correct.
    f. Answers (b) and (c) are both correct.
    g. Answers (a) and (c) are both correct.

32. The Wall Street Reform and Consumer Protection Act, often referred to as the Dodd-Frank bill, addresses which of the following four key elements?
    a. consumer protection, derivatives regulation, limits on interest rates, and regulation of shadow banks.
    b. consumer protection, derivatives regulation, subprime lending limits, and regulation of shadow banking.
    c. consumer protection, derivatives regulation, regulation of shadow banks, and resolution authority.
    d. consumer protection, derivatives regulation, subprime lending limits, and resolution authority.

ANSWER KEY

Answers to Problems and Exercises

1. **a.** The total amount of deposits at First Bank is equal to the amount of each deposit ($10,000) times the number of depositors (1,000), or $10,000,000.

b. The amount of reserves at First Bank is equal to 20% of $10,000,000, or $2,000,000.

c. The total number of mortgages issued by First Bank is equal to the amount of money available for mortgages ($8,000,000) divided by the amount per mortgage ($100,000), or 80 mortgages.

d. If 50% of First Bank's depositors demand their funds back, then First Bank will need 500($10,000), or $5,000,000 to meet this demand. Since First Bank only has $2,000,000 in reserve, the Bank will find that it has a shortage of $3,000,000.

e. Since First Bank needs to raise $3,000,000 in funds to meet depositor demands, it will need to sell $3,000,000/$75,000 per mortgage, or 40 mortgages.

f. Since 50% of depositors have withdrawn their funds from the bank, this implies that First Bank now has deposits of only $5,000,000. First Bank sold 40 mortgages to raise the needed funds to meet depositor demand, so it still owns 60 mortgages. If each mortgage is now valued at $75,000, this means that the value of First Bank's mortgages is now equal to 60($75,000), or $4,500,000. First Bank's reserves are now equal to $0, since the bank used the $2,000,000 it had in reserve plus the sale of 40 mortgages to raise the funds necessary to honor depositor demand for funds.

g. First Bank's assets are now equal to $4,500,000 (the value of the mortgages it holds), while its liabilities are equal to $5,000,000 (the value of deposits at the bank). First Bank is not solvent.

2. The deposits made at the bank are short-term in nature: that is, the depositors place funds in the bank where these funds are available whenever the depositor demands them. These deposits represent liabilities to the bank, since the bank owes these funds to the depositors who made the deposits. The bank takes these funds and uses them to finance mortgages that have a maturity of 30 years: that is, the mortgage amount borrowed does not have to be repaid in full until 30 years have elapsed. These mortgages represent assets to the bank, since the bank owns these mortgages. The bank has transformed a short-term liability, the deposits, into a long-term asset, the 30-year mortgages. Maturity transformation is the conversion of short-term liabilities into long-term assets.

3. Shadow banking refers to a diverse group of financial firms including hedge funds, money market mutual funds, and investment banks. Like depository institutions, shadow banks borrow short-term funds and use these funds to create long-term assets. Shadow banks create long-term assets by borrowing funds in the short-run and then lending or investing these funds over the longer term. This process is referred to as maturity transformation. Shadow banks are different from depository institutions because shadow banks do not accept deposits. Shadow banks, like depository institutions, are subject to bank runs because both types of banking institutions provide the same economic task of allowing their customers to make a better trade-off between rate of return, or yield, and liquidity. If the shadow bank lenders decide that it is no longer safe to lend to the shadow bank, then the shadow bank will find this loss of credit means it can no longer fund its operations. Unless the shadow bank is able to quickly sell its assets to immediately raise cash, it will fail. This failure to get funds to finance its operations is what happened to Lehman Brothers.

4.   When a bank run occurs, many people are adversely impacted: the shareholders of the bank, the creditors of the bank, the depositors at the bank, the loan customers at the bank, and the bank employees. A bank run that spreads like a contagion affects many more people: it can cause a loss of confidence among depositors at other banks, and this can lead to a cascade of events that creates more bank failures and even a bank crisis. In a bank crisis, a significant portion of the banking sector ceases to function. Often a banking crisis also precipitates a severe economic downturn, resulting in higher rates of unemployment and lower levels of aggregate production that persist for many years.

5.   There are two broad types of regulation that governments can implement to reduce the likelihood of banking and financial crises. Government can act as a lender of last resort so that financial institutions have a source of funds or credit when they are unable to borrow from private credit markets. This lender of last resort protects solvent financial institutions from engaging in fire sales to raise needed funds when the private credit markets are not functioning well. The government can also provide guarantees to depositors and others with claims on banks. These guarantees effectively mean that when a financial institution becomes insolvent, the government will step in and take on the bank's risk. When the government does step in, it often demands the temporary ownership of the bank until the government can "reprivatize" the bank. This guarantee is a method for restoring depositor confidence in troubled financial institutions.

6.   The Dodd-Frank bill called for consumer protection, derivatives regulation, regulation of shadow banks, and resolution authority.

      Consumer protection was deemed necessary after the financial crisis of 2008 because there was recognition that many borrowers prior to the crisis had accepted offers they did not understand. One of the goals of the Dodd-Frank bill was to reduce abusive financial industry practices while protecting borrowers.

      The bill called for regulation of derivatives because these complicated financial instruments were seen as a means of concealing risk. The new legislation calls for more transparent markets in derivatives.

      The Dodd-Frank bill legislated regulation of shadow banks in recognition that these institutions, although they did not fit the traditional definition of a bank, played a major role in the banking crisis. Shadow banks will be regulated with regard to their levels of capital and their investments.

      The Dodd-Frank bill provided for resolution authority that empowered the government to seize control of financial institutions that require a bailout. This would be an extension of the government's resolution authority over not just depository institutions, but also over the shadow banking industry. Recognizing that government guarantees can lead institutions to take excessive risk, the provision for resolution authority allows the government to reduce its exposure to backing these overly risky institutions through the government's ability to seize these errant institutions if necessary. Knowing the government can do this will likely reduce risk taking on the part of financial institutions.

Answers to Chapter Review Questions

1.   **Answer b.** This is just a definitional question: commercial banks accept deposits from customers, while investment banks do not accept these deposits. In addition, investment banks trade in financial assets.

2.   **Answer a.** A subprime mortgage is a mortgage issued to a homebuyer who lacks the level of income and/or assets that would allow him or her to qualify for a standard or prime mortgage. Because the borrower lacks the income and/or assets to qualify for a standard mortgage, he/she represents a greater threat of defaulting on, or not paying back, the loan.

3. **Answer a.** In a credit crunch, borrowers would like to borrow funds, but they find it either impossible to get credit because lenders are unwilling to lend, or it is very expensive to get credit because lenders are only willing to lend at very high interest rates. In a credit crunch, lenders have funds but are reluctant to make these funds available unless they receive unusually high interest rates on the loans they make.

4. **Answer e.** *Shadow banking* is a term coined by Paul McCulley to refer to a diverse group of financial firms including investment banks, hedge funds, and money market funds that prior to the crisis of 2008 were not closely watched or effectively regulated. Commercial banks are not considered shadow banks; commercial banks are highly regulated.

5. **Answer f.** Banking reduces the need to hold cash in the event of a financial need because the existence of banks provides a means of borrowing funds if they are needed. In addition, the banking system provides liquidity for lenders while simultaneously providing a means for those individuals with surplus funds to make those funds available to those with productive opportunities but a deficit of funds. Thus, it is possible to have liquidity while earning an interest return on your assets because of the banking system. The banking system, however, does require regulation in order that asymmetric information issues like moral hazard and adverse selection can be addressed.

6. **Answer a.** Deposits at depository institutions are available at any time and are thus short term. Depository institutions lend out these funds to those seeking funds for productive purposes: these loans are due at some point in the future, but because they are not immediately due they are viewed as long term. This borrowing on a short-term basis and lending on a long-term basis is called maturity transformation.

7. **Answer c.** Maturity transformation refers to the conversion of short-term liabilities to long-term assets. Both depository institutions as well as shadow bank institutions engage in maturity transformation.

8. **Answer d.** These are all definitional or descriptive statements that are covered in the text.

9. **Answer a.** Shadow banks are in the business of maturity transformation: they borrow on a short-term basis and lend or invest longer term. If lenders decide that the shadow bank is not a safe place for their funds, then this mismatch between short-term borrowing and long-term lending can result in a bank run as other lenders decide they also do not want to place their funds at the shadow bank. Shadow banking, prior to the banking crisis of 2008, was not regulated. The government does not issue warnings about the stability of the shadow bank institutions.

10. **Answer d.** Banking crises are typically the result of an asset bubble or financial contagion. With an asset bubble, financial institutions make a similar mistake in valuing an asset at a level greater than its true value. With financial contagion, the financial problems of one institution spread to other institutions and create problems for these other institutions. Government regulation is not a source of banking crises.

11. **Answer a.** Answer (a) describes what happens when a financial institution is forced to sell its assets quickly in order to reduce debt and raise cash. These quick sales drive the price of these assets down, and other institutions holding similar assets find that these assets are no longer as valuable. This causes these institutions to need to similarly sell assets to reduce their debt and raise cash. The data suggest that Lehman's did suffer from a downward spiral of asset prices. The shadow banking system prior to 2008 was not regulated. The shadow banking system is especially prone to fear- and rumor-driven contagion.

12. **Answer d.** These are all true statements and are discussed in the text.

13. **Answer c.** Between the Civil War and the Great Depression, the United States had frequent bank crises despite the fact that banks were regulated. This regulation focused on reserves and capital but did not provide for guarantees for depositors. As a result, bank runs were common as were bank crises.

14. **Answer e.** The banking crises of the early 1930s were much more severe than earlier banking crises, resulting in GDP falling by a third and the overall level of prices also falling. During this period, about 40% of banks in the United States failed. President Roosevelt eventually declared a temporary closure of all banks—this was termed a "bank holiday"—in order to end the vicious circle.

15. **Answer f.** These are all descriptive statements that are discussed in the text of the chapter. From 1970 to 2007, there were no fewer than 127 "systemic banking crises" in the world. Most of these crises were in small, poor countries and were not as severe as the earlier panics of 1873 and 1893. The crises in Finland, Sweden, and Japan in the early 1990s were due to heavy lending into a real estate bubble.

16. **Answer c.** The term "Celtic Tiger" was used during the 1990s and 2000s to refer to Ireland and its economic success. Ireland's impressive economic performance, however, came to an abrupt halt in 2008 due to a huge banking crisis.

17. **Answer a.** Banking crises typically are associated with recessions and, often, severe banking crises result in prolonged, and significant, economic slumps.

18. **Answer d.** These statements are from the text: a severe banking crisis results in many bank failures, a loss of confidence in the financial system, the need for government intervention, and a prolonged and deep recession that lasts for an extended period of time.

19. **Answer d.** The severity of recessions following banking crises is typically explained by the credit crunch, the debt overhang, and the loss of monetary effectiveness. Economic activity slows as credit becomes difficult to get, consumers and businesses slow their spending in order to reduce their debt and rebuild their assets, and monetary policy is not effective in stimulating the level of aggregate spending.

20. **Answer d.** These are all reasons for why monetary policy is ineffective following a banking crisis. Banks fearful of bank runs or a loss of confidence by their investors will want to hold excess reserves in order to have more of a cushion against a bank run or reluctance on the part of investors to provide funds. The vicious circle of deleveraging reduces the value of financial assets held relative to debt: consumers and businesses will be reluctant to increase their spending until they have reduced their debt levels relative to the value of their financial assets. Finally, a low interest rate when consumers and businesses are recovering from a vicious circle of deleveraging may not provide sufficient incentive to get these groups to borrow and spend.

21. **Answer e.** When financial institutions cannot borrow from private credit markets, they must find a source of credit. This source of credit can come from these institutions selling their assets, but this sale of assets typically is only possible if the financial institutions offer these assets at greatly reduced prices. This selling of assets at fire-sale prices starts the vicious circle of deleveraging and worsens the balance sheet for all the financial institutions. The central bank can prevent this from happening by stepping in as a lender of last resort and providing a means of credit for solvent, but credit-strapped, institutions. For a financial institution where the value of the assets is insufficient to cover its debts, the central bank's willingness to lend as a last resort will not be sufficient to restore the public's confidence in the financial institution: in this case, the government may choose to step in and guarantee the institution's liabilities.

22. **Answer b.** Bank regulation goes back a very long way, to 1776, when it was first advocated by Adam Smith. Although Adam Smith was a strong proponent of the free market, he recognized that bank regulation was necessary in much the same way that fire standards are necessary in the building code. There was more comprehensive banking regulation after the banking crisis of the 1930s. Deregulation of many markets occurred toward the end of the Carter presidency and continued, at a faster rate, during the Reagan administration.

23. **Answer c.** Banking regulation from the 1930s to the crisis of 2008 consisted of three primary elements: deposit insurance on the funds deposited by bank customers, which effectively eliminated bank runs; capital requirements to reduce irresponsible bank behavior that might result from the existence of deposit insurance; and reserve requirements, which also aid in reducing bank runs.

24. **Answer a.** The existence of bank deposit insurance means that depositors no longer fear that their funds might not be safe at a banking institution: effectively, the deposit insurance reduces the occurrence of bank runs because of the guaranteed protection of depositor savings. However, when these deposits are insured, it creates an incentive for bank owners to engage in riskier behavior with regard to the use of these funds, since the bank owners know that these funds will be guaranteed by the government even if a speculative bet does not pay off. Bank owners know that the government, and therefore taxpayers, will cover the cost of any bad bet on their part.

25. **Answer a.** Financial regulation has traditionally been concerned with depository institutions. However, shadow banking also functions like depository banking because shadow banks engage in maturity transformation. It is the rise of shadow banking that has created the greatest problem in financial regulation.

26. **Answer e.** A repo, or repurchase agreement, is a very short-term loan whereby the seller of the asset (for example, a corporate bond) agrees to buy back the asset at a higher price a short time later. Often repos are sold back the next day. In effect, the seller makes a short-term loan to the buyer, with the asset being sold acting as collateral on the loan.

27. **Answer e.** The repo market prior to the crisis of 2008 expanded, as many investors with excess cash put their funds in this market rather than in commercial banks. The repo market yielded a higher rate of return than that paid by depository institutions. Shadow banks recognized that they could use the repo market as a means to get short-term loans to purchase other assets, and then they could return to the repo market with these newly acquired assets and use them as collateral for additional loans.

28. **Answer d.** These are all descriptive statements about the shadow banking system in the 2000s, prior to the financial crisis of 2008.

29. **Answer a.** When a homeowner is "underwater," this means that the value of the house is no longer worth as much as or more than the amount owed on the mortgage. When a homeowner is "underwater," this often results in the homeowner being in default: that is, the homeowner may not be making mortgage payments sometimes because the homeowner has chosen to walk away from the property, and sometimes because he or she could not keep up with mortgage payments and could not sell the home for enough to pay off the mortgage. When a homeowner is "underwater," this may result in the home being foreclosed: the lending institution may repossess the home as a result of the failure of the homeowner to make mortgage payments. With a housing bubble, lending institutions may fail, as the value of the mortgage-backed securities that they hold fall in value.

30. **Answer a.** This is just the definition of a subprime mortgage.

31. **Answer a.** Bank regulation had failed to keep up with financial innovation, and this became evident with the banking crisis of 2008, particularly with the recognition of the growth of shadow banking. In the aftermath of the banking crisis of 2008, it was recognized that bank regulation would need to be extended to cover more than traditional banking and that shadow banking also needed to be regulated.

32. **Answer c.** The four elements of the Wall Street Reform and Consumer Protection Act are delineated and discussed in the chapter.

chapter 19

International Trade, Capital Flows, and Exchange Rates

BEFORE YOU READ THE CHAPTER

Summary

This chapter discusses international trade and the gains from trade that are possible through specialization according to comparative advantage. The chapter explores the sources of comparative advantage, and also provides a model to illustrate the distributional consequences of trade. This model provides a method for considering who benefits and who loses from international trade and why the benefits from trade outweigh the losses from trade. The chapter also considers the impact of tariffs and quotas and how tariffs and quotas create market inefficiencies and reduce the area of total surplus. The chapter discusses why governments engage in trade protection and the effect of international trade agreements on the international flow of goods and services.

This chapter also introduces the balance of payments and explores its measurement. In addition, the chapter considers the determinants of international capital flows and the role of the foreign exchange market and the exchange rate in the macroeconomy. The chapter explains the distinction between nominal and real exchange rates and emphasizes the importance of the real exchange rate in the current account.

Chapter Objectives

Objective #1. Trade is beneficial to both parties that engage in the trade, whether they are individuals or countries. Countries that specialize in producing different goods and then trade these goods with other countries benefit from this trade. Goods and services purchased from abroad are called imports, and goods and services sold abroad are called exports. Countries trade goods and services with one another, but they also invest funds: this linking of the markets for goods and services as well as financial assets between different countries is referred to as globalization.

Objective #2. A country has the comparative advantage in producing a good or service when that country can produce the good or service at a lower opportunity cost than can other countries.

703

A simple way to model international trade is to use linear production possibility frontiers to analyze trade between two countries. The straight-line production possibility frontier implies that the opportunity cost of producing the two goods does not change as the level of production of these two goods changes. This model is known as the Ricardian model of international trade.

Objective #3. Autarky refers to the situation in which a country does not engage in trade with any other countries. The Ricardian model of international trade allows a comparison to be made between a situation in which two countries trade with one another versus a situation in which the two countries act as autarkies and do not trade with one another. The Ricardian model of international trade results in the following conclusions:

- When countries specialize according to comparative advantage and then trade with one another, the total amount of goods and services produced is greater than when the countries do not engage in specialization and trade.

- No country will engage in trade unless the relative price of the good traded is less than the country's opportunity cost of producing the good in autarky.

Objective #4. For example, consider two countries, country A and country B, that have linear production possibility frontiers for the production of two goods: good X and good Y. These two countries and their production possibility frontiers are illustrated in Figure 19.1.

Figure 19.1

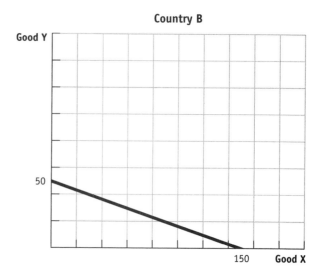

The opportunity cost of country A's producing one more unit of good X is equal to 1 unit of good Y, since country A must give up 1 unit of good Y to produce an additional unit of good X according to its production possibility frontier illustrated in Figure 19.1. The opportunity cost of country B's producing one more unit of good X is equal to 1/3 unit of good Y, since country B must give up 1/3 unit of good Y to produce an additional unit of good X according to its production possibility frontier illustrated in Figure 19.1. Comparison of these two opportunity costs reveals that country B can produce good X at lower opportunity cost than can country A, since country B gives up fewer units of good Y to get one more unit of good X. Country B has the comparative advantage in producing good X. Country A has the comparative advantage in producing good Y, since the opportunity cost of producing 1 unit of good Y for country A is 1 unit of good X, while for country B the opportunity cost of producing 1 unit of good Y is 3 units of good X. Both countries can benefit by specializing in the production of the good they can produce at lower opportunity cost and then trading.

- As an example, suppose the two countries initially do not trade and that country A produces 50 units of good X and 50 units of good Y while country B produces 75 units of good X and 25 units of good Y. Total production without trade is summarized in the table below.

	Production of good X	Production of good Y
Country A	50	50
Country B	75	25
Total production	125	75

- Now, suppose the two countries specialize according to their comparative advantage: country A produces 0 units of good X and 100 units of good Y while country B produces 150 units of good X and 0 units of good Y. The table below summarizes the result of this specialization. Notice that the total production of both goods increases when the two countries specialize.

	Production of good X	Production of good Y
Country A	0	100
Country B	150	0
Total production	150	100

- Let's digress a moment and consider what would happen if the two countries specialized, but produced those goods for which they did not have the comparative advantage: this implies that country A produces good X while country B produces good Y. The table below summarizes what happens when countries do not specialize according to their comparative advantage: total production decreases! Specialization is beneficial only when countries produce those goods for which they have lower opportunity cost of production.

	Production of good X	Production of good Y
Country A	100	0
Country B	0	50
Total production	100	50

- Once countries decide to specialize according to comparative advantage and to trade, they then need to decide on the price of these traded goods. In our example, country A will be willing to trade good Y for any price between 1 unit of good X (country A's opportunity cost of producing good Y) and 3 units of good X (country B's opportunity cost of producing good Y). Within this range of relative prices, country A benefits from trading with country B rather than producing the good itself. Using similar reasoning, country A will be willing to trade good X for any price between 1/3 unit of good Y and 1 unit of good Y.

Objective #5. Gains from trade depend on comparative advantage and not on absolute advantage. Comparative advantage is based on the opportunity cost of producing the good and not on the absolute amount of resources used to produce the good. A country with low wage rates generally reflects low labor productivity, while a country with high wage rates reflects high labor productivity.

- One fallacy with regard to trade is the pauper labor fallacy, which is the belief that when a high-wage country imports goods produced by workers in a low-wage country, this is an action that results in harming workers in the high-wage country.

- A second fallacy with regard to trade is the sweatshop labor fallacy, which is the belief that trade must be bad for workers in low-wage countries since the wages paid to workers in these countries is so much lower than the wages paid to workers in high-wage countries.

- Both the pauper labor fallacy and the sweatshop labor fallacy fail to recognize that trade is to the advantage of both the high-wage and the low-wage country, because both are able to achieve a higher standard of living through trade with one another.

Objective #6. Comparative advantage arises because of differences in climate, differences in factor endowments, and differences in technology.

- Climate and seasonal differences (northern hemisphere versus southern hemisphere) play a significant role in comparative advantage, since some goods can only be produced in certain climates or during certain seasons.

- The Heckscher–Ohlin model finds that a country has a comparative advantage in producing those goods whose production is intensive in the factors that are abundant in that country compared to other countries. This finding arises because the opportunity cost of a given factor is low when that factor is relatively abundant. This argument also helps to explain incomplete specialization, which is the situation when a country continues to produce a good that it also imports. A country will engage in incomplete specialization whenever that country has factor endowments that make it economically feasible for the country to produce the good. A country can still gain from trade even if it does not completely specialize.

- Technological differences can also drive comparative advantage. Technological differences may arise due to accumulated experience or because of innovations that one country has made that other countries have not adopted.

Objective #7. The model of demand and supply can be used to analyze the benefits of international trade. Figure 19.2 illustrates a market for a country that does not trade. In this figure, domestic demand represents the total demand for this good from individuals who live in this country, while domestic supply represents the total supply of this good from firms producing this good in this country. In autarky, the equilibrium in this market would be determined by the intersection of the domestic demand curve with the domestic supply curve: P_A is the equilibrium price and Q_A is the equilibrium quantity under autarky. Consumer and producer surplus are indicated in the figure, and total surplus in this market equals the sum of consumer and producer surplus.

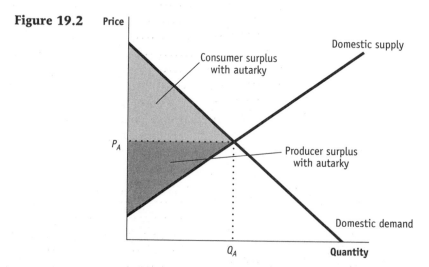

Figure 19.2

Consider what happens in this market if this country opens to trade. Suppose the world price for this good is lower than the autarky price (P_A) for this good. In Figure 19.3, this world price (P_W) is drawn on the graph. Notice that if the country opens to trade, the quantity of the good demanded domestically in this country at the world price (Q_D) will be greater than the amount of the good supplied domestically at this price (Q_S). This excess demand will be satisfied by the country importing ($Q_D - Q_S$) units of the good. Trade will also change the areas of consumer and producer surplus in this country: consumer surplus will increase as consumers get more units of the good at a lower price, while producer surplus decreases as domestic producers sell fewer units of the good at the lower price. Study Figure 19.3 carefully and recall that consumer surplus is the area that is beneath the demand curve but above the equilibrium price, while producer surplus is the area that is above the supply curve but below the equilibrium price. In this example, total surplus increases. Domestic producers of this good, however, see a reduction in their producer surplus, while domestic consumers see an increase in their consumer surplus. In the case of an imported good, domestic consumers benefit while domestic producers lose. Trade is beneficial since total surplus increases, but trade has distributional consequences, as you can see from what happens to the areas of consumer and producer surplus.

Figure 19.3

We can use the same analysis to consider the situation when the world price is greater than the autarky price. Starting from Figure 19.2, a market under autarky, let's consider a situation in which the world price exceeds the autarky price. Figure 19.4 illustrates this example: P_W is the world price, and in this case, when this country opens to trade, it finds that the quantity demanded domestically at the world price (Q_D) is less than the amount supplied domestically at this price (Q_S). This excess supply of ($Q_S - Q_D$) will be exported to other countries. Figure 19.4 also identifies the areas of consumer surplus and producer surplus once trade is allowed. As in Figure 19.3, we find that the area of total surplus is larger than in autarky. However, the distribution of the surplus has changed: in Figure 19.3, domestic consumers benefited from trade while domestic suppliers were hurt; in Figure 19.4, domestic suppliers benefit from trade while domestic consumers are hurt. In both of these examples we find that trade is beneficial since it increases total surplus, but that trade has distributional consequences.

Figure 19.4

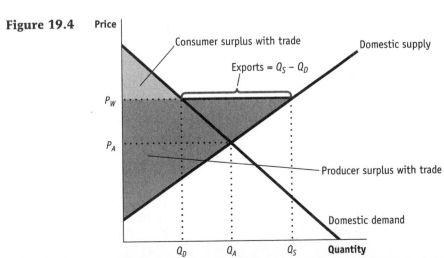

Objective #8. A country's industries can be broken down into two broad categories: exporting industries that produce goods and services to be sold abroad, and import-competing industries that produce goods and services also imported from abroad. When a country opens to trade, this leads to higher production in the exporting industries and lower production in the import-competing industries, and these changes affect the demand for factors of production in these two types of industries. The Heckscher–Ohlin model posits that international trade increases the demand for those factors of production that are relatively abundant in the country and decreases the demand for those factors of production that are relatively scarce. Thus, the price of abundant factors tends to rise while the price of scarce factors tends to fall. This price movement redistributes income toward a country's abundant factors and away from a country's less abundant factors.

Objective #9. Countries engage in trade protection, or protection, to limit the level of imports with the idea of protecting domestic producers in import-competing industries from foreign competition. Tariffs are a form of excise tax levied on the sales of imported goods, while quotas are legal limits on the quantity of a good that can be imported.

- Figure 19.5 illustrates a tariff placed on the good represented in this diagram. The tariff raises the world price of the good and therefore reduces the level of imports while simultaneously reducing the overall domestic demand for the good and increasing the domestic supply of the good. In Figure 19.5, the domestic supply and domestic demand curves are illustrated. P_W is the world price for the good with open trade, and P_T is the price of the good once the tariff is applied. At P_T, the quantity supplied domestically is Q_{ST} while the quantity demanded domestically is Q_{DT}. Thus, the level of imports with the imposition of the tariff is ($Q_{DT} - Q_{ST}$). The tariff results in a decrease in consumer surplus, an increase in producer surplus, and the capture of some of the consumer surplus as tariff revenue that the government earns. These areas are marked on the graph. In addition, the tariff results in deadweight loss: some mutually beneficial trades fail to occur and the economy wastes some resources on inefficient production since some producers produce the good even though their costs are greater than the world price of P_W. These two areas of deadweight loss are also identified on the graph. Study Figure 19.5 carefully and then compare it to Figure 19.3 to see how a tariff changes the outcome in this market. Notice that the tariff redistributes part of the consumer surplus to domestic producers and to the government as well as creates the areas of deadweight loss.

Figure 19.5

- Imposition of a quota in a market with free trade creates a limit on the number of units of the good that can be imported into the domestic market. This legal limit is typically administered through a license whereby the license holder purchases the legal right to import a certain number of units of the good into the domestic market. A quota results in a similar outcome as the tariff, but with one crucial difference. With a quota, the area labeled "tariff revenue" is now license-holder revenue. Instead of the government's earning tax revenue from the imposition of the tariff, the quota results in the license holder's earning quota rents equal to the area $(P_Q - P_W)(Q_{D\ QUOTA} - Q_{S\ QUOTA})$. The quota results in an increase in the domestic producer surplus and a decrease in the domestic consumer surplus. In addition, the quota results in the same two areas of deadweight loss that occurred with the tariff. Figure 19.6 illustrates the impact of a quota of $(Q_{D\ QUOTA} - Q_{S\ QUOTA})$ units on the market.

Figure 19.6

Objective #10. The balance of payments accounts summarize a country's transactions with other countries.

- The balance of payments on financial account is the difference between a country's sales of assets to foreigners and the country's purchases of assets from foreigners during a given period of time. This is also referred to as the capital account. The financial account can be broken into subaccounts, including the private net purchases of assets by private individuals and the official net purchases of assets, which represent transactions made by central banks.

- The balance of payments on current account is the difference between a country's exports and its imports plus net international transfer payments and factor income during a given period of time. Net international transfer payments is the difference between the payments foreigners send into the country and the payments that are sent out of the country to foreigners, while net international factor income is the difference between income payments received from foreigners and payments paid to foreigners.

- The sum of the balance of payments on current account (*CA*) and the balance of payments on financial account (*FA*) must equal zero. Thus, if *CA* is a positive number, then *FA* must be a negative number; conversely, if *CA* is a negative number, then *FA* must be a positive number.

Objective #11. A modified circular flow diagram can illustrate the flows between a country and the rest of the world.

- One flow represents the payments that are counted in the balance of payments on current account: here, the rest of the world sends payments into the country for goods and services (this would be payments for the country's exports), factor income, and transfers, and the rest of the world receives payments from the country for the goods and services (this would be payments for the country's imports), factor income, and transfers.

- A second flow represents payments that are counted in the balance of payments on financial account: here, the rest of the world sends the country payments for assets the world purchases from the country, while the country sends the rest of the world payments for assets it purchases. The country's balance of payments on financial account is a measure of the capital inflows or the amount of foreign savings that are available to finance domestic investment spending.

- Since the total flow into the country must be equal to the total flow out of the country, this implies that the balance of payments on current account plus the balance of payments on financial account must equal zero.

Objective #12. The merchandise trade balance, or trade balance, is the difference between a country's exports and imports of goods. It does not include the value of services traded.

Objective #13. In recent years, the United States has had a massive current account deficit with resultant huge capital inflows during this period. This capital inflow was attributed to the financial crises that caused investors to be unwilling to invest funds in poorer countries, which prior to the financial crises had been the recipients of substantial capital inflows. In addition, many governments started amassing large levels of foreign exchange reserves: this led these countries to have massive capital outflows that primarily flowed into the United States.

Objective #14. Currencies can be exchanged for one another in the foreign exchange market. This market determines the exchange rate, or the price for which two currencies exchange. When one currency becomes more valuable in terms of another currency, we say that the first currency has appreciated. When one currency becomes less valuable in terms of another currency, we say that the first currency has depreciated.

- The foreign exchange market brings together demanders and suppliers of currencies, and it is the interaction of this demand and supply that determines the equilibrium exchange rate. For instance, in the foreign exchange market for dollars, the demanders in this market are giving up foreign currency in order to acquire dollars. Their demand for dollars is influenced by the price they must pay for these dollars: this price is the exchange rate expressed as foreign currency per dollar. In the foreign exchange market for dollars, the suppliers of dollars provide dollars in exchange for the foreign currency; the supply of dollars they provide to this market depends on the price, or the exchange rate, they receive for those dollars. In the foreign exchange market for dollars, as the exchange rate increases, holding everything else constant, the quantity demanded of dollars will decrease, while the quantity of dollars supplied will increase. The equilibrium exchange rate is that exchange rate for which the quantity of dollars demanded equals the quantity of dollars supplied in the foreign exchange market.

- When there is an increase in capital inflows into a country, this increases the balance of payments on financial account. An increase in a country's exchange rate makes imports more attractive and exports less attractive for this country: this leads to a reduction in the balance of payments on current account for that country, which exactly offsets the increase in the balance of payments on financial account for that country. To generalize, a change in the balance of payments on financial account for a country must generate an equal and opposite reaction to that country's balance of payments on current account.

Objective #15. The real exchange rate is the exchange rate adjusted for international differences in aggregate price levels. The real exchange rate of country X's currency to country Y's currency equals the nominal exchange rate of country X's currency for country Y's currency times the ratio of the aggregate price level in country Y to the aggregate price level in country X. For example, the following equation gives the real exchange rate between the Mexican peso and the U.S. dollar:

$$\text{Real exchange rate} = (\text{Mexican pesos per U.S. dollar})(P_{US}/P_{MEX})$$

- The current account responds only to changes in the real exchange rate, not to changes in the nominal exchange rate. A country's products become cheaper to foreigners only when that country's currency depreciates in real terms, and a country's products become more expensive to foreigners only when that country's currency appreciates in real terms.

Objective #16. Purchasing power parity refers to the nominal exchange rate between two countries at which a given basket of goods and services would cost the same in each country. Nominal exchange rates almost always differ from purchasing power parities. Sometimes this difference is due to systematic differences; for example, prices are lower in poor countries because services tend to be cheaper in poor countries than they are in rich countries.

Objective #17. The real exchange rate affects exports and imports. When a country's real exchange rate rises, or appreciates, that country's exports fall and its imports rise. When a country's real exchange rate falls, or depreciates, that country's exports rise and its imports fall.

Key Terms

imports goods and services purchased from other countries.

exports goods and services sold to other countries.

globalization the phenomenon of growing economic linkages among countries.

Ricardian model of international trade a model that analyzes international *trade* under the assumption that *opportunity costs* are constant.

autarky a situation in which a country does not trade with other countries.

factor intensity the difference in the ratio of factors used to produce a good in various industries. For example, oil refining is capital-intensive compared to clothing manufacture because oil refiners use a higher ratio of capital to labor than do clothing producers.

Heckscher–Ohlin model a *model* of international trade in which a country has a *comparative advantage* in a good whose production is intensive in the factors that are abundantly available in that country.

domestic demand curve a *demand curve* that shows how the quantity of a good demanded by domestic consumers depends on the price of that good.

domestic supply curve a *supply curve* that shows how the quantity of a good supplied by domestic producers depends on the price of that good.

world price the price at which a good can be bought or sold abroad.

exporting industries industries that produce goods and services that are sold abroad.

Notes

Key Terms *(continued)*

import-competing industries industries that produce goods and services that are also imported.

free trade *trade* that is unregulated by government *tariffs* or other artificial barriers; the levels of *exports* and *imports* occur naturally, as a result of supply and demand.

trade protection policies that limit *imports*.

protection an alternative term for *trade protection;* policies that limit *imports*.

tariff a tax levied on *imports*.

import quota a legal limit on the quantity of a good that can be imported.

balance of payments accounts a summary of a country's transactions with other countries, including two main elements: the *balance of payments on current account* and the *balance of payments on financial account*.

balance of payments on current account (current account) transactions that do not create liabilities; a country's *balance of payments on goods and services* plus net international transfer payments and factor income.

balance of payments on goods and services the difference between the value of *exports* and the value of *imports* during a given period.

merchandise trade balance (trade balance) the difference between a country's *exports* and *imports* of goods alone—not including services.

balance of payments on financial account (financial account) international transactions that involve the sale or purchase of assets and, therefore, create future liabilities.

foreign exchange market the market in which currencies can be exchanged for each other.

exchange rate the price at which currencies trade, determined by the *foreign exchange market*.

appreciation a rise in the value of one currency in terms of other currencies.

depreciation a fall in the value of one currency in terms of other currencies.

equilibrium exchange rate the *exchange rate* at which the quantity of a currency demanded in the *foreign exchange market* is equal to the quantity supplied.

real exchange rate the *exchange rate* adjusted for international differences in *aggregate price levels*.

purchasing power parity (between two countries' currencies) the nominal *exchange rate* at which a given basket of goods and services would cost the same amount in each country.

AFTER YOU READ THE CHAPTER

Tips

Tip #1. Students often struggle with the concept of comparative advantage and how it relates to the opportunity cost of producing the good. One fail-safe method for analyzing this type of problem is to follow these steps. (1) Identify the two individuals or the two countries (for the rest of this tip we assume that we are analyzing the comparative advantage with regard to two countries) that are involved in the problem. (2) Identify the two goods that are being produced. (3) For each country, draw a graph that illustrates the production possibility frontier for that country. Make sure you label the graph with the country's name and label each of the two axes with the good being produced. This labeling is very important since it helps ensure that you do not confuse the two countries or the two goods. (4) Find the slope of the production possibility frontier and then use this slope to calculate the opportunity cost of producing one more unit of the good measured along the x-axis. You can use the slope in this manner since the slope equals the "rise over the run"—that is, the slope tells you the change in the y-variable divided by the change in the x-variable. So, for example, if one more unit of the x-variable was produced, the slope of the production possibility frontier would tell you how many units of the y-variable must be given up to produce this additional unit of the x-variable. (5) Under each country's graph, write a statement using this slope measure that says "OC of producing 1 good X is equal to [slope value] good Y." This statement just reminds you of what the opportunity cost of producing that additional unit of good X is. Below this statement write another statement that says "OC of producing 1 good Y is equal to [1/slope] good X." (6) Compare the opportunity cost of producing good X between the two countries, and decide which country can produce good X at the lowest opportunity cost. Circle the label on the x-axis for this country to identify the country that has the comparative advantage in producing good X. Then, on the other country's graph, circle the label on the y-axis to identify the country that has the comparative advantage in producing good Y. Figure 19.7 provides an example of this method. Note the labels, the OC statements, and the circling of the relevant labels as a means of identifying the country's comparative advantage. Faithful adherence to this method will certainly assure you of getting this concept right.

Figure 19.7

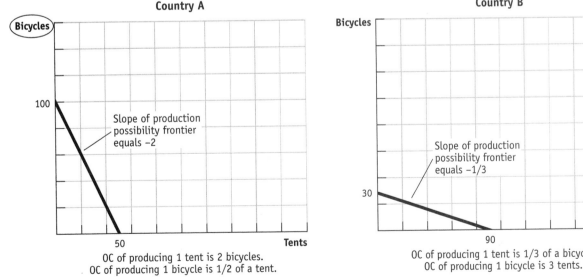

Country A

OC of producing 1 tent is 2 bicycles.
OC of producing 1 bicycle is 1/2 of a tent.

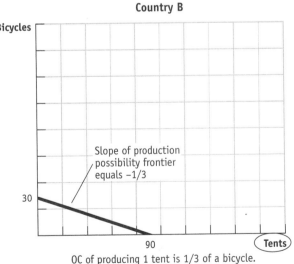

Country B

OC of producing 1 tent is 1/3 of a bicycle.
OC of producing 1 bicycle is 3 tents.

Tip #2. Students struggle with deciding what the relevant range of relative prices is for a good when countries specialize and then trade. Let's use the information in Figure 19.7 to work through a method for calculating this range of relative prices. Start with the good measured on the *x*-axis: tents. From the OC statements below the two graphs, we can see that the OC of producing 1 tent is between 1/3 of a bicycle (country B's OC) and 2 bicycles (country A's OC). You can think about placing these two limits on a number line and noting that the relative price of 1 tent must fall somewhere between the lowest possible relative price of 1/3 of a bicycle and the highest possible relative price of 2 bicycles. Figure 19.8 illustrates this number-line approach.

Figure 19.8

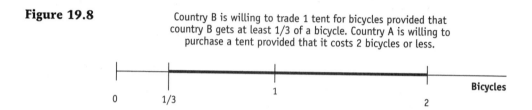

Country B is willing to trade 1 tent for bicycles provided that country B gets at least 1/3 of a bicycle. Country A is willing to purchase a tent provided that it costs 2 bicycles or less.

Tip #3. Working with quotas is often difficult for students: a quota is a legally established limit to the amount of imports a country allows during a given period. An alternative way of thinking about this legal limit is to recognize that the quota is the amount of imports that leads the sum of the quantity supplied domestically plus the quota amount to equal the quantity demanded domestically. Thus, if you are told the quantity demanded domestically and the quantity supplied domestically at a given price, you can then calculate what the necessary quota would be in order for the total quantity supplied of the good (both the domestic production plus the world production) to equal the quantity demanded domestically. With this thought in mind, go back and revisit Figure 19.6 to see if you can apply this concept to the graph.

Tip #4. An exchange rate is the price of one currency in terms of another currency. When a country's exchange rate increases, or appreciates, this makes its domestically produced goods relatively more expensive than goods produced by other economies. This will decrease exports and increase imports for the domestic economy: the balance of payments on current account will decrease, while the balance of payments on financial account will increase. The following table summarizes this relationship.

Appreciation of country X's currency ⟶ Country X imports more, exports less

Depreciation of country X's currency ⟶ Country X imports less, exports more

Tip #5. You will want to be thoroughly familiar with the terminology and the relationships represented in the balance of payments. The balance of payments (illustrated in Figure 19-12 of your text) shows the flow of money between national economies. It illustrates why the balance of payments on current account must equal the balance of payments on financial account. It illustrates the relationship in a domestic economy between the payments from the rest of the world for goods and services, factor income, and transfers, and payments to the rest of the world for goods and services, factor income, and transfers.

1. Bob and Mary are the only inhabitants of Littleburg. Both Bob and Mary spend their time planting vegetables and looking for berries. They currently do not trade with one another. The following graph shows their production possibilities for a day. Assume that both goods are measured in terms of some type of unit measurement (e.g., rows of vegetables or pints of berries) and that Mary and Bob have equal amounts of resources and technology available to them.

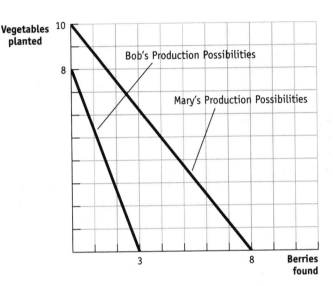

You are asked to determine who has the absolute advantage in planting vegetables and who has the absolute advantage in finding berries. You are also asked to identify who has the comparative advantage for each of these tasks. What is Mary's opportunity cost of finding berries? What is Bob's opportunity cost of finding berries? Finally, suppose that Bob and Mary decide to specialize according to their comparative advantages and then trade. What is the range of amounts of vegetables planted that both would agree to trade in exchange for one unit of berries found?

STEP 1: Review the definition of absolute advantage and then determine who has the absolute advantage in the production of each good.

Review the section "Comparative Advantage versus Absolute Advantage" on pages 576–578.

From the available set of resources, Mary can produce more planted vegetables and found berries than can Bob: Mary has the absolute advantage in the production of both goods.

STEP 2: Review the definition of comparative advantage and then determine who has the comparative advantage in the production of each good.

Review the section "Comparative Advantage and International Trade" on pages 572–581, as well as Figure 19-2 on page 574, Tables 19-1 and 19-2 on pages 574 and 575, respectively.

The opportunity cost of producing a unit of berries is 8/3 units of planted vegetables for Bob and 10/8 units of berries for Mary. Mary has a lower opportunity cost of finding berries than does Bob: for each unit of berries that she finds, she gives up less than does Bob. Mary therefore has the comparative advantage in finding berries. Bob, in contrast, has the comparative advantage in planting vegetables: his opportunity cost of planting vegetables is 3/8 unit of found berries, while the opportunity cost of planting vegetables for Mary is 8/10 unit of found berries.

STEP 3: From the above graph determine the opportunity cost of finding berries for each of these individuals.

Review the section "Comparative Advantage and International Trade" on pages 572–581, as well as Figure 19-2 on page 574, Tables 19-1 and 19-2 on pages 574 and 575, respectively.

In Step 2, the opportunity cost of finding berries is given. Remember that you can find the opportunity cost of the good measured on the *x*-axis by using the slope measure if the production possibility frontier is linear. Thus, the slope of Mary's production possibilities curve is equal to −10/8: this indicates that for every unit of found berries she must give up 10/8 units of planted vegetables. The slope of Bob's production possibilities curve is equal to −8/3: this indicates that for every unit of found berries he must give up 8/3 units of planted vegetables. It is more costly for Bob to produce found berries than it is for Mary to produce found berries. Thus, Mary has the comparative advantage in finding berries, while Bob has the comparative advantage in planting vegetables.

STEP 4: Apply your knowledge of the opportunity cost of finding berries for each of these individuals to determine a range of amounts of vegetables planted that both would agree to trade for one unit of berries found.

Review the section "Comparative Advantage and International Trade" on pages 572–581, as well as Figure 19-2 on page 574, Tables 19-1 and 19-2 on pages 574 and 575, respectively.

Bob is willing to give up 8/3 units of planted vegetables for a unit of found berries, while Mary must receive 10/8 units of planted vegetables to be willing to give up a unit of found berries. Any time Mary can receive more than 10/8 units of planted vegetables for a unit of found berries, she is willing to trade; any time Bob pays less than 8/3 units of planted vegetables for a unit of found berries, he is willing to trade. The trading range for one unit of found berries is thus somewhere between 10/8 units of planted vegetables and 8/3 units of planted vegetables.

2. Suppose there are two individuals: Trent and Sue. Both Trent and Sue produce two different goods: clarinets and drums. Each of them has the same amount of resources, the same technology, and the same amount of time to spend producing clarinets and drums. If Trent devotes all of his time, resources, and technology to producing clarinets, he is able to produce 1,000 clarinets and 0 drums. When Trent devotes all of his time, resources, and technology to producing drums, he is able to produce 500 drums and 0 clarinets. If Sue devotes all of her time, resources, and technology to producing clarinets, she is able to produce 800 clarinets and 0 drums. When Sue devotes all of her time, resources, and technology to producing drums, she is able to produce 500 drums and 0 clarinets. Assume that the production possibility frontiers for both Trent and Sue are linear. You are asked to provide graphs of Trent's and Sue's production possibilities on which clarinets are measured on the vertical axis and drums are measured on the horizontal axis. After drawing this graph, you are asked to determine who has the absolute advantage in producing clarinets and drums. In addition, you are asked to determine who has the comparative advantage in the production of each of these goods. Suppose initially that Trent and Sue each devote half of their time and half of their resources to the production of clarinets. The rest of their time and resources goes toward producing drums. Currently Trent and Sue do not trade with one another. Fill in the following table given this information.

	Clarinets	Drums
Trent		
Sue		
Total Production		

Suppose that Trent increases his production of clarinets by one unit relative to his initial production level, while Sue decreases her production of clarinets by one unit relative to her initial production level. They both adjust their production of drums so that they stay on their respective production possibility frontiers. Complete the following table, based on these assumptions.

	Clarinets	Drums
Trent		
Sue		
Total Production		

Did total production increase or decrease when Trent and Sue altered their allocation of resources? Explain your answer. Suppose instead that Trent decreases his production of clarinets by one unit from the initial level, while Sue increases her production of clarinets by one unit from the initial level. They both adjust their production of drums so that they stay on their respective production possibility frontiers. Complete the following table, based on these assumptions.

	Clarinets	Drums
Trent		
Sue		
Total Production		

Did total production increase or decrease when Trent and Sue altered their allocation of resources? Explain your answer. When Trent and Sue adjust their production of these two goods, total production is impacted: explain how their adjustments and their impact on total production are related to specialization, comparative advantage, and trade.

STEP 1: Draw graphs of Trent's and Sue's production possibilities on which clarinets are measured on the vertical axis and drums are measured on the horizontal axis.

Review the section "Production Possibilities and Comparative Advantage, Revisited" on pages 573–575, and Figure 19-1 on page 572.

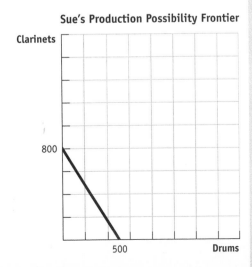

STEP 2: Determine who has the absolute advantage in the production of clarinets and who has the absolute advantage in the production of drums.

Review the section "Comparative Advantage versus Absolute Advantage" on pages 573–575, and Figure 19-1 on page 572.

Trent can produce more clarinets than can Sue: Trent has the absolute advantage in the production of clarinets, since he is more productive than is Sue. Neither Sue nor Trent has an absolute advantage in producing drums, since each of them can produce an equivalent amount of drums from the same amount of resources.

STEP 3: Determine who has the comparative advantage in the production of clarinets and who has the comparative advantage in the production of drums.

Review the section "Production Possibilities and Comparative Advantage, Revisited" on pages 573–575, as well as Figure 19-3 on page 575, and Table 19-1 on page 574, and Table 19-2 on page 575.

To determine who has the comparative advantage in producing drums, you first need to determine the opportunity cost of producing a drum for both Trent and Sue. Trent's opportunity cost of producing a drum is equal to 2 clarinets, since each time he produces a drum he must give up the production of 2 clarinets. Sue's opportunity cost of producing a drum is equal to 8/5 clarinets, since each time she produces a drum she must give up the production of 8/5 clarinets. Trent's opportunity cost of producing a drum is greater than Sue's opportunity cost: Sue has the comparative advantage in producing drums.

To determine who has the comparative advantage in producing clarinets, you will need to determine the opportunity cost of producing a clarinet for both Trent and Sue. Trent's opportunity cost of producing a clarinet is equal to 1/2 of a drum, since each time he produces a clarinet he must give up the production of 1/2 of a drum. Sue's opportunity cost of producing a clarinet is equal to 5/8 of a drum, since each time she produces a clarinet she must give up the production of 5/8 of a drum. Sue's opportunity cost of producing a clarinet is greater than Trent's opportunity cost: Trent has the comparative advantage in producing clarinets.

STEP 4: Fill in the following table based on the assumption that Trent and Sue each devote half of their time and half of their resources to the production of clarinets. The rest of their time and resources go toward the production of drums.

	Clarinets	Drums
Trent		
Sue		
Total Production		

Review the section "Production Possibilities and Comparative Advantage, Revisited" pages 573–575, as well as Figure 19-3 on page 575, and Table 19-1 on page 574, and Table 19-2 on page 575.

To fill in the table you can consult the figures you drew in Step 1 and find the midpoints of each production possibility frontier. The results are given in the following table.

	Clarinets	Drums
Trent	500	250
Sue	400	250
Total Production	900	500

STEP 5: Fill in the following table based on the assumption that Trent decides to produce one more clarinet than he did initially, while Sue decides to produce one fewer clarinet than she did initially. Make sure that the new levels of production are on Trent's and Sue's respective production possibility frontiers.

	Clarinets	Drums
Trent		
Sue		
Total Production		

Review the section "Production Possibilities and Comparative Advantage, Revisited" on pages 573–575, as well as Figure 19-3 on page 575, and Table 19-1 on page 574, and Table 19-2 on page 575.

From the earlier discussion on comparative advantage (see step 3), you know what the opportunity cost of an additional clarinet is for Trent: to produce one more clarinet he must give up 1/2 of a drum. Thus, Trent can produce 501 clarinets and 249.5 drums. A similar calculation is performed for Sue: when she produces one fewer clarinet, she is able to increase her drum production by 5/8 (this is the same as 0.625) of a drum. The following table summarizes these results.

	Clarinets	Drums
Trent	501	249.5
Sue	399	250.625
Total Production	900	500.125

STEP 6: Determine the effect on total production of the change in resource allocation in Step 5. Explain your result.

Review the section "Production Possibilities and Comparative Advantage, Revisited" on pages 573–575, as well as Figure 19-3 on page 575, and Table 19-1 on page 574, and Table 19-2 on page 575.

When Trent moves toward more clarinet production and less drum production, while Sue moves toward more drum production and less clarinet production, we see that total production increases. Notice that in this example both Trent and Sue are moving toward specializing in the production of the good for which they have comparative advantage, and this leads to greater overall production of the goods.

STEP 7: Fill in the following table based on the assumption that Trent decides to produce one fewer clarinet than he did initially, while Sue decides to produce one more clarinet than she did initially. Make sure that the new levels of production are on Trent's and Sue's respective production possibility frontiers.

	Clarinets	Drums
Trent		
Sue		
Total Production		

Review the section "Production Possibilities and Comparative Advantage, Revisited" on pages 573-575, as well as Figure 19-3 on page 575, and Table 19-1 on page 574, and Table 19-2 on page 575.

Do the same type of analysis that you did for Step 5, but this time have Trent produce one fewer clarinet while Sue produces one more clarinet. Use the opportunity costs that you calculated in Step 3 to help you figure out what happens to drum production for both Trent and Sue. The following table summarizes these results.

	Clarinets	Drums
Trent	499	250.5
Sue	401	249.375
Total Production	900	499.875

STEP 8: Determine the effect on total production of the change in resource allocation in Step 7. Explain your result.

Review the section "Production Possibilities and Comparative Advantage, Revisited" on pages 573-575, as well as Figure 19-3 on page 575, and Table 19-1 on page 574, and Table 19-2 on page 575.

This time total production decreases from its initial level: Trent and Sue are specializing, but they are not specializing according to their comparative advantage, and their decisions here result in less overall production than would be possible if they specialized according to their comparative advantage. It is best for overall production if Trent produces clarinets and Sue produces drums.

STEP 9: Given your analysis in Steps 6 and 8, explain how these adjustments and their impact on total production are related to specialization, comparative advantage, and trade.

Review the section "Production Possibilities and Comparative Advantage, Revisited" on pages 573-575, as well as Figure 19-3 on page 575, and Table 19-1 on page 574, and Table 19-2 on page 575.

This example illustrates how specializing in the production of the good for which you have comparative advantage can result in greater overall production than is possible if there is no specialization. For specialization to be advantageous, two things must happen: you must specialize according to your comparative advantage, and you must engage in trade with others who are also specializing according to their comparative advantage.

3. The small economy of Newville produces chocolate, and this market for chocolate is characterized by the following equations:

    Domestic Demand for Chocolate: $P = 100 - Q$
    Domestic Supply of Chocolate: $P = Q$

    You are asked to determine the equilibrium price and quantity in this market if Newville continues to be a closed economy with regard to the chocolate market. You are also asked to provide a measure of the consumer and producer surplus when this market is closed to trade. Newville is considering opening this market to trade and imagines two possible scenarios: in the first scenario, the chocolate market is open to trade and the world price of chocolate is $80 per unit. Newville's government wants you to analyze the effect of opening this market to trade given this price: the government in particular wants to know the impact of opening the market on the level of imports or exports of chocolate it could anticipate as well as on the values of consumer and producer surplus when there is trade. In the second scenario, the chocolate market is open to trade, and the world price of chocolate is $20 per unit. You are also asked to provide an analysis of the impact of opening the market on the level of imports or exports of chocolate as well as on the values of consumer and producer surplus if the world price for chocolate is equal to $20 per unit. For both scenarios, you are asked to illustrate your answer with a graph to help the government officials understand the impact of opening the market to world trade. The government also wishes to understand if opening its market to trade is beneficial whether it is confronted by the first or the second scenario. Who (domestic consumers or domestic producers of chocolate) in Newville is more likely to favor opening the chocolate market to trade if the world price is anticipated to be $80 per unit?

STEP 1: Start by drawing a graph of the market for chocolate in Newville when its economy is closed to trade. Use this graph to calculate the levels of consumer and producer surplus if there is no trade.

Review the section "Supply, Demand, and International Trade" on pages 581–588, and Figure 19-5 on page 582.

Graph the two equations and then use these two equations to find the equilibrium price and equilibrium quantity in this market when the market is closed to world competition. Using the demand and supply equations—$P = 100 - Q$ and $P = Q$, respectively—we can solve for the equilibrium quantity and then use this quantity to find the equilibrium price. Thus, $100 - Q = Q$, or $2Q = 100$, and therefore $Q = 50$. Plugging $Q = 50$ back into either the demand or the supply equation, we can find that the equilibrium price is equal to $50.

The value of consumer surplus is equal to $(1/2)(\$100 \text{ per unit} - \$50 \text{ per unit})(50 \text{ units})$, or $1,250. The value of producer surplus is equal to $(1/2)(\$50 \text{ per unit} - \$0 \text{ per unit})(50 \text{ units})$, or $1,250. These areas are marked on the above graph.

STEP 2: Modify your graph from Step 1 by adding in a line that represents a world price for chocolate of $80 per unit.

Review the section "Supply, Demand, and International Trade" on pages 581–588, and Figure 19-8 on page 585.

STEP 3: Analyze the impact on this market if the world price is equal to $80 and Newville opens its chocolate market. Be sure to identify whether or not Newville will export or import chocolate. In addition, determine the impact of this decision on consumer and producer surplus. Finally, analyze whether trade is beneficial if the world price of chocolate is equal to $80 per unit.

Review the section "Supply, Demand, and International Trade" on pages 581–588, Figure 19-8, and Figure 19-9 on page 585.

When Newville opens its chocolate market to international trade and the world price of chocolate is $80 per unit, domestic suppliers will be willing to supply 80 units of the good, while domestic demanders are willing to buy only 20 units of the good. This excess supply of 60 units will therefore be exported into the world market for chocolate.

To find the consumer surplus, first recognize that it is the area that is under the domestic demand curve but above the world price for chocolate. Then, calculate the value of this area: consumer surplus is equal to (1/2)($100 per unit − $80 per unit)(20 units), or $200.

To find the producer surplus, first recognize that it is the area that is under the world price for chocolate but above the domestic supply curve. Then, calculate the value of this area: producer surplus is equal to (1/2)($80 per unit − $0 per unit)(80 units), or $3,200.

The following figure illustrates the impact on consumer and producer surplus when the world price is equal to $80 per unit.

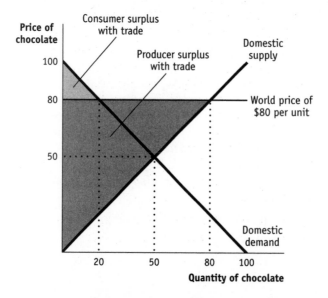

Trade is beneficial to Newville when the world price is $80 per unit since the value of total surplus, the sum of consumer and producer surplus in this case, is greater than the value of total surplus when Newville has a closed chocolate market.

STEP 4: **Redraw your graph from Step 1 and revise it by adding in a line that represents a world price for chocolate of $20 per unit.**

Review the section "Supply, Demand, and International Trade" on pages 581–588, and Figure 19-6 on page 583.

STEP 5: **Analyze the impact on this market if the world price is equal to $20 and Newville opens its chocolate market. Be sure to identify whether Newville will export or import chocolate. In addition, determine the impact of this decision on consumer and producer surplus. Finally, analyze whether trade is beneficial if the world price of chocolate is equal to $20 per unit.**

Review the section "Supply, Demand, and International Trade" on pages 581–588, Figure 19-6 on page 583, and Figure 19-7 on page 584.

When Newville opens its chocolate market to international trade and the world price of chocolate is $20 per unit, domestic suppliers will only be willing to supply 20 units of the good, while domestic demanders want to buy 80 units of the good. This excess demand of 60 units will be met by Newville's importing 60 units of chocolate from the world market.

To find the consumer surplus, first recognize that it is the area that is under the domestic demand curve but above the world price for chocolate. Then, calculate the value of this area: consumer surplus is equal to (1/2)($100 per unit – $20 per unit)(80 units), or $3,200.

To find the producer surplus, first recognize that it is the area that is under the world price for chocolate but above the domestic supply curve. Then, calculate the value of this area: producer surplus is equal to (1/2)($20 per unit – $0 per unit)(20 units), or $200.

The following figure illustrates the impact on consumer and producer surplus when the world price is equal to $20 per unit.

Trade is beneficial to Newville when the world price is $20 per unit since the value of total surplus, the sum of consumer and producer surplus in this case, is greater than the value of total surplus when Newville has a closed chocolate market.

STEP 6: Review your analysis in Step 3 to determine whether domestic demanders or domestic suppliers of chocolate will be more likely to favor opening the chocolate market to trade when the world price is $80 per unit.

Review the section "Supply, Demand, and International Trade" on pages 581–588, Figure 19-8 and Figure 19-9 on page 585.

Domestic producers will favor opening the chocolate market to trade when the world price is equal to $80 per unit, since they will be able to sell more units at a higher price. We can easily see the benefits to these producers by comparing the area of producer surplus when the economy is closed to trade (see Step 1) to the area of consumer surplus when the economy is open to trade and the world price is $80 (see Step 3). In contrast, domestic consumers of chocolate will be opposed to opening this market to trade, since their consumer surplus will shrink once the market is open to trade.

4. The small economy of Newville produces chocolate, and this market for chocolate is characterized by the following equations:

$$\text{Domestic demand for chocolate: } P = 100 - Q$$
$$\text{Domestic supply of chocolate: } P = Q$$

Furthermore, you know that the world price for chocolate is $20 per unit. Newville has decided to open its market for chocolate, and although recognizing that this will allow domestic consumers to consume more chocolate at lower prices, it has also determined that it will levy a tariff that raises the price of chocolate in Newville to $40 per unit. You are asked to compare the areas of consumer surplus with and without the tariff, the areas of producer surplus with and without the tariff, the amount of tax revenue the government of Newville will earn from this tariff, and the deadweight loss or efficiency cost of this tariff. The government of Newville has asked that you provide them with graphs that depict what happens if the market is opened to trade and what happens if this tariff is imposed.

STEP 1: Start by drawing a graph of the market for chocolate in Newville when its economy is closed to trade. Then, use the two equations to solve for the equilibrium price and quantity in this market. Once you have plotted the equilibrium price and quantity in your graph, you will then be able to use this graph to calculate the levels of consumer and producer surplus if there is no trade.

Review the section "Supply, Demand, and International Trade" on pages 581–588, and Figure 19-7 on page 584.

From Step 5 of problem 3, we can review the graph that represents this market if it opens to trade and the world price of chocolate is $20 per unit. In addition, we know from problem 3 that consumer surplus is equal to $3,200 and producer surplus is equal to $200.

STEP 2: Draw a graph of the market for chocolate in Newville showing the effect of a tariff that raises the price of chocolate to $40 per unit. In this graph, indicate the areas that represent consumer surplus, producer surplus, tariff revenue for the government, and deadweight loss from the tariff. Calculate the values of these different areas.

Review the section "Supply, Demand, and International Trade" on pages 581–588, Figure 19-7 on page 584, the section "The Effects of a Tariff" on pages 588–590, and Figure 19-11 on page 590.

The tariff raises the price of chocolate to $40 per unit. This increase in price will reduce the quantity of chocolate demanded by domestic consumers while increasing the quantity of chocolate supplied by domestic producers. When the price of chocolate is $40, domestic consumers demand 60 units while domestic producers are willing to provide 40 units. Newville will import that difference, or 20 units of chocolate. The government of Newville will collect $20 from every unit of chocolate that is imported and will therefore earn $400 in tariff revenue.

The deadweight loss for the tariff will equal $400. To find the area of deadweight loss, you first need to recognize that it is the sum of the areas of two triangles. Then, calculate the area of each triangle. From the following graph, we can see that the area of deadweight loss is equal to (1/2)($40/unit − $20/unit)(20 units) + (1/2)($40/unit − $20/unit)(20 units), or $400.

The following graph depicts the impact of this tariff on the market for chocolate in Newville.

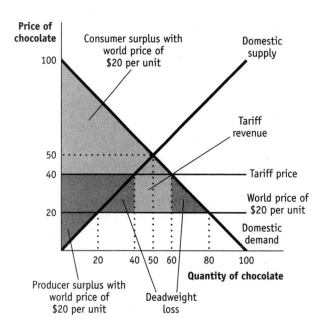

5. Suppose that Newville is still considering opening the market for chocolate that was described in problem 3, but is also now considering imposing a quota in the market once it is opened to trade. Suppose the government of Newville wishes to achieve the same outcome that it did with the tariff in problem 4, but now uses a quota instead. What limit on imported chocolate would achieve the same outcome as the tariff described in problem 4, and what should the government of Newville charge the importer for the license to bring these imported chocolates into the Newville economy?

STEP 1: Review the graph in Step 2 of problem 4 to determine how many units of the chocolate are imported into Newville when there is a tariff that raises the price of chocolate to $40. This amount of imports is the amount that the quota must be set at in order to achieve the same outcome as under the proposed tariff.

Review the section "The Effects of Trade Protection" on pages 588–592, and the section "The Effects of an Import Quota" on pages 590–591.

From the graph we can see that Newville imports 20 units of chocolate when the price of chocolate is raised to $40 per unit. Thus, if the government of Newville limits imports to 20 units, this will cause the price of chocolate to rise to $40 per unit, since it is only at this price that the difference between the quantity demanded domestically (60 units) and the quantity supplied domestically (40 units) is exactly equal to the amount of allowed imports (20 units).

STEP 2: Determine the price of the license for importing the chocolates by looking at the tariff revenue.

Review the section "The Effects of Trade Protection" on pages 588–592, and the section "The Effects of an Import Quota" on pages 590–591.

The tariff revenue represents the revenue the government receives when it places a tax on the imported good. With the quota, the government places a limit on how many units of the good can be imported, and it limits these imports by selling the right to bring the imports into the market. By selling the rights for the same price as the tariff revenue, the government imposes a quota limit that has exactly the same impact as the proposed tariff. The government of Newville should sell the rights to import chocolate for $20 per unit, or a total of $400 for all the rights.

6. Suppose a country runs a trade deficit, which implies that it imports more goods than it exports. Using the balance of payments, explain what this trade deficit implies about this country's financial accounts.

STEP 1: **Start by discussing the implications of a trade deficit on a country's current account.**

Review the section "Balance of Payments Accounts" on pages 592–596, and Figure 19-12 on page 591.

When a country runs a trade deficit, this implies that there is a positive balance in the current account for the rest of the world and a negative balance in the country's current account. The balance of payments reminds us that the total flow of funds into a country must equal the total flow of funds out of a country: thus, when the country runs a trade deficit, this implies that the current flow of funds out of the country is greater than the flow into the country if you only examine the current account, and this therefore implies that there must be some other source of funds flowing into the country.

STEP 2: **Connect the discussion of the country's current account in Step 1 to a discussion of the country's financial account.**

Review the section "Balance of Payments Accounts" on pages 592–596, and Figure 19-12 on page 591.

From Step 1, we know that the balance of payments requires that the flow of funds out of a country must equal the flow of funds into the country: when a country runs a trade deficit, this implies that it also is receiving payments from the rest of the world for assets. Another way of stating this is that the country that runs a trade deficit must also be receiving funds for the purchase of financial assets.

Problems and Exercises

1. Paula and Harry both produce lawn care and window washing services, and they both have an equal number of hours available to them each week to engage in providing these services. Paula is able to clean 1/2 of a window or care for 1 yard per hour, and Harry can clean 1 window or 1/2 of a yard per hour. Currently Paula and Harry divide their work time evenly between cleaning windows and doing yard work. Both Paula and Harry work forty hours a week.

   a. Suppose that Paula and Harry initially work independently of each other. Draw two graphs, with one graph illustrating Paula's production possibility frontier and the other graph illustrating Harry's production possibility frontier. Measure windows washed on the vertical axis and yards cared for on the horizontal axis.

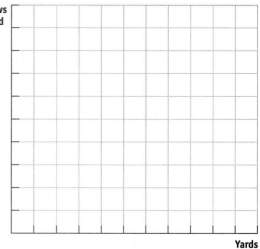

b. Who has the absolute advantage in performing yard care? Who has the absolute advantage in window washing?

c. Suppose both Paula and Harry divide their available time evenly between washing windows and doing yard care. Fill in the following table based on this assumption.

	Number of windows washed	Number of yards cared for
Paula		
Harry		
Total		

d. What is Paula's opportunity cost of washing a window? What is Paula's opportunity cost of caring for a yard?

e. What is Harry's opportunity cost of washing a window? What is Harry's opportunity cost of caring for a yard?

f. Who has the comparative advantage in washing windows? Who has the comparative advantage in caring for a yard? Explain your answers.

g. Assume that both Paula and Harry specialize according to comparative advantage and that both Paula and Harry produce only one type of good. Fill in the table below based on this specialization. What happens to total production of lawn care and window washing when Paula and Harry specialize according to their comparative advantage?

	Number of windows washed	Number of yards cared for
Paula		
Harry		
Total		

h. If both Harry and Paula specialize according to their comparative advantage and then trade with one another, what is the range of prices they will both accept for 1 washed window?

2. Titania and Phoenix are two countries that both produce steel and oats from their available resources. The production possibility frontiers for both countries are linear, and the following table provides information about the number of labor hours (the only resource either country uses in producing these two goods) it takes for each country to produce 1 unit of steel or 1 unit of oats. Assume that Titania and Phoenix both have 60 hours of labor available to produce either steel or oats or some combination of steel and oats.

	Number of labor hours needed to produce 1 unit of steel	Number of labor hours needed to produce 1 unit of oats
Titania	5	2
Phoenix	4	3

a. On two separate graphs, draw the production possibility frontiers for Titania and Phoenix. Place steel on the vertical axis and oats on the horizontal axis.

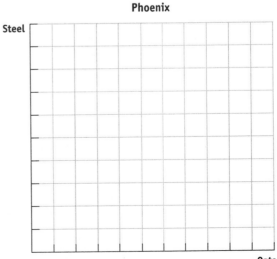

Titania

Steel

Oats

Phoenix

Steel

Oats

b. Which country has the absolute advantage in producing steel? Which country has the absolute advantage in producing oats?

c. What is the opportunity cost of producing 3 units of steel for Titania? What is the opportunity cost of producing 3 units of steel for Phoenix?

d. What is the opportunity cost of producing 5 units of oats for Titania? What is the opportunity cost of producing 5 units of oats for Phoenix?

e. Which country has the comparative advantage in producing steel? Which country has the comparative advantage in producing oats? Explain your answers.

f. Suppose that Titania and Phoenix both specialize according to their comparative advantage and then trade with one another. Furthermore, suppose that when they specialize these two countries only produce one type of good. What is the range of prices that steel will trade for once this specialization takes place? What is the range of prices that oats will trade for once this specialization takes place?

g. Titania proposes that Phoenix accept 1 unit of oats for 1 unit of steel. Will Phoenix agree to this trading price? Explain your answer.

3. Finlandia and Sweetland are two autarkies possessing equal resources. Both Finlandia and Sweetland produce two goods: food (*F*) and clothing (*C*). The table below provides information about the maximum amount of these two goods that these two countries can produce if they devote all of their resources to the production of just one good. Assume that the production possibility frontiers for both Finlandia and Sweetland are linear.

	Food	Clothing
Finlandia	1,000 units	2,000 units
Sweetland	600 units	1,800 units

a. On two separate graphs, draw Finlandia's and Sweetland's production possibility frontiers. Place units of food on the vertical axis and units of clothing on the horizontal axis.

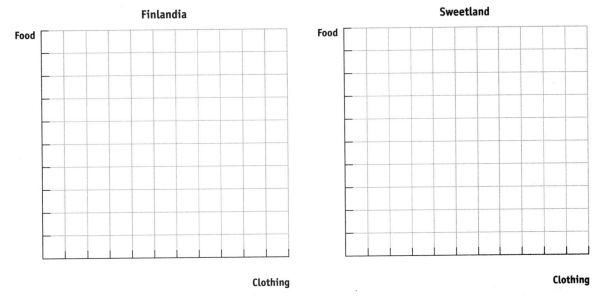

b. Both Finlandia and Sweetland currently produce at points that are located on their production possibility frontiers. Based on this information, fill in the table below. (Hint: You may find it helpful to write an equation for each country's production possibility frontier.)

	Food	Clothing
Finlandia	500 units	
Sweetland		900 units
Total production		

c. Suppose Finlandia and Sweetland open their economies to trade, but neither country fully understands the concept of comparative advantage. Suppose Finlandia and Sweetland adjust their production as given in the table below. Fill in the rest of the table assuming that both countries produce at points that are on their production possibility frontiers. Are Finlandia and Sweetland specializing according to their comparative advantage? Explain your answer.

	Food	Clothing
Finlandia	250 units	
Sweetland		390 units
Total production		

d. Finlandia and Sweetland alter their production once again in hopes of reaping the benefits of specialization and trade. Fill in the following table based on both countries producing on their production possibility frontiers.

	Food	Clothing
Finlandia		400 units
Sweetland		
Total production	892 units	

e. Given the production possibility choices Finlandia and Sweetland make in part (d), do these countries reap the advantages of specialization and trade?

4. Do you agree or disagree with the following statement: "Comparative advantage depends on the amount of resources used to produce a good." Explain your answer.

5. Do you agree or disagree with the following statement: "If two workers have different labor productivity, then their wage rates will usually differ from one another, with the worker with greater labor productivity earning a higher wage rate." Explain your answer.

6. What are the major sources of comparative advantage?

7. The Heckscher–Ohlin model predicts that a country has a comparative advantage in producing those goods whose production is intensive in the factors that are abundantly available in that country compared to other countries. What does the Heckscher–Ohlin model predict about factor prices for abundant resources versus less abundant resources? Explain your answer.

8. Use the following graph to answer this next set of questions. The graph depicts the domestic demand and domestic supply of bicycles in a small closed economy.

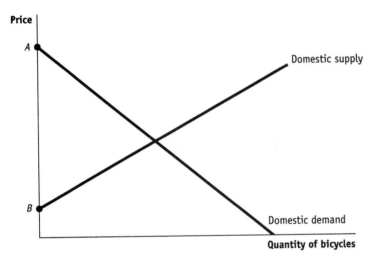

a. In the preceding graph, label the equilibrium price (P_e) and the equilibrium quantity (Q_e) for this autarky. Label the areas that correspond to producer surplus and consumer surplus.

b. Provide a mathematical expression for the areas of producer and consumer surplus based on the symbols and labels in the graph.

c. The same graph is replicated below, but this time the world price is also drawn on the graph. Suppose this autarky opens to trade. On the graph, indicate the quantity supplied domestically ($Q_{S_{dom}}$) and the quantity demanded domestically ($Q_{D_{dom}}$) when this country opens to trade. Identify how many bicycles this country will import or export when it opens its economy to trade.

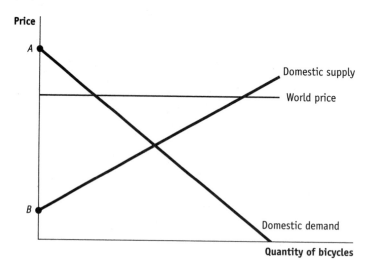

d. On the graph in part (c), label the areas that correspond to producer surplus with trade and consumer surplus with trade. Who benefits in this example from trade? Explain your answer.

e. The initial graph is replicated below, but this time the world price is also drawn on the graph. Suppose this autarky opens to trade. On the graph, indicate the quantity supplied domestically ($Q_{S_{dom}}$) and the quantity demanded domestically ($Q_{D_{dom}}$) when this country opens to trade. Identify how many bicycles this country will import or export when it opens its economy to trade.

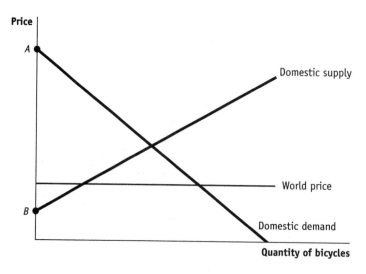

f. On the graph in part (e), label the areas that correspond to producer surplus with trade and consumer surplus with trade. Who benefits in this example from trade? Explain your answer.

9. Suppose the market for TVs in the small closed economy of Kennet can be described by the following domestic demand curve and domestic supply curve:

$$\text{Domestic demand: } Q = 1{,}000 - (1/2)P$$
$$\text{Domestic supply: } Q = (1/2)P$$

(Hint: For this question you will find it helpful to sketch graphs of the market.)

a. What is the equilibrium price and quantity in the market for TVs in Kennet? What is the value of consumer surplus, producer surplus, and total surplus?

b. Suppose Kennet opens to trade and the world price for TVs is $1,200. What is the quantity supplied domestically, the quantity demanded domestically, and the number of TVs imported into or exported out of Kennet, given this world price? What happens to the value of consumer surplus, producer surplus, and total surplus when Kennet opens to trade?

c. Given the information and the analysis you did in part (b), who benefits from trade in the television market when Kennet opens its economy? Explain your answer.

d. Suppose Kennet's economy is still open to trade, but domestic demand in Kennet has significantly increased so that at every price domestic demand is now 500 units higher than it was initially. Although domestic demand in Kennet has increased, this has not impacted the world price for TVs since Kennet is a small economy. Given this change in demand, how many TVs will be domestically supplied and domestically demanded? Will Kennet import or export TVs? Calculate the numeric value of Kennet's imports or exports. What is the value of consumer surplus, producer surplus, and total surplus given this change in demand? (Hint: You will find it helpful to draw a sketch of these changes in the market for TVs and to calculate the new domestic demand equation.)

10. Pepperville is a small economy that currently operates as an autarky. In the market for green peppers, domestic demand and domestic supply can be represented as $P = 5,000 - 0.5Q$ and $P = 1.5Q$, respectively, where P is the price per ton of green peppers and Q is the quantity of green peppers measured in tons.

    a. Identify the equilibrium price and quantity of green peppers in Pepperville. What is the value of consumer surplus and producer surplus?

    b. The current world price of green peppers is $3,000 per ton, and domestic producers of green peppers are lobbying the government of Pepperville to remain an autarky. Explain why domestic producers of green peppers are not in favor of open trade in the green pepper market.

    c. Domestic consumers of green peppers in Pepperville successfully lobby the Pepperville government to open trade in the green pepper market. How many tons of green peppers will be imported into or exported out of Pepperville, given the world price of $3,000 per ton when this market opens to trade? What is the value of consumer surplus and producer surplus with trade?

    Domestic producers wage a successful campaign to enact a tariff in the market for green peppers. The tariff effectively raises the price of green peppers to $3,450 per ton. Answer questions (d) through (g) based on this tariff. Assume the world price for green peppers is unchanged and equal to $3,000 per ton.

    d. How many tons of green peppers will be imported into Pepperville once this tariff is enacted?

    e. What is the value of consumer surplus and producer surplus once this tariff is implemented?

    f. What is the tariff revenue the government earns with this tariff?

g. What is the deadweight loss associated with this tariff?

h. Pepperville is considering replacing the tariff on green peppers with a quota. If consumer surplus and producer surplus are to remain the same under the quota as they are with the tariff, what must the amount of the quota equal?

i. From the domestic consumers' perspective, which trade policy—closed economy, open economy, or open economy with a tariff or quota—would they prefer? Explain your answer.

j. From the domestic producers' perspective, which trade policy—closed economy, open economy, or open economy with a tariff or quota—would they prefer? Explain your answer.

k. Given your answers in (i) and (j), why do governments frequently adopt tariffs or quotas in particular markets?

11. Evansville is a small closed economy. The domestic demand curve for shoes is given by the equation $P = 200 - Q$, where P is the price for a pair of shoes and Q is the quantity of pairs of shoes demanded. The domestic supply curve for shoes is given by the equation $P = 10 + Q$. Currently the world price of shoes is \$40 a pair. Evansville is considering opening its economy to trade, and the government is debating three possible trade positions. Option I is to open the economy to trade with no trade protection intervention in the market. Option II is to open the economy to trade but limit the amount of pairs of shoes imported to a quota of 50 pairs of shoes. Option III is to open the economy to trade but impose a tariff on the shoe market that would increase the price of shoes to \$80 a pair.

a. Analyze these three policies and enter your findings in the following table.

	Option I	Option II	Option III
Pairs of shoes imported			
Consumer surplus			
Producer surplus			
Tariff revenue or quota rent			
Deadweight loss			

   b. From the perspective of domestic consumers, which is the best option?

   c. From the perspective of domestic producers, which is the best option?

   d. Which option results in the greatest efficiency cost? Explain your answer.

12. Use the following table of information to answer this question.

	Payments from foreigners (millions of dollars)	Payments to foreigners (millions of dollars)	Sales of assets to foreigners (millions of dollars)	Purchases of assets from foreigners (millions of dollars)
Goods	$200	$80	—	—
Services	50	20	—	—
Factor income	70	10	—	—
Transfer payments	10	20	—	—
Official sales and purchases	—	—	$100	$300
Private sales and purchases	—	—	80	80

   a. Provide a definition or an equation for each of the following items.
      (i.) Merchandise trade balance

    (ii.) Balance of payments on goods and services

    (iii.) Net international factor income

    (iv.) Net international transfer payments

    (v.) Balance of payments on current account

    (vi.) Balance of payments on financial account

b. Given the previous information, compute the value of each of the terms given in part (a).

c. Explain why the sum of the balance of payments on current account and the balance of payments on financial account must equal zero.

13. a. Calculate the missing values in the following table.

	U.S. dollars	Funland dollars	Macroland dollars
1 U.S. dollar exchanged for			1.05
1 Funland dollar exchanged for	0.005		
1 Macroland dollar exchanged for			

Suppose that the above exchange rates change as shown in the following table.

	U.S. dollars	Funland dollars	Macroland dollars
1 U.S. dollar exchanged for	1	210	
1 Funland dollar exchanged for		1	
1 Macroland dollar exchanged for	1.02		1

b. Fill in the missing values for this table.

c. Which currencies appreciated against the U.S. dollar?

d. Which currencies depreciated against the U.S. dollar?

e. Holding everything else constant, what do you expect will happen to the level of U.S. exports to Funland?

f. Holding everything else constant, what do you expect will happen to the level of U.S. exports to Macroland?

14. Suppose you are shown the information in the following table. Assume net international transfers and factor income equal zero for this problem.

Funland purchases of Macroland dollars in the foreign exchange market to buy Macroland goods and services	3.0 million Macroland dollars
Funland total purchases in the foreign exchange market of Macroland dollars	5.0 million Macroland dollars
Macroland sales of Macroland dollars in the foreign exchange market to buy Funland assets	1.5 million Macroland dollars
Macroland sales of Macroland dollars in the foreign exchange market to buy Funland goods and services	3.5 million Macroland dollars

a. Given the information in this table, compute the values in the following table.

Funland purchases of Macroland dollars in the foreign exchange market to buy Macroland assets	=	_____
Total sales of Macroland dollars in the foreign exchange market	=	_____
Macroland balance of payments on current account	=	_____
Macroland balance of payments on financial account	=	_____

Suppose that the capital flows to Macroland from Funland decrease and this causes Macroland's currency to depreciate against Funland's currency, holding everything else constant.

b. How will this affect the demand and supply of Macroland dollars in the foreign exchange market? Use the following graph to illustrate your answer.

Exchange rate
(Funland dollars
per Macroland
dollar)

Quantity of
Macroland dollars

c. How will this depreciation affect Macroland's balance of payments on current account? Explain your answer.

d. How will this depreciation affect Macroland's balance of payments on financial account? Explain your answer.

15. Suppose initially the nominal exchange rate is 20 Macroland dollars per 1 Funland dollar, and the aggregate price index in both countries has a value of 100.

   a. What is the real exchange rate expressed as Macroland dollars per Funland dollar?

   b. Suppose the real exchange rate increases to 25 Macroland dollars per Funland dollar when the aggregate price index in Funland increases to 150. Assuming the nominal exchange rate is unchanged, what is the aggregate price index in Macroland?

   c. Suppose the aggregate price index in Funland is 150 and the aggregate price index in Macroland is 125. If the nominal exchange rate increases to 25 Macroland dollars per Funland dollar, what is the real exchange rate?

   d. If the real exchange rate measured as Macroland dollars per Funland dollar increases, holding everything else constant, what happens to the level of exports and imports in Macroland?

16. Suppose that currently the cost of a standardized market basket in Macroland is 300 Macroland dollars, while the same market basket in Funland costs 150 Funland dollars.

   a. If purchasing power parity holds for the two countries, what must the nominal exchange rate, expressed as Macroland dollars per Funland dollar, equal? Explain your answer.

   b. If the actual nominal exchange rate equals 4 Macroland dollars per 1 Funland dollar, what do you expect will happen to the nominal exchange rate over the long run, holding everything else constant? Explain your answer.

17. Consider each of the following transactions and identify how the transaction would be categorized in the U.S. balance of payments accounts. For each transaction identify whether it would be counted as part of the balance of payments in the current account or the financial account. Lastly, identify whether the transaction will increase or decrease the relevant account.

   a. An American company purchases machinery that is produced in Germany by a German company.

b. An American donates money to the foreign group organizing an international sporting event in another country.

c. A French citizen purchases cheese produced in the United States.

d. An American purchases 100 shares of a Swiss company.

■ BEFORE YOU TAKE THE TEST

Chapter Review Questions

1. International trade based on comparative advantage is
   a. beneficial to some of the countries involved in the trade, but not beneficial to other countries.
   b. beneficial to all of the countries involved in the trade.
   c. rarely benefits any of the countries involved in the trade.
   d. only beneficial to relatively rich countries.

2. Sarah purchases wine from France, cheese from Italy, wheat crackers from Minnesota, potatoes from Idaho, and lamb from Australia. Sarah lives in New York.
   a. Sarah purchases imports of wine, cheese, and lamb.
   b. Sarah purchases only domestically produced goods, since she can purchase all of these goods at her local grocery store.
   c. The wine, cheese, and lamb represent exports from the perspective of the United States.
   d. Answers (a) and (c) are both true.

Use the following information to answer the next seven questions. The table below gives information about the production possibility frontiers for two countries, Smallville and Gooseville, that each produce two types of goods, bicycles and cheese. Two possible production points on each country's production possibility frontier are given in the table. Both countries have linear production possibility frontiers.

	Bicycles	Tons of cheese
Smallville	1,000	0
Smallville	0	2,000
Gooseville	1,500	0
Gooseville	0	1,500

3. Suppose that Smallville and Gooseville have the same amount of resources and technology. Which of the following statements is true?
   a. Smallville has the absolute advantage in producing bicycles, and Gooseville has the absolute advantage in producing cheese.
   b. Smallville has the absolute advantage in producing bicycles and cheese.
   c. Gooseville has the absolute advantage in producing bicycles and cheese.
   d. Smallville has the absolute advantage in producing cheese, and Gooseville has the absolute advantage in producing bicycles.

4. The opportunity cost of producing one more bicycle in Smallville is
   a. greater than the opportunity cost of producing one more bicycle in Gooseville.
   b. less than the opportunity cost of producing one more bicycle in Gooseville.
   c. equal to 2 tons of cheese.
   d. Answers (a) and (c) are correct.
   e. Answers (b) and (c) are correct.

5. Suppose that both countries are in autarky and do not engage in trade. In autarky, both countries choose to produce at the midpoint of their production possibility frontiers. Total cheese production is equal to _____ and total bicycle production is equal to

   _____.
   a. 1,750 tons of cheese; 1,750 bicycles
   b. 1,750 tons of cheese; 1,250 bicycles
   c. 1,250 tons of cheese; 1,750 bicycles
   d. 1,250 tons of cheese; 1,250 bicycles

6. Suppose that both countries decide to specialize according to their comparative advantage and trade with one another. Then
   a. Smallville will produce cheese and Gooseville will produce bicycles.
   b. Smallville will produce bicycles and Goosevillle will produce cheese.

7. When the two countries specialize according to their comparative advantage and then trade with one another, the price of a bicycle measured in terms of cheese will be
   a. less than 1/2 ton of cheese.
   b. greater than 1 ton of cheese.
   c. between 1 ton of cheese and 2 tons of cheese.
   d. between 1/2 ton of cheese and 1 ton of cheese.

8. Suppose both countries specialize according to their comparative advantage and then trade. Which of the following represents the maximum possible amount of total production given this specialization?
   a. 3,500 tons of cheese and 2,500 bicycles
   b. 2,500 tons of cheese and 2,500 bicycles
   c. 2,000 tons of cheese and 1,500 bicycles
   d. 1,750 tons of cheese and 1,250 bicycles

9. When a production possibility frontier is linear, this implies that
   a. the opportunity cost of producing either of the two goods represented is constant and does not change.
   b. the country will have both a comparative and an absolute advantage in producing both of the goods depicted relative to its trading partner.
   c. trade of either good to other countries will always be beneficial for this country.
   d. this country cannot have a comparative advantage in the production of either good.

10. When a country does not engage in trade with other countries, this is referred to as
    a. independence.
    b. autarky.
    c. Ricardian economics.
    d. Heckscher–Ohlin economics.

11. Which of the following statements is(are) true?
    I. Gains from trade depend on absolute advantage.
    II. Comparative advantage depends on the amount of resources used to produce a good.
    III. A country's comparative advantage is translated into world markets through its wage rates: a country's wage rate typically reflects that country's labor productivity.
    a. Statement I is true.
    b. Statement II is true.
    c. Statement III is true.
    d. Statements I, II, and III are true.
    e. Statements II and III are true.

12. Which of the following situations illustrates one of the three sources of comparative advantage?
    a. A country produces olives that can only grow in a Mediterranean climate.
    b. A country specializes in producing medical equipment whose production relies on the use of highly productive labor resources.
    c. A country in the southern hemisphere specializes in providing grapes to the northern hemisphere during the winter season.
    d. A country uses its extensive network of fiber-optic cable to produce information technology for countries located throughout the world.
    e. All of the above answers illustrate at least one of the sources of comparative advantage.

13. Which of the following statements is *not* supported by the Heckscher–Ohlin model?
    a. A country specializes in producing the good whose production is intensive in the factors that are abundantly available in that country compared to other countries.
    b. After they specialize, countries find that those factors that are relatively scarce in their country compared to other countries command higher factor prices than those factors that are relatively abundant in their country.
    c. Countries that are labor abundant produce goods that are labor intensive relative to countries that are less labor abundant.
    d. Countries that are capital abundant produce goods that are capital intensive relative to countries that are less capital abundant.

14. Which of the following statements is(are) true?

    I. Countries with highly skilled labor will tend to import goods whose production requires high levels of human capital.

    II. Countries whose exporting industries focus on using a higher ratio of highly educated workers to other workers are human capital intensive.

    III. Countries will find that their exporting industries utilize their relatively more abundant factors of production.

    a. Statement I is true.   d. Statements I and II are true.

    b. Statement II is true.   e. Statements II and III are true.

    c. Statement III is true.   f. Statements I, II, and III are true.

Use the following graph to answer the next four questions. The graph shows the market for bicycles for the country of Pedalland. The demand curve indicates the domestic demand for bicycles and the supply curve indicates the domestic supply of bicycles.

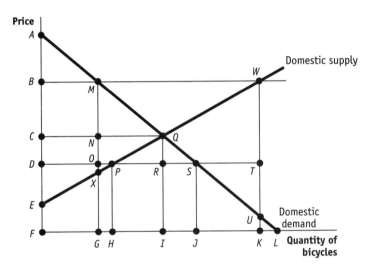

15. Suppose Pedalland is initially an autarky. In the graph, the area that corresponds to consumer surplus is equal to area _____, and the area that corresponds to producer surplus is equal to area _____.

    a. *ACQ; CQIF*   c. *ACQ; CQE*

    b. *ADS; DPE*   d. *BMNC; CNOD*

16. Suppose this country opens to trade and that the world price is equal to *B* in the above graph. Then we know that Pedalland will

    a. import the number of bicycles represented by the distance between points *M* and *W*.

    b. import the number of bicycles represented by the distance between points *W* and *T*.

    c. export the number of bicycles represented by the distance between points *M* and *W*.

    d. export the number of bicycles represented by the distance between points *W* and *T*.

17. Suppose this country opens to trade and that the world price is equal to *D* in the above graph. Then we know that Pedalland will import the number of bicycles represented by the distance between points

    a. *R* and *S*.   c. *P* and *R*.

    b. *P* and *S*.   d. *P* and *T*.

18. Suppose this country opens to trade and that the world price is equal to B in the above graph. Consumer surplus is equal to area _____, and producer surplus is equal to area _____.

a. *ABM; BWE*

b. *ABM; BMNE*

c. *ACNM; CNXE*

d. *ABM; BMQE*

Use the following graph to answer the next four questions. The graph shows the market for bicycles for the country of Pedalland. The demand curve indicates the domestic demand for bicycles, and the supply curve indicates the domestic supply of bicycles.

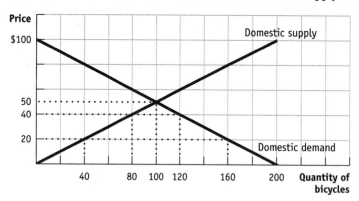

19. The world price in this market equals $20. If the market opens to trade,

a. Pedalland will import 120 bicycles, and the area of total surplus will increase by $6,800.

b. Pedalland will export 120 bicycles, and the area of total surplus will increase by $6,800.

c. Pedalland will import 120 bicycles, and the area of total surplus will increase by $1,800.

d. Pedalland will export 120 bicycles, and the area of total surplus will increase by $1,800.

20. Suppose the world price for bicycles is $20 and Pedalland opens its bicycle market to trade. Domestic producers successfully lobby the government of Pedalland, and the government imposes a quota on the number of bicycles that can be imported into Pedalland. Suppose license-holder revenue from the quota is equal to $800. Which of the following is(are) possible quota limits that result in this license-holder revenue?

a. 20 bicycles.

b. 40 bicycles.

c. 60 bicycles.

d. 80 bicycles.

e. Answers (b) and (d) are both possible answers.

21. Suppose the world price of bicycles is $20 and Pedalland opens to trade. Domestic producers of bicycles in Pedalland successfully lobby for a tariff on imported bicycles, which results in the price of bicycles being $40. The deadweight loss associated with this tariff is equal to

a. $400.

b. $800.

c. $1,600.

d. $2,000.

22. The world price of bicycles is $20 and Pedalland opens its economy to trade. A quota of 60 bicycles is imposed in Pedalland. This will result in consumer surplus increasing by _____ relative to the level of consumer surplus when Pedalland was an autarky.
    a. $1,725
    b. $2,500
    c. $4,225
    d. $6,725

23. A country that engages in international trade will find that this international trade increases the demand for the factors used by the exporting industries and decreases the demand for the factors used in the import-competing industries.
    a. True
    b. False

24. Which of the following statements is true?
    a. The balance of payments on goods and services is the difference between the value of imports and the value of exports during a given period.
    b. The merchandise trade balance includes the sale of goods as well as financial assets.
    c. A country's international transactions are tracked by the balance of payments accounts.
    d. Answers (a), (b), and (c) are all correct.
    e. Answers (a) and (c) are both correct.
    f. Answers (b) and (c) are both correct.

25. The balance of payments on goods and services plus net international transfer payments and net international factor income
    a. equals the merchandise trade balance.
    b. equals the balance of payments on current account.
    c. equals the balance of payments on financial account.
    d. plus the balance of payments on financial account equals zero.
    e. Answers (a) and (c) are both correct.
    f. Answers (b) and (c) are both correct.
    g. Answers (b) and (d) are both correct.

26. For a hypothetical economy, if the balance of payments on financial account equals –$100 million, then the balance of payments on current account must
    a. equal –$100 million.
    b. be greater than –$100 million.
    c. be less than –$100 million.
    d. equal $100 million.

27. The balance of payments tracks the
    a. flow of payments into a country from the rest of the world as well as the flow of payments from the country to the rest of the world.
    b. flow of payments for goods and services, factor income, and transfers in the balance of payments on current account.
    c. flow of payments for assets in the balance of payments on financial account.
    d. Answers (a), (b), and (c) are all correct.

28. Which of the following statements is true?

    a. A country that receives capital inflows will have a matching financial account surplus.

    b. The exchange rate is always measured as the price of a dollar in terms of the foreign currency.

    c. The more euros it takes to buy a dollar, the fewer dollars Europeans will supply.

    d. When a country's currency appreciates, exports fall and imports rise.

29. Suppose a U.S dollar trades for 0.9 euro. Which of the following statements is true?

    a. A euro trades for $1.11.

    b. If the exchange rate changes to 1 U.S. dollar in exchange for 0.95 euro, then the euro has appreciated.

    c. If the exchange rate changes to 1 U.S. dollar in exchange for 0.95 euro, then the dollar has appreciated.

    d. When the exchange rate changes to 0.95 euro per dollar, the United States will export more goods to European Union countries.

    e. Answers (a), (b), and (d) are all correct.

    f. Answers (a), (c), and (d) are all correct.

    g. Answers (a) and (b) are both correct.

    h. Answers (a) and (c) are both correct.

30. An increase in capital inflows into a country, holding everything else constant, will

    a. result in an increase in net exports for the country.

    b. result in a decrease in net exports for the country.

    c. result in an increase in the balance of payments on financial account for the country and an equal and opposite reaction in the balance of payments on current account.

    d. Answers (a) and (c) are both correct.

    e. Answers (b) and (c) are both correct.

Answer the next two questions using the following information. Suppose the aggregate price level for a given market basket of goods in Macroland is 125, while the aggregate price level for the same market basket of goods in Funland is 150. Suppose that currently the exchange rate is 10 Macroland dollars for 1 Funland dollar.

31. Given the previous information, what is the real exchange rate initially?

    a. 10 Macroland dollars for 1 Funland dollar

    b. 1 Macroland dollar for 10 Funland dollars

    c. 1 Macroland dollar for 1 Funland dollar

    d. 10 Macroland dollars for 10 Funland dollars

    e. 12 Macroland dollars for 1 Funland dollar

32. If the aggregate price level of the market basket in Macroland increases to 150, what must the exchange rate be in order for the real exchange rate to be unchanged from its initial level?

    a. 10 Macroland dollars for 1 Funland dollar

    b. 1 Macroland dollar for 10 Funland dollars

    c. 1 Macroland dollar for 1 Funland dollar

    d. 10 Macroland dollars for 10 Funland dollars

    e. 12 Macroland dollars for 1 Funland dollar

33. When the purchasing power parity rate is greater than the nominal exchange rate, then over time we can expect the

a. purchasing power parity to fall.

b. purchasing power parity to rise.

c. nominal exchange rate to rise.

d. nominal exchange rate to fall.

34. Which of the following statements is true?

a. When a country's currency undergoes a real depreciation, this causes exports to fall and imports to rise.

b. Nominal exchange rates almost always equal the purchasing power parity rate.

c. The current account is affected by changes in the nominal exchange rate as well as the real exchange rate.

d. None of the statements is true.

35. Which of the following represents a payment from foreigners to the hypothetical economy called Macropedia?

a. the dollar value of corn that Macropedia imports from Cornucopia

b. the dollar value of bicycles that Macropedia exports to Pedalland

c. the fees that engineering firms in Macropedia receive for bridge designs they provide to the foreign country of Islandville

d. the fees that companies in Macropedia pay to Islandville in compensation for the financial services Islandville provides

e. Answers (a), (b), (c), and (d) all represent payments from foreigners to Macropedia.

f. Answers (b) and (c) both represent payments from foreigners to Macropedia.

g. Answers (a) and (d) both represent payments from foreigners to Macropedia.

36. Which of the following statements is(are) true?

I. The sum of the balance of payments on current account (*CA*) and the balance of payments on financial account (*FA*) must equal zero.

II. The balance of payments accounts illustrate the concept that the flow of funds into a country's economy must equal the flow of funds out of that country's economy.

III. A country that imports more than it exports must by definition have negative capital inflows.

a. Statements I, II, and III are all true.

b. Statements I and II are both true.

c. Statements I and III are both true.

d. Statements II and III are both true.

37. Suppose that currently the exchange rate is 1 U.S. dollar to 5 Mexican pesos. If the exchange rate changes to 1 U.S. dollar for 10 Mexican pesos, then the peso has

a. appreciated against the dollar.

b. depreciated against the dollar.

38. Suppose there are only two currencies in the world: the U.S. dollar and the Mexican peso. Furthermore, suppose that the foreign exchange market for U.S. dollars is initially in equilibrium. If the demand for U.S. dollars increases, holding everything else constant, this will result in a movement along the supply of U.S. dollars curve and

a. an increase in the peso–U.S. dollar exchange rate.

b. a decrease in the peso–U.S. dollar exchange rate.

39. Holding everything else constant, if the U.S. dollar rises against the Mexican peso, then
   a. U.S. goods will look cheaper to Mexico.
   b. U.S. goods will look more expensive to Mexico.
   c. Mexico's goods will look cheaper to the United States.
   d. Mexico's goods will look more expensive to the United States.
   e. Answers (a) and (d) are both correct.
   f. Answers (b) and (c) are both correct.

ANSWER KEY

Answers to Problems and Exercises

1. a.

b. Paula has the absolute advantage in yard care since she can clean more yards than Harry with the same amount of resources (40 yards versus 20 yards), and Harry has the absolute advantage in window washing since he can wash more windows than Paula with the same amount of resources (40 windows versus 20 windows).

c.

	Number of windows washed	Number of yards cared for
Paula	10	20
Harry	20	10
Total	30	30

d. Paula's opportunity cost of washing a window is 2 yards cared for, since she must give up caring for 2 yards to free up enough resources to clean 1 window. Her opportunity cost of caring for a yard is 1/2 of a window washed since she must give up washing 1/2 of a window to free up enough resources to care for a yard.

e. Harry's opportunity cost of washing a window is 1/2 of a yard cared for, since he must give up caring for 1/2 of a yard to free up enough resources to clean 1 window. His opportunity cost of caring for a yard is 2 windows washed since he must give up washing 2 windows to free up enough resources to care for a yard.

f. Harry has the comparative advantage in washing windows, and Paula has the comparative advantage in caring for yards. Harry's opportunity cost of washing 1 window is only 1/2 of a yard, and Paula's opportunity cost of washing 1 window is 2 yards, so Harry can produce a washed window at a lower opportunity cost than can Paula. Paula's opportunity cost of caring for 1 yard is 1/2 of a window washed, and Harry's opportunity cost of caring for 1 yard is 2 windows washed, so Paula can care for a yard at a lower opportunity cost than can Harry.

g.

	Number of windows washed	Number of yards cared for
Paula	40	0
Harry	0	40
Total	40	40

Through specialization according to comparative advantage, total production of both goods increases.

h. The range of prices for 1 window washed falls between 1/2 of a yard cared for and 2 yards cared for. Paula is willing to trade up to 2 yards cared for to get a single window washed, while Harry is willing to wash a single window provided he is compensated by 1/2 of a yard cared for.

2. a.

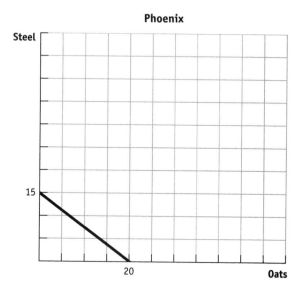

b. Phoenix has the absolute advantage in producing steel since, from the same amount of resources, Phoenix can absolutely produce more units of the good than can Titania. Titania has the absolute advantage in producing oats since, from the same amount of resources, Titania can absolutely produce more units of the good than can Phoenix.

c. The opportunity cost of producing 3 units of steel for Titania is equal to 7.5 units of oats. From the graph, the slope of the production possibility frontier for Titania is –2/5, which implies that the opportunity cost of Titania producing 1 unit of oats is 2/5 unit of steel. We can take the reciprocal of this measure and get that the opportunity cost of 1 unit of steel is equal to 5/2 units of oats. But since we want to know the opportunity cost of 3 units of steel, we need to multiply the 5/2 units of oats by 3 to get 15/2 units of oats, or 7.5 units of oats. The opportunity cost of producing 3 units of steel for Phoenix is equal to 4 units of oats. From the graph, the slope of the production possibility frontier for Phoenix is –3/4, which implies that the opportunity cost of Phoenix producing 1 unit of oats is 3/4 unit of steel. We can take the reciprocal of this measure and get that the opportunity cost of 1 unit of steel is equal to 4/3 units of oats. But since we want to know the opportunity cost of 3 units of steel, we need to multiply the 4/3 units of oats by 3 to get 12/3 units of oats, or 4 units of oats.

d. The opportunity cost of producing 5 units of oats for Titania is 2 units of steel, and the opportunity cost of producing 5 units of oats for Phoenix is 3.75 units of steel.

e. Titania has the comparative advantage in producing oats, while Phoenix has the comparative advantage in producing steel. Titania's opportunity cost of producing 1 unit of oats is 2/5 unit of steel, and Phoenix's opportunity cost of producing 1 unit of oats is 3/4 unit of steel, so Titania can produce oats at lower opportunity cost than can Phoenix. Titania's opportunity cost of producing 1 unit of steel is 5/2 units of oats, and Phoenix's opportunity cost of producing 1 unit of steel is 4/3 units of oats, so Phoenix can produce steel at lower opportunity cost than can Titania.

f. One unit of steel will trade for between 4/3 units of oats to 5/2 units of oats, and 1 unit of oats will trade for between 2/3 units of steel and 3/4 units of steel.

g. No, Phoenix is only willing to trade 1 unit of steel if the price is at least 4/3 units of oats.

3. a.

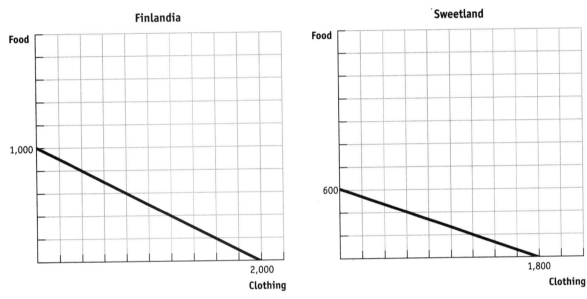

b. The equation for Finlandia's production possibility frontier is $F = 1{,}000 - (1/2)C$. When $F = 500$ units, then $C = 1{,}000$ units. The equation for Sweetland's production possibility frontier is $F = 600 - (1/3)C$. When $C = 900$ units, then $F = 300$ units.

	Food	Clothing
Finlandia	500 units	1,000 units
Sweetland	300 units	900 units
Total production	800 units	1,900 units

c. Use the equations you calculated in part (b) to fill in the table.

	Food	Clothing
Finlandia	250 units	1,500 units
Sweetland	470 units	390 units
Total production	720 units	1,890 units

Finlandia and Sweetland are not specializing according to their comparative advantage since their total production of the two goods has fallen as they altered their production.

d.

	Food	Clothing
Finlandia	800 units	400 units
Sweetland	92 units	1,524 units
Total production	892 units	1,924 units

e. Yes, by specializing according to their comparative advantage and then trading, the total level of production of the two goods increases.

4. Disagree. Comparative advantage depends on the opportunity cost of producing the good rather than the amount of resources used to produce the good.

5. Agree. Workers with lower labor productivity will earn a lower wage than workers with higher labor productivity since the competition for less-productive workers is less intense, resulting in a lower wage rate.

6. The major sources of comparative advantage are differences in climate, differences in factor endowments, and differences in technology between countries.

7. The Heckscher–Ohlin model predicts that factors of production that are abundant in a country that trades with other countries will command higher factor prices than factors of production that are less abundant. This is the result of the country's specialization in the production of the good whose production is intensive in the abundant factors of production. This specialization increases the demand for these factors and therefore increases the price of these factors.

8. a.

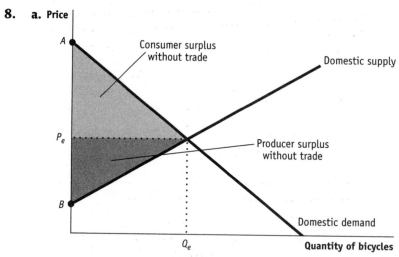

b. Consumer surplus $= (1/2)(A - P_e)(Q_e)$
Producer surplus $= (1/2)(P_e - B)(Q_e)$

c.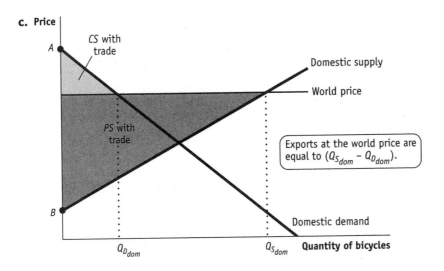

d. Domestic producers benefit from this trade because they can produce more units of the good and sell each unit at a higher price relative to the initial autarky equilibrium. Compare the graphs from part (a) and part (c) and note that the area of producer surplus is larger with trade than without trade.

e.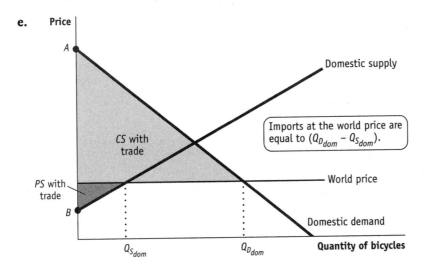

f. Domestic consumers benefit from this trade because they can consume more units of the good and purchase the good at a lower price relative to the initial autarky equilibrium. Compare the graphs from part (a) and part (e) and note that the area of consumer surplus is larger with trade than without trade.

9. a. Here is a sketch of Kennet's market for TVs.

The equilibrium price is $1,000 and the equilibrium quantity is 500 TVs. Consumer surplus is equal to $250,000; producer surplus is equal to $250,000; and total surplus is equal to $500,000.

b. When Kennet opens to trade, it will buy and sell TVs at the world price since it is a small economy. Since $1,200 is greater than the domestic equilibrium price when Kennet is a closed economy, domestic demand will fall and domestic supply will increase. The quantity demanded domestically will equal 400 TVs, and the quantity supplied domestically will equal 600 TVs. Kennet will export the excess supply of 200 TVs. Consumer surplus with trade will decrease to $160,000 while producer surplus with trade will increase to $360,000; total surplus with trade will increase to $520,000. The sketch below illustrates this answer.

c. Domestic producers of TVs benefit from trade when Kennet opens its economy, because trade increases their producer surplus and decreases consumer surplus. The gain to producers is greater than the loss to consumers, so the net gain from trade is positive.

d. The sketch below provides a helpful guide to solving this problem.

The equation for the new domestic demand curve is $Q = 1,500 - (1/2)P$. The domestic supply curve is still $Q = (1/2)P$. Use these two equations to analyze the effect on this market of the increase in domestic demand for TVs. At a world price of $1,200, the domestic demand for TVs is 900 while the domestic supply of TVs is 600. Kennet will import 300 TVs to meet this excess demand. Consumer surplus will now equal $810,000; producer surplus will equal $360,000; and total surplus will equal $1,170,000.

10. a. The equilibrium price of green peppers is $3,750 per ton, and the equilibrium quantity of green peppers in Pepperville is 2,500 tons. Consumer surplus is equal to $1,562,500 and producer surplus is equal to $4,687,500.

b. Domestic producers are currently selling 2,500 tons of green peppers at a price of $3,750 per ton. If the market opens to trade, each ton of peppers will sell for a lower price: domestic producers will sell fewer tons of peppers as the price falls (2,000 tons instead of 2,500 tons), and they will receive a lower price per ton than they do when the green pepper market is closed ($3,000 versus $3,750).

c. When the green pepper market is open to trade, the domestic demand for green peppers at $3,000 per ton is equal to 4,000 tons of green peppers. At a price of $3,000 per ton, the domestic quantity supplied is equal to 2,000 tons of green peppers. There is an excess demand for peppers when Pepperville opens to trade, and this excess demand will result in Pepperville importing green peppers to make up the difference between the amount domestically supplied and the amount domestically demanded. Pepperville will import 2,000 tons of green peppers. The value of consumer surplus with trade is equal to $4,000,000 and the value of producer surplus with trade is equal to $3,000,000.

d. At a price of $3,450, the quantity of green peppers demanded domestically is equal to 3,100 tons while the quantity supplied domestically is equal to 2,300 tons. Pepperville will import 800 tons of green peppers.

e. The value of consumer surplus is equal to $(1/2)($5,000 \text{ per ton} - $3,450 \text{ per ton})(3,100 \text{ tons})$, or $2,402,500. The value of producer surplus is equal to $(1/2)($3,450 \text{ per ton})(2,300 \text{ tons})$, or $3,967,500.

f. The government earns the difference between the tariff price per ton of green peppers and the world price of green peppers on every ton of green peppers imported into Pepperville. The tariff revenue is equal to ($3,450 per ton – $3,000 per ton)(800 tons), or $360,000.

g. The deadweight loss is the difference between the total surplus with open trade and the sum of consumer surplus + producer surplus + tariff revenue, or $7,000,000 – ($2,402,500 + $3,967,500 + $360,000) = $270,000. Alternatively, the deadweight loss can be calculated as the sum of the areas of two triangles, which is equal to (1/2)($3,450 per ton – $3,000 per ton)(2,300 tons – 2,000 tons) + (1/2)($3,450 per ton – $3,000 per ton)(4,000 tons – 3,100 tons), or $270,000.

h. The quota has to equal the number of units Pepperville imports when the tariff raises the price of green peppers to $3,450 per ton. That is, the quota must be 800 tons of green peppers.

i. Consumer surplus is greatest when the trade policy is one of an open economy. Consumers rank these choices from best to worst in this order: open economy, open economy with a tariff or quota, closed economy. This ranking occurs whenever the world price is less than the closed economy price for the good.

j. Producer surplus is greatest when the trade policy is one of a closed economy. Producers rank these choices from best to worst in this order: closed economy, open economy with a tariff or quota, open economy. This ranking occurs whenever the world price is less than the closed economy price for the good.

k. Governments can successfully provide a benefit to both consumers and producers by choosing this option. If you review the consumer and producer surplus under each of these options, you will see that the middle option gives consumers a greater consumer surplus than they would get with a closed economy and it gives producers a greater producer surplus than they would get with an open economy. It is a compromise position for the government to take between these two constituencies.

11. a.

	Option I	Option II	Option III
Pairs of shoes imported	130 pairs	50 pairs	50 pairs
Consumer surplus	$12,800	$7,200	$7,200
Producer surplus	450	2,450	2,450
Tariff revenue or quota rent	0	2,000	2,000
Deadweight loss	0	1,600	1,600

b. From the perspective of domestic consumers, the best option is the option that results in the greatest value for consumer surplus: option I, the open economy option.

c. From the perspective of domestic producers, the best option is the option that results in the greatest value for producer surplus: option II and option III result in equivalent values for producer surplus, with the license holder earning a quota rent for option II and the government earning tariff revenue for option III. If the license holder is a domestic producer, then option II would be the best option.

d. Options II and III result in the largest, and equivalent, efficiency cost as measured by the deadweight loss that occurs with the imposition of these two trade-protectionist policies.

12. a. (i.) Merchandise trade balance = (exports of goods) – (imports of goods) = (payments from foreigners for goods) – (payments to foreigners for goods)

(ii.) Balance of payments on goods and services = (exports of goods and services) – (imports of goods and services) = (payments from foreigners for goods and services) – (payments to foreigners for goods and services) (iii.) Net international factor income = (factor income payments from foreigners) – (factor income payments to foreigners)

(iv.) Net international transfer payments = (transfer payments from foreigners) – (transfer payments to foreigners)

(v.) Balance of payments on current account = (balance of payments on goods and services) + (net international transfer payments) + (net international factor income)

(vi.) Balance of payments on financial account = (sales of assets to foreigners) – (purchases of assets from foreigners)

b. (i.) Merchandise trade balance = $200 million – $80 million = $120 million

(ii.) Balance of payments on goods and services = $250 million – $100 million = $150 million

(iii.) Net international factor income = $70 million – $10 million = $60 million

(iv.) Net international transfer payments = $10 million – $20 million = – $10 million

(v.) Balance of payments on current account = $150 million + (–$10 million) + ($60 million) = $200 million

(vi.) Balance of payments on financial account = –$200 million

c. This reflects a basic rule of balance of payments accounting for any country: the flow of money into a country must equal the flow of money out of the country.

13. a.

	U.S. dollars	Funland dollars	Macroland dollars
1 U.S. dollar exchanged for	1	200	1.05
1 Funland dollar exchanged for	0.005	1	0.004762
1 Macroland dollar exchanged for	0.952381	210	1

b.

	U.S. dollars	Funland dollars	Macroland dollars
1 U.S. dollar exchanged for	1	210	0.980392
1 Funland dollar exchanged for	0.004762	1	0.004669
1 Macroland dollar exchanged for	1.02	214.2	1

c. Macroland dollars appreciated against the U.S. dollar since in part (a), 1 Macroland dollar was worth 0.952381 U.S. dollar, and in part (b), 1 Macroland dollar was worth 1.02 U.S. dollars.

d. Funland dollars depreciated against the U.S. dollar since in part (a), 1 Funland dollar was worth 0.005 U.S. dollar, and in part (b), 1 Funland dollar was worth 0.004762 U.S. dollar.

e. U.S. exports to Funland, holding everything else constant, will fall because, as Funland's currency depreciates against the U.S. dollar, this makes U.S. products more expensive to the residents of Funland relative to Funland's products. Funland will export more to the United States and the United States will export less to Funland.

f. U.S. exports to Macroland, holding everything else constant, will increase because, as Macroland's currency appreciates against the U.S. dollar, this makes U.S. products cheaper to the residents of Macroland relative to Macroland's products. Macroland will export less to the United States and the United States will export more to Macroland.

14. a.

Funland purchases of Macroland dollars in the foreign exchange market to buy Macroland assets	=	2 million Macroland dollars
Total sales of Macroland dollars in the foreign exchange market	=	5.0 million Macroland dollars
Macroland balance of payments on current account	=	−0.5 million Macroland dollars
Macroland balance of payments on financial account	=	0.5 million Macroland dollars

b. The depreciation of the Macroland currency against Funland's currency will cause the demand for Macroland dollars to decrease at every exchange rate (measured as Funland dollars per Macroland dollars). This will, for a given supply of Macroland dollars, cause the exchange rate to decrease. This is illustrated in the following figure.

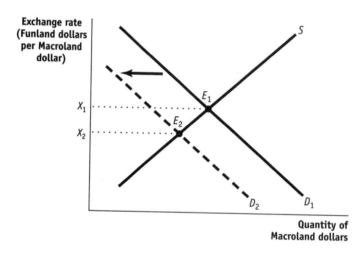

c. This depreciation of Macroland's currency against Funland's currency will cause Macroland's balance of payments on current account to increase, since Funland will now find Macroland goods and services relatively cheaper.

d. This depreciation of Macroland's currency against Funland's currency will cause Macroland's balance of payments on financial account to decrease, since any increase in Macroland's balance of payments on current account must be offset by an equal and opposite reaction in the balance of payments on financial account.

15. a. Real exchange rate in Macroland dollars per Funland dollar = (20 Macroland dollars per Funland dollar)(100/100) = 20 Macroland dollars per Funland dollar

b. To answer this question, we will want to use the equation:

Real exchange rate = (nominal exchange rate)[(price index in Funland)/ (price index in Macroland)]

Thus, 25 Macroland dollars per Funland dollar = (20 Macroland dollars per Funland dollar)[(150)/(price index in Macroland)], and solving for the price index in Macroland, we find that the price index in Macroland equals 120.

c. To answer this question, we will want to use the equation given in part (b):

Real exchange rate = (nominal exchange rate)[(price index in Funland)/ (price index in Macroland)]

Thus, the real exchange rate = (25 Macroland dollars per Funland dollar) [(150)/(125)], and solving this equation for the real exchange rate yields a real exchange rate equal to 30 Macroland dollars per Funland dollar.

d. When the real exchange rate increases this is an appreciation of Macroland's currency, and this appreciation will make Macroland's products more expensive to foreigners: Macroland will export less and import more when the real exchange rate increases, holding everything else constant.

16. a. If purchasing power parity holds in the two countries, then the price of the market basket in the two countries is 300 Macroland dollars equals 150 Funland dollars. This implies that the exchange rate must equal 2 Macroland dollars per Funland dollar or, equivalently, 1 Macroland dollar per 0.5 Funland dollar.

b. If the actual exchange rate is greater than the purchasing power parity exchange rate, one would anticipate that the exchange rate will fall over time, since nominal exchange rates between countries at similar levels of economic development tend to fluctuate around levels that lead to similar costs for a given market basket.

17. a. When the American company purchases machinery that is produced in Germany by a German company, this transaction enters the U.S. balance of payments on current account as an import. This transaction will reduce the balance of payments on the U.S. current account.

b. When the American donates money to the foreign group organizing an international sporting event, this enters the current account as a transfer payment to a foreigner. This transaction will reduce the balance on the U.S. current account.

c. When a French citizen purchases cheese produced in the United States, this transaction enters the U.S. balance of payments on current account as an export. This transaction will increase the balance of payments on the U.S. current account.

d. When the American purchases 100 shares of a Swiss company, this transaction is categorized as part of the U.S. balance of payments on financial account. The balance of payments on the U.S. financial account will fall.

Answers to Chapter Review Questions

1. **Answer b.** International trade is a source of mutual benefit to the countries involved in the trade.

2. **Answer a.** The wine, cheese, and lamb are all imported goods into the American economy since these goods are produced elsewhere in the world and then brought into the American market. Exports refers to those goods produced in the domestic economy and sold in a foreign economy.

3. **Answer d.** Since Smallville can absolutely produce more cheese than can Gooseville, Smallville has the absolute advantage in producing cheese. Gooseville, on the other hand, can absolutely produce more bicycles than can Smallville from the same resources, so Gooseville has the absolute advantage in producing bicycles.

4. **Answer d.** The opportunity cost of producing one more bicycle in Smallville is equal to the number of tons of cheese that must be given up to produce one more bicycle. In this case, 2 tons of cheese must be given up to produce one more bicycle in Smallville. The opportunity cost of producing a bicycle in Smallville is 2 tons of cheese, while the opportunity cost of producing a bicycle in Gooseville is equal to 1 ton of cheese.

5. **Answer b.** If Smallville produces at the midpoint of its production possibility frontier, it will produce 1,000 tons of cheese and 500 bicycles. If Gooseville produces at the midpoint of its production possibility frontier, it will produce 750 tons of cheese and 750 bicycles. Total cheese production will equal 1,750 tons and total bicycle production will equal 1,250 bicycles.

6. **Answer a.** Smallville will produce cheese since the opportunity cost of producing cheese for Smallville is 1/2 bicycle while the opportunity cost of producing cheese for Gooseville is 1 bicycle. Smallville gives up fewer bicycles to produce a ton of cheese and therefore Smallville has the comparative advantage in producing cheese.

7. **Answer c.** The opportunity cost of producing a bicycle is 2 tons of cheese for Smallville and 1 ton of cheese for Gooseville. Smallville will be willing to pay up to 2 tons of cheese for 1 bicycle, while Gooseville is willing to trade 1 bicycle for any amount of cheese greater than 1 ton. The price of a bicycle will be in the range of 1 to 2 tons of cheese.

8. **Answer c.** If both countries fully specialize, then Smallville will produce only cheese (2,000 tons of cheese) and Gooseville will produce only bicycles (1,500 bicycles).

9. **Answer a.** A linear production function is a production function with a constant slope. This constant slope tells us that for a given change in the good measured on the x-axis there will be a given change in the good measured on the y-axis. Another way to express this idea is that the opportunity cost of producing either good is constant: for the good measured on the x-axis, the opportunity cost of producing one more unit of that good is equal to the absolute value of the slope of the production possibility frontier; for the good measured on the y-axis, the opportunity cost of producing one more unit of that good is equal to the absolute value of the reciprocal of the slope of the production possibility frontier. A country cannot have the comparative advantage in producing both goods: one country must have the comparative advantage in producing one of the goods while the other country must have the comparative advantage in producing the other good. Trade is beneficial, provided that countries specialize according to their comparative advantage. Trade without regard to comparative advantage results in lower total production.

10. **Answer b.** This is the definition of autarky. A country may be independent of other countries when it decides not to trade, but that is not the term used to describe this trade position. Answers (c) and (d) refer to models used to analyze international trade, but they are not direct references to the term describing a closed economy.

11. **Answer c.** Gains from trade stem from a country's comparative advantage and not its absolute advantage (statement I is false). Absolute advantage focuses on the amount of resources used to produce a good (for example, the number of hours of labor it takes to produce a shirt) while comparative advantage focuses on the opportunity cost of producing the good—that is, what must be given up to produce a unit of this good (statement II is false). When a country has a comparative advantage in producing a good, this means that its opportunity cost of producing the good is lower than the opportunity cost of producing the same good in some other country: this advantage in terms of opportunity cost is translated into wage rates. When a country has less-productive labor, then the wage rate for this labor is lower than it is for a country that has more-productive labor.

12. **Answer e.** The main sources of comparative advantage are differences in climate, differences in factor endowments, and differences in technology. Answers (a) and (c) illustrate a country's specialization based on climate differences, answer (b) illustrates a country's specialization based on factor endowments, and answer (d) illustrates a country's specialization based on differences in technology.

13. **Answer b.** According to the Heckscher–Ohlin model, country has a comparative advantage in producing those goods and services whose production is intensive in the factors of production that are relatively abundant in that country compared to other countries. Thus, a country that has an abundance of labor relative to other countries tends to specialize in producing labor-intensive goods and services, while a country that is capital abundant specializes in producing capital-intensive goods and services. This specialization bids up the factor price of the factors that are abundant in a country due to the increased demand for these factors, and the factor price of the factors that are scarce in a country tends to fall due to decreased demand for these factors. Answer (b) is not true because the prices of the factors are moving in the wrong direction.

14. **Answer e.** Countries will tend to import those goods that are produced using factors of production that are relatively scarce in the importing country (statement I is therefore false). Countries that utilize a high ratio of highly skilled workers to less skilled workers are countries that tend to produce goods that are intensive in human capital (statement II is true). Countries will export goods whose production takes advantage of the relative abundance of the factor (statement III is true).

15. **Answer c.** The area of consumer surplus is the area beneath the demand curve but above the equilibrium price, or in this example, area ACQ. The area of producer surplus is the area above the supply curve but below the equilibrium price, or in this example, area CQE.

16. **Answer c.** When the world price of the good is greater than the autarky price and the country opens to trade, Pedalland will export the good to other countries in order to sell the good at the higher world price. In this case, domestic suppliers are willing to supply the amount represented as the distance between points B and W while domestic consumers are only willing to consume the number of bicycles represented by the distance between B and M. Thus, domestic producers will export the number of bicycles represented by the distance between points M and W.

17. **Answer b.** When the world price is below the domestic equilibrium price and the country opens to trade, the country will import goods. The country will import the number of goods that represents the difference between the amount domestically supplied at the world price and the amount domestically demanded at the world price. In this case, the country will import the number of goods represented by the distance between points P and S.

18. **Answer a.** The area of consumer surplus is the area beneath the demand curve and above the equilibrium price, while the area of producer surplus is the area above the supply curve and below the equilibrium price. When this country opens to trade and the world price is equal to B, the country will export the good, which benefits domestic producers, who are able to sell more units of the good than they could when the country was closed to trade.

19. **Answer c.** When the world price of the good is less than the autarky price, the country will import the good if it opens its economy to trade. In this case, the country will import the difference between the quantity demanded domestically at a price of $20 and the quantity supplied domestically at a price of $20, or 120 bicycles. The area of total surplus is initially equal to $5,000, and when the country opens to trade, the area of total surplus has a value of $6,800, so the increase in total surplus is $6,800 − $5,000, or $1,800.

20. **Answer e.** To calculate the license-holder revenue from the quota you first need to rewrite the supply curve taking into account the quota. So, for example, if the supply equation is initially $P = (1/2)(Q)$, then with a quota of 40 units this supply equation will be $P = (1/2)Q − 20$. Using this new supply equation and the demand equation, $P = 100 − (1/2)Q$, you can find the new price with a quota of 40 units. The price with this level of quota is $40 per bicycle. The license-holder revenue is equal to the difference between the price with the quota and the world price times the number of bicycles imported with the quota: ($40/bicycle − $20/bicycle)(40 bicycles), or $800. This argument, however, also works for a quota of 80 units: when the quota is 80 bicycles the supply curve can be written as $P = (1/2)Q − 30$, and the new price with this quota limit is $30 per bicycle. The license-holder revenue is equal to the difference between the price with the quota and the world price times the number of bicycles imported with the quota: ($30/bicycle − $20/bicycle)(80 bicycles), or $800.

21. **Answer b.** The deadweight loss associated with this tariff is the result of two forces: (a) mutually beneficial trades do not take place because of the imposition of the tariff, and (b) the bicycles sold are produced at a price that exceeds the world price for bicycles. The area of deadweight loss can be calculated as the sum of the areas of two triangles: (1/2)($40 per bicycle − $20 per bicycle)(80 bicycles − 40 bicycles) + (1/2)($40 per bicycle − $20 per bicycle)(160 bicycles − 120 bicycles) = $800.

22. **Answer a.** This is a tough problem! You first need to figure out the price with the quota, the quantity supplied domestically with the quota, and the quantity demanded domestically with the quota. From the graph you know that if the quota price was $40, the quota would be equal to 40 units. From the graph you also know that, at the world price, 120 bicycles are imported into Pedalland. So, logically you know that the quota price must be lower than $40 and higher than $20. When the quota price is $35, the quantity demanded domestically is equal to 130 bicycles and the quantity supplied domestically is equal to 70 bicycles, for a difference of 60 bicycles. This difference is the same as the quota amount given in the question. Now you need only compute the original consumer surplus (equals $2,500) and the consumer surplus with the quota ($4,225) and subtract the original consumer surplus from the new consumer surplus to get the change in the value of consumer surplus that occurs with the imposition of the quota.

23. **Answer a.** When countries engage in trade, they produce those goods and services for which they have a comparative advantage. This specialization according to Heckscher-Ohlin advantage results in these countries producing those goods and services for which they have an abundant amount of resources. Thus, the exporting industries in the country will bid up the price of these resources as they increase their production of the good. The country will tend to import goods and services that are intensive in the factors that are scarce in its economy. This effectively decreases the demand for the relatively scarce factors and increases the demand for the relatively abundant factors. Trade will cause the factor price to increase for the relatively abundant factor and to decrease for the relatively scarce factor.

24. **Answer c.** The balance of payments on goods and services is the difference between the value of exports and the value of imports during a given period. The merchandise trade balance does not include the sale of financial assets, but does include the sale of goods. The balance of payments accounts provide a set of numbers that describe a country's international transactions.

25. **Answer g.** By definition, the balance of payments on goods and services plus net international transfer payments and net international factor income equals the balance of payments on current account. In addition, the sum of the balance of payments on current account plus the balance of payments on financial account equals zero.

26. **Answer d.** The sum of the balance of payments on current account and the balance of payments on financial account must sum to zero: thus, if the balance of payments on financial account equals –$100 million, then the balance of payments on current account must equal $100 million.

27. **Answer d.** Figure 19-1 in your text reviews this concept: the balance of payments tracks flows of goods and services, factor income, transfers, and assets between a country and the rest of the world. Transactions involving goods and services, factor income, and transfers are measured in the balance of payments on current account, while transactions involving assets are measured in the balance of payments on financial account.

28. **Answer d.** A country that has capital inflows will have a matching current account deficit. The exchange rate may be measured as the price of a dollar in terms of the foreign currency, or it may be measured as the price of the foreign currency in terms of dollars. The more euros it takes to buy a dollar, the fewer dollars Europeans will demand in the foreign exchange market for dollars. When a country's currency appreciates, this means that the exchange rate for that currency in terms of the other currency has risen: this increase in the exchange rate makes goods and services produced in the country whose currency has appreciated more expensive relative to goods and services produced elsewhere. This will lead to a decrease in exports and an increase in imports for the country whose currency has appreciated.

29. **Answer h.** If 1 U.S. dollar trades for 0.9 euro, this is the same as 1 euro trading for $1.11 (to see this, simply divide 1/0.9 to find how many dollars it takes to purchase 1 euro). If the exchange rate changes to 1 U.S. dollar in exchange for 0.95 euro, this means that dollars have appreciated and that euros have depreciated in value, since 1 dollar initially was worth only 0.9 euro and now is worth 0.95 euro. This means that a dollar has greater purchasing power in European Union markets and, therefore, imports of European goods to the United States will increase and exports of American goods to European Union countries will decrease.

30. **Answer e.** When a country has an increase in capital inflows, this causes the exchange rate to increase, leading to an appreciation of that country's currency. With this appreciation of its currency, the country will find that its goods and services become relatively more expensive and, therefore, its net exports will decrease. Furthermore, the increase in capital inflows will cause the balance of payments on financial account to increase, and this increase will be met by an equal, but opposite, reaction in the balance of payments on current account.

31. **Answer e.** To find the real exchange rate, we need to know the nominal exchange rate (in this case, 10 Macroland dollars per 1 Funland dollar) and the aggregate price level in the two countries. We can plug them into formula 19–4 in your text: real exchange rate equals (10 Macroland dollars/1 Funland dollar)(150/125) = 12 Macroland dollars per 1 Funland dollar.

32. **Answer e.** To find the exchange rate, we need to know the real exchange rate (in this case, 12 Macroland dollars per 1 Funland dollar) and the aggregate price level in the two countries. We can plug them into formula 19–4 in your text: 12 Macroland dollars per 1 Funland dollar equals (the exchange rate)(150/150). Solving for the exchange rate yields an exchange rate of 12 Macroland dollars per 1 Funland dollar.

33. **Answer c.** Purchasing power parity between two countries' currencies is the nominal exchange rate at which a given basket of goods and services would cost the same amount in each country. When the purchasing power parity rate is greater than the nominal exchange rate, we would anticipate that the nominal exchange rate must increase over time in order for the two countries to have similar costs for a given market basket.

34. **Answer d.** When a country's currency undergoes a real depreciation this causes exports to rise and imports to fall, since the depreciation reduces the price of the country's goods and services relative to the prices for goods and services produced in other countries. Nominal exchange rates almost always differ from purchasing power parity rates: the nominal rate tends to fluctuate around the purchasing power parity rate. The current account responds only to changes in the real exchange rate, not the nominal exchange rate: it is a change in the real exchange rate that alters the relative cost of domestic goods and services in comparison to foreign-produced goods and services.

35. **Answer f.** Payments to Macropedia from foreigners are represented by dollars that flow into Macropedia. For example, the farmers in Macropedia will receive compensation from abroad if they export their agricultural commodity to another country; or the providers of a service will receive compensation from abroad if they provide their service to people residing in another country. Thus, answers (b) and (d) both represent flows of funds into Macropedia, while answers (a) and (c) represent flows of funds out of Macropedia.

36. **Answer b.** Statements I and II state the same idea: if the sum of the balance of payments on current account (*CA*) and the balance of payments on financial account (*FA*) equal zero, then this implies that the flow of funds into a country's economy must equal the flow of funds out of that country's economy. If a country is importing more than it is exporting, this means that its balance of payments on current account is negative and, therefore, implies that its balance of payments on financial account is positive. When the balance of payments on financial account is positive, this implies that the country has positive capital inflows.

37. **Answer b.** Five pesos originally are worth 1 U.S. dollar, but when the exchange rate changes, five pesos are worth only $0.50 in U.S. dollars. The value of the peso in terms of U.S. dollars has fallen, and thus the peso has depreciated against the U.S. dollar.

38. **Answer a.** When there is an increase in the demand for U.S. dollars, this causes the demand curve for dollars to shift to the right. The subsequent move along the supply of U.S. dollars curve will cause the equilibrium exchange rate of pesos to U.S. dollars to increase.

39. **Answer f.** If the U.S. dollar rises against the Mexican peso, this means that it takes more pesos to buy a U.S. dollar: this then implies that U.S. goods are now relatively more expensive to Mexico than they were before the dollar rose against the peso. If U.S. goods are now relatively more expensive to Mexico, then Mexico's goods are now relatively cheaper to those of the United States.